WINNING TRAINERS
Their Road to the Top

The lives and success secrets
of the world's trainers of
Quarter Horses
Standardbreds
Thoroughbreds

WINNING TRAINERS
Their Road to the Top

The life stories, training methods, feeding, and
strategies of the leading trainers of
Thoroughbreds, Quarter Horses and Standardbreds
from around the world. A thorough analyis of how
they made it to the top of their game and how
they stay there.

D. Wayne Lukas, Quarter Horses then Thoroughbreds, USA.
Caesar Dominguez, Quarter Horses, USA.
Tommy 'TJ' Smith, Thoroughbreds, Australia.
Fred Kersley, Standardbreds, Australia.

by *Ross Staaden* B.V.Sc., Ph.D.

Headway International Publishing, Perth, Western Australia, and Lexington, Kentucky, USA.

ISBN No. 0 646 09154 9

Main entry under title:
Winning Trainers: Their road to the top

Typeset by CTS Inc, Minneapolis.
Printed and bound by Everbest Printing Company Ltd of
Hong Kong

Published by Headway International Publishing

To order more copies of this book, write to:

Headway International Publishing

4 Gillon St, Karawara, Western Australia, 6152
PO Box 1907, Barr St, Lexington, Kentucky, USA, Zip 40593-1907

Dedicated to my sister Joy,
a source of caring and strength in our family
through some tough years;

to her husband Rob,
a wonderful guy,
who passed away in February 1990;

AND ...

To battling two-horse trainers everywhere,
who take their many setbacks
and plug on with optimism and humor.

Contents

D. WAYNE LUKAS

D. Wayne Lukas continued

CAESAR DOMINGUEZ

Caesar Dominguez continued

TOMMY SMITH

Tommy Smith continued

Tommy Smith continued

FRED KERSLEY

Fred Kersley continued

Fred Kersley continued

Preface — What makes a trainer successful?

What is it that enables some trainers to rise like a rocket to the top of their profession and stay there? What do they have that the thousands of other trainers DON'T have? How much of this rise is due to luck, to having that first champion horse? How much is hard work? Talent? Which talents count the most? Is there a formula? Are there some common factors, some important talents or personality traits that ALL the top trainers have?

For as long as I can remember, racegoers in Australia have argued about just what made "TJ" Smith such a phenomenal success as a trainer of racehorses. A lot of beer flowed over the topic but not much real information. If you raised the subject in any of the state capital cities you would soon have the usual spectrum of views:

> "He has so many horses he has to have the most winners."
> "Good at 'conning' owners, he can really dish up the bulldust."
> "He steals horses after other trainers develop them."
> "Because he fills them to the eyeballs with anabolics."
> "He's a very smart man Tommy smith, very quick off the mark."
> "He's the best trainer so he gets the best horses."
> "Very good eye for a horse."
> "TJ Smith uses something, he's got the golden needle."

You will hear some of these points in any dispute about the merits of trainers anywhere in the world, in Quarter Horses, Standardbreds or Thoroughbreds. I have no doubt that for as long as horses have been raced against each other, and one trainer had more success than others, there have been arguments about the reasons for that trainer's success. In Roman times there were claims of doping in the chariot races. The latin equivalents of 'Golden Needle', 'Golden Tongue' and 'Just Damned Lucky' were doubtless muttered around the Hippodrome stables.

To the best of my knowledge, in spite of thousands of years of speculation, there has never been any serious effort to determine the ingredients needed for success as a racehorse trainer. This book is an attempt to evaluate some of the ingredients. In order to sharpen my observations and steer my questions in the right directions, I thought hard about how someone might go about becoming the 'perfect trainer', then I set off around the world to find the answers to the questions.

I had not really expected trainers to be *keen* to tell their secrets but neither had I anticipated that it might have been easier to learn about the Mafia or the KGB. Top trainers are incredibly busy people and their idea of an 'in depth' interview is 10 minutes squeezed in between lots of incoming phone calls. To be granted such a 'lengthy session' you have to be from a prestige racing magazine and be able to exhibit at your elbow a professional photographer, bristling with a clutter of cameras and multiple megalength lenses.

It soon became obvious that to do the job at all well it would take numerous world trips, with a lot of 'hanging around', waiting for lulls in the bedlam. Such trips are not cheap from Perth, Western Australia. It is the only regional capital city in the world that is more isolated than the capital of Siberia!

It has proven to be an expensive but interesting project and I hope you enjoy the results as much as I did collecting the information. One note of caution. This volume contains the biographies of just four trainers. Do not become too certain of the trends and conclusions from these four. I have looked closely at 32 trainers and there were many differences and some interesting surprises.

Acknowledgements

First and foremost I have to thank my lovely wife Anita. She has had to put up with someone who often went away for many weeks at a time. Someone who usually didn't go to bed until 1am, 3am or 5am for upto a week before leaving.

Someone who catches planes by the skin of his teeth after a nerve-wracking dash in the car.

Someone who arrives back at the home airport at 2am, clears customs at 4am, but only leaves at 6am after establishing that the camera bag is in Italy. Someone who then continues to eat and sleep as though in some other time zone for another week.

In spite of that she has been very supportive of the project, contributing as an editor and constructive critic. She hasn't even made me promise that there will be no more after this one!

My daughters Emily and Kate have also shown great tolerance. 'Father' has come to mean a very preoccupied, possibly still living ancestor, who hunches endlessly over a computer keyboard. The only signs of life are those noises associated with word-processing: Tapping sounds interspersed with sudden, loud, unnerving cries of 'Oh no!' and 'Bloody stupid thing!' They know this could all be mechanical but believe that there is real protoplasmic life present because he grunts in response to questions.

To get over the boredom associated with their father's state of upright walking coma, they have written a couple of terrific children's books at ages 15 and 11! I'm very proud of them but now they want to know why my book is taking so long. Emily also typed in a lot of tedious training tables for me. She types a lot faster than me.

Then there is Jasmine, my constant companion and stress consultant. She whiskers my foot at 10pm every night to tell me it's time to pay her fee by feeding her sunflower seeds. She used to sleep all day at my feet but lately has preferred to doze elsewhere. Any time I feel stressed I just look at Jasmine and I realize the stupidity of it all. Rabbits are like that.

I also wish to thank:

Some very tolerant typists who transcribed thousands of pages from tapes, including Ann Holder, Jenny Williams, Chris Murray and especially Sue Isles.

Ahmet Bektas, a friend and one of the nicest people I know, who helped whenever the computer got out of hand in Australia. A poorly trained computer is capable of unbelievable displays of insensitivity and ignorance.

Chris Nielsen of Minneapolis, also a nice human being, who rescued four years of work from a disc crash that took the backup with it. He turned anguish into joy in the Easter resurrection of 1990.

Gloria Jiminez who researched in American libraries for me.

People who read manuscripts for me, including Joy, Rob and Gary Edgar; Athol Staaden, Flora and Lindsay Dutton, Dr Kal Kobluk, Dr Ray Geor, Dr Jane Quandt, Jeff LaPoff, Joe Merrick, Pat Cuccurullo, James 'Junior' Fortner, Tom Winkle, and Wilson Brown.

James Bester of Sydney, Douglas Saunders of Lexington, and Frank Dunn of Ireland, who were very helpful with accommodation and information.

Pat Styles who knew a lot about Australian trainers and loaned me old, hard-to-find magazines.

A swag of publicity people and racing secretaries including Paul Macchia, at The Meadowlands, New Jersey; Ed Burgart at Los Alamitos, Los Angeles; Mark Doth at Ruidoso Downs, New Mexico; Jim Peden at Hollywood Park, Los Angeles; Jane Goldstein at Santa Anita, Los Angleles; Steven Schwartz at Belmont Park, New York; and Ray Holloway at Gloucester Park, Perth.

Journalists Max Agnew, Gino di Mori, John McGrath, and Bill Whittaker in Australia; Brad McKinzie, Pete Axthelm, Steve Davidowitz, Leslie P. Ford, and others in America.

Richard Chamberlain at the American Quarter Horse Association in Amarillo, Texas.

Dean Hoffman and David Carr at the U.S. Trotting Association in Columbus, Ohio.

The team at Cold Type Setters: Bill Simpson, Jeff Munson, Ann DuChaine, Dean Dutcher and Doug Herkenhoff.

George Dick and Bobby Dean at Four Color Imports.

Wyn Jones and the Animal Protection Society, whose dedication to helping the stray dogs of Perth provided me with inspiration and a source of income.

My bank managers at the National Australia Bank in Booragoon, who have been very helpful when I have needed overdrafts, foreign currency and overseas transactions. I wish I could say nice things about all of my travel agents but some owe me refunds which they don't get around to paying.

Most importantly I wish to thank some trainers, and although I hate to have to draw a line, I must mention Fred Kersley, Luca Cumani, John Gosden, Jeff LaPoff, Caesar Dominguez and Jack Brooks. Their willingness to answer questions and the impressive commonsense intelligence of those answers kept me believing the project was feasible and worthwhile.

Introduction

How the trainers were chosen

I started by asking people, especially trainers, for suggestions. Many people suggested famous trainers of the past. I said that it would be difficult to obtain details of their training. The trainers (particularly) said, "Well you won't get training details from a living trainer anyway."

There were some other reasons to go for trainers of the deceased type. Journalists told me that living relatives and connections of past trainers could afford to be more honest and forthcoming because the subject trainer was not going to tackle them about what they had let out of the bag. In addition, I learned, you can't be taken to court for defaming the dead. Neither can they punch you on the nose.

The retired trainers, I decided, were my greatest hope for some training detail. I thought as a test run I would look at a mixed bag of historic, retired and still training. I set about compiling a list of names. One point that emerged was that not many top trainers retire. They seem to keep going until they are mentally incompetent or they die on the job. Failing that, they have a son or daughter or favorite assistant and they want to preserve the secrets for them.

The first trainer I looked hard at was Australia's Tommy Smith. He is much better known in Australia than any American trainer could hope to be known in America. He was a legendary figure when I was a vet student in the 1960's and he still is.

From that study of TJ Smith I learned some valuable lessons. First and foremost, I found that some widely believed stories about him were not quite right - or at least you needed Tommy's view to have the true perspective.

My conclusion was that someone researching Tommy's life by interviewing associates a decade or two after his death would believe they had the facts - after all three different associates told them the same thing - when they did not. Often the people right up close to Tommy did not know his reasons for doing certain things.

I also found that when dealing with connections of the past trainers, there was usually no way to check the egomaniac claims of some as to how much they had contributed to the success of that past trainer. When I could check, I found the accounts of some to be very wide of the mark. I had been inclined to the view that men's egos declined somewhat with age, chiseled down in size by relentless reality. Not so. Down at the old men's home there are some who are still grasping at a thread of undeserved immortality by wildly exaggerating their role in the past triumphs of someone else.

All this confirmed a long held view of mine that history is a very inexact science. The attitude of many historians, that 'History' somehow or other, in the end, will always comes up with the true and correct perspective, has never washed with me. It is more a matter of what bits of the evidence survive, *whose* accounts, who lives longest etc. Then there is the twist applied by the personal life, times and views of the historian. 'History' is probably wrong very often. "History will judge" they say pompously. History *will* judge but I doubt it will get to the truth of the matter any more often than that great ass the legal system deals out true justice.

So there I was, stuck with the living, currently training trainers. My training and racing associates were not impressed. "They won't tell you if they are using drugs." Obviously you couldn't publish hotel bar or backstretch allegations of drugging, nor should you unless a) it is a widely expressed opinion (in which case you describe it as just that - unsubstantiated opinion) or b) there is some concrete corroborating evidence. As I went further into the project I found that a great many of my potential top trainers were, in the opinions of many of the public and backstretch personnel, users of illegal drugs. There was nothing to do but investigate the matter as far as I could and report what I found.

"They either won't tell you anything about their training or they will tell you lies to mislead you." As far as I could check and double check with assistant trainers, jockeys, clockers and even rival trainers, no one told me lies about their training. If trainers didn't want to talk about training, they either said so, or simply looked astonished at the gall of the question. In particular I was able to obtain training sheets from some trainers the day they finished with them, or straight out of a desk draw or from one of those books that hold a whole year's records. They were not something cooked up.

The top trainers seem less concerned about hiding their training details than the lower ones. Some saw my book as a way of going down in history and wanted to look their best. (Hopefully the book will still be read in a hundred years, just as some hundred-year-old horse books are today.) Not a few believed giving some real information would show that they were smart, on the ball. This would help them in the publicity game and bring in new owners. One or two didn't want to give anything away, but also could not bear to be left out because rivals were going to be in it.

Unfortunately some trainers would agree to an interview and promise to discuss their training, but when the time arrived, told me little or nothing about their training. They will be left out, replaced with some who did. A waste of air fares, time and photos. In fairness, there were a few who promised nothing, to whom I went in hope. When insufficient information was forthcoming, that was my problem. A gamble that sometimes worked out, sometimes not. For some trainers I have a lot of pretty pictures but not enough gutsy information to make their inclusion worthwhile.

At all times I was conscious that I would have to defend my choices, so I was trying to stick with those who had won a training title at some time, preferably a string of them and/ or some major races. Some way into the project however, I found that these were not necessarily the trainers that other trainers respected the most. Conversely there were trainers who did not make it into the top three regularly, but who were held in very high regard by everyone at the track. Bob Gilbert, a Quarter Horse trainer at Los Alamitos was an example of this.

Some trainers did not care about Derby-winning trainers. They wanted to know about top claiming trainers, a group they saw as more at their level. There was also a group of trainers who loathed dealing with owners. They wanted to know of anyone who was making a good living training just their own horses. I'm still looking for a few more trainers in these two categories.

There were also some young trainers who were reckoned to be on their way up, acclaimed as probable top-cockys of the future. Talking to this category of trainer I found that they were really hot - plotting, scheming, thinking - right in their prime. There seems to be a time-lag factor in getting to the top. That may be the time taken to be recognized by a lot of owners, the time during which a previous generation of trainers holds sway through sheer reputation. Whatever it is due to, it does seem to me that many make it perhaps a decade later than when they were at their innovative mental best. Then it is another decade or two before they are household names.

Talking to some in their 30s and 40s who were pointed out as probable stars of the future, but who have not won a training title, I was struck by the ongoing changes. They were changing things in their overall strategy, in their training programs and so on. They could tell me why they changed something and what happened. With a rapid rise already behind them they were in the thick of the battle. They were 'on fire', continually reassessing tactics, thinking hard every day about how to bridge that gap, how to make it over the last few trenches to the top of Glory Hill.

This contrasted with the inability of some, who had already made it up Glory Hill, to recall details. I know as a vet I have sometimes had difficulty explaining to students why I used a particular method of treatment. Perhaps 10 years before I had tried three possible solutions to some nasty condition. At the time, one method gave better results, and that was retained, but the other methods and their deficiencies have often slipped out of the memory banks. So I understand why a trainer cannot recall some things after 40 years.

Some at the top of Glory Hill had a disinterested attitude. Some of the top trainers were simply not very communicative. I decided to include some of the very articulate 'rising rockets' on the grounds that it may be at this point of their career that they have the most information to pass on. They are still facing, or have recently overcome, challenges that some of the most revered names have forgotten, but which are more relevant to the multitude of lesser-known trainers.

Last but not least in choosing trainers, I tried to go to major centers where I could look at a number of 'name' trainers at one time, simply to minimize time and costs. I have not included a list of the trainers to be included in future volumes, because the list is still subject to addition and subtraction.

Why mix Thoroughbred, Quarter Horse and Standardbred?

Many trainers switch from one breed to another. Many train more than one type of horse. Three of the four trainers in this volume train, or have trained, more than one breed of racehorse. Hans Adielsson had been the leading Thoroughbred trainer in Sweden for 10 years when I interviewed him in 1987. Since then he has switched to Standardbreds entirely, because it is the dominant racing form there. He has already slugged his way into the top 25 in the country in his new code of racing.

Secondly, many trainers are curious about various aspects of other racing breeds - what age they start youngsters, how they train them and so on. Few trainers outside America have the opportunity to read about the training of Quarter Horses. Thoroughbred trainers in England, where there is no Standardbred racing, would ask me if it was true about the 'huge' amounts of work they heard a trotter or pacer could stand.

I also found a curiosity about the great names of training in other codes. Thoroughbred trainers were interested in Stanley Dancer. Quarter Horse trainers were interested in Vincent O'Brien.

I would add a few reasons of my own. I find all forms of horse racing fascinating, and the differences and similarities are often the most fascinating part of all. More than that, the differences and similarities are illuminating, they tell us things. For example, the long gaps between serious workouts in Quarter Horses are serious food for thought for the Thoroughbred trainer who has a few sprinters in his stable. The Quarter Horse trainer preparing a horse for an 870 yard race, or for the Jeep Challenge (a 1000 yard race series between Thoroughbreds and Quarter Horses) could use a peek at some Thoroughbred trainer's tables.

Careful observation can lead to some interesting questions, and quite often to valuable conclusions. For example, in Australia, Standardbred trainers feed a lot less iron than Thoroughbred trainers. Standardbreds in Australia mostly race around a mile and a half, and the race time is much longer than for Thoroughbreds.

Is iron more necessary at the sprinting end of the spectrum? Should a five furlong runner get more iron than a mile and a half runner? A very valuable clue would be - how much iron do Quarter Horse trainers feed?

I wanted to determine the ingredients of success in trainers of the racing breeds. Most factors - luck, personality type, business approach, how they acquired training skills and so on - we can expect will be similar in all breeds. The BEST examples of some of the variations - e.g. forming public companies, dividing the responsibility for yearling selection , training and public relations - occur in one breed or another.

The trainer who doesn't think they can learn anything from reading how the top trainers in another breed made it to the top, is, in my opinion, a dolt. The trainer who doesn't see how looking over training programs from other breeds can give a new perspective on their own programs is suffering from a lack of imagination.

Why all the headings and numbers?

I have tried first and foremost to produce something that will help ordinary everyday trainers. It should also interest anyone else who wants to understand the ingredients of success in the top trainers. The numbering system will allow the reader to easily find and compare different trainers under any topic. A standard treatment, moving through time with the fortunes of the trainer, is much more readable but less useful. Within the limits of a cross- referencing number system, I have tried to preserve the fascinating lives of these people as stories.

Conclusions

Conclusions about individual trainers are in the individual sections but most comparisons and overall conclusions will be left to the last volume. The uniform layout makes finding topics simple. It is easy to run through the role of any one factor by going to that heading for each trainer. Most trainers covered later will be abbreviated to reduce the length but still convey the most interesting information. For this volume I wanted depth and detail, particularly for trainers as controversial as Wayne Lukas and Tommy Smith. I wanted to lay out the questions and the answers, show you all the evidence - not tell you I investigated and these are my conclusions. Those journalists who looked at the manuscript told me it needed tightening up, condensing. But the trainers and horse people seemed to find it fascinating in all its detail. Even those who found it a bit long would list different sections as the most suitable to be cut. In several instances, the section one person found least interesting was the bit another found most interesting. I now understand why, when journalists do condense something, there is always *someone* who cries butcher!

When I was interviewing English trainer Michael Stoute, (over a good white wine), he asked me, "Of all the trainers you've interviewed, which would you give a horse to train?" Of course he also wanted to know why. To decide at that time would have been premature, but at the end of all the interviews I will take up Michael Stoute's challenge.

Some other trainers, freezing in a New York January, wanted to know where I'd train if I was to take up training. So at the end I will take up that challenge too. I will stick my neck out and say where I'd train, what I'd train and why.

How To Become The Perfect Trainer?

Before interviewing any trainers, I thought hard about how someone would set about becoming a perfect trainer. The result was seven typed pages of questions. When I found out how little time I was to have with these very busy people I used the list to focus my attention on the most interesting questions for that particular trainer.

How to (try to) become a perfect trainer

A very good start is to be a descendant of a multi- generation dynasty of top trainers. This can be difficult to arrange *after* you are born. You should also be endowed with good health, tons of energy, a reduced need for sleep and a slowness to anger, as this is helpful around horses. Grow up adjacent to the stables, help as a strapper (groom) and become a jockey/ driver.

This might be squeezed in around a degree in business or vet science. Mostly the budding supertrainer keeps the wallet healthy by successful gambling at a racetrack near the university/ college. Upon graduating, let's say as a vet, you work for a short while with some top equine vets and then spend a year or two each with some of the most successful trainers around the world. Keep careful notes on their feeding and training. Meet some very wealthy horse owners. Impress them with your knowledge and enthusiasm.

At the same time you are going to major sales, selecting a phantom string of yearlings, and following their progress. Make notes on the anatomy of horses that win the major events. These activities are to sharpen the 'eye for a horse'. Study pedigrees. Devour books on horses - new and old. Shout knowledgeable old-timers a few ales in return for some useful clues from their lifetime of experience.

Decide where you would most like to set up as a racehorse trainer, then proceed to interest some clients in the buying of horses. Look around for an experienced head lad/ foreman, someone who has had a decade or two with a successful trainer or two. Someone who has fed and coddled a lot of winners. Etc.

Interviewing some of the world's leading trainers for this book I found a few that came surprisingly close to this 'formula'. Others came in from the strangest side tracks. Some had a poor start but surprised everybody by making it to the top. Clearly a lot of the 'perfect' track is not essential.

Some of the areas investigated may seem unimportant to the reader, so a brief explanation of their relevance follows.

2) What start in life did they have?

Some of the attributes and skills that would make up a perfect trainer are matters of heredity, parental example, early conditioning and early exposure. The best way to ensure that the right genes, attitudes and experiences are there would be for the parents to be top racehorse trainers themselves. The child ideally would live with the parents on or next to the stabling area. The growing child in such a case would see the way horses are handled, how staff are treated, how owners are managed - by someone who has succeeded and therefore has a proven approach to all these things.

Compare that start to one where the parents are bricklayers, accountants, shop assistants, teachers etc. A farming start would probably be second to an outright horsy background. Or would a business background be better?

Which are more frequently successful - children of top trainers, children of trainers, or children of 'outsiders'?

Birth Order

First-born children have been found in much larger than expected numbers in positions of corporate leadership. The rationale given is that they learn early to plan for, manage and manipulate the younger children. Second and later born go less for leadership and more for center stage activities. They will take risks to get attention. They are over- represented in dangerous sports and make 'more effective' fighter pilots. This is said to be because they have to compete with the oldest child for attention. Because the oldest child is always doing new things, the oldest is more interesting to the parents. The younger child has to try much harder to get parental attention. While young they often become some kind of entertainer or throw tantrums to get attention.

Where would 'racehorse trainer' fit in all this? To be a successful trainer means taking risks to be in the spotlight a lot, classic later child stuff. But to run a large business means managing staff and money. Is there a predominance of first-born among successful trainers? Or very few of them?

2.1 How much help were their parents?

Parents can help with obvious things like money and an education. There are less obvious ways - the directions they steer us in for example. When mothers are a strong influence, certain character traits, ambitions and professions predominate. Mothers especially like junior to go into occupations with high community status, low risk of injury and little unemployment;

occupations in which they wear a suit. Mother's notoriously steer their children into medicine, teaching and banking.

2.3 How far did they go at school?

Is it important to get a university degree to become a trainer? Is it important to be able to digest all that 'sports medicine'? Arguably such an education would also help in dealing with the wealthy class of people that usually own horses. They are often very well educated. Ideally the degree would have to have some relevance to be worth the time. I would go for a vet degree, possibly marketing or business management, as the most useful degrees. (Some of my cynical mates would suggest pharmacy or chemistry.)

Or would the time spent gaining that degree mean passing up a lot of valuable experience in stables, working with horses and trainers? Is it worth going past a basic education? Historically, racehorse training has been seen as an apprenticeship; start young at the bottom and work your way up. How much use is an education beyond basic reading, writing and arithmetic, to a trainer? Could it be that the three R's are enough?

2.4 What were their early ambitions?

Is training a primary ambition or something to do if you fail to qualify for something else?

3) How did they get their training skills?

How much is there to know about horses? Handling them, feeding them, keeping them happy and disease-free. As a vet in mixed practice, I have seen all levels of competence with horses and the results can be spectacularly different. Some clients regularly create calm manageable horses, others regularly create excitable problem horses. What is more, the first group can usually take the unmanageable product and make it docile. By extension, give two people the same horse and one year later you can have two very different horses. There is a lot to know, but it is not only a matter of time. Much depends on who you work for and who you work with. Small bits of information can drastically improve your ability to manage problem horses and problem people.

3.1 Is early experience with horses essential?

The best start would be to work with people who have a proven record with horses, be they trainers or just backyard horse owners. The age at which a person is exposed to these skills may have some significance. In our youth, we absorb like blotting paper when we first encounter something new - like horses. What we learn then becomes second nature. The worst scenario is to work with someone who gives bad advice and encourages sloppy habits in this same impressionable period ie. first exposure when young, to someone who is lazy or stupid.

At the extreme, has anyone who had nothing to do with horses until adulthood, made it to the top?

3.2 Experience as a rider/ driver/ jockey

Many jockeys, when they become old, overweight, or simply because they can't make a living as a jock, turn to training. Many Standardbred trainers drive their own but put a catch driver in the sulky on race night. A spell on or behind horses would give a trainer a useful insight into the problems of riders and drivers, and of race tactics.

3.4 Acquiring training skills

3.4-1 Did they work with a top trainer?

Training skills can be acquired by working at various levels for trainers of varying ability. The ideal? Assistant with a top trainer, eventually running the show or a branch for long periods. Even better, work with many top trainers. Each will usually have a 'specialty' - stayers, sprinters, feeding, conditioning etc. If you feed like A, fast work like B, and slow-work like C, will you obtain better results than any of them? Or will that only lead to a confusing hodge-podge? Is each successful trainer a single integrated solution, or do bits add up like so many wooden blocks to 'higher' results?

An alternative is having horses and learning by trial and error. This would seem to me to have the disadvantage of being a very slow way to learn, but does have three advantages - you are not constrained by 'tradition', you have seen the signs and experienced the results of too little work and too much work etc., and you will be a more careful observer.

I well remember how much progress I made whenever I worked with top vets early in my career. I doubt I could ever have made that much progress by myself, even in triple the time. For a self-taught trial-and-error trainer there are the additional hazards that some good horses (and clients) may be lost during the more incompetent trial and error period. Can a bad early reputation be overcome? Does one outstanding horse and a few eye-catching wins wipe all that out of potential owners' minds?

4) Starting off - how to obtain those first owners and horses (and dollars)

Work two jobs, save money, then start full time? Or one job and work a small string of horses before or after work? Work for a trainer until you can find enough clients of your own? Work for a trainer and apply for jobs as a private trainer to a big owner? How did the success stories start off?

4.1 How they got their first horses

Start with a few horses YOU have paid for? This would seem like suicide if you still have a lot to learn about selection and training. Even the top guys' clients are seldom in front. It reminds me of people who represent themselves in court. They are said to have a fool for a client. Perhaps a beginning trainer who is his own owner has a foolish owner. So how many have started that way?

4.3-1 Did they bet on horses?
This is the road to ruin unless you know your horses and study the form. But provided the gambling is small while it is 'unproductive', it can be a very useful form of education for a future trainer. Outside of the connections of the horses in the race, nobody watches a race as intently as someone with money on it. A diligent punter learns a lot about race tactics, pace as a destroyer of horses, the effect of weight etc. Once into full-time training there may not be time to study the form and bet successfully, but the lessons learned are applied placing horses in races they can win, giving instructions to jockeys, mapping a horse's campaign etc.

4.5 Age married and role of spouse
In many careers a spouse is almost an impediment to success - pop music, acting, sailing, professional golf. In others a spouse is indispensable, politics for example. Are singles able to concentrate more on the effort and do better?

Most trainers are men, but I think women will become a steadily increasing proportion of trainers. It might be thought the role of a wife in training horses would be very small, but many American trainers rely on the wife to run a farm and a family while they follow the racing circuit, sometimes a thousand miles away. Other wives have to live a gypsy existence, moving around with their husbands, shifting children from school to school many times per year. Sometimes the trainer's wife is an important part of his public relations, talking to the owners at the track, entertaining clients at home and dealing with out of hours phone calls. Some are right there at the stables in some role or another.

Then there is the emotional and financial disaster of divorce. With each divorce assets and incomes are split. So how many of the top guys have a wife at the stables every morning, how many stayed single, how many have been divorced many times?

8) Training
I had several pages of questions on this subject, an area of great interest to me, but it was the hardest on which to squeeze out answers.

8.3 Greater success with ?
2yo, 3yo or Older Horses?
Sprinters Or Stayers (Routers)?
Tied in with training programs, this gives clues to the ideal program for various categories of horse. For example if a trainer trains his horses often and hard and his best results are with older stayers, it would give you some clues about how to train your older stayers.

8.5 Placing horses in races.
One of the training greats of last century warned that a trainer, "must not become enamored of his own horses - bad betting and bad placement follow."

8.7-1 Shinsoreness
In some breeds all trainers have some cases but some have consistently more than others, possibly reflecting differences in programs. Do any trainers have ways of avoiding it? What do the breed differences tell us?

8.7-2 Tying up
Training programs and electrolyte mixtures have considerable bearing on the frequency of this condition.

8.10 Have they produced any good trainers?
Some top trainers produce other top trainers. Some don't. Why?

9.5 Additives
I tried to interest advertisers in giving information and illustrating products used by the trainers in the book, but the response was varied, and I decided to leave it until all the trainers have been covered.

13.3 The formulated approach
Whereas our personality is largely out of our control, something decided by the interaction of our genes and our upbringing, our business approach can to some extent be modified by conscious adoption of certain practices, responses, rules. Books abound in this field - on business management, staff motivation, time management, and how to sell yourself and your product. These self-molding practices are common in business, but how many of the top trainers are 'naturals' and how many have read the books and remade themselves?

Personal philosophy and religion might seem strange bedfellows for management techniques and how to make the best use of your time, but I have included them because someone with a personal philosophy has consciously reviewed their life and set its direction, and churchgoers do the same. At the other extreme is the theoretical possibility of a trainer who has never gone to church, never thought out a set of personal goals, never read any of the kind of books mentioned above. Has anyone made it to the top by just doing what they have to do, day by day, without long-term planning?

13.4 Any record of a positive swab?
This was a tricky area but one that had to be looked at. Some people in racing believe that everything they see on a racetrack, and everything a trainer does, revolves around the use of drugs. These people attribute everything - a trainer having a good patch, form reversals, improvements with age - everything - to drugs.

At the other extreme are the naive and the wishful thinking - the ostriches. Part of this group believes no sporting person would use such things. Another part comforts itself with the notion that there isn't anything that can make a horse race faster. The argument goes that nothing has been *proven* to improve performance.

Suffice to say that from my investigations it is my belief that some drugs DO improve racing performance. Trainer George Lambton, skeptical at first, proved it to himself and the English Jockey Club back in 1903. That led to the original ban on doping. I wish it wasn't true. I wish nothing but good feed and good training could make a horse run faster, but the evidence convinces me otherwise.

The natural consequence of that is to believe that trainers who use drugs and get away with it have a considerable advantage. I believe some trainers use drugs all their racing lives, at least until each particular drug becomes testable.

I also believe some trainers use drugs when they are small operations - but quit when they have some success. As their operation grows, using drugs becomes less attractive. Secrecy is more difficult and they have more to lose. As they become better known, more notice is taken of form reversals and the like. With better quality horses, in better quality races, they no longer need drugs to survive. As they win better grades of race at better tracks, the standard of detection technology increases. The stress of waiting for the swabs to clear is not worthwhile.

Some reformed dopers, forced by the size of their operation to stop using drugs themselves, join the cleanskins in their calls for more stringent drug testing. They may be very strong in their campaign because they *know* people are using 'gear' and they *know* the horses go faster.

That does not mean that a top trainer who campaigns hard against drugs in racing was once a drug user - the reformed drunk turned wowser. If you think you are the best conditioner of a racehorse at your track, then you know that if someone can stop the use and abuse of 'rocket booster juice' - *you will rule the roost.*

There is also a school of thought that says you can use drugs and get away with it if you are big. If you are a big fish, the authorities will only warn you, because they wouldn't want the bad publicity of ruling off a publicly known name. It is the little guys they jump on and make examples of. I have been told (and 95% convinced) of several examples of this, and if it is true, I think it is very unfair.

Even the non-user of doping drugs in horses has reasons for fear. The trainer, under the rules found in most parts of the world, is held liable for a positive swab in that trainer's horses regardless of the circumstances. This makes the trainer the 'absolute insurer', the one who will pay the penalty even if someone else gave the horse dope without the trainer's knowledge.

The object of the law is to make the trainer responsible for preventing doping by others, and therefore force the trainer to take every precaution - a good objective. The alternative, where a trainer could be penalised only if the authorities could prove the trainer was responsible, would make it nearly impossible to counter doping trainers.

The present absolute insurer rule, however, puts trainers at the mercy of 'over the wall dopers', of defective forensic labs, and of drug users in the forensic system. They are also at the mercy of their own employees and even vets, who may want to send the horse along a little faster to bet it themselves - unbeknown to the trainer. Employees could be approached by rivals to commit sabotage. Employees might do it for revenge over discipline, pay disputes etc., or out of jealousy. They may simply give the butazolidin sachet or other normal medication to the wrong horse.

Then there is the lack of a definite line between doping and legitimate use of additives or drugs for treatment. This is best seen in the area of vitamins. Vitamins are naturally occurring components of the diet. Horses take in vitamins in the feed and they also manufacture a lot in their bowel. Almost all trainers add vitamins to the feed. Some give vitamins periodically by injection. A few inject vitamins in megadoses on race day. They all do it to improve performance. Where is the line?

The same problem occurs with anti-inflammatory drugs. A horse has a sore knee after a race. It can be treated as close up to the next race as the rules allow, or it can be given a few days extra treatment knowing the test will still not pick it up, as is often the case. A trainer may switch the horse to a different anti-inflammatory, something that is seldom tested for. Says he's doing it for the horse or the owner.

Trainers have to wander about in a quagmire of gray areas on the edge of black, areas where there is often no clear demarcating line between legal and illegal. The progression from gray to black can be a gradual unintended thing or a deliberate decision. It can be a deliberate decision for quick profit, or to avoid failure.

The claiming trainer is particularly vulnerable when the drug detection system is failing. Horses claimed from a battling trainer improve dramatically for the trainer who claimed them, a man believed on the track to have 'something'. The improvement is seen by the battler's owners, fellow trainers, and family. With a tattered reputation, a mortgage to pay off, kids to educate, and owners defecting - what is this poor wretch going to do when someone offers him a drug that may improve his few remaining runners by 5 lengths? The same 'something' that a half dozen others have been rumored to be using with impunity for years.

A good example is cortisone given intravenously the day of the race. It goes on in Australia and America and probably the world. The drug policing bodies know it goes on, but find it very difficult to stamp out. This is because cortisone is produced naturally in the body, and when positive drug tests for cortisone are challenged in court, it is difficult to convince a judge or jury that it couldn't all have been produced by the horse. "This horse must have gotten a fright and produced all that cortisone."

"This horse must have had a bout of Cushing's Syndrome."

Whatever the excuses, there is an element of doubt and the result is a failure to get a conviction. The result is a widespread use of cortisone, which disadvantages the honest trainer. One study in Australia, reported in 1979, found traces of dexamethasone in 188 out of 206 post-race urine samples.

It is easy enough for the trainer to rationalize the use of illegal drugs. Hell man, it's not as if this is an ethical question involving human life and death! (Although when doped horses fall or breakdown it can be.) It is just getting on equal terms with rivals. It is protecting the family, providing for them. The only losers are some gamblers the trainer will never meet, some trainers who are already using the stuff - and a lot who aren't. But honor wasn't paying the bills. Heck if the authorities can't protect me from the chemical racing fraternity, then I have to protect myself by using the same thing.

So - have any top trainers had a positive swab? Or does the stigma ruin a trainer's chances of making it to the top? If any have had a positive drug test, was it in their lean and hungry days, or later? What is their side of the story?

13.5 Luck and other reasons for success

Is luck important in the rise of these trainers - or would they have risen to the top with the inevitability of cream? Do they make luck by hard work, by ingenuity, by refusing to give up? Or is it like the Bible says: ' . . . the race is not to the swift, nor the battle to the strong . . . but time and chance happeneth to them all.' Are there a dozen trainers on the backstretch, just as capable as the glamour boy, but unheard of and uncelebrated because they never had one or two of those great horses fall into their hands at the right time in their career?

13.8 What drives them?

The main motivations of achievers in the business world have been classified into:

> Social - status from social contacts and social standing; they love to socialize
>
> Fortune - they'll respect me because I have made a lot of money; they love money
>
> Independence - no one can tell me what to do
>
> Uniqueness - no one is quite like me, I can do something they can't

Any of these could be a motivation to become a trainer, but being your own boss seems to be a particular attraction. However, those seeking independence seldom feel a strong need to achieve anything more than a good living. Those seeking social fame or monetary fortune can seldom get enough. Studies of businessmen have shown that men who rely mainly on one of these four drives have different chances of success, depending on which one it is. Which drive or combination of drives produced the top trainers? Are there other forces at work such as love of horses, of the excitement of winning, of gambling? Luca Cumani of Newmarket, England describes himself as needing a 'fix' of racing and winning, preferably every day.

I hope you enjoy reading the book. I hope you find things to stimulate your interest, increase your understanding, and improve your chances of success.

Hollywood Park Racetrack from the air. The horses are still going to the post, so the patrons are at the betting windows. There are plenty of cars. Older barns among trees lower right. Newer barns middle right. Wayne's stable is in the newer barns.

A turf race at Hollywood Park. Turf races are not common in America, and many tracks don't have a turf course. Dirt tracks are favored because American tracks usually race 4 - 6 days per week, 9 - 12 races per day, for months. Turf cannot stand up to that much work.

D. WAYNE LUKAS

Wayne Lukas is the most amazing phenomenon in any kind of horse racing in the world today. He left teaching at 31 years of age to train racehorses full-time. After becoming the king of wins, stakes races and money in Quarter Horses, he switched over to Thoroughbreds and has again taken the throne in wins, stakes races and money. He has dominated Thoroughbred racing in North America since 1983 and dominated it so thoroughly that there is no visible challenger to him at this time. What personality traits, skills and strategies have enabled him to rise rapidly to the top of two very competitive racing arenas, one after the other?

**Was: No. 1 Quarter Horse
Trainer in U.S.A.
Now: No. 1 Thoroughbred
Trainer in U.S.A.**

LOS ANGELES, CALIFORNIA, U.S.A.

Lukas has achieved his successes without family wealth or a family background in horses. He has never worked for any other trainer, yet he has developed the skills of racehorse training and yearling selection to a very high level.

Starting at age seven, with a pony called 'Queenie,' he progressed to horse trading to make money while attending high-school and university. He graduated from university with a master's degree thesis in physical education. He knows in detail the structure of muscle, the role of lactic acid and the advantages and disadvantages of interval training.

More importantly, Wayne studied the anatomy of the horse and now has a considerable understanding of what determines a horse's gait and running speed. By observing the speed of thousands of horses, he has been able to catalogue anatomical traits according to their usefulness in producing winners on the track.

Armed with that mental catalogue, Lukas has gone to the public auctions, and year after year, bought horses that have proved to be amongst the cream of their crop. Not surprisingly, he has been able to find wealthy backers. With them to sign the checks, he has challenged Robert Sangster and the Sheiks at the megabuck select Thoroughbred yearling sales. It is a game they all enjoy and one in which Lukas at least, is coming out financially ahead.

Not everyone will agree with the above summary. Wayne Lukas has many detractors, many critics. Some criticize the man, some his methods. "D. Ranged Lukas," they like to call him. Some say he can't train and attribute his success to a smooth tongue and large numbers of horses. They argue that from such large numbers anyone would produce some champions.

There was another 'explanation' of Lukas's success, an explanation I encountered frequently around the barns in 1987. One common version started off, "Do you know why Wayne Lukas can't win a Kentucky Derby?" The story said he had bought someone off in the swabbing boxes in New York and in California. Samples containing drugs were swapped for uncontaminated ones. Naturally he could use whatever drugs he liked in those states, but his horses had to run on their merits in Kentucky. "He has had a positive swab you know." I heard these stories before the victory of Winning Colors in the 1988 Kentucky Derby. Her win seemed to discredit the drugs story a little.

Then, early in 1989, cocaine and one of its metabolites were found in stored swabs, including one from a Lukas horse.

Wayne Lukas at Hollywood Park Race-track, Inglewood, Los Angeles.

These samples were tested at the request of the Horsemen's Association. The presence of the metabolite implied the drug had not been added after sample collection, that it must have gone through the horse's system.

Read on and make up your own mind about what makes Wayne Lukas the most successful trainer in horse racing today.

2. What start in life did Wayne have?

Wayne's early years are well docu-

---

mented in racing magazines. His rapid and seemingly inexplicable rise, his willingness to talk, and his flair for saying controversial and quotable things have attracted journalists to his stables like horses to oats. There have been articles on Lukas in just about every Thoroughbred and Quarter Horse magazine in the world. Much of the information on his early years traces back to one thoroughly researched article by Sports Illustrated senior writer William Nack.

Darrell Wayne Lukas was born on September 2, 1935 in Antigo, Wisconsin. Antigo is a small town. Its population nowadays is 8,600. When William Nack went there in 1985 to talk to Wayne's parents and to dig up some background on the emerging superstar of racing, he found an area known primarily for potato farms, dairies and lumber yards.

It is an area of dense forest. The pines and the white-barked birch remind an Australian of pictures of Canada. This is hardly surprising when Canada is just a few hundred miles to the north. It is a region of rich silted meadows set in the floors of valleys. The expanses of flat country are small, limiting farming to small operations. Tourism is a major summer industry, the main draw being the many fish-filled lakes. In winter all trees except the conifers lose their leaves, the lakes freeze over, and snow lies several feet deep. Of the few people who keep horses, most kept them in barns in winter. Some shipped them south.

Such was the countryside in which Wayne grew up. Wayne was the second of three children. The oldest was a sister, Dauna, 18 months older than Wayne. Brother Lowell was two and a half years younger.

I asked Wayne's mother why he was officially called Darrell, but known as Wayne. "That is strange," she said, thinking hard. "It seems we just started calling him Wayne. We never did start calling him Darrell, I don't know why."

2.1 How much help were his parents?

Wayne's parents were not wealthy, but they put time into their children while they were still young. They gave them the kind of freedom that develops a child's independence and from that other abilities develop.

Mother Bea (Beatrice) is of English and Irish descent. The surname Lukas is found in a belt across Europe including Sweden and Germany. Wayne's father was the son of Czechoslovakian immigrants. "My husband's mother and father met over here but they were both from the province of Bohemia. You could say Wayne's father was a purebred Bohemian." Father Ted Lukas drove heavy construction equipment and delivered milk when Wayne was young. Later he worked for the government in the construction industry. Ted Lukas was described by Bea as a brilliant person, a very progressive man with a good business head on his shoulders. The family lived on 10 acres (4 hectares) near the town.

All three children went on to college (university). That suggests Mr and Mrs Lukas were doing something right when it came to turning out bright children. They gave their children a very solid work ethic and the ambition to aim high. They were very successful parents in this regard, because all three children achieved a master's degree or better at university. Ted and Bea must have been what you might call a very good 'nick' in breeding terms.

The main ingredients for raising academically successful children are lots of reading to them, lots of talking to them and lots of the parent's time, especially in the pre-school years.

"You have raised three impressive children. Did you read to them a lot when they were little?"

"Yes. Oh yes." Her voice implied *lots*.

"Did you treat them like adults?"

"I treated them as my equal. I never talked baby talk to them. We let them assume responsibility at an early age. They were running riding camps - stables -for the big holiday resorts when they were 14. Wayne's brother did the same thing, but he did it for the monetary reward. If Wayne had not been paid he would still have done something in the same line for nothing. He said he was doing what he wanted to do and being paid for it."

"Was Wayne competitive or cooperative as a child?"

"Everything that he faced was a challenge to him and he faced every challenge head-on. He never ever was too dependent on anyone." Each was allowed to do their own thing, no one told them what they had to do. The kids were cooperative when they needed to be.

2.2 Was Wayne's family in racing?

Wayne's parents were not at all involved in horses or racing, but they let Wayne develop his talent for working with horses.

Clyde Rice was a schoolboy who lived nearby. He also became a racehorse trainer. When he was 7 or 8 years old he met Wayne who was several years older. What was Wayne like then? "Wayne was very outgoing, always. He was very positive. He was a natural leader. We rode our ponies around together." Clyde's family was much more involved in horses, and raced some Quarter Horses at fairs.

2.3 How far did Wayne go at school?

Bea and Ted only completed high-school themselves, "But," says Bea, "We were determined that each of the three children would have a college education. At that time that was a great sacrifice." (College in America is the same as university in other countries, and university fees in America run between 2,000 to 20,000 dollars per year.) Even if it was a sacrifice, the family has continued the drive to education.

"My daughter has five doctors in her family -three are PhD's and two are MD's (doctors)."

"What made you so determined to push your children

"We realized it was an essential part of getting along in this world today. We saw what schooling did for them not only in education but socially in learning how to deal with people and cope with situations."

"It's funny though. Wayne's grade-school teacher said he would never graduate from the 8th grade. His high-school teacher said he would never graduate from high-school. He had a habit of getting by with his jokes, but he wasn't doing very well. He learned to study at college. You learn to study or you get out at college."

"Was watching TV a factor?"

"No, we didn't have a TV at that time. The day he got his master's degree we were at the ceremony. He came up afterward and said, 'I have my master's degree and neither my grade-school teacher nor my high-school teacher have theirs.'"

2.4 What were Wayne's early ambitions?

Wayne's early activities were saturated with horses. Bea will proudly tell you that from the age of 14, Wayne worked every summer on a farm, ranch or racetrack. He ran a stable of horses for a holiday ranch. It was a sign of things to come. Wayne wanted to do something in horses but felt teaching was a safer, surer career path. Also his mother wanted him to do something useful; make a contribution to society. She didn't want him hanging around the horse barns all the time. Today she says his foresight in going into the horse business was greater than his mother's.

The Lukas family is still close. Wayne speaks of his parents, his brother and his sister with great admiration. In recent years Wayne always took his parents to California for Christmas. "He sent his jet to pick us up and take us to Arcadia. We were there for a couple of weeks and his jet would take us back. Our Christmases were . . . spectacular is the only word I can think of, because Christmas was one of the highlights of Wayne's life. Second to horses."

Bea gets *The Blood-Horse* and another magazine whose name she couldn't remember to help her keep track of her famous son.

3. How did Wayne get his training skills?

Wayne's home state, Wisconsin, helps to keep Lake Superior and Lake Michigan from becoming one big lake. It is part of swathe of country settled predominantly by Lutherans. In Wayne's youth Wisconsin allowed some organized horse racing, but not with betting. What racing there was, was small-time fairground stuff.

Although there was no interest in horses in Wayne's family, Bea told me proudly: "Wayne has a natural God-given talent with horses. From the time he was an infant he had a way

with horses, an understanding with horses. I like to say he spoke their language. But he could do things with horses that more accomplished horsemen couldn't. He could relate to them in such a way that they responded."

"Any idea how that talent came about?"

"My mother was a horsewoman from Kentucky, and I believe that talent was passed down in the genes. Neither of the other children had that talent. They have their own talents but neither had Wayne's talent with horses."

Much of Wayne's animal management skills were acquired in the process of his entrepreneurial advances, which occurred at an astonishingly early age. One of his first efforts was to sell young rabbits as Easter bunnies at Easter. He did his best to arrange the matings so that the little rabbits would be the right age at Easter. Wayne was so young at the time that he himself doesn't remember doing it, but his mother does and it is a well established part of Wayne's 'legend' within the family.

Amongst Wayne's early animal husbandry experiences was the hand-rearing of calves, a common thing in dairy areas. It is a good way to learn about feeding and disease control if large numbers are reared.

3.1 Any early experience with horses?

When Wayne was seven years old (according to Bea - but four or five years old according to some reports), his parents acquired a pony called Queenie, on which he did many of the usual 'kid and pony' things - exploring the district, racing other kids and their ponies etc. He also used her to deliver newspapers, one round in the morning and one round at night.

While as young as eight or nine he began to buy and sell horses. He was so young and so small his father had to instruct the auctioneer to take his bid. He was fortunate in being able to go to many sales with an older friend of his father's. According to his mother, he developed more than a commercial interest in horses. After a short introduction, he would have the horse following him around. He seemed to have a very real and mutual affinity for them.

Wayne's father told Bill Nack he particularly remembered Wayne's early self-confidence: "He was just SO sure of himself." A trait that has certainly continued to the present day, and an essential one for rapid progress and daring exploits.

Wayne advanced swiftly at an age when many children would not know how to spell the word 'profit,' let alone 'entrepreneurial'. Aged just nine, he rented a two acre paddock from an uncle and planted string beans. These he harvested with paid help from other children and sold to a local cannery at a good profit.

"If his father had a good business head he'd have been delighted with this effort of Wayne's."

"Oh yes, oh yes."

This is what you call a crowd. They were there to see Ferdinand and Alysheba clash on Hollywood Gold Cup day 1988. In a wealthy area like California, this crowd creates a big betting turnover and consequently big prize money. Even so, Hollywood has had to experiment with evening racemeets to combat falling crowds.

Wayne was usually in bed by 7pm so he could rise at 4am to tend his calves and horses, and deliver his papers before schooltime. Even without television, The Great Time Absorber, he didn't have enough hours in the day.

3.2 Experience as a rider or jockey?

Wayne began racing his pony at the Antigo County Fairgrounds. As he got older he went to fairgrounds 30 to 50 miles away. He developed a teenage fascination with horses and horsemen. His idols at the time had cheap horses on what was known as the 'leaky roof circuit,' but the young Wayne was plenty happy to hang on every word of their horse wisdom.

Being admired probably wasn't a common experience for some of these guys, so they were pleased to answer Wayne's questions. They showed him their tricks for handling difficult horses and patching up their legs. The class of horses this circuit attracted probably needed a lot of patching up. Wayne recollects: "I'd sit there and listen to those guys tell stories by the hour, and I'd pick their brains."

Wayne and his friend Clyde Rice were training and breaking a few horses for friends when Wayne reached high-school. From that they went into minor buying and selling of horses, then turned 'professional' to help pay their way through university. One of their problems was finding enough horses, so they turned to an unusual source of supply.

Hundreds of miles to the west of Wayne's home in Wisconsin, in the Dakotas, there were hundreds upon hundreds of wild horses, the famed mustangs. These animals were something of a pest to farmers, ranchers and national parks, and they were being trapped in big roundups and sold. They didn't make good riding horses unless expertly and completely broken in. Consequently most were bought for petmeat. Many ended up in Wayne's home state because there were mink ranches there.

Mink are a meat-eating, ferret-like animal, the skin of which produces that ultimate status symbol so much loved by status-conscious women, the mink coat. The Great Lakes area is one of the largest mink farming areas outside Russia.

Wayne and Clyde attended the sales and saved many a horse from becoming 'mink meat'. Clyde's wife told me they bought up to 30 or 40 at a time, enough to fill a railway truck, which was how they got them home. This experience was invaluable. Breaking and gentling the wild, frightened mustangs from the Dakotas took 5 or 6 months, but gave Wayne great insight into the minds of horses. In Clyde's words, "We served our dues. We didn't make much money on each one, but on those numbers, we made some money." Even then Wayne was buying 'typey' horses with good conformation.

Wayne and Clyde graduated to better horses at the grade horse auctions where the trade was in ranch and riding horses. They didn't take as much time to break and train or retrain, but they cost more and were more likely to be carrying

Wayne's Quarter Horse days show clearly in his horse and equipment, as he rides back from the track to the barn.

some chronic leg problem than the Mustangs. Wayne began to learn about things like ringbone and spavin. The prices and risks were greater, but if you were smart, so were the turnover and profits. Clyde Rice maintains that he made enough to pay his way through his university training to become a teacher.

Wayne and Clyde would make trips to sales in a pickup truck with a two-horse trailer behind, selling the horses they took and buying another couple to improve. Some just needed a good brush up, some needed more.

"We went down into Iowa and Nebraska . . . buying and selling. We'd buy two at one sale, shampoo'em, clip'em, pull their manes, clean'em up and sell'em the next day. We'd go through Friday, Saturday and Sunday, and we'd roll the money over two or three times and then try to beat the first check to the bank. I got streetwise in a hurry about horses. You learn to judge what a good one looks like and what a bad one looks like and what somebody will pay and won't pay." Today Wayne's barns have shelves and more shelves of different shampoos, presumably a legacy of skills he developed shining up horses for the sales.

Although it meant a lot of travel to nearby states, he went to a lot of racetracks too. Wayne took out his Quarter Horse trainer's license at 16 and his Thoroughbred trainer's license for bush tracks when he was 17. It was at this time that Wayne's appreciation of a horse's anatomy and conformation began to take shape. He was assessing horses for a multitude of purposes - racing, comfortable all-day riding, cutting out cattle, jumping etc. Later this assessment of conformation

would be very deliberately sharpened when he went into Quarter Horse racing.

Wayne was not aiming for a career as a horse trader, it was simply his most successful means of making money. Nor was racehorse training on his career agenda. He had given training some thought but it had not been financially feasible at the time. With mother Bea urging the Lukas kids, "do something useful with your life," education was still first on the list of priorities. Becoming a teacher had the great advantage that there was enough time in the summer vacation for Wayne to train and deal in horses.

In addition, Wayne, like millions of other teenage boys, desperately wanted to make it as some kind of athlete. When Wayne wants to achieve something he tries a lot harder than almost anyone else, but the natural talent was not there. It was a disappointment to him but later he would try for the next best thing -coaching. Coaching would still allow him to be a factor, to apply his great energy and intensity. Wayne could never be a mere spectator.

His idol of long standing was that model motivational coach, the legendary Vince Lombardi. At the summit of his career Lombardi coached the Green Bay Packers, an American Football team, to take out the first two Super Bowls. Green Bay was the nearest big town to Antigo, some 90 miles away.

If Wayne was disappointed to miss out on the school sporting scene, he was completely unfussed to miss out on the school social scene. Even at university he had little time for girls and none for beer swilling although he did sign up with one of the notorious fraternity houses. "I didn't have any time for that . . . I was always working, always hustling, always trying to hit the sales."

When I asked Clyde about those years - was Wayne that disinterested in the girls and the social life -he paused for a long time: "Well, I would only say he wasn't as dedicated as he is now."

College, teaching and coaching

Wayne attended the University of Wisconsin at the campus in La Crosse, less than 100 miles from his home. It is a small city of around 40,000 on the magnificent Mississippi River, which at that point forms the border with Minnesota.

"You did your major in physical education?"

"I did education, but I have a major in physical education. I only taught physical education one year, then I taught in the class room."

"Muscle structure, lactic acid, interval training, exercise prescriptions-" Wayne was nodding his head emphatically.

"Yes, all of that."

"Was that useful later when you were learning how to train horses?"

"Yes, it sure was, and it still is."

After graduation in 1958, the 22 year old Wayne took a post as teacher at the high-school in the small farming town of Blair - population 900. He also was appointed basketball, football and track (athletics) coach. For Wayne, an important thing about Blair was that it was only some 25 miles from the university in La Crosse. Wayne wanted to stay close because although he continued to buy, sell and race horses, his major ambition at this time was to become a University basketball coach. So he stayed close to the University town and he studied every known strategy and system.

To pursue his coaching ambition he left Blair after two years to go back to the University of Wisconsin at La Crosse. There he became assistant to basketball coach Johnny Orr. In his two years there he completed a master's degree and developed a training shoe for athletes.

"What did you do your thesis on?"

"I did my Master's degree on the overload principle. I invented a basketball shoe that was one ounce per size heavier than a normal shoe. I wrote my thesis on that."

The training shoe was identical to the competition shoe except it was heavier than the competition shoe, so that players felt extra nimble and fleet-footed during the game. This concept was taken by coach Orr to Converse, a company that produced athletic footwear.

"I eventually sold the shoe to the leading basketball shoe company in the country. I did very well on that by the way. I designed it in the basement."

Orr summed up Lukas this way for William Nack: "Wayne was a very energetic guy, very intelligent, articulate and neat as hell . . . When I got my first head-coaching job at Massachusetts, I couldn't take an assistant. If I could have I'd have taken Wayne with me."

Where would Wayne be now? Big league basketball coach?

Wayne Lukas as a teacher and coach

But Johnny Orr couldn't take an assistant coach, so in 1961 Wayne became head basketball coach at Logan High-School, in La Crosse. In the classroom Wayne taught a course called American Problems. It looked at the whole gamut - economic, civic and social problems.

The diligent detective Nack dug up Wayne's assistant coach from those days and some of the student players. He found that Lukas is remembered from this era as a firm disciplinarian, in the class and on the court. With coach Lukas, if you didn't play the game his way you didn't play at all.

Logan was a blue-collar working area and Wayne became well known for his efforts to upgrade his players in all departments, especially off the court. He regularly brought in a lady to instruct the players on how to dress, how to eat, how to order and tip in a restaurant. His players had to be polite to umpires. When Wayne arrived at Logan, many of the students were aimless. He changed that, giving his players objectives. "He didn't just coach you on the floor, he taught you how to run your life," one of his players told the reporter years later.

Around this time he was heavily into motivational techniques and he led by example. He was always on time, prepared, organized and well dressed - like someone out of Esquire. Said one of his players, "You went to a game, you felt you were on Mount Everest, even if you had three tubes of Clearasil [acne cream] in your pocket. He made you feel like a special person."

According to the assistant coach, most of the other teachers in the school envied Wayne because of the respect the students showed him. This was not only because of his athletics coaching, but also his classroom work. "The others did not feel they could get close to him. He was on a pedestal as far as they were concerned. We felt he was on a level higher than us."

By the time he left, Wayne was known as a tough coach with a man-to-man defense style, but a record of 44 wins to 95 losses. Nobody, however, considered that poor record to be any fault of Wayne's. Wayne in fact showed a great ability to motivate people, in the class room and on the sportsfield. But the major determinant of success in high-school basketball is the number of tall boys. This is a function of school size and ethnic composition. In addition, wealthy schools may bring in talent with that American phenomenon 'athletic scholarships'. (an oxymoron?)

Someone from a neighboring school told me of a game

against Wayne's team. "If we could have found him after the game we would have lynched him," he said smiling ruefully. "His top players were a lot better than our top players, but we still rotated our ordinary and better players. Not Wayne - he played his five best players right through the game and beat us 100 to 25."

"Was there a points bonus in winning by a wide margin?"

"No."

Unable to find Wayne and lynch him, they contented themselves with nasty rumors about coach Lukas and one of the cheerleaders.

Right through this period Lukas continued with his Quarter Horses. He rose at 4am to drive 60 miles to Rochester, which was over the Mississippi river in Minnesota. After working his horses, he drove home to shower, change and begin a day's teaching. That was followed by coaching in the basketball season. Energy and drive in abundance.

During this time Wayne married and his wife Janet had a son they named Jeffrey. Wayne raced his horses around Minnesota and the Dakotas during the spring months of the teaching year. Kenny Schoeph was a jockey who rode for Wayne then. He's now a horse identifier and patrol judge at Canterbury and other tracks. He remembers Wayne ran a string of 20 horses which he often left in the care of a trusted employee during the teaching week. Even when Wayne went training full time, Kenny recalls Wayne being away a lot. He remembers Janet driving up for weekends and the Lukas's staying at motels.

As a teacher, Wayne was able to get around the country every summer during the long American school vacation - 12 to 14 weeks of it! The short, intense racing seasons of the numerous American tracks made it easy to find one that ran during the break. Wayne raced both Thoroughbreds and Quarter Horses at this time. He would settle into the Park Jefferson racetrack some 300 miles west in South Dakota, or Centennial 800 miles away in Denver, Colorado. Jefferson's season suited perfectly - July and August. He lived out of his camper, which he parked right by his stables.

Wayne's barn at this time already carried two of his hallmarks - it was spotlessly clean and it was landscaped with grass, potted shrubs and bright flowers. In classic Quarter Horse style, Wayne wore blue jeans. Every day he wore a shirt fresh from the cleaners. When Janet was not with him he lived on the barn site, using the side mirror of his pick-up truck as a shaving mirror. He learned heaps about his horses and did much of the work himself. While he did all that work, Wayne had a lot of time to think.

3.3 Why did Wayne become a trainer?

Wayne was very successful as a teacher and basketball coach at this time, but he was also very successful as a racehorse trainer. With a few wins he got more and better horses. Then he won stakes races and set records. Every year at the end of summer, he had to pass a team of fit racehorses to other trainers and go back to school. Every year he was more successful and every year going back to school was harder.

One of Wayne's pupils from those years, Terry Mueller, told me Wayne would sometimes set the history class an assignment, then settle into some horse-racing books at his table out the front. Terry was not impressed.

Wayne's problem was that most of the Quarter Horse action - and virtually all of the money - was 800 to 1600 miles away. While teaching, Wayne had been able to test himself out as a trainer during the long summer vacations. He had great self confidence and he could see a future for himself in this exciting and increasingly wealthy sport. How much of the draw was excitement and how much was monetary, only Wayne knows, but there can't have been a lot of Quarter Horse trainers making more than a teacher at that time.

When Wayne quit teaching in 1967 he knew very well what he was going into. He also knew that with his excellent reputation in teaching, he could always go back to it. It was no risk - or so it must have seemed.

Speaking many years later, Wayne was quoted as saying that he left basketball coaching and went into racing because he realized he had made a mistake going into basketball: "Racing is a captivating business, I don't know anyone who's ever left it for good after they've been involved to any degree. I know people who have tried, but once you're involved you never really leave fully. There is a certain lure there. It's the challenge, the competition, the excitement. And if you're successful it's a very lucrative business."

I think it is very revealing that Wayne speaks of 'why he left basketball coaching' and not 'why he left teaching.'

Why Quarter Horses?

In 1967 Wayne was training Quarter Horses and Thoroughbreds, but Quarter Horse racing was booming. In that year, when Wayne Lukas was wondering whether or not to quit teaching, the gross purse for the All-American Futurity was $486,600 and the dramatic annual increases meant it would be appreciably higher the next year. In the same year the Kentucky Derby was worth only $162,200 - a decrease on the previous year. Quarter Horse sales were enjoying record entries and record prices. Rich futurities, imitations of the booming All-American, were sprouting everywhere.

Wayne had success with his Quarter Horses and so he was given more Quarter Horses to train. It was a time of very rapid expansion in the breed. It was not so much a decision between the two by Wayne, more a matter of which way the numbers went in the barn. Thoroughbreds were simply squeezed out of

Wayne's operation.

3.4 Acquiring his training skills
Wayne had developed some buying and selling skills as a horse trader. He had learned some skills as a teacher and coach. How did he learn the skills of racehorse training?

3.4-1 Did he work with a top trainer?
Wayne did not work for another trainer, in Quarter Horses or Thoroughbreds.

3.4-2 Did he watch other trainers?
Wayne told me specifically - No. Deliberately - No. Wayne is adamant he has worked out everything himself, although he did mention watching others in an early magazine interview.

"Did you go and watch specific Thoroughbred trainers at any stage?"

"Never. Never in my life. I never watched them, I never worked for anybody."

"You were never curious - oh, there's a big name. I must go and see how he works his horses?"

"No. I've been observant of people, you know, over the years, but I've never really tried to pattern myself after any style."

"Well, not necessarily pattern, but just go and see what they do."

"No. Never happened. Always been trial and error."

3.4-3 Did he try published workouts
I don't know of any regular published track workouts in Quarter Horses. The Equine Research book *Conditioning to Win* contained some general guidelines on training but did not come out until 1974. By then Wayne was already dominating Quarter Horse racing.

3.4-4 Reading, seminars, asking questions
Wayne must have asked a few questions, certainly he had some for Jack Brainard, but later he was more interested in the results of his own training experiments.

3.4-5 Experiments and experience
Wayne has a good scientific understanding of training. He uses that to learn from his own observations: "Everything I know about horses I formulated in my own mind or learned from trial and error. I never worked for another trainer, I never watched another trainer, I never even discussed training with another trainer. Jeff has never worked for another trainer either. (Wayne's son Jeff later became an assistant trainer to Wayne)"

"Have you had employees tell you what trainers they had previously worked for, would do in a certain situation?"

"Yes, but we don't take any notice. We've hardly ever employed anyone who has worked for another trainer. Even if they have, they are so overwhelmed by our organization that they never say anything. Charlie Perez, my foreman here (at Hollywood Park at the time), he worked for Charlie Whittingham, for about a year I think, but he never ever mentions it."

4. Starting out on his own

4.1&2 How he got his first horses and clients
There were people around Wayne's home who had racehorses. Wayne's friend Clyde was from a family that trained racehorses, mostly Quarter Horses, in a small way. But Wayne's first racehorses came from a man in a neighboring state, a man who was looked up to by Wayne and many other horsemen. Jack Brainard not only helped Wayne get his first horses, he helped him understand horses.

Jack had a Quarter Horse training establishment in Rochester Minnesota. There he trained pleasure horses, roping horses and reining horses. He recalls meeting Wayne around 1959 when Wayne was "a schoolteacher at La Crosse."

"Wayne had a horse, a cutting horse, and he was having some problems with it, so I invited him up to my ranch. He came up on weekends and hung around and I helped him and he told me he'd like to train a racehorse. I told him, 'If you want to train racehorses I'll find some horses for you'. I went to the phone and got him the first five horses he ever trained and he trained them at my ranch. I got those horses from friends of mine."

"Where did Wayne race them?"

"We'd organized a Minnesota Quarter Horse Racing Association and we built a track at our house. We had a starting gate and we had the first Minnesota Racing Futurity right there at our house. The prizemoney was $3000."

"How well did Wayne's horses do?"

"Wayne didn't train the winner of that futurity, but he later trained horses for the winning owner."

In 1967, going training full-time was on Wayne's mind, but Janet, with a nine-year-old son at foot, was far from keen.

"One day he came to me and said, 'I'd like to quit teaching school and go to training horses permanently, but Janet doesn't think I should. She's raising hell with me. What do you think about it?' So I said, 'If I was you I'd give that school board two months notice and I'd bid them goodbye because you can make it in this business."

"Where did Wayne start off?"

"He raced out at Park Jefferson in South Dakota and then he said he needed to go to a warmer climate, so he went down to a little old track somewhere in Oklahoma. He hung around there that winter with 2 or 3 horses and of course starved out there. Then he went down to Uvalde, Texas and starved out there. From there he went over to Sunland Park in El Paso,

New Mexico and that's when he started to get some better clientele and some better horses."

Wayne's high regard for this older horseman shines through when he talks about Jack. "He just knows so much. He could understand what went on in a horse's mind, tell you why it did things. That is essential for racing or anything you do with horses." These days Jack Brainard lives in Texas but they are still 'old buddies'.

In 1967 Wayne was rising 32 years of age when he left teaching for full-time Quarter Horse training. It wasn't an easy decision. He told one journalist that he anguished over it, wrote letters and tore them up. But eventually he made the decision and left teaching. He chose Oklahoma, possibly because it was central to the Quarter Horse region of New Mexico, Oklahoma and Texas. Later he shifted to Uvalde, Texas.

In 1968, Wayne's first full year of training, he made it into second place for number of winners. Included was a win in the Northeast Kansas Futurity, total purse $11,060. Almost topping the wins table was without doubt a good effort, but perhaps not as amazing as it might sound. In those days there were not many full-time trainers, able to follow the action over Texas, Oklahoma, New Mexico and surrounding states. Prizemoney in Oklahoma and Texas was hard to come by. A trainer could win a lot of races and starve.

Wayne moved to El Paso which is also in Texas, but right at the western end, on the border with New Mexico. He was trying to find the best base. El Paso was the nearest city to Ruidoso Downs, which was about 140 miles north. Ruidoso had fat purses and the Quarter Horse was king. Owning, racing and talking Quarter Horses was a way of life.

Wayne did not wait to build up a name at lesser tracks, acquire a strong team of talented horses and *then* move to the top tracks. In a very short span of time he tried out the backwaters and then moved to Mecca. Bob Moore remembers Wayne having only a very few horses when he first met him at Ruidoso.

In 1969 he failed to make even the top ten in winners, but he may have earned more money than the previous year. He was learning and he wasn't easily discouraged.

Wayne started to make real progress when he arrived in New Mexico. Janet and Jeff joined him. At Sunland Park in El Paso and at the home of the All-American, Ruidoso Downs, he began to meet some of the wealthiest people in America. One of his earliest wealthy owners was Mr Bunn. Mr Bunn had been in Quarter Horses for years, but when he joined up with Wayne he had a lot of success. Bunn paid for a lot of horses and won a lot of races. He unfortunately died young, but not before giving Wayne a very good start.

Wayne began to make a name for himself. In 1970 he notched up 73 wins from 347 starters. Nowadays that doesn't seem like a real lot of wins, but back then there were fewer meets, fewer days in a meet and perhaps 6 or 8 races on the day. Today there are often 10 or 12 races on a day's program. In 1970, 73 wins was enough to make him leading trainer nationally on number of wins - in just his 3rd full season. That same year, 1970, he met owner Bob Moore. Sitting in the office of his Cadillac dealership in Oklahoma City, Mr Moore remembered meeting Wayne at Ruidoso: "Must have been 1970."

"How did you meet Wayne?"

"I guess we just introduced ourselves."

"What was your first impression of him?"

"He was a very good handicapper. He watched the horses and did a good job."

"Did he use that information for betting or for buying the horses?"

"In those days he didn't have that much to do."

"He didn't have many horses?"

"No."

"Did he hustle you to get some horses?"

"No he didn't."

"Did he watch other trainers work their horses?"

"Well, Wayne gets up very early."

"You did put some horses with Wayne though."

"He took Mr Jet Moore to California for me, in a trailer, and later the horse became a champion." Mr Jet Moore was trained by Newt Keck at Ruidoso, and by Earl Holmes at Los Alamitos in 1972, the year the horse was World Champion.

Wayne seems to have had horse and business dealings with Mr Moore, but Wayne did little training for him.

Wayne met Melvin Hatley, who made his money in oil, construction, land development and banking. I asked Wayne if he approached Hatley or the other way round. "He approached me. I trained some horses for him, we became friends and eventually partners."

Melvin Hatley had already been in Quarter Horses for some years when he took up with Wayne. I asked Mr Hatley how they got started. He said, "I bought a stakes-winning mare that Wayne was training and I left her with him to train. That's how I got to be close friends with him."

"If you left your horse with him for training, you must have known something about him?"

"I knew he was one of the top trainers in the country, had been for several years. I wouldn't have left her with him if I hadn't known that."

Clearly Hatley came on the scene when Wayne was well on his way.

"What was your first impression on meeting him?"

"I don't recall, but I always liked Wayne. He's a very impressive young man, highly educated, very articulate and enthusiastic. I guess the outstanding thing about him is his enthusiasm for what he does. He's a very interesting person to be around. We just hit it off. I have a lot of respect for people who work hard, have enthusiasm and pride in what they are doing."

Melvin Hatley bought into Mr Jet Moore in his three-year-old year when the horse went on to become 1972 World Champion Quarter Horse. Hatley also owned the Lukas-trained Native Empress at one time. In one interview some years back, Lukas said of Hatley: "He's not only a business associate but probably as close a friend as I have in the world."

Some other very rich owners Wayne recruited in his days in New Mexico included Barry Beal and Lloyd R. (Bob) French Jr., an oilman. They are often said to be two of the wealthiest men in Texas, but neither made it into the Forbes magazine list of the 400 wealthiest Americans for 1989, although some other residents of Midland and a lot of Texans did. That may be because the price of oil had been down for some years, and French is an oilman.

French had already been in Quarter Horses a long time. He had Panama Ace which ran 2nd in the very first All-American Futurity in 1959. I asked Wayne how he met French. "Bob French sent me some horses to train. Beal I met through Bob French. Beal has usually taken a 5 or 10 percent interest in our operation." Bob Spreen Sr., who owned Spreen Cadillacs, the biggest Cadillac dealership in southern California, was another Lukas owner. He owned many big winners including Sold Short, Flight 109, Easy Treasure and Game Plan.

According to Wayne, all of these people approached him. As far as I can determine, that was because of his reputation and the powerful impression he made.

4.3 Financing the start

In the beginning, training during the summer vacations, Wayne slept in his pick-up truck, parked at the barn. "I never slept in a motel," he told one reporter. That doesn't necessarily mean he couldn't afford one. Perhaps he simply had better uses for the money.

When he went into training full-time, things didn't go according to plan. Jack Brainard laughs as he recounts the trials and tribulations of Wayne's start: "He had 3 or 4 years of pretty rough going. It was extremely hard to get going in the Quarter Racing game at that time."

"Around the racetrack in Minnesota there are stories about Wayne borrowing money to buy a saddle he was so broke."

"Oh yes. There is no doubt about that. We financed him and loaned him money, hell! Wayne's a good horseman but he didn't have quite enough practical experience. He spent too much time in school. But once he got away from school and basketball, he became an excellent horseman. He's as good a conformation judge as there is and he always has been."

An interesting side to the stories of Wayne borrowing money to buy a saddle, or, as the story sometimes went, bor-

rowing a saddle, surfaced at Canterbury racetrack in Minnesota. Racing journalist Loren Vantries told me he knew a man who had loaned a saddle to Wayne, and that at Arlington Park one year Wayne had confirmed the story.

That man was another pioneer of racing in Minnesota, Ron Resch. But according to Ron, it wasn't poverty that forced Wayne to borrow a saddle, but a desire to win. It would seem the Quarter Horse trainers of Minnesota in that far-off day were racing their horses in western saddles, which weigh a ton. They are solid enought to tie down the other end of a lassoo (lariat) so that it will stop cattle when the rope whips taught. Wayne approached Ron because Ron taught English Riding and he wanted to try the comparitively very light saddle in a race.

Was that the origin of all the stories? The urban myth? Even if it was, from what Jack says, Wayne was pretty well broke at times.

One who remembers Wayne's days in New Mexico is José Dominguez, who worked for Wayne from when he first arrived, until Wayne left to set up in California. José is now a successful trainer at Ruidoso Downs and other New Mexico tracks. (Before he turned 21 he had trained one Quarter Horse and one Thoroughbred to win $100,000 races.) José is an earnest, energetic man and a rapid-fire talker.

"Wayne arrived here in a little red Volkswagen. When he started racing he did good right off the bat, but then all of a sudden it was kind of hard. His horses could only run 120 yards. But he had good owners, he bought good horses and he had a very good year before he decided to go to California."

"I went everywhere the stable went - Pyke's Peak, all the tracks in New Mexico, Centennial in Denver. We were leading trainer in Denver, we always did good in Denver. One year Wayne had more winners than the leading jockey and that is hard to do."

"When did he start the flower beds round the stable - was he doing that then?"

"He had that already. His first wife Janet, she liked flowers and helped him out with that. He always liked his barn nice and neat and he was good at that. They used to call him 'Mister Clean.'"

"How did he get those good owners?"

"He was a good promoter. He could sell a refrigerator to an Eskimo in a New York minute."

"Did he lay out the royal treatment? I don't suppose he could offer them a coffee because he doesn't allow coffee machines in his stables."

"He used to have a coffee machine then because he had an owner who made coffee machines, Jacob Bunn. He always had coffee when he was here."

"Was Wayne buying horses then?"

"Yes."

"Was he considered good at picking horses then?"

"Oh yes. He bought Carlotta 2 which won the Sun Country Futurity. He bought Go Maggie Go and all them big producers. He could pick a horse."

"How long did it take for him to get that reputation for being able to pick a horse?"

"I guess right off the bat, because he had them good owners following him around. I guess he already had that reputation. He's real sure of himself. He knows he ain't going to make a mistake - and if he does he'll try to cover it up. If you're always doubting your judgment - I guess you're not that good."

"But he never won the All-American Futurity."

"No, the All-American is every Quarter Horse owner's dream and it's tough, very tough to win."

"Was he considered a good trainer?"

"That falls into place with the quality of the horses and the quantity. He could get the owners. I've seen good horsemen look bad as a trainer. You can't make miracles if you ain't got the stock. He could do anything he wanted."

"He was the first person to sell a Quarter Horse yearling here in Ruidoso for a hundred thousand dollars. He took the horse out of his barn, took it to the All-American Sale, sold the horse for $100,000 and he brought the horse back to his barn. Now that's pretty damn good because he probably not only got 10% to sell the horse, but another 10% to come back to his barn. It was the year after a horse called Rocket Wrangler won the All-American. This horse was a half brother to Rocket Wrangler, a black horse, pretty son-of-a-bitch, but if I remember rightly he had trouble breaking his maiden (winning his first race). Broke his maiden in Tucson, Arizona."

"I tell you what Wayne did one time - he's awesome, just awesome - he can go out there and claim a horse for three or four thousand and by the time he gets back to his barn he's done got him sold for ten. And it stays right there in his barn. Jacob Bunn, he had a lot to do with where Mr Lukas is at right now."

"Bought a lot of horses did he?"

"Whatever Wayne said, he bought the horse. And from him came Mr Moore, from Moore came Hatley, from Hatley came French."

"Where did Wayne meet Mr Bunn?"

"That I do not know. I know that Wayne came from up north and he was here and before we knew it, we had Mr Bunn buying horses right and left. Hell he even built the most beautiful barn in Lexington, Oklahoma."

"Wayne went to Los Alamitos and if he didn't have the horse he would buy the horse. At one time, in every stake race he would have 5 or 6 horses - in every stake race! So he automatically dominated. When he made owners pay 30, 40, 50 thousand for a 5, 6, 7 year old gelding, that didn't matter. What mattered was they were going to get their picture taken, and

he was going to dominate that stakes race. At that time they ran for 10, 15, 20 thousand dollar pots and he just took all of them."

"He had a mare. She used to run for 3500 dollars here. When he got done with her he, she got sold 5, 6 times and every time she got sold she went from 20 to 50 to 150,000 dollars. She turned into a stakes winner. I think at the end the people that owned her were a hockey team from California."

"We knew his little boy Jeff. He used to steal our Burritos (Mexican food) . . . not steal them, just take a bite. We used to make our Mom put some hot chili in them and then he'd burn up. Buck-teeth kid, good kid. I'm very happy to see him up there."

"When Wayne left out of here - just the tack man, Johnny Bean - he owed him 10, 15 thousand. When he got to Los Alamitos, he made those other trainers go broke trying to keep up with him, because he's got a style all his own. When he left here they used to call him 'Mister Clean'. We used to have three different rakes: a rake for the shedrow, a rake for the rocks, a rake for this. Every horse, individually, had its own brushes, its own blankets: day blanket, night blanket and whatever kind of blanket. People at Los Alamitos, trying to keep up with him on tack, and on how pretty he kept his barn - they went broke."

"When Wayne was here in Ruidoso he was politicking - getting his owners. He knew there was a lot of money in the state of Texas. That's when the price of oil was sky high. He knew that all these people from Oklahoma and Texas were here to see their Quarter Horses race. It was the richest race in the world. And that's how he picked up all these Texas and Oklahoma millionaires. They were right here in Ruidoso."

"And they ended up with Wayne?"

"In due time. It's his charisma, his way of speaking to people. He's just got so much class, style. He makes people feel important."

4.3-1 Did Wayne bet?

If they were at good odds and he really fancied the horse's chances, then Wayne would bet.

4.3-2 Did Wayne borrow?

In the Minnesota horse set you will hear that Wayne had to borrow money to buy a saddle at one stage. That, as we have seen, may have been a myth. Wayne borrowed from Jack Brainard and from Mel Hatley. Mel Hatley financed some horse people and Wayne went to him with some ideas about buying some colts and developing them. Mel loaned him the money. They made lots of money and they have had a close relationship ever since.

One who remembers Wayne well from the early days is Blane Schvaneveldt, who would become Wayne's main rival and yet a close friend. Blane Schvaneveldt would remain in

Quarter Horses after Wayne left, and be the leading trainer in the nation for over a decade. Blane was already at Los Alamitos when Wayne arrived. "When Wayne came from New Mexico to here, he couldn't buy Coca Cola. He was bust. He owed everybody in Ruidoso, and he had to bum money to get out here, and that ain't no lie."

At Ruidoso Downs a number of people including José Dominguez and a journalist told me that when Wayne left to go to Los Alamitos he owed the tack store owner a lot of money - amounts from $10,000 to $20,000 were mentioned but $20,000 was the most popular figure.

That tackman was Johnny Bean, now semi-retired in El Paso. I asked him if the story was true: "Oh that's ridiculous," was Johnny's reaction. "Nobody had $20,000 in those days. People just say those things."

"Did he owe any amount? $2,000 perhaps?"

"I don't remember." Cynics will say he is covering up for Wayne, but Johnny's memory of some other things about those times was also poor. If it is just a matter of memory, I think Johnny *would* have remembered if Wayne had owed him $10,000 or $20,000. Besides, what tack store owner in his right mind ever let horsemen build up debts like that?

Johnny said he liked Wayne from the time he first met him, way back when Wayne was based in Texas. When Wayne journeyed to Ruidoso with a few horses, from his base in Texas, he stayed at Johnny's farm. Johnny never raced horses, but after Wayne moved to Ruidoso, Johnny spent a lot of time in what he called the 'hospitality room' at Wayne's barn. There was a coffee machine there in those days.

When I asked Johnny why he spent time there if he didn't race horses, he told me it was because Wayne was a very interesting man to be around. Conversely, you didn't have to be a horse owner to be around Wayne's barn. Not then anyway. At the time I talked to Johnny, he had recently been visited by Wayne, who was in the general area and couldn't leave without seeing his old friend. (I think that should show some cynics that Wayne would put the effort into seeing a friend who was very unlikely to buy a horse.)

In summary, Wayne did borrow in his early days. How much of that was because he was broke and how much due to expansion (extra equipment etc) I do not know, but talking to José Dominguez, Jack Brainard and Blane Schvaneveldt, Wayne sounded broke. This can't have been very pleasant for Wayne. He had a wife and child and they were all accustomed to a reasonable standard of living after nearly a decade on his steady income as a teacher.

Many years later Wayne would tell a writer from the Milwaukee Journal, "I've been through hard times. I've slept in the back of a pickup truck and I've been overdrawn at the bank, so today I don't apologise for my Rolls Royce or my tailored suits. Luck had nothing to do with it. I've been poor and I earned what I have."

4.4 Steady rise or sudden breakthrough?

Leaving Wisconsin to pursue his dream, Wayne floundered around Texas and Oklahoma, but only for a short while. Oil prices were good and there were lots of oil millionaires in the region. The money that flowed with the oil made other millionaires. But Texas is big and the money men were scattered. When Wayne shifted to New Mexico, in particular to Ruidoso Downs, he found a concentration of wealthy men with a passion for racing Quarter Horses. Ironically, many were from Texas.

Why do these rich Quarter Horse fanciers travel hundreds of miles to this tiny town? The land for many hundreds of miles around is dry, arid, hot and sometimes humid. Summer temperatures may reach 120°F (49°C). But Ruidoso is set in a valley, thousands of feet up in a mountainous region that is perpetually cool, moist and pleasant. They come because it is an elevated oasis. Ruidoso is a wonderful, wonderful place to relax, have a summer holiday, and watch the races.

The other attraction is the All-American Futurity, which has made the track famous. The man who took over the little rundown track in 1952, Gene Hensley, was a good promoter. His track already had one big plus -permission to have betting on races, something few surrounding states allowed then. A friend of his suggested he take the futurity concept a step further than others by guaranteeing a purse of $50,000. That friend, a Californian named Carl Mercer, also suggested the name.

It was a gamble that paid off. It lured so many nominations that Hensley didn't have to put any money of his own into that purse. That made his main race, the All-American Futurity, THE race to win. It became the richest horse race in the world for some two decades.

With Wayne's compelling personality, this concentration of wealthy owners at a small track town must have seemed like heaven to the young ambitious trainer. Wayne's breakthrough was moving to New Mexico and meeting truly wealthy men with a passion for horses, particularly Jacob Bunn. It was a breakthrough, but with an owner rather than a horse.

Blane recalls, "Mr Bunn was one of the main owners he come out here from Ruidoso with. Mr Bunn was a very rich man and he had a lot of good horses, and Wayne bought him some of the best mares in the business."

"Wayne trained for a man named Chuck Nicholls from Montana that was a banker. Him and Wayne were kind of partners on those horses. He trained them on a deal with that guy. They had some old claimers and they had Native Empress, which he'd bought cheap - $3500. They sold her the first time, for Chuck, I think, he sold her for about $15,000. Chuck was always kind of mad at him, because Wayne sold her to his own owners in the barn. She went on and he sold her about five times and she never ever left his barn. The last time she sold, she sold for about $200,000. She never ever left his barn. He kept selling her, kept keeping her. Yes, he sold her to Melvin Hatley, and they sold in turn to Warnerton Farms. Warnerton has all the good Thoroughbred horses now. They sold her back to Melvin, and then Melvin ended up selling her again. Wayne had her in his barn and sold her about six times. She never left his barn. And when he first got her, he give $3500 for her. But he was smart enough to keep her in his barn, and she just kept winning."

"But then he met Mr Spreen, and Spreen had two or three claimers around here (Los Alamitos) then. Wayne did him some good, and then they bought the highest priced horse ever sold, for about $110,000. Wayne sold the horse to Mr Spreen and he belonged to Jake Bunn who was Wayne's owner too. Then Mr Bunn died and Wayne bought all the horses and sold them to Spreen. Wayne is a sharp dealer."

"Spreen was Wayne's main man here when he was in Quarter Horses. He was like Klein was later in Thoroughbreds. Mr Spreen'd buy three or four hundred thousand dollars worth of Quarter Horses every fall. Two-year-olds. Spreen gave Cuckoo money for horses -hell, they'd buy half a dozen of those high-priced yearlings every year, and Wayne went all over for them. Studs bought a lot of them when Spreen got out. Wayne never did win the All-American, but he qualified for it. He won a lot of the big races. He was very competitive."

So Wayne's second breakthrough was moving to Los Alamitos, where he met more men with money. Jacob Bunn died while only in his fifties apparently, but by then Wayne was firing at Los Alamitos.

It is interesting to speculate: how well would Wayne have done in Thoroughbreds without his millionaires from his Quarter Horse days?

4.4-1 How long until first progress?
After leaving teaching in 1967, Wayne made considerable progress as a trainer, but it didn't pay well and initially he was 'starving'. He must have struggled financially from 1967 until 1970 at least, unless betting or horsetrading made exceptional amounts of money. But the progress must have outweighed the setbacks, because he didn't go back to teaching.

In 1970, Wayne's horses won $185,206, enough for him to be listed in the table of top ten moneywinning trainers in Quarter Horses. His cut would have been the standard trainer's 10% or $18,520. Wayne probably didn't hit the real comfort zone until 1974.

YEAR	WINNINGS
1970	$185,206
1971	$113,608
1972	$56,214
1973	$157,186
1974	$497,205

4.4-2 Did one horse provide a sudden lift?
Even in the early years Wayne made rapid progress, in training winners if not in making money. He won the Northeast Kansas Futurity in 1968, as mentioned, with a horse called Trouble Straw.

In 1970, with Carlotta 2, which José says Wayne chose, he won the Sun Country Futurity Grade 1 at Sunland Park in El Paso. The gross purse was worth $75,300 but the winning horse might only get $25,000 of that, and the trainer 10% of that winner's prize, ie $2500. (I have seen it reported that Wayne's salary as a teacher had been $5,200.) Carlotta 2 went on to achieve a very creditable speed index of 97 (see glossary) and win $67,685. That was a lot of money for a Quarter Horse to win back then. (Note: the horse may not have spent its whole career with Wayne, because of claiming races or sale. The same applies to any horses in America - they change ownership during a racing career more often than in Austalia or the U.K.)

With a horse called Reller he won the Kansas Derby - also in 1970. The race was at Ruidoso Downs. This is now a $200,000 plus race rated Grade 1, but back then it was only worth $12,043. The gradings were not in place in those days and grades were retrospectively awarded to the races that now carry those grades. If the prizemoney is any guide, the race enjoyed a sudden lift in class in 1975. Reller went out of racing with a speed index of 92 and winnings of $18,870.

Another good horse for Wayne was Native Empress, which won 5 races now classed as graded stakes, the first one in 1973. She went on to achieve an outstanding speed index of 101, and lifetime earnings of $207,365. Since then Wayne has usually had more than one big-name horse to carry his banner into the publicity wars. In summary, his was not a one-horse rise to stardom.

4.4-3 Important helpers
There is no single person who was essential to the rise of Wayne Lukas in Quarter Horses, but many helped. Jack Brainard brought horses, owners, and an insight into horse's minds. Then followed a growing band of wealthy and loyal owners - Bunn, Moore, Hatley, Beal and French.

4.5 Age married and role of spouse
Wayne married when he was about 21. His first wife, Janet, was a very nice, talented lady but she was not into racing. When Wayne left teaching and headed off south, their son Jeff would have been nine years old. Wayne told a reporter that the lifestyle of a horse trainer was too much for Janet. They had to shift every few weeks and they were living in motels and campers. The marriage was pretty much over when Wayne shifted from New Mexico to Los Alamitos in 1970.

Wayne's second wife, Pat, was the daughter of a trainer. "Wayne is still good friends with the trainer," was Jack Brainard's cryptic comment.

Shari, his third wife has children of her own from a previous marriage. Shari met Wayne while studying the exacta odds on a screen at Santa Anita. They married during Kentucky Derby week of 1984. (One story said there was not even one day off for a honeymoon.) She is a sharp lady who used to teach gifted children. She became a pretty good handicapper and that is how she met the man who makes a lot of the odds. She has had some business involvement in racing, as an agent for aerodynamic jockey silks. In the words of one of Wayne's friends, "she has to be admired for putting up with his regimen."

Wayne's wife Shari studies The Racing Form. She is an ardent handicapper.

4B) The switch to Thoroughbreds

Wayne's years as a Quarter Horse trainer

We have seen that after a somewhat stumbling start in 1967, Wayne led the country in winners in 1970, and his winnings totalled $185,206. However during the next two years his winnings fell away to $113,607 in 1971 and $56,213 in 1972.

Wayne was still not very settled. In New Mexico his mar-

riage was falling apart. He went to Los Alamitos, the track on the outskirts of Los Angeles in California, for one week in 1970, to run a horse in a stakes race. He liked what he saw and he shifted there permanently the next year, 1971. It was a richer and more concentrated racing circuit on the west coast of California.

He had barely set up there when he made a serious attempt to break into Thoroughbreds at Hollywood Park and Del Mar with a string belonging to Eugene Cashman. This was presumably the reason his number of Quarter Horse wins fell away in 1972.

To race Thoroughbreds *and* Quarter Horses, Wayne was commuting daily between Los Alamitos and whatever track the Thoroughbreds were racing at. Mostly that was Hollywood Park. He was supervising the training of both strings. This meant rising at 3:30am, driving to Hollywood Park, (probably a half hour drive for Wayne!) working his Thoroughbreds, then driving back to Los Alamitos to work his Quarter Horses. Trainers don't have to be off the track at Los Alamitos until late in the morning. That was a help.

If Wayne had starters at Hollywood, he would be back to saddle them up around mid-day. Late in the afternoon he would head back to Los Alamitos to saddle up his runners for the night racing there. Finally he would head home as Los Alamitos closed down around 10pm to midnight. It was too much even for superman Lukas in his prime. He had to pull back and concentrate on the Quarter Horses. It would be 1978 before he would try to break into Thoroughbreds again.

Back into the Quarter Horses, it was to be four years from his first training championship before he was to lead the Quarter Horse trainer rankings on numbers again. Lee Young would take the title twice and "Bubba" Cascio once before Wayne would take his second numbers title in 1974.

At the end of the 79 nights of that season at Los Alamitos in 1974, Wayne had shattered every single season record. The next year, 1975, he was leading trainer in a big way. He was leading money earner with $926,340 - a huge figure for the sport at that time. His 152 wins was more than double the win total of any other Quarter Horse trainer.

In 1976 Wayne won the most money, but his new arch rival Blane Schvaneveldt took away the training title for number of winners. In 1977 Blane won again, as he did every year until 1988. Wayne topped the money winners table in 1974, 1976 and 1977. As New York trainer Woody Stephens would say, he took ALL the money. But in 1977 Wayne decided to have another try at the Thoroughbreds.

Why did he leave Quarter Horses?

It seems odd to leave a sport when you have just established yourself as its king. Wayne would seem to have been in his element in a sport suited to a specialist juvenile trainer. The biggest prizes are in futurities, which are for two-year-olds. Even so, he never won some of the biggest of these plums like the All-American Futurity. But he won a lot of the major plums and won them often. He won the Bay Meadows Futurity three out of four consecutive years, including 1978.

He demonstrated that he could train older horses by winning the richest race for older Quarter Horses, the Vessel's Maturity, three years in a row. An event named after the founder of Los Alamitos racetrack and designed to keep top stock racing instead of retiring, he won it in 1975 with She's Precious, in 1976 with another mare, Little Blue Sheep and in 1977 with the first male to win it since its inception in 1973, world champion Dash For Cash.

Was it for better prizemoney?

In 1977 Quarter Horse racing had some very plump plums. The All-American Futurity was worth $766,000, the All-American Derby $591,000 and the Kansas Futurity $394,000 - all run at Ruidoso Downs in New Mexico. Closer to Wayne's base, the Bay Meadows Golden State Derby was worth $236,600, the Los Alamitos Golden State Futurity $228,000, the Los Alamitos Derby $75,000 added and the Bay Meadows Futurity $160,000.

Seattle Slew's Kentucky Derby that year was worth a gross purse of $267,200, the Oaks $60,888. It would seem Wayne was already right where the money was. But is it harder for a trainer to get his hands on the best Quarter Horses? It has been my impression that there are more Quarter Horse breeders who race their own homebreds than is the case in Thoroughbreds. A great many Quarter Horses compete and many of them have never been on open sale. However, as far as I can determine, of the 18 winners of the All-American Futurity to that year, 11 were owned by the breeder. This is 61% - very similar to the Kentucky Derby figure of 60%.

However, in futurities the money itself is spread among a long list of heat winners, finalists and consolation winners - 20 to 30 horses. An important monetary factor in many of the futurities is the cost of getting a horse into the event. Way back in the first All-American in 1959, the owner of a horse going into the trials had put up $2,000 over the previous two years. Where there is legal betting, the purse is usually topped up with some of the betting handle. In non-parimutuel (non-betting) states, the Quarter Horse owner is "running at his own money". Whatever the gambling situation, the winner in a Quarter Horse Futurity typically gets a lot less than half the total purse. In the Kentucky Derby Seattle Slew got $214,700 out of that total purse of $267,200.

Was it profitability?

Quarter Horse trainers charge only a bit over half the training fees that Thoroughbred trainers do. I asked Caesar Dominguez, who trains both in California, for typical 1989 training fees. He believed $30 per day was about average for the Quarter Horse trainers at Los Alamitos, and $50 was typical for Thoroughbreds at Santa Anita/Hollywood Park.

Any businessman can tell you that if the basic costs are similar for staff, feed, etc., the profitability on these two rates would be vastly different. A few years earlier, Caesar had worked out his costs and concluded his net profit on the daily rate was $3 for his Quarter Horses. Trainers of Thoroughbreds have to pay slightly more on feed, track riders and insurance. But it would be reasonable to suggest that a trainer of Thoroughbreds nets much more profit on daily charges.

In addition, although the prizemoney on major events seems to have been better in Quarter Horses at the time, the top Thoroughbred trainers were winning around double what the top Quarter Horse trainers were. The trainer gets 10% in both cases. Purses are pretty much a percentage of the handle (betting turnover). In 1978, the average daily handle at Los Alamitos was $922,979 compared with $4,047,969 at Hollywood Park. On that basis, Thoroughbred trainers had four times as much to aim at. (But a Thoroughbred cost a lot, lot more to buy.)

A trainer is also entitled to one mare service a year to any of his racehorses that become breeding stallions. Once again, the service fees in Thoroughbreds were much higher.

However prizemoney and profits were probably not the only factors in Wayne's decision to change. The greater prestige on a national scale may have also been an attraction. He might also have wanted to 'show 'em'. The Thoroughbred brigade have always looked upon Quarter Horse racing as a poor country cousin.

Wayne himself says it was just a new challenge. To most reporters asking why he changed, his reply was couched in terms of different basketball competitions: College versus professional.

"I'd won the NCAAs and I wanted to try it in the NBA."

To another reporter he said: "I wanted to see if I could stand toe to toe with the Barreras and Whittinghams."

Clyde Rice, his friend from his horse-dealing days, was already in Thoroughbreds and he was having some success, but not as much as Wayne was having in Quarter Horses. Was his contact with Clyde a factor? Clyde says, "Wayne and I both knew, always knew, that Thoroughbreds, at the top of the game, was where the real money and the real challenge was."

Was it because Blane was beating him?

In money and races won, Wayne led nationally in 1974 and 1975. He was undisputed King for two years. But in 1976, Blane won the numbers battle, although Wayne still topped the money. In mid-1977, Wayne went to the Thoroughbred select sales to buy a horse. At the end of 1977, Blane was top in money ($1,012,362) and numbers (151). Wayne was third in money with $526,296 and ninth in winners with 70, a colossal falling off. Was it simply too difficult to maintain the physical or mental effort necessary to hold off Blane, or was Blane too good to be held off? Certainly the number of starts over those years tell a story:

RACE STARTS

	WAYNE	BLANE
1976	690	776
1977	414	825

In 1978, Wayne began his second attempt to break into Thoroughbreds. Did he leave to avoid Blane? When I asked Blane, he shrugged in a way that suggested yes. "I was in front. He couldn't get past me," he said. But it's hard to tell when Blane is joking too, and he and Wayne like to have humorous digs at each other. Certainly with Lukas out of the way, Blane Schvaneveldt completely dominated the trainer standings in Quarter Horses over the next 11 years. If Wayne *did* leave because he felt he could not hold Blane out, it paid off for both of them.

But the way Wayne tells it, much as he respects and likes Blane, he had Blane's number. He shifted on a whim, not to avoid Blane Schvaneveldt. He was at the Quarter Horse races in the middle of 1977 and he suddenly decided to go to the select sales and buy some Thoroughbreds. He just asked who else wanted to come along, who wanted to be in. It was an impulsive thing. Some of the wealthiest people in Quarter racing went with him. In one interview in 1978, a year after the event, he said it was Hatley's idea. It certainly doesn't seem that it was a carefully premeditated plan.

I asked Melvin Hatley about it. He said, "Wayne had trained Thoroughbred and Quarter Horses one season. I noticed a change in the Quarter Horse market. I went to Wayne and I mentioned that, and I said, 'Wayne we need to transfer over into the Thoroughbred business.' He said, 'Why would I want to do that, I'm at the top of the heap in Quarter Horses and have been for five years."

"He'd never been to Keeneland up to that point. I said, 'The difference is that we've got an international market for Thoroughbreds; they're at a different level; there's more money to run at; it isn't a sucker's game, you don't run at your own money.' I said, 'We've got to go into Thoroughbreds and get to the same point you're at in the Quarter Horses now.' We'd bought and we'd sold some of the highest priced horses in the Quarter Horse industry. We got over into the Thoroughbreds and it didn't take him long to accomplish the goal, even go a little further, because you're dealing with more money and more powerful people; there is an international market, international racing; it's just a better game really. No comparison."

"So you made money at it?"

"I've made money since the first year I was in horses: twenty some odd years. I made money every year."

"But you made more money in Thoroughbreds than in Quarter Horses?"

"Oh yes, much more."

When Wayne made his second attempt to move into Thoroughbreds, he did not close down his Quarter Horse stable in 1978 as many people were led to believe by some press articles. Although he got some publicity with the Thoroughbreds he campaigned in 1978, he remained in the top ten Quarter Horse trainers for both wins and money that year.

He was able to concentrate on his small Thoroughbred string because he had a very capable lieutenant, Tom MacKenzie, who ran the Los Alamitos operation whenever Wayne was absent. MacKenzie had been with Lukas since 1971 and had looked after the Lukas pre-training and lay-ups at San Luis Rey. Wayne travelled up and down between the tracks a lot, but often MacKenzie trained the Quarter Horses - 80 at one stage - by himself. The good results probably gave Wayne the confidence to set up branch stables later on.

In 1978 Wayne still had Quarter Horses he hoped would win the All-American Futurity that year, but the great prize continued to elude him. The Thoroughbred string grew and his Quarter Horse string shrank. His Quarter Horse operation only started 342 times in 1978, the lowest number since 1974 and far below his peak year, 1975, when he had 863 starts. But in 1979 he had only 49 starts - he was effectively out of Quarter Horses and full-on into Thoroughbreds.

During that transition year he put in a lot of long hard days. At the time of this display of sheer physical stamina Wayne Lukas was 42 years old.

Second entry into Thoroughbreds

In 1977 when he impulsively went to the Keeneland July Selected Yearling Sales, Lukas bought one youngster, which was later named Terlingua after a town in Texas, like so many of his Texan client's horses. She was the only horse he bought at those sales. Terlingua was a well-bred entry point for Lukas. She was by the great Triple Crown winner Secretariat out of the speedball mare Crimson Saint, which in 1973 had set a record of 56 seconds for five furlongs at Hollywood Park. Terlingua cost $275,000.

Terlingua's sire Secretariat had won the Triple Crown in 1973 after being syndicated for over $6m BEFORE he had even won the Derby. He was retired at the end of his third year and his first yearlings averaged a record $371,000 at the summer sales of 1976. When the sales rolled around in 1977, very few of Secretariat's first crop had raced, but the word in the inner circle was that they didn't look like justifying their high price tags. Wayne may not have heard the whispers, but if he did, they did not put him off.

Indeed, at $275,000 she represented an all-eggs-in-one-basket approach. The average for the Keeneland summer sales that year was $87,000. Wayne could have had three at the average price. At the Fasig-Tipton sales the average was $24,000. Clearly the policy was to buy as far up the quality scale as possible, and to hell with quantity.

An important helper - Albert Gift Yank

Albert is a shortish, solidly built man with a swarthy skin and curly silver hair. And he's quite a character. He grew up behind ploughhorses, and owned his first broodmare in 1934 at 14 years of age. From that beginning he progressed into the breeding, training and trading of bloodstock in California. I asked if he was best described as a bloodstock agent. "No," he said, "These days everyone is calling himself a bloodstock agent." He prefers to be called a horseman. Albert speaks very slowly and deliberately, using lines you feel he's spoken before. He speaks in a somewhat gravelly voice, and that may have something to do with how often he has a cigar in his mouth.

"I first met Wayne Lukas at Keeneland. I was standing under a Pin-oak tree smoking a cigar and he walked up to me. He was wearing blue jeans that had creases SOWN in them; cowboy boots; a belt with a big buckle; and a hat. He said, 'Are you Mister Albert Yank?' - he was very polite - and I said, 'Yes I am'. He said, 'I'm Wayne Lukas'. I said, 'I've never heard of you.'"

"Wayne said, 'I'm in the Quarter Horses. Every year I've gone to your sales, especially at Del Mar, and I've never wanted to bother you but I've looked down your shed row and I've thought: This has to be an exceptional man, the way he keeps his stable'. He said, 'I pattern the way I keep a stable after you.' I said, 'You just inflated my ego."

"He next said, 'What have you bought out of the sale?' I said, 'Nothing." He said, 'Well I have a line on some horses that I really like and I have a very good eye for a horse'. He was hustling pretty good."

"I said, 'Mr Lukas I don't know anything about you. I like my own eyes." Albert went on to tell Wayne he had purchased an older horse called Effervescing, which was supposed to be unsound. Wayne asked how much.

"Well over a million dollars," said Albert.

"How much?" Wayne asked again.

"Million and fifty thousand."

"Strange number," said Wayne.

Albert sent the horse to California, to a long-time friend. Lukas phoned to say he had a friend from Oklahoma that loved the horse.

"He wants to buy him," said Wayne.

"Money can't buy everything," said Albert. But Albert did say he would sell an option to buy half of the horse.

"Sure enough," said Albert, "Mr Melvin Hatley showed up and bought an option on him and I made a quarter of a million dollars on him the minute he walked through the door. Hatley insisted that if he bought half of him, that Wayne should train him. That horse opened the door for D. Wayne Lukas to come to Santa Anita with a racing stable of Thoroughbreds. I brought Great Lady M to his stable. I sold the filly to Bob Spreen. She won 11 races for Wayne and was the dam of Lady's Secret, a champion."

"I also brought Tartan Farm to D. Wayne Lukas when he needed horses. I brought 16 or 18 horses - I picked them out of a book that my friend John Nerud had. We were playing Gin Rummy and drinking Scotch whisky. I told him Tartan Farm should be represented on the west coast. I told him I had a cowboy, a star-spangled cowboy, that didn't know that much about Thoroughbreds, but would work his way through; that I was his mentor. He sent the 18 horses out and that was the start of D. Wayne Lukas."

"D. Wayne Lukas used to come to my house - just outside the gates at Santa Anita - once a day, twice a day. He has plenty ego - that's what makes him work. He has guts, he's been good for the horse business, he's a more than average trainer, and he's a friend of mine."

Albert did tell me that at one time Wayne suddenly stopped calling in at his house: "He must have thought he'd learned everything I could teach him." After some estrangement, the two have renewed their friendship, but are not as close as during the buddy days.

In those days of close friendship, Wayne described Albert as his "booster" and acknowledged that he was invaluable in getting contacts, clients and horses. In the move into Thoroughbreds, Albert may well have been the difference between the failure of 1972 and the success of 1978.

Tartan Farms

Tartan Farms, near Ocala Florida, belonged to Mrs James Binger. For Tartan Wayne would train many horses including such standouts as Codex and Muttering. At that time, Tartan Farms was managed by John Nerud. He had trained the mighty Dr Fager for Tartan before 'retiring' to manage the breeding operation. Lukas must have impressed Nerud as a trainer because he later put one of his own horses with him, a filly by Dr Fager called Movin Money.

So in 1978 Lukas arrived at Hollywood Park with six horses. By August he was reported to have 20 at Hollywood Park and the same number at San Luis Rey Downs training center. By then the number of Quarter Horses at his Los Alamitos stables had fallen to 32. Terlingua, Effervescing and Great Lady M. were his Thoroughbred contenders that year. That year, 1978, Wayne was able to buy 4 or 5 at the yearling sales according to one report, although in his book 'Lukas at Auction', Joe Bagan could find no purchases in the name of Lukas for that year. If he did buy some, they must have been under clients names, or Albert may have signed for them.

One of Wayne's first eye-catching training efforts in Thoroughbreds was his preparation of Effervescing, the five-year-old that was considered sore (having a painful area or lameness) when he took him over. He was able to win the $100,000 American Handicap on grass, at Hollywood Park on July 4 1978 - the big Independence Day meeting. He went on to run the horse just five days later to win another biggie - the $100,000 Citation Handicap - on dirt.

"I've always had good luck running horses right back when they are good," he told reporters afterwards. Another report said that after winning the Hollywood Handicap with the previously sore horse Effervescing, everyone expected a layoff for the horse. It said that Wayne stunned one of the owners, bloodstock agent Albert Yank by announcing that the horse would run five days later in the Citation Handicap, another 'hundred grander'. Yank's retort was to ask Wayne, "Are you drinking your bathwater?"

"Absolutely not," declared Wayne, according to the report.

Albert Yank however, says running the horse back was his idea. "I, personally, walked the horse after the first race." Even if it was Albert's idea, Wayne already had a reputation in the Quarter Horse game for running a horse often when it was at its peak. Blane Schvaneveldt, the leading Quarter Horse trainer and a friend of Wayne's was quoted as saying;

"He'd run his horses back every five days. Wayne has a motto - 'When they're hot they're hot. You better run them because tomorrow they might be dead."

When it came time to race Terlingua, Lukas showed the Thoroughbred boys his aggression and confidence. He put the two-year-old first-time starter in a stakes race at Hollywood Park. She had some powerful morning works behind her but that didn't stop the critics having a say about "the Quarter Horse trainer". Terlingua went out on the day and drew away from the field in the home stretch, winning the 5½ furlong Nursery Stakes in the time of 1:03 3/5. It was a new record for a 5½ furlong stakes race.

A month later Terlingua ran away with the Hollywood Lassie in the fastest time ever run by a two-year-old filly over six furlongs at that track. Cary Grant made the presentation. Wayne fronted in a luridly checked coat. Just one week later she went out to beat the colts in the Hollywood Juvenile, which really set the local trainers abuzz. Starting a filly against the colts was regarded as bordering on insanity!

So Wayne managed the switch to Thoroughbreds on his second try. Wayne didn't see it as that much of a change.

"You were in and out of Thoroughbreds all the way?"

"Yes, I was, on and off. Sure. The Quarter Horses became so successful they pushed the Thoroughbreds back for a few years there and we were very successful, but I've always been in both."

The major ingredients in this success appear to have been Albert Yank, who brought Effervescing and Tartan Farms; Tom MacKenzie who managed the Quarter Horse training; and his choice of Terlingua with the help of Clyde Rice.

At about the time Wayne was switching breeds, his son Jeff decided he would become a full-time trainer in his father's organization. He was just finishing his college degree, and had enjoyed working with his father during vacations. Already close, father and son had worked well together.

5A. Achievements as a Quarter Horse trainer

Wayne claims that by the end of his Quarter Horse racing career in 1979, he had trained 23 champions, including Dash For Cash, twice Horse Of The Year. I could not find that many, but Richard Chamberlain of *The Quarter Racing Journal* tells me that the definition of a champion has changed with time. In Wayne's Quarter Horse days there were many regional champions, regional divisional champions, and track champions. Even the winners of certain races were designated champions. (Wayne won the Los Alamitos Championship Gr 1 in 1975, 76, and 77.) The national divisional championships are a recent idea and many of the awards are somewhat retrospective. Wayne's national divisional champions are listed below.

When he left, Wayne was second behind Blane Schvaneveldt in total victories, but had a reputation for creaming off the big-money stakes races. He had won the most stakes races, 50 to Schvaneveldt's equal second place score of 39.

It is often said, or written in articles on Wayne Lukas, that he won the six 'hundred granders', the six races worth $100,000 in California, in each of three consecutive years. I checked the records in the annual review issue of *The Quarter Racing Journal*. I could not find 18 such wins. I asked Wayne about it, and Wayne still makes that claim. Wayne said they had to be in the records somewhere. It could be that some of the $100,000 races have been discontinued. After all, many races listed in the 1990 review have increased dramatically in value, while some have halved in value. So it is possible some may have been worth $100,000 once, but declined so much in value they don't make it into the list of major races now.

Sometimes journalists will say Wayne won the *six richest* races in California three years straight. That is demonstrably incorrect. There are, in each year, top money Californian races Wayne *did not* win.

In the table are his major race wins that I could find, and they add up to a staggering achievement over such a short period.

Wayne's record in major Quarter Horse races

All-American Futurity	G1	- none	
All-American Derby	G1	- none	
Anne Burnett Inv H'cap	G2	- 1974, 75, 76	$25,000
Bay Meadows Futurity	G1	- 1975, 76, 78	$165,000

It is sometimes written that Wayne won this event 4 consecutive years, but for 1977 the trainer of record was Kenneth Teutsch. The owner was Robert Spreen Sr. See sec. 13.4

Champion of Champions	G1	- 1976, 77	$100,000

This could be part of the confusion. Dash For Cash won this in 1976 and 1977. After eight wins from ten starts at two, under the training of Charles 'Bubba' Cascio, the great horse was sent to Los Alamitos. He was trained by Wayne at Los Alamitos 'under the direction of Bubba.' The records show Bubba as the 'trainer of record' for these wins but Wayne for some others listed below. Wayne may have trained other horses without being the trainer of record, under this kind of arrangement.

Double Bid Handicap	G3	- 1975, 77	$16,300
Ed Burke Memorial Futurity	G1	- none	$155,000
El Primo Del Ano Derby	G1	- none	$131,000
Go Man Go Handicap	G1	- 1976, 77	$50,000
Golden State Derby	G1	- none	$236,625
Golden State Futurity	G1	- 1975	$152,950
Horsemen's QHRA Championship	G1	- none	$50,000
Kindergarten Futurity	G1	- 1978	$336,180
La Primo Del Ano Derby	G1	- 1979	$181,000
Las Damas Handicap	G1	- 1978	$ 38,900
Los Alamitos Championship	G1	- 1975, 76, 77	$100,000

Dash For Cash won in 1977 and Wayne was the trainer of record.

Los Alamitos Derby	G1	- 1975, 76	$90,200

Dash For Cash won in 1976 and Wayne was the trainer of record.

Miss Peninsula Handicap	G3	- 1977, 78, 79	$21,950
Miss Princess Handicap	G2	- 1974, 75, 76	$24,375
Peninsula Handicap	G1	- 1973, 75	$17,625
Pomona Invitational Handicap	G2	- 1973	$10,000
Vandy's Flash Handicap	G3	- 1975	$11,350
Vessels Maturity	G1	- 1975, 76, 77	$100,000

Dash For Cash won in 1977 and Wayne was trainer of record.

As you can see, in these records Wayne had six events with 3 wins, but they were not all over the same three year period, and many were not worth $100,000. These represent the MINIMUM of his achievements as a Quarter Horse trainer - he may have won others that are no longer recorded in the annual History of Major Stakes Races in *The Quarter Racing Journal,* and some may be under other trainer's names. Nevertheless, his record was outstanding.

Wayne's Quarter Horse Champions

Pass Over	- 2yo Filly	1973
Flight 109	- Aged Gelding	1974
Pass Over	- 3yo Filly	1974
Maskeo Lad	- 3yo Colt	1975
She's Precious	- Aged Mare	1976
Dash For Cash	- World Champ'n	1976, 77
	- 3yo	1976
	- 3yo Colt	1976
	- Aged Horse	1977
	- Aged Stallion	1977
Little Blue Sheep	- Aged Mare	1977, 78

Miss Thermolark was down as trained by Tom MacKenzie and owned by Mel Hatley in races in 1979, but in 1978, when she won the Champion of Champions race, she was listed as trained by Blane Schvaneveldt and owned by Ronny Schliep. When I asked Wayne if he considered her one of his champions, he said emphatically, "Oh yes. Mel Hatley and I bought her and I think it was part of the way through the year when she became a champion."

Miss Thermolark	- World Champ'n	1978
	- 3yo	1978
	- 3yo Filly	1978

5B. Achievements as a Thoroughbred trainer

- Almost Unbelievable!

5.1 Training titles, money and stakes

Money won - single season

1977 - 1980 Laz Barrera was the leading money winning trainer.

1978 Lukas won $942,786. Big figures for a 'rookie'.

1979 Lukas had winnings of $1,360,772.

1980 Lukas was 5th - in his third year - with earnings of $2,010,841

1981 Lukas was 2nd to Charlie Whittingham with winnings of $2.6m

1982 Charlie Whittingham set a North American money won record of $4,587,457. Lukas was not far behind with $3.5m

1983 Wayne hits the front - leading trainer on winnings with $4,267,261.

1984 Wayne again - setting a record, with winnings of $5,835,921.

1985 Another record - $11,155,188

1986 Yet another record - $12,345,180. More than double Whittingham's second place total.

1987 $17,502,110 What more can be said?

1988 $17,842,358 from a staggering 1500 starts.

1989 $16,103,998 A plateau? Or a crouch before the next leap? Beginning of a decline without Klein?

Of Wayne's first 12 years in Thoroughbreds, he was leading money earner for the last seven. It is claimed that Wayne has sometimes earned more than all the other trainers at a track combined! He is that rare trainer whose winnings can exceed the top jockey's in this era when the top jockeys fly wherever the big money is, ride nearly every day, and may ride in every race on the card.

Before the arrival of Wayne Lukas on the scene, the climb up the ladder of successive million dollar steps was something of a crawl.

1947 H. A. (Jimmy) Jones was the first to pass $1m, with $1,334,805.

1966 Eddie A. Neloy passed $2m earning $2,456,250 (Gap of 19 years.)

1978 Laz Barrera passed $3m with a total of $3,307,164

1982 Charlie Whittingham passed $4m. (16 years after passing $2m.)

1984 Wayne Lukas passed $5m.

1985 Lukas passed *$11m*, an astonishing lift for just 12 months and more than doubling the $4m in just three years.

Lukas has dramatically lifted the standard required to top the money list. Part of this has been due to higher rates of inflation, but there are other important factors. One has been a generally increasing concentration of pursemoney into the more prestigious events. (I don't have figures but Joe Average trainers constantly complain that the tracks do it, and no one seems to refute the claim. The tracks do it to attract big-name horses, patrons and television. Small trainers complain because they seldom have horses good enough to go for the big pursemoney events.) The Breeders' Cup has added more money to the available pool while definitely adding to that trend, i.e. the best horses can win more nowadays.

Lukas has gone after an unprecedented percentage of that top money by having 'battalions' based in carefully selected regions of the country, and by doing whatever vanning or flying was necessary to have his horses in any significant stakes races. This adds to the costs and worries and weak points, but it sure adds to the gross.

Starts, wins and stakes

1978	194 starts	37 wins	
1979	440 starts	63 wins	
1980	466 starts	64 wins	
1981	526 starts	71 wins	
1982	561 starts	89 wins	
1983	595 starts	78 wins	21 stakes
1984	801 starts	131 wins	32 stakes
1985	1140 starts	218 wins	70 stakes
1986	1509 starts	259 wins	64 stakes
1987	1735 starts	343 wins	92 stakes
1988	1500 starts	318 wins	82 stakes
1989	1398 starts	305 wins	89 stakes

His record of 92 stakes was set by 40 individual stakes winners.

To put the number of these annual stakes wins in perspective, I should point out that some Hall of Fame trainers have only won 40 to 80 stakes *in their whole career*. H. A. (Jimmy) Jones set a one year record of 46 stakes victories in 1947, when he was training for Calumet Farm at its peak. On records such as stakes winners for the year, Wayne often knows the score. He is not one for being told he has set some record - he usually knows. "That's number 49 for us," he told reporters in 1985 when a win put him three over Jimmy Jones' single season stakes record.

When Wayne led in BOTH wins and money in 1987, he was the first to do so since Jack Van Berg in 1976.

5.2 Important races and awards

Historically the top breeding and carnival event of the American Thoroughbred racing scene is the Kentucky Derby, held on the first Saturday in May. Two weeks later the Preakness Stakes is run in Baltimore, some 400 miles east, followed three weeks later by the Belmont Stakes in New York. All these races are for three-year-old's and a horse winning all three is said to have won THE Triple Crown.

5.2-1 Wayne's Triple Crown record

Wayne Lukas never made any secret of his strong desire to win the Kentucky Derby. He calls the Derby the 'gold ring', an analogy to the rings given out to the winning team in the Super Bowl, the grand finale of American football (gridiron). Yet at the start of 1988, in spite of setting five successive money-won records as a trainer, he had not won a Kentucky Derby. Pressmen loved to write about this at Derby time. As a result Lukas was embarrassed and frustrated at the way Thoroughbred racing's most sought-after prize had eluded his battalions.

Once, when the press were hassling him about his failure to win the Kentucky Derby, he made the public relations blunder of calling it, 'just another race'. The press dived on that and made him look like a spoilt brat. His team's frustrations came to the surface when son Jeff had some angry exchanges with critical pressmen. Lukas made excuses as optimists always do but he also continued to make plans.

Going through Wayne's history in the Derby it is obvious he is trying to win a race that does not suit his strengths. His best results as a trainer have been with two-year-old sprinters and fillies; the Kentucky Derby is a staying race (1¼ miles) for three-year-old's, won almost entirely by colts. Many of his Derby entrants had faded badly, encouraging the jeers of those who say he can't train and inviting the question: Does he really expect to win?.

It looks like he wants a runner in the Derby at all costs, even one with next to no chance, presumably to get some attention and publicity. Who is to say that is not a worthwhile publicity strategy for a public trainer? It has certainly brought him a lot of publicity, but much of it has not been flattering. If you believe any publicity is good publicity, then Wayne has done well.

It is probably true as, many believe, that Wayne has sometimes gone into the Derby with horses that he knew had poor chances of winning, simply because he knows an entry will put his name in front of potential megamoney clients. But I think he also takes the view that quite often the Derby is not won by the best horse: to have a starter is to have a chance. His horse might steal off to an uncatchable lead. It might come through after the hot prospects have duelled each other into the ground. Hell - half the field might fall down. It has happened in the English Derby. Wayne, I believe, has definite strategies with his Derby runners: patterns emerge.

1980

This was the year of Wayne's first Triple Crown entry. Wayne had no starter in the Derby which was won by the filly Genuine Risk. As the first filly to win since Regret in 1915, she became a public hero. Wayne's colt Codex then won the Preakness, beating Genuine Risk into second place. (Codex was reportedly not entered in the Kentucky Derby because of some unwillingness on the part of the owners and because Lukas did not rate the colt highly at an early nomination round.) Codex won after a bumping exchange with Genuine Risk that sent her in a wide orbit at the last turn. The stewards ruled the bumping legal, but Eddie Arcaro, a famous ex-jockey was the commentator on ABC TV, and he disagreed. The press said the colt "mugged" the filly. Angel Cordero rode Codex and he already had a reputation for rugged rough-and-tumble riding tactics. A colt bullying a filly, and a public heroine at that! Lukas and Cordero faced some public hostility over it.

At the stable gate the next morning there was a bag of 50 or 60 telegrams. It was Lukas's first win in one of the Triple Crown classics and he expected congratulations. "I thought the whole world would congratulate me." But the telegrams were overwhelmingly against him and his star. "They said things like, 'You Quarter Horse trainer, what are you trying to do?" Wayne swept it under the carpet as 'part of the fun'.

Then Genuine Risk's owners challenged the steward's decision. They were very wealthy but said they would donate the prize money to a racing charity, should they win an appeal. There were three weeks of inquiries and appeals before Wayne could feel sure his horse was the official winner.

By then it was Belmont Stakes time. Codex was the 8 to 5 favorite. Genuine Risk drew the inside gate position at number one, with Codex alongside at number two. A slugging rematch was anticipated by the public, but on the day Temperance Hill ran off by two lengths from Genuine Risk. Codex was fourth at one stage but faded to eighth.

Since Codex beat Genuine Risk over a distance only slightly less than the Derby, Wayne no doubt felt that the colt must have been a good Kentucky Derby chance gone to waste. Wayne has had a Kentucky Derby entry every year since.

1981

Partez started at the longshot odds of 34/1 but gave Wayne an exciting first Derby. Partez broke well and trailed a big bunch led by speedball Top Avenger at a suicidal pace. Between the ¾ and mile poles Partez went around the pack to be second as they came into the straight. By the time Partez had mown down the last of the tiring front-runners however, they were all passed by the eventual winner, Pleasant Colony. Partez hung on for third but was almost out of a place when the jockey mistook the the 1/16th pole for the finish, a blunder Shoemaker had made famous some years before.

1982

Wayne's Derby entry was Muttering, owned by Tartan Stable, the racing arm of Tartan Farms. Muttering's preparation included the San Rafael Stakes on March 6, his first start since December 23rd. In the San Rafael Muttering was 2nd, beaten by Prince Spellbound which had been deliberately *not* nominated to the Triple Crown events by an owner who believed the Triple Crown events were too severe for a three-year-old. The San Rafael was followed by the Santa Anita Derby on April 4.

Wayne had another top three-year-old, Stalwart, pointed at the Derby, but the horse went amiss. It was reported that Stalwart's last three recorded workouts were ⅝ mile Jan 23, ½ Feb 17 and ½ March 6. The gaps of 25 and 17 days strongly suggest some of the horse's workouts were missed by the clockers, but many would consider them short works for a Derby preparation.

Muttering went off 3rd in the betting with top jockey Laffit Pincay up. They sat 4th in a race with a fast early pace and hung on to run 5th, while Gato Del Sol came from last at the half mile to win by 2½ lengths. Wayne went on record as saying Muttering was a "superhorse". The name Muttering is appropriate: he was a son of Drone.

Lukas won the Kentucky Oaks, the fillies-only equivalent of the Derby. He saddled up Blush With Pride, owned by Stonereath Farms who bred the filly. This no doubt did the job in the eyes of Stonereath Farms. It was a Grade 1 win of great sales and pedigree value plus $126,000 to the winner. Wayne however may have contrasted that with the $428,000 that Gato Del Sol won in the Derby, and the immensely greater publicity that the Derby-winning horse and its trainer received. Comparatively speaking, the Oaks was nowhere, completely overshadowed by the Derby. This could only have increased Wayne's existing propensity for running top fillies against colts. In later years he would run his best fillies in the Kentucky Derby.

Fillies carry only 121 pounds to the colts' 126, but when Genuine Risk won the Derby in 1980, she was only the second filly to win in 106 runnings. Genuine Risk was, however, the first filly to start in 21 years and Lukas no doubt had taken note of her win. He may well have seen that the belief that fillies cannot win was at least partly responsible for their poor record.

1983

In the Derby, Lukas entered Marfa, winner of the Santa Anita Derby, and two other horses, Balboa Native and Total Departure. This was the first triple entry since 1946. Lukas now had a very large stable of horses and could find and afford a multiple entry. (Running in the Kentucky Derby is not cheap. For 1987 it was $10,000 entry fee and $10,000 starting fee. All fees go to the winner.) Marfa was noted for his erratic racing but had some dramatic wins when he did run straight. Marfa was owned by Lukas with French and Beal. In the Derby, the Lukas team went out as favorites, at 2.4/1. Under American betting rules, all three horses are bet as one entry and having three horses in the race has to make you some kind of a chance. However Marfa was considered by some experts to be the best shot in the race.

With the favorite and two other runners it was good publicity for Lukas. Total Departure, owned by Rebalot Stable, set the early pace and although that was not very fast, dropped rapidly out to last after the ¾ mile mark and remained last at the post. Marfa, like Partez the previous year, sat back off the pace and went wide around the pack after the ¾ mile mark. In the home straight Marfa got to within one and a half lengths of the leader and eventual winner, Sunny's Halo, but faded back to be 5th. Balboa Native, owned by Spreen, sat even further back but could only move up to be 9th. Marfa went on to the Preakness but was not successful.

1984

Lukas showed up with a smaller Derby team, Althea and Life's Magic, both fillies. Fillies had become a rarity in the Kentucky Derby and this was the ultimate rarity: two fillies on the one entry, the first in its history. Note: in the Derby instead of the Kentucky Oaks. Again one of the Lukas horses took off and set the pace. Althea led all the way until she was passed after the ¾ mile pole. Like Total Departure the year before, her pace was fast but not suicidal, perhaps designed to improve another entrant's chances, but if unchallenged, to steal the race from in front. This gives Team Lukas (As Wayne was now calling his organization) a chance of winning whether the pace is slow, true or fast.

After being passed by a few fresher rivals, Althea faded rapidly out to be 19th and last. Total Departure had done the same thing the previous year. Clearly there was no instruction to flog a tired horse.

Life's Magic sat back behind two-thirds of the field, then moved up to 8th after the half mile. She was probably meant to come from off the pace and may have been a factor if the lead horses went too fast, but with a true pace she just didn't have enough left and that's where she stayed - eighth to Swale.

But the carnival was not all bad for Wayne. He won the Oaks again with Lucky Lucky Lucky, defeating Woody Stephen's Miss Oceana by a nose. If he had won the Derby, it would have been a unique double with fillies.

Four years later in 1988, with a lot more experience preparing horses for the Derby, Wayne would say that he ran Althea too close up to the Kentucky Derby. In that prep race Althea won the Arkansas Derby by seven lengths (four in another report), setting a new track record. That was two weeks before the Kentucky Derby.

1985

Wayne's Derby prospect was a horse called Tank's Prospect, owned by Mr and Mrs Eugene Klein. Eugene Klein was a very wealthy man who had suddenly developed a passion for racehorses. With Wayne advising him, he had invested tens of millions of dollars and become one of the major owners in the sport. Tank's Prospect was well bred and already had some

Eclipse Awards won by some Lukas-trained horses hang on the wall of his Arcadia office.

big wins behind him. The Kleins had already knocked back an offer of $5m for the horse. On Derby day, Tank's Prospect went out 6th in the Kentucky Derby betting. Chief's Crown was the short-priced favorite. Tank's Prospect ran midfield early, made some ground to be 3rd at the mile but faded back to midfield in a race that Spend A Buck led from start to finish to win by 5 or 6 lengths.

Then Lukas had some luck: Spend A Buck had won two Derby prep races at the reconstructed Garden State track in New Jersey. If Spend A Buck could win the Jersey Derby he would collect a two million dollar bonus. Spend A Buck's connections decided to bypass the chance of winning the Preak-

World's Leading Trainer. Sounds good doesn't it. The secretary said this one was commissioned by 'our home office.'

ness (and the Triple Crown), and go for the bonus in New Jersey. (This action later led to the massive Triple Crown bonus scheme, funded by Chrysler. Chrysler guaranteed a $1m bonus to the winner of the most points in the three races and in the event of one horse winning all three races, the three wins would be topped up to a total of $5m.)

In the Preakness, Tank's Prospect sat way back off a cracking pace. Even money favorite Chief's Crown swept to the lead in the home straight. He looked to have it sewn up but Tank's Prospect came with a flying finish to make it a photo decision. Tank's Prospect was announced the winner, breaking the record by 1/5 of a second. Lukas and Klein were ecstatic. In the Breeders' Cup Juvenile the previous year, it had been Chief's Crown 1st, Tank's Prospect 2nd and Spend A Buck 3rd. This result went a long way to lifting Tank's Prospect back into contention in the big money matter of which was the best stallion prospect of the three-year-old crop. As a top racing son of the sire phenomenon Mr Prospector, Tank's Prospect was an excellent sire prospect.

However the spotlight was now turning back to Spend A Buck and the Jersey Derby, to be run the following Saturday. Lukas entered a sprinter, Huddle Up (a coaching term no doubt). The opinion going around was that this horse had no show of winning at the distance, but was in the race to challenge Spend A Buck's early lead, force his pace and wear him out so some other horse could win. This would greatly enhance Tank's Prospect's stud value. Eugene Klein owned both Tank's Prospect and Huddle Up.

Spend A Buck stumbled as he broke but still went for the lead. Huddle Up challenged him from the very start and the two went head and head for six fast furlongs in 1:09. Huddle Up faded and it seemed Spend A Buck must do likewise, but as fresher challengers came from back in the field, he doggedly fought them off. He went on to win in a rousing display of sheer heart.

If Lukas and Klein did put Huddle Up in the race specifically to cut down Spend A Buck's stud value, then it backfired something awful. A show of 'fighting heart' by a tired horse when challenged is something many breeders rate very highly. Spend A Buck's earnings leapt up another $2.6m.

Tank's Prospect's (and Chief's Crown's) faint hopes of squaring the slate lay in the Belmont Stakes, the remaining leg of the Triple Crown. Only an outstanding win by Tank's Prospect would suffice. But it was not to be. Lukas's horse ended the race with a fetlock injury that would shift him from track to stud. The critics had a field day, saying Tank's Prospect had not been right for the race, had no chance in the race and had been risked for the sake of the glamour and publicity.

Fortunately for Lukas, Chief's Crown had a poor showing in the Belmont and later in the Breeders' Cup, indirectly raising the stud value of Tank's Prospect. Spend A Buck would go to stud at an unofficial value of 12 to 20 million dollars while Chief's Crown had already been syndicated for $9m immediately before the Breeders' Cup races of the previous year, i.e. of his two-year-old year. Tank's Prospect was syndicated for $16m and in 1989 was standing at Mare Haven Stud Farm for $30,000 stud fee.

1986

Wayne's Derby entry was Badger Land, sired by his 1980 Preakness Winner Codex. Badger Land was bred by Mel Hatley and part owned by Wayne and Jeff. Wisconsin is called Badger Land, so the Lukases must have named him. Owned, bred and trained by such a close group of friends, it must have been a very exciting time for the trio. Fancied by many respected observers, Badger Land had to scramble for position and had very little fire left by stretch time. It was Ferdinand's Derby. In the Preakness, Badger Land fared no better.

1987

Lukas brought War, Capote and On The Line to the Derby track at twin-spired Churchill Downs. His best chance for '87 had been an Alydar colt called Talinum, but the horse came up lame after a morning gallop just a week before the Derby.

Capote was the two-year-old Champion of the previous year. In America there is no racing layoff for the winter as there is in England and Ireland, but there is a "winter book favorite" for the Derby and that winter it was Wayne's Capote. However Capote ran in the Gotham Stakes and the Wood Memorial on muddy tracks at Aqueduct and faded in both. Lukas blamed the mud but was sharply criticized for Capote's training schedule. Lukas was also being criticized for taking the horse to the Derby after his poor showings. To the skeptical pressmen Wayne said, "The question is - have I got him tight enough to go a mile and a quarter next Saturday? Since the Wood he's had the best four days of his life. I like him better than at any time that I've been around him. He could be a tremendous surprise."

War had won the Blue Grass Stakes on April 23 after a hard scrimmaging finish in which the first horse across the line was disqualified. On The Line earned his start in the Derby with a win in the one-mile Derby Trial.

The press were having a field day with Wayne as the losingest Kentucky Derby trainer, 9 starts for 0 wins, and Wayne wasn't enjoying it. He ordered a journalist from his barn, threatening novel anatomical placement of the journo's most recent writing. Things deteriorated to the point where Wayne called upon his friend, basketball coach Bob Knight, to keep things cool with the press. To counter his image as a failure in the Derby, Wayne described how his team was setting records in stakes and money won. "We're over $5m right this minute." The press studiously ignored that. They preferred to needle Wayne, make him writhe.

Exasperated, Wayne explained and finally became caustic: "All you can do is believe in yourself, believe in the horse … work your plan … and if you are right, everyone will write that it was a bad field, that the pace was slow and you got lucky. But if you are wrong, Lord help you, you've got your head on the chopping block. But that's the nature of it. We get paid very well. A lot better than you do."

In the race, On The Line and Capote jumped to the lead and stayed there at a good speed until the ¾ mile mark. War had been further back but fought his way up to be third at the ¾ mile mark, so for a moment the Lukas team was 1- 2- 3 in the Kentucky Derby, but they ended up 10th, 13th, and 16th in a 17 horse race in which Demons Begone bled and had to be pulled out of the race. Alysheba got up from near last to improve steadily and win in the last furlong. Capote had ended up a virtual last but may have been intended as a pacemaker anyway, or to help cover the pace possibilities. Some of the critics had a field day. They took great delight in pointing out that this brought to 12 the number of unsuccessful Derby contenders sent out by Wayne. The Lukas team did not have much to celebrate, but that was not going to deter Wayne.

At the end of the year, after Success Express won the 1¼m Breeders' Cup Juvenile, Wayne was asked if the horse was a Derby prospect: "I will say he has the dosage (see glossary) and the numbers to be a Derby horse. Eventually we will get the right horse on the right day in Kentucky. I'll take odds that we'll win it one of these days. And if we ever win, I'll invite everybody from the press corps to my post-Derby party."

In January 1988, Klein was announced the Eclipse Award winning owner of 1987. He told Joe Hirsch of the Daily Racing Form, "There are still a lot of goals to achieve. One of them is the Kentucky Derby. We'd love to win it, and I think we will some day. We've got several chances this year, with colts like Success Express, and Notebook, which won the Kentucky Jockey Club Stakes at Churchill Downs. We also have a lightly raced colt named Sir Lightning, by Sir Ivor, who shows promise, plus a number of unraced colts which have the breeding to be any kind." In the last days of 1987, Notebook won the Bongard Stakes by 18 lengths.

1988

Lukas brought just one contender to the Derby, a filly, called Winning Colors. After supervising in the saddling paddock, he watched the race on the TV set in the racing secretary's office. Winning Colors broke on the lead and went off at a steady pace. Surprisingly, the others left her alone on the lead even though the pace was not fast - the half in 46 4/5 and the 6 furlongs in 1:11 2/5. According to the ever diligent William Nack, as she was loping down the backstretch Lukas was yelling, "Switch your leads baby, switch your leads." Fortunately for him, she did, because even so she got the wobbles after putting

in a solid effort in the last part of the race.

Two hundred yards out from the finish, the Woody Stephens-trained Forty Niner began to cut into her lead. Forty Niner was alongside her rump, then her flank, then her shoulder. The crowd was going berserk. Winning Color's jockey, Gary Stevens was thrashing about with whip and heels, but she was fading. Wayne was yelling at the TV set, "Stay with them Gary! Come on! Gary, Gary, Gary, Gary, Gary!" Forty Niner was alongside her neck when the two of them flashed past the post.

Klein's Winning Colors had led all the way to become only the 3rd filly in history to win the Derby. Everyone knew she would win it if she was allowed to get away to an easy lead. But everyone knew they would ruin their own chances if they tried to run with the giant speed machine.

Wayne was jubilant. The Kentucky Derby 'monkey' was off his back. The Lukas planning and determination had prevailed in the end. Wayne gave much of the credit for the training of Winning Colors to his son Jeff. But this success did not seem to win over his critics, rather it seemed to antagonize some of them further. At this point Winning Colors' clear win seemed to give her a stranglehold on the possibilities for the Triple Crown races. Apart from the glory of the Triple Crown itself there was a bonus put up by Chrysler which would bring the total winnings to $5m. Should she fail to win all three races, Chrysler offered a bonus of $1m for the horse amassing the most points (5 for a win, 3 for second and 1 for third) over the three runs. With her front running style considered the most suited to winning the Preakness because of the Pimlico Track's sharp turns, she appeared a moral certainty to win the most points even if she were to later prove not up to the 1½ miles of the Belmont.

In the Preakness the Woody Stephens trained entry Forty Niner went with Winning Colors to prevent her having the same stress-free lead she had in the Derby. Forty Niner was on the inside of Winning Colors and held her way out off the rail. There was a lot of bumping. Forty Niner faded to the rear of the field but the job was done. Winning Colors could not win, but she did hang on courageously for a place behind winner Risen Star.

All hell broke loose as spectators and press argued about what they had just witnessed. There were any number of points to argue about but the main ones were - A) would Winning Colors have won without the interference of Forty Niner? - B) was Forty Niner's action legal? - and C) was it fair? The stewards soon confirmed it was legal which left the other two points for weeks of discussion and editorializing. To the majority it seemed a deliberate and unfair "spoilsport" action by Forty Niner's jockey. Forty Niner's jockey was reported to have apologized to Winning Colors' jockey saying he was sorry but he was riding to orders. Winning Color's feisty owner Eugene Klein and the equally fiery Woody Stephens got into some mutual character sketching. Everyone had plenty to say, but Wayne, most uncharacteristically, refused to comment -for a while anyway. The press labeled the now ongoing hostilities and debate the "Woody and Wayne Show".

Wayne started Winning Colors in the Belmont even though she perhaps looked a little light, a bit drawn on the day. Presumably he did that because she was still the major contender for the $1m bonus. As the horses left the beautiful treed parade ring, Risen Star's trainer and co-owner, Louis Roussell III went over to speak very solicitously with Wayne. A wag in the crowd yelled, "Don't kiss his ass Louis." The crowd laughed. Louis and Wayne hesitated in a moment of embarrassment. "Don't kiss his ass Louis," the man yelled again. Another ripple of laughter. Wayne and Louis decided to split up and meet somewhere else.

In the Belmont the splendid son of Secretariat, Risen Star, became just that, a risen star, winning the race and the $1m bonus. For the Lukas camp it was an anticlimax after the euphoria of the Derby.

1989

Wayne's stable put up $12,000 ($600 each) to enter 20 horses in the first round of Triple Crown nominations. Open Mind was one of 10 fillies nominated. But on Derby day, Wayne's main contender was the much heralded Houston, a magnificent looking horse for which Wayne had paid $2.9m as a yearling. Houston led for a large part of the race but then was passed by the stars of the 1989 Triple Crown series, Sunday Silence and Easy Goer. Houston finished 8th. Wayne's other starter, Shy Tom, owned by Wayne's new main owner W.T. Young, finished 10th.

Open Mind did not run in the Derby, but she helped Wayne take a quinella in the Kentucky Oaks, with Open Mind 1st and Imaginary Lady 2nd. Said Wayne, "I own 50% of Imaginary Lady and 22 shares in Marfa (Her sire). It would have been better for me if Imaginary Lady had won, but I don't play the game that way."

1990

Wayne came with 3 contenders, one from Calumet Farm and two which he owned jointly with Overbrook Farm. Lukas was co-breeder of one of them, Real Cash. This Kentucky Derby showed how far Wayne had come in the racing world. Once 'starving' in the dry, wide, harsh expanses of Texas, he was now linked to two of the most powerful breeding establishments in the lush green grass and white-mansioned world of Kentucky.

There was, however, a nightmare lurking in the background - in the field for the race to be precise. Video Ranger, a long shot, had been in Wayne's stable, but was claimed for $40,000 out of a maiden claiming race in January. If Video Ranger was

to win, Wayne would be known as the man who sent battalions to the Derby but lost a winner in a claiming race just 5 months before it won. I mean, you're talking about a real trainer's nightmare here, possibly the ultimate American Thoroughbred trainer's nightmare. If the ultimate dream is to have a Kentucky Derby winner, the ultimate nightmare would be to lose such a horse in a claiming race shortly before it won the Derby.

There was a bad omen before the race. On the way into a VIP parking lot with his pal and onetime public relations man, Indiana basketball coach Bobby Knight, a guard stopped the car.

"D. Wayne Lukas," said a voice from the car.

"Never heard of you," said the guard. "Move on."

This is the time to be Adolf Hitler or Joseph Stalin - when you are trying to get a parking spot at a Kentucky Derby attended by 128,000 people. Wayne parked elsewhere. Bobby Knight thought it was hilarious.

In the race, Wayne's horse Real Cash duelled with the unbeaten favorite, Puerto Rican-owned Mr Frisky. The two set suicidally fast fractional times and began to fade by the time they had gone a mile. Video Ranger was one of a bunch that swept around them. It would have been interesting to monitor Wayne's heart rate and blood pressure at this point. But Unbridled swept to the lead and held it, with Video Ranger fourth. Wayne's horses finished 7th, 10th and 11th. The duelling Real Cash was 11th while Mr Frisky hung on to be 8th in a field of 15.

Wayne's entries in the Preakness and the Belmont did little better.

No doubt the Kentucky Derby win of Winning Colors in 1988 has taken most of the pressure off - but there is still THE Triple Crown.

5.2-2 Wayne's Breeders' Cup record

The Breeders' Cup is a new arrival on the scene. It concentrates $10m in prizemoney and a welter of championship events onto one track, on one day. Breeders' Cup day was the brainchild of breeder John Gaines, who believed that racing needed a televised equivalent of the Superbowls and Grand Finals of other sports. It needed something concentrated, something that would be a big television occasion - live all afternoon on a major network. After all, if you are not on TV, some would say you don't exist.

Gaines was successful in persuading the industry to back the idea. Large amounts of money were collected. Stallion owners had to pay one service fee to make the stallion's offspring eligible. Owners of young contenders had to pay to maintain that eligibility. Horses not paid up had to pay huge sums to become eligible. Of the money raised, $10m would be distributed on the day. (The rest is spread over many races and dates and tracks.) Final order of eligibilty was determined by points which were allocated for winning or placing in graded stakes races during that year.

The Breeders' Cup races:
$1m $1^1/_{16}$ mile for 2yo colts
$1m $1^1/_{16}$ mile for 2yo fillies
$3m $1^1/_4$ mile classic for 3yo and up
$1m $1^1/_4$ mile mare's race, the distaff
$1m 6 furlong open sprint
$1m 1 mile on turf
$2m $1^1/_2$ mile on turf
A steeplechase at another venue

1984
The first year of the Breeders' Cup. The big question was - would it work? Because of doubts, a lot of good sires were not nominated. There was a wait-and-see attitude by some breeders. Because it is held in November, many top horses were not kept in training for it, or they were too tired and there wasn't sufficient time to freshen them up. As a result, a lot of good racehorses were not nominated. That helped Wayne get away to a good start and so did the venue - Hollywood Park in Los Angeles.

Juvenile Stakes, Fillies
Fiesta Lady 7th, Tiltalating 8th
Juvenile Stakes, Colts
Tank's Prospect 2nd to Chief's Crown. $225,000
Distaff Stakes
Life's Magic 2nd, Lucky Lucky Lucky 6th. $225,000 and $10,000

Lukas Stable's take-home? $560,000 without a winner! At the end of the decade it would be the only Breeders' Cup meeting at which he *didn't* have a winner.

1985
This was the second year of the event and attitudes had changed. The doubts had gone and the entries were up. The sheer weight of prizemoney was enough to make each race a true championship event. Lukas arrived with 10 horses to contest 4 of the 7 races on the program. The races were held at the Aqueduct track in New York.

Juvenile Stakes, Fillies
Twilight Ridge 1st, Family Style 2nd Arewehavingfunyet 8th (A visitor to Lukas's stables in August had claimed there were no outstanding two-year-old's about. Lukas's top two-year-old for the year to that time was Klein's Sovereign Don with whom he had won two New York stakes races. "Just stay in the buggy," said Lukas. "In the next 60 days, your eyes will be popping out. We're still running our 'B' team. We haven't even put

the first team in yet." That tells you how important Wayne considers the Breeders' Cup.)

Juvenile Stakes, Colts
Ketoh 8th, Louisiana Slew 11th
Distaff Stakes
Life's Magic 1st, Lady's Secret 2nd, Alabama Nana 4th
Sprint
Mt Livermore 3rd, Pancho Villa 5th (5th still paid $50,000!)

Lukas Stables won $1,688,000. Klein's four earned $1.35m on the day.

1986
Juvenile Stakes, Fillies
Sacahuista 4th, Anything For Love 10th
Juvenile Stakes, Colts
Capote 1st, Pledge Card 10th
Distaff Stakes
Lady's Secret, by 2½ lengths, Twilight Ridge 6th
Sprint Stakes
Pine Tree Lane 2nd

Wayne's brigade made off with $1,195,000

1987
Juvenile Stakes, Fillies
Dream Team 3rd, Classic Crown 6th, Over All 7th, Lost Kitty 10th, Blue Jean Baby 11th. Wayne provided the field - almost. Four of Wayne's starters were Klein horses. Klein had owned the San Diego Chargers, and his racing colors were similar. This prompted one wag to suggest that the cluster of jockeys looked like a San Diego Chargers huddle. With five runners, the result left Wayne shocked and disappointed, but he still won $118,000.
Juvenile Stakes, Colts
Success Express 1st, Tejano 3rd, Contempt 10th
Distaff Stakes
Sacahuista 1st, Clabber Girl 2nd, North Sider 6th
Sprint
High Brite 5th, On The Line 10th, Pine Tree Lane 11th

1988
Juvenile Stakes, Fillies
Open Mind 1st, Darby Shuffle 2nd, Lea Lucinda 3rd, Some Romance 6th, One Of A Klein 11th. Doing poorly with bulk last time obviously didn't change Wayne's approach. This time it paid off with the first three placings, and a lot of money.
Juvenile Stakes, Colts
Is It True 1st, beating Easy Goer. One of the upsets of the year.

Distaff Stakes
Winning Colors 2nd, just beaten by Personal Ensign in what at year's end was voted Race of the Year. Classic Crown 5th.
Sprint
Gulch 1st, High Brite 12th
Classic
Slew City Slew 9th
Mile
Steinlen 2nd

A record three wins, plus three seconds and a third. $2,133,000

1989
Juvenile Stakes, Fillies
Stella Madrid 3rd, Special Happening 4th, Voodoo Lilly 11th
Juvenile Stakes, Colts
Grand Canyon 2nd. If he had beaten Shug McGaughey's Rhythm it would have been four in a row for Lukas, and a major win for a major new client.
Distaff Stakes
Open Mind 3rd, Highest Glory 5th, Winning Colors 9th, Wonder's Delight 10th
Sprint
On The Line was injured within 25 yards of the start and had no chance.
Classic
Slew City Slew 6th
Mile
Steinlen 1st. This win rescued the day for Wayne and made it winners for five consecutive Cup Days.

Wayne believes in sending a lot of horses to this event, including a lot that finish near the rear -obviously the same approach as he has to the Derby. The result: he has more winners by far than any other trainer - 10. Those wins were worth $450,000 each.

Almost all of these wins have been in just 3 of the 8 races - the two Juvenile's races and the Distaff. These races for two-year-old's, and the Distaff for fillies three-year-old and up, are over more distance than ideal for Wayne. In fact the Juvenile races seem rather long (1 1/16m) for two-year-old's in America. Maybe they set the distance with Wayne in mind! Nevertheless they have been good races for Wayne, much better than the Kentucky Derby, and he may go on to have his name associated with one or several of these races (or indeed the Breeders' Cup), in the same way as the Jones brothers are associated with the Kentucky Derby, Charlie Whittingham with the big Californian handicap races and Woody Stephens with the Belmont Stakes.

In particular Wayne's record in the Breeders' Cup Distaff is already worthy of comment. In the first five years he had first or second or both in every running for a total of three wins and four seconds.

Wayne's attitude is clear: "When else are you going to get a day when every breeder and person that even knows they run racehorses is going to be watching you? You've got to point them for it. They're the most important races in the world and you've got to look good."

All things considered, the Breeders' Cup was a gift to Wayne. It was started just after he hit the front in money, so he was ready for it. It had four divisions for which his training and selection skills were suited. Horses qualify by winning or placing in stakes races which he already chased all over the country, for black type breeding value. Apart from the huge prize money and breeding value, it has been a better showcase for him than the Kentucky Derby.

Eclipse Awards
These awards are named (I presume) after two famous horses, the original Eclipse of England, and another in the United States, known as American Eclipse. In 1970 J. B. Faulconer of Kentucky suggested at a convention of Thoroughbred Racing Associations that racing needed something akin to the Academy Awards. A committee was set up to consolidate existing awards into one set. The result was the Eclipse Awards, voted on by a body of writers and journalists across the country. Naturally there are fewer awards after this consolidation but the result has been greater prestige and greater publicity for those who do win them. There is however an element of popularity with the voters in winning an Eclipse award. It is not decided by some objective test, but then the same thing is true of the Academy Awards.

This popularity factor would not be in Wayne's favor. For whatever reasons, he is not popular with the racing fraternity. Even after winning the most money for 1983 and 1984, Wayne did not win the Eclipse Award for outstanding trainer. The welcome mat was not out. A lot of the Eclipse votes are from the New York area and they regard Californians as upstarts.

One year Wayne led in money, stakes and wins, but still didn't get the trainer's Eclipse Award. "We did everything," he told an interviewer. But the Eclipse Award that year went to Jack Van Berg. Lukas recognised that Van Berg had also been slighted and passed over previously, so he hoped that eventually he would get the Eclipse.

Eventually they had to give it to him in 1985, and that broke the ice. He won it again in 1986 and 1987. In 1988 the award went to Shug (as in sugar) McGaughey, trainer of Easy Goer. Shug looked like making it two in a row, but Sunday Silence put Easy Goer away 3 races to 1, and Charlie Whittingham won the 1998 Eclipse Award for best trainer. If the Eclipse Award went with money won or stakes, Wayne would own it.

5.3 Some major horses

Wayne's Eclipse Award-winning horses

1982	Landaluce	Champion 2yo Filly
1983	Althea	Champion 2yo Filly
1984	Life's Magic	Champion 3yo Filly
1985	Family Style	Champion 2yo Filly
	Life's Magic	Champion Older Handicap Mare
1986	Lady's Secret	Horse Of The Year
	Capote	Champion 2yo Colt
1987	Sacahuista	Champion 3yo Filly
	North Sider	Champion Older Handicap Mare
1988	Open Mind	Champion 2yo Filly
	Winning Colors	Champion 3yo Filly
	Gulch	Champion Sprinter
1989	Open Mind	Champion 3yo Filly
	Steinlen	Champion Turf Male

To attempt a full list of significant Lukas horses would require a lot of space. Below are some of his more interesting horses, in chronological order.

LANDALUCE: By Seattle Slew. Cost $650,000 at the sales in 1981. This filly was a very important horse in the rise of Wayne Lukas. In 1982 this filly generated more excitement and crowd interest than any horse since Secretariat in his Triple Crown Wins of 1973. She was featured in an ABC newscast with footage of two of her crushing victories. As a result mail poured in for her and Lukas had to hire a secretary to answer it. Considered one of the best fillies of the decade, she won the Hollywood Lassie by 21 lengths. 21 lengths!

Unfortunately Landaluce died with a viral infection while still a two-year-old, her head cradled in Wayne's lap. Wayne wept then and on at least one occasion when speaking of her in an interview. Posthumously she was awarded the Champion Two-Year-Old title for 1982 and later a major race was named after her.

MARFA: Bought at the 1981 Keeneland Sales for $300,000. Started twice as a two-year-old for one third placing. Three wins from 13 starts at three, including the Santa Anita Derby by 3 lengths and the Jim Beam Spiral Stakes by 8 lengths. Ran 5th in the Kentucky Derby and 4th in the Preakness. Career earnings of $407,944 from 15 starts with three wins. Injured a check ligament in the middle of his three-year-old year. The injury returned to end Marfa's career. He was retired to stand at Hancock Place for the 1985 season at $5,000 per live foal, still owned by French, Beal and Lukas. In 1987 he was moved to North Ridge Farm, where he was to continue at $5,000 live foal. When the owner of North Ridge ran into financial trouble, Marfa was moved to Lane's End, to stand the 1990 season at $10,000.

MOUNT LIVERMORE: By Blushing Groom. Cost $150,000 in 1982. Had 30 starts for 11 wins (4 stakes), making $610,000. Syndicated in 1986 for $4m. In 1989 he was 28th in the Sires of two-year-old's list.

LIFE'S MAGIC: By Cox's Ridge and bought at the Keeneland Fall Sale in 1982, but she still cost $310,000. She won $2,255,218. Her biggest win was in the 1985 Breeders' Cup Distaff, which she won by six lengths. In foal to Alydar she was included in the sale of Klein stars. One year earlier this bay mare had been put up at auction as the fairest way for Klein to buy out his partner Melvin Hatley. The Maktoums bought into the action and Klein had to bid $5.4m to retain the mare, although he doubtless had a mental reserve at which he would have been happy to let the Maktoums have her and bank his share of the sale price. At the second sale however, the Maktoums took her away, in foal to Alydar, for $4.4m.

Lukas was part owner of three that sold for more than a million dollars in the same sale. Two were still in training with Lukas for the Breeders' Cup, which was only weeks away - an interesting time to sell a horse!

ALTHEA: A homebred campaigned by the operations manager at King Ranch Thoroughbreds, Helen Alexander, in partnership with her mother, Mrs Helen Groves and Englishman David Aykroyd. Althea was in Alydar's first crop. She was Champion two-year-old filly of USA for 1983. She won over $1.25m. Lukas ran her in the Arkansas Derby 1984 (Approx April 20) in which she set a course record of 1:46 4/5. It was a nice Group 1 prep race for her shot at the Kentucky Derby and another example of Lukas beating the colts with a filly.

TANK'S PROSPECT: A son of champion sire and sire of sires, Mr Prospector. Bought for Eugene Klein by Lukas at a cost of $625,000 at the 1983 Keeneland yearling sales.

1984 2nd in the Breeders' Cup Juvenile to Chief's Crown.

1985 1st El Camino Real Derby (Grade 3) at Bay Meadows. Ran last in the Santa Anita Derby on April 6th, due to epiglottic entrapment. In this condition the airway is obstructed. Operated by Dr Greg Ferrraro with only a local anaesthetic, the horse was cantering two day's later and did a serious 5/8ths of a mile five days later. Lukas sent him the same track to the Kentucky Derby as Althea the year before, i.e. via the Arkansas Derby - run April 20 1985. Lukas worried how the horse would run after its choking experience in the El Camino Real Derby.

"In my mind the only question was Tank's Prospect's mental condition. Sometimes if a horse runs a race without getting air, he is hesitant to put out (try) the next time. After the first five furlongs I knew he was going to finish big." Tank's Prospect won the Arkansas Derby. Nevertheless, even days after the Arkansas Derby, Lukas cannot have been certain he would take Tank's Prospect to the Kentucky Derby in Louisville.

"I filled out three health certificates today for Tank's Prospect,' he told reporters. 'One was for Louisville, one was for California, and one was for New York. I've got them all laying on the trunk in the tack room, so tomorrow morning I can pick up the one I need. I think we will pick up the Louisville one." Tank's Prospect did poorly in the Kentucky Derby but won the Preakness.

Syndicated for $16m although it was said Klein was left with more shares than he wanted.

SARATOGA SIX: By Alydar. Cost $2.2m in 1983. An outstanding colt which broke down early in it's career. Syndicated for $16m.

PANCHO VILLA: By Secretariat out of the Crimson Satan mare Crimson Saint. A full brother to Terlingua, bought in 1983. Did he buy this horse on conformation or consanguinity i.e. on its appearance or its blood relationship to Terlingua? Probably both because he paid $1.8m. Pancho Villa won some major sprints and set a track record on a muddy track. Syndicated for $6m.

TWILIGHT RIDGE: By Cox's Ridge. A Lukas selection purchased by Klein at the 1984 Fasig-Tipton Kentucky summer yearling sale for $350,000. Wayne Lukas had a chance to buy this filly for LESS THAN ONE THIRD of this price just months earlier. Because Lukas was having great success with Life's Magic and she was by Cox's Ridge, a bloodstock agent asked him if he would be interested in looking at another filly by the same sire. At the time, Wayne was in Hot Springs, Arkansas, to race Althea in that year's Arkansas Derby.

"I asked how far away the farm was, and the man told me about an hour, so I didn't bother to go take a look at her." (Isn't it heartening to know that even the gods make mistakes.)

Helen Alexander, part-owner of Althea, did take the time, liked what she saw and bought the filly for $90,000. When Wayne and Eugene bought the filly, Helen Alexander made nearly $240,000 profit - because of a two hour car trip! When you're hot you're hot.

This filly was broken at San Luis Rey Downs, a pre-training centre about 60 miles south of Santa Anita and Hollywood Park. Wayne kept his off-track horses there before Klein built a training center. She was then sent to Jeff at Belmont Park, New York. She suffered bucked shins after winning under pressure in the Astoria Stakes (Grade 3) at Belmont on July 30.

Lukas outlined his thinking: "99 out of 100 you might keep in training with her kind of injury, but you have to do what is best for the horse. If you don't have a barn full of good fillies,

you might say, 'Let's paint her (shins) and send her out in the Spinaway.' We decided the best thing to do with her was to rest her and get her ready for the Breeders' Cup in the fall."

Lukas did have a barn full of good fillies and sent out Family Style to win the Grade 1 Spinaway. Twilight Ridge however did not race for 3½ months. By mid-October Lukas was looking for a race before the Breeders' Cup. An allowance race at Meadowlands failed to fill so she was vanned the next day to Philadelphia where she ran against fillies in the Critical Miss Stakes, in which she ran second. She was then vanned back to Belmont to await the Breeders' Cup.

"We sent her to Philadelphia to get a race into her," Klein was quoted as saying. "I'm not saying we weren't trying to win, but a minor stakes victory at Philadelphia Park wasn't the goal we had set for a filly we felt was one of the best in the country. Our goal was the Breeders' Cup." She won the Breeders' Cup Juvenile Stakes for Fillies, worth $450,000.

Sold at the 1987 Night of the Stars, in foal to Saratoga Six, for $1.325m.

LADY'S SECRET: By Secretariat out of Great Lady M., a mare Lukas owned. This amazing mare raced at two and lasted to run at five, for a career record of 45 starts and 25 wins. Her total of over $3m in prizemoney was a record for a mare. In 1986 she won a record eight Grade 1 stakes races, for which the four-year-old was named Horse Of The Year.

Towards the end of 1987 the Fasig-Tipton sales company's president, John Finney guaranteed Klein that Lady's Secret would sell for $6m. Finney wanted Klein's outstanding grey mare as the focus of his 'Night of the Stars Sale'. She could give Finney's sale title a great deal of credibility. Klein agreed and eventually eight of his horses brought in $14,525,000. Bidding on Lady's Secret went up in million dollar leaps to $5m then went on in $100,000 steps but the bidding did not reach $6m and Robert P. Levy of Fasig-Tipton signed for her at $5.4m.

LIFE AT THE TOP: By Seattle Slew. Cost $800,000 in 1984. Won a few thousand less than a million. Sold for $1.1m.

CAPOTE: By Seattle Slew. Cost $800,000 in 1985. Won the Norfolk Stakes (Gr 1), Breeders' Cup Juvenile for Colts, and one other race from four starts at two. Named Champion Two-Year-Old Colt of 1986, and given top weight of 126 pounds in the Experimental Free Handicap for two-year-old's, but failed to win a race in six starts at three. His career ended with winnings of $714,470. A half interest was bought by a stud for $6.4m, presumably Calumet where he went to stand at stud.

SUCCESS EXPRESS: by Hold Your Peace from a Canadian Oaks winner. Ran 6 furlongs in 1:8.4 at Belmont. Won the $213,000 Sport of Kings Futurity at Louisiana Downs by 15

This is Wayne's beautiful home. Many of the trademarks of the Lukas stables are there - a passion for white paint, trim green lawns, shaped trees, and lots of bright flowers. The flowers are impatiens in the foreground and begonias along the front of the house.

lengths, beating Risen Star. The time was one second outside the record and the fastest by a two-year-old. Won the Breeders' Cup Juvenile at Hollywood Park in 1:35.2 Won $835,359 and then sold for $1.25m to onetime corporate octopus Robert Holmes à Court, to stand at his studs in Australia. Only cost $150,000.

WINNING COLORS: A very big filly, 16.3 hands high, by Caro Lukas is not afraid to buy them big. Cost $575,000 at the 1986 Keeneland Summer Sale. beat the colts by 7½ lengths in the Santa Anita Derby, then went on to win the Kentucky Derby, making her one of the most important horses in Wayne's career. Won $1,379,146. Sold in the 1989 Klein wind-up sale for $4.1m

OPEN MIND: By Deputy Minister, a sire with little to recommend him until this filly. Selected by Wayne, Klein paid only $150,000 for her, won $1.8m with her, then sold her for $4.6m, making her one of the bargains of the decade. Champion two-year-old Filly of 1988. Wins included the Breeders' Cup Juvenile for fillies. At three, won the Kentucky Oaks, the New York Fillies Triple Crown (three Grade 1 events), along with many other stakes races. Went on to win an Eclipse award as Champion three-year-old Mare of 1989,one of only nine fillies to top

the list at two and three, since 1936.

5.4 Where was Wayne at age -

20 - 1955 In college, training to become a teacher and coach.

30 - Still in Wisconsin, teaching, coaching and training Quarter Horses.

40 - 1975 At the top of the game in Quarter Horses at Los Alamitos.

50 - Top of the money in Thoroughbreds for the third year straight.

In 1990 Wayne turned 55.

6. His operation now

6.1 Home

Wayne's home is in sunny California. He has a beautifully kept house on a large block of land in a suburb of Los Angeles close to Santa Anita racetrack. Most trainers in Los Angeles live in that area in preference to living near Hollywood Park track. Santa Anita is set in nice suburbs with trees, hills and the mountains behind. Hollywood Park is set in a low, flat, hot area of less desirable suburbs with lines of landing aeroplanes overhead every minute of the day. Wouldn't an airport be useful to Wayne? Yes, but there IS a smaller airport, Ontario, not far from Santa Anita. At times he has kept a plane there.

In the grounds of the house is an office which houses much of Wayne's large collection of training awards. In a rear corner is a children's play house. Behind the house is an elegant poolside entertaining area, complete with fountains and arched bridges.

6.2 Organization, stables and staff

Corporate headquarters for Team Lukas is Norman, Oklahoma, a hangover from his Quarter Horse days and his connections with Mel Hatley and Bob Moore. General Manager J. David Burrage heads a group there who look after all the accounting, financial planning and legal matters. Burrage has a degree in accounting. He went to work for Wayne in 1981, whom he met when he worked for an associate of Wayne's. He describes himself as carrying Wayne's briefcase.

This is also the management base for the many racing partnerships and for Wayne's venture into the stock market through the publicly traded Mid-America Stables Inc. In this company Wayne is Chairman of the Board and Jeff is President. In June 1987 the company raised $4m and at the Keeneland sales Wayne spent $402,000 of that on four Thoroughbred yearlings. Wayne has found answering to so many small bosses a bit tedious. He has also been hit with a lawsuit by shareholders, who claim the share offering individually benefited the Lukas's and Burrage. Mid-America acquired the assets of Melvin Hatley, which included about 56 horses. The horses were valued by an auditing company at $1.7m but were later sold at a book loss of $710,000. This was largely due to a decline in the Quarter Horse market. The suit alleges the prospectus did not disclose that the Lukases and Burrage held interests in the Hatley Partnership. So don't expect a big expansion of the public company side of the business.

Adjoining the headquarters building is the Lukas farm where Wayne maintains a large broodmare band. Wayne bought the property from Mel Hatley. As you would expect, the farm is an upto-the-minute showplace facility. Wayne originally bred Quarter Horses here. In 1981 he was reported to have sold $2m worth of mares to a buyer and was arranging Quarter Horse sires for them. Now Wayne and his clients, as a group, have become a major consignor of Thoroughbreds at the fall broodmare sales, and the mares and foals are prepared here. According to Burrage, they have sold an annual average of about $20m worth of horses at these sales, over the last three years. Presumably these are mostly mares he has trained, often in foal to stallions in which he has shares, sold at sales like the Night of the Stars Sale.

Stables

In America, trainers house their horses in stables (they call them barns) at the track. These are provided by the track owners. There usually aren't enough boxes so most trainers have their young horses, injured horses and excess horses at special training tracks where they rent stalls.

Wayne has year-round stables in California and New York as well as seasonal racing stables each year in the states of New Jersey, Kentucky, Nebraska, Florida, Ohio, Arkansas, Illinois, Louisiana and Alabama. The new track at Remington Park in Oklahoma will also have a seasonal representation. Any track with a decent stakes race can expect a visit from some of his better horses.

The New York division became permanent around 1983, and in 1985 was run by Kevin Rodine in the winter and by Wayne's son Jeff teaming with Rodine in Summer. Kiaran McLaughlin runs it in winter now. When Jeff takes over for the summer, Kiaran runs summer stables like Monmouth Park. In the Midwest, after starting as a low key operation, a more permanent Midwest division was started around 1986 when the new Canterbury Downs track looked promising but it went back to a low key operation as Canterbury staggered towards bankruptcy.

Wayne's operation is perhaps best known for the impact his barns have on visitors. This is something of an achievement because the barns are the property of the track owners and at most grounds are made of dull gray concrete, or of timber that is now old and tatty. He achieves this visual jolt with beds and windowboxes of colorful plants which are invariably in flower; potted trees with glossy bright green leaves; healthy, flat, neatly trimmed lawns; engraved, white painted, wooden signs; plenty of white painted railings; white saddle racks all carefully aligned; and everything surrounded by clean soil in carefully raked patterns.

The white trim around doors and stalls and sometimes much of the building appears to have had a recent coat of paint. At Santa Anita Wayne had a smart varnished timber door to his office, the grain showing through. The door was so out of character with the age and condition of the rest of the building that he must have brought it with him.

The horses' stalls have a white, freshly-painted door frame and all the tack, equipment and haynets are in good order. The bedding is first class hay, deep, fluffy and fresh. The combination of lots of white paint with lots of strong light bulbs gives a bright, well lit appearance to the corridors and stalls. There are no gloomy corridors or grubby stalls, no traces of moldiness anywhere to be seen. And no worrying smells. The tack rooms are orderly and clean with a place for everything and everything in its place. The gear itself is all oiled and soaped and polished.

In the cupboards where detergents, shampoos, hoof treatments, bandages and medications are kept, there are labels to indicate what belongs where and what is more, the label and the goods immediately above them usually correspond. Containers are in neat orderly rows with spaces between the rows, something that doesn't happen by accident.

On any ordinary day after the main business of working the horses, taking care of legs and feeds and so on is over, Wayne and his enthusiastic Mexican bee-swarm turn their attention to the appearance of the stables. People are hosing and hanging mats, dusting walls and shelves, removing any hay and debris. The final phase consists of a lot of sweeping, shoveling, brushing and raking to achieve a uniformly flat, soft, earthen surface. The only ugliness left at the end of their efforts are the small mountains of soiled hay and dung which sit awaiting the trucks from the mushroom farms.

Usually the clean-up takes less than an hour and by 10 or 11am the stable looks like Royalty is due any minute for a tour of inspection. Part of the impact is due to the comparison with the stables that surround Wayne's. Most of the trainers understandably take little pride in buildings that are something of a natural eyesore, which they do not own, often only occupy for a matter of months before moving on, and may not even be allocated next season at the same track. All this titivation and embellishment, this dressing up, takes time and money. Most of the trainers can think of things they'd rather do with both.

Nevertheless the immediate impression on owners, of conspicuous orderliness, uncommon attention to detail and a healthy surgical ward cleanliness, could only be a good one. To get to Wayne's equine Hilton owners have had to pick their way through horse dung, soiled hay and peculiar looking liquids of dubious origin. Owners are often in footwear more suited to a carpeted bar. Their reaction can only be one of, "thank God my expensive horse is in this man's stables and not those other dirty dingy dungeons".

Many horsemen take the attitude that any worthwhile owner will know that the Lukas trimmings are just unnecessary show - extra glitz and worker's time that ultimately goes on the owner's bill. One thing is for certain, Wayne does not have many imitators among the trainers around Belmont Park, Hollywood Park or Santa Anita.

Trainer Willard Proctor is quoted as saying, "It's important you keep the barn clean and neat, sure, but if he wants to go into the landscaping business he should do that." I suspect that any trainer trying to tart up his stables to become a Lukas clone would cop one hell of a rubbishing from his colleagues. Possibly a new generation of trainers will follow suit and only then will Wayne's display lose its impact.

Staff

Wayne was reported to have 267 employees in 1987. That may have been a turnover number or an average number. His workforce in the barns is almost entirely Mexican. They work hard and willingly, although there are a lot of broken shifts with some staff returning to race horses in the afternoon, some for evening feeding etc.

Border-hopping is rife and many of the Mexicans in California are illegal 'aliens'. In 1983 Wayne had to suffer the indignity of being one of five southern California trainers charged with harboring illegal aliens. Two raids by the U.S. Immigration and Naturalization Service at San Luis Rey Downs netted over 250 illegal aliens. The trainers entered guilty pleas and cooperated with the authorities. Repeated or deliberate offenses could have serious consequences. Conviction of a felony would automatically disqualify a person from holding a racing license. Lukas therefore has to be very careful about employee's papers. Charlie Whittingham on the other hand employs mainly African-Americans (formerly negroes), and whites.

Lukas's barns have several differences to most of the barns around his where working conditions are concerned. There are no coffee dispensers, the lifeblood of many barns as grooms and riders try to wake themselves in the early morning darkness. He is on record as saying this is because people stand around coffee machines and talk and waste time. It no doubt helps that he only wants one shot of coffee a day himself, and that he drinks it before he gets to work.

Profane language is not allowed. Wayne tells the help that this is a place of business and that work is the activity required. There are no loud radios, because they might frighten the horses, distract the workers or make it hard for people to communicate with each other.

There are card-punch time-clocks. Every employee has to put their card in on arrival and departure and have the times punched in. The clock is an Acroprint, made by Time Recorder Company. There are names on the cards - like Perez, Garcia, Cerano, Olivez, de la Lobos. There's a date 28/6 to 4/7. Sections for regular time and extra time .

Such clocks are almost unique in American racing barns in my experience. For Wayne the clocking system is just part of running his stables like any other well-run business. The clock and cards are very close to the office of Wayne or whoever is in charge and there would not be too much punching of cards for late friends.

Clocking devices are usually used when an employer has a lot of employees, isn't always there to check up on their presence or absence, and doesn't trust them to turn up on the dot. However NOT having them is not necessarily a sign of benevolence. Sometimes not having a time clock allows a trainer to exploit his employees, working them for a longer period than he pays them for, not an unusual practice in racing. Wayne obviously prefers to police the punctuality of his employees, but also to pay accordingly. He has an almost entirely Mexican workforce, but there is little 'fiesta', 'siesta' or 'maniana', just lots of hard work.

Organization of the staff through the day is controlled by daily lists, which Wayne or his on the spot chief make up the

This is the kind of back yard the average slacker dreams about. Such wonderful places to relax are usually owned by workaholics like Wayne. More of the Lukas style.

The Lukas stable at Hollywood Park. Note signs, welters of white paint and a profusion of potted plants. There are lots of begonias, trimmed trees and lush lawns.

previous evening or before training starts. These lists detail who amongst the workers will do what. There are lists showing which horses are doing fastwork, jogging, walking, etc. The list of horses racing in the afternoon also details who will take the horse over to the track and what gear has to go with it. Anyone unable to carry out their listed job is to arrange a replacement and notify someone higher in the hierarchy.

All these lists go on a bulletin board outside the main office in the stable, along with a treatment list, vet list and a staff list. The staff list specifies who is coming back for evening feed up, who's day off it is next day etc. There is a list in the feed room of how many dippers of grain to put in each horse's feed.

Phones play a large part in the day by day management of Wayne's far-flung equine empire. Not long after he arrives at 4:30 - 5:00am he receives phone calls from all the people in charge of his racing stables around the country (the number of which varies), and from David Burrage in Norman, Oklahoma. Because of the timezone differences, the hour is a little more civilized for the others. At Wayne's stable the phone rings frequently during the morning, and if it doesn't he gets on and makes calls himself. The callers seem to know when Wayne will be between sets of horses. The phone bill of his organization must be massive but he obviously thinks it is worthwhile.

By late morning the stables are immaculate. The curved bales are called 'puffs' by some people. Each has a mat under it - a neat, re-usable display. All the horses seem to be asleep. Note one halter per stall. Striped bags hold feeds.

Wayne has a number of assistant trainers, but one of the most important people in his organization is his son Jeff.

Son - Jeffrey Wayne Lukas

Wayne's son Jeff was born on November 29 1957, when Wayne was 22. Wayne, like many a sportsfan father, encouraged Jeff to try hard in the directions of football and basketball. Jeff did well but was not major league. He attended the University of Wisconsin like his father, but he did a business major at the River Falls campus.

Helping out at his father's Quarter Horse barns over the summer vacations, Jeff found he liked the work and liked working for his father. He joined his father full-time in the spring of 1979, taking out his trainer's license. "When my dad switched to Thoroughbreds in 1978, I figured it would be a good opportunity to grow with the business."

After a number of years under Wayne's intense tutelage in California, Jeff was sent off to help Wayne's assistant trainer with the horses the stable sent to New York. The Lukas assault on the rich plums of New York racing has a summer seasonal peak. This allows Jeff to move home to Arcadia each winter, near his father, as the snows fall on New York.

Since the fall of 1983 Jeff has been listed as overseer of the Lukas New York division. He has supervised many of the top Lukas stable horses to major wins and is highly regarded by

Jeff Lukas enjoys a January joke at Hollywood Park. He has good reason to laugh. When the winter snow blows in, he leaves New York and moves to sunny California.

D. WAYNE LUKAS

John Gosden and other trainers. For a few years John Gosden was in the barn next to the Lukases at Hollywood. John has worked with Vincent O'Brien in Ireland and with the late Noel Murless in Newmarket. John has studied Charlie Whittingham closely and is himself regarded as a top trainer: Highly regarded enough to be chosen by Sheik Mohammed bin Rashid al Maktoum to train his horses in Newmarket, England.

John got to know Jeff fairly well. In Gosden's opinion Jeff could go out on his own and train really well. He has an eye for conditioning a horse and is not dependent on instructions from Wayne. The Lukas stable set records for New York in the number of stakes wins in 1985, 1986 and 1987. Like his father, Jeff lists his hobbies as "horse racing". He is married and his wife's name is Linda.

Jeff can be a little tense and a scuffle between him and another trainer occurred during preparations for the Kentucky Derby one year. It was over the parking of a car too near to where the Lukas horses were being washed down. The press were there in droves for the Derby and many of them didn't know much about horses. So Jeff's connection with Wayne - 'the trainer who tries hardest but can't win a Kentucky Derby' - and a fistfight, made for a good story about the frustrations and tensions in the Lukas barn. That hasn't done anything for Jeff's attitude to pressmen nor for the attitude of some of them to him.

D. Wayne Lukas Training Center
This magnificent facility was built by Eugene Klein on a large property on the edge of expanding San Diego, not far from the Del Mar racecourse. Wayne rented the stables and the training track behind them. He used this center for breaking and training and to lay-up any turned out, sore or injured horses.

Horse transportation is a very large concern for Lukas. Apart from shuttling horses back and forth between divisions and between pre-training facilities, he takes horses all over the country in an effort to win stakes races. He has four monster horse transportation trucks in California and 33 licensed vehicles in all. They are part of his own horse transportation company, but are used only to transport his and his clients horses - "The less we have to depend on anyone else the better". Squeezing every dollar possible from the business according to his critics.

6.3 Number of horses
Wayne told a reporter in mid 1989, when the summer-only divisions were in full operation, that he had 40 horses at Monmouth in New Jersey, 36 at Belmont in New York, 40 at Arlington in Chicago and 32 at Del Mar near San Diego. That is 148 horses - *at the track*. Probably just the tip of the iceberg! To this you would have to add smaller unmentioned divisions - horses virtually 'on the road', and those at the training center.

Before Klein built the D. Wayne Lukas Training Center, Wayne kept his off-track racehorses at the San Luis Rey Downs training center. A 1987 article about the San Luis Rey Downs center said Wayne had kept over a hundred horses there. However that might have been a peak number during the winter when many tracks are closed down, and you could not simply add that 100 to the 148 in the racing stables.

Another factor is turnover. Two trainers can have 30 stalls with 30 horses in them. One is principally a trainer of two-year-old's, who tests them quickly, and if they fail, go sore, or need more time they are out. New horses are brought in. Such a trainer might 'test' 90 horses in one year, while maintaining a core of 10 well-known horses. The other might have older horses and have hardly any turnover for the year.

The essential factor is how many horses a trainer has the opportunity to test per year, and that is a very hard figure to obtain. Only a broad estimate is possible.

Trainers tend to understate their numbers and rivals tend to overstate them. The figure given most often for Wayne is 300 but I suspect that is one of those 'guesstimates' that eventually becomes accepted as fact because - Hey! - I've heard it from 10 different people! No matter that we and they all heard it directly or indirectly from the same unreliable source. How many he would train in a year only he and his book-keepers would know. How many he might be offered and refuse only Wayne would know. Suffice to say he gets his hands on BIG numbers.

"How many horses do you train in a year?"
"We average out about 145 -150."
"Is that the number of stalls you have?"
"We have about 145 in the stables round the country and 60 or 70 at the training center. Those are horses laying off or coming back."
"That totals around 210. The most popular figure, the consensus figure for the number of horses you have would be 300."
"No way. Never in my life have we ever even gotten close to that figure."
"What sort of numbers did you have in your Quarter Horse days?"
"35 to 40. Total."

6.4 His typical day, week and year
For most of the last few decades Wayne has risen every morning at 3:20am.
"Where do you have breakfast?"
"I don't. I just get a cup of coffee and a donut on my way over."
"That's your one daily cup of coffee?"
"Yes. I don't ever eat breakfast."
When Jeff and Wayne are in the same town they usually

meet for breakfast at 4.20am in some place like an all-night diner or doughnut place. Understandably Shari and Linda don't feel like socialising or cooking brekkie for the boys at that hour.

Depending on the plans for the day, they will then go to the same or different barns, for instance Wayne to Santa Anita and Jeff to Hollywood Park. Because of limitations on space at whichever track is racing, the bigger trainers usually have a second string in work at the 'other' track i.e. the one with no racing. At the barn Wayne checks his problem horses and begins organizing the day's work.

His ranch foreman in Oklahoma calls around 5am. Wayne and the foreman go over the ranch plans for the day. His trainers around the country call in one after the other. He discusses the work each horse is to do, treatments for any ailments or leg problems, and any problems his assistant trainers have.

Wayne takes out horses for fast works in sets of 3 to 6 at regular intervals until around 9am. Time between sets is spent supervising or on the phone. From about 9am to 10am he finalizes things around the stables, getting right into the work. Wayne gives a lot of orders but he also gets his hands dirty. He's in there digging and scraping, raking or whatever. He works harder than anyone. He then checks the horses and makes preparations for the afternoon's racing. Between 10am and 11am he goes home to eat and spend time in the office.

"I eat one main meal, sometimes in the afternoon, and I don't ever eat dinner. That snack in the morning, and one major meal. The rest of the time I may snack at night. If I feel a little bit hungry I'll have a bowl of cereal or something."

Wayne frequently flies interstate - to sales, or to watch his horses in important races. He always goes to the races when he has horses racing, unless he is involved in sales. After the races finish he goes back to the barn for one or two hours. This time is spent checking on the horses, especially those that raced. He also talks to his assistant trainers and gets the race results of his horses around the country.

He heads for home near Santa Anita racetrack around 6pm to 8pm. If he's leaving Santa Anita it is less than five minutes, if he leaves Hollywood Park it could take half to one hour depending on the traffic. For the month-long season at Del Mar, 90 miles south, he sometimes commutes and sometimes stays overnight near the track.

At home he eats and unwinds by watching cable television replays of the day's races. He might go down to his office (which is in the grounds of his home) for some paper work and usually some more phone calls. Some evenings he dines with horse dealers, owners, prospective owners and business associates. If he does go out, he told me, he is usually back at home by 11:30 or 12:00.

His day has shortened from the 20 hours he budgeted as a hard driving younger man to a mere 16 or 18 hours in his 50s.

He often takes short catnaps, "particularly nowadays". He once told his wife Shari, "I'm going to take a nap. Wake me in seven minutes."

In California, Wayne's week consists of racing every day except Monday and Tuesday. There are usually big meetings on any Monday public holidays. From June to November a lot of Wayne's time is spent preparing for, or at sales.

When Wayne visits New York, Jeff or one of his staff usually collects him at the airport. Wayne has a house in New York but Jeff or assistant trainer Kiaran McLaughlin have the use of that. Wayne stays at a hotel. His business must be mainly at the barn because he seldom hires a vehicle, making do with the barn Jeep, which is also used by Jeff.

The racing year in California begins with four months at Santa Anita, starting the day after Christmas. In late April racing moves to Hollywood Park. In Late July it moves to Del Mar for some seaside summer sport. This is followed by a two week stint at Pomona Fairgrounds, then a month at Santa Anita called the Oak Tree Meet. The Oak Tree profits go to racing charities and research. The last six weeks before Christmas, racing is at Hollywood Park again.

The month at Del Mar may be as near as Wayne gets to a vacation. It's best to stay overnight for a few nights at least; relax and get into the swim of things. Clyde Rice says Wayne does not take vacations, never has. He can reach Wayne 365 days a year at whichever barn Wayne is at, at 5am local time, "and Wayne answers the phone."

6.5 His car

In recent years Wayne has driven a large Mercedes Benz, usually black or white. His Mercedes 500 is stacked with country and western music tapes. One report said he gets a lot of speeding tickets, indeed it said one of them was for doing 110 miles an hour, which was twice the speed limit. "He drives like he's crazy," a trackworker told me.

At one time Wayne had a Rolls Royce *as well* as two Mercs. Presumably the Rolls for special occasions and the Mercs for running down to the barn or the shops. He used to have a share in a jet at nearby Ontario Airport, a Jet Commander apparently, but found that expensive. He now leases one, presumably for the peak of the season, and uses commercial flights more. A private jet must make a big impression on owners. How many trainers could phone an owner, and say, "Your horse is running Saturday in a stakes race in Louisiana, why don't you join us on the jet?"

If the cars and so on seem a little excessive, Wayne has his reasons. He told the Milwaukee Journal Magazine, "I've been through hard times. I've slept in the back of a pickup truck and I've been overdrawn at the bank, so today I don't apologise for my Rolls Royce or my tailored suits. Luck had nothing to do with it. I've been poor and I earned what I have."

Mid morning at Belmont. The trench dug by horses being walked and cooled out has not yet been raked level. Note large fan in use at right and one against the wall at the left end. There is another small one at the top of the first stall. The heat and humidity can become very oppressive in New York in summer. Many of the workers are attending to their horses' legs.

WAYNE'S MORNING: Riders and a saddle pony wait for Wayne. It was after 5am. Wayne was LATE! It is still very gloomy when he takes his first set out.

Later in the morning Wayne takes another set out. He was on the phone and the horses waited. Note white bridle on waiting horse. Also, the horses being hand-walked in the background.

Wayne escorts his set to the track, then waits as they go around. He is watching one of his horses finish, and is so intent he doesn't notice a horse that nearly runs him over.

He doesn't wait for the troops, they have to jog about and calm down. He has too much to do. He heads back. Note observation platform from which many trainers and grooms watch the works. Many trainers watch from the clocker's box, out of sight to the left.

Up the alley and 'home'.

Wayne confers with Charlie Perez about the horses in their care. Note neatly trimmed trees in large white 'pots'.

Out behind the barns, Wayne checks on the progress of some his horses on the small training track. Wayne had an angry exchange with Tony Matos, jockey's agent for Laffite Pincay.

7. Does he get good horses?

This is generally considered one of the most important ingredients of Wayne's success and consequently one of the most interesting to assess.

7.1 Where does he get his horses from?

In his Quarter Horse days Wayne was given horses by owners and he proved himself in the claiming ranks (see claiming races in the glossary). According to Blane Schvaneveld, Wayne was tough to beat at the claiming game. He was soon buying horses in the big Quarter Horse Sales.

Nowadays Wayne buys most of his horses in yearling sales. These horses are for clients although he retains a share of many of them. Few are sent to him by breeders. This is whispered to be because he uses drugs, trains them too hard and/or breaks too many down. But the number of big breeders connected with Wayne is growing, and includes industry leaders like Calumet and Overbrook Farm.

7.2-1 Who chooses?

Wayne appears to be pretty much a one-man band in horse selection. Major clients like Klein, Hatley, Beal, French and Peter Brant are allowed to accompany him at sales, but it is essentially Wayne who chooses. There is however a number of people with whom Wayne consults. They constitute a network or grapevine of information about young horses on the studs. They are mostly people whose opinion Wayne respects and on whose recommendation Wayne will look closely at a horse. The main one is his old friend from his teens, his horse trading partner Clyde Rice.

Clyde and Wayne went around the Thoroughbred sales together when Wayne began going in 1977. Clyde had already been going for some years. They compare notes with each other about the horses they look at.

Some articles have contrasted Wayne's phenomenal success with Clyde Rice's obscurity, training at little-known Penn National track, near Harrisburg, Pennsylvania. The implication is that after an identical start, Clyde had ended up at the other end of the spectrum - a failure.

That is far from true. They certainly had a parallel start; Clyde and Wayne rodeoed and bought and sold horses together; they both went into teaching and coaching; they became fed up with teaching at about the same time and left it for racehorse training. They both started in Quarter Horses but Clyde went into Thoroughbreds sooner than Wayne. Both wandered like the proverbial gypsies for some years. Finally Clyde settled at Penn National in 1973, not long after Wayne settled at Los Alamitos.

Like Lukas, Clyde Rice has a reputation for picking good horses. His philosophy is that his horses are always for sale. He horse-traded his way to ownership of a nearby property called Riverview Farm, then built a huge 52 horse barn at Penn Na-

tional in return for a 75 year lease on the building. To that he has added a large farm near Indian Prairie in Florida. Certainly he was no failure.

He came to public notice because Wayne respects his eye. It was Clyde who picked Life's Magic at Keeneland in 1981. But he doesn't just advise Wayne, he sells horses to him. In 1984 he won first up with a horse then sold it through Lukas to Klein. Some 15 or 20 people had looked but considered it was too much like a Quarter Horse. It went on to win stakes races.

In 1985 Clyde tried to interest Wayne in a whole package of horses. Wayne only bought seven of them, but one was Family Style, one of Wayne's most successful horses. Clyde had paid $60,000 for Family Style at the Keeneland Fall Sale. He also bought Sovereign Don at the Hialeah Two-year-old Sale for $40,000 and many other horses that became winners for Wayne. The fame that followed has enabled him to get more and wealthier clients. Now Clyde leaves training to his sons and spends his winters on his horse breaking property in Florida.

7.2-2 Can Wayne pick the best yearlings?

There are many pitfalls in assessing a trainer's ability to pick the best horses. When we see the lists of a trainer's champion horses, we usually do not know if they were selected by the trainer, by the trainer with help and advice, or by other people. An owner or breeder may have simply sent the horse to the trainer. We also do not know if he trained his champions from 100 horses, 500 horses or a thousand. For example, around the racetracks you will hear estimates of how many horses Wayne Lukas has in training ranging from 60 to 300, mostly the latter. Last but not least, we do not know how many he was outbid on. There must be some trainers with an excellent eye for a racehorse but not enough financial backing to buy their selections. Then of course there is luck.

In the case of Wayne Lukas, there have been two detailed studies of his results buying Thoroughbred yearlings in sales, to help us. The first study was by David L. Heckerman, Joyce Fogleman and John Tolson of the Thoroughbred Record. They have compared his results with those of Sangster and the Sheiks. They looked at the yearling crops sold through the Keeneland Select Sales of 1980 to 1984 inclusive, in their July 1987 issue. This meant the last crop especially, had not completed their careers, the survey being done in the December of their three-year-old year. The horses do not include all the horses purchased in this period by these buyers, because they bought other horses at other sales, for example Lukas purchased Saratoga Six at the Saratoga sales during this period.

The study found spending by Lukas rose from $845,000 in 1980 to $5,680,000 in 1984, an indicator of the rapid rise of the man in the Thoroughbred world. Over the period Lukas spent a total of $17.85m, Sangster $67.7m and the Maktoum family

$124m. The Lukas purchases cost an average of $482,000 compared with $1.3m for Sangster and $912,000 for the Maktoums.

Wayne's had average earnings of $164,125, about four times those of the Sangster and Maktoum horses, but prizemoney in England and Europe where most of the Sangster and Maktoum purchases raced is so low a realistic comparison cannot be made.

Lukas, despite his greater racing success with fillies, bought 19 colts and 18 fillies. Sangster bought 90% colts.

Perhaps the most revealing comparison was in the percentage of winners, stakeswinners and Grade/Group 1 winners, compared to the breed and sale average.

SELECTION STATISTICS

Thoroughbred Record study

	Breed Average	Keeneland Select Av	Lukas	Sangster	Maktoums
Winners	54%	62%	62%	71%	62%
Stakes Winners	3%	12%	27%	35%	17%
Grade 1 Winners	0.2%	2.1%	18.9%	5.8%	4.4%

In summary Lukas bought 37 horses, 31 started, 23 were winners, 10 won a stakes and seven won a Grade/Group 1 event. Again, the Sangster and Maktoum horses had to earn their stakes and Grade 1 wins in a different part of the world, but we can realistically compare Wayne's figures with the sale and breed averages. The findings are quite startling. At the highest level, Group 1, in which the breed average is one in 500, he chose almost one in 5! In case you think all it takes is the money to buy at the select sales, that was nine times the average of the Keeneland Select!

The comparison with Sangster and the Maktoums is tenuous since Lukas campaigned his horses in a different region of the world. However it does allow some measure of the success rate of Wayne Lukas and the level of his yearling selection skills, since both Sangster and the Maktoums have assembled teams of expert advisers to do the same job. Sangster is reputed to have spent a fortune on scientific advisers. Sangster and the Maktoums are also given lists of the choices of their many trainers. The amounts of money spent suggest that if any of the three has had to pass up a selection through being outbid it would usually have been Lukas.

Some things have been in Lukas's favor, notably that both Sangster and the Maktoums have been chasing highly pedi-

greed stock which can run on turf, especially Northern Dancer yearlings. They tended therefore to compete with each other and force up the prices of stock Wayne was not interested in. He wanted dirt runners, so he did not buy any Northern Dancer yearlings while the others bought 23. They also chased stock by Northern Dancer's sons. In addition to buying different stock, Sangster and the Maktoums helped Wayne by taking almost all of their horses out of the North American arena, which meant that of those yearlings left, Wayne was training a lot of the highest-priced.

One factor that swung expenditure statistics Wayne's way was that he was the underbidder on a $13.1m colt bought by Sangster. Had he bought this horse it would have meant an extra $13m had to be made if he was to end up in profit. Would he have made $13m out of this horse? It was an exceptional individual. The consensus of observer's guesses was that Lukas thought this colt might be a dirt and turf horse. Named Seattle Dancer, it went on to win two Group 2 events in Europe. This horse ended a run of sales-topping bummers ie, high-priced horses that could not run out of sight on a dark night. If, as many have suggested, Lukas went after Seattle Dancer in mid 1985 with the intention of running it in Europe, his judgment was good. Wayne would have had a good chance of breaking even on this purchase, perhaps even making a profit from a stallion syndication.

For an American comparison, here are some figures from the Thoroughbred Owners and Breeders Association, given by Edward Bowen in *The Blood-Horse* in 1990. To give buyers some idea of what to expect from buying horses chosen by agents offering their services, he lumped together about 5 respected names in the game and came up with some average figures over a number of years. The figures are not strictly comparable for at least two reasons: the years and sales are not exactly the same, and the agents were probably working in a lower section of the market because of their client's finances. On the other hand, they (or some of them) may have deliberately opted for a strategy of greater numbers at the expense of quality. The Lukas figures are from the Thoroughbred Record study above.

	AGENTS	LUKAS
Average Price	$156,886	$482,000
Average Earnings	$36,084	$164,125
Winners	45%	62%
Stakes Winners	7%	27%

The second major study of Lukas's results filled a whole book, 339 pages, called *Lukas at Auction*. Joe Bagan pulled together all the details: sales prices; breeding and race results; data on number of starts. He also looked for patterns in Wayne's purchases: patterns in sires, dams, dosage, and nicking. Dosage

Lukas's auction sales purchase record

(Compiled from Lukas at Auction, by Joe Bagan, Sachs-Lawlor Co. 1717 S. Acoma St, Denver Colorado, 80223.)

YEAR	No.	COST	EARNINGS	NOTABLE BUYS with winnings
1977	1	275,000	423,896	TERLINGUA Hollywood Juvenile Ch
1978				
1979	8	514,000	76,340	NONE
1980	17	2,006,000	1,261,906	BLUSH WITH PRIDE Kentucky Oaks
1981	24	6,024,000	1,700,084	LANDALUCE Champion 2yo filly
				MARFA $407,944 Derby fav.
1982	27	3,649,000	3,871,864	MT LIVERMORE $610,644
				LIFE'S MAGIC Breeders' Cup Distaff

(That year Seth Hancock of Claiborne Stud decided to hold his nine yearlings out of the Keeneland Sale because they would not sell his horses on the Monday, which he regarded as the strongest day of the sale. Three of those, including first pick by Seth Hancock, went to Woody Stephens to train. That trio included 1984 Kentucky Derby winner Swale and the best two-year-old of the crop, Devil's Bag. Would Wayne have bought them?)

YEAR	No.	COST	EARNINGS	NOTABLE BUYS with winnings
1983	23	9,470,000	3,124,810	SARATOGA SIX Hollywood Juv. Ch.
				TANK'S PROSPECT Preakness Stakes
				PANCHO VILLA Gotham Stakes
1984	28	8,382,000	3,144,258	TWILIGHT RIDGE Breeders' Cup Juv Fillies
				LIFE AT THE TOP $989,504
1985	53	17,374,000	6,093,488*	Underbidder on $13m SEATTLE DANCER
				SACAHUISTA Breeders' Cup Distaff $1.298m
				CAPOTE Breeders' Cup Juv Colts
1986	46	14,081,000	5,850,759*	WINNING COLORS Kentucky Derby
				SUCCESS EXPRESS Breeders' Cup Juv Colts
1987	63	16,434,000	3,455,300*	OPEN MIND Breeders' Cup Juv Fillies
				HOUSTON
1988	64	20,029,000		

*Indicates winnings thru 1988. 1987 crop in particular will win more.

and nicking are both somewhat controversial. Dosage is a mathematical calculation, based upon the capabilities of well known sires in the pedigree, that gives some idea of the distance limitations of a horse. Nicks are crosses of two particular bloodlines that produce exceptionally good results. Bagan's nicking data was obtained from the 'King of Nickers,' Jack Werk of Fremont, California, and the book ends up something of a promotion for Jack.

One of Bagan's conclusions is that Wayne's purchases made a profit after training costs, when resale for breeding and residual values are estimated. He notes that the high syndication prices of the mid-80's helped.

Joe Bagan compares Lukas purchases with those of some other leading names in various years and finds Lukas to have the better results by far. From the details given it is clear that Lukas is not afraid to buy the progeny of first-season sires, unpopular sires, or dams with a poor producing record. Many 'type' buyers don't care if a sire is unsuccessful, but Bagan

makes a case that Wayne does not continue to buy from sires if he gets poor performers. It is also obvious Wayne does not care about dosage or nicks, but Bagan argues that Wayne's results would be even better if he consulted Jack Werk about the nicks.

Clearly Wayne can pick good racehorses and he can do it better than a lot of moneyed and knowledgeable people in the game. He can do it well enough to make a profit on average. But the ultimate aim for a North American trainer is to choose and train a Kentucky Derby winner - as many as possible.

How easy is it to buy a Kentucky Derby winner?

It depends which era you tried. Going through the history of the event, the minimum number of Derby winners kept by breeder's can be determined by checking winning breeder's names against winning owner's names. If they are the same, or if the horse is owned by a person listed as the owner of the breeding farm, I have considered that to be one kept by the breeders. Where there is a stud of unknown ownership, and some entity other than the stud is listed as owner of the horse, I considered the horse to have been sold. Since some of these may actually have been owned by the breeder under another name, or been sold privately rather than by auction, these figures reflect the *minimum* retained by breeders and may overestimate the opportunity for purchase at auction.

In the first 40 years, until the win of Regret did a lot to popularize the race, only 10 out of the 40 winners had been kept by the breeder i.e. 25%. As the Derby became the one to win, the wealthy breeders began to hold onto those yearlings with superior chances. In the 1930's, 40's, 50's, and 60's they kept an average of over 60%. In the 1970s there seemed to be a reversal because only 40% of that decade's winners had been kept by the breeder.

Was this a real difference, a trend due to changing habits or a bit of poor guesswork on the part of the breeders? Because of the upsurge in the number of Derby winners sold in that decade, many commentators went on record saying the change was real. They wrote about the opening up of "the really good blood" to the outsiders in the sale ring. The reason they gave for this opening up was the escalating prices, making it too tempting not to sell. The yearling represented too much money in a very risky form to not at least spread the risk.

Ironically, in the 1980s, it was while the prices were high that the breeders kept the yearlings that became Derby winners. Later in the eighties when the prices fell, the future winners went through the ring. The 1980's have seen five wins by horses bought from the breeder, or 50%.

So, overall, less than half the eventual Derby winners ever go through the sales ring. This makes Wayne's quest quite difficult. If the horses with Derby-winning potential don't go through the sale rings, he has little chance to buy them.

Let's look at Wayne's selection record in the Derby in the 1980s. In 1978, the year 1980 winner Genuine Risk was probably sold, Wayne was not very active in the yearling market. This filly did change hands, presumably through the yearling sales of 1978. The next four winners were all owned by their breeder. The 1985 winner, Spend a Buck, was bought in a private deal, as a yearling, in March of 1983. Ferdinand, winner in 1986, changed ownership from breeder Howard B. Keck to Mrs Elizabeth A. Keck. I doubt there was any real opportunity for Lukas to buy this horse!

I have read that Lukas did not have a chance to look over 1987 winner Alysheba at the 1985 yearling sales because he had stomach trouble, the result of a "bad egg" at breakfast. The article said this was the only Alydar yearling in the sale he did not look at. However Wayne DID look at Alysheba. When I asked him at the Keeneland Sales in 1989, he said he had looked the horse over. He bought the 1988 winner, Winning Colors. He saw the 1989 winner Sunday Silence in the 1987

sales, last chance for the decade, but did not buy him.

I asked Wayne why he didn't buy Alysheba or Sunday Silence. He said it was because they did not score highly enough in his rating system.

"If you buy those kind of horses, if you make those kind of concessions, you will be wrong more often than you'll be right. It's not an exact science, there are always exceptions to the rule, so I don't worry about that. Alysheba made a much better horse than I thought he would. Sunday Silence still fails me when I look at him. If Sunday Silence was in the sales tonight I still wouldn't buy him."

Plenty of people passed up Sunday Silence including everyone connected with him as a yearling. One bloodstock agent who saw Sunday Silence as a yearling described him as being so cow-hocked you could not pass a sheet of paper between his hind legs. Horses sired by Halo also have a reputation for being 'ornery' (difficult). His breeder Arthur Hancock III was part owner only because he got stuck with the horse. He has never claimed he saw anything wonderful about this horse as a yearling.

Clearly it is a numbers and percentages game to Wayne. He does not believe as some do that there is some near infallible formula to be cracked. Only four of the decade's ten Kentucky Derby winners went through the sales ring and Wayne bagged one of them.

The anatomy of a purchase - Saratoga Six

According to a magazine article, Lukas may never have bought Saratoga Six were it not for the resourcefulness of the yearling's owner, Lee Eaton. The well bred colt was in Alydar's second crop, coming up for sale at Saratoga in August 1983, and there was plenty of interest. His dam Priceless Fame was a full sister to champion Bold Forbes. Her first three foals had been stakes winners, including Dunbeath, the early favorite for the recent English Derby. Dunbeath had been bought by the Arabs for a reported $10.2m.

At the sale a rumor went around that one of the major European buyers had found fault with Eaton's colt. Sensing a fall off in interest in his horse, Eaton gambled and won in a standout piece of marketing. He had expected some interest in his horse from Wayne Lukas because Lukas was having great success with Althea, a champion filly from Alydar's first crop. Less than a month before she had won the Hollywood Juvenile Championship (Grade 2), beating a bunch of colts by 10 lengths. But far into the sale there was still no sign of Lukas.

Eaton however knew Lukas's taste in yearlings and felt certain he would want the colt. He persuaded Lukas to come to the sale, chartered a jet and arranged a chauffeur-driven car to bring him to the sales complex. (Perhaps these were merely precautions to keep Lukas from hearing the rumor!) Eaton was right about Lukas liking the colt. That night, in the last session of the sales, Lukas paid $2.2 million for the Alydar colt.

Naming the horse was easy - Saratoga for the place of the sale and Six for the number of friends in the syndicate. One of those in the owner syndicate was Lee Eaton. The others were Eugene Klein, Sam Lyon, Mel Hatley, Bob French and Wayne Lukas.

Lukas said: "Everybody has his own taste and this one fit my particular taste. He's not so rangy that he won't be able to adapt to the demand for speed we place on our horses, and to some of the hard tracks he will have to run over. And he has the pedigree to carry his speed as far as he'll have to go."

(A photograph taken at the time shows a rather immature-looking colt with four white feet, long upright pasterns and no great depth through the chest. Top price filly at the sales has similar conformation.)

I asked Lee Eaton about Saratoga Six and Wayne's taste in horses.

"Its been 7 or 8 years. We sell here at Keeneland and then at Saratoga. My first obligation is to sell these then start selling Saratoga. We had a lovely Mr Prospector. I think I'm correct in saying the Arabs bought him for $2.7m. Wayne was the underbidder and he had never bid that kind of money. Wayne came down here and he was just sick, because when Wayne Lukas sees a horse that he likes, he really wants to buy him. He said - I think I'm correct - 'That's the most I've ever bid on a horse and I didn't get him'. This sale was over and I said, 'Wayne I've got a better one I promise you. In fact I think it will be the best colt sold at public auction in North America this year. Just save your money and come on up to the sales at Saratoga.' And he said that he would."

"When I got up there, we were selling on Friday and by Tuesday I had not seen any Wayne Lukas. So I went into town - there's only a few decent hotels in the town - and I said, 'What about Wayne Lukas, is he coming?' They said he was but he had canceled. I thought, 'Man Alive!' I knew I had one man who would pay a pretty healthy price for him, one of the sheiks who had his brother, Dunbeath, a Group 1 winner, but I thought, 'Who's going to bid against him?'"

So I called Wayne up and I said, 'Wayne, I thought you were coming up to buy this colt'. He said, 'I'm in Del Mar and I'm busy and we've spent our money'. I said, 'Well you're going to miss the best colt that sells in North America this year,' which is a stupid statement, but I really felt he was that good. He said, 'Is he really that good?' I said, 'Yes I really believe he is'. He said, 'Well let me think about it.'"

"Then I believe he called me. Wayne had talked to another California trainer who had just returned from the sales and he looked at his notes and said yes he was a very good colt. Wayne called me and said, 'If I come, the problem is that we have already spent the money we had to spend,' and I'd guess in those days Lukas spent about 5 or 6 million at the sales. He said, 'How quick do you have to be paid?' I said, 'As long as we're paid by the end of the year so that we get it into this year'. He said, 'That'd be fine. What kind of interest?' I said, 'How about 10 percent'. He said, 'That's fair. That interests me, I may come."

"Well then I get another phone call from Wayne and he says, 'Do you really like him? And I believe at this point he was calling me, after he had talked to the other trainer, whereas before I was calling him. I said, 'You bet I like him'. He said, 'Do you like him well enough to keep half of him?' He was apparently having trouble finding the kind of money that he thought it would take to buy him. I said, 'I, meaning we, Eaton Farms and Redbull Stables, we like him enough we'd keep up to half of him."

"So that afternoon it had been a pretty good sale. On the Friday night, the first good thing I see is Alan Paulson. He had wanted to buy the horse privately before the sale. He had said he did not have time to come back for the sale. A little bit later, about 4 o'clock, I see Wayne and Shari. By now we'd been showing this horse since Sunday and he was sick of it. Wayne said, 'Would you mind taking him down there in front of that empty barn?' where the horses had already been sold, and boy he picked his head up when he got in that new spot and he looked like what he was. Wayne looked at him and I'm scared to death because I'm thinking, 'Man, if he came all this way and doesn't like this horse, I've lost my credibility with him forever."

"So Wayne sits there all night, never bids on anything and then he and the Sheik's man - that was Richard Warden then - go at it and Wayne gets the horse. I had to wait a week to find out what share we had. We were committed up to half. Wayne divided him up. The good thing is that I ended up owning more than anybody."

"The next year, Wayne phoned me after Saratoga Six won his maiden. I said, 'Was he impressive? And he said, 'Yes he ran OK'. I was puzzled because he'd won his first start and I knew how high Wayne was on him. About thirty minutes later Wayne phoned again, and he said, 'I apologize. I didn't want to say in front of some people here what I really think. This horse did some things I don't see many horses do. He's impressive."

"Next thing, Wayne's standing here in Lexington, just flew in for the yearling sale, and he's running Saratoga Six in the Hollywood Juvenile, and he's flying back out to be there. He says, 'Why don't you come with us?' 'I said I can't leave my partner'. He said, 'John Williams can do this better than you can'. So we went. Wayne told me - must have told me about six times - that Saratoga Six might be beat today because there was a lot of speed and this was a 6 furlong race or so and this horse would be better at a mile. 'But,' he said, 'if they don't beat him today, they'll never beat him'."

"Well at the start Saratoga Six got left behind - here to the fence (about 10 yards) - and Wayne put his glasses down and said, 'We came out here for nothing'. But then the horse he come on and won by 3 or 4 lengths. He came through on the inside and Wayne said generally two-year-old's won't come up between that rail and those horses."

"We were so excited we didn't need that plane to come back. I fell asleep on the plane coming back. We got in at - might have been 5 o'clock or 6 o'clock in the morning. I took a shower, laid down and had a little sleep and at 8 o'clock I was out here and I felt terrible. Lukas comes walking out and he's just as crisp as though nothing's happened. He only needs 3 or 4 hours sleep but of course he didn't even get that."

That day back at the sales, still high on the win of Saratoga Six, Wayne paid $1.6m for another by the same sire. It was to that time the highest price for an Alydar. Named Santiago Peak, he could win only one race and $16,000 from 14 starts.

Saratoga Six, however, was undefeated in four starts as a two-year-old in his only racing season. He won three graded stakes and was in training for a race in which he was to meet his arch rival Chief's Crown, when he fractured both sesamoids in his left foreleg. Wayne Lukas, just across the track on his Quarter Horse pony, heard a loud crack. Surgery restored Saratoga Six to breeding soundness and the horse was syndicated to stand at Franklin Groves' North Ridge Farm in Lexington.

Wayne said, "He was the next Seattle Slew in my mind. In a couple of years his crops will get to the races and we'll find out." The night of the mishap, Angel Cordero, who had ridden Saratoga Six in all four of his starts, called from New York. "Don't worry, Daddy," he told Lukas, "You can pick them out of a crowd."

The European expert who found fault with Saratoga Six certainly did Wayne Lukas a big favor, forcing Eaton to drag Lukas to the sale and at the same time depressing the price of the horse. The top price a short while before at the Keeneland sales was $10.2m and at the same sales a yearling went for $3m.

7.2-3 Does he favor type or pedigree?
At the 1981 California Thoroughbred sales, Wayne bought some high-priced horses. Ruth Crosby Bunn, widow of Jacob Bunn, paid $275,000 for a daughter of Nijinsky out of a stakes-winning mare on the advice of Lukas, who was to train it. In an interview at the time, the reporter asked if Wayne was buying the fillies on pedigree, so they would still have some breeding value if they failed on the track. But Wayne was adamant that he bought fillies as racehorses, not for their residual value. Type comes first for Wayne.

Wayne Lukas had made the final full-time transition to Thoroughbreds in 1978. Looking back in an interview with Sharon B. Smith in The Quarter Racing Journal of 1988, he admitted he found it a bit of a struggle to adjust his eye to the new breed. Quarter Horses need explosive speed out of the gates, but they only need to sustain that speed for about 200 to 800 yards, mostly about 400 yards.

"What happens is that you'll have a tendency to look for a Quarter Horse type - with a little more muscle. I think even I was guilty of that the first year. But what you've got to remember is that while muscle is beautiful and while we like it on a Thoroughbred too, they've got to drag it around with them for a mile and a quarter. It tires them out."

Gene Klein told a reporter that looking at yearlings with Wayne was a chore because Wayne looks at them all.

"I let the horse sell me," Lukas said. "I look at every one. I don't look at pedigrees first. I look for the equine athlete. If I'm impressed with an individual, I will look at his pedigree. Sometimes I have to make a judgment call. If an outstanding individual has no pedigree, I might buy him feeling that he will be the one to give the mare a better produce record. If a pedigree is outstanding, I will make some concessions on the individual. There are certain things I will never allow, but I'm not going to give away all my trade secrets. At this point (Nov. '85) I feel you have to spend about a quarter of a million dollars to buy an 'A' individual with a 'B' pedigree."

Wayne bought Life's Magic for $310,000 and the horse went on to win an Eclipse Award. Everyone said "Jesus, what kind of a price is that for a Cox's Ridge?" But Wayne didn't buy by the sire's reputation. "She was a good-looking yearling, she balanced out and checked out as well as anything else in the Fall Sale. Price doesn't matter, not when they are that good. She was like Landaluce, Can't-Miss, Blue-Chip, a First Round Draft Choice." Wayne will look over every yearling at a sale, but will only pay attention to the ones that really stand out, "that really grab me", he said. "I go for the dead-centre ones that jump out."

Wayne rates the sales yearlings out of 10. There have apparently been no tens, and only 3 nines. Wayne was reported to have been attracted to the mighty Landaluce by her tremendous heart girth.

One of his top purchases was Winning Colors, for which he paid $575,000 at the 1986 Select Yearling Sales. He told an unnamed journalist from The Backstretch, "She had it all. When she walked out, I went around her twice and I didn't want to draw a lot of attention [to her]. I said, 'Put her away.' It's like when Liz Taylor walks in a room, you don't have everybody tell you that's a pretty woman. She had the highest score with me of all the horses in the sale, and I looked at every one of them. I gave her an eight-plus and the highest marks I've ever given were nines for Landaluce and Saratoga Six [and later Houston in 1988]. I grade all the horses that interest me and I try to buy all those rated at seven or above." Lukas doesn't claim infallibility, pointing out that not all of his top picks made the track. One of his 1985 purchases, named Moon Light Miracle, cost $2.5m but had never made it to a race by 1989. Day Light Robbery might have been a better name, but it must have been at least an 8 for Wayne to pay that much for it.

Success Express, winner of the 1987 Breeders' Cup Juvenile, was a $150,000 Fasig Tipton yearling. "He was a seven-plus,' Wayne told Robert Henwood of *The Blood-Horse*. "He has the dosage to be a Kentucky Derby winner. He's a nifty-made colt who, to look at, some people might think won't stretch out. But he's a Snow Chief-type; he'll go on. With his speed he might go to the Derby through Arkansas." Success Express was sold to Australia.

Houston attracted Wayne's attention - again with the help of Lee Eaton. There were other interested parties. Lee Eaton no doubt saw to that. A multimillion dollar price was expected. Wayne's backers were not keen to have so many eggs in one basket. Moon Light Miracle might have been on their minds. They preferred half a dozen at $500,000 each to the risks of one at $3m. Wayne ended up arranging the finance and signing at $2.9m himself. He was later able to sell 'about half' of the horse to French and Beal.

Did Wayne set about cleaning up the two-year-old races with his star? The Breeders' Cup Juvenile? No. Houston had very few two-year-old starts. He broke his maiden with a 12 length win in July at Belmont Park. The lack of starts for such a highly touted horse brought questions about Houston's soundness. Wayne may have been remembering Saratoga Six.

"This would be the best horse I've ever had. He's perfectly sound. No horse in America has had a more consistent work tab than this horse." Lukas said he took his time because, "there was no sense winding him up. We already knew what kind of horse we had." Wayne obviously felt that Houston would do his best running at three.

As a three-year-old Houston won the $115,000 Bay Shore by 10 lengths on March 25th. The wonder-horse label appeared to be deserved. The unusually low number of two-year-old starts and the preparation appeared to be a repeat of his handling of Winning Colors. Wayne looked a chance to take back-to-back Kentucky Derbies. A win with this magnificent-looking and well-bred horse would be a stallion syndication bonanza.

Then the horse ran a dismal race in the April 8th Santa Anita Derby. Wayne said it was just an off day. Blood tests showed the horse was dehydrated and had some electrolyte disturbances. He ran a fading 8th in the Kentucky Derby and later in the year, a 2nd in a stakes.

At the yearling sales, even an 8 is so rare that on one occasion when Wayne found one, he was all excited, but thought it would be by Mr Prospector or some other expensive stallion. He asked one of his entourage to sneak a look in the catalogue.

It was by Raja Baba. "Is it true?" asked Wayne. He still had to go to $650,000. It raced as Is It True to a great victory in the Breeders' Cup Juvenile Colt's Stakes. Although Wayne tries to buy anything he rates 7 or above, it was reported that most of what he buys he rates a 7 or less.

The comments of an astute horsewoman cast some light on Wayne's favorite 'type'. Helen Alexander, who gave Althea to Wayne to train, is manager of the Thoroughbred operations for King Ranch. Her family owns King Ranch. She is only in her thirties but has run that Thoroughbred operation since 1974. Helen also races and breeds her own horses. Interviewed by the Thoroughbred Record in 1987, she had this to say about why she put Althea with Wayne: " . . . sometimes you'll see a horse that seems like the type a particular trainer has had success with . . . Overall, a lot of the horses Wayne has bought are pretty muscular, well-developed in the shoulder, well-developed hindquarters, a nice long neck, well-balanced . . . a bit blockier kind of horse than the old traditional distance horse, the one that stood over a lot of ground and had a bit longer back and was a bit leaner."

Wayne is understandably proud of the fact that he chose most of his champions as yearlings. He likens this to looking for Liz Taylor at age eight. I asked Wayne how he developed his impressive selection abilities:

"Did you develop this skill when you were a teenager?"

"Yes. I decided early on that I would study the mechanics, and of course this goes back to performance horses, and Quarter Horses. Not race-horses, but performance horses; reining, cutting - horses of that type. I decided that I would study all the good horses and see if there was a common line that ran through them. When I got into racing, every time a horse ran well I looked at it. I'm not talking about looking at champions, I'm talking about looking at the horse that excelled in the third race, or excelled in a claiming race - any horse that showed some ability. I looked to see if there was a common thread, a common line, that ran through every one of those horses. Believe it or not, I started to find that there were certain things that all of them had, and if they didn't have it, their chances of success went down."

"I started making very very visual pictures of certain anatomy traits in horses, that seemed to give them a chance to excel. I refined my eye over and over and over and over. Then I tested it, and I think I've been successful. For example, one year while I was training both Quarter Horses and Thoroughbreds, I went to three major sales. Two Quarter Horse sales and one Thoroughbred sale. I only bought one horse in each sale, and I bought the best horse in all three sales, so I feel very confident. But our record, I think, speaks for itself. We are very confident that we can find a runner in a crowd. I am very confident, and that's one thing I've never wavered on. I don't want to sound over-verbose, but given a hundred yearlings, without knowing pedigrees or anything, I'm confident that I can find the best two or one."

"The best two or one?"

"Yes, out of a hundred. Without a doubt. Given the fact that they all get an equal chance, you know. Of course there are other variables. But I have gone down to farms where there'll be forty or fifty babies, in various pastures, and all they have is a number on a neckstrap. I did this on two or three Kentucky farms, without mentioning names. I've walked out there and walked through them for a couple of hours and come back and given the guy four numbers - wrote 'em right on my hand with a pencil - and said, 'They'll be your four best horses' and then said thank you and left, and have the guy call me a year later and say, 'Three of those were multiple stakes winners; the other one got hurt.' Something to that effect. 'The rest of them - I never had another one in the barn that did anything.' I felt confident I could do that."

"You're very good at selecting horses, and obviously you don't want to give away secrets, but it does interest me how people like you can select the biomechanics, ratios etc., so accurately by eye."

"A lot of people don't see it. I've stood there by the hour showing people [what to look for] on a horse - and then [on another horse] I've said, 'Where's the weakest part of this horse?' Even with my people, my employees, trying to help them, but they couldn't get it right. I'm thoroughly convinced that I could hold a seminar on choosing horses, for two weeks, and then lead the next horse out and they wouldn't see it. Some people do not see it. What I see, and what are certain 'un-negotiables' I'm going to call them, things I have to have in a horse, I have tried to point out but they just don't see it. Once in a while when it's really exaggerated in a horse, I'll say, 'Now this horse shows what I was showing you in the other horse,' and then they'll pick up on it."

"But then I'll bring another horse and they won't see it, which always amazes me. I don't know if you've heard the story I use so much: It's like when you were a child and they had the coloring books in the school. They would show a farm scene, and hidden in the picture would be a cat. They would say, 'Find the cat in this picture,' and you'd look and look and look and you can't find the cat, and then somebody says, 'Okay, here's the cat right here'. Now when you look back at the picture, the only thing you see is the cat. That's all. Your mind focused right away on the cat. After you look at hundreds and literally thousands of horses, like Wayne Lukas - I see the cats very quickly in a horse, and I can judge a horse in three to four seconds in many cases, where he'll fail me. On a marginal one it takes longer, but I don't have to watch them walk. I don't have to watch them move. I don't have to watch their foot

placement or anything. Because the anatomy of a horse will only let him do certain things. His neck-set on his shoulder will tell me how he's going to carry his head at a full gallop. It doesn't make any difference if you walk him off or not. As soon as I walk around him three times, motionless, standing there, I'll tell you how he's going to walk before he moves."

"You can tell if he's going to overstep?" (Overstep means that the hind hoof lands ahead of the imprint in the ground of the hoof of the foreleg.)

"Sure, because I can tell by the anatomy and the musculature. Of course, I've made a study of it all my life. And I've done that many times to the amazement of people. I'll say, 'Stand him there,' I'll walk around him three times and I'll say, 'Okay, when this horse walks off now, he's going to overstep a full foot. He's going to be slightly out on his right, and he's going to place that foot there, and he's going to be a little bit shorter on his right and not as free as he will be on his left. He'll break great over the knee on the left, he will not on the right. His head carriage will be such and such.' I'll go through it, and when he walks off, that's what he'll do, because the anatomy only lets him do that."

"Do you ever see people measuring horses in Kentucky? Are they on the same track?"

"That's another parameter. I respect what they do because they're measuring heart-girth, gaskin, you know, things like that."

"They're doing slowly and tediously, with a tape and a computer, what you can do by eye quickly?"

"Yes, I've been on some sessions with those guys. When they measure a horse, which will take 'em thirty minutes, and they say, 'This horse measures up very well' I can say that in three seconds, I can tell you exactly that. They'll say, 'This one doesn't measure' and I'd say, 'Well, that's obvious.'"

"That must be very discouraging for them."

"Yes. But I respect 'em for what they're doing. I think what they've done is they've taken a set of all the measurements of great horses and then tried to apply those principles to what they're looking at there. But there are a few measurements they can't make with a tape."

"Which you look very pleased about. What do you do about heart size, since that must be such a large factor."

"Okay. Years ago, some people found that heart size was a determining factor in the success of high-caliber horses. And I believe that. I believe that, and I think that it is another variable that could be used, but what happened to the heart size people is they got caught up in their own game."

"They started to think it was the be-all and end-all."

"Yes. I had guys telling me how great the heart size was. What I could see was that the anatomy of that horse would not allow that horse a) to train or b) to be physically able to coordinate himself. I mean, just the way he was put together. So that's it - you have to put it all together."

"I would say if you are choosing these horses so successfully - best one out of a hundred - you must have some handle on their heart size."

"Well I think that would be great. I think that would be helpful. If there was some kind of independent agency that went through the yearlings at all the select sales, and said here are all the heart scores and heart sizes on all these yearlings, I would factor that in. I think that is a very big factor. Unfortunately or fortunately, depending on which side of the fence you are on, nobody is doing it."

"But there are people doing it." (Mostly by Echo)

"Oh sure there are people doing it privately. That is the same as the old measurement deal. You know when guys were going around measuring different lengths of hip and backs and necks and stuff. The consignor says well if he falls into a great pattern tell me; if he doesn't I'll pay you and you don't tell anybody."

"In Australia we have a lot of people who are keen on heart score, and averaged over 50 horses it is better than guess work but it is fairly inaccurate on an individual basis."(Echocardiographic estimation can also be inaccurate.)

"There are some things in conformation, if it doesn't have them, it doesn't matter what size his heart is."

"Nevertheless I am surprised that you don't go into the heart size."

"Well there was a little flutter there a few years ago. They were really getting into it, measuring heart beat and pumping. I think it will come to that as a variable. I don't think it will be a bottom line deal but as we get out of the stone ages in the horse business, which we're having trouble with, we'll get to the point where we will start paying attention to size of hearts - all that sort of thing."

"I don't vet horses at the sales either. I never let a veterinarian influence me in any way shape or form. I have no luck with those guys at all."

"Vets are taught at vet school that certain faults are a big no-no but no one tells them to evaluate the overall worth of the animal. Add good features and subtract bad features is not what they are taught. We were taught that any animal with an inherited defect should not be bred from. If it is a dog or cat it should be castrated or spayed. It's this all-or-nothing Nazi approach. What is really required is an evaluation of that animal's overall worth, fault and all. There are severe faults, medium faults and harmless faults. Sometimes an animal with a fault is still worth breeding from. They would castrate the best specimen - say the fastest horse in a breeding program for speed - because it has developed a splint. They would keep something with great thick legs and no speed, probably an equally heritable 'defect'. Vets don't

wake up unless they go into breeding something themselves. But no one, not the breeders nor vets who have woken up, can shift the vet schools on that. It is part of the vet school dogma, part of the academic dogma syndrome which makes academics a joke in so many industries."

"If you take a veterinarian - if he turns them all down he'll never be wrong. You know that he's going to be right most of the time because most of them don't make it to the races. I don't ever get a vet's opinion."

"Well some vets will look at it as an athlete but most see their job as finding any existing or potential veterinary problems. They are not trained to think of the overall assessment. You would have to specify what you want."

This reminded me of John Gosden's comments on Wayne's selection methods. John believes that Lukas is a really fine judge of horses. He can go to the sales and come out with the top horses. He also says that Lukas walks around the horse, and examines it from quite a distance, and stands off and looks at the front legs from something like about forty five degrees, and the same at the back. Doesn't like a really close inspection of them. *"Doesn't have any veterinary inspection either. He'll pay over a million dollars on a horse that has not had a veterinary inspection."*

I asked Wayne: *"What about the horse's best distance? How much can you work that out from its conformation?"*

"Well, I think I can predict that. I think I can look at a yearling and pretty accurately give you - I'm not talking about saying he's a perfect miler - but I think I can tell you if he's going to go beyond a mile, or under a mile or what, by looking at him. That is based on angles, muscle tones and body blending."

"Another thing that surprises me is that you can get a horse's distance without its muscle fiber-type percentages."

"The horse's fiber-type I think I can tell."

"So you feel them for muscle tone? Are you a poker and pusher?"

"No. Look at them. You can see that. Very obvious. Very obvious. I know that someone who is scientifically in there would laugh, but I think that muscle tone and muscle fiber are very apparent in the racehorse."

"I've been around too long to laugh at anything simply because it can't be explained by the current dogma. We have some muscle prodders in Australia. To see it by eye - at a guess - I suppose it would be that fast twitch stay more tense than slow twitch or look more tense."

"Correct."

(Muscle tone might be greater in muscles with a higher percentage of fast twitch fibers, or it may be that strong resting muscle tone is simply a sign of athleticism, one of more importance to sprinters than stayers.)

"I like to operate by taking the theory and matching it up with what people have found by sheer experience, and when the two things fit, then I think I've probably got it right."

"That is what I'm doing with my conformation in horses. By trial and error and trying different types and things over the years, I know there are certain things that they all have. If they don't have it they don't succeed. And I've refined my eye down. It's like I tell Jeff. I look at a horse and he looks at a horse - and he looks and he looks - but I'm done in minutes because I go to the heart of the problem. I can look at 4 or 5 things and if the horse doesn't have them - 'scusi' [excuse me]."

"Can a horse's neck be too long?"

"No."

"It can't be too long? The longer the neck, the better?"

"Well, I didn't say that. I just said I didn't think it could be too long. I never saw one that I said, "This horse's neck is too long.""

"And the same about the length of the shoulder?"

"Well that I couldn't answer in one answer."

"Because it's also the slope?"

"The slope and the length of the shoulder are all relative to the other parts of it. I don't think the length is the key. What I would say to that is, I've seen a lot of long-shouldered horses with a good slope to the shoulder, that can't run because it doesn't fit other places. So I would never make that generalisation. I'd have to see the rest of the horse to tell you if his shoulder was too long or too short."

"When you choose on angles, muscle tone and body blending, how sure are you of their best distance. Do you get any surprises?"

"Pretty close now. Over the last 4 or 5 years I think I am getting so I can really zero in on it. After I have once scored them high enough conformation-wise that I know I like that horse, then I take a look at the pedigree. If it is by a horse that absolutely does not get anything that runs over a mile then you would be crazy to think you can beat the system, but on the other hand I don't get many surprises like that any more either. I think over the last couple of years it has become extremely easy for me to pick them quickly. I can go through a hundred horses so quickly that people think I'm not looking. Most of the time now, when I go to a consignment and they walk up and back -that's a courtesy walk. That's because I don't want to be an asshole. He has only gone a few yards and I know that horse fails me in so many places. But I don't say well turn that around and bring me the next one."

"The anatomy of the horse absolutely dictates the limits of it's gait - and I really believe this: If you blindfold me, take a yearling and lead him out of the stall, stand him on a spot and square him up, then unblindfold me, I'll walk around him four times and I'll tell you how he's gonna move. I really believe that in my heart."

"Well you'd have had enough experience to know if you can. You didn't get any surprises?"

"No. The anatomy of the horse will only let him do certain things and I will even go so far as to say when this horse is in full stride his head carriage is going to be too high, he's going to have far too much motion on his front end, he's going to have a lot of wasted motion, he'll have no speed or he'll have a lot of speed. I think I've got it covered. I really feel confident. The other thing, and I've proved it over and over up there with Jeffrey - (Wayne leans down, hangs his arms down and clenches his fists to imitate an imaginary horse) - when this horse moves off he's going to overstep 6 to 8 inches, and he'll absolutely place his left front here (demonstrates outward swing and fall of the foot) and he'll do this etc. The anatomy of the horse will only let him do certain things."

"That overstepping, a lot of trainers in Australia believe that the more they overstep the better they are. Do you believe that? Or can they overstep too much?"

"I'll say the thing I've been quoted on so much and that is;

They should have a head like a princess,
    a butt like a washerwoman,
    and a walk like a hooker.

If they walk like a hooker they'll overstep."

"I saw a horse that overstepped by about 18 inches. Until then I'd only seen them overstep by 10 inches or a foot."

"You've got to be a little careful with that because the length of the back is going to dictate that."

"Yes this was very short-backed and long-legged."

"That is what I was going to say - sometimes a perfectly balanced horse won't overstep at all. He'll put 'em right in place. Depends on the length of the back and it all has to blend in - what you have to learn about conformation is that you cannot just take one thing. For example you can't just say, 'I like low hocks' because it is how the hock ties into the rest of the angles of the hip and the front end of the horse."

"My horses all have speed lines even if you take a filly like Winning Colors, which we were able to run at a mile and a quarter against the colts; she definitely had speed lines and speed. It is hard for me - when I select a yearling they will have what I call speed lines. I can't buy a horse that doesn't have muscle."

"What do you mean by speed lines?"

"There are certain things in the conformation that will let a horse be quick and show speed - without regard to the pedigree. I've seen some Vaguely Nobles and some Allegeds and

This is one Wayne bought for $150,000 at the 1989 sales. The session average was $355,000 so this was a 'cheapie'. It was by Devil's Bag out of Burst Of Colors by Crimson Satan. Note long pasterns, average depth of girth, rounded muscular rump, and 'downhill' to withers.

things like that, which are definitely pedigreed to go a mile and a half even, and yet they will show great speed lines for me, and I will still buy them."

"You can obviously tell an awful lot by looking at these horses."

"I've made a living at it since I was about seven years old, so I learned to study them. You know what I think happens to a person in life, is that all of us learn - but the intensity factor is the motivation for learning. If there is no real sincere reason to learn anything - computers, carpentry, how to fix cars, foreign language, anything in life - if there is no real intensity factor, you're not going to learn. When you are like I was, started out in the sales ring dealing with virtually no money, and knowing that every horse I bought I had to make a profit on and turn it into another sale, well then the intensity factor goes way up and you start paying attention a lot more. I went to Keeneland in 1978 and bought one horse and that horse was Terlingua. Now I knew I was only going to get one chance and so I had to be careful to make sure I got the right one. But I've been studying these horses for a long time and there are certain common threads that run through the good ones."

"Was that a steady progression or did you suddenly see some big things - breakthroughs?"

"No. That's been from refining my eye over a period of twenty-five years. You just keep working at it and you keep trying to find the hidden qualities."

"If you can do it really quick, is it because there's not that many factors in it, or is it an overall impression?"

"It's an overall impression, but I think I can do it quickly because I know what I'm looking for. I know what I want, and I think after you look at thousands - I probably look at five thousand yearlings a year - you get to the point where the obvious things come out and you scan through it. I can judge ninety-nine, or ninety-five percent of them, in three seconds."

"How early can you pick them?"

"I think I can pick a runner out at four months. I think it's all there. I think at four months, I can predict a good colt."

"Had you been to any sales previously and 'imagined' you could buy some and followed them to see how they turned out?"

"No. No I was at Los Alamitos one Saturday night, running in a Quarter Horse meet and we had a Championship Mare

"That's all thank you." Wayne finishes assessing another yearling at the sales in Lexington, Kentucky. I think this was a second look. Note tall, leggy, with long pasterns, average girth, muscular rump and 'downhill' to withers. This diagonal view is favored by Albert Yank and Wayne.

and Filly race that night. The Keeneland sales were on Monday and Tuesday. I turned to my client and I said I'm going to Keeneland to buy a Thoroughbred yearling - I'm going to switch over so I'm going to get one and get started. He said well what are you going to do? I said I'm going to go over and buy the best one I can buy. He said who's going to pay for it? I said I don't know, I'll pay for it or maybe someone else will, but I'm going to go buy a good yearling. He said will you buy one for me? I said I'd be glad to."

"It would be interesting if you were ever to put pen to paper on this selection business."

"I don't think I'll ever do that."

"No it wouldn't pay you."

"It serves no purpose. In fact I've had numerous opportunities to discuss that at seminars and lectures and whatnot. The Maryland Thoroughbred Association asked me to come back and judge thirty-some yearlings and rate them from one to thirty and then explain why I like this one more than that one. I said, 'I don't think there is enough money in Maryland for me to do that."

"The only person I've ever really intently sat down with at

a sale and talked with is Jeff. I've schooled him. In fact last summer I bought him to Keeneland and he came two days after I'd been there. I said, 'I'm going to test you a little bit'; we've been doing this for a number of years. I've always schooled him in the saddling paddock. Like today we'll go over there and I'll say, 'Look at the shoulder on that filly,' in just a horse going back. I'll say, 'That is a perfect shoulder in relation to that horse's pasterns'. I'll say, 'Study that'. When it catches my eye I'll say, 'See the set of that horse's hocks' - it won't even be our horse - I'll say, 'Study the set of those hocks because that is a perfect set."

"So he came to Keeneland and I said, 'I am going to give you four numbers, and I want you to go look at them and score them from 1 to 10'. These are numbers of horses that I've looked at and I like, and so he was gone about an hour and he came back and I said, 'What are your scores'? He gave me three of them - they were sevens. And I had asked him to make a comment and he was right on target on the three of them. On the fourth one he said, 'I looked at that filly and for the life of me I cannot see the things that you like in a racehorse. That one got by me and I don't see it at all'. I said, 'Good because that's a five. If you had come back and told me you liked that one, I'd have been terribly disappointed. The reason you couldn't see it is because it is not there'. So I was very proud of him on that."

"So out of however many horses you buy in a year, what sort of a strike rate do you get?"

"I think that our percentage of winners is in the 70s or 80s. Our stakes winners, I think run in the high 30s."

"Well, that would explain your great confidence."

"Yes. Given any kind of budget, and a chance to look at two or three thousand yearlings every year, we're always going to be tough. Our whole program, all these records that we have, are all built out of buying horses, untried yearlings. We've trained very few horses that were raised and given to us, and virtually all of our champions were bought in. I had twenty-three world champion Quarter Horses and they were all bought in sales. Every one of them. So we're looking at thirty, forty world champion horses, all bought because I said, 'That's a good horse."

It's easy to call a top American Quarter Horse a World Champion, but a Thoroughbred - that's another matter. Incidentally, Wayne did not buy Dash For Cash. Bubba Cascio trained the horse to some big wins, then it was sent to Los Alamitos, to Wayne. He did not buy Miss Thermolark as yearling, but after some of her big wins, and he did not buy Little Blue Sheep - she was bred by French. No doubt Wayne had a role in determining if the horse should be kept or sold.

How does Clyde Rice choose yearlings?

Clyde told Steve Haskin from *The Backstretch* that he and Wayne liked the same things in a yearling. "They have to be good individuals, sound well balanced athletes. We're not picky about pedigree, but more interested in soundness and good legs. We would prefer well-bred yearlings but it's not number one on our list of priorities."

I asked Clyde if he and Wayne developed their selection skills separately or together. He told me that Wayne developed his skills when he was off racing, rather than when they were trading together. Because Clyde had picked Life's Magic, when Wayne was at the same sales, I asked Clyde if they chose different horses after they got past the basics.

"No, because we taught each other and we complement each other. We work together."

"Did you see much of each other in Wayne's Quarter Horse days?"

"Yes. We were very close friends."

"Were you there when he went the first time to the Thoroughbred sales, when he chose Terlingua in 1977?"

"Yes."

"Did you have a role in choosing her?"

"Yes."

Clyde told me that when he and Wayne first went to the

Thoroughbred sales, everyone bought on pedigree. "You would not believe the faults some of those high-priced yearlings had. We have revolutionized the sales business. We showed that the right individual could run, even if it didn't have the best pedigree. Of course we won't buy if the dam has had eight foals and none of them have run. But if there are just a few holes, or maybe we know that some of those foals did not get much of a chance, we will buy if we like the individual - because a lot of good horses fall through the cracks. You see so many great horses - they go to a trainer and the next thing you hear they are hurt, sick or unsuccessful for so many reasons."

"Are your best results with two-year-old's, like Wayne's?"

"Yes. I make my money by re-selling the horses."

"So you want something that gets ready quickly, that shows something quickly."

"Yes."

"Wayne has better results at picking fillies, do you also have better results with fillies?"

"Yes."

"The type of masculine filly that wins races, have there been any problems breeding those fillies after racing?"

"If you choose very good fillies they will race a lot. They have a lot of stress from that racing so there will be some problems. They love to race, they are bred for it, but it is hard on them."

"How much of the Thoroughbred crop does Wayne try to look at? Does he go only to the main sales or does he go to the cheaper sales as well?"

"I still go to the cheaper sales but Wayne doesn't."

"He used to go to the cheaper sales, but now that he can afford the better pedigreed horses he only goes to the main sales?"

"That's right."

"Wayne said he'd had good results with his own breedings."

"Breeders were breeding winner to winner, or pedigree to pedigree, without looking at the animals. You have to match up the two individuals."

"Wayne is not afraid to buy a horse with a long upright pastern."

"What we say is that the pastern has to match the shoulder."

"Would you buy one with a short upright pastern if it had a short upright shoulder?"

"No that's a Quarter Horse-type of pastern. They can't carry their speed and they would break down if you asked them to. You'll see good horses in all shapes and sizes, but some things are the bottom line. I like a horse with a long hip. I like a short cannon."

"You make your living by re-selling these horses after

you have demonstrated their ability?"

"That's correct. And I'm not afraid to sell a horse either. A trainer who gets a good horse, he'll hang on to it because it's a once-in-a-lifetime thing for him. You have to remember, some people have spent fortunes and come up with nothing. But not me - I know there are more good horses out there and I know I can find them."

"Has it become easier with experience?"

"To someone who has not been in it all their life, it is a very difficult thing. To someone like me it is easy. Lately it has become easier to buy the ones I like."

"Simply because you can afford to pay the price?"

"Yes."

"How much do you charge to select a horse for someone?"

"Most people charge 5%, but I charge 10%, in fact even at 10% I'd rather buy the horses myself."

"And resell them?"

"Yes. This is a very interesting time for me. (Feb. 1990. Clyde had 156 youngsters in work at his property in Florida.) The young horses are doing their first works. There is nothing more interesting than a two-year-old."

Clyde's reputation has given him problems bidding. His wife told me that people watch him at the sale and bid on horses if he bids. If he delegates the job it makes it difficult to react to other bidders, to the way the sale is going. He should take a few bidding lessons from Wayne.

After my discussion with Wayne about his selection methods, I told him I wondered how he could bid without others bidding higher, just because he was also interested. Surely it would encourage other buyers to bid more if they found Lukas also had a high opinion of the horse. Someone with NO ability to judge a yearling could simply watch Lukas and buy one he started bidding on?

"Oh yes, that happens," said Wayne, "but I bid on it all by signal. I arrange a signal with the bid spotters."

"Wouldn't that signal become known?"

"I change the signal every session. Nobody could ever tell I'm bidding anyway."

"Wouldn't the bid spotter get confused?"

"No. That's their job. That hasn't happened. I have my own set of spotters; I have three or four spotters who work with me, and I may be bidding right now, talking to you; there's no way you could tell. My hands are in my pockets; my arms are folded; I'm in conversation; I'm talking to you: I'm in the bidding up there. Now I'm out. Nobody's ever going to be able to do that (ie bid in because Wayne is)."

"One of these days one of the guys might screw it up and you might buy a horse when you scratch your eye."

"It's happened once. They had the in and out signals reversed, and I bought one. It went too far and I was out and

they thought I was in, but it was still a good horse. It didn't matter."

I had the opportunity to watch Wayne bidding at the 1989 Fasig Tipton Kentucky Selected Yearling Sales. These sales are not as important as the Keeneland July Select Yearling Sales, which follow straight after, and Wayne didn't go to any great lengths to hide his bidding. Wayne was bidding mainly from the crowd of people in the center of the holding area at the back of the sales pavilion. By standing in the center, the buyers can watch the yearlings as they are walked around the ring just prior to going into the pavilion. There are two bid spotters in a raised stand in the middle of this ring. They are surrounded by people.

Wayne did some of his bidding while in conversational groups. Sometimes he would walk around to the other side of the crowd to bid. He would nod his head or flick his catalogue. It would have been easy to get in on his bids at this sale. Even so, on one occasion the bid spotter was already taking bids from a determined looking buyer. Wayne was off to one side and further back. He made several progressively less subtle bids with his catalogue, but the spotter missed them. Wayne rapidly became incensed and threw his catalogue in an arc towards the spotter. The spotter still didn't notice. Wayne retrieved his catalogue, by which time the horse was sold. The spotter finally noticed Wayne who gave him a furious glare.

At the Keeneland Sales, where the prices were much higher, Wayne was all over the place, and his bidding was much harder to detect. I watched him during the bidding on one I thought he might be interested in. He must have been subtle, or else he had Jeff or some other person bid, because I saw nothing, yet he was listed as the buyer at the end of the day. In the pavilion it is difficult for another person to get a good enough vantage point from which to see all possible signals, but Wayne does seem to have a good system.

The system he uses requires very few signals. When he wants to, he signals that he is in the bidding. As others bid and the spotters shout the prices, Wayne's spotter simply ups the bid immediately. With loudspeakers everywhere, and the auctioneers calling the price every few seconds, it is easy to know the price. Wayne could have his back turned. He could successfully buy the horse while in earnest converation, without any further signal. What if someone puts in an immediate raise with Wayne's spotter? I'm sure Wayne has debugged his system by now, and has a way around any possible hitches.

When a Robert Sangster - Vincent O'Brien syndicate bought one yearling for $13.1m at the 1985 sales, Sangster was surprised to find that Wayne, rather than the Arabs, had been the competing bidder. Sangster said the bidding had been much faster than the usual Maktoum bidding pace. Even so, it seems Wayne's usual group of backers was involved and there was no hidden signalling on this occasion. The auctioneer, Tom

Caldwell, said, "How about $13m and end all this." Lukas waited a few seconds and then nodded. Sangster finally went to $13.1m. Each of the bids was followed by frantic discussion amongst the Lukas syndicate. Some time after the sale, Lukas said that if they opened the bidding back up, "We'd be right back in there". Wayne's next step might be a private bidding room like the Maktoums have.

The yearling they were bidding on was by Nijinsky II out of My Charmer, dam of Lomond which won the English 2000 Guineas, and of Seattle Slew. Seattle Slew won the Triple Crown and was Champion two-year-old, three-year-old and older horse. Lukas considered the yearling had a breeding residual backup of about $10m, "If he went to hell in a handbasket." He used one of his sporting analogies. "We had the singles hitters, but we were looking for our clean-up hitter with that one."

I discussed Wayne's yearling selection abilities with a lot of people, but one man cast a lot of well-researched light on the subject:

Paul Mostert, Equix Biomechanics Corp.

Suite 400, 380 Corporate Drive, Lexington, Kentucky.
Paul Mostert has a PhD in mathematics and is a world authority on cluster analysis which is very useful in understanding the relationship of racing and breeding success to horse 'types'. He has measured many many horses and uses computers to examine relationships between conformation types and what happens on the racetrack. He has had sufficient success to be offering his system as a commercial service around the world. North Ridge Farm, which has been a major client for years, was the top breeding farm in North America for 1989. His most complete assessment of a yearling crop was in South Africa in 1989. In 1990 his top yearling picks of 1989 are coming first and second in South African racing.

Paul has classified horses by the ratios of their weight, muscle power and stride length.

TYPE 1: When all three factors are close to the ideal balance. The best race distance of the type 1 is 5½f to 1¼ miles.
TYPE 2: Nearly in balance.
TYPE S: Have a longer stride in relation to their weight and power. They run more on rhythm than power, usually a come from behind type but the best at the classic distances, which in America are 1 and 3/16 to 1½ miles.
Type P: More power relative to their weight and stride. Usually sprinters, occasionally win classics.
TYPE E: Slight excess of weight. Occasionally make good filly sires.
TYPE W: Excess of weight to the point of being a handicap.

"You classify horses into six basic types. Does Wayne pick one type or a range of types?"

"Wayne chooses an early maturing type with a fair amount of power."

"He chooses the power or 'P' type in your classification."

"He's moving towards the classic type, his eye is changing a bit, but you can still look at a horse and say, 'That is a Lukas-type horse." Here is what Paul Mostert's booklet on biomechanical analysis has to say about the power type:

TYPE P: This type is divided into two subcategories, P1 and P. The Type P horse has great power in relation to its trunk size and stride length. So much power that it seldom survives its two-year-old year unless it is very well balanced and has no appreciable leg faults, or unless the K-factor is present. (The K-factor is a set of conformational traits in the hind quarters.) It runs on power and therefore can generate speed quickly. Power can overcome many biomechanical faults, so these horses will be in the winner's circle more often than their basic biomechanical efficiency rating would indicate - provided they can stay sound.

The type P1 horse is not quite as powerful and is not as likely to break down as the pure type P. This type produces early runners with consistency, but not classic distance horses unless the K-factor is present. Some type P1 horses have won Triple Crown events (one even won a Belmont Stakes), but such horses had excellent biomechanical efficiency scores and the K-factor to go with their power.

"Is Wayne tolerant of conformational faults, things like being toed out?"

"Oh yes. He has a very good eye for the total athlete. In particular, upright pasterns don't seem to bother him."

"I've heard his choices described as tall, upright and narrow."

"Yes but very muscular in front. If you look at them from in front they generally have a nice 'V' in front where they have these nice forearms, and a lovely oval front end to them."

"Is he equally interested in muscle at the back end?"

"Moreso there than anywhere. He likes to have a good ischium [a bone at the corner of the rump] on a horse with plenty of muscle back in there and plenty of muscle on the thigh - well . . . enough - doesn't like *too* much muscle on the thighs. So it's not one of these horses that will go quick but be finished after a certain time."

"Have you ever picked one out that you thought maybe no one else would notice, and Lukas has come along and bought it?"

"No, but he has picked some out that I thought would mature much too fast, and I thought their career would be over before they ever got to the track."

"And did that happen?"

"Yes."

"That might be a hangover from his Quarter Horse days."

"Yes I think so. But he has an eye for early-maturing horses that are going to make it as a two-year-old."

"In your opinion does he have a better eye for colts or fillies?"

"I think he has a better eye for fillies. There is no question there."

"When a trainer selects his own horses, good racing results with fillies could be due to either a better eye for fillies or a better training method for fillies."

"Let me say this: I have a lot of respect for anyone that can train fillies. Basically fillies run for you. Colts run for themselves. You can mistreat a colt and he will still run."

"Wayne does talk about how much he 'babys' them."

"It shows. His horses are always well-fed with plenty of flesh on them."

"So do you think his success with fillies is due to choosing better fillies than colts?"

"I've seen him pick more good fillies than I've seen him pick good colts, I'll say that. There are fewer good fillies to choose from. But he has chosen some awfully nice colts."

"Does he ever surprise you with his selections?"

"Yes. Usually they are colts and they are very good looking horses. One was, as I mentioned, way too early maturing. Another one, I thought he should wait a little longer than he did to run him. He ran it early and it didn't do very well. He let it go home for a while and then brought it back and it did a little better."

"Would you say you could do better than Wayne Lukas at selecting racehorses?"

"I would hate to say that I can do better than Wayne Lukas, with the success he's had. What I would say is - no matter who it is, if they use us in addition to what they already have, and then make their mind up as to whether we are calling attention to something they should be concerned about, then they will do better. And we would do a whole lot better too, if we had him choosing, and then we went out and measured those. We would do better than we do by ourselves. We would love to have him on our team!"

Wayne seems to deliberately select horses which have a best distance on the short side of 1¼ miles rather than right on that distance. This may be because, as Paul Mostert's analysis at Equix shows, the classic distance type doesn't do very well at winning in the bulk of everyday races. Wayne buys horses to win money, some of which, with a little luck, will carry their speed to a Kentucky Derby win at 1¼ miles. It is unlikely that any of that type will win a Belmont Stakes at 1½ miles.

Wayne's chances of winning a Triple Crown are quite low with his present strategy. Some of his critics would say his training doesn't help him win longer races.

Did anyone help Wayne develop his eye?

Blane Schvaneveldt believes starting in Quarter Horses helped. I asked him if Wayne had his incredible eye for a horse in the Quarter Horses?

"That's where he learned it."

"He could buy the best horse in the sale every time?"

"Sure. And he learned it through the Quarter Horses. That's where he learnt to have an eye for the horse, for conformation. That's more important in the Quarter Horse than it is in the Thoroughbreds. They run faster, it's more important." Blane is quite a humorist. He turned to a horse with awful feet. "It's like this little club-footed thing. Taking her to the races is like going to Vietnam with a flyswatter."

Melvin Hatley, when he met Wayne, had been standing stallions and breeding horses for sale for many years. Mr Hatley told me he had made a profit every year he'd been in Quarter Horses, so he was no mug. Mr Hatley selected those horses so he must have known something about picking horses. I asked him if he was any help to Wayne in the development of his ability to choose good horses. "Definitely not," said Mr Hatley. Wayne already knew much more, and from the time they hooked up, Wayne chose the horses and the profits improved markedly. "We always looked together, but I had complete faith in what he was doing."

Albert Yank's contribution

Albert Yank buys and sells horses as an agent. One of his magazine advertisements says: "My eye can put a champion in your barn".

"Albert, what are some horses that you have selected?"

"I bought Vaguely Noble as a two-year-old in Newmarket England; TV Lark; Argument, which won the International; Glorious Song; and I trained two two-year-old's: Risen Star and Sunday Silence." Risen Star went on to win the Belmont Stakes and Sunday Silence the Kentucky Derby and Preakness.

In spite of everyone else's low opinion of Sunday Silence, Albert advised Arthur Hancock III (who had sent him the horse to prepare for the sale) not to sell the horse for less than $150,000. Arthur put $50,000 reserve on it, which it didn't reach. So Arthur sold half to Charlie Whittingham and ended up as a part owner of a horse worth millions. Albert also advised the present owners of the now successful stallion Halo that it would be a smart move to buy him, well before Sunday Silence put him on the map.

Albert once saw a three-year-old horse he liked, in a paddock in New Zealand. He bought it for $US15,000 for a Californian client who respected his eye. Called Oriental Nip, the horse went to Australia, won the Geelong Derby Trial at 100 to 1 with 600 of Albert's money riding on him. Albert and the owner flew out to see it run in the VRC Derby in Melbourne. The pace did not suit and he finished out of the real money. Taken to California, he ran in San Francisco's Bowling Green Stakes and he romped in. Then he took sick and died. I think we can say Albert knows a few things about choosing yearlings. Did he teach Wayne anything?

ALBERT:"Wayne told someone today, 'This is the man that taught me how to look at a horse'. They said, 'What did he tell you?' He said, 'To always look at them on the oblique. Only idiots look at them from the front and back only."

"Did you have a lot to do with teaching him how to look at Thoroughbreds?"

"He knew a lot about how to look at a Thoroughbred before I met him but I taught him all I knew."

"Why do you look at them from that oblique angle? Is it simply that you can see what you can see from the front and the side from one position?"

"You can shoot'em on the angles as they're walking away. I can tell every fault in a horse."

"Is that just practice? Did you start out looking at them from the front and the side?"

"I don't remember how I started out, I only know what I do now. But I taught him other things too. Or I helped him learn."

Albert likes a horse's cannon bones to be like axe handles: flat in front and tapered back towards the tendons.

"Those horses with round cannons are apt to be coarse-boned horses.   You can start out with the 20th best horse and with the wear and tear on the two-year-old's, you may end up with the best horse of the year. It doesn't matter how brilliant a horse is, if he doesn't have soundness he's no good."

"Do you like thick tendons then - for soundness?"

"No I like nice tight, well defined tendons. Good definition everywhere. I don't like a heavy neck. Good profile. No short-necked horses."

"Can a neck be too long?"

"It could be possible. I've never seen one too long. I like a long neck. Horses that have a nice neck on them cover the ground. They cover more ground. There may be some faster (striding) horses, but they're losing their action, they're not covering the ground."

"So you get a longer stride out of a longer-necked horse."

"Sure."

"What about hocks?"

"Horses that are not correct, when they hit the ground, there is a shearing action, like a plane landing in a cross wind. There is a shearing action in the knees, in the ankles, in the hocks. We get most trouble in the knees. Shearing causes knee fractures, chips. It takes its toll."

"So what do you look for in a knee?"

"Some width, flat, not back. I won't put a horse down if he's over at the knee as long as he's not too bad. There is a lot in how you feel about the horse, how you relate. But good horses think differently. When you take them to the paddock, a good horse will look at the other horses with utter disdain."

Albert clearly was a help to Wayne, who even now considers himself to be still learning. I was very impressed and told Wayne so.

"If I had a horse, that wasn't doing much I'd probably sell it and get you to buy a replacement."

"Well, that's a nice compliment."

I'd probably ask him to buy a filly.

In summary, Wayne clearly has a proven ability to choose outstanding horses. He has bought million-dollar duds but his overall percentages are very good. He proved he could buy good horses even when his buys averaged below the sale average. He chooses primarily on physical type and therefore has often gotten bargains.

8. How Lukas trains

As mentioned earlier, Wayne has developed his own training methods. Rather than spying on other trainers, he has deliberately avoided imitating them. Below are some of Wayne's comments on training, collected from interviews in various magazines:

Why he runs numbers in a race

With Tracy Gantz in the Thoroughbred of California, in 1983, speaking on the number of times he has 2, 3, or even 4 contenders in one major race: "I think it's a numbers game . . . It's so easy to plan these things out but the thing that happens is the horses don't cooperate".

One of the advantages of the large numbers, that Wayne didn't mention, is some control of the pace. That was because on his mind at this time was Marfa, a horse he owned with French and Beal, that had proven almost unsteerable in some of his early races. Lukas persevered because once or twice the horse had shown something in morning workouts.

"My theory has always been with a horse, that if he shows a sign of brilliance at some time - in the morning, in the afternoon, in a six furlong work or whatever - that the talent is there and you just have to fool around by trial and error until you can get it to come out."

Marfa took five races to hold enough of a straight line to win his maiden, but eventually went on to win the Santa Anita Derby, in which Lukas typically had two other starters, Easy Cash and Total Departure. The three horses were ridden by Jorge Velasquez, Angel Cordero Jr and Laffit Pincay Jr respectively, three of the best jockeys in the country. The $198,000

Marfa earned, when added to his previous winnings, guaranteed him a start in the Kentucky Derby.

The key: Mental preparation

Wayne told Paul Haigh, "Number one: The mental preparation of an athletic team is as important as the physical preparation, and that has come through in horseracing too. I think that everyone who is training horses is getting them physically fit to run their distance. I mean their blood count, their muscle tone, all the things that go into the physical end of winning a horserace. But I think the thing that separates the Woody Stephens's, the Whittingham's, the Wayne Lukas's, if you will, is that consciously or unconsciously the good trainers are into a program where they're preparing those horses mentally to perform at their peaks - and I think that's highly overlooked by a lot of trainers. I venture to say that all successful trainers, whether they realize it or not are doing something mentally with their horses to prepare them for peak performance. It has always been my contention that there is a very fine line between physical fitness and mental staleness. I think it's a delicate balance and we try to dwell on the fact that we not only want our horses physically fit but we never want to take the try out of a horse ... Since the horse can't talk, the only way you're going to pick up that communication is through observation and the only way you're going to be able to observe your horse is to put in a lot of time with him. There are many, many signs that a horse will give off, if in fact you're aware of them and observing them. Many people feel that if they spend an hour with the horse they spend enough time with him. We feel that you cannot train horses without spending more time with them."

Lukas has a large staff and is well known for asking them to spend plenty of time with their horses: "We watch them cool out. We watch them when the boys are cleaning them up after they are done in the morning, brushing them and so forth, to see what kind of reaction they have to that. We observe them in every way to try to pick up on them."

In another interview: "An athlete's an athlete. You can get them ready physically, but you'd better also pay attention to the mental aspect as well. Nothing is more discouraging to an athlete than to be asked to do something he can't do. All horses naturally want to run. You'd better know your individual so that you can take that native desire and work with it and keep that 'want to' in them. Bringing a horse up and getting him ready physically and mentally for the sixth race on Saturday is the key."

Commenting on his reputation for giving a horse a lot of starts (for example the fillies Gene's Lady and Life's Magic both started over 50 times) Wayne said, "I think we've got quite a good record of getting a horse good and then keeping it good for a long time. I think that comes partly from being observant as to their mental balance ... but I think it also comes from fulfilling their needs ... Too many people train defensively. They train the horse along, then when the problem occurs ... they try to right the problem. We try to be ahead of the problem."

"We feel we can make many mistakes in our training schedules, but if they are physically fit and mentally happy they will overcome them. You can gallop them too far or too little. You can work them when you should have walked them. You can work them five-eighths when you should have worked them a mile ... "

"If he's running out on the turns do not immediately go through a number of equipment changes to correct it. Get to the bottom of the problem instead and find out why he's running out in the turns."

"Then one more thing ... there is no difference (in the level of care) between Lady's Secret and the cheapest horse in the barn. We absolutely base it on the ultimate care."

In another interview with Tracy Gantz after the win of Movin Money, ridden by Patrick Valenzuela in the Del Mar Oaks, Wayne explained some more of his thinking: "Our horses like to run free and Pat lets them run. We didn't want to be laying worse than third or fourth into the first turn. I told Pat to let her go if he had to, and if we die in the stretch we die in the stretch. Then he did what he does so well - he let her run easy on the backside (backstretch)."

"When they came to the stretch she was on the outside where I think you have to be on this track." Lukas explained that a jockey cannot afford to override this filly. "As soon as you override her she loses her stride. Some who rode her got to bootin' and scootin' on her and she didn't respond. You also can't work her too much. Once I realized that, I gave her long gallops and got to babying and loving her."

Wayne has been known to give his horses ice water on very hot days: "Some of these races are won by a photo finish. If they enjoy fresh ice water on hot days, it might make them stick their noses out a little further. I do every little thing I can to make these horses happy." (This ice water thing caught the press fancy and has been repeated in many articles about Wayne.)

"Some of them you love and cuddle and bring along; others you kick their ass," was another published comment.

Lukas believes tension is a major problem in racehorses especially on raceday: "Anytime you create tension in a person or a horse, you lose performance. The tension wears them out." The signs are profuse sweating and high-strung behavior. Lukas had a horse called Partez in the Kentucky Derby of 1981. Rival runner Pleasant Colony lathered up so much the sweat was just running off him. His son Jeff pointed out Pleasant Colony saying, "There's one we don't have to worry about". Pleasant Colony won. There are exceptions. Seattle Slew lathered up before almost every race but only lost one.

Back in his Quarter Horse days Lukas had a very fast but green young horse in a futurity heat. He begged top jockey Bobby Adair to fly to Emporia Kansas to ride it. The young horse was fast but shied and ducked at the cheers of the crowd and almost lost a place in final, to be run the following week. Adair was not impressed. The youngster was so rank he had feared it might try to make a U-turn in a field of racing Quarter Horses.

"I'll take care of this," Lukas told him. "Be back here next week to get your picture taken (Implying the horse will win)."

Lukas rounded up children from the local grade-school, paying them 50 cents each to appear at the empty racetrack grandstand. Like Cecil B. de Mille with movie extras, he asked them to shout, cheer, run, jump, wave and later to throw paper cups as he led the young horse past them again and again. He repeated the dose the next day until he was happy with the horse's response. As many "takes" as necessary until the scene was just right. The horse won the futurity.

On Turning a Horse Out (Spelling)

After Success Express won the Breeder's Cup Juvenile on November 21st 1987, Wayne announced that the 2yo horse would go on to a million dollar futurity even though he believed the horse was a Kentucky Derby prospect for May the next year. (Woody Stephens had already passed up the Juvenile with Forty Niner because he believed it would harm his horse's chances for the Derby.) Wayne explained: "After the Futurity we'll keep him in light training. You have to let a horse down for at least 90 days for him to get any benefit out of it. So I'll keep him in my barn or send him down to my training center at Del Mar and put him in a jogging program."

Success Express injured himself pulling up after that futurity, and was out of Derby contention.

On Transporting Horses

Moving horses around a large country is something Lukas has had a lot of experience with. He has experimented with different approaches. Some he ran fresh off the plane, some he gave as much as a month in the new surroundings. In the new spot, some were worked hard, some lightly. He believes from his results that horses run better than usual when they are raced within 1 or 2 days of arriving by plane. Tank's Prospect was flown from the east coast to the west and back again prior to the Preakness which he won, to benefit from this effect. Not a cheap training aid.

In the 1988 Breeders' Cup magazine Lukas was quoted as believing that the uniformity of the way he sets up his stable - presumably the feed bins, the stall fronts, the hay 'puffs,' the potted trees and saddle racks etc. - helps his horses adjust when they are moved around in the quest for wins. The new surroundings have a lot of 'home' markers.

Equipment

Jon White interviewed a number of trainers on their approach to equipment in the *Thoroughbred Record* of August 1981. One was Wayne: "What we do on equipment is try to keep everything very basic and very simple. We've got a horse that is bearing out on the turn, we feel there's a reason for that and that the equipment will certainly help. For example we can put on an extension blinker or use a run-out bit. But generally speaking, there's a physical or mental problem that causes this because we know, if everything is normal and in proper order, a horse isn't going to bear out. He'll go round turn on a mile oval pretty good."

"So before we get into equipment, we try to go to the basics and see if we can't figure out why. Maybe he's got an ankle that's bothering him a little bit or maybe he's got a tooth that's bothering him. So rather than put on a run-out bit, we might check his teeth merely to find out if he's having trouble when he takes a hold of the bit."

"Some horses just absolutely need a blinker or certain cup or certain bit in order to get the best performance out of them. Ideally we like to run all of our horses in a standard D-bit. We like to use a copper covered D-bit. The reason we like to do that is copper induces saliva in the mouth . . . and it keeps a horse's mouth a little bit better, a little bit longer. They don't get what we call a hard mouth from constant wear and tear . . ."

"We like to put a lot of our fillies in a rubber D-bit, a leather D-bit, rubber snaffle or a leather snaffle. We find that many of them respond to a little bit of cushion."

"We try to stay away from blinkers on a young horse as long as possible . . . Quarter Horses . . . most of them do run in blinkers, I would say 8 out of 10 do. They're in close quarters going straight in an all-out dash, and blinkers seem to get their mind more on speed and heading down the racetrack. So they do stay in blinkers and most 2yo's use them right away."

Wayne ran Grand Canyon, one of his top 2yo's of 1989, in a white shadow roll. This was reportedly to get him to keep his head down to improve his action.

Training Fillies

Wayne has had amazing success with fillies. For example in 1987 he won his 5th Santa Anita Oak Leaf (G1) in six years, and his 6th Del Mar Debutante in 10 years. What is more he has sent out fillies to win many races formerly regarded as the province of colts, such as the Del Mar Futurity and the Santa Anita Derby. So what is his secret?

In 1984 Lukas won the Kentucky Oaks (1⅛ mile) with Lucky Lucky Lucky, defeating Woody Stephen's Miss Oceana by a nose. Lukas, the man with big successes with fillies and

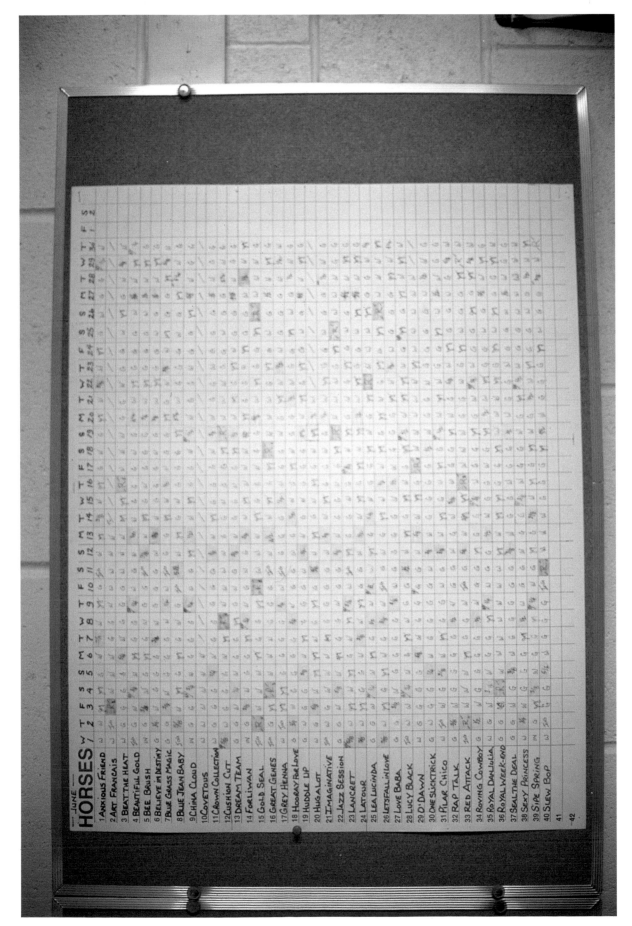

Wayne's training chart on the wall of his Hollywood Park stable office, June 1988. Unaware at that time of how solidly he worked his horses on 'gallop' days, I was staggered at the long times between works/races. Tommy Smith, Australia's most successful trainer, fastworks his horses 2 or 3 times per week. G = gallop, but in Australia or England it would be called a canter. R = race, W = walk.

mares, gave her two sharp ⅝ mile workouts in preparation for the race. "I wanted to get her interest back in racing. You have to get the try back in a filly if they throw a bad race. Fillies don't run races unless it's fun for them. If it becomes work they'll quit."

Lukas revealed that winning the Oaks had been his long term goal for Lucky Lucky Lucky. While he had planned early to run her in the Grade 2 Ashland Stakes (in which she had finished 4th in a field of 4), he decided to give her a run even earlier than that race, opening her 3yo campaign in the Jim Beam Stakes (Grade 3). In the Jim Beam she raced just off the pace and faded in the straight to finish 9th. Asked if the Jim Beam was to some extent a preparation for her later races, Lukas replied, "I thought she was a legitimate shot. Certain races are important to win in a horse's career, and you have to plan for them. You win the Oaks and Derby in March and April, not in May."

In 1987 Wayne cleaned up the Grade 1 Del Mar Futurity with a filly. He told Robert Henwood of The Blood-Horse, "You can take a shot with a filly against colts in July, August and early September, but then the maturity and strength factors start to even out unless you've got a Landaluce." I presume his comment applied only to 2yo's.

Running fillies against colts is something Wayne learned in Quarter Horses. Quarter Horse trainer Don Essary, in his 1980 book *Training Quarter Horses* has this to say: "If you have a filly keep her in races restricted to fillies whenever possible. However . . . this is less important than in Thoroughbred racing because fillies and mares are more equal to males in short sprints that do not require as much stamina. It is even more so with 2yo's. As a rule fillies develop faster than colts and are quicker . . . as a result 2yo fillies and colts are more or less equal." Fillies have won a lot of All-American Futurities, but it's not just the youngsters - mares won the first five runnings of the Vessels Maturity, a major race for older Quarter Horses.

Lukas has explained how he decides if he will run a filly in the Kentucky Derby: "You must be sure in your heart that she is an exceptional filly. The bottom line is you must believe she is the best racehorse of her year regardless of sex. She must be superior physically, strong enough to handle the training program for the Derby. It's too hard for some colts. She must have natural speed so she can always be in the race. A filly does not have the power and stamina to fight her way through a 20 horse field."

"You must also consider what the consequences will be, because this is a step out of the norm. If you fail, some members of the media will pounce on that and there will be a lot of second guessing."

It is worth noting that Regret, the first filly to win the Derby, did so in 1915 by leading throughout. Genuine Risk won in 1980. The chances of a filly winning were considered so poor she was the first filly to start for 21 years. Genuine Risk settled midfield initially before working her way five wide around the field to take the lead at the mile. Winning Colors led throughout her Derby.

Despite his results and obvious ability with fillies, Wayne has had some failures. In 1987 Lady's Secret, after a string of poor performances, embarrassed Wayne by trying to run off the track. The jockey's boot scraped the *outside* rail. "Physically, she's absolutely perfect," Wayne told reporters, "but if she was human, we'd take her to the psychiatrist in the morning."

Lukas believes his greater success with fillies has come from two factors. First, he has bought more fillies, especially early on, presumably because the monetary loss if they fail on the racetrack is much less. Second, he believes that the high level of individual care and the extra individual attention in his stable brings out the best in fillies.

"I think that they are like women. They like the attention . . . they respond to it a little more than a stud horse."

8.1 Wayne's training chart

This analysis is based on the June 1988 training chart at Wayne's office at Hollywood Park track. The study was helped by comparison with the statistical analysis of his race results by Bloodstock Research Information Services (B.R.I.S.) in Lexington, Kentucky. The information contained in their Trainer Summary is useful to bettors, for obvious reasons, but also to trainers who wish to study the great trainers, their rivals records, and of course their own record. It provides Thoroughbred racing in North America with one of the best tools there is for analyzing a trainer's strengths and weaknesses. The data is there for the current year and six previous years, showing their success rates on dirt and turf, over sprints and routes, with fillies and colts etc. There are 74 categories of starts.

Having grown up hearing about Tommy Smith's training in Australia, and having seen the training charts of Woody Stephens, Charlie Whittingham and John Gosden in America, I found Wayne's chart astoundingly different. The gaps between fast works were much longer than anything I had seen or heard of in Thoroughbred racing anywhere in the world. In the 1970's and 1980's there has been a worldwide interest in interval training to *increase* the amount of work horses do. Wayne's training seems to be a push in the opposite direction, and his success gives much food for thought. Wayne was reluctant to discuss training in any detail, but one morning, when I asked if I could photograph the chart for this book, he surprised me by saying, "I suppose so".

The camera had 400 ASA film in it, suited to the weak early morning light, but I decided not to try his patience by asking if

I could bring a tripod and finer grain film the next day. I took some shots with the 400 ASA film. The next day I did have the camera loaded with fine grain film and I had a telescoped tripod, but Wayne's first words were, "You know I'm a little uncomfortable with letting you take a picture of that," - indicating the chart. He didn't rescind his permission, but I didn't ask if I could take a better set of shots.

I think other trainers should be grateful to Wayne for the opportunity to see the chart, because his training represents a very different approach, which he developed. In the spacing of fast works it is similar to Caesar Dominguez's Quarter Horse charts, no surprise considering Wayne's years in Quarter Horses.

Wayne has every reason not to let anyone see the charts, considering that many trainers insist he can't train. They say his extraordinary results are due to sheer numbers or drugs, but I believe his horses have won so many races, by such wide margins, and set so many track and race records that only a fool would ignore Wayne's training methods.

See:
Photos of Wayne's training chart.
Arrangement of the chart by age and sex — see next page.
Extended racing history and training chart of individual horses — see page 92.

NOTE: Winnings given for each horse in the charts are from January 1st to October 1st 1988. The horses were in Wayne's training program at Hollywood Park in Los Angeles in June. Jeff was in New York, so the chart is Wayne's own work. Wayne does not claim horses out of claiming races (4 are listed since 1982, the last in 1987), so horses listed as running in claiming races upto June were almost certainly with Wayne. Horses run in a second or later claimer after June may have been with other trainers. Kiaran McLaughlin said that about 15 to 20 horses are claimed off the New York barn each year.

Walk Days
On a walk day the horses don't leave the barn. They are hand-walked round and around the barn verandah, led by grooms and hot-walkers. The horses hooves dig a trench in the dirt, which the workers rake level again later in the morning. It's the same in practically every trainer's barn when it comes to walking.

Jog Days
On a jog day the horses jog and trot for one or two miles.

Gallop Days
What happened on a gallop day varied a lot, according to people who had ridden track work for Wayne. I asked the riders waiting for Wayne one morning. *"Gallops -what sort of distance and speed do they go?"*

"It depends. Each horse is an individual."
"Average, roughly."
"An average gallop here is about a mile and a half, a mile and five-eighths. As far as speed, like I said, I couldn't even answer that because every horse is different, and you don't know what's going to happen on a day-to-day basis."
"Wayne tells you?"
"Yes. An average gallop for us is about eighths (furlongs) in eighteens, so if you figure eighths in fifteens is what they call a two-minute lick, eighteens is kind of a nice open gallop, as long as a horse is doing it comfortable. It might be twenties or it might be eighteens or it might even be sixteens. Not very often, sixteens."
"The spacing is like Quarter Horse training."
"Well, it might look like it on paper but it's very very far from Quarter Horse training."
"Because they're going further?"
They're going further and they're generally going a little faster. A Quarter Horse has generally got to run 350 yards. Some of them it's 870 yards. To train a horse to go 400 yards is sometimes as strenuous as it is to train a horse to go a mile and a half, because they're a different makeup of a horse. You want a Quarter Horse that is more keyed, for going 350. Got to fire them away from there. These horses here, you want them to fire away from there too, but you've got to save a little reserve for that last quarter of a mile or eighth of a mile. They say the basic rule that we go by, which doesn't always hold true for all horses, is that a horse can usually run all-out for about three-eighths of a mile, whether it's in the first part or the middle part or the last part. Somewhere during that race."

In New York a regular track observer told me that at Belmont Wayne's horses do one lap of a canter, which is one mile, and one lap at a two minute lick, which is 15 seconds per furlong or 200m, and they do that every day or every second day. Kiaran McLaughlin said the gallops are a mile to a mile and a half.

Work days
On work days, Wayne's horses will go out and warm up by jogging three-eighths or even a whole mile if they are big tight-muscled horses. A work out of the starting gates is indicated on the chart by the little G in the upper left hand corner of the yellow work day boxes. A gate school, when the horse is walked in and out, backed in, stood in the gates, all those kind of things, then worked, is indicated by a GS. Most of that kind of training would have already been done at the training center.

The work itself is at 12 to 13 seconds per furlong (a furlong is equal to 220yds, ⅛ mile or 201m). Even though Wayne's horses don't fast-work very often, they still don't go very fast.

WAYNE LUKAS'S TRAINING CHART

For his Hollywood Park stable, June 1988. This was weeks after his Kentucky Derby win. June 11th was Belmont Stakes day at his New York stable.

¼, ⅜, ½ = quarter mile work etc.
4½ = four and a half furlongs

g = gallop (canter)
j = jog
R = race
w = walk.

Two-year-old colts						Sat							Sat							Sat							Sat			
Date June	1	2	3	4	5	6	7	8	9	10	11	12	13	14	15	16	17	18	19	20	21	22	23	24	25	26	27	28	29	30
Crown Collection	w	g	g	g	¼	w	g	g	g	g	g	⅜	w	j	g	g	g	w	⅜	w	g	g	w	g	g	g	½	w	g	g
Great Genes	j	g	j	R	w	w	w	g	g	g	j	w	4½	w	j	g	j	R	w	w	w	g	j	g	w	g	½	w	j	g
Latour	⅜	w	j	g	g	w	⅜	w	j	g	g	w	½	w	j	g	j	w	j	½	w	j	g	g	w	j	⅝	w	j	g
Roving Cowboy	g	½	w	g	g	g	g	½	w	g	g	j	g	g	⅞	w	g	g	j	g	w	½	w	g	g	j	g	j	⅝	w
Sports Call	g	w	g	g	¼	w	g	g	g	w	g	⅜	w	g	g	g	g	½	w	g	g	g	g	B	w	g	g	½	w	g
Texian	g	g	g	½	w	g	g	¼	w	g	g	j	⅝	w	g	g	g	g	½	w	g	g	B	g	R	w	w	j	g	g
Upstart	g	B	w	g	g	⅝	w	g	g	g	g	R	.	.	.	.	.	.	.	.	.	.	.	.	.	.	.	.	.	.
Winning	⅜	w	g	g	g	g	½	w	g	g	g	g	4½	w	g	g	w	w	w	j	g	g	g	w	g	g	g	½	w	g

Two-year-old fillies						Sat							Sat							Sat							Sat			
Date June	1	2	3	4	5	6	7	8	9	10	11	12	13	14	15	16	17	18	19	20	21	22	23	24	25	26	27	28	29	30
Anxious Friend	w	w	j	j	g	w	⅜	w	j	g	j	w	j	⅜	w	j	g	w	g	j	w	⅜	w	j	g	w	g	g	½	w
Beautiful Gold	j	g	w	⅜	w	j	g	g	¼	w	g	w	½	w	g	g	g	w	g	4½	w	j	g	g	g	w	⅝	w	j	¼
Beebrush	IN	g	⅝	w	g	j	g	w	g	g	j	⅜	w	j	g	w	g	g	g	⅜	w	j	g	g	g	w	½	w	j	g
Forliwan	IN	g	⅜	w	g	g	j	¼	w	g	w	g	⅜	w	j	w	w	w	j?	j	g	g	w	j	g	g	w	½	w	j
Lea Lucinda	g	g	w	¼	w	j	g	½	w	B	w	j	g	⅝	w	g	g	j	w	g	j	R	w	w	w	j	g	g	w	⅝
Lucy Black	j	w	w	¼	w	g	j	w	g	g	½	w	j	g	j	w	g	j	½	w	j	j	w	g	j	g	j	w	j	w
Royal Danjulia	w	g	w	⅜	w	g	g	j	¼	w	g	g	½	w	g	g	w	g	j	½	w	j	g	g	w	g	⅝	w	j	g
Super Baba	g	j	½	w	g	g	g	¼	w	g	g	w	⅝	w	g	g	g	⅜	w	g	j	R	w	w	w	j	g	g	g	⅝
Wonders Delight	w	j	g	½	w	g	g	¼	w	g	½	w	j	g	g	w	g	⅜	w	g	g	w	g	g	½	w	j	g	g	¼

Three-year-old colts						Sat							Sat							Sat							Sat			
Date June	1	2	3	4	5	6	7	8	9	10	11	12	13	14	15	16	17	18	19	20	21	22	23	24	25	26	27	28	29	30
Cougarized	.	.	.	.	.	.	.	.	.	.	.	.	.	.	.	.	.	.	g	j	g	w	½	w	j	g	g	g	w	w
Rap Talk	g	⅜	w	g	g	g	g	½	w	g	g	w	g	w	⅝	w	g	g	j	w	g	⅝	w	j	g	g	w	g	⅝	w
Slewbop	w	j	g	g	⅝	w	g	g	g	j	R	w	w	w	g	g	g	j	4½	w	g	g	g	j	w	g	g	⅜	w	R
Success Express	w	g	j	j	g	w	⅝	w	j	g	g	w	g	g	j	⅝	w	j	g	j	w	g	j	g	j	R	w	w	w	j
White Mischief	w	w	w	w	j	g	g	j	½	w	g	g	w	g	j	g	¾	w	j	g	g	w	g	j	R	w	w	w	j	g

Three-year-old fillies						Sat							Sat							Sat							Sat			
Date June	1	2	3	4	5	6	7	8	9	10	11	12	13	14	15	16	17	18	19	20	21	22	23	24	25	26	27	28	29	30
Beat The Heat	w	g	g	g	g	⅝	w	g	g	g	w	w	w	j	j	R	w	w	w	g	g	w	g	g	w	j	g	w	⅝	w
Blue Jean Baby	j	⅝	w	j	g	j	g	w	g	j	5½	w	j	g	w	g	g	g	j	5½	w	g	g	g	w	g	j	5½	w	g
Cushion Cut	⅝	w	g	g	g	w	j	R	w	w	w	w	g	g	w	g	g	j	R	w	w	w	g	g	w	g	g	5½	w	g
Dream Team	g	g	w	¼	w	g	g	j	g	w	g	⅜	w	g	g	w	g	j	½	w	j	g	j	w	g	g	4½	w	g	g
Gold Seal	j	R	w	w	w	j	g	g	j	R	w	w	w	j	g	g	w	g	g	⅝	w	j	g	g	j	R	w	w	w	g
Grey Henna	w	j	j	j	g	g	g	g	⅜	w	j	g	g	g	½	w	g	g	w	g	j	w	½	w	g	g	g	w	½	w
Hooray For Love	g	¼	w	g	g	g	g	⅜	w	g	g	w	g	½	w	g	j	w	g	g	½	w	g	g	j	w	g	½	w	g
Hugalot	w	g	⅝	w	j	j	w	g	j	g	⅝	w	j	g	w	j	g	w	j	½	w	.	.	.	.	.	.	.	.	.
Imaginative	j	w	g	w	w	w	j	g	g	g	g	w	⅜	w	j	g	g	w	g	½	w	j	g	g	w	g	g	½	w	g
Jazz Session	g	g	w	⅝	w	j	g	g	w	g	g	⅝	w	g	g	w	g	j	R	w	w	w	g	j	R	w	w	w	g	g
Lets Fall In Love	⅜	w	j	g	j	w	g	⅜	w	j	g	w	g	j	w	½	w	j	g	j	w	g	j	w	j	R	w	w	w	j
O'Dawn	w	g	g	g	g	⅝	w	g	g	g	g	w	⅝	w	j	g	R	w	w	w	w	w	j	w	w	w	w	w	.	.
Over All	.	.	.	.	.	.	.	.	.	.	.	.	.	.	.	.	.	.	⅝	w	j	g	g	g	j	j	j	w	w	w
Royal Weekend	g	g	j	R	w	w	w	w	w	w	w	j	w	j	j	g	g	j	w	w	w	j	g	j	w	j	g	g	j	w
Smarterthanilook	j	j	g	g	g	⅜	w	j	g	g	g	½	w	g	g	g	w	⅝	w	g	g	w	g	g	g	⅝	w	g	j	g
Tap Your Toes	w	g	g	j	g	⅝	w	j	g	g	j	w	⅝	w	g	g	g	w	g	5½	w	j	g	j	R	w	w	w	j	j

Four-year-old colts						Sat							Sat							Sat							Sat			
Date June	1	2	3	4	5	6	7	8	9	10	11	12	13	14	15	16	17	18	19	20	21	22	23	24	25	26	27	28	29	30
Seal The Deal	g	g	w	g	⅜	w	g	g	g	g	g	⅜	w	g	g	w	g	g	½	w	g	g	w	g	g	w	½	w	g	g
Gulch		.	.	.	.	.	.	.	.	IN	g	3½	j	R	w	w	w	g	g	g	w	g	5½	w	g	g	g	w	g	g

Five-year-old colts						Sat								Sat								Sat							Sat							
Art Francais	w	j	R	w	w	w	g	g	w	w	w	w	w	.	.	.	.	.	.	.	.	.	.	.	.	.	.	.	.	.	.	.	.			
Love Baba	g	g	⅜	w	g	g	g	g	⅜	w	g	g	g	g	w	½	w	g	g	g	j	w	½	w	g	g	g	j	w	4½						
Steinlen	w	g	g	j	⅝	w	g	j	g	g	w	g	¾	w	j	g	j	g	R	w	w	w	j	g	j	g	g	⅝	w	g						
Synastry	w	j	w	j	g	½	w	j	g	g	g	w	⅝	w	j	R	w	w	w	j	g	w	g	g	g	w	⅝	w	j	g						

Six-year-old colts						Sat								Sat								Sat							Sat							
Huddle Up	g	w	g	g	⅝	w	j	g	g	g	w	½	w	g	w	g	g	g	4½	w	j	g	j	g	w	g	w	g	⅝	w	j	g				
Red Attack	j	R	w	w	w	j	g	g	w	j	g	⅝	w	j	j	R	w	w	w	g	g	w	g	j	w	g	g	j	R	w						

Unraced in 1988 to October

Age/ Sex unknown					Sat								Sat								Sat							Sat			
Date	June 1	2	3	4	5	6	7	8	9	10	11	12	13	14	15	16	17	18	19	20	21	22	23	24	25	26	27	28	29	30
Believe In Destiny	g	¼	w	g	g	g	⅜	w	g	g	g	w	⅜	w	g	g	g	w	g	⅜	w	j	g	g	w	g	½	w	j	g
Blue Grass Magic	g	g	⅜	w	g	g	g	w	½	w	j	g	g	g	j	w	½	w	g	g	j	g	w	⅜	w	j	g	g	j	⅝ w
China Cloud	IN	g	g	⅜	w	g	g	g	¼	w	g	j	½	w	j	g	g	w	½	w	g	g	g	w	g	g	j	⅝	w	g g
Count Aly	.	.	.	g	½	w	w	j	g	g	g	w	g	IN	g	½	w	g	g	g	g	w	½	w	g	g	g	j	½	w
Space Cup	.	.	.	g	½	w	w	j	g	g	g	w	g	IN	g	½	w	j	g	g	w	g	j	¼	w	g	⅝	w	j	g
Latour	⅝	w	j	w	j	g	w	j	⅝	w	j	j	g	g	w	g	¾	w	j	g	w	g	j	g	w	g	⅝	w	j	g
Sexy Princess	w	¼	w	g	g	g	j	½	w	g	g	w	g	g	⅜	w	g	g	w	g	j	½	w	g	w	g	w	w	w	w
Sipe Spring	IN	g	j	⅜	w	g	g	j	¼	w	g	j	g	⅜	w	j	g	j	w	g	½	w	j	g	g	g	w	g	½	w j

Wayne was reported to have said, "When you see one of our horses break 48 seconds in half mile, a minute in five furlongs, or a 1:14 for six furlongs, it's because of one of three things: The horse is a very exceptional horse, the reins broke, or the exercise rider fell off. The fitness I think you can get without the hard works. You can instead put a lot of 'bottom' in them and save them a little bit."

Each fast work the horse goes a little faster than the last outing at that distance and while the first furlong might be 13 seconds, the last will be the fastest, around 12 or even a little less. Typical training times for his horses at Belmont Park would be 36 to 37 sec for ⅜ of a mile, 48 to 50 sec for ½, and 1 min to 1:02 perhaps 1:03, for ⅝. Hollywood Park being a faster track, they might go 59 sec to 1:01 for ⅝ there. The time would depend on the ability of the horse, but the stick (whip) is not used in morning works - with rare exceptions.

Typically, most of a set of Wayne's horses is out on the track for about 7 minutes. For example one set came out and some horses were out for seven minutes, some for 11 minutes and one for 14 minutes. Horses going slow paces go round the outer fence of the Santa Anita track clockwise. Horses doing canters or gallops go round the inner fence counter-clockwise, just the same as in races. Wayne's horses start by walking and trotting around the outer track fence. After a while one might peel back and do a lap at a gallop (canter). Another one might turn and go at race speed a half mile.

As far as warming the horse down - cooling out in American parlance - an article in 1981 reported his horses, "walking for the full 45 minutes and cooled out properly".

I asked Wayne about his unusual training pattern.

"In your training chart, you seem to fast work them fairly infrequently."

"I never fast work them. In other words, we don't let our horses work. At five-eighths we very seldom break a minute; we very seldom break one-fourteen in six furlongs, and very seldom ever ever ever break a forty-eight work at a half mile. You'd have to take individual horses, but to make a generalisation, we very very seldom work under eight days."

"That's pretty unusual in Thoroughbreds. It's like Quarter Horse training."

"Not only do we work 'em infrequently; sometimes we'll go twenty and thirty days. We ran Winning Colors in the Kentucky Derby, she had two works in thirty-seven days."

"I find that amazing."

"We don't work horses."

"So you really have a very Quarter Horse style of training your Thoroughbreds?"

"No, no. I don't think it would be fair to make that generalisation. I don't do anything here that I did over there. You're trying to correlate the infrequent works with the Quarter Horse training - but that's not true. What I do every day with these horses is entirely different to what I did with those Quarter Horses."

"What would be the difference?"

"Well, I do more work with them every day. I do spend some time in putting the miles into my horses, I just don't believe in fast works or frequent works. It wouldn't be fair to say that I'm training them like Quarter Horses. That's not true at all. You don't win mile-and-a-quarter, or mile-and-an-eighth races like that. If I did with these what I did with a Quarter Horse, we wouldn't win any races."

When I said to Wayne that his training chart still looked like a Quarter Horse trainer's in the spacing of the fastworks and races, he looked pained.

"Don't say that. What we do - particularly on the other days - is a lot different to what a Quarter Horse does."

"So you believe the canters - you call them gallops - have some critical distance and speed?"

"I stress with my exercise riders that when I get a horse to a certain speed, galloping, I'm very fussy about how far he keeps him at that speed, and how constant he keeps that speed because I know he's getting aerobic exercise at that point. They take it lightly and I get all over them, I say, 'Hey Goddammit when I tell you to go from that pole to that pole, I don't want you to vary it, I want it perfect. There is a reason for that."

"I believe that is one of the critical things in racehorse training. There are the three fiber types in the horse, and I am convinced that some trainers, by just taking the horse's aerobic speed a little too far, take away some of its speed. One possibility is that they tire the fast twitch high aerobic fibers, so the horse begins to use the fast twitch low aerobic fibers. Those fibers learn to use more oxygen, but they are probably horrifically inefficient. In adapting to use more oxygen, they lose some of their diameter, some of their power, so the horse loses some of it's peak speed and acceleration."

"You're absolutely right. That is so important to me. See, my exercise riders, I drill on them and drill on them and drill on them, because I know that is a fact. The thing about it is, there are a lot of guys around here doing this, but they don't know why."

Kiaran McLaughlin, his assistant trainer for five years, agreed that Wayne's training was different to that of other trainers he had worked for. It took him some time to adjust, but whenever he asked Wayne why he did something, Wayne had a reason. Kiaran said that Wayne likes to keep the horses fresh, wanting to run. "Why run them every four days if you can get the same result running them every seven days? Why run them ¾ of a mile if you can get the same result running them half mile?"

"Other trainers would say that won't get a horse fit. Does Wayne do more on the canter days - you call them gallop days - than other trainers?"

"Yes. That helps a lot to get them fit. Wayne believes all you do if you drill on them is risk breaking them down."

Here is a comparison of Wayne's Thoroughbred training with Quarter Horse training, by one of the riders.

"Quarter Horses you keep everything in, basically you do nothing with them. Quarter Horses would do (gallop ie canter) one lap (5/8 mile) at Los Alamitos. Thoroughbreds, you really let them gallop along. Some of Wayne's would go a mile and five eighths. They go 18 maybe 17 seconds to the furlong. He lets them warm up, then go along and then go faster at the end. Make them extend themselves, get them tired."

"He gets them tired even on the gallop days?"

"Yes. They move along. They would do the last furlong in 17, 16 seconds."

"And they go somewhere between a mile and a mile and five-eighths?"

"Yes, Wayne's do, but some Thoroughbreds at the same tracks go two miles."

"Is Wayne very specific in his instructions for each horse?"

"Yes, each horse he tells each rider what he wants done."

"Is it different each day?"

"Sometimes. Off a fastwork or a race he won't gallop them quite as far. Then the next day he'll gallop them a little further. Then the next day he'll gallop them a little further and a little harder. Just builds back up to it."

"And before they race does he back-off?"

"The day before they run they just jog everything two miles. Just trot. He might have one horse he gallops race day because he gets upset."

"Some of the Thoroughbred trainers will give a horse a blowout on the raceday or a few days before."

"The ones that eat pretty good, he'll work them a lot closer to a race than he will light fillies. And he lets them recover better."

Patterns in the chart
In the training sheets certain patterns are evident. The overall program can be pieced together for the 2yo's. Forliwan and Beebrush both started with an IN, and did a ⅜ work within three days. This would indicate that they had been given preliminary 'legging up' work before arrival. They may also have done some ¼ mile works. This would have been at the D. Wayne Lukas Training Center.

Pre-conditioning at the Training Center
I asked one of the riders, *"When the horses come here to Hollywood Park, have they already done a few months of slower work at one of these pre-conditioning places?"*

"It depends. Most all of them have. The two-year-olds, they have been. We get horses from Calumet Farm, and they've already done something. Most everything that we get here will have, because we just don't have the time and space."

Kiaran McLaughlin said the youngsters from the sales begin galloping in November, at the Training Center. They gallop every day and go for one or two miles. Some do fast-works. So these youngsters may have done up to seven months of work already.

How long to first race?
From those first ⅜ works, it was 66 and 72 days until the fillies raced. The colts Crown Collection and Sports Call raced 77 days after working ¼ mile, and they might have had earlier works in May. From first fast work at Hollywood Park to first race, 9 to 12 weeks looks to be typical, with 6 to 8 weeks from first ½ to first race. Anxious Friend may have had a more rapid preparation, because it is 53 days from the first ⅜ on the June chart and 32 days from the first ½, until she raced. Beautiful gold has 29 days from ⅜ and 20 from the ½ but there must have been a lot of earlier works.

The first works for the 2yo's were sometimes ¼, sometimes ⅜. The rise to the first ½ took many forms: Crown Collection went ¼, ⅜, ⅜, ½; Sports Call a steeper ¼, ⅜, ½; Beebrush went 3 x ⅜; Forliwan went ⅜, ¼, ⅜ and then after a gap of 15 days, ½.

"How do you go first up with your horses? Do you have a good winning rate on your horse's first time on the track?"

"We always run a horse a little bit wanting, if you want to put it that way. We do not try to win first crack out of the box. We feel that a horse may need a race and we let him have it."

Before and after works
For the horses on the chart, the works were preceded the day before by walks, gallops or jogs. After a work there was one day of walking followed most often by two to four gallop days, but many other patterns are present.

Days between works
The interval between works is 6 or 7 days in the 2yo colts and 5 or 7 days in the 2yo fillies. There are quite a few four day gaps from work to work, but in those cases the horse only breezed or went ¼ mile. The older horses were worked at 6, 7, 8 and 9 day intervals, the average being a little over 7 days.

Having built up to ½ mile works, the horses mostly did ½ or ⅝ works until they raced. Occasional breezes, ¼ or ⅜ works occur and there are two ¾ and one ⅞ work.

Many trainers have a longer distance for the last work or two if there is a longer race involved. It would seem from these tables that Wayne's horses do ⅝ as a last work for races of 5 furlongs to 9 furlongs -unless the work is close to the race. If it is three or four days before the race, the work may be less than 5/8 and if it is two days, the work may be only ⅛. This may be a factor in the ⅝ before the 8 and 9 furlong races. The two ¾ works were before 8 furlong races. The 9f race of Cougarized is preceded by a half mile work 10 days before, but there may have been a short work in the previous days. The 9f

races of O'Dawn and Gulch were preceded by ⅝ four days before and 3½f two days before.

In his attack on the 1990 Kentucky Derby, Wayne worked all three of his contenders ⅝ of a mile on the Monday, 5 days before the 1¼ mile classic. Real Cash and Land Rush went in 1:00.4 and Power Launch in 1:03.

On the June chart, the time from last work to race varied from 2 to 10 days. The period after a race until the next work, on the other hand, was fairly constant at 8 or 9 days with occasional examples of 10, 11 or 12 days.

The day before a race
Races were almost invariably preceded by a jog day. The exceptions were gallops before 4 of the 29 races and on one occasion a walk. Races were followed by three days of walking with one exception when it was two days of walking and then a jog.

The interval between the first and second races for the 2yo's certainly didn't indicate that Wayne felt they were underprepared. There were only 16 examples so conclusions are wobbly. The time between races for the 2yo's was on average shorter than for all his horses in racing that year according to his Bloodstock Research Information Services figures (BRIS). Considering the 1039 starts separated by 30 days or less in the BRIS data for 1988, Wayne's figures were as follows:

Days since last start	BRIS 1988	CHART 2yo
1 - 5	0.1%	0.0%
6 - 10	11.3%	31.25%
11 - 21	64.8%	68.75%
22 - 30	23.9%	0.0%

In the chart, the shortest interval between the first and second races was 6 days for Beautiful Gold and the longest 20 days for Roving Cowboy. In between were one 7 day interval, two 8 day intervals, one 9, one 12, four 14's, two 16's, two 17's and one 18. The two starts in six days for Beautiful Gold may have been too close for her. After finishing 3rd in her first maiden, Wayne ran her in a stakes race. That would indicate he thought she had potential, but she then disappears, for several months at least.

The win rate for the first race of the 2yo's was 2 from 16, for the second race 4 from 16. The numbers are too small for any conclusions. The BRIS figures indicate Wayne has a 17% win rate for debut as a 2yo. Wayne's overall first start win rate for 1983 to Oct 1988 was 14%, for the second start 21%. The figures from year to year jump about. For instance his second start win rate varies from 8% in 1983 to 70% in 1988. The perils of conclusions from small numbers.

Stepping out in distance

There are two schools of thought about the ways a poorly pre-pared horse can go when it begins racing or begins to race over-more ground. It may perform poorly at first but win as it races itself fit, or it may win through freshness but rapidly become sour or lame. Either way there should be a trend up or down in the stats. That is why punters want the figures for each trainer. These are from the Bloodstock Research Information Service. They define a sprint as 7 furlongs (1400m) or less, and a route as 7½ furlongs or more. Most would be going from 6 to 8 or 9 furlongs.

Wayne's stats are:

Sprint to route   20%
Sprint to route to route 21%
First race at a route   19%
Second race at a route 20%

These figures certainly don't indicate any defects in Wayne's training skills. Another way poor preparation might show up is differences in the win rate for different times since the last race. There are many possible scenarios, but for example, un-der-prepared horses will benefit from a longer gap between races so they can freshen up again. They may benefit from a fittening effect of closer races but won't usually win until the third or fourth race. Over-raced horses may also benefit from a wide gap between races. So many factors are involved that some may cancel each other out. The result is that similar win rates over a range of intervals between races usually indicates a good trainer, but not always. On the other hand, wide differences on large numbers usually point to some fault in the training. So what are Wayne's figures?

Days since last start	% winners
1 - 5 days	18%
6 - 10 days	21%
11 - 21 days	19%
22 - 30 days	20%

These are very consistent results.

I will leave you with this snippet from Wayne: "What sepa-rates good trainers from average trainers is . . . studying those signs and getting that feedback, then making a judgment or opinion. The good trainers are in sync. They're doing what the horse needs."

WAYNE'S CHARTS EXPANDED

Two-year-old Colts

CROWN COLLECTION
SIRE Alydar - DAM Avowal

3 starts 2 wins 0 2nd 0 3rds $31,350
No starts prior to June.

June
1 W 1st race 81 days later
2 G
3 G
4 G
5 WORK ¼
6 W
7 G
8 G 7 days between works
9 G
10 G
11 G
12 WORK ⅜
13 W
14 J
15 G
16 G
17 G
18 W
19 WORK ⅜
20 W
21 G
22 G
23 W
24 G
25 G
26 G
27 WORK ½ 55 days to 1st race
28 W
29 G
30 G

Date	Track		Distance		
Aug 20th	Del Mar	Maiden	6f	won	$14,300

9 days between races

Aug 29th	Del Mar	Allowance	6f	won	$17,050
Sep 14th	Del Mar	Stakes	8f	9th	

GREAT GENES
Saratoga Six - Delightful Vie
4 Starts 1 win 1 0 $20,235
No starts prior to June.

June
1 J
2 G
3 J

4 RACE	Hollywood	Maiden	5f	2nd	$5,200

5 W
6 W
7 W
8 G
9 G
10 G
11 J
12 W
13 WORK 4½
14 W
15 J
16 G
17 J

18 RACE	Hollywood	Maiden	5f	won	$14,300

19 W
20 W
21 W
22 G
23 J
24 G
25 W
26 G
27 WORK ½ mile
28 W
29 J
30 G

Jul 6th	Hollywood	Allow.	6f	5th	$825
Aug 17	Del Mar	Stakes	6f	-	$0

    failed to finish

LATOUR
Desert Wine - Carefree Lass
3 starts 0 wins 0 1 $2,825
No starts prior to June.

June
1 WORK ⅜
2 W
3 J
4 G
5 G
6 W
7 WORK ⅜
8 W
9 J
10 G
11 G
12 W
13 WORK ½
14 W
15 J
16 G
17 J
18 W
19 J
20 WORK ½
21 W
22 J
23 G
24 G
25 W
26 J
27 WORK ⅝
28 W
29 J
30 G

Jul 28th	Del Mar	$32,000 Mdn Cl	6f	9th	$0
Aug 25th	Del Mar	$32,000 Mdn Cl	6f	3rd	$2,400
Sep 2nd	Del Mar	$40,000 Mdn Cl	8f	5th	$425

ROVING COWBOY
Well Decorated - Pound Foolish
4 starts 0 wins 0 0 $0

No starts prior to June.

June
1 G
2 WORK ½
3 W
4 G
5 G
6 G
7 G
8 WORK ½
9 W
10 G
11 G
12 J
13 G
14 G
15 WORK ⅞ G 3 or 5
16 W
17 G
18 G
19 J
20 G
21 W
22 WORK ½ G 5 or 6

23 W
24 G
25 G
26 J
27 G
28 J
29 WORK ⅝
30 W

Date	Track	Race	Dist	Fin	Earn
Jul 4th	Hollywood	Maiden	6f	10th	$0
Jul 24th	Hollywood	Maiden	6f	8th	$0
Aug 6th	Del Mar	Maiden	6f	11th	$0
Aug 27th	Bay Meadows	Mdn	6f	-	$0

   failed to finish

SPORTS CALL
Spectacular Bid - Our Bidder
2 starts 0 wins 0 1 $4,550

No starts prior to June.

June
1 G
2 W
3 G
4 G
5 WORK ¼
6 W
7 G
8 G
9 G
10 W
11 G
12 WORK ⅜
13 W
14 G
15 G
16 G
17 G
18 WORK ½
19 W
20 G
21 G
22 G
23 G
24 BREEZE G 6
25 W
26 G
27 G
28 WORK ½
29 W
30 G

Date	Track	Race	Dist	Fin	Earn
Aug 20th	Del Mar	Maiden	6f	3rd	$3,900
Aug 28th	Del Mar	Maiden	6f	5th	$650

TEXIAN
Majestic Light- Simple English
8 starts 2 wins 1 1 $155,225

No starts prior to June.

June
1 G
2 G
3 G
4 WORK ½
5 W
6 G
7 G
8 WORK ¼ G
9 W
10 G
11 G
12 J
13 WORK ⅝
14 W
15 G
16 G
17 G
18 G
19 WORK ½ G 3 or 5
20 W
21 G
22 G
23 BREEZE 100 yds G 3 or 5
24 G

25 RACE	Hollywood	Maiden	6f	6th	$0	

26 W
27 W
28 J
29 G
30 G

Jul 13th	Hollywood	Maiden	6f	8th	$0
Jul 27th	Del Mar	Maiden	5f	2nd	$5,000
Aug 7th	Del Mar	Maiden	8f	Won	$14,850
Aug 17th	Del Mar	Stakes	6f	4th	$4,500
Aug 31st	Del Mar	Stakes	7f	5th	$1,875
Sep 14th	Del Mar	Stakes	8f	3rd	$39,000
Sep 25th		Cant'y Stakes	8f	Won	$90,000

UPSTART
Saratoga Six - Kitchen Window
2 starts 0 wins 0 0 $1,950

May 26th	Hollywood	Maiden	5f	4th	$1,950

June
1 G
2 BREEZE
3 W
4 G
5 G
6 WORK ⅝
7 W
8 G
9 G
10 G
11 G

12 RACE	Hollywood	Maiden	5f	-	$0

  failed to finish
13 -
14 - etc.

WINNING
Nijinsky II - Little Happiness
3 starts 0 wins 0 0 $2,775
No starts prior to June.
June
1 WORK ⅜
2 W
3 G
4 G
5 G
6 G
7 WORK ½
8 W
9 G
10 G
11 G
12 G
13 WORK 4½
14 W
15 G
16 G
17 W
18 W
19 W
20 J
21 G
22 G
23 G
24 W
25 G
26 G
27 G
28 WORK ½
29 W
30 G

Aug 7th	Del Mar	Maiden	8f	5th	$675
Aug 21st	Del Mar	Maiden	8f	4th	$2,100
Sep 30th	Belmont Pk	Maiden	8f	6th	$0

Two-year-old Fillies
ANXIOUS FRIEND
Mr Prospector - Leave Me Alone
2 starts 0 wins 0 0 $0
No starts prior to June.
June
1 W
2 W
3 J
4 J
5 G
6 W
7 WORK ⅜
8 W
9 J
10 G
11 J
12 W
13 J
14 WORK ⅜
15 W
16 J
17 G
18 W
19 G
20 J
21 W
22 WORK ⅜
23 W
24 J
25 G
26 W
27 G
28 G
29 WORK ½ G ?
30 W

| Jul 30th | Del Mar | Maiden | 9th |
| Aug 7th | Del Mar | Maiden | 11th |

BEAUTIFUL GOLD
Mr Prospector - Before Dawn
2 starts 0 wins 0 1 $3,900

No starts prior to June.

June
1 J
2 G
3 W
4 WORK ⅜ G 3 or 5
5 W
6 J
7 G
8 G
9 WORK ¼ G 3 or 5
10 W
11 G
12 W
13 WORK ½ 14 W
15 G
16 G
17 G
18 W
19 G
20 WORK 4½
21 W
22 J
23 G
24 G
25 G
26 W
27 WORK ⅝
28 W
29 J
30 WORK ¼ G 3 or 5

Date	Track	Race	Dist	Fin	$
Jul 3rd	Hollywood	Maiden	6f	3rd	$3,900
Jul 9th	Hollywood	Stakes	6f	7th	$0

BEEBRUSH
Storm Bird - Queen's Bid
3 starts 1 win 1 0 $19,500

No starts prior to June.

June
1 I
2 G
3 WORK ⅜
4 W
5 G
6 J
7 G
8 W
9 G
10 G
11 J
12 WORK ⅜
13 W
14 J
15 G
16 W
17 G
18 G
19 G
20 WORK ⅜
21 W
22 J
23 G
24 G
25 G
26 W
27 WORK ½
28 W
29 J
30 G

Date	Track	Race	Dist	Fin	$
Aug 14th	Del Mar	Maiden	6f	2nd	$5,200
Aug 28th	Del Mar	Maiden	6f	won	$14,300
Sep 12th	Del Mar	Stake	6f	6th	$0

D. WAYNE LUKAS

FORLIWAN
*Forli - Lisawan

2 starts 0 wins 0 0 $0

No starts prior to June.

June

1 I

2 W

3 WORK ⅜

4 W

5 G

6 G

7 J

8 WORK ¼ G ?

9 W

10 G

11 W

12 G

13 WORK ⅜

14 W

15 J

16 W

17 W

18 W

19 J

20 J

21 G

22 G

23 W

24 J

25 G

26 G

27 W

28 WORK ½

29 W

30 J

Aug 8th	Del Mar	Maiden	8f	9th	$0
Aug 22nd	Del Mar	Maiden	8f	6th	$0

LEA LUCINDA
Secreto - Linda Lea

6 starts 3 wins 1 2 $351,000

No starts prior to June.

June

1 G

2 G

3 W

4 WORK ¼ G ?

5 W

6 J

7 G

8 WORK ½

9 W

10 BREEZE G

11 W

12 J

13 G

14 WORK ⅝

15 W

16 G

17 G

18 J

19 W

20 G

21 J

22 RACE   Hollywood   Maiden   5f   Won $14,300

23 W

24 W

25 W

26 J

27 G

28 G

29 W

30 WORK ⅝

Jul 9th	Hollywood	Stakes	6f	2nd	$21,750
Aug 6th	Monmouth	Stakes	6f	3rd	$20,812
Aug 22nd	Del Mar	Stakes	7f	3rd	$11,250
Sep 9th	Del Mar	Stakes	8f	Won	$193,850
Sep 24th	Canterbury	Stakes	8f	Won	$90,000

This filly really covered some miles, from California to New York, back to California and then up to Minnesota.

LUCY BLACK
Alydar - Black Eyed Lucy
2 starts 0 wins 0 0 $0
No starts prior to June.
June
1 J
2 J
3 W
4 WORK ¼ G 3 or 5

5 W
6 G
7 J
8 W
9 G
10 G
11 WORK ½
12 W
13 J
14 G
15 J
16 W
17 G
18 J
19 WORK ½ G 3 or 5
20 W
21 J
22 J
23 W
24 G
25 J
26 G
27 J
28 W
29 J
30 W

| Aug 8th | Del Mar | Maiden | 8f | 10th | $0 |
| Aug 22nd | Del Mar | Maiden | 8f | 7th | $0 |

ROYAL DANJULIA
Believe It - Royal Tease
3 starts 0 wins 0 0 $0
No starts prior to June.
June
1 W
2 G
3 W
4 WORK ⅜
5 W
6 G
7 G
8 J
9 WORK ¼ G ?
10 W
11 G
12 G
13 WORK ½
14 W
15 G
16 G
17 W
18 G
19 J
20 WORK ½
21 W
22 J
23 G
24 G
25 W
26 G
27 WORK ⅝
28 W
29 J
30 G

Jul 25th	Hollywood	Maiden	6f	7th	$0
Aug 10th	Del Mar	Mdn Cl	6f	9th	$0
Aug 25th	Del Mar	Mdn Cl	6f	6th	$0

SUPER BABA
Raja Baba - Super Zone

2 starts 0 wins 0 0 $1,950

No starts prior to June.

June
1 G
2 J
3 WORK ½
4 W
5 G
6 G
7 G
8 WORK ¼ G ?
9 W
10 G
11 G
12 W
13 WORK ⅝
14 W
15 G
16 G
17 G
18 WORK ⅜ G ?
19 W
20 G
21 J
22 RACE   Hollywood   Maiden   5f   4th $1,950
23 W
24 W
25 W
26 J
27 G
28 G
29 G
30 WORK ⅝

Jul 9th	Hollywood	Stakes	6f	11th	$0

WONDER'S DELIGHT
Icecapade - Ambry

6 starts 3 wins 0 0 $170,847

No starts prior to June.

1 W
2 J
3 G
4 WORK ½
5 W
6 G
7 G
8 WORK ¼ G
9 W
10 G
11 WORK ½
12 W
13 J
14 G
15 G
16 W
17 G
18 WORK ⅜ G ?
19 W
20 G
21 G
22 W
23 G
24 G
25 WORK ½
26 W
27 J
28 G
29 G
30 WORK ¼ G ?

Jul 3rd	Hollywood	Maiden	6f	7th	$0
Jul 10th	Hollywood	Maiden	6f	Won	$14,300
Jul 23rd	Hollywood	Stakes	6f	4th	$7,500
Aug 3rd	Saratoga	Stakes	6f	Won	$67,680
Aug 29th	Saratoga	Stakes	6f	4th	$14,112
Sep 17t	Turfway Pk	Stakes	6f	Won	$67,000

Three-year-old Colts

COUGARIZED
Cougar II - Jolie Jolie
9 starts 1 win 1 2 $89,333

Date	Track	Type	Dist	Fin	Purse
Jan 2nd	Hialeah	Stakes	9f	5th	$7,500
Feb 12th	Aquaduct	Stakes	8f	3rd	$9,918
Mar 5th	Aquaduct	Stakes	9f	2nd	$25,784
Apr 2nd	Gulf Stream	Stakes	8f	4th	$6,000
Apr 28th	Keeneland	Stakes	9f	4th	$14,681
May 7t	Churchill D	Stakes	8f	3rd	$5,650

June

Date	Track	Type	Dist	Fin	Purse
11th Jun	Belmont Pk	Allow.	8f	Won	$19,800
18 -					
19 G					
20 J					
21 G					
22 W					
23 WORK ½					
24 W					
25 J					
26 G					
27 G					
28 G					
29 W					
30 W					
Jul 3rd	Hollywood	Stakes	9f		$0
failed to finish					
Aug 11th	Del Mar	Allowance	8f	9th	$0

RAP TALK
His Majesty - Save a Minute
5 starts 0 wins 1 1 $1,291

No 1988 starts before June

June

1 G
2 WORK ⅜
3 W
4 G
5 G
6 G
7 G
8 WORK ½
9 W
10 G
11 G
12 W
13 G
14 W
15 WORK ⅝
16 W
17 G
18 G
19 J
20 W
21 G
22 WORK ⅝
23 W
24 J
25 G
26 G
27 W
28 G
29 WORK ⅝
30 W

Date	Track	Type	Dist	Fin	Purse
Jul 6th	Hollywood	$16,000 Clmg	6f	5th	$375
Jul 21st	Hollywood	$25,000 Clmg	8f	7th	$0
Aug 27th	Atlant Cit	$10,000 Mdn Clmg	6f	8th	$0
Sep 3rd	Atlant City	$9,000 Mdn Clmg	8f	2nd	$580
Oct 1st	Atlant Cit	$10,000 Mdn Clmg	8f	3rd	$336

D. WAYNE LUKAS

SLEWBOP
Seattle Slew - Full Card
15 starts 2 wins 2 1 $104,675

Date	Track	Type	Dist	Fin	Purse
Jan 2nd	Santa Anita	Maiden	6f	8th	$0
Jan 24th	Santa Anita	Maiden	8f	10th	$0
Feb 7th	Santa Anita	Maiden	8f	Won	$14,850
Mar 6th	Santa Anita	Allow.	8f	6th	$0
Mar 19th	Santa Anita	Allow.	9f	2nd	$7,200
Apr 8th	Santa Anita	Allow.	8f	Won	$19,800
Apr 23rd	Golden Gate	Stakes	9f	2nd	$50,000
May 30th	Hollywood	Allow.	8f	4th	$3,000
June					
1 W					
2 J					
3 G					
4 G					
5 WORK ⅝					
6 W					
7 G					
8 G					
9 G					
10 J					
11 RACE	Hollywood	Handicap	8f	6th	$0
12 W					
13 W					
14 W					
15 G					
16 G					
17 G					
18 J					
19 WORK 4½					
20 W					
21 G					
22 G					
23 G					
24 J					
25 W					
26 G					
27 G					
28 WORK ⅜ ?					
29 W					
30 RACE	Hollywood	Allow.	8f	3rd	$6,000
Jul 14th	Hollywood	Allow.	8f	11th	$0
Aug 7th	Del Mar	Allow.	8f	4th	$2,475
Aug 19th	Del Mar	Allow.	6f	7th	$0
Aug 26th	Bay Meadws	Allow.	8f	5th	$450
Sep 5th	Del Mar	Allow.	8f	5th	$900

SUCCESS EXPRESS
Hold Your Peace - Au Printemps
9 starts 0 wins 1 3 $98,152

Date	Track	Type	Dist	Fin	Purse
Jan 27th	Santa Anita	Stakes	7f	3rd	$11,250
Feb 27th	Santa Anita	Stakes	8f	3rd	$18,750
Mar 26th	Aquaduct	Stakes	7f	2nd	$36,102
Apr 9th	Aquaduct	Stakes	8f	4th	$18,150
Apr 27th	Hollywood	Stakes	7f	4th	$5,625
June					
1 W					
2 G					
3 J					
4 J					
5 G					
6 W					
7 WORK ⅝					
8 W					
9 J					
10 G					
11 G					
12 W					
13 G					
14 G					
15 J					
16 WORK ⅝					
17 W					
18 J					
19 G					
20 J					
21 W					
22 G					
23 J					
24 G					
25 J					
26 RACE	Hollywood	Handicap	6f	5th	$1,375
27 W					
28 W					
29 W					
30 J					
Jul 10th	Hollywood	Allow.	6f	3rd	$6,900
Jul 27th	Del Mar	Stakes	8f	8th	$0
Aug 21st	Del Mar	Allow.	6f	7th	$0

WHITE MISCHIEF
Roberto - Arachne
12 starts 1 win 1 1 $51,031

Feb 11th	Santa Anita	Allow.	8f	8th	$0
Mar 16th	Santa Anita	Allow.	8f	6th	$0
Apr 6th	Santa Anita	Stakes	6f	5th	$1,406
May 7th	Hollywood	Stakes	8f	4th	$5,625
May 20th	Hollywood	Allow.	8f	2nd	$8,000
May 29th	Hollywood	Stakes	8f	8th	$0

June
1 W
2 W
3 W
4 W
5 J
6 G
7 G
8 J
9 WORK ½
10 W
11 G
12 G
13 W
14 G
15 J
16 G
17 WORK ¾ G 3 or 5

18 W
19 J
20 G
21 G
22 W
23 G
24 J

25 RACE	Hollywood	Allow.	8f	3rd	$6,000

26 W
27 W
28 W
29 J
30 G

Jul 13th	Hollywood	Handicap	9f	Won	$27,500
Jul 24th	Hollywood	Stakes	10f	9th	$0
Aug 7th	Del Mar	Stakes	8f	5th	$2,500
Aug 21st	Del Mar	Stakes	9f	7th	$0
Sep 8th	Del Mar	Allow.	8f	6th	$0

Three-year-old Fillies

BEAT THE HEAT
Talc - Ganadora
8 starts 1 win 0 0 $12,375

May 6th	Hollywood	$32,000 MdnCl	6f	5th	$375

June
1 W
2 G
3 G
4 G
5 G
6 WORK ⅝
7 W
8 G
9 G
10 G
11 W
12 W
13 W
14 J
15 J

16 RACE	Hollywood	$32,000 MdnCl	6f	5th	$375

17 W
18 W
19 W
20 G
21 G
22 W
23 G
24 G
25 W
26 J
27 G
28 W
29 WORK ⅝
30 W

Jul 7th	Hollywood	$32,000 MdnCl	6f	Won	$8,250
Jul 22nd	Hollywood	$20,000 Clmg	6f	4th	$1,275
Aug 8th	Del Mar	$16,000 Clmg	6f	4th	$975
Aug 17th	Del Mar	$16,000 Clmg	6f	4th	$1,125
Aug 31st	Del Mar	$16,000 Clmg	6f	7th	$0
Sep 8th	Del Mar	$16,000 Clmg	6f	6th	$0

BLUE JEAN BABY
Mr Prospector - Jones Time Mac
3 starts 2 wins 0 0 $62,350

Apr 9th	Santa Anita	Stakes	6f		Won	$34,350
Apr 30th	Hollywood	Stakes	7f	6th		$0

June
1 J
2 WORK ⅝
3 W
4 J
5 G
6 J
7 G
8 W
9 G
10 J
11 WORK 5½
12 W
13 J
14 G
15 W
16 G
17 G
18 G
19 J
20 WORK 5½
21 W
22 G
23 G
24 G
25 W
26 G
27 J
28 WORK 5½ ?
29 W
30 G

7th Jul	Hollywood	Allow.	7f		Won	$28,600

CUSHION CUT
Raise a Man - Julie Prince
11 starts 1 win 0 2 $37,475

Jan 6th	Santa Anita	Stakes	6f	3rd	$11,250
Feb 3rd	Santa Anita	Stakes	7f	7th	$0
Feb 8th	Santa Anita	Allow.	6f	3rd	$5,250
Mar 23rd	Santa Anita	Stakes	6f	6th	$0
Apr 30th	Hollywood	Stakes	7f	9th	$0

June
1 WORK ⅝ ? ?
2 W
3 G
4 G
5 G
6 W
7 J

8 RACE	Hollywood	Allow.	8f	9th	$0

9 W
10 W
11 W
12 W
13 G
14 G
15 W
16 G
17 G
18 J

19 RACE	Hollywood	Allow.	8f	6th	$0

20 W
21 W
22 W
23 G
24 G
25 W
26 G
27 G
28 WORK 5½ 29 W
30 G

Jul 16th	Hollywood	Allow.	8f	4th	$3,000
Aug 1st	Del Mar	Allow.	8f	7th	$0
Aug 6th	Del Mar	Allow.	6f	Won	$17,050
Aug 22nd	Del Mar	Allow.	7f	5th	$925

DREAM TEAM
Cox's Ridge - Likely Double
1 start 0 wins 0 0 $0

No 1988 starts before June

June
1 G
2 W
3 W
4 WORK ¼
5 W
6 G
7 G
8 J
9 G
10 W
11 G
12 WORK ⅜
13 W
14 G
15 G
16 W
17 G
18 J
19 WORK ½
20 W
21 J
22 G
23 J
24 W
25 G
26 G
27 WORK 4½
28 W
29 G
30 G

| Jul 25th | Hollywood | Allow. | 6f | 6th | $0 |

GOLD SEAL
Mr Prospector - 'N Everything
13 starts 2 wins 1 1 $54,794

Jan 23rd	Santa Anita	Maiden	6f	4th	$1,875
Feb 6th	Santa Anita	Maiden	6f	Won	$13,750
Mar 5th	Santa Anita	Allow.	6f	Won	$17,600
Mar 23rd	Santa Anita	Stakes	6f	4th	$4,219
Apr 1st	Santa Anita	Allow.	8f	8th	$0
Apr 30th	Hollywood	Allow.	7f	5th	$1,875

June
1 J
2 RACE   Hollywood   Allow.   6f   9th $0
3 W
4 W
5 W
6 J
7 G
8 G
9 J
10 RACE   Hollywood   Allow.   6f   2nd $7,200
11 W
12 W
13 W
14 J
15 G
16 G
17 W
18 G
19 G
20 WORK ⅝
21 W
22 J
23 G
24 G
25 J
26 RACE   Hollywood   Allow.   6f   6th $0
27 W
28 W
29 W
30 G

Jul 10th	Hollywood	Allow.	6f	7th	$0
Jul 27th	Del Mar	Allow.	8f	4th	$2,475
Aug 18th	Del Mar	Allow.	6f	3rd	$4,950
Sep 4th	Del Mar	Allow.	6f	5th	$850

D. WAYNE LUKAS

GREY HENNA
Grey Dawn II - Henna
10 starts 1 win 3 0 $33,525

Feb 14th	Santa Anita	Maiden	8f	-	$0
Failed to finish					
Mar 12th	Santa Anita	Maiden	8f	2nd	$5,400
Apr 9th	Santa Anita	Maiden	8f	6th	$0
Apr 29th	Hollywood	Maiden	8f	2nd	$5,600

June
1 W
2 J
3 J
4 J
5 G
6 G
7 G
8 G
9 WORK ⅜
10 W
11 J
12 G
13 G
14 G
15 WORK ½
16 W
17 G
18 G
19 W
20 G
21 J
22 W
23 WORK ½
24 W
25 G
26 G
27 G
28 W
29 WORK ½
30 W

Jul 2nd	Hollywood	Maiden	6f	7th	$0
Jul 10th	Hollywood	Maiden	6f	2nd	$5,200
Jul 23rd	Hollywood	Maiden	6f	6th	$0
Aug 4th	Del Mar	Maiden	8f	Won	$14,850
Aug 14th	Del Mar	Allow.	38f	6th	$0
Sep 2nd	Del Mar	Allow.	8f	4th	$2,475

HOORAY FOR LOVE
Believe It - Dancing Damsel
5 starts 1 win 1 1 $24,625
No 1988 starts prior to June

June
1 G
2 WORK ¼
3 W
4 G
5 G
6 G
7 G
8 WORK ⅜
9 W
10 G
11 G
12 W
13 G
14 WORK ½
15 W
16 G
17 J
18 W
19 G
20 G
21 WORK ½
22 W
23 G
24 G
25 J
26 W
27 G
28 WORK ½
29 W
30 G

Jul 10th	Hollywood	Maiden	6f	3rd	$3,900
Jul 24th	Hollywood	Maiden	6f	Won	$14,300
Aug 8th	Del Mar	Allow.	6f	2nd	$5,600
Aug 22nd	Del Mar	Allow.	6f	6th	$0
Sep 2nd	Del Mar	Allow.	8f	5th	$825

HUG A LOT
Raise a Cup - Hugable
6 starts 0 wins 2 4 $16,450

Jan 7th	Sant Anita	$40,000 MdnCl	8f	3rd	$2,700
Feb 4th	Santa Anita	$32,000 MdnCl	8f	3rd	$2,550
Feb 25th	Santa Anita	$32,000 MdnCl	7f	2nd	$3,200
Mar 31st	Sant Anita	$32,000 MdnCl	6f	3rd	$2,550
Apr 27th	Hollywood	$35,000 MdnCl	6f	2nd	$3,200
May 13th	Hollywood	$32,000 MdnCl	6f	3rd	$2,250

June
1 W
2 G
3 WORK ⅝
4 W
5 J
6 J
7 W
8 G
9 J
10 G
11 WORK ⅝
12 W
13 J
14 G
15 W
16 J
17 G
18 W
19 J
20 WORK ½
21 W
22 -

IMAGINATIVE
Exclusive Era - Cancaniere
6 starts 3 wins 1 0 $67,725

Jan 17th	Santa Anita	Maiden	6f	4th	$1,875
Jan 31st	Santa Anita	Maiden	8f	Won	$14,850
Feb 20th	Santa Anita	Stakes	8f	4th	$7,500
Apr 14th	Santa Anita	Allow.	8f	2nd	$7,200

June
1 J
2 W
3 G
4 W
5 W
6 W
7 J
8 G
9 G
10 G
11 G
12 W
13 WORK ⅜
14 W
15 J
16 G
17 G
18 W
19 G
20 WORK ½
21 W
22 J
23 G
24 G
25 W
26 G
27 G
28 WORK ½ ?
29 W
30 G

Jul 9th	Hollywood	Allow.	6f	Won	$18,150
Jul 27th	Del Mar	Allow.	8f	Won	$18,150

D. WAYNE LUKAS

JAZZ SESSION
Secretariat - Juke Joint
8 starts 0 wins 0 0 $2,100

Mar 27th	Santa Anita	Maiden	6f	12th	$0	
Apr 23rd	Santa Anita	Maiden	6f	9th	$0	
May 21st	Hollywood	Maiden	6f	8th	$0	

June
1 G
2 G
3 W
4 WORK ⅝
5 W
6 J
7 G
8 G
9 W
10 G
11 G
12 WORK ⅝
13 W
14 G
15 G
16 W
17 G
18 J
19 RACE Hollywood Maiden 7f 11th $0
20 W
21 W
22 W
23 G
24 J
25 RACE Hollywood Maiden 8f 7th $0
26 W
27 W
28 W
29 G
30 G

Jul 23rd	Hollywood	Maiden	8f	4th	$2,100	
Aug 4th	Del Mar	Maiden	8f	9th	$0	
Sep 5th	Bay Meadows	Maiden	8f		$0	

failed to finish

LETS FALL IN LOVE
Northern Baby - Humming (GB)
8 starts 0 wins 0 1 $12,525

Feb 14th	Santa Anita	Allow.	6f	5th	$800	
Mar 3rd	Santa Anita	Allow.	8f	5th	$850	
Apr 1st	Santa Anita	Allow.	8f	4th	$3,150	

June
1 WORK ⅜
2 W
3 J
4 G
5 J
6 W
7 G
8 WORK ⅜
9 W
10 J
11 G
12 W
13 G
14 J
15 W
16 WORK ½
17 W
18 J
19 G
20 J
21 W
22 G
23 J
24 G
25 J
26 RACE Hollywood Allow. 6f 4th $2,475
27 W
28 W
29 W
30 J

Jul 14th	Hollywood	Allow.	9f	3rd	$5,250	
Jul 28th	Del Mar	Allow.	8f	9th	$0	
Aug 7th	Del Mar	Allow.	8f	7th	$0	
Aug 25th	Del Mar	Allow.	8f	7th	$0	

O'DAWN
Alydar - Before Dawn

5 starts 0 wins 1 1 $14,650

Mar 20th	Santa Anita	Allow.	6f	7th	$0
Apr 14th	Santa Anita	Allow.	8f	6th	$0
Apr 28th	Hollywood	Allow.	6f	4th	$2,400
May 13th	Hollywood	Allow.	8f	2nd	$7,000

June
1 W
2 G
3 G
4 G
5 G
6 WORK ⅝
7 W
8 G
9 G G?
10 G
11 G
12 W
13 WORK ⅝
14 W
15 J
16 G
17 RACE Hollywood Allow. 9f 3rd $5,5250
18 W
19 W
20 W
21 W
22 W
23 J
24 W
25 W
26 W
27 W
28 W
29 -
30 -

OVER ALL
Mr Prospector - Full Tigress

2 starts 0 wins 0 0 $5,328

May 8th	Aquaduct	Stakes	7f	4th	$5,328
May 21st	Belmont	Stakes	8f	6th	$0

June

Brought to Hollywood Pk from Belmont.
19 WORK ⅝
20 W
21 J
22 G
23 G
24 G
25 J
26 J
27 J
28 W
29 W
30 W

ROYAL WEEKEND
Secretariat - A Status Symbol
6 starts 1 win 1 0 $26,125

Date	Track	Type	Dist	Fin	$
May 14th	Hollywood	Allow.	6f	6th	$0
June					
1 G					
2 G					
3 J					
4 RACE	Hollywood	Allow.	6f	6th	$0
5 W					
6 W					
7 W					
8 W					
9 W					
10 W					
11 W					
12 J					
13 W					
14 J					
15 J					
16 G					
17 G					
18 J					
19 W					
20 W					
21 W					
22 J					
23 G					
24 J					
25 W					
26 J					
27 G					
28 G					
29 J					
30 W					
Jul 20th	Hollywood	Allow.	8f	4th	$2,625
Jul 31st	Del Mar	Allow,	8f	Won	$16,500
Aug 13th	Del Mar	Allow.	8f	2nd	$7,000
Sep 8th	Del Mar	Stake.	8f	7th	$0

SMARTERTHANILOOK
Smarten - Sarah Percy
6 starts 0 wins 2 0 $5,680

Date	Track	Type	Dist	Fin	$
Jan 21st	Santa Anita	$50,000 MdnClmg	6f	9th	$0
Feb 10th	Santa Anita	$50,000	6f	10th	$0
June					
1 J					
2 J					
3 G					
4 G					
5 G					
6 WORK ⅜					
7 W					
8 J					
9 G					
10 G					
11 G					
12 WORK ½					
13 W					
14 G					
15 G					
16 G					
17 W					
18 WORK ⅝					
19 W					
20 G					
21 G					
22 W					
23 G					
24 G					
25 G					
26 WORK ⅝					
27 W					
28 G					
29 J					
30 G					
Jul 15th	Hollywood	$25,000 clmng	6f	2nd	$3,800
Jul 29th	Los Alamitos	Maiden	6f	5th	$1,100
Aug 20th	Atlantic Cty	Mdn All	6f	2nd	$600
Sep 11th	Atlantic City		?f	4th	$180

TAP YOUR TOES
State Dinner- Lesley's a Dance
5 starts 0 wins 0 0 $7,500

Date	Track	Type	Dist	Pos	Prize
Jan 6th	Santa Anita	Stakes	6f	5th	$1,875
Feb 3rd	Santa Anita	Stakes	7f	4th	$5,625
Mar 2nd	Santa Anita	Stakes	8f	7th	$0

June
1 W
2 G
3 G
4 J
5 G
6 WORK ⅝
7 W
8 J
9 G
10 G
11 J
12 W
13 WORK ⅝
14 W
15 G
16 G
17 G
18 W
19 G
20 WORK 5½
21 W
22 J
23 G
24 J

25 RACE	Hollywood	Stakes	8f	8th	$0
26 W					
27 W					
28 W					
29 J					
30 J					
Aug 21st	Del Mar	Allow.	8f	10th	$0

WINNING COLORS
Caro (Ire) - All Rainbows
8 starts 4 wins 2 1 $1,109,546

Not on the chart but included to show Wayne's successful race path to the Kentucky Derby of 1988. He told Bill Nack from Sports Illustrated that he knew he had something special when she won her only two races as a 2yo. He wanted to bring her along slowly and kept what was probably the best 2yo filly in the country in her barn when all the big 2yo races were being run. That meant passing up the Breeders' Cup 2yo fillies race. At the time Wayne probably felt he could win that race

WINNING COLORS continued
anyway: he started 5 fillies in the Juvenile Fillies race of 1987. The best any of them could do however was 3rd. Wayne was described as shocked and disappointed. He probably went back and looked at Winning Colors in her stall and wondered if he'd blundered. Early in 1988 Gene Klein listed a heap of Lukas/ Klein Derby contenders but Winning Colors was not mentioned.

Her Santa Anita Derby preparation consisted of three races against fillies. In the second race she lost by a neck. "We got a little over- confident. We hadn't put any real good work into her." He changed that and in the third race she came out and beat the fillies by eight lengths in the Santa Anita Oaks.

Date	Track	Type	Dist	Pos	Prize
Jan 20th	Santa Anita	Stakes	8f	Won	$47,100
Feb 20th	Santa Anita	Stakes	8f	2nd	$26,750
Mar 13th	Santa Anita	Stakes	8f	Won	$89,900

In the Santa Anita Derby she beat the colts by 7 ½ lengths.

Apr 9th	Santa Anita	Stakes	9f	Won	$275,000

Between this race and the Derby, Winning Colors worked three times: 6f in 1:13 3/5, 5f in 1:01 4/5 and 4f in 49 sec.

May 7th	Churchill D	Stakes	10f	Won	$611,200

Wayne had won the Kentucky Derby. After the Derby he told Bill Nack of *Sports Illustrated*, "It was difficult. It takes a lot of mental discipline to wait on one like this, but I feel good about it now." Wayne told *The Blood-Horse*: "She certainly did not come into the Derby dead tight fit. One thing we did for a lot of years was win all the prep races and then we'd stub our toe here. This year we won the right ones, but we left her a lot of time to get ready for the Derby. There is a fine line between physical fitness and staleness and I was given the choice of having her over the edge or a little bit short. I wanted her fresh so I took the latter position with her. We like to leave our horses with a little bit of spring in their step. **It seems to me I've won more good races when I thought I ran a horse short than I ever did when I ran one dead fit.**"

She then went into the Preakness.

May 21st	Pimlico	Stakes	9½f	3rd	$35,000

Followed by her poor run in the Belmont Stakes.

Jun 11th	Belmont	Stakes	12f	6th	$0

Sent for some restful rebuilding.

Sep 10th	Belmont	Stakes	8f	2nd	$24,496

May have raced between Sep 10th and Nov 5th. On Nov 5th in the Breeders' Cup Distaff, she led all the way against unbeaten Personal Ensign. Personal Ensign got up in the last strides of the race to win, in what was later voted The Race of the Year.

Four-year-old Colts

SEAL THE DEAL
Northjet (Ire) - Hanina (GB)

2 starts 0 wins 0 0 $0

No 1988 starts prior to June.

June
1 G
2 G
3 W
4 G
5 WORK ⅜
6 W
7 G
8 G
9 G
10 G
11 G
12 WORK ⅜
13 W
14 G
15 G
16 W
17 G
18 G
19 WORK ½
20 W
21 G
22 G
23 W
24 G
25 G
26 W
27 WORK ½
28 W
29 G
30 G

| Jul 22nd | Hollywood | $32,000 MdnCl | 8f | 9th | $0 |
| Aug 1st | Del Mar | $32,000 MdnCl | 8f | | $0 |

failed to finish

GULCH - Changing a Horse's Distance
Mr Prospector - Jameela

9 starts 4 wins 3 2 $861,736

Peter Brant switched top sprinter Gulch to Wayne's stable. Wayne told Brant it would be hard to stretch the horse but easy to shorten him up. Ironically the Bloodstock Research Information Services figures show his win rate to be 20% going from sprint to route, but 18% going from route to sprint. The horse was given longer stronger gallops. After a win at 6½ furlongs in a Grade 3 race, he went to a Grade 1 race over 1⅛ mile in which he ran 3rd.

| Mar 18th | Santa Anita | Allow. | 6f | Won | $30,250 |
| Mar 30th | Santa Anita | Gr3 | 6½f | Won | $44,050 |

That was the Potrero Grange Handicap

| Apr 16th | Oaklawn Pk | Gr1 | 9f | 3rd | $50,000 |

Oaklawn Handicap

| May 7th | Aquaduct | Gr 2 | 7f | Won | $174,300 |

Carter Handicap

| May 30th | Belmont Pk | Gr 1 | 8f | Won | $351,600 |

Metropolitan H'cap

June
8 IN
9 G
10 WORK 3½
11 J

| 12 RACE | Hollywood | Gr 1 | 9f | 2nd | $60,000 |

Californian Stakes

13 W
14 W
15 W
16 G
17 G
18 G
19 W
20 G
21 WORK 5½
22 W
23 G
24 G
25 G
26 W
27 G
28 G
29 To New York
30 -

| Jul 16th | Belmont | Gr 2 | 7f | 2nd | $37,026 |

Tom Fool Stakes

| Aug 6th | Saratoga | Gr 1 | 9f | 2nd | $59,510 |

Whitney Handicap

GULCH continued

Aug 27th   Monmouth   Gr 1   9f   3rd $55,000
Philip H Iselin Handicap

After wins at 7f and 8f and then placings at 1⅛ miles in Grade events it was time to consider that he really was a sprinter and bring him back in distance for the Breeders' Cup Sprint. This race was due on November 5th of 1988. To sharpen Gulch, Wayne gave him no races in September and opened the new campaign with a 2nd placing in the 7f Grade 1 Vosburgh Stakes. The horse was still a bit dull and dropped off the pace too much. But Wayne had the horse spot on for the big one and Gulch cleaned up the 6f Breeders' Cup Sprint on November 5th. The horse retired to stud with winnings of over $3m.

Five-year-old Colts

ART FRANCAIS
Lyphard's Wish(Fr) - Abala(Fr)
4 starts 1 win 1 $51,400

Mar 20th	Santa Anita	Allow.	8f	1st	$26,400
Apr 29th	Hollywood	Allow.	8f	3rd	$7,500
May 13th	Hollywood	Allow.	8f	3rd	$7,500
June					
1 W					
2 J					
3 RACE	Hollywood	Allowance	8f	2nd	$10,000
4 W					
5 W					
6 W					
7 G					
8 G					
9 W					
10 W					
11 W					
12 W					
13 W					
14 T					
15 -					

LOVE BABA
Raja Baba - Lov Tov
4 starts 0 wins 0 0 $104

No 1988 starts prior to June.

June
1 G
2 G
3 WORK ⅜
4 W
5 G
6 G
7 G
8 G
9 WORK ⅜
10 W
11 G
12 G
13 G
14 G
15 W
16 WORK ½
17 W
18 G
19 G
20 G
21 J
22 W
23 WORK ½
24 W
25 G
26 G
27 G
28 J
29 W
30 WORK 4½

Sep 4th	Atlant City	$12,500 MdnCl	6th		$0
Sep 13th	Atlant City	$8,000 MdnCl	6f	6th	$0
Sep 17th	Atlant City	$4,000 MdnCl	6f	5th	$52
Oct 1st	Atlant City	$3,600 MdnCl	6f	5th	$52

STEINLEN (GB)
Habitat - Southern Seas
10 starts 5 wins 3 1 $463,270

Jan 21st	Santa Anita	Allow.	9f	3rd	$8,250
Mar 12th	Santa Anita	Allow.	8f	7th	$0
Mar 26th	Santa Anita	Allow.	8f	Won	$29,700
Apr 10th	Santa Anita	Stakes	8f	Won	$88,760
May 1st	Hollywood	Stakes	8f	Won	$80,200
May 15th	Hollywood	Stakes	9f	2nd	$30,000

June
1 W
2 G
3 G
4 J
5 WORK ⅝
6 W
7 G
8 J
9 G
10 G
11 W
12 G
13 WORK ¾
14 W
15 J
16 G
17 J
18 G

19 RACE	Hollywood	Stakes	8f	Won	$66,200

20 W
21 W
22 W
23 J
24 G
25 J
26 G
27 G
28 WORK ⅝
29 W
30 G

Jul 4th	Hollywood	Stakes	9f	2nd	$40,000
Aug 14th	Saratoga	Stakes	9f	2nd	$26,620
Aug 27th	Saratoga	Stakes	8f	Won	$93,540

Five-year-old Colt

SYNASTRY
Seattle Slew - Municipal Bond
10 starts 2 wins 1 0 $77,295

Mar 18th	Aquaduct	Allow.	6f	4th	$2,295
Apr 9th	Aquaduct	Hcap	6f	7th	$0
Apr 27th	Aquaduct	Hcap	8f	7th	$0

June
1 W
2 J
3 W
4 J
5 G
6 WORK ½
7 W
8 J
9 G
10 G
11 G
12 W
13 WORK ⅝
14 W
15 J
16 RACE Hollywood Allow 8f 6th $0
17 W
18 W
19 W
20 J
21 G
22 W
23 G
24 G
25 G
26 W
27 WORK ⅝
28 W
29 J
30 G

Jul 4th	Hollywood	Allow.	6f	4th	$3,900
Jul 30th	Del Mar	Stakes	7f	2nd	$12,000
Aug 8th	Del Mar	Allow.	6f	Won	$23,100
Aug 14th	Del Mar	Stakes	8f	4th	$7,500
Aug 24th	Del Mar	Stakes	6f	5th	$1,875
Sep 2nd	Del Mar	Allow.	6f	Won	$26,400

Six-year-old Colts

HUDDLE UP
Sir Ivor - Huggle Duggle
5 starts 1 win 1 1 $19,650
No 1988 starts prior to June.

June
1 G
2 W
3 G
4 G
5 WORK ⅝
6 W
7 J
8 G
9 G
10 G
11 W
12 WORK ½
13 W
14 G
15 W
16 G
17 G
18 G
19 WORK 4½
20 W
21 J
22 G
23 J
24 G
25 W
26 G
27 WORK ⅝
28 W
29 J
30 G

Jul 2nd	Hollywood	$50,000 Clmg	6f	6th	$0
Jul 23rd	Hollywood	$32,000 Clmg	6f	3rd	$3,750
Aug 3rd	Del Mar	$32,000 Clmg	6f	2nd	$4,400
Aug 10th	Del Mar	$25,000 Clmg	6f	Won	$11,000
Sep 3rd	Del Mar	$25,000 Clmg	7f	h	$500

RED ATTACK
Alydar - Miss Betty
13 starts 0 wins 2 6 $100,285

Jan 3rd	Santa Anita	Allow.	8f	3rd	$9,000
Jan 16th	Santa Anita	Allow.	8f	5th	$1,375
Feb 10th	OP	Allow.	8f	3rd	$3,000
Feb 27th	OP	Stakes	8f	3rd	$5,805
Mar 12th	OP	Stakes	8f	3rd	$7,280
Mar 26th	OP	Stakes	8f	2nd	$26,750
Apr 16th	OP	Stakes	9f	6th	$0
May 22nd	Hollywood	Stakes	8f	4th	$15,000
June					
1 J					
2 RACE	Hollywood	Allow.	8f	4th	$4,500
3 W					
4 W					
5 W					
6 J					
7 G					
8 G					
9 W					
10 J					
11 G					
12 WORK ⅝					
13 W					
14 J					
15 J					
16 RACE	Hollywood	Allow.	8f	3rd	$8,250
17 W					
18 W					
19 W					
20 G					
21 G					
22 W					
23 G					
24 J					
25 W					
26 G					
27 G					
28 J					
29 RACE	Hollywood	Allow.	8f	2nd	$11,00
30 W					
Aug 1st	Del Mar	Allow.	8f	3rd	$7,200
Aug 29th	Del Mar	Allow.	8f	5th	$1,125

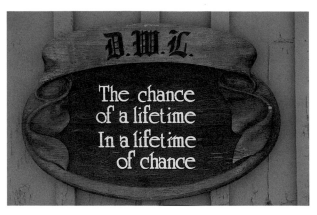

Wooden sign with a line from the popular song about the Kentucky Derby - 'The Run For The Roses'.

8.2 Hard or soft trainer?
Wayne is soft on his horses in their fast works, but hard on them in their gallops (canters). Around the tracks they say he breaks a lot of horses down.

Does Wayne break down too many horses?
To answer this we would need to know the breed average and Wayne's breakdown rates. This is not a simple thing to measure. When a horse breaks down and can hardly walk like Saratoga Six did, it is easy to know in which group that horse belongs. When a horse retires after a big campaign, aged 4 or 5, to a previously announced stud, we can be reasonably sure it was sound.

But the in-betweens come in all shades of gray. Some disappear because they lack ability, some because they are irretrievably damaged, and some are just a bit sore; nothing permanent, but the horse is not good enough to be worth a spell and a return to training. Wayne may have a lot of breakdowns simply because he has a lot of horses. Because he is well-known, they are all brought to public notice. As a proportion of his number of horses, those breakdowns may be less than the two breakdowns among the horses of some less noteworthy smaller trainer. However the track-watcher's consensus is that he DOES break down a lot of horses.

One clue is the 'failed to finish' category in the racing records of the horses in the chart. Of the 46 horses that raced, six were listed as failing to finish their race. These presumed injuries occurred between June 1 and October 1, a period of five months. One of those raced 6 weeks later. I was told that Upstart had broken down. The number of horses is so small that conclusions would be very uncertain.

I asked Greg Ferraro, a highly respected veterinarian who did Wayne's work in Los Angeles:

"One of the accusations that you hear all the time about Wayne is that he breaks heaps of horses down."

"I think if you look at his percentage, he's probably somewhere in the middle."

"So he doesn't break heaps of horses down?"

"Not considering the number of horses he's got. He's got three times as many horses as anybody else, so sure, he's going to break more down. But I don't think his percentage is any worse than anybody else. No worse, certainly. I'd say he's average. Average. At least, in my book."

When Saratoga Six broke down, Hall of Fame trainer Laz Barrera told Lee Eaton not to blame Wayne, that it was the track. Wayne however, declined to use the track as an excuse. He told Lee that he had horses running on many tracks and that horses broke down on all of them. Wayne is a realist. He does not permit himself any delusions, nor it would seem, does he encourage them in his owners.

Does Wayne prepare his horses poorly? There are those who say he cannot train. Does he race them too often or for too long? He has a reputation for getting what he can while he can. Over All and Lost Kitty both ran in 10 races, many of them graded stakes, over six month periods as 2yo's. Does he run them when they have signs such as soreness? He is certainly accused of it.

These things are seen as a damning indictment of Wayne Lukas by some. What could Wayne do about it? He could, first and foremost, select a more solid-legged or less powerful type of horse. But they don't win many races. Wayne's perspective could be viewed this way. YOU are at the yearling sales and there are two horses paraded in front of you. The first goes past with an assessment as follows: Lovely thick legs. Absolutely guaranteed not to break down. Three years training costs, $60,000. Winnings $20,000 in claimers from 101 starts. Stakes races won - nil. Residual stud value - nil. The second parades past with this assessment: Muscular body, fine-boned lightweight legs. Very likely to breakdown after 5 or 10 races. But note: it will possibly win $500,000 including stakes races. Residual stud value - millions.

What is YOUR choice?

OK you are a horse's rights activist and you choose the first and call it Rugged Legs. You line it up in a maiden and Rugged Legs is beaten by a fine-legged type that will probably break down sooner or later. That happens start after start. The fine-leggeds are going sore, even breaking down, but there are all degrees of them and a lot of them, and at the end of the 2yo year, they have managed to take ALL the money. Eventually,

at four, Rugged Legs wins his first race. Everything with fine legs has finally retired from the scene, broken down, gone off to the stud, or both. How much money is there for slowish four-year-olds? Precious little. Down the tubes for the purchase price plus some $60,000 in training costs, you retire from racing.

I believe that is pretty much how it is. If you want to avoid injury altogether, you have very little chance of winning. People will leap from their chairs and shriek the names of horses that stood up to 50, 100 even 150 starts. Fine. If such horses were the road to racing riches, they would be bred from and similar horses would be everywhere. Lots of well-intentioned people *have* stood tough campaigners at stud. But at some points, notably I would say in leg thickness, but in other ways as well, what makes for toughness detracts from track speed. The long term result is that the top stakes winners are not, in general, the soundest or toughest horses.

Wayne has focused on the type of horse that wins the most money, and there is a high injury rate among those horses. But those horses are in the sale and if he doesn't buy them someone else will. The trainer who buys this type and sets it aside until it is three, lets its bones harden a little more, will miss nearly all the money because many horses that could have won at two, change so much biomechanically that they are unlikely to win at three.

There is no doubt a middle course. If they race it less often, train it differently, it will probably last longer but will earn less at two. Some will go on to win for many years if trained with care. But any trainer who wants to maximize the horse's winnings would probably have a breakdown rate little different to Wayne's.

We know Wayne's choice: the 'power' type in the classification of Paul Mostert at Equix Biomechanics. A type that seldom survives its 2yo year in any trainer's hands, but which makes it to the winner's circle rather frequently. A type that seldom wins Triple Crown events. Wayne Lukas has come into racing with a scheme, a plan, to continually train his eye to select what he sees most often in the winner's circle. That he has been successful in this is very clear. The price he has paid has been a sizable slice of heart-break, because along with their winning ways, this type of horse has a high risk of a sudden end to its racing career. And that is nothing new; for as long as I can remember trainers have told me that more good horses break down than slow horses.

It may be no accident that Lukas 'can't train' in the estimation of many trainers. He may be selecting within such a narrow range in the type spectrum that he has specialized his training to that sub-type: widely spaced runs for horses with high power and weak legs. It fits nicely. However Australian trainer Tommy Smith has also been able to select 2yo winners and has a similar reputation for breaking horses down, but his fastworks are close together, and Tommy is regarded as very hard on his horses.

There will be those who say these horses would stand up to the racing if they had a longer, more solid preparation, and they might, but would they win as much money? By that I don't wish to seem callous and money-oriented. I'm simply pointing out that in the industry the measure of success is prizemoney and wins. If you want to be considered as successful as Wayne Lukas or Tommy Smith then you have to have as many wins and accumulate as much prizemoney as they do.

If anyone seriously wants to do anything about the breakdown rate in racehorses' legs, they would have to end 2yo racing and short races. Then they would probably find out why the old-timers gave up on three and four mile races for older horses in the first place. But while racing is the way it is, Wayne will continue to select the money-winningest type - arguably a trainer's duty - and his breakdown rate, whatever it is, will continue.

8.3 Best with what category of horse?

2yo, 3yo or older horses?

When it comes to age, 5 of Wayne's 14 Eclipse winners to early 1990 were 2yo's, 4 were 3yo's and 5 were older horses. Two-year-olds however made up only 22% of his starts in the Bloodstock Research Information Service figures, while 3yo's were 47.5%, but then 3yo's do have a lot more starts on average. His record in the Breeders' Cup is best by far in the 2yo's. Conclusion: he does best with 2yo's.

Fillies, colts or geldings?

There is no argument Wayne's best results are from fillies and mares. Of his 14 Eclipse Award winning champions to early 1990, all but Capote, Gulch and Steinlen were female. A sex ratio of 11 to 3. He won his Kentucky Derby with a filly. His Horse of the Year, Lady's Secret, was a filly.

In the Experimental Free Handicap for 1988, published in *The Blood-Horse* early in 1989, six Lukas-trained fillies made it into the top 30 2yo fillies list. These included Open Mind, 1st and Some Romance 2nd. In the 2yo colts, Lukas could only manage one in the top 30, Is It True at equal third. One year the top five juvenile fillies were all in the Lukas team. All except one belonged to Klein.

He often has multiple entries in important filly races; for example in the Grade 1 Oak Leaf Stakes, 1 1/16 miles, run at Santa Anita in October 1987, Lukas had Dream Team 1st (a Klein purchase at $500,000), Lost Kitty 2nd (Klein $775,000), and Blue Jean Baby 4th (Klein $850,000). In America all a trainer's horses race as one entry. The Lukas trio went out at 1 to 5 and took home $227,771 of the $264,850 total prizemoney. Lukas had won *five of the last six* runnings of this prestigious fillies race, starting with Landaluce in 1982.

Clearly he does best with females. He dominates the filly stakes races. Does he buy more fillies? No. He may have in his early days, but the statistics over all the years show he buys close to half fillies and half colts. His Bloodstock Research Information record from 1983 to August 1989 (from which the figures below are quoted) stood at 4063 filly starts to 4052 colt starts. This would differ significantly from the industry average, where more colts than fillies are sold and there are many more colt starts per year than filly starts.

Are his better results with fillies due to his selection methods or to his training or both? In section 7.2 on selection, Paul Mostert of Equix was of the opinion Wayne is better at choosing fillies. But his training style or 'babying and cuddling' level of care may contribute. We won't know until more people train like him with a range of horses Wayne didn't choose. **It would certainly pay any trainer to look hard at how Wayne trains fillies.**

Sprinters or stayers? (routers in the US)

Wayne has had better results at the sprint end. Short sprints of less than 6½ f made up about ⅜ of his starters. Wayne's win rate for these was 20% His win rates decline slightly as the distance of the race increases then drop markedly at the classic distance. Over the classic distance, 1 and 3/16 to 1½ miles, Wayne's win rate has been 14%. So poor was Wayne's reputation at the classic distance, that in 1988 Kelso Sturgeon, a respected newspaper handicapper, dismissed Winning Colors' chances in the Derby precisely because Wayne trained her. (Ah, sweet revenge.)

Claiming, stakes, handicap.

North America is claiming race territory. Each year over 80,000 races are run for Thoroughbreds, and over 70% are claiming races. Claiming races are classified by how much it costs to claim a horse out of the field. If you put a good horse in a weak field, chances are that after the race you will have the prize but someone else will have the horse. The better class of horse runs in handicap, allowance and stakes races. Not only is the prize money higher, but you can't lose the horse. Of course it has to be good enough to qualify, and there is no point running the horse if it has no chance of winning. The figures below will give an indication of what type of race Wayne aims for. The North American figures for 1989 appeared in The Blood-Horse in 1990. The numbers for Wayne are from Bloodstock Research Information Services.

The higher level of Maiden races is an indication of the number of horses Wayne starts off, horses he bought in the sales. Some trainers seldom start a maiden, obtaining all their horses by claiming them out of claiming races. If allowance, handicap and stakes are the elite races, the bigmoney events,

NORTH AMERICAN AVERAGE		LUKAS 1988
Maiden	8.6%	20.4%
Starter Allow.	1.2%	incl in clmg
Claiming	73.9%	18.3%
Allowance	12.1%	33%
Handicap	0.7%	incl in allow
Stakes	3.3%	28.3%
Other	0.2%	
	100.0%	100.0%

then although they represent only about 16% of all races, they were 61% of Wayne's starts.

Wayne's specialty in race type is stakes races. Not only are they high prizemoney races, they add great breeding value to the horse. In sales catalogues, the names of stakeswinners in the pedigree are printed in bold letters. The horse is said to have 'black type'. Wayne has won an amazing number of stakes, with a win rate of 18%. He has nowhere near Charlie Whittingham's record in the big handicaps, but they are mainly for older horses.

It might seem that Wayne is limited by his concentration on 2yo races. After all, they only made up 11.9% of the prizemoney in 1989. But over one third of that money, $31m of it, was crammed into just 512 stakes races.

Turf races are only a small part of the program in America, but when Wayne's critics wanted something to rubbish Wayne about after Winning Colors' Kentucky Derby win, they focused on his record in turf races. In the first four Breeders' Cups, Wayne had a total of 36 starters, but not one in the two turf races. In 1984 he had 96 turf starts for just 2 wins. Two percent in round figures. His win rate on dirt the same year was 18% The low win rate on turf was not for want of trying - in that year almost 12% of Wayne's starts were on turf.

These dismal turf results did not stop Lukas. Rather he seems to have set out to improve his record on grass. In 1987 he was greatly helped in this effort when major European owner Daniel Wildenstein began to send him horses. Five of the horses had already won group races in Europe! Wayne's turf results improved to 14% in 1988 and to 16% for the first eight months of 1989.

Then in September 1989 Lukas clubbed his detractors severely by winning the Arlington Million, 1¼m on turf, with Steinlen. In the race were top turf horses from Europe and three entries from Charlie Whittingham. Wildenstein had to pay an extra $50,000 to get Steinlen in the race, and the horse only got a start because several others were scratched.

The gloating pundits who had written off Steinlen and Lukas were left with a mouthful of loose teeth. Wayne likes to give the impression that he takes no notice of critics, but I think he would have greatly enjoyed the result of his first Arlington Million entry. Nevertheless he has a way to go. His turf

results, even at 16%, are only two thirds as good as his 23% on dirt in 1989 and below the likes of Woody Stephens who averaged 19% wins in turf races from 1983 to August 1989.

Wayne's Record in the varied races of six Breeders' Cups add to the overview of his strengths and weaknesses.

Breeders' Cup Results Including 1989
Juvenile Stakes, Fillies
Two wins from 20 starters.
Juvenile Stakes, Colts
Three wins in a row from 8 starters.
Distaff Stakes
Three wins in a row from 16 starts.
Sprint
One win from 9 starts.
Classic
Slew City Slew ran twice without placing.
Mile (Turf)
One win and a second by Steinlen.
Turf (1½m)
No starters

That is a total of 10 wins from 57 starts, a respectable 17.5% wins. Two-year-olds accounted for over half the starts - 30 of 57. They also made up half the wins. Females made up 63% of his starts, and half the wins.

8.4 Jockey policy
In Wayne's Quarter Horse days, there were two outstanding jockeys and Wayne already had one under his control. The other, Bobby Adair, rode mostly for Wayne's arch rival Blane Schvaneveldt. Blane said that Wayne was always trying to monopolize both of them. "He told me he would get both of them."

"He told you?"

"Yes he said, 'If I can get Adair too, I'll have you by the ears."

In the Thoroughbreds, Wayne uses a large number of the very best jockeys. He chooses jockeys for the individual horse and race, according to what a jockey's talents are and what the horse and the race require. Jockey's agents follow him around and court him because he has the largest number of starters and winners around.

One agent told me in June 1988 that Wayne was booking jockeys for the Breeders' Cup, which is in November. No other trainer, he said, was even thinking about it yet. Wayne improves his chances of having the best jockeys by planning and booking so far ahead.

Wayne often has more than one horse in a race. He gives each jockey separate instructions and tells them they are on their own. 'Team tactics,' i.e. having jockeys help each other is illegal. Nevertheless, having multiple horses in many of the races gives him some opportunity to determine such things as the early pace. But he has never to the best of my knowledge been accused of teaming his jockeys. He uses so many different jockeys that team tactics would soon be well known if he did use them. His use of so many jockeys, rather than the same two or three has, helped him avoid any accusation of team tactics.

Wayne's basic race strategy
Making the transition from Quarter Horses, Wayne said he had to learn more about pace and how to relax his horses. "You really have to know your horse. If he wants to lay back off the pace and make one big run at the end, you had better find that out early. If he wants to go wire to wire and doesn't want to be rated, like Great Lady M., let him do it."

Wayne's horses do seem to run in all parts of the field in the early part of the race. Obviously the jockeys are not sent out with a blanket policy for 95% of Wayne's starters, such as the 'be near the front' instructions of TJ Smith. He often has Angel Cordero on his front runners. Angel is one of the all-time great jockeys, but is infamous for one aspect of his front-running strategy. *Thoroughbred Record* writer Timothy Capps described it this way:

"Cordero has the lead turning for home. He takes one or two backward glances over either shoulder; then, depending on where the most serious competition lies, slides his mount in a direction that will . . . compromise the pursuing horse's chance to take the shortest path to the wire." For connections of the second horse, Capps called it being 'Cordero-ized'. But Cordero doesn't move out enough to allow action by the stewards.

While some trainers refuse to use Cordero because of this tactic, Wayne makes frequent use of the champion jockey. Wayne obviously believes if the stewards can't stop Cordero, better to have him on a Lukas horse than cutting off a Lukas horse. Better to Cordero-ize than be Cordero-ized.

One morning at Hollywood Park Wayne was very angry with Tony Matos, agent for jockey Lafitte Pincay. "I can fix it up with McCarron but that woman is worth a billion dollars and you messed it up," said Wayne. Later, Matos said to me, "He's always like that. He's difficult, but you get used to it."

8.5 Placing horses in races
A useful guide to the ability of a trainer to place horses where they can win is their strike rate or win rate, i.e. wins as a percentage of starts. Again we have the advantage of the Bloodstock Research Trainer Summary. This gives the percentage of winners in each year, in each of 74 categories.

What is the ideal percentage of winners for a whole year? Wayne has an overall win rate of 19%, i.e. about one in five of his starters wins its race. His arch-antagonist Woody Stephens had a win rate of 32% in 1984. Does this mean Woody is nearly twice as good? Is win rate determined by the quality of the horses or the judgment of the trainer?

Let us start with some presumptions, the first being that we are speaking here of trainers with a sizable string of reasonable horses. Not a one horse string consisting of unbeaten Colin, nor a clutch of cursed clumpers. Whether the horses are good or very good, the trainer should be able to put them in races they can win. That is the art of placing.

If a trainer was able to predict precisely which races his horses could win and did not need to give them some races as a form of schooling or conditioning, he would have a 100% win rate. He would also be able to bet like a demon and never lose. Such a trainer may have existed, but retired rich so early we've never heard of him.

Moving a little closer to reality, we have to accept that while good trainers have a good idea of which races their horses can win, there is a lot of luck involved in any race, so the win rate will be well below 50%. With the size of factors like pace and luck, it would be reasonable to say a trainer who wins more than 50% of starts over a large number of races is not winning all the races he could win. He is leaving them out of races against worthwhile rivals even when they have a chance, and in claiming races he is running his horses in lower class races than they should be in. This means the horse can be claimed at a low price and is winning smaller purses than it should be. To have such a high win rate the trainer has passed up many other wins and much money.

At the other extreme, if a trainer keeps putting his horses in races they have only a very poor chance of winning, his win rate will be very low, say 5%. Wayne, as mentioned, has a win rate of 19% since 1983. That rate has risen steadily from 13% in 1983 to 22% for the first eight months of 1989. Wayne is no dummy and says he is still learning, so we can assume the trend indicates steadily improving placement skills on his part.

His results on turf show this trend clearly. In 1984 he tried 37 horses to find 2 winners. In 1989, to August, he had tried 49 horses to find 16 winners. An improvement from 5% to 33%, a definite indication that he has a better idea which horses will win on grass. Not good news for his rivals.

As more trainers are covered, the many factors involved in determining a trainer's win rate, such as testing horses over different surfaces and distances, will become clearer.

From reading the press clippings it would seem that if Wayne has a fault in his placing of horses it would be in running some horses with poor chances in stakes races - especially (going on where they finished), some of his Triple Crown starters. But this is a calculated policy on Wayne's part. Some of his Kentucky Derby starters have finished last or close to it after leading. These were probably attempts to steal the race or set a pace for another of his contenders. When they were obviously going to finish out of the money, they have not been kept slogging.

It is hard to argue with his results. He has won 18% of the graded stakes his horses have run in since the start of 1987. He believes the variables are so great that not running a horse because it has poor chances of winning means you will miss out on some money and some black type.

Mr Bruno, jockey Eddie Maple's agent in New York: "I think the thing that makes Wayne Lukas so tough is that he is very very aggressive and he is not afraid to challenge anyone. He will bring horses from Saratoga or California on a heart beat. He will put them on the plane and two days later they're running. He's got horses all over the country right now. If a horse doesn't fare well on a deep track then maybe he'll come east because he feels that the horse may appreciate the speed here."

Presumably referring to race tactics, Wayne was reported to have said, "When you run an entry (ie multiple horses in one race) you want to be sure they complement each other". Wayne, as we saw in his Kentucky Derby history, often runs one on the lead and one well back in the field, covering the pace possibilities.

I doubt if it matters to run two come-from-behind horses in one race, but it sure would be stupid to run two horses that will want to lead, against each other.

That Wayne can place horses with some skill shows clearly in the Bloodstock Research Information Services trainer summary. His overall win rate is 19% over seven years, but when he steps a horse up two or more classes, his win rate is 38%. A trainer has to have a good reason to promote a horse several levels, because it passes up some opportunities at lower levels. Obviously he knows how good they are and what he has to beat. There would be a lot of trainers who have 0% on large step-ups because they are more optimistic than their horse is able.

When he demotes a horse two or more classes they win 24% of their races. If they won 50% then he would be demoting horses that shouldn't be demoted. If he won 5% he would be demoting too late or down too few levels, indications that he was not facing reality or was not a good judge of the relative ability of his horses and those in the likely fields. A 24% win rate on large drops in class suggests Wayne knows what he is doing.

On the score of traveling, there can be few trainers as willing to travel a horse, and not just to one of the big tracks either; he'll send a horse wherever there is a stakes race.

8.6 Claiming strategies

Blane said that Wayne was very much into claimers when he first arrived at Los Alamitos from Ruidoso, but within a few years was concentrating on stakes and allowance horses. I asked Wayne about his claiming days.

"In the Quarter Horses, Blane Schvaneveldt said you were tough to beat at claiming."

"Yes I did very well at that. My theory was that there was not a horse in the world, that if I liked the look of him, I couldn't move up. That was action claiming. In 1972 -3 -4, round then, I was just claiming to keep the stable active, setting records and so on. It was an action program. The horses I anchored the stable with, the stakes horses and so on, I still bought at the sales."

"So your claiming strategy was that you liked the look of them."

"If they showed a little brilliance or something, if I thought I could move 'em up I claimed them. Sometimes I claimed 3 or 4 a night if I felt like it."

"Was it horses you thought you could improve -their gear, their action?"

"I always claimed a horse I thought I could move up. Most of the time we did but not always."

The Bloodstock Research Trainer Summary indicates that in the Thoroughbreds, Wayne was not into claiming horses out of claiming races. (4 are listed since 1982, the last in 1987). Wayne did however, put horses in claiming races, averaging several hundred claiming races per year. This is not much more than a way of unloading his lesser horses, perhaps of earning some money with them. His win rate in claimers has been about the same as his overall 19%.

Kiaran McLaughlin said that about 15 to 20 horses are claimed off the New York barn each year. They usually only win 3 to 8 races between them for the year. However one was claimed for $50,000 and went on to win $200,000 in a string of $50,000 claiming races. "You have to have one do well like that to be able to have the others claimed." (Putting horses in claiming races is one way to sell them off in America.) But Kiaran says none have really come back to haunt the Lukas operation. I'd guess for a claimed horse to haunt Wayne it would have to win a stakes race. I haven't heard of that happening, and I'm sure Wayne's enthusiastic detractors would have been trumpeting it around it if it had.

Video Ranger, the Lukas horse claimed months before it ran in the Kentucky Derby, may go on to become just such a ghost.

8.7 Injuries and therapies

The backstretch rumor mill classifies Wayne as a trainer who breaks a lot of horses down. The presumption is that he doesn't bother to patch them up, just sends them out and gets new ones in to replace them. Blane Schvaneveld told me that in his Quarter Horse days, Lukas never cortisoned many horses. "He was a great ice man," said Blane. "He iced every horse. But he goes through different things - a couple of years ago he had fifteen of those magnetic machines, put it on every horse, before they run. I know it worked for them - then he said they don't use it much any more. They cost a lot. But he goes through surges of that stuff."

Leg care in America is an extraordinary business compared to Australia or England. Here, one of Wayne's workers prepares to use a white clay-like paste that is smeared all over the legs, either from pastern to knees, or pastern to mid forearm. The paper the worker has in his left hand is wrapped over the 'poultice', and then bandages are applied. Most stables do most horses every day or every fastwork day. The poultice is considered to be a preventative and a curative for inflammations and infections. It is said to 'draw' fluid from the tissues and thereby reduce swelling and filling. For this reason these products are sometimes called 'tighteners'.

8.7-1 Shinsoreness

"With the way you train, do you get much in the way of bucked shins?"

"None at all hardly, virtually none. Shins in our barn are virtually non-existent. The only sore shins we get are the ones we aren't able to start off in training for some reason or other. Somebody will break them on the farm and send them to us and then we do. The horses we get at the beginning and start, we hardly ever get any sore shins. That's a judgment call first of all and common sense. If you put the foundation in it does not have to happen. I'm not saying it won't happen, we have some rare cases where one will surprise us and just show up with a shin. We haven't fired or blistered a sore shin in years. We may have a shin heat up, but we don't have any what you would call buck shins, where you point at them and he drops to his knees."

Twilight Ridge bucked her shins and Houston, Wayne's 1989 Derby hope was reported to have bucked at two. But from my enquiries it does seem that Wayne has a very low rate of sore shins in his 2yo's. I believe that is due to his slow, controlled preparation for racing, with no big step-ups in the stress load of the cannon bones, either during the preparation or in the

first races. His feeding may have something to do with it, but talking to Wayne I got the impression he believes, as I do, that the secret is in the conditioning program.

Low rates of shin soreness in 2yo's are a sign of a careful trainer, usually one who takes time in the preparation, and who has good riders who ride to instructions. Trainers who are aiming to do the most with their horses at 3yo are generally the ones with the low shin soreness rate. It is unusual to find such a low rate in a trainer who is considered to push his 2yo's along. I have no doubt minimizing this problem helps Wayne get such good results with his youngsters.

8.7-2 Tying up

"I don't know what would be average. We have a few horses tie up but not very much."

I found this interesting, since fillies are more prone to this problem, and he trains a lot of fillies. Electroyte losses are an important factor. Considering the amount of galloping he gives his horses, they must lose a lot of electrolytes in their sweat. Although he says he is not fussy which electrolyte he uses, he must be using some that help. A lot of tying up is triggered by nervous excitement. Wayne's great attention to the mental state of his horses must contribute to his minimization of this problem.

8.7-3 Most common lameness

"What would be your most common injury?"

"I think the same as any trainer, it's knee chips. I think if you go around the whole grounds you'll probably get that answer. I think chips are still the biggest problem and by that I mean known and unknown."

"Yes, there are plenty of undiagnosed knee chips."

"Never take a picture (X-ray) of a horse. You might find out something you don't want to know. There are a lot of cold tight knees, and ankles, where there are spurs and chips. Then there are the ones where I have a horse for sale and they vet them and they say this horse has a spur and I'm astounded because it has never shown anything. Some of them may occur as yearlings even."

Wayne's passion for muscular horses, along with his preference for racing horses fresh, horses that break fast from the gates, would contribute to the level of knee chips.

Impulse Corporation advertise a product called the IC Combo, which combines transcutaneous electrical stimulation (TENS) and pulsating electromagnetic field (PEMF). The advertisements claim that Lukas uses five of these machines. They are priced at $1795 each, and are claimed to be effective treatment for a range of leg problems.

Around Wayne's cupboards were:
Ultrasound coupling gel, for using ultrasound therapy; Beta-

dine Solution, a disinfectant; Two green Equine Transpirators ET-100's, for horses with respiratory problems.

8.8 Role of the vet

Wayne is not very impressed with veterinarians as some of his comments have already shown, although any horse he buys has its airways examined by endoscope within the hour.

8.8-1 How much does he blood test?

"Only if I think there's something critically wrong. Then we do a complete blood-count. We do not routinely draw blood on horses to see how they're doing. If we can't tell by looking at them, we feel like we're missing the boat anyhow."

8.8-2 Jugs (intravenous drips)

I spoke with a past employee:

"Does he jug (intravenous drip) many horses?"

"Yes, jugs and vitamins, but if it weren't for vitamins the vets would starve to death in Wayne's barn. They give the jugs the morning after the races. You watch horses and if they are a little flat you give vitamin boosters. If they are a little flat in between [races] they'll hit 'em a couple of days in a row with shots. A horse might run real hard and he might hang a jug on them three days in a row. Usually he uses one bottle but if a race has been a real stress to a horse he might double up or even triple up the bottles."

"What vitamins does he use?"

"Just B vitamins to pick them back up."

"A lot of trainers use B1 for nervous horses, does Wayne do that?"

"There might be half a dozen that get nervous before a race and they get a shot of B1 before a race. But he uses hardly any other medication, hardly any bute (butazolidin). I knew when they came out with those drug charges that that was wrong. I worked for him and hardly anyone uses less medication."

"But lots of horsemen think he uses something."

"He has pedigree and pedigree will run. That's what he uses."

Dr Greg Ferraro gives the 'jugs' at Wayne's Hollywood barn. At the time he was using bottles of Dexolyte with some calcium levulinate added. Greg said the calcium levulinate helped restore the calcium balance.

"He's like Charlie Whittingham in the sense that he probably uses as little medication as anybody. Good trainers don't need veterinary medicine."

"So he's low on steroids or is he average?"

"I would say he's probably below average. Wayne's below average. Charlie's probably way below average. You know, the good trainers don't need as much. Good trainers train successfully year after year after year. And those guys, the longer they're in the business, the less they use the veterinary medicine. They don't need it. I mean, they take care of the sick ones and the cripples."

"Is he strong on the pick-me-ups in those jugs after racing?"

"Yes, he does that. He likes to see his horses eating well and feeling good, and so he'll give them that just to ensure."

I asked Wayne's New York assistant trainer Kiaran McLaughlin what they did with bleeders, since Lasix is not allowed in New York. He told me they send them down to the California division and put them on Lasix.

"But we don't get many bleeders."

"Do you think that is because of the way you train?"

"Yes. We put less stress on our horses."

Wayne was quoted as saying that with bleeders he starts them on Lasix, but likes to move them off it after 2 or 3 races, if they haven't bled again.

This is Wayne's standard stall front. The 'V' is widely used and considered to minimise weaving and wind-sucking. The positioning of the hay net diminishes these problems even further.

Unusual Therapies

"Alternative medicine: I am interested, because as a vet, I have had great results with a few things that some vets frown on, such as herbal treatments. A lot of the people in herbal medicine are quacks or anti modern medicine, but I keep an open mind and if there is no other treatment or a herbal treatment works better, I use it. There are some rather closed-minded fools among the vets, who won't use herbal remedies even if they work, but I'm after results."

"We're that way too."

"So have you had any success with chiropractors?"

"No. Had one woman come that was very interested in doing that and adjustments and spines and hand-massages and everything. I let her work there one day. She wanted to do it for nothing, just to show me. I thought the horses ran average. I decided I wasn't interested. We've experimented a little bit with acupuncture."

"Freaky but can be an excellent thing."

"A friend of ours recommended a guy and we had some horses that I thought he helped with acupuncture and we have done some acupuncture."

"There are some horse chiropractors that are impressing what I would call some fairly skeptical trainers in Sydney. I'm watching it with interest -the chiropractic thing in horses."

There are numerous reasons for my interest in these 'alternative medicine' approaches. The first reason for my interest in chiropractic and acupuncture in animals is to know just what conditions they will be useful for. Another is to see if they end up outside the veterinary profession, as chiropractic has ended up outside the medical profession in humans. With chiropractic in humans, the medical profession was really stupid. In spite of millions of people obtaining great relief, medicos wouldn't believe in it because the explanation given by the manipulators was not anatomically possible. The chiropractors said they put the discs back in. Medical anatomists - anyone with a knowledge of anatomy really - would look at a dissection and say they couldn't possibly be moved by manipulation. So they said it was a lie etc.

The fools did not pay attention to the RESULTS -the manipulators fixed heaps of people. I have walked into chiropractor's offices in great pain and walked out relieved. You have no idea how stupid a medical doctor sounds to me when he says chiropractors are quacks who cannot cure anything. Straight away I think of the doctor concerned as a dogmatic idiot, someone taken in by the myth the medical profession wants to believe, and perpetuated around the medical schools. It is a staggering example of blindness because questioning even a small random sample of their patients would soon establish the fact that most chiropractors can greatly help many people with certain back problems. I have met doctors who know this, but who say they avoid stating their point of view in medical circles because of the flack they will cop.

Today there are a few medicos trying to bring it back into medicine. One medico told me it was originally started by doctors but it became a no-no to do it. It is a classic example of the 'medieval' academic mentality - throwing out the observation when it disagrees with the theory, the dogma. It is the theory that should have been re-assessed.

The mechanisms by which chiropractic works are being slowly worked out. It will suddenly become respectable then, and the medicos will want it. It should have developed as a branch of medicine but the dogmatists threw it away. I'd rather go to a medical doctor who was a manipulator, someone with a sound medical degree, than someone who just manipulates. They would be less inclined to attribute everything to disc problems, less likely to oversell weekly manipulations. But I suppose we have to be grateful that someone kept it going and developed it when it was being ridiculed by the idiot zealot factor amongst academics and medicos.

So far I have heard of two vets who manipulate horses and have met or heard of eight non-vets. Many vets repeat the medical myth, saying horse chiropractors can't possibly be moving anything and therefore they are quacks. They seem to discount any success stories totally. Those who don't know history are condemned to repeat it.

Another reason for my interest was as an indicator of open-mindedness in trainers. For years I have heard trainers described as unimaginative people still using methods that were in place in the 1800's. This view is a favorite with some of the 'sportsmedicine' set and people trying to sell high tech equipment to trainers. I *have* known trainers who did things exactly as they had learned when they were boys in the stables 40 years before. But I have also met a lot of trainers who were far from that image. They were cautiously experimental, keen to try anything new. A few seemed too experimental, either changing too many things too often, or trying things that seemed bizarre to me.

To which of these groups would the top trainers belong? - conservative, experimental or highly experimental? For that matter, would they all fall into the one group? So I was keen to know if these top trainers had tried chiropractic or acupuncture in horses.

Every trainer with large numbers has some chronically lame horses. A conservative trainer would not try such unconventional therapies. An experimental trainer would try them at least once on lame horses that have not responded to conventional treatment. The trainer I would classify as too experimental would try it on horses before trying established treatments.

Wayne certainly tried them, although in the case of the lady chiropractor, results on one session with the horses are not enough to form a negative opinion. If something works on one horse when everything else has failed, then barring a coincidental self cure, one case is reasonable cause for a *provisional* belief that it works.

One failure however, particularly with the sort of problem for which nothing else works, means very little. In my experience as a vet, particularly in referral practices, if something works on one in five of cases regarded as incurable, it can be very worthwhile. How many cases do you have to try to come to such a conclusion? You could easily have three failures in a row and decide the treatment doesn't work. You could, if you were a little unlucky, have ten failures in a row. If it seems surprising that someone with Wayne's scientific training seems to be making a premature conclusion on one result, I can only say that it is a very common failing even in people with such training.

When I was a recent graduate, and I worked with older, more knowledgeable vets, I would go to them with the more difficult cases, cases where my treatment hadn't worked. They would tell me of some less well-known treatment, and in some instances, warn me that it didn't have a high success rate. I found that after just one or two failures for a particular treatment, that I really did not believe it ever worked. Through a lack of any alternative I might have to treat more of these cases, with almost no faith in the remedy. Suddenly - Bingo - a cure, maybe two or three cures.

I had played my share of cards and flipped coins. I had even studied statistics and probability theory. I should have known that it might take 3, 5 maybe 10 cases to get a result in such one-in-five situations. But my subconscious had an opinion of its own after a few unsuccessful cases, and it had a big say. From those experiences however, I learned to persevere, and in a few years found myself in the position of recommending such treatments to other vets who asked me for advice on difficult cases. Very few vets, I found, will have faith after just one or two failures, even if you tell them it is a one-in-three (or whatever) proposition.

Anyway, to conclude on this point, on the acupuncture and chiropractic test, Wayne was experimental. He tried them.

8.9 Shoeing - what Wayne does differently

When I first inquired around the barns about Wayne's shoeing, I was told he used horseshoes with very long toe grabs on the front feet. These were perhaps double the height of the toe grabs other trainers use. (Toe grabs of any kind are outlawed in Australia on the grounds that when a horse gallops up on another horse from behind, the toe grabs greatly increase the possibility of damage to the horse in front. Almost all racing in Australia is on turf.) In America it seems there is no limitation for dirt tracks but a maximum (low) size for turf.)

I asked one of the farriers who shod Wayne's stock in California, how high Wayne's toe grabs were. He guessed about ¾ inch (1.9 cm). Asked if Wayne used them to give his horses a better grip he replied that he thought it was, "just his little gimmick - to be a little different than anyone else".

A more likely explanation is that Wayne used long toe grabs in his Quarter Horses. They are common on racing Quarter Horses. They need as much grip of the track as possible for their powerful muscles to push against. Since they mostly run flat as a strap down straight tracks there is rarely much 'coming from behind'. Quarter Horses run parallel, almost like runners in lanes, over the 200 to 440 yard courses. Only over longer distances like 870 yards do they form tight bunches.

Presumably Wayne used these grabs routinely on his Quarter Horses, has tried them on Thoroughbreds and preferred them to the usual low toe grabs. The farrier said, "He uses them on all the horses all the time here in California". Not just for certain track conditions. A few other trainers have switched to the same grabs, but at a later date, another farrier in New York told me Wayne had pretty much given up his long toe grabs.

"Your toe grabs were a source of amazement to the Thoroughbred people in New York."

"We still run our horses with standard Quarter Horse toe grabs behind. All our horses run with those. We don't use stickers or block heels or wedges or any of that stuff. Regular shoes in front."

"Are they the same as a Louisiana grab?"

"No a Louisiana grab is a lot longer. There is a lot of confusion there. A Louisiana grab would horrify you. A regular Quarter Horse grab is maybe quarter of an inch - just a little longer than a Thoroughbred shoe. We've never put those Louisiana grabs on - ever - even when we were in the Quarter Horses."

"No grabs on the front?"

"Not much."

8.10 Has he 'produced' any good trainers?

Wayne has turned his son Jeff into a widely respected trainer, and from their results, his foremen at the scattered outposts do pretty well too.

"Are there any people who have worked for you in your Quarter Horse days or your Thoroughbred days who have gone on to become good trainers in their own right?"

"I've never had any assistants leave me that I didn't fire and those were the ones that I didn't think would make it anyhow. The ones that I think would make top trainers, like Kiaran McLaughlin, Jeff, Randy Bradshaw, they are still with us."

"Is Tom MacKenzie is still with you?"

"No I fired him. He got complacent, lax. I don't tolerate that."

"He must have been with you a long time?"

"Yes, probably too long. That was probably his downfall."

I was unable to find Tom for his side of the story, but it will be interesting to see if he sets up as a trainer. But to return to Jeff Lukas, there are those who believe Jeff is a better trainer than his father. For some it is a means of taking some of the credit away from Wayne, a means of defending their opinion that Wayne is an awful trainer, 'A butcher' etc. They can attribute the good results of the Lukas stable to Jeff. However some are astute trainers, and some, like handicapper, journalist and author Steve Davidowitz, can say they have studied the results, and that horses last longer and do better for Jeff. How much of that is due to the bleeders and sore horses being sent from New York to California, as well as improvers in California being sent up to New York, I don't know.

8.11 Analysis of his training

Most trainers consider that Wayne cannot train. In an article, Pete Axthelm reported that Charlie Whittingham, the revered Californian trainer, praised the Lukas business management but joked: "Imagine how he'd dominate the game if he was a great trainer?" Wayne prefers to let his results speak for themselves, but the other trainers attribute his results to numbers, hustling, hype, drugs and business management.

One measure is how successful he is with horses he takes over from other trainers, and vice versa. But there are not a lot that go to Wayne from other trainers. He took on Peter Brant's sprinter Gulch, previously trained to some great wins by Leroy Jolley, and tried to win quality mile races with it. Gulch turned in some good performances, but had to go back to the sprints. Gulch won the Breeders' Cup Sprint, so Wayne did well with the horse. The horses he lets go in claiming races don't go on to show him up. Imported horses are very tricky to use in assessing a trainer, because there are many freaky results. Wayne's biggest bust, according to one report, was South American sensation Triny Carol, imported from Venezuela, which failed to beat a horse in four U.S. starts for Wayne. His biggest training success with an import would be Steinlen, detailed in section 8.3.

Commonly heard criticisms

Running fillies against colts - Wayne wins a lot of big stakes races with fillies running against colts. He often has another filly that will win the parallel fillie's race anyway, if there is one. The black type resale value and winnings speak for themselves.

Running large numbers of horses in the same race - Some trainers will put Wayne down by talking about him having five horses in a race and then still not winning. Certainly the long standing ideal of the mythical Great Trainer is a trainer who has five horses he could put in a race - but he puts in one horse and it wins. I think that is as mythical as the Great Trainer himself. Any handicapper will tell you that the best horse is often beaten. Wayne believes there are considerable lottery factors in any race and so if he has five prospects, he puts them all in. It solves problems about which owner's horses should be left out, and in high value races, second is still better money than a win in ordinary races. Every trainer that qualifies a horse for the Breeders' Cup, runs it if it is still sound and in form, to the best of my knowledge. While I consider the perfect trainer would leave in only those with a chance, there are other considerations, like pleasing owners

and getting publicity. I think many of the same trainers rubbishing Wayne for putting in five, wish they could qualify one, and if they did qualify five, they'd probably run five.

Running his horses too frequently - Wayne believes that when a horse is hot you should keep it going and going often. He's happy with the results of that.

Running unsound and sore horses Nearly every trainer on the backside has run sore horses. Several trainers said Wayne took it a bit further than most. It can be argued that, like trainers for wealthy private stables, Wayne doesn't have to succumb to the financial pressure. But profitability is one of his key selling points. He may also consider that many of his horses have a limited time as top horses, even if they remain sound. Paul Mostert of Equix in Lexington, after careful research, believes the biomechanical efficiency of many horses peaks early and then declines. Many trainers have similar beliefs, derived from years of experience, but there are also some top trainers who immediately let up on horses that go sore, and certainly won't run them.

Kiaran McLaughlin explained that there is a very fine line between when you run a horse and when you don't. "We get a lot done with horses that are maybe a little bit sore or they don't eat all their meal." He believes the thing others overlook the most about Wayne as a trainer is his great horsemanship.

"He is a great horseperson. Nobody talks about that. I could tell you story after story about his ability with horses. One time we had a horse sent to us that was a 3yo, and it was difficult in the starting gates. I took it down to the gates, and I think I'm a reasonably good horseman, but it just would not go in. The gate crew, they wanted to blindfold it and lead it in. I knew Wayne would not want that, so I took it back up to the stable."

"Wayne took the horse down and said to the gate crew, 'This is going to take a while, but you have had a year to train it to the gate and it won't go in. Just let me have some time.' He put the shank over its nose, and led it up and down until it showed him some respect. Then he led it up to the gate for about half an hour. Back and forth, back and forth. Eventually it went in."

"This horse's problem was that the gate crew had been whipping on him to get him to go in the gate. He had no respect for people leading him. He was so worried about being hit from behind that he would walk all over you. That's why Wayne led it around before-hand. He wanted it to pay attention to him."

"After he got it to go into the gate, he wanted it led out, but the gate crew were too worried about the horse walking over them to do it. So Wayne did it himself, over and over. The next day he took the horse down, and it went straight in. Perfect. That was a horse called Mathew's Keep. It went on to win $400,000."

"What did the gate crew think of him doing that?"

"Half of them were happy he solved the problem for them, but some of them didn't like it. Another example is the way his horses are in the saddling paddock. With other trainers, I was taught to dominate the horse. Hold it there and don't let it move. The horse gets more and more agitated. You put on chains and bits to control the horse. It is not natural. Wayne has his horse on a loose lead, just clipped to its bridle, and he lets it walk around. It stays relaxed."

"We had another horse that would just sweat up 'til it poured off her. No matter what I did, even letting her move around like that, she sweated up, got all washy and ran poorly. I went and asked Wayne what I should do. He told me just to leave her alone next time she was to race, and he would be the groom. He told me not to let anybody near her. Well he put on his blue jeans and did that, and that's how we went to the saddling paddock. I was the trainer. Wayne brushed her and groomed her and she did not sweat a drop. She ran third."

"We had a horse come to us that had won a lot of money, called Bordeaux Bob. This horse didn't like the gates and he had to be backed into them. He had always been backed in. The horse was entered for a race that was going to start right in front of the grandstand. It was like - this horse is already a problem - what will it do right in front of a crowd?"

"Wayne does not like his horses 'gimmicked' into the gate. He was in Quarter Horses, and if they don't come out of the gate right, you lose the race. He organized a session at the gate and he trained the horse to go in from the back like all the other horses. On the day of the race the horse went in without a problem. Next day the assistant starter came down to the barn. He thanked Wayne. He said he wished some of the other trainers would come down and do that with their horses. That is what Wayne does. He is just like that. It is amazing what he can do with horses."

Blane's assessment

Blane had this to say: "I'll guarantee you, and you can quote me: I can watch races on television and I can pick Wayne Lukas's horse out, and not even know he's got one in the race."

"How?"

"The way they look. They stand out over other people's horses. He takes firm care of them and those horses look- the hair and everything. They've got more flesh on them, and that's why he beats those other guys." I looked unconvinced. "It is! The condition. He may not be as smart as Whittingham - I think Charlie Whittingham's the greatest. I don't think there'll ever be a trainer any better. Charlie's like O'Brien, you know, they're great horsemen. But on the other hand, Wayne beats them on condition, because he's a great feeder and caretaker."

Blane had some interesting comments on Wayne's reputa-

tion for breaking horses down: "They harp on that about Wayne, but Wayne runs a lot of young horses. If Whittingham ran a lot of young horses, if he had all 2yo's, he'd get breakdowns too. Whittingham doesn't develop all those horses of his, they are sent to him when they are three and four years old, foreign horses and so on. Whereas Wayne develops all his horses."

Clyde's assessment

Wayne's old school friend and sales partner Clyde Rice had no doubts about Wayne's ability as a trainer. Speaking of the things he saw as a horse trader, he said, "A lot of good horses fall through the cracks. You see so many great horses - they go to a trainer and the next thing you hear they are hurt, sick or unsuccessful for so many reasons. I'm very critical of so many people's pre-race training programs. That doesn't happen often if they go to Wayne. He runs such a good tight ship. He's a great horseman. He's grown up with it and he's dedicated."

"The horses have a better chance with Wayne training them? Most trainers say he can't train. They say he breaks a lot down."

"I have sold a lot of horses, and I can tell you that they have a better chance if they go into Wayne's program. The same caliber of horses. Because of that, Wayne has helped me make my reputation."

Clyde is in an unusually good position to compare Wayne's results with those of other trainers. He buys something like 50 to 100 horses per year, and re-sells most of his horses after a race preparation or a race win. He has a good idea of the ability of each horse he sells. He follows them with interest because he can trumpet their success to help him sell more of his horses. In Clyde's view Wayne offers owners, "awful good value for their money."

I would have to say that analysing Wayne as a trainer, getting opinions from all and sundry, was like a rerun of my experiences collecting information on TJ Smith. Uncannily so.

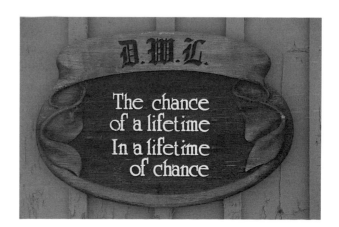

9. Wayne's feeding and additives

"Any differences between the feeding of Quarter Horses and the feeding of Thoroughbreds?"

"No, we feed 'em exactly the same. We haven't changed our program. What we try to do is we try to get as much into 'em as we can."

9.1 First ration

Wayne's first feed mix 'evolved' in his youth and continued to evolve.

9.2 Grains

"We feed any kind of grain, anything that we think has got to be good for them."

"So they get fed oats, corn-"

"Corn, barley, wheat - we give them every grain there is. You name it, it's probably in there. Figuring it can't hurt them if they'll eat it."

The feed bay certainly contained a variety of grains: flax, cracked corn, wheat flakes, barley flakes, whole oats and something the groom called 'black seed.' Wayne feeds as much grain as he can get them to eat, at 10:30am, 4:30pm and 3am. Some get four feeds a day. The night watchman feeds them at 3am, followed by one scoop of oats plus sweet feed (a mix of grains and molasses) in the morning, three scoops in the afternoon, and one in the evening.

Sweet feeds in Wayne's feed stall

Magnum Sweet Feed, US Grain Co, Minneapolis, Minnesota.
Barker's Equine Sweet Feed - lots. Equitech Inc., Minneapolis, Minnesota.
Respond - Specialty Feed Products, Ada, Minnesota.

9.3 Hay

"We don't draw horses (take away the hay and water on raceday). We try to give 'em all the hay. If the feed company that's supplying the track has eight varieties of hay, we use all eight. We have confined the horse and taken away the liberty to have free choice in its feed. If a horse is turned out in its natural environment, it can pick and choose. We can't give him that option, so we try to compensate."

"You make different hays available to them?"

"You bet. We change the hays up all the time. We're merely trying to get as much roughage in them as we can."

9.4 Cut green grass or grazing.

No cut grass is brought to the stables. However, a lot of Wayne's press interviews in the lead-up to the Kentucky Derby each year took place while he was grazing his candidates. After his wedding in 1984 he left to get back and 'graze those fillies' - which were candidates for the Derby.

Wayne's attitude is simple. He told Ann Boughton from the Oklahoma Thoroughbred Racing Fans Society, "It's not the nutrition," he said, watching Family Style drop her head to graze, "We could do more for her nutritional well-being in the stall. But we think the afternoon out, letting her sun on a sunny day . . . will relax her and get the tension out." Family Style was getting ready to run in the Kentucky Derby week of 1986.

9.5 What additives does he use?

"Do you have an additive that has vitamin A and D in it? It's probably in that general vitamin supplement."

"Yes, we do."

"I'm interested in iron because the Quarter Horse people tend to use a fair bit of it."

"We don't inject. Everything we do is always in a feed supplement. We keep it very natural. We do very little. Our vet bills are absolutely minimal. We usually put some multiple vitamin in the feed and that's it. Nothing special."

"Did you find that Quarter Horses have a greater need for iron than Thoroughbreds?"

"No, I don't think that at all."

"The reason I ask is that there seems to be a trend. Generalizing a bit, Thoroughbred trainers use more iron than harness horse trainers, and there seems to be even more of an emphasis among some of the Quarter Horse people I've talked to. I thought I'd ask you because you have worked with both."

"Maybe they are right. Maybe it's something to look into. I don't think I used iron when I was in Quarter Horses, to that degree"

"In Australia, I know the Thoroughbred trainers use a lot more iron than the Standardbred trainers. I wonder if that's some physiological difference, because Thoroughbreds generally have a higher red cell count than Standardbreds."

"I think the red cell count, in a blood-test on a Quarter Horse, should be higher than a Thoroughbred horse, for that explosive action."

"Interesting. There probably is a trend there. I'll keep asking questions about that. Do you use electrolytes?"

"Use them all the time."

"Did you find there was a difference between Quarter Horses and Thoroughbreds in the need for electrolytes?"

"Yes. Definitely more in Thoroughbreds. More dehydration, more body fluid loss. We always use electrolytes. That's one of the things we try to do, put the body fluid back."

"We have in Australia a thing called a saline drench, which you hardly use in America. It is a mixture of various salts in water. They use a stomach tube to run it in. Do you do that?"

"No. IV (intravenous), or in the drinking water. We use a jug, an electrolyte jug - we jug 'em IV - and we give it in their drinking water all the time."

"And do you have any particular mix that you use for that?"

"No. Just a commercial mix. What is on the shelf. We don't get too caught up in it. Whatever's there."

"Do you have much of a problem with tying up?"

"Literally none. I would say we have a horse with it occasionally, but of the number of horses we deal with, I would say that it's less than one half of 1%."

VITAMIN AND MINERAL SUPPLEMENTS

Clovite in each feed. Fort Dodge Labs, Fort Dodge, Iowa.

707 - a lot of containers. John Ewing Co., LaSalle, Colorado.

Equine X Power Formula, Equine Enterprises, Beverley Hills, California.

Wayne features in a number of endorsements of this product:

"I've been using Equine X-2 Power Formula for four years and have found it is state-of-the-art in equine nutrition. It is palatable . . . my horses like it . . . The horse's blood counts increase and maintain at a high level. The horse's coats have more sheen and their stamina has been increased. There is no doubt that for a high quality supplement you have the lowest per day cost per horse on the market . . ."

"They all appear to be more alert . . ."

"I've been using Equine X-2 Power Formula for almost five years and have concluded it is the state of the art in equine nutrition. I recommend this vitamin-mineral supplement to all trainers and horsemen."

The number of dark green plastic buckets indicates that Wayne certainly does use a lot of this product. Perhaps he buys it because the the buckets are the same green as his stable colors. It contains vitamins, minerals and amino acids in an alfalfa (lucerne) powder base.

Supreme by Vitaflex NY. Sample?

Calf Manna, Manna Pro, Inglewood, California.

ELECTROLYTES

Race trace mineral salt. They get a little bit of that.

Apple A Day Electrolyte, Finish Line, Prospect Hts Illinois.

Applelytes, made by Grade 1

MISCELLANEOUS FEEDS

Corn Oil, Mazola brand

Carrots

FOOT AND LEG TREATMENTS

Antiphlogistine, Colorado Chemical, Moanachie, NJ.

BAL - Brace Antiseptic Linament - lots, Zirin Labs.

Absorbine, WF Young, Ontario, Canada.

70% Isopropyl Alcohol

Bickmore Super H Poultice

Vita-Hoof - Wayne has appeared in ads: "We get a good, safe, flexible foot that stands up to a lot of hard racing. It really works!"

Baby Oil, Johnson and Johnson

Tuttle's Elexer - a liniment containing ox gall, pure grain alcohol, and essential oils. Rubbed in or added to water as a body wash.

Furazone - antibiotic

OTHER

Listerine Mouth Wash

Red Pepper Rosebud - to put on bandages to discourage chewing.

Buchu Leaves - Kiaran McLaughlin said they were a digestive aid.

SHAMPOOS

Wayne had an amazing array of shampoos, to get the horses gleaming and glowing, a legacy of his buying and selling days.

> **Corona Shampoo Concentrate**
> **Grade 1 Shampoo**
> **VIP 20 Iodine Shampoo**
> **Body Wash Concentrate**, Quick Products
> Others

All the shampoos, medical supplies, bandages, antiseptics etc. were set out in cupboards and shelves in very neat fashion. Labels were set out indicating where things should go, and everything was extremely clean. The cleanest and most organized stable I have ever seen.

10. His management and how he makes money

How much of Wayne's success is due to skillful management of men and money? The performance of his teams, racing in other parts of the country, is an indication of his management skills. It demonstrates the ability to choose responsible people, the ability to set up a control system that works, the ability to delegate. Wayne's teams have notched up a multitude of wins in as many as 16 states in a given year.

Wayne's task as a manager is made easier by his proven ability to pick top horses. Good horses make his assistant trainers look good. It brings in money and raises staff morale. How good would his management be if his horses were not always winning races? From my observations his management is superb, but it would be interesting to compare Jack Van Berg's situation in the 1970's. Jack ran teams that were predominantly claiming horses, right across the country. Running a claiming team by remote control would have to be the ultimate management challenge.

Wayne's management approach was first brought into focus by Sports Illustrated writer Bill Nack. His thoroughly researched article made the muddy waters much clearer. The 'mystery' of Wayne's success became much less of a mystery. He was clearly a top notch manager who would be at home in

When I went to photograph the feed room, this employee suddenly appeared and began to sweep vigorously - employee pride. On the left, almost totally obscured, is the wall chart that tells employees how much to feed each horse. Below that on the left are yellow bins with a variety of grains. What comes in those green buckets? Equine X Power Formula.

charge of the workers or in the boardroom of any top company.

10.1 Wayne's business philosophy

Lukas has a definite interest in management. He has no doubt read some of the business bibles. How would he stand up under the scrutiny of a business management analysis? In a study of the top American corporations, business writers Tom Peters and Robert Waterman found certain attributes in common among those corporations. They listed eight in their bestseller *In Search of Excellence* which is now on the bookshelves of every aspiring entrepreneur and manager. Let us examine Wayne's outfit under those eight hallmarks of excellence.

1) A bias for action - as opposed to indecisiveness or paralysis by analysis. Wayne is a doer, seldom still, never indecisive.

2) They are close to the customers. They find out what the customer wants. Wayne talks to his owners frequently.

3) Autonomy and entrepreneurship. Leaders are encouraged. Team Lukas has respected assistant trainers, with some autonomy. They are clearly not paralyzed, waiting for instructions.

4) Productivity through people. Every individual is respected and motivated. The lowest levels of Wayne's workers are very motivated and work very hard.

5) Hands on, value driven. Wayne Lukas visits all parts of his empire regularly, but the outstanding feature is intense phone contact. Goals and objectives are set - be the best.

6) Stick to the knitting. Stick with the business you are good at. Wayne doesn't move out of horses.

7) Simple form, lean staff. Avoid complex command structures. Wayne has three levels at most. He deals mainly with assistant trainers and an office manager, who deal with everyone below them. Under the assistant trainer there is sometimes a Mexi-

can foreman who helps manage the Mexican workers, which makes four levels. But when Wayne is around, all levels get their orders (and their hands on example) from him.

8) Simultaneous centralized and decentralized properties. The top companies are fanatical about having common *values* throughout the organization, but allow the *decisions* to be made without head office permission. Wayne's assistants know what the guiding philosophy is and can make decisions within those guidelines. Son Jeff and Kiaran McLaughlin both spent over a year under Wayne's direct tutelage before they were sent off to control branches of the empire.

The cupboards were a picture of organization. The number of different shampoos was astounding.

The feed room board at the Hollywood Park stables. The horses are grouped by grooms. The feed board at the New York stables was similar, with notes like - no vitamins, no carrots, no Clovite. Simple, effective organization that does not rely on anyone's memory.

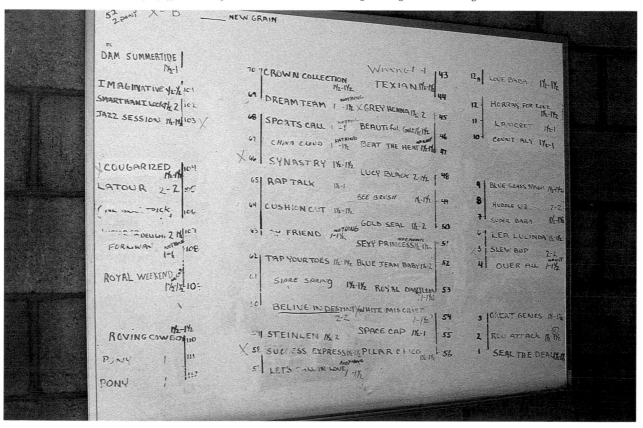

D. WAYNE LUKAS

Lukas has no doubt read *In Search of Excellence*, or books like it. Many of it's findings, e.g. stick to the knitting, pep talks and motivational sayings, have been around for many years. Some were used by Lukas in his basketball coaching days. His idol, football coach Vince Lombardi, was a motivational coach. Wayne told a reporter from the *Milwaukee Journal* that after he met Lombardi, the man became a personal hero: "He stood for principles that I respect. I saw what he was trying to do in motivating his team and striving to be the best, and I have tried to apply that in my own life and work."

Lukas used to tell his basketballers: "Just because you win doesn't make you a winner; just because you lose doesn't make you a poor person. It's how you prepare and dedicate yourself, how much you improve."

But it is hard to see how he can use pep talks effectively with an almost entirely Mexican stable crew at Santa Anita, because many of them cannot understand English. How well can Wayne speak Mexican? One day Wayne was speaking Mexican, and he could not get through to a new employee that he was to, 'go now (11am) and be back at 3pm,' eventually asking another Mexican to explain it to the fellow. Maybe it was just a problem with a dialect, but trainer John Gosden, for example, seems to have made a better job of learning Mexican. Maybe the Mexicans who can speak English translate for their fellow Mexicans.

Whatever way he does it, Wayne says he constantly talks to his staff to motivate them. Observing them around his stables, his employees work hard and work happily. There is very little bickering and needling among them. Their numbers and energy are reminiscent of bees in a hive. There is very little standing around and chatting in Wayne's barn, least of all by Wayne.

That doesn't mean the workers are afraid of Wayne. Most show a healthy but relaxed respect, a few joking with him in spite of his usually preoccupied, serious state of mind. It seems to take a second or two for the joke to register, he smiles briefly, then the serious face returns. Nothing distracts him long from the job in hand.

On several occasions, individuals amongst Lukas's Mexican shedrow workers cornered me to tell me what a 'great' or 'wonderful' man Lukas was. They were convinced that if they work hard, they too can one day make something of themselves. Clearly he DOES get the message through. Cynics might consider that verbal motivation comes cheap, but Lukas puts his money where his mouth is with a profit sharing scheme. With the level of success he has had, there has been a lot of profit to share.

In trying to raise morale and spread the credit, Lukas has gone for the outfit title of Team Lukas. It seems to be the trend, like Team Nordin in the Standardbreds, another father and son success story. Obviously he prefers it to D. Wayne Lukas, Son & Co.

If anyone asks the reasons for his success, Wayne is quick to give the credit to his assistants and his client. When he received his first Eclipse award he said he wished there were three so he could give one each to Jeff and Laura Cotter, his stable manager at the time. The praise is often for attributes that are useful to the team's success. Don't just say what a good fellow the employee is: praise the laborer for hard work, the skilled worker for skill and the manager for good management.

"We've got young, aggressive assistants who aren't afraid to work. We've also been extremely blessed with clients who have backed us on our decisions, both in the sales ring and in where we want to run their horses." Classic corporate managerial stuff. It is logical and it works.

Whenever he spoke of the training center at Rancho Santa Fe, Wayne spoke of how much control he had. He could select and control everything from the track surface, the pop-up sprinklers along the inside rail of the turf track, and the hay bedding, all the way through to the people. This is not someone afraid of work. This is a perfectionist for whom no detail is too small and yet who has the time for it all.

One of the ways Wayne makes time is at the expense of time spent socializing with other trainers. This does however foster an element of separateness and secrecy that is grist to the mill of those who say Wayne uses drugs.

Veterinarian Dr Greg Ferraro had this to say about Wayne's philosophy: "He and Charlie [Whittingham] have the same thing in common, in the sense that they're extremely dedicated; that's the only thing they think about. Other than that, they're probably as opposite as two people can be. They both like horses and they're both good trainers, but their style is totally different."

"Charlie is the old style, consummate horse trainer. He's the quiet guy you have in mind when you think about what a trainer was like in old stories about horses."

"Wayne is more a professional businessman. He's a good horse trainer too, but he runs a very efficient operation, he ships horses all over the country, he's on top of it. He runs it more as a business, whereas Charlie - his attitude might be to make the consummate individual. That's maybe Charlie's goal: to train the best horse that could ever be developed, or to try and beat a better horse with a lesser horse, as a trainer."

"I think Wayne's concept probably would be to have as many horses as possible, be as successful as he can, have his owners be as successful as they can in terms of the numbers of winners, the pleasure of winning a lot of races, and be financially successful. So that at the end of the year, he's made them a profit and he's given them a lot of enjoyment. He looks at the whole picture, total investment, where Charlie probably looks at the individual horse. It's just a different perspective."

10.1-1 Ownership of horses and premises

Wayne owns some horses outright and a share of many others as a deliberate policy. Premises are a different story. In America all horses in active racing are stabled on the track, with few exceptions. The tracks are privately owned and the track owns the stables. There is usually no charge but usually there are not as many stalls as the trainer wants. Wayne rented his main off-track training center, which was owned by Eugene Klein. When that was sold in 1990 he moved his horses to the ranch in Oklahoma.

10.2 Personality and management style

Wayne lives by his own hard taskmaster's precepts. He leads by example and is indeed an outstanding example of 'The American Dream'. That Dream is to find fame and fortune by hard work. None of his staff works harder than he does. Wayne has a pre-occupied, intense expression on his face which is quite forbidding at times, but in spite of this, his workers are not afraid of him.

Wayne delegates, but at the same time maintains close watch on his empire by frequent visits. He has a say in everyday decisions because all his lieutenants MUST make contact with him twice a day. He may phone them or vice versa. The first call is early in the morning to report all OK and check on the works for the horses. The second is after the afternoon's racing to let him know how any runners performed.

Some of Wayne's offices had a wall sign headed;

THE TRAINER'S DAILY DOZEN
The value of time.
The success of perseverance.
The pleasure of working.
The dignity of simplicity.
The worth of character.
The power of kindness.
The influence of example.
The obligation of duty.
The wisdom of economy.
The virtue of patience.
The improvement of talent.
The joy of originating.

Businesses, like suppliers, that deal with Wayne's stables are always impressed with the efficiency and organization. They don't want to be quoted because other trainers may be offended. A typical example was vet Brad Brown, who has dealt with Lukas stables at a number of tracks around the country.

"They are very business-like. Everyone at the stable knows what is happening, and what is supposed to happen. They always know which horse has to have an Xray, or whatever.

Their stables are so organized it is a pleasure to work with them. You send the bill in to their headquarters, and you get a check - in a day - it seems. I guess it's return mail. They are the best pay in the world."

10.3 Staff selection and delegation

Wayne chooses key staff and delegates authority well, as his success with scattered training divisions shows. While he pays attention to every little detail, nearly every little job is delegated, particularly the routine ones. For example, in 1981 his stable manager Laura Cotter handled a lot of things. On the social side, she arranged the clients' hotel reservations, airplane tickets, and owners' licenses. On the stable side, she organized registration papers, health certificates and identification tattoos for the horses, as well as ordering stable supplies. (Women are rare in the Lukas stables. Some years back Wayne told a reporter that he respects women grooms and exercise girls, but he won't hire them for fear an employee romance would interfere with work.)

At that time Jeff's responsibilities, under his father's direction, were to learn as much as possible, as fast as possible, about the training. He was also looking after legs and leg treatments, checking the feeds, and having the right horse, in the right gear, at the right time, in the mounting paddock. Jeff was also in charge of the personnel. This left Wayne relatively free of hassles, free to concentrate on the horses in their morning training, free to spend time with owners (and potential owners) in the Turf Club in the afternoons.

Wayne delegates, and he gives praise readily, but he also gives pretty good bonuses. This has kept talented people working for him who could easily have gone out on their own, such as Kiaran McLaughlin. McLaughlin is highly respected in the east but has stayed with Wayne.

Wayne is on record saying that enthusiasm is the main requisite, that it is more important than experience. "If they don't have that we just get rid of them. Doom and gloom mumbling makes for doom and gloom mumbling grumbling horses. We give them everything they need to work with except excuses."

Wayne has no doubt read company organization manuals and studies that say a company should weed out those who do not subscribe to the company's aims, beliefs and mythology.

Another article said Lukas looks for two important qualities in those he hires as assistants. "First, they have to have a high level of ambition. They can't be afraid to work. They'd better be excited. Second, they have to have blind faith. They have to totally believe that this is the best way to win races. They're brainwashed into my system. They can't revert to what they think is best. You can't be afraid to work. If you don't put in an eighteen hour day, you don't want to be around me. I don't want you around me. They have to work a year under me before they'll go out on their own. I tell all my new help, 'Don't buy a new set of clothes because you'll be a size smaller

Total 52   To Track 51

                    July 4th. Mon

WALKS · 18   GALLOPS 22

★ ANX. FRIEND   BLUE JEAN BABY   5
★ BEAT THE BEAT   CROWN COLLECT   5
★ BEAUTIFUL GOLD Jug+V   ★ CUSHION CNT   2
★ BLUE GRASS MAGIC   ★ FORLIWAN
  GREY NEVVA   / GOLD SEAL   3
  JUDDLE UP   GREAT GENE'S   5
★ JAZZ SESSION   ★ HOORAY / LOVE
  LA. TOUR   ★ IMAGNOTIVE
★ PILAR CHICO   LANCRET   4
★ ROYAL WEEKEND   /   LER LUCINDA   3
★ SEAL THE DEAL   /   LET'S FALL LOVE   3
★ SEXY PRINCESS CK/VET   LOVE BABA   4
  SMART / LOOK   ★   RED ATTACK   2
★ WHITE MISCHIEF²   ★   SIFE SPRINGS   2
★ WINNING   ★   SCEW BOP
  WONDER'S DELITE Jug+V /   SPORTSCALL   9
★ CONGARIZED Jug+V (SCOPE) ★ SUCCESS EXPRESS   2
★ OVER ALL   /   SUPER BABA   3
                             TAP / TOES   5
  IN TODAY. 5   ★   TEVIAN   2
                             SPACE CUP   4
★ STEINLEN — OK   /   COUNT ALY.   3
★ SYNASTRY. 5L
★ ROVING COWBOY OK   JOGS. 2

  GATE— BREEZE 1   LUCY BLACK   4
                             ONE SLICK TRICK 4

  RAP. TALK. ¼   WORKS · 6
              ★ SUMMER TIDE ½   ★ BEE ARISH ½
              ★ CHINA CLOUD 5/8 ★ BELIEVE IN DESTINY ½
              / DREAM TEAM 4½   ★ ROYAL DAN 5/8

The day's main activities are all boiled down to one sheet of paper. The numbers are added up to ensure no horse is forgotten.

in thirty days." Another time he said, "We hired on a few that were fat, but they didn't stay fat."

From what I saw around Wayne's stables, the work load and pace would weed out a lot of less dedicated souls.

Wayne says a lot of people can train but they can't teach, and he thinks that teaching your staff is important. "We're highly organised," he said. "If we've done one thing right, it's that. It's a neat, tidy, military operation. No nonsense. Businesslike. It's the same at every stable we have at any track. Each one is a mirror of the others. You don't see any coffee pots, no radiators, no one sitting down, sitting around reading the *Daily Racing Form*. Everyone knows that they do the job that's expected of them, or they're gone. It's a black and white operation. I'm there to make sure it's done right."

I found it interesting that a number of ex-Lukas employees that I met considered him the best boss they'd ever had. They said he paid well and was very fair. They would work for him again if the opportunity arose. They had left because of seasonal closures or shifts to cities they didn't want to go to.

Out of town assistants check in constantly. They call to plan the training regime. They call to go over what happened in the morning's training, and they check in again after their day's racing has finished. "And that's the minimum," Lukas said. "I want to keep on top of everything. I don't want any surprises. I want everything that's done with a horse to come across my desk. I don't want them to say, 'Oh, he was flying all night and he's in a bad mood. Let's not tell him about this until tomorrow.' I don't want anything shielded from me. It's better to die small than shield something from me."

Kiaran McLaughlin, in 1990, had been with Wayne for five years. He was working for a trainer in Chicago when Wayne stabled a visiting stakes horse there. "I told him I had started walking horses for $85 a week and I was working my way up." Some time later Wayne came again with Tiltalating, and Kiaran again inquired about a position in Wayne's stables. Wayne told him to keep in touch, and four months later he got a call. He packed up and drove to California. After a year of intensive learning he was sent off to New York.

"They all call Wayne a teacher and a basketball coach, instead of a trainer, but that is part of what makes him what he is. He IS a great teacher, a great coach and a great horseman. He teaches you. He has an answer for everything. When I am running things, I make my own decisions because I know what to do. If I don't know, if I am having trouble with something, I just ask Wayne and he has an answer."

"You feel confident you know what Wayne would do? Do you think, 'What would Wayne do?' when you are making decisions?"

"Yes, I do."

"How does Wayne motivate the Mexicans when so many of them don't seem to understand English? Does he give them pep talks?"

"No he doesn't give them talks. He talks every day to the assistants and the riders. The others . . . they just are affected by his example. The Mexican people, we find, are very disciplined, very honest, very correct, they want to do right. They have relatives back home in Mexico. They send them money. They don't go out at night, they don't drink. They are very, very disciplined."

"Wayne has about the only time clocks I have ever seen in a stable. Why does he have those?"

"They were put there because there was a problem with people saying we were not paying them properly. That can cause trouble with the INS (Immigration and Naturalization Service). After forty hours they have to get time and a half and double time. The clocks were put in to solve that problem, because we want to do everything right. David Burrage had more to do with that. But they are very well paid, and they share in 1% of all prizemoney. That was $170,000 or so last year."

I asked Kiaran if he planned on setting up on his own as a trainer. He told me he is so well paid and so hassle free - not having to pay all those wage and feed bills - that he intends to stay working for Wayne. "If I started training, my income would go way down."

"Wayne pays well?"

"Very well."

10.4 Training arrangements

Wayne told me, "We don't train for anybody that we don't like. We judge the people. We don't care what the horse is like."

"How many clients do you have?"

"Nineteen. Maybe don't have that many."

10.4-1 Training rates

"How much do you charge per horse per day?"

"Sixty five dollars per day with no add-ons. The owners can work out their monthly bill easily. Take 65 times 30 days or whatever. Taking them to the gate, shoeing, vet bills - all that is included. The veterinarians would starve to death if they had to rely on my barn. We average out at something like 19 dollars per horse per month."

"What if they develop a colic?"

"Well *then* they get a vet bill."

How does this day rate compare with other American trainers? Two years earlier, in 1987, Louis DeFichy had canvassed New York trainers for an article in the Blood-Horse. He found a range from $65 to $100 per day. Trainers charging $60 were considered lucky to break even. Woody Stephens recommended $65 or more, and never less. Grooms were paid $250 to $275 a week, hotwalkers $150, exercise riders $350 to $400, foremen and assistant trainers $400 to $500.

Obviously Wayne was not aiming to make his money on the daily training fee. Kiaran believed Wayne might not be breaking even, at least in New York. In 1990 Wayne raised his daily rate to $75, still on the low end. For their money Wayne's clients get a high staff to horse ratio. At Santa Anita when he had 34 horses he had 14 hot walkers (people who walk horses for twenty minutes to one hour after exercise, often paid per horse), 13 grooms, five exercise riders and a management team. That team consisted of an assistant, a foreman and a roving trouble-shooter.

10.4-2 Debt collection

Wayne said that the small number, and careful selection of his clients meant there was no debt problem.

10.5 Investments outside racing

As far as I can see Wayne pours his money back into owning horses, particularly colts. I asked David Burrage if Wayne invests in anything outside racing, and the answer was no. Wayne clearly believes he can make a profit buying and racing horses, and the two analyses of his record back that view. From an owner's point of view, he backs his yearling selections with his own money.

10.6 What is Wayne worth?

There is no hard information on Wayne's net worth. He likes to project an image as a wealthy, successful man. One day he wore a gold watch with what looked like about 45 or so diamonds around the face. Shari has a matching watch but with a smaller face - only has about 30 diamonds on it! In the shops these matching his-n-hers Rolex watches cost around $30,000 for the pair.

Wayne is reported to have homes in San Diego and New York as well as the one in Arcadia, near Santa Anita racetrack. At one time at least he had a Rolls Royce and two Mercedes. He was also part-owner of a helicopter with Gene Klein. Now he leases a small plane. He presumably owns his home in Arcadia, the house in New York, and the farm in Norman, Oklahoma, but then again he just might have mortgages to enable him to buy more horses.

What he owns in racehorses, stallion shares and broodmares would be anybody's guess but my guess is that it must be worth over ten million dollars. In mid 1990 Wayne had interests in over 100 horses in training, 65 mares and foals, and about 30 yearlings for which he had just paid $11m - mostly from Keeneland's Select Sales. Added to these are his stallion interests.

How does that compare with Wayne's earlier career ambition, basketball coaching? Top basketball coaches can earn big money, of the order of a million a year, but they are at the mercy of fickle team owners and fans.

Wayne earns the same money and can't be sacked. Most basketball coaches have their first heart attack at 50 some-

thing, and are retired by 60. Trainers like Woody Stephens and Charlie Whittingham have gone from strength to strength in their 50's and 60's. I doubt if Wayne feels he missed the boat, except that basketball coaches are known to perhaps ten times as many Americans as horse trainers are.

10.7 How did he make his money?

We have seen that Wayne would not make much profit from his daily charges. His 10% of prizemoney in Thoroughbreds passed $10m in May 1990. Does Wayne have any other income, and how does he invest his income?

In 1981 he was reported to be on a retainer to three of his owners, in their Quarter Horse business. In addition, said the article, he markets their foals through the Heritage Sales Company, of which he is part owner. When I asked Wayne's manager David Burrage about this, he said that Wayne and Mel Hatley had been part owners, but had sold their interest.

Wayne owns part of some very useful breeding stallions and mares, and shares in many racehorses. It is the custom that the trainer of a racehorse that becomes a stallion receives an annual service to that stallion as long as it is at stud.

"Looking at trainers, the ones that have done the best financially are the ones that have been able to make stallions and own a big share in them. Is that something that you've had a good look at?"

"I think that the icing on the cake for a trainer is that if you can survive this business, and develop-"

"Are you feeling the strain?"

"No not really, but I think it is a survival-type business because there are many many knocks and very few wins in it. If you can last and become a survivor in the business over a number of years AND be lucky enough to develop a number of sires, even at a moderate level, it has a mushrooming effect. Those seasons accumulate and at some time in your career you should be able to sit back and say, 'I've got 6 or 8 or 10 sires working for me out there. I have a breeding right to each one and that is X amount of income.' You're not going to make it on day money, training horses, and I doubt seriously if anybody is going to make any more than a living out of the 10% of the purses, even the way Lukas is running at $18 million."

"You have an amazing idea of a LIVING by some people's standards!"

"I don't know where the $1.8 million that we have collected in 10 percents goes but I know it's not around. I don't know what the hell happens. So I think there are two chances for a trainer to make a certain amount of wealth in the industry and that is a) to develop a number of nice sires where those stud fees are going to accumulate and be very profitable and b) if you really believe in yourself, you have to take a financial interest in every horse you train. I've taken both of these positions."

"You own a part of every horse you train?"

"Almost, almost. Not all of them. But I own a substantial portion of almost every horse I train now. Of course it takes a long time to work yourself into that financial position. If you are not able to do that you can take it to a different level. The ones that you really believe in, if you are able to, you say well I'll take 25%. That's what's happened to me with Pancho Villa, Capote, Saratoga Six, Tank's Prospect and Mount Livermore - all those horses I had substantial pieces of."

"So your retirement benefit is building up."

"Oh sure. Not only did I get a breeding right as a trainer, but like Saratoga Six - I think I had eight shares of him also. At $75,000 apiece that is sizable income. A guy could stop right there and say, 'That's enough I'll just go along on that.' But of course that's not our style."

Wayne's income from stud fees is large and growing every year. The growth is mainly due to added stallion numbers. Overall, stud fees in Kentucky have been falling for the last 5 years, but some of Wayne's have risen. In 1987, single seasons to Pancho Villa were traded at $25,000, in 1990 at $30,000.

The list is not complete, because many lesser sires are not advertised in *The Blood-Horse Sire Book*. It is not known if Wayne still has his trainer's breeding right to all these sires, because a lot of trading goes on: Sometimes the horses are sold and the trainer takes a part of the sale price. The trainer may sell the annual right each year, or the trainer may sell the 'share' ie all future annual services, on the open market. Below are the service fees for some stallions Wayne raced.

Service fees for 1990 live foal

Badger Land	$7,500
Capote	$35,000
Codex	dead
Gulch	$50,000
Marfa	$10,000
Mt Livermore	$20,000
Muttering	$2,500
Pancho Villa	$30,000
Roo Art	$5,000
Saratoga Six	$30,000
Slew City Slew	$12,500
Stalwart	$15,000
Success Express	sold to Australia
Synastry	$2,000
Talinum	$15,000
Tank's Prospect	$10,000
Tejano	$7,500
War	$2,500
	$254,500

Note: Gulch was trained by Leroy Jolley for part of his career and I presume he shares the trainer's annual breeding right, but owner Peter Brant may have given them one each.

Wayne's annual income from his trainer's gratuities, if he has kept them all, can only be estimated. The gross would be around $150,000 because only about 60 to 70% of mated mares produce a live foal. Then there is the fee the stud charges to agist the stallion and mate the mares. Advertising is an expensive part of sire management. There are discounts for early payment on some sire's stud fees, and of course there are bad debts. So at a guess Wayne's annual income from his trainer's breeding right would be around $100,000. It would vary a great deal depending upon which sires produced a live foal that year. If the service cannot be sold, Wayne has enough brood mare interests to make use of it.

In addition , Wayne often owns a sizable share in the horse besides the trainer's single share gratuity. That's where Wayne invests his money. After the 1988 Kentucky Oaks, Wayne said he owned 22 shares in Marfa. Marfa has been fully booked for a number of years. Wayne would make $220,000 per year, less about 1/3 for barren mares and less some management and agistment fee. The profit to Wayne would be over $100,000 per year from Marfa.

One of the nice things about stallion income is that it goes on year after year. Some stallions do die young, but a few serve mares until 25 years of age. Most sires are active for 10 to 15 years. Codex died young, after siring Badger Land and Lost Code. Lost Code, winner of four Derbys lifted Codex into the top twenty on the general sires list, a bonanza if he'd lived. Most of the top ten in the general sires' list have service fees of $100,000 to $300,000. Mr Prospector seasons sold at $250,000 for 1990, with no live foal guarantee. The ultimate is to train a stallion like Northern Dancer, as Horatio Luro did. A single share in him was worth around $750,000 *per year* in the early 1980's.

None of Wayne's stallions were in the *The Blood-Horse* 1989 Leading Sires List, which came out early in 1990, and lists the top 65 sires. Not surprisingly Wayne's best showing was in the Sires of two-year-old's list. Mt Livermore was 28th and Marfa at 55th. Ironically, Mt Livermore did not have any starts at two.

It is interesting to imagine what Wayne's income might be if he had the same success with colts as he has had with fillies. He would have four times as many stallions at stud, and of a higher class, if his ratio of Eclipse Award winners is any guide.

In 1989 Wayne bought quite a few offspring of stallions he had raced. That may be because he liked those sires as racehorses, because their offspring are like their sire and therefore a type he likes, or because he wants to help raise the average price of yearlings by these stallions. He may also feel he will do the best job of making those yearlings add to the sire's produce record. Probably a bit of all four, but I have no doubt that they have to look like racehorses first of all.

In addition to service fees, Wayne might receive a cut for buying horses. Joe Bagan, in his book, added an 'assumed 5%' for commision on purchases - a cool $4.89m. It may be that like some trainers, Wayne doesn't charge for a horse bought to race in his stable. He might receive a percentage of the sale price of any horse he sells out of the stable, but again in Joe Bagan's book, he says the Lukas organisation said there were no fees on sales, except for 2.5% on sales at the Night of the Stars Sale. Traditionally, the trainer is paid part of the sale price if he finds the buyer or negotiates the sale.

Wayne's Quarter Horse connections give him an extra outlet for his horse sales, because Thoroughbreds are often bred into the Quarter Horses. It is not just a way to unload speedy squibs, horses with no market value on the Thoroughbred scene. For example a Grade 1 multiple stakes winner of $442,588 - Total Departure - wound up at stud at Flag Is Up Farms. Total Departure was advertised in *The Quarter Racing Journal* at an introductory fee of $3,500 and a guaranteed maximum booking of 80 mares.

Wayne's comments on the horse as publicized by the stud were: "He's probably the fastest horse we've had in a long, long time . . . he's genuine, loves to run . . . that's really a sign of a good sire . . . as good a speed horse as I've ever been associated with, Quarter Horse or Thoroughbred . . . I think Total Departure is a can't miss sire of both speed and conformation."

Wayne's recommendations would doubtless carry a lot of weight in the Quarter Horse world. Monty Roberts, at Flag Is Up Farms, says Total Departure has done well, but primarily as a Thoroughbred sire. He has stakes winners.

In summary, it can be seen that Wayne makes hundreds of thousands a year from his stallion interests. His huge turnover in horses must make him some tidy profits from sales at career end. From his daily training rate it would seem there is not much profit, although the Quarter Horse trainers make do with a lot less. His income from the standard 10% of purse winnings in the 10 years 1979 through 1988 would have averaged out at $785,013 per year. For the three years 1987 - 1989 it would average over $1.7m per year.

The Lukas money-making strategy

Klein stated Wayne's philosophy when they sold Lady's Secret. Klein was criticized for peddling a horse that had been very good to him, like a piece of meat. Hard-nosed businessman Klein was not having any of that. His explanation makes the basic strategy very clear.

"You syndicate stallions, so why not sell the mares? The object is to get the money back so you can keep pouring it into buying the yearlings. Oh I'll breed some to race and I hope I can get lucky. But in my book the odds are much more against you when you breed your own, because you never know if you'll breed a crooked-legged foal. At the yearling sales you can see what you get."

This was expected to be a feature of Wayne's operation to the point that the Night of the Stars Sale would be an annual event. So said John Finney, president of the Fasig-Tipton sales company.

Wayne Lukas's strength is first and foremost the ability to choose the best yearlings in the sales. This ability is worth millions - if you can find a backer or backers with the money to buy numbers in a market in which Sangster, the Arabs and various other wealthy groups are competing.

These groups have advisors who specialize in picking athletic yearlings and good pedigrees. When the two qualities are present in the same individual, the bidding will be fierce. These horses at the top end of the sales prices represent the greatest money making potential.

A "cheap" athlete with a poor pedigree might only cost $100,000. It might win a million dollars, but then sell at a low price whether colt or filly. If it wins nothing it will be worth nothing, but will cost a lot to train. Compared to their numbers, very few cheap horses win a million.

A well-bred athlete might cost a million dollars and still only win a million - but then - if it is a filly it is worth millions and if it is a colt, tens of millions. The overall percentage increase in the starting stake is about the same but the chances of winning a million are much higher with these well-bred horses. Besides, the big boys like to bet in millions. Breeding income can not only be very large, it can be spread over many years and has assorted tax perks. If a well-bred horse wins nothing, it still has some stud value because it is 'well-bred', and 20%, maybe even 100% of the purchase price may be recovered.

The Lukas policy of buying yearlings, racing them and then selling them, was a radical departure from the time-proven formula of the industry's wealthy elite. Their strategy has been to keep anything that raced well, especially the mares. These were used as the nucleus of a home-breeding operation. Many, like Ogden Mills Phipps, would take great pride in having owned and bred the dam and grand-dam of one of their winners. (Ideally, Grand-daddy bred the great-great-great-great- grand-dam.)

But breeding had too many uncertainties for Wayne. Compared to HIS ability to pick winners at the yearling sales, breeding IS very uncertain. Compared to other people's abilities however, keeping winners and breeding from them was probably less risky. In fact the prevailing view was that you could not get the really good horses out of sales, because the breeders 'kept the good blood.' Wayne has shown that the breeders do not have a good enough eye to 'keep all the good ones'. Klein put it this way to Joe Hirsch of *The Daily Racing*

Form: "Purchasing from the sales permits a stable to pick and choose. Breeding your own stock is like owning an NFL football team, and doing all your drafting from one college."

As Wayne has found wealthier clients, he has been able to buy the same physical type with better pedigree. This should improve his success rate in picking stakes winners. It also forces the breeders to meet and deal with him. He has stallion connections to perhaps a dozen Kentucky studs. Naturally he wins some of them over, and he gets some of the breeder's select stock to train. The Lukas machine rolls forward gathering momentum and size like a snowball rolling down a hill. All of which should further improve his profitability and increase his dominance.

Getting credentials - black type

Wayne goes after stakes races harder than anyone else. In 1987 his horses won 22 of the 118 Grade 1 races run in North America. Stakes wins usually have a high level of prizemoney and they add a lot of breeding value to a horse. Stakes wins add to the value of its relatives for generations above, generations below - and sideways to about the second cousin twice removed. To win a stakes race, Wayne will ship a horse anywhere anytime.

Wayne gave some costs: "It's very, very expensive to ship horses - it can cost $15,000 to $20,000 to get a horse to a stakes - and shipping a horse to someone else's ball park can be very tough. Fortunately, we've had clients who have been willing to take the risks."

Chasing stakes wins was probably a factor in Wayne's decision to branch out. New York has long been considered to have more than its fair share of stakes races, certainly many more than California. (This is a result of the earlier start of racing there, but New Yorkers consider this to be a natural consequence of the superior quality of the racing in New York.)

As all trainers do, Wayne tries to match his weaker stakes candidates to the less well-known and less moneyed stakes, reserving the better horses for the top stakes races. The idea is to get the black type that indicates a stakes winner on as many horses as possible rather than a heap of it on one horse. Having large numbers of horses helps. "With our options increased, we've been able to place our horses where they fit."

He has been especially successful at winning stakes races for two-year-old's. Wayne learned how to assess and exploit precocity in the world of rapidly maturing Futurity prospects in the Quarter Horses. An example was his campaign with Sovereign Don in 1985. Lukas assessed the horse as inferior to some others in his stable. Reserving the superior performers for the classier but tougher end of the season, he hunted down some early stakes wins with Sovereign Don. By the time the other trainers began to wheel out their carefully prepared

stakes candidates, Lukas had won three stakes races and over $300,000 with Sovereign Don and had his own top candidates ready for battle. Sovereign Don went off to a stud career.

This has helped Lukas set a new annual stakes winning record. Wayne has had more stakes wins than the top stakes-winning jockey in some years, an almost unheard of phenomenon. There is an additional and very important plus in the great stakes hunt nowadays - graded stakes wins and placings earn the points for entry into the Breeders' Cup.

Did wayne use the same strategies in Quarter Horse racing?

Things are a little different in Quarter Horses. There are still many thousands of small Quarter Horse breeders who want to see a horse they raised run at the races in their own name - many more than are left in Standardbreds, let alone in the Thoroughbreds. So I suspect a smaller percentage of the annual Quarter Horse crop goes through the sale ring. Many of a trainer's horses are sent to him by breeders. Trainers have to accept or reject what these breeders offer.

Young trainers starting off took everything offered. This was probably very educational for Wayne since he would end up with all sizes and shapes, and eventually see how they ran. Trainers starting off in Thoroughbred and Standardbred racing in most parts of the world, select most if not all of their racing stock themselves or in consultation with their owners. They are therefore likely to be working with a narrower range of conformational types, making it more difficult to learn what anatomical traits beget what gaits and speeds.

Wayne also served time in claiming. All manner of horses go through a claiming trainer's hands.

So while it was educational for Wayne's eye, once he developed his eye, he needed to be where as many as possible of the horses that would race are in sales. Initially that meant shifting from New Mexico to Los Alamitos. There, fewer horses were trained by the breeder or a home town friend. It was still difficult to buy the young horses before the futurities, but after the futurities, the good horses are sent on to Los Alamitos. When Wayne went to Los Alamitos he had connections at Ruidoso Downs.

Caesar Dominguez on Wayne Lukas in Quarter Horses

"I've known Wayne Lukas, since way back, when he was in El Paso, at Sunland Park racetrack in New Mexico. That's where we met. The reason I know Wayne Lukas so well is because all our family worked for Wayne Lukas. My oldest brother was his foreman at Sunland Park. I had a lot of cousins and uncles, that were trainers, and lost their horses - they were claimed. They were getting to the age now where clients want younger trainers. They came back and they were working for Wayne Lukas. Wayne Lukas knows all my family, probably since the seventies, when he first started training."

"What was it that made him so good in Quarter Horses?"

"What drives Wayne is that Wayne tries to be number one at anything he does. He's a workaholic, for one thing. He thrives on work. He must not sleep at all because - I never worked for Wayne Lukas, but my brothers, my cousins, my uncles, everybody did - and I was always around them, and I know for a fact that he was always there. Any time you come to the barn, Wayne Lukas was there. You hear the people talk: 'He don't let us stop work, he don't let us sleep, he's always at the barn, he's always this and that.' He always had a first-class barn, which he still does. He's very clean, he's a perfectionist, and guys like that always make it big, because he wants to be perfect and he does it perfect."

"He did a lot of amazing things in Quarter Horses, didn't he?"

"He was the first man to go out to a public auction and buy a horse for $100,000, when $100,000 was never even thought of. If you bought a Quarter Horse for $10,000, you thought you were a millionaire. He was the first one that paid $100,000 and I think he was the one that made them go to $13m for that Thoroughbred ."

"So part of his thing is he'll pay big big money. What's he like with owners?"

"He had some owners like Jacob Bunn. He was probably one of his biggest owners. He was the inventor of the Bunn coffee percolator. He's dead now, but when he come to the barn, Wayne Lukas always treated him very well. Wayne, he's a man that expects a lot. He's no different to anybody that's successful, he demands and he gets."

"So what would you say was his secret in Quarter Horses? Was it his training methods, his organization, his ability to get owners, or his ability to pick horses?"

"I tell you what, with Wayne Lukas, it's all the above. He can pick horses, he can talk to owners, he can get the clients with money."

"How did he get those clients with money? Does he have any special tricks there?"

"No, I guess he's a good talker. He can talk you into anything and at the same time he's a good horseman. He knows what he's doing. In my eyes, he is Mr Thoroughbred, Mr Quarter Horse. He is the horseman of horsemen."

Why the large numbers?

Attempting to discover when Wayne started his emphasis on numbers, I started with Blane. Wayne used to send him horses from New Mexico. Blane was already at Los Alamitos when Wayne arrived there. Wayne didn't have many horses when he came to Los Alamitos, but he steadily wound up his numbers.

"When Wayne came out, he made us all get tougher. I swear I didn't want over twenty horses until he beat me one year for the trainer's title. I decided I wanted more because he had more. He made me have what I've got today."

Blane said Wayne built up his numbers in those days by claiming horses. In the claiming ranks you can get wins, but winning big money requires a better class of horse.

"How many horses do you have today Blane?"

"I keep about a hundred in training."

"I hear estimates of your number of horses anywhere up to about four or five hundred."

"Yes, they estimate it. They tell lies sometimes. We keep around a hundred in training."

I suppose the way Wayne sees it, if he can run one stable at a profit, largely because of his ability to choose outstanding horses in the sales, then why not run lots of stables? If he can recruit or train staff capable of training horses under his direction he can achieve all the business benefits of size: Better prices on bulk buys, a turnover that makes a fully staffed office, training center and trucking company pay etc.

There are some training benefits too: Wayne can send horses to cooler or warmer areas; he can send them to tracks with different soils, bends, lengths of straight; he can send bleeders and sore horses to states where medication is permitted. The overall results are larger profits.

I asked Caesar Dominguez: *"Did Wayne have huge numbers racing in his Quarter Horse days?"*

"He always had as many Quarter Horses as he's got now in Thoroughbreds. He always had a lot of horses."

"Two or three hundred?"

"Yes. He always had a lot of horses."

"To end up with so many horses - does that mean that he was less selective? Was he willing to take ANY horse?"

"No. Now, he's probably very selective, because he's got so many, but before, he wasn't. Like me now, even though I've got a lot of horses, I'm still accepting horses, but I'm selective to a point."

Wayne Lukas and Blane Schvaneveldt were fighting for the number one spot on the trainer's ladder and both went after numbers to get winners. They both went into the hundreds according to some people, but no one seems to know for certain or have accurate numbers. Wayne says he had 35 to 40 total in his Quarter Horse days. The trainer is usually speaking of the number of stalls at the track. His rival trainers tend to think of those plus any youngsters, layups, cast-offs and maybe retired horses and breeding stock.

There are people at Los Alamitos who say they remember Wayne having a lot of horses, a lot more than Wayne remembers having. It seems to me you can always expect trainer A's estimate of trainer B's horse numbers to be a multiple of the number trainer B says he has.

I asked Caesar about the branch stables: *"When Wayne was in Quarter Horses, did he get into that business where he had stables at three or four tracks, like he has with the Thoroughbreds?"*

"No. He always stayed in one place. He was in Bay Meadows or Los Alamitos, but one place at a time."

"He didn't have branches with assistant trainers and he didn't go everywhere?"

"No. He didn't start that till he got into Thoroughbreds, then he started branching out."

11. How he gets and keeps owners

The practical aim of the trainer is to get more owners, with more money, so the trainer can have more, or at least better horses. Wayne has some of the wealthiest owners in racing. Let's see how he has arrived at that point and by what means he is still climbing rapidly.

11.1 What is his public image?

In my experience there are two sub-groups in the population when it comes to opinions of Wayne Lukas:

The first group, almost everyone who has worked with him, dealt with him, interviewed him or met him for more than a few minutes, has a very high opinion of him. Totally awesome (Rhymes with Australian pronunciation of blossom) is currently a favorite expression with the American public, and Wayne can make that sort of impression on people he meets. Some have a few reservations, making statements like, 'Wayne is pretty good with the bullshit,' or, 'He can be a rude son of a gun at times,' but they all - ALL - hold him in high regard.

The second group consists of those who have not met him, or have had little to do with him. They mostly have negative views of him and his achievements. The phrases used are often the same. "He wins because he has the numbers," "the money," "the big owners," "because he uses drugs." They don't like him because he is too big, has so many stables he couldn't possibly supervise them, he breaks horses down and he's aloof, even arrogant.

Many people say Wayne has been good for the image of the game because he looks like a businessman, he's articulate, he projects a good image for racing. However, talking to the peripheral people of racing I would say they have absorbed mostly the views of the group that doesn't like him.

11.1-1 Opinion of other trainers

Many of the backstretch population had little except derogatory things to say about Wayne and were adamant that he uses drugs. Another common statement by other trainers is that Wayne can't train. One humorous anecdote that went the rounds of the tracks has Mel Stute, Laz Barrera and Charlie Whittingham in a conversation about the dreaded newboy on the block after about his third consecutive topping of the money table. Stute supposedly says, "The bastard can't train you know." Whittingham says, "Well we better hope he doesn't

damn-well learn." (I asked Charlie if this conversation actually occurred but he steered our conversation elsewhere.)

Whittingham's view of Wayne, as expressed to me, is that Wayne has paid his dues, he's in the game and he's 'one helluva a player'. Charlie knows better than to whinge in public.

Another joke the trainers like to tell about Wayne has Charlie Whittingham arriving in heaven. He's being shown around personally by St Peter, as befits a multiple winner of the Santa Anita Handicap (Remember this is a Californian view of heaven). Charlie suddenly stops in his tracks.

"There's Wayne Lukas!" exclaims Charlie.

"No it's not," says St Peter, "that's God. He just thinks he's Wayne Lukas."

The Thoroughbred trainers, in general, wish Wayne had stayed in Quarter horses, although a great many of them do not know he was at the top in Quarter Horses. The information is a surprise to them. They should be grateful he spent 10 years in that game first.

How much of their criticism is valid and how much is envy? Envy is defined as the coveting of something someone else has. Studies by Peter Salovey of Yale University have shown that you feel envy or jealousy most in those areas where you stake your own reputation and pride.

In one of his studies 82 undergraduates took part in what they thought was a study of personality and career choice. They filled out questionnaires about themselves and their career choices. They were then given a score which was said to represent their aptitude for their career, BUT some had their scores artificially raised and some had them lowered. They were then asked to evaluate the writers of some essays. Some of the essays, they were told, were written by a person who was doing well in the career they had chosen. Those given the lowered scores, who had been made to feel insecure about their aptitude for this career, gave the writer from their career choice a low mark. Neither those given low scores nor those given higher scores were prejudiced against the essayists who were in other careers. The conclusion was that the more insecure someone is about their own skills in a field related to their self esteem, the more prone to envy they will be.

Certainly in my experience, the lesser trainers were the most critical, some offering very weak or illogical arguments, but some very successful trainers also have strong feelings about Wayne. Is it envy or is it justified? After all, very few show the same feelings towards Charlie Whittingham. It is hard to argue with Wayne's training success unless he does use drugs, so we'll leave that to section 13.4.

11.1-2 Relations with the Stewards

I have never heard of Wayne having major problems with the stewards, only the occasional horse late in the saddling paddock, or incorrect gear. Pretty much the little errors that have to happen occasionally with a large organization.

11.2 How does he get publicity?

Wayne does not seem to go out of his way to court the press. Not now anyway. Many trainers will regularly buy certain press 'mates' a drink, but not Wayne. He seems to rely more on sheer results and perhaps a little unorthodoxy to get attention. When he started in Thoroughbreds at Hollywood the second time, his training and racing antics with the successful duo of Terlingua and Effervescing were very useful in bringing him to the notice of the writers and owners. They won four stakes races for him in the month of July.

Albert Yank, a bloodstock agent was a very important booster for Lukas at that time. Apart from bringing Effervescing and other horses to Wayne's door, Albert Yank was a mobile advertising billboard. He was widely known and respected in the Thoroughbred world.   "He believed in what we were trying to do . . . I can't say enough about how helpful he's been. His expertise, his contacts. He's opened doors for us, moved us up two or three years in developing our stable."

Wayne's eye-catching barns help. He carries the showiness all the way from the neat barns and 200 sports coats through to his horses. His horses usually look well fleshed with gleaming coats and white bridles. It has to impress owners and it gives the press positives to talk about. Being different is important in the publicity game. In many magazine photos Wayne is wearing sunglasses. I wondered if they were a calculated part of an image building effort. They have certainly become part of Wayne's image.

"Are those sunglasses prescription sunglasses - for an eye problem?"

"No I don't need glasses, but I live in a very sunny state and I feel more comfortable in them."

As a person who has a lot of trouble with the glare in sunny Western Australia I can understand that.

11.2-1 Wayne and the press

The regular racing press are, with a few exceptions, most impressed with Wayne and his organization, even if they personally have a soft spot for some other trainer. It is hard not to be impressed by Wayne and his organization. One journalist said to me, "I flew home with him from Keeneland one day, sitting next to him for two hours. Hell, by the end of the flight I thought he was the greatest horseman that ever lived." I did get the impression though, that some reporters are not keen to say good things about Wayne in print, because it will annoy other trainers, trainers they have to deal with every day.

As for the negative things about Wayne, wherever they come from, they are given plenty of press because journalists like to put both sides of a situation. That means they're being fair and balanced - right? It also means they can dish-up unsubstantiated tripe and spread a baseless rumor further. Controversy breeds readers, as newspaper and other publishers

well know. Saying nasty things sells more copies than saying nice things.

The 'once a year' writers who do their stuff for daily papers at Derby time or local meet time are the most likely to give Wayne a bashing. They don't have to deal with Wayne on a regular basis, and they have discovered that many of the public and the horsemen love to read something that rubbishes him. It is a natural part of the 'Tall Poppy Syndrome' - people love to see the great go-getters stumble, preferably fall down flat.

Once when filling in a questionaire that was to be used by the New York Racing Association's Press Guide, Wayne wrote under Dislikes, "Sports writers who try to train my horses."

"One of the things that I would have to say after meeting you, is that I think you're greatly misrepresented by the press. Some journalists seem to feel obliged to snipe at you, to get in a few barbs."

"We feel that way too. There was a journalist from Sports Illustrated, Bill Nack, came to me, and wanted to do a profile. I consented to do it and his idea was to stay with me for eight to ten days, right at my elbow and see everything. He lasted about two days and then he gave that up, but the bottom line was that he told me that he had come with the idea that he was going to write an exposing, critical article. On the last day, after he had spent the eight days picking his spot, and I gave him hours and hours of interview, he said, 'You have completely changed my whole way of thinking. If I had a horse, you would train it. I consider it has been an enlightening experience and I consider you a good friend.'

"He wrote the article, changed the whole format of what he was going to originally write. I think if most people would take the time to spend eight days with us, I think we can win 'em over to our program. It's the guy that won't research it and look into it, or takes the hearsay."

"Of course I have an enormous amount of confidence, and a large ego. Sometimes that's very much confused by my colleagues. My intensity is so intense that it's sometimes confused with rudeness or even being aloof. I'm not aloof at all."

"That runs through many of these trainers. Like Vincent O'Brien. He just wants to concentrate on the job."

"Now when you're intense, and when you're attuned to what you're doing, sometimes it comes off as arrogance and aloofness. I have had people write in different articles that I'm arrogant and aloof, only to get to know them later, and they will say nothing could be further from the truth."

"Yes, I found you rather forbidding, hostile even."

My experience is that Wayne is very suspicious of any press person and his feelings show in a rather fiercely disdainful facial expression. He doesn't trust them until they have shown some empathy, or at least the willingness to research and report accurately. Even then he can be abrupt if he's not in the right mood, or in a hurry.

Was the 'Woody and Wayne show' a publicity stunt?
Woody Stephens and Wayne have traded increasingly less subtle barbs, and the press has had a field day reporting it all word for word. Was this staged?

I well remember listening to Muhammed Ali reminisce about his early days in the boxing game. He was at his peak, and when Ali was at his best he was among the most intelligent and articulate people around. Ali told how he modeled himself on a wrestler known as "Gorgeous George" who dressed outrageously and said shocking things - absurd things if necessary - whatever it took to get press attention.

Poncing about with long blond hair and an elaborate red dressing gown, George would declare he was going to 'moider dis bum'. 'He's not fit to fight someone of my class.' Ali noticed that when 'Gorgeous George' wrestled, the place was packed to the rafters. Mostly the enraged fans paid in the hope they'd see George's gorgeous hair ripped out, but win lose or draw, 'Gorgeous George' went home with his share of a monster pile of gate money.

Ali became a consummate artist at stimulating controversy and increasing interest in his fights. Nowadays, nearly everyone in boxing and wrestling does it, and mostly it is a boring farce. Was the 'Woody and Wayne show' racing's attempt to enter the world of publicity by hyping a bit of verbal fisticuffs between two trainers? Well, it wasn't intentional and they are not friends behind it all, but it certainly roused some interest.

It had all the right ingredients. Woody represented New York, the wealthy, old establishment east vs. Wayne, the new, brash cowboy upstart from the west coast. There were elements of east coast vs. west coast, old vs. young, perhaps of established horsemen vs. Wayne. The feeling had grown and simmered long before the public outbreak in the 1988 Preakness.

Back in 1983 Woody had the best Alydar filly on the east coast, Miss Oceana when Lukas had the best Alydar filly on the west coast, Althea. Althea went on to be champion juvenile filly for that year. The sniping was low key.

In 1985 Klein and Lukas noted after their victory with Family Style in the $437,000 Arlington -Washington Lassie (Gr. I), that in the two previous runnings they had come second to Woody's entries, i.e.:- 1983 Woody's Miss Oceana had beaten Wayne's Life's Magic. 1984 Woody's Contredance had beaten Wayne's Tiltalating.

As late as 1986 or early 1987 Wayne told reporter Paul Haigh: "We don't have the jealousy or the feeling of animosity from everybody . . . The people that are most critical are the people that are threatened. Woody Stephens, Charlie Whit-

tingham, Laz Barrera, Mack Miller, Leroy Jolley - I never feel it from them because they are confident and secure in their profession."

In 1987, the Lukas stable set a record by winning 92 stakes races. Without Lukas in the orchard, many of those plums would have been picked by Woody. What consoled Woody was the feeling that he had the 1988 Kentucky Derby by the throat. He had won it before, the last time with Swale, and he knew what kind of horse it took. He had that kind of horse in Forty Niner. Forty Niner had won many top races in his two-year-old year. On October 30 he won the Breeders' Futurity over 1 and 1/16 miles, just like Swale did.

Woody announced that Forty Niner would pass up the Breeders' Cup Juvenile, a giant plum, because he wanted to give the son of Mr Prospector plenty of rest before he embarked on a three-year-old campaign. Wayne's Success Express carried off the Breeders' Cup Juvenile, but Forty Niner was still voted Champion Two-year-old Colt by a comfortable margin.

In early 1988 things went right along with Woody's high hopes, but the Kentucky Derby itself unfolded like a nightmare. Wayne's Winning Colors was allowed to get off to a long comfortable lead. Woody's Forty Niner surged up the straight and was cutting her lead rapidly, but failed by the smallest of margins. One or two strides past the post Forty Niner was in front, but at the post, he was second.

The Preakness is considered to be gift to a frontrunner. Woody promptly predicted that his horse would not let Winning Colors have an easy lead in the Preakness. In the race, Forty Niner dueled with Winning Colors for the lead but also held her very wide and the two bumped numerous times. The duel certainly ended the chances of both horses. There was an uproar in the crowd and in the racing press.

"I saw a lot of comment by everyone else, but I never saw any comment by you on that business in the Preakness, when Woody's horse Forty Niner held your horse (Winning Colors) out wide. I mean, you might have made comment but I never saw any."

"I didn't make any."

"You didn't make any!!!??"

"I made none. And most people noticed that too. Usually I'm very outspoken. But I didn't make any statement, because I thought everybody was going to do it for me, and that's just what happened. I made a decision when I went down to get the horse, I knew it was not going to be an unnoticed or uncontroversial race. I knew it was going to be very controversial, and I just took the position, walking back to the barn with the filly, that most of the things I would say, they're going to say for me, and that's exactly what happened."

In the turmoil and press exchanges that followed, Wayne was seen by most as the good guy wronged. Even Woody's supporters directed most of their venom at statements by Klein and the *Daily Racing Form*. Woody is one of the most-loved trainers in racing, and he copped some harsh press, even when the other guy was Wayne, arguably the least popular trainer in racing. If Wayne had sent one of his horses out to spoil Woody's chances, he might have been lynched, at least in New York.

The Woody and Wayne show was not staged. It was a result of Wayne invading Woody's territory and doing too well for Woody's liking. Both men are quick to advertise themselves, ultra-competitive, outspoken men. The rivalry became too great and the thin veneer of diplomacy was eventually worn through.

11.3 Getting owners and horses

Wayne will certainly approach potential owners just as he did Albert Yank. Albert says, "He was hustling pretty good." Many however, have been attracted from afar by his results, and from near by the impact he has in a face to face meeting. Wayne has long known the value of making a big impression and what's more he knows how to make a big impression.

One of Wayne's fellow students from his college and teaching days, told the Milwaukee Journal: "He used to dress like something out of Esquire; wore three- piece suits when the rest of us were dressing more like labourers. He got matching coats for his basketball players."

One of the journalists at Hollywood Park told me he was seated next to Wayne Lukas on a plane flight. "It was a three hour flight, and gee it was hard not to buy a horse and have it with him by the end of that flight."

Many of his clients have been with him a long time. When he went from the Quarter Horses to the Thoroughbreds, the late Mrs Ruth Crosby Bunn, Mel Hatley, Bob French and Barry Beal went too. That to me is an indication that they were well satisfied. (Bob Moore didn't. He still races Quarter Horses and told me with just a hint of sarcasm, "I guess I haven't graduated.")

What does Wayne 'sell' to his owners? His 1985 business card reads "Bring your dreams to us." In 1988, he had a presentation folder based upon the Thoroughbred Record study of his profitability (see 7.2-2). It also listed his champions. This guy can take you right to the top. Have fun in racing AND make a profit. That is a strong message.

Now Wayne says he can pick and choose his owners. They can approach him but then he checks them out. They have to have 'acceptable attitudes', which largely means accepting the main points of Wayne's business strategy.

11.3-1 Personality and social skills

Around the barn, Wayne does not have a life-of-the- party personality. I found he can be pretty grumpy, but if you are vitally interested in horses he is very interesting to be around. He is all business and you probably have to be important to his business to see the full flow of charm. I'm sure his social skills are of the highest order in that situation. You could take him home to Mum or to Buckingham Palace without worries. (You would probably find that Mum and the Queen both had horses with him a little later.)

Bill Nack was told a good tale about Wayne's epic reputation as a silver-tongued talker. The source was onetime leading Quarter Horse jockey Bobby Adair. At the stables one day, Lukas was holding forth to a bunch of owners. The blacksmith told Adair, "I hope I die the same day he does." Adair asked the blacksmith why. "Between now and when I die, no matter how bad I screw up, when we reach them pearly gates, I know that Wayne can talk the both of us in."

Many people have names for Wayne that reflect his prowess with the spoken word. Telingua's jockey, Darryl McHargue, for example, called Wayne 'Golden Tongue'.

11.3-2 Social stamina and alcohol

Wayne's name is almost synonymous with stamina. Talking does not exhaust him. Cynics will say its the training his voice gets.

"I was going to ask you about alcohol, but you say the strongest thing you drink is coffee."

"Never ever drank. Never tested a cigarette behind the barn as a kid. Don't even take an aspirin."

11.3-3 Social class of owners

Wayne's big-name owners are mainly self-made men like himself, many from out of his cowboy Quarter Horse past. He has never been fully accepted by the blue- blooded hereditary money brigade, but that does not seem to cause Wayne any lack of sleep. While there are enough self-made squillionaires around, Wayne can do without the Eastern Establishment's III's IV's and hyphenated name set. In that corner of America, a person's middle name can be more important than their christian name or their surname, signifying links to Mayflower families or great fortune-makers of the past. If Lukas ever starts picking Triple Crown winners, they'll be queuing up at his barn.

11.3-4 Does he steal owners?

Peter Brant switched his champion horse Gulch from leading trainer Leroy Jolley to Wayne but explained to the press that it was because he wanted to run his horses in different parts of the country and that he would continue to have horses with Leroy. He also said he liked Wayne's operation.

Daniel Wildenstein had his turf horses with Bobby Frankel but switched most of them to Wayne. That was presumably Wildenstein's decision. I have not heard of Wayne trying to steal horses that are already winning.

This is a typical scene on the walking machines at Hollywood Park. I never saw any near Wayne's stable. He can afford to have all his hand walked, which is less hazardous and keeps the horse calm. A selling point with owners.

11.3-5 Has Wayne ever advertised?

I have not seen any direct advertising by Wayne. He wouldn't need it at this stage of his career anyway.

11.3-6 Does he give talks?

He does give lectures to clubs and groups, sometimes in aid of charity, but at the same time exposing Lukas to potential clients. For example he was scheduled to be keynote speaker at the annual Texas Thoroughbred Breeders' Association meeting on January 25, 1986, at the La Mansion Hotel in Austin, Texas. Think of all those rich, horse-mad Texans, about to have pari-mutuel racing legalized. When pari-mutuel racing was legalized in Texas, Wayne was specifically mentioned as an important part of the campaign.

On the charity side he was due in August 1985 to be guest speaker at a benefit at Heritage Place in Oklahoma City. The proceeds were to go to capital improvements at the Rogers State College Horse and Ranch Management program.

He also gives motivational speeches to business clubs, conventions and company personnel. This can be big business in America. "I tell them what I think are the ingredients to make you a winner." Giving a talk to a banquet crowd, Lukas told them, "Dream great dreams." He also said that falling in love with your work is the magic ingredient to success.

Those who have heard him, describe his performance as very good, not an overly hard sell (by American standards) and in one word - impressive.

Wayne likes to chew the fat with old Quarter Horse buddies like Blane Schvaneveldt and likes to participate in events like a roast for his friend Bobby Adair, a Quarter Horse jockey retiring because of injury. No doubt it is a dual purpose exercise. Wayne enjoys himself, enjoys his hero status, and possibly a greater acceptance than he has had from the Thoroughbred fraternity, plus he is exposed to people who have an interest in racing horses. People who might just be thinking about making the same change from Quarter Horses to Thoroughbreds.

When I first interviewed Caesar Dominguez, I asked if he tried to get into the lecture thing. He replied that he couldn't. "They invite Wayne Lukas to give lectures BECAUSE he is Wayne Lukas."

11.3-7 Any affiliations with studs?

Soon after switching to Thoroughbreds, Wayne had a very useful connection with Tartan Farms, a Florida based stud, which sent him large numbers of yearlings at the urging of Albert Yank. It was dispersed by sale in 1987, but by 1989 he had connections with two major Lexington studs, Calumet Farm and Overbrook Farm. Overbrook is owned by a major new Lukas client, W.T.Young.

An interesting point: if Tartan had not been disbanded, the owners would in all probability have sent Unbridled, winner of the 1990 Kentucky Derby, to Wayne.

11.4 Managing owners

Wayne is not known as a highly social trainer. He doesn't do his owner management at the bar. He will eat out but he doesn't drink. On the other hand he is not a recluse dealing only over the phone. He maintains good phone contact with his owners.

He doesn't have a dictatorial manner with his clients. When Wildenstein was sending him turf horses from France, Wayne was quoted as saying that since the Europeans don't like white bridles, those horses would run in leather. It was up to Wildenstein. Kiaran McLaughlin said if Wildenstein wanted yellow bridles he was sure Wayne would get them for him. Wayne has no need of a dictatorial style. He is too good at persuading people of the logic of his plans to need that approach. He gets his way without the bossiness of TJ Smith.

11.5 Main owners

Some of Wayne's main owners have been with him for many years. Ruth Crosby Bunn, widow of Jacob Bunn, had Quarter Horses and later Thoroughbreds with Wayne, pretty well upto her death. Hatley, Beal and French go back a long way into Wayne's Quarter Horse days. French and Beal, both from Midland Texas, have been partners in Landaluce, Terlingua, Capote, Tejano, Sacahuista and many others. But the most visible, most publicized owner of the 1980's was comparative latecomer Eugene Klein.

Who was Eugene Victor Klein?

Klein was born in an unfashionable part of New York in 1920 or 1921, the youngest of six children of a Russian immigrant. By Klein's account his family were half- starved during the depression. He sold encyclopedias door to door to get himself started in night school, eventually earning enough to start electrical engineering at university.

The war intervened and Klein signed up the day after Pearl Harbor for aviation training. He flew in many parts of the world during his 4½ year stint. During the war Klein married and his wife had a baby.

When the war ended Klein settled in California, eventually starting his own used car lot. In 1951 he brought in the first Volvos. Later, with a partner, he became Volvo distributor for the Western United States. Eugene Klein was really on his way. In 1957 he sold the Volvo distribution rights for $2.6m. He was a 39 year old millionaire.

The next step was into banking in the late 1950's, from where he bought into a failing theatre chain, finally taking it over in 1961. He took it out of the red, and in a series of corporate raids transformed it into a conglomerate with assets of more that $1 billion. During this time he turned down the American rights to a rising British pop group called the Beatles.

In 1966 Klein organized a group of investors and bought the San Diego Chargers, a football team, for $10m. Klein had a 20% interest and although it was small potatoes compared with the corporate game, it was more fun. Later he bought into a basketball team as well.

In the mid 1970's Klein sold out of the conglomerate to concentrate on the football team because it was more exciting! Klein built up his original investment until he owned 53%, but by then it was no longer fun. In fact it had become a legalistic nightmare with anti-trust suits, lawsuits and drug problems. His football team was the first ever singled out and fined for a drug problem.

In 1981 Klein suffered his first heart attack while testifying in his own defense in a lawsuit. He had another during the next year's football draft round. It was not long after that he met Lukas. He moved out of football and into racing. In August 1984 he sold his $10m investment in the football team for $50m ($70m according to some).

Klein was often quoted on the difference between owning a football team and owning a racing stable: "Horses don't have agents and they don't ask for renegotiated contracts or more money or an interest- free loan."

What was Klein worth?

Eugene Klein was wealthy. Not wealthy enough to make the Forbes 400 richest in America. That required a net value of $275m. But he was very comfortable and had the trappings of big money - an art collection that included Picassos and various planes including a helicopter. However he was not all money and ego. He served on some 14 civic and charitable organizations, most of them medical - hospitals, American Cancer Society and the like.

How Klein and Lukas came together

It was towards the end of Klein's 18 year involvement with the San Diego Chargers. He had bought into the football team for the fun and excitement. He had been through the highs and the lows, but his team had not won the top prize in the game, the Lombardi Trophy for winning the Super Bowl. By the time he met Wayne, Klein's heavy involvement in the football team was giving him frustrations, headaches and heart attacks.

He was introduced to Thoroughbred racing when friends of his wife Joyce invited them to be partners in a broodmare. Klein wound up buying an interest in three but it was still Joyce's hobby. Shortly after this Joyce took Gene to Del Mar racetrack, on the southern coast of California. The track was just a few miles from their home in Rancho Santa Fe, and they went to watch a friend's horses in morning work. They ran into an old football acquaintance of Gene's, Dick Butkus, former middle line-backer for the Chicago Bears.

Butkus had a horse in training with Lukas. The group ended up at Lukas's barn, where Klein and Lukas were introduced. Gene knew enough about the scene to make small talk regarding Wayne's outstanding filly of that time (1982), Landaluce. Gene liked Wayne, gave him his phone number (Let's face it - you only give your phone number to a racehorse trainer if you really want to end up with a horse!) and told him, "When you get a chance, why don't you give me a holler."

Not surprisingly Wayne paid Gene a visit. The two hit it off. Wayne told Gene, "You'll get a fair shake from me if you want to do some business. I'm not going to cheat you. I don't need full stalls." Walking Lukas to his car after lunch, Klein was surprised to find he was driving a Rolls Royce. "I said I wasn't going to cheat you," Lukas said, "I didn't say I was going to work for nothing." Gene told Wayne, "If you've got a horse available and you think it can run, give me a call."

Lukas came up with a two-year-old filly called Cassie's Prospect by New Prospect. Klein bought her, went to watch her at her first start, but was disappointed when she ran 5th. Lukas pointed out that it was only her first start.

Next time out, January 30th 1983, Cassie's Prospect won and Klein was hooked. Here was something with thrills, highs and lows, but without the hassles of a lot of temperamental coaches and athletes. In fact Klein only had one person to deal with in his racing interest - Wayne Lukas - with whom he got on like a house on fire. Klein's words to Lukas were predictable - "If you come across any other good horses let me know."

At the March sale in 1983, Lukas bought 3 horses for Klein for $275,000.

The bug must have really bitten Klein because late in 1983 Klein took Lukas to see a barn built on a steep slope on rocky ground. Lukas advised him that the barn was OK but the ground was unsuitable for Thoroughbreds. Later Klein took Lukas to a paddock of Lima beans.

"This is just what you need."

"Good because I've already bought it."

The paddock of some 350 acres was to form the bulk of what was to become Klein's Rancho Del Rayo, Del Rayo being the Spanish term for a lightning flash. Klein has a lightning flash on his jockey's helmets and sleeves. His racing silks - gold shirt with blue sleeves - are based on the Charger's colors.

Klein bought the land parcels totaling 410 acres next to Fairbanks Ranch around 1982 and 1983 for an estimated $15m. In 1985, conservative estimates valued it at $40m. Within a few years, the subdivided lots sold off had paid for a large part of, if not the whole, of the acreage he had retained. Once a good businessman, always . . .

At about the time of the land purchases, one of Wayne's clients died, leaving a stable of ten horses for sale. Klein asked how much. Wayne gave him a price and Klein wrote out a cheque. One of them was Miss Huntington, which went on to become Klein's first stakes winner and accumulator of $794,000.

Next Lukas sold him three weanling fillies for $600,000. One died, one named Gene's Lady won nearly a million dollars and then was sold for $600,000 and the third was Lady's Secret. Lady's Secret was Horse Of The Year for 1986 and won over $3m. Klein was having a ball.

In the five years after 1983 he is said to have spent $40m on yearlings. (A trainer's wildest dreams come true, you say, such luck to find this owner! But Klein was only spending because he was making a profit. His horses won $5,743,134 in 1987, and he had large interests in the stallions Tank's Prospect, Saratoga Six, Sovereign Don and Capote.)

D. Wayne Lukas Training Center

Variously given as 100, 110 or 140 acres, the D. Wayne Lukas Training Center was designed by Wayne, built by Klein and named in honor of the trainer. It had stalls for 120 horses. The center was run for a number of years by Tom MacKenzie, who had been with Wayne for 10 years in Quarter Horses. It has a six furlong dirt track and nine furlong turf course.

It was used exclusively by horses in training with Wayne. Because the facility was not open to the public like the training track 15 miles further north in San Luis Rey, horses trained at the Rancho Santa Fe facility could not have track times clocked there. They had to go to a public track and have some public works recorded (as must all racehorses in America), before they could start in a betting race. Wayne usually sent them to the track at which they were going to race to do their recorded works. It became part of the settling in period for the horse.

When he was racing a large number of horses, Klein kept them in his own part of this beautiful development, the Del Rayo Racing Stables, set on 140 acres. Rancho Santa Fe is a select fringe-suburban area, about 20 miles north of downtown San Diego. In an area where land is expensive, Klein's horses had acres to run in. Where mechanical walkers are common, Klein's horses were walked by hand.

Klein could not lose with his real estate investment. The Del Mar Racetrack is expected to become a much more significant track with a longer season. If that didn't make the land and facilities valuable the sheer expansion of San Diego would.

Klein thrived on competition, sought "every legitimate edge," and had a team approach. He had total confidence in Wayne Lukas - and why shouldn't he? In 1985 he was quoted as follows: "Why did I buy 40 (yearlings)? Because I have total confidence in D. Wayne Lukas, who selected them and because I believe this is a business of averages. We certainly don't think all 40 of them are going to be superior runners. We would not have bought any of them however, if we did not believe they had a chance to become good runners. We feel reasonably confident we will get our share of winners from the 40."

Although few people knew it, Klein, Hatley and Lukas campaigned a Quarter Horse called Some Power Play, a son of Easy Jet. In 1986 it contested the finals of the All-American, Rainbow and Blue Ribbon Futurities. The horse earned $200,000. If it had won the All- American it would have made Eugene Klein unique, as far as I know, in being the owner of winners of the premier events of two different codes of racing.

Lukas on Klein

At the peak of their friendship, Wayne had this to say of Eugene: "If I feel there is something we need to win . . . he will get it. He does not second guess those who work for him. He does not dwell on failures or mistakes. He looks to the future."

Klein retires from the field of battle

Klein had set many owner records in a very short time and enjoyed some of the greatest highs racing has to offer. By 1988 his horses had won more than $19m and 300 races - owner records. To July 1988 he had won three Eclipse awards as owner and had six Eclipse winning horses. In 1988 he had a Kentucky Derby win. But in mid 1989 it was announced he was going to pull back and sell off a lot of his stock. He'd had two coronary bypass operations and the need for a quieter life was given as the reason. For some time his towering figure had been absent at many of his horse's victories. Rather than travel around the country to watch his runners, the canny Klein would fly to Las Vegas. There, in the air-conditioned halls of Caesar's Palace, he could bet on his horses and see them run - on the TV screens.

Not everyone believed it was Eugene's health that caused him to retire from active racing. There was speculation that it was because after the attempts to sell his best stock had gone poorly, Eugene felt the establishment was against him. (A factor in the sale prices might have been the belief that Lukas uses anabolics on his fillies. Many breeders believe anabolics ruin fillies for breeding.) Some said Klein now realized he was not going to come out ahead financially and was cutting his losses. In mid 1988 Klein's monthly bill for horses in work was $300,000. He told Pete Axthelm of The Thoroughbred Record, "We'll ship anywhere to win a good race. My shipping bill alone is over $1m a year." How much the decision was due to his health, how much to economics and other matters, only Eugene really knew.

He did say that he and his wife, "have enjoyed our experiences in racing more than I can describe. We've met a lot of wonderful people in racing and that too has enriched our lives." To another reporter he said, "If I get the urge to go racing again, all I've got to do is pick up the phone and say, 'Lukas, let's go to the yearling sales and buy some horses."

Sadly, the big man who loved to see his horses win, died early in 1990.

11.5-1 How well would Lukas have done without Klein?

Klein was a risk-taker, an action man and a very wealthy one. He was without doubt a major factor in the Lukas success story. Wayne was in contention for the Number 1 Trainer spot before Klein came on the scene, but Klein was a great publicity draw for Wayne. He was great copy for the journalists, saying very quotable things, rather than the predictable, boring diplomatic drivel so many owners come out with. He also provided millions to buy horses.

In summary Gene Klein was very helpful to Wayne's rise, and to the setting of many of his records, but Wayne would have made it to the top anyway.

11.5-2 Are Wayne's big owners winning Or losing?

Wayne uses the lure of high profits to bring him more owners. One of the sheets his manager sent out to prospective owners in 1989 showed an internal rate of return, or profit, of 37% on past performances. That calculation allowed for the cost of the yearlings and the training costs.

Notes on the reverse said the rate was calculated on a Lotus Symphony Spreadsheet, an accounting package for computers. It would seem they could hardly believe it themselves because it went on to say they checked the calculations with a calculator. So overall, Wayne can claim to make money for his owners.

In their calculations, some of the 1986 horses had not yet completed their careers, but it is worth noting that half the total profits for the six year period came in 1983 when Wayne had two excellent stallion syndications. Nevertheless, his calculations and outside studies of his profitability make investing in a horse with Wayne Lukas seem like a good proposition, *especially when contrasted with the overall results in the industry.* Those results usually show overall rates of return of about 10%. That is not interest, that's how much of the capital the average investor in Thoroughbred ownership gets back. $1 back for every $10 you invest!

Over the years, many people wondered if Klein was ahead or behind. From when he got into the game in 1982, according to one report, he had spent $39m on weanlings and yearlings, mostly at public auction. At Derby time 1988, Klein's training bill was $300,000 a month. If that was typical for the main racing months, it suggests a training bill for the year around three million dollars. Transport was $1m for one year.

What is on the income side of the equation? His total prizemoney was reported at the time of his sell- off to be over $27 million. 1987 was his best year. He won 41 stakes races and $5.7m in prizemoney. 21% of that would go to Wayne and the jockey and the help. That would leave over a million in operating profit for that year. The big unknown was the value of Klein's stock, but it was generally conceded that his horses increased in value. Wayne's general manager David Burrage told a reporter at one point that by his estimate, if Klein sold out,

The buildings and track at the magnificent D.Wayne Lukas Training Center just north of San Diego. The center was built by Eugene Klein. It has since been bought by a European group.

he would be ahead by about $31m after expenses.

Such estimates are difficult. Much depends on overall market conditions. Sale prices of individual broodmares, racing stock and stallion shares change with every major race win. Sunday Silence won the Kentucky Derby and every horse closely related to him doubled and tripled in value. A lot of the guess work was removed when Klein called it quits and sold most of his stock in 1989.

The most successful owner of the 1980's sold 114 horses, including 11 Grade 1 winners, for a shade under $30m. Open Mind topped the sale at $4.6m. She was Champion two-year-old filly, won the Kentucky Oaks, the New York Fillies Triple Crown, and two months after the sale was voted Champion three-year-old mare. Open Mind was bought by a Japanese buyer who put the mare back with Lukas to race as a four-year-old.

Kentucky Derby winner Winning Colors brought $4.1m. Lady's Secret, the leading money-winning mare ever with a total of $3,021,325 sold for $3.8m. Seven sold for over a million dollars each. That might have been eight if On The Line had not been withdrawn because of injuries sustained in the Breeders' Cup race two days before.

But there are still uncertainties in the accounting columns. Tank's Prospect, a son of Mr Prospector, cost $625,000 as a yearling. He won the Preakness and in total earned $1,355,645. Klein sold nine shares at $400,000 each, i.e. for $3.6m and kept 31 shares himself. This valued the colt at $16m. Now that Tank's Prospect has runners, is he still valued at $16m? A mating to him in 1990, with a live foal guarantee cost $10,000. That would put Klein's gross from the stallion at a little over $200,000 per year, allowing that about 2/3 of matings produce a live foal. He would have to pay a management fee to the stud farm. I asked Burrage after the sale if Klein had come out ahead. He said the figures were being withheld at Klein's request.

At the time of the sale, Wayne told Billy Reed in an interview "I've always preached that you can make money in this game and have fun too, and I think that's what we've done with Gene Klein."

Beal, French and Hatley have large independent sources of wealth so the fact that they are still in the game after so many years does not necessarily mean they are ahead. But Mel Hatley certainly said he was.

Then at Ruidoso Downs for the All-American Futurity in late 1989, I was told Mel Hatley was going bankrupt. Several months after that, I asked him if he was going broke. He laughed and said it was not true, that he 'might oughta be' but no, he was very happy with his position.

Hatley did not know what was happening about the legal action over Mid-America Stables, but said it didn't involve him anyway. He had bought horses out of the Klein sale worth $700,000. He wanted to get in at the top end. "You have to play in the top 5% to make money. There is no money in the bottom end of the horse market."

Wayne's manager also told me the bankruptcy story was not true, that Mr Hatley had just built a new home worth perhaps $1.5m and had bought horses worth $700,000 at recent sales. Ah, the rumors . . .

12. Lukas and the breeding game

When Wayne Lukas was starting off in racing, the prevailing philosophy was that racing a stable of horses lost money, but you could, if you kept the well-bred ones that did well on the track, make a profit out of breeding. That meant the money was tied up for a long time before making a profit - IF it made a profit.

Wayne turned that approach around: "You can absolutely make money out of racing horses, you don't have to wait until breeding time to make a profit." He proved that, but nevertheless has become steadily more involved with breeding. He has stated his priorities: "Breeding does not dictate what you do during the racing year." That would seem to be at odds with the way he chases stakes races across the country, but perhaps he sees stakes races as nothing more than high purse races that add value to the horse at resale time.

12.1 Lukas as a stallion maker

"How have you rated at picking horses that became good stallions?"

"Most of ours are just starting out (June 1988). Saratoga Six has just got his first crop and he's going to be the leading juvenile sire this year. Tank's Prospect has got his first crop. Mount Livermore. The rest are going to have their first crops next year - Pancho Villa, Badger Land, Capote. More significant is that the mares that we have picked and raced are having phenomenal success with their offspring. Someone has done a study and we're really getting a lot of graded winners out of them, even the ones that didn't turn out very well on the track. So I guess the theory holds true that a good-looking yearling makes a good racehorse and makes a good broodmare - so it follows through. But Saratoga Six was the first sire we sent out and he's doing exceptionally well."

"The reason I was asking is that Paul Mostert at Equix has done a study that shows that although there are a number of body-types that can win at the races,

only one of those types goes on to great success at stud. He has had great success predicting the top first-season sires, so he knows what he is talking about. We have some top trainers in Australia that can pick horses, but none of them can repeatedly get good stallions. Vincent O'Brien repeatedly got top stallions. I presume trainers will choose a body conformation type consistently and so they'll get winners and stallions accordingly."

"Well obviously they're picking horses that have got- I like to pick horses that are very very precocious at a mile. I think they make the best sires. I don't think that's any secret in the industry. Horses that seemed to have brilliance at a mile seemed to do very well at stud."

"Were there any similar trends in the Quarter Horse? Were there some types that could breed on and some that couldn't?"

"Not as clearly as in the Thoroughbred. Not at all. In fact I don't think there is any correlation of that because they're running so short."

"And the range of distance is so narrow?"

"Yes it's a narrow band and the range of conformation is going to be narrowed down. In the Thoroughbred you're looking at one type from six furlongs to a mile and an entirely different type when you get beyond that. That doesn't happen in the Quarter Horse."

"If you're trying to win a Triple Crown, does that affect the type of horse you choose?"

"Yes it does. You have to adjust your eye a little bit in trying to pick a horse that is going to definitely go a mile and a quarter. I think also when you are buying horses you end up liking a particular body-type or horse. If in fact it's going to cost a lot, meaning he's got a good pedigree and he's good-looking, then you have to look at the pedigree and see if it will carry you to a classic distance."

"If you are going to pay $700,000 for a horse that might not get over a mile, you are going to get into trouble sooner or later. It goes back to what you were talking about. You are going to win some races but you're not going to have the syndication or stud value on those particular horses. You take a big risk. I think if you pay over a half a million dollars for a horse you better have a pedigree that will get him at least beyond a mile and possibly would be appealing to a group of breeders."

"Did you find that when you started to think about ending up with sires, that it altered the physical type of the horses you were buying?"

"I think early on, that I might have looked at a horse that maybe had a conformation type to be a miler or a little bit less. Over the years - I still have certain things that I have to see in a horse - but I may be looking towards horses that are maybe going a little further because the money in the game is at a mile and a quarter and maybe even beyond. We're running in so many of these big races that I'm looking at horses that can do that, but I still have an affinity for a horse that can run 7/8 to a mile. I love those horses, I love speed."

Paul Mostert of Equix has gone on record predicting the success or failure of first season sires and has an excellent score card. I asked him what he predicted for the success at stud of the Lukas selections.

"Is he choosing the very best sire type, the optimum type in your opinion?"

"Well I don't believe that Lukas thinks in terms of a sire at all. He's choosing a racehorse. Same with broodmares. In fact with the masculine type of filly that he likes, I don't think they will do very well as broodmares, but the type of horse that he likes tends to make a more consistent sire. The likelihood is that most of the sires that he chooses will be able to reproduce at a fairly high level but most of them will not produce *great* horses. So you will seldom have something like Cox's Ridge, which produces a great horse and then nothing, then another great horse and then nothing."

"His sires will be more consistent, but will produce very few really top horses?"

"The early maturing miler or just below miler - 7/8 - those make good sires, but generally they don't produce the classic horse, or very rarely."

"It was claimed to me that he chooses a hybrid type of horse that will not breed true. Is there a hybrid type that doesn't breed on?"

"If you you mix your horses - say you breed a sprinter and a stayer and it just happens to work out right, that horse may breed in either direction. Depending on his opportunities he might or might not make a sire. Depends if he's got one end of one, and one end of the other, or not. But I think that with the type of horse Wayne chooses, it's not generally a mixed up horse, quite the opposite."

"Are his selections at the sprint end?"

"I wouldn't say they are at the sprint end, they are a little higher than that. He's moved out of the sprint end."

"Many people believe that staying ability comes mostly through the mare and that the most successful breeding plan is sprint sires to staying mares. On that basis, if it's true, his colt selections should have a good chance of making it as sires, but perhaps his fillies may not do so well."

"The fillies he chooses may not do as well as his colts because the type of athletic fillies he chooses have a tendency not to be so good as producers."

"As good in numbers of foals or quality of foals?"

"Quality and numbers."

"It would seem odd in the sense that if masculine fillies win races, then you should breed from masculine fillies to get more winners."

"The thing about the female is that it is made for reproduction. If it has all the things that make for good reproduction, she herself may not be a good athlete. If she was an athlete in spite of that, well so much the better. Whereas if you have a kind of masculine filly, she might not have a well developed uterus or as well developed ovaries and so forth; just doesn't have the right environment to produce that foal. Plus some of the very masculine ones have a kind of an odd sex chromosome anyway."

12.2 Record as a breeder

"I always breed the qualities I like in a stallion with the qualities I like in a mare without regard to whether she's got three dosages of Nasrullah or anything like that. That stuff is for guys in libraries. I always look for good running characteristics first."

"Wayne, you are obviously going to move into the breeding game a bit."

"I hope not but I'm already into it a bit."

"Well, you have stallion shares and you bred-"

"And we've got some mares back and I have some brood mares. I mean it happens but I don't emphasize it." (Wayne's voice drips with his reluctance. It sounds like he has either been dragged into breeding or fell into it by unfortunate accident.)

"What has happened, American International Bloodstock - Norm and Phil Owens in Kentucky - they ran a little study. I've only bred about 20 or 30 horses - and I've had the Horse Of The Year and I think something like seven Grade 1 winners out of something like 14 foals. I've raised some awfully good horses, Lady's Secret for one, Badger Land, Tejano. I bred those and raised those horses. My record is better than Claiborne's for the number of horses."

"You know how I'm breeding them? I don't look at a page of the pedigree or nothing. I look at the horse I've got in front of me and the quality and the things that I like. Then I think of the sires that are available that have the qualities I like and I mate them that way. And you can't believe the success I've had. Even with horses like Badger Land which had a very very moderate $25,000 mother, but I thought that she and Codex complemented each other so much - and the mating was just exactly what I thought - a multiple Grade 1 million dollar winner. Lady's Secret - I bred her. The same year I bred three million dollar winners - out of four tries."

" Is complementing the largest part of it?"

"Sure. That's exactly what it is. I never looked at the pedigrees. I could have been inbreeding - if you talk about inbreeding, I could have really messed it up. Afterwards people made studies and said you did that and you did this. Well you know all I did was to complement the two horses. I couldn't care less about all that other stuff they found out. They said, 'Jesus you are breeding some really top flight horses without any thought. We have a guy we pay sitting there all day plugging that stuff in there."

"Now I'm working with W. T. Young [Overbrook Farm] and he's got Ken McLean [Author of *Tesio: Master of Matings* and *Quest for a Classic Winner*] who is outstanding. He's sitting there all day fooling with this stuff. Of course my comment to Ken was - he's saying this is this and that is that - and I say, 'You know what you had better do? If you breed that mare to Alydar, you're going to be in trouble, I don't care what that computer says. I'll tell you why: because Alydar's tend to be a little long in the back and their weakness is over the loin. So any time you breed a mare that has weakness over the loin to Alydar you are not going to get a racehorse. You must, YOU MUST take a strong loin mare. And you have to be careful of the hocks on Alydar's. I know this from experience. If you breed that mare to Alydar you will get a foal you will not like."

"Ken is also a strong advocate of Devil's Bag. When Devil's Bag went to the stud I predicted he would be one of the biggest disasters ever to hit the breeding market." (Devil's Bag was raced to the Two- Year-Old Championship by Woody Stephens. At the Keeneland sales in 1989 Wayne bought two Devil's Bag yearlings for a total of $350,000 - but then that was a low price for that sale.)

"There was a leading sire here about three years ago, [that would be about 1985] made a big splash - sensational - and I told my clients and I told Lee Eaton and John Williams, if they don't quit breeding to this horse, it's going to take 50 years to overcome it. And I mean he was sensational. They were knocking the doors down to get to him. Sure enough . . . well he's not zero but he's certainly not where he was."

"So he already had proven race winners?"

"Yes, he had a very strong first year. But even when he was right at the height, I was saying, 'This horse will not make a good sire, will not sustain that level'. I have a whole theory about that too. It's like Secretariat."

"A reason a sire can go downhill?"

"Take a horse that maybe wasn't a sensational racehorse but he has enough pedigree that somebody wants to try him. And of course he gets a lesser mare, what I call a cold blood mare. They are usually a little bit soggier, a little hardier, a little stronger, a bit more bone. That's what keeps them from being brilliant on the racetrack - they are a little bit crude."

"Now, suddenly, boom - he comes out of the woodwork with good runners - bam, bam, bam. And everyone says, 'Wow, this horse never had a chance, they bred all these nickel mares to him and he got runners. What will happen when we breed these good ones to him?' When they breed the good ones to

him they don't help him one little bit. The foals one after another have no bone, no feet, no knees. You can write him off because they are taking those million dollar mares to him and it's over."

"What happened to Secretariat was - you didn't dare breed just an old cold half-mile mare to Secretariat. He was too great. So they bred the classic mares to him and they didn't complement him. So the best runners came from-"

"Second grade mares."

"Yes. The mare I bought, Terlingua, her dam raced in New Mexico in the bush tracks and ran the fastest half mile in the world. I knew that that was what Secretariat had to have. And she looked the part. I've had 13 stakes winners by Secretariat, that I've trained personally, and that's far more than anyone else has had. He's only had something like 26. All of them are out of soggy, speedy, solid mares."

"What exactly do you mean by soggy?"

"Stout, got a lot of substance. But with a lot of my breeding I go completely against the grain of present breeding theory. In fact I am breeding types to types. My other theory is that you absolutely have to breed light types to light types to get a uniform foal. The conformation must complement but they must be similar types. To put it in the extreme, you don't put the tall big horse to the little mare and hope to get the happy medium. That never works. What you do is you breed a sire and dam that look similar, then you have got a great chance of getting a uniform foal. Otherwise you get one that looks like it was made by a committee in three days."

13. What makes Wayne Lukas successful?

13.1 How he acquired his skills and knowledge

Clearly Wayne did not learn from some great master. He listened, asked questions, observed and deduced from a very early age. Because of this he probably knows most of what most horsemen and trainers know plus some things that very few know, and a few things that only he knows.

13.2 Personality Traits

Intelligence

All those who work with Wayne consider him very very bright. Melvin Hatley has said, "Wayne is not only my trainer but a good friend and an outstanding person. He's highly intelligent and has unending energy that enables him to work on things to a fine detail. I honestly believe he would be a success in any field he put his mind to."

Memory

"A lot of these top trainers have a phenomenal mem-

ory. What's yours like?"

"Good. I can look at two hundred and fifty yearlings and re-call the pedigree on every one of them the next day."

"I'd like to go to some sales with you and test you out."

"I have no problem when it comes to horses. I can't remember three items at the grocery store to bring home, but I can remember horses. That's the interest level thing, of course. My memory is really good. I can see a horse that I'd seen run two or three years ago, and see it on the racetrack and call it by name, and breeding. But if someone asked me to remember four items, I probably won't, I'll mess that up."

Racing journalist and publisher Loren Vantries, speaking of Wayne and Jeff: "Even though they have so many horses, they keep track of them, they know what's going on. Even if they didn't see the race, they know what happened, how their horse did, what it's going to do next. I don't see them that often, maybe once a year, but they know who you are, and you can pick up where you left off."

Sleep and energy

For most of his adult life Wayne Lukas has only slept for three hours a night - from midnight to 3am. Even now, in his fifties, he rises at 3:30am.

"You only need about three or four hours sleep a night. Do you get that from your parents - do they need much sleep?"

"No, I don't know that it came from them. I always had a high energy level, and it's been something that just more or less developed. I used to think that sleep was necessary, but when I got really into my career and got intense, it seemed like . . . well, for about a seven or a nine-year-period there, I would take one of these legal pads every morning, and budget twenty hours of work out of it before I'd sleep. Every night before I went to bed, or every morning when I got up, I would budget. I would get up at 3.30 - still do - and by 4.00 I'd be on the job and then I'd budget as the hour, thirty minutes for lunch, and I would budget twenty hours."

"As an adult, did you at one stage need, or get, seven or eight hours sleep?"

"I got to the point in my career where I was driving, trying to get some things done and some goals met, and I slept whenever I needed it. I even got to the point where I would go, you know, days. I would train during the day, race at night. Quarter Horse racing was always at night, and in the afternoon, when most of the guys were taking naps, I would get in the truck, drive to a training center, switch some horses - I never stopped. And it was hard on me. I dropped way down in weight and everything, but the ambition and the drive within, I think carried me then. I didn't need sleep. When I got just too tired, I'd stop."

"Tommy Smith, a trainer in Australia, was very like

that. According to his vet, Percy Sykes, when Tommy went to a new carnival in a different city in his heyday he sometimes would not sleep for the next two or three days."

"That's the way I used to be."

"For Tommy Smith it was great for socializing with the owners until late at night or early in the morning and being at the track at 4am in the morning."

"I never socialized very much. Most of mine was at the barn."

"Do you drink coffee and Cola to stay awake?"

"Just one cup in the morning. That's it. After the first cup, I hardly ever - unless I get really pushing, driving a lot. Years ago, when I was driving a lot at night, had a lot of horses and I used to do all my own work because I didn't have any money - then I used to drink coffee."

I find it interesting that a hard driving go-getter like Wayne is careful with coffee consumption. In the course of four years writing this book I have discovered that I can write until 1am most nights of the week if I have a big drink of Coca Cola before the evening meal. My normal bedtime was 10 - 11pm. It's a little harder to wake up but I can rise at the usual time.

If I drink it too often - eg a glass with each meal, it doesn't work. Too much caffeine makes it difficult to sleep when I go to bed, I feel dozy a lot during the day, and can't stay up late. Anyone trying to get a lot done in a day should monitor their coffee, tea and cola intake.

Back in his early days at Ruidoso Downs, Wayne told José Dominguez that all he needed was 15 or 20 minutes of sleep. Racing was in the afternoons and Wayne did not have to use this talent much. José didn't believe him. "I said, 'That's a bunch of bullshit Wayne'. But I guess he did that out in California."

Wayne is able to take advantage of any lull in the day's rushed proceedings to catch up on sleep by 'catnapping'.

The Lukas energy level is legendary, and so is the desire to get the job done. Journalist Loren Vantries again: "I've approached Wayne and Jeff, and you can talk to them, but they keep on working. Jeff grabs a pitch-fork and cleans out a stall. They don't stand around, neither of them, but if you're willing to walk along, they'll talk to you."

If Wayne or Jeff were conversationally inclined, there are plenty of people who would help them waste time. But then you might never have heard of them if they weren't so driven to get it done.

Health

"Hard-driving people are prone to heart disease. Do you go and get a cardiogram and a stress test every couple of years?"

"I hadn't seen a doctor in twenty-nine years, for anything. Anything. No checkup, anything. No sickness or anything else.

A year ago, a couple of my clients wanted to take out 'Key Man' insurance on me, because they thought my knowledge to do certain things was tied to many millions of dollars of their business. So two or three of my key clients - Gene Klein, Bob French and some other people, wanted to take out a multi-million dollar insurance policy on me, and pay for it, because if something happened to me, they felt that their business would suffer by millions of dollars. That test, at my age, - at that point, 51 - they took me to a place and it was almost an all-day deal. And they put me through it. I mean, the treadmills, the running uphill, all the stuff, you know what they do. And I hadn't seen a doctor in twenty-nine years and I came through it just perfect. No high blood-pressure, no heart, nothing."

"No high cholesterols?"

"Nothing. Just perfect. The guy couldn't believe it. This doctor, when he sat down to give me the results, said to me, 'I know what you do. I know a lot about you. Nothing on these records, nothing, shows any stress.' He said, 'That's amazing, because I know you've got to be in terribly stressful situations."

"But it doesn't bother me. I thrive on the toughest situations, and I try to shield my assistants, but the tougher, the bigger the challenge, the better I enjoy it, it's not a stressful thing, it's more of a challenge to me."

Wayne may not have called a doctor but his friend Mel Hatley did. When Wayne was going through his second divorce he lost 33 pounds. "He was feeling very bad. Fact is I was very concerned about him. I hired a doctor and sent him out to stay with Wayne for two weeks."

Stress Management - Type A or B?

"You'd be interested to know the classification of personality types has been changed. Type A people were people who worked too hard. There's a guy who subdivides the old type A people, who work enormous hours, into two groups. The old-term 'workaholics' he reserves for those who don't like their work - and now he has a classification called 'workaphilics' who enjoy their work so much that it's not a stress on them."

"That's me - yes."

Wayne thinks that he's handling criticism better now because, he says, "We've outlasted the detractors. Our record stands: we've put a lot of criticism to bed. A lot of guys who criticized our methods and what we do with a horse have had to back up."

Celebrates successes?

"Do you celebrate your wins?"

"No. No. Never do. The night after the Kentucky Derby win, a friend of mine - Bobby Knight - who is our Olympic basketball coach, and who had won the NCA championship - was with me. He and another Olympic coach, Pete Newall, were my guests. The track had sent tubs of champagne to the barn. We gave a bottle to everybody that came by; the news, the media, guys like yourself, because we didn't even open them."

"After everything quieted down, after standing around the barn and making sure everybody cleared away from the horses, we went. I think it must have been right after eleven o'clock we got back to the hotel. We went in and we asked them and they opened up the kitchen, which had closed. We sat there and ate Kentucky stew and drank chocolate milk until about one, two in the morning, just talking about the race and everything. That's as close as it came."

"When I won my first classic, which was Codex's Preakness, I went back to the motel, and there's a wooded area behind the motel in Baltimore, where I stayed, and I remember getting to the motel about ten- thirty, and I think I walked out through that wooded area till about one-thirty in the morning, by myself, just soaking it up."

Hobbies and interests

Wayne told Joanne Stover of *The Thoroughbred of California*, "I don't have any interests outside horses. My vacation . . . is spending four days at a horse sale in Keeneland. Riding my horse in the morning is all the relaxation I need, and winning races is all the stimulation I need."

Retire?

I didn't ask, but he seems too driven to stop.

Drive and application

Wayne is famous for hard work and long hours. Trainer John Nerud told Bill Nack, "He works like a goddam dog. He's a different piece of work from you and me. At dinner, he sits down and says, 'Bring me a Coke and a menu.' He eats in five minutes and wants to go home."

"Wayne, what influence did your parents have, if any, in the development of your very powerful drive? Were they hard-driving people?"

"Yes, all of our family are very ambitious. My brother and sister are both in education, both college graduates, masters degrees or beyond. My sister has a doctorate. My folks were very supportive. We come from mid-west, medium backgrounds. No wealth in the family or anything like that, but as far as the horse connection, there was very little. I had the horse interest, and I was supported early on."

"You developed that philosophy of ambition and hard work?"

"Yes. I would say that came from both my parents pretty much, and even when I was in grade-school and high-school, I was up at 4am and out doing things. I had two or three jobs - had two paper rounds when I was a little kid. One in the morning and one at night. So that has never been a problem. My son Jeff seems to have those same qualities. His work ethic, I think, is very strong."

"I never socialized very much. Most of mine was at the barn. I socialize at the barn a lot. I've always been a person that stays very very close to the horses. Not so much in these years, because I have top assistants and so forth, but early on in my career, I used to always, ALWAYS spend seventeen, eighteen, nineteen hours a day at the barn, and hardly ever left. Used to send out for food. I used to do a lot of the work myself, but I think it made me a better horseman."

" I can see that it would be a very thorough way to learn about horses. You were the second in the birth order. How much older was your sister?"

"She was two years older and my brother was two years younger. My sister is an amazing story in herself. She's a very very high-achieving person; was number one in her class, from about the third grade, all the way through to university. She was very very talented. She's so book-smart she's dumb."

"Yes I know the type. The universities are plagued with them. Obviously there was something in the home environment there. Did your parents push you or reward you? Did they urge you on or did they just praise what you did?"

"I think more just giving us the opportunity. Nobody had to push me. I think my ambition level was far beyond . . . it might even have been to the point where they were trying to slow me down. I had these tremendous projects going."

"You don't know how many parents wish they had that problem."

"Yes. I had so many projects going when I was a kid. My mother tells me that when I was seven years old, I used to raise rabbits and try to have them all birthed so they'd be ready at Easter and I could sell them. I always had my cattle, my calves that I was raising, and sold at the fair, and my other projects. I think most of the time my folks were trying to slow me down."

This strong drive causes Wayne to concentrate on the job and since he works all day, his concentration has 'stamina'. I think this is a factor in his success at the sales. Many trainers are unable to concentrate after looking at their first 20 or 50 yearlings for the day. 'I'm worn out,' or 'They're all starting to look the same.' Not so with Wayne. The other thing that helps Wayne's concentration is his use of 'disqualifiers'. If the horse does not have certain things, it is ruled out and he rests his concentration until they bring the next one out.

An example of Wayne's single mindedness is his 'honeymoon' after his third marriage. He married Shari on May 1st 1984, appropriately in Lexington, Kentucky. When is the Kentucky Derby? First Saturday in May. What did they do after the ceremony? They hightailed it back to the barn to graze Al-

thea and Life's Magic, Wayne's prospects in the Derby which was just four days away. One report claimed he married then in the hope it would change his Derby week luck.

Wayne's first two marriages would have been under the severe pressure of his desire to succeed, first in basketball coaching, later in racing. If his current lifestyle is anything to go by, being the best in racing is still the biggest thing in his life. Shari Lukas obviously can spend more time with Wayne because her own kids are older, and she has an interest in racing. She has gotten into the entrepreneurial thing too - a business selling aerodynamic jockey silks. The idea is to have clinging material like downhill skiers, cyclists and 100 meter runners. She has been involved in selling franchises around the country for these silks.

Willingness to travel

Wayne is plenty willing to travel. He used to visit his branches frequently, but leaves it more and more to his proven lieutenants. That allows him more time to travel to the sales.

Optimist or pessimist?

An out and out optimist.

Socializing - Loner or Outgoing?

One of the largest pitfalls a trainer can fall into is over-socializing. But it's a very enjoyable trap, it keeps owners very happy, and many trainers don't want to get out of it anyway. Ambitious trainers have to.

Wayne enjoys company but limits it so that it does not interfere with his work output. He certainly does not feel any compulsion to socialize. Most of his friendships seem to be with owners, and to a lesser extent, people in his workplace. In his Quarter Horse days he seems to have mixed with other trainers a bit more, indeed he was great friends with arch rival Blane Schvaneveldt. Blane says of Wayne, "I think he's a good fellow and as good a friend as I've ever had. Good person. Yeah, I'm tickled for his accomplishments over there. He's a hell of a guy. He earns what he gets."

But Wayne remains primarily competitive. Trainer John Gosden's name came up one day. I said, *"He's a really good guy."*

"He's a great guy," said Wayne, "Great guy. Wonderful person. Very positive. I like him a lot. You don't get too close to these guys though, because you're battling them all the time, one on one. But it's like when I was in the Quarter Horses, Blane and I were very close friends. We liked each other, and we respected each other. We went at it tooth and nail every night, but we still-"

"I think that's one of the anti-stress factors. The guys who let it all get to them, they suffer."

"The guys who let it get to them, I don't have anything to do with. There's guys on the grounds who have extreme animosities and when you beat them, it shows up very obviously.

Wayne's day at the races.

Post time at Hollywood Park was 1.30pm. Wayne did not have an entry until the 6th race, in which he had two.

The handlers couldn't get the filly Wonder's Delight into her bay. Wayne took charge and soon persuaded her to move in. Note conformation.

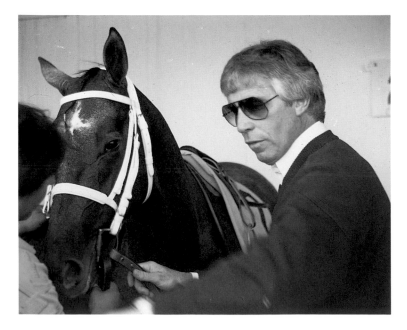

Wayne makes all the equipment changes. Note the white bridle, a Lukas trademark.

Wayne waits with the jockey for his other entry, Chris McCarron, who wears the fuschia and lime colors of Calumet Farm. Wayne is still giving orders to his horse handlers.

Wayne retreats to the private boxes to watch the race. Those with binoculars watch the field, those without, except for Wayne, watch the race on the giant screen in the infield. Also present are his wife and a jockey's agent. Obviously neither of Wayne's horses is winning.

After the race Wayne told the jockey of Wonder's Delight, 'Gary I'll take the blame for that one'. Back in the boxes, Wayne was buttonholed by two jockey's agents.

I don't have anything to do with those guys. I don't waste my time with them. John can beat me or I can beat John, and we'll walk down to the winner's circle together and laugh about it and kid each other and shake hands, and it's over."

Inborn talent or something learned?

It would seem Wayne had a talent with horses at a very young age. It is difficult to assess the importance of that to his success. Wayne has used his intelligence and memory to learn how to pick good horses, and that has been his greatest selling point.

In summary, Wayne showed energy, application and intelligence to an extraordinary degree. Some might consider that made it too easy for him. But he did have his failures. A trainer at Canterbury, who grew up racing horses at the same fairs, remembers some setbacks for 'Luke' as they called him then. He remembers when Wayne and Clyde took up rodeoing, and Wayne was pitched off time and again - a failure. The man said Wayne remained confident, saying, 'I should be able to do this, I'm an athlete.'"

He recalled Wayne bringing a bunch of horses to a fair in a fancy gooseneck trailer - he already had an owner with money. Wayne was oozing confidence that he was going to win races. But the horses were 'only show horses and cowbreds'. Over the whole fair he managed only one score - a third place. I asked if that dented Wayne's confidence.

"No. There was a Futurity and Wayne's horses were not in it, wouldn't have had a chance anyway. But Wayne was telling everyone his horses would have had a great chance. Nothing stopped his confidence. He eventually worked it out that you needed at least a couple of crosses of Thoroughbred in those cow horses to win races."

13.3 The formulated approach

How much of Wayne's success is due to things outside inborn talents and personality? How much is deliberate application of learned rules?

Planning and method

Wayne Lukas has a very carefully thought out approach to everything. Nothing much happens around him that is not planned. It is interesting therefore to ponder his preponderance of successes at the two-year-old game. Is it an extension of his origins in Quarter Horses, a historical accident? Does his training favor the two-year-old? Is it exactly where he wants to be in the Thoroughbred world? Or would Wayne prefer to be a trainer of three-year-old classic winners and older horses?

Much of Wayne's success is due to his ability to pick yearlings that become winners. Wayne chooses primarily on the yearling's build. A horse's proportions, and consequently its ability to win, change with age. The yearling's shape is much closer to its two-year-old shape than its three-year-old shape. So he can choose two-year-old winners with more accuracy, but would he swap that to be more successful with older horses?

If Wayne is sticking with a preponderance of two-year-old winners, I believe it would be planned and the reason would be to make a profit from racing. It is generally accepted that three-year-old's make more money than two-year-old's, in their prime year, in the United States. That usually shows in the greater number of three-year-old's that win $1m for the year. If you were going to make money at racing, shouldn't you therefore aim to select the type of horse that does its best at three? Breeding is part of the equation: it comes into the resale value.

The winnings plus sales value of a three-year-old have to be about 40% more than the two-year-old, to make the same percentage profit per year. That is primarily because it has taken $2 = 4$ years to determine its worth, versus $1 = 4$ for the two-year-old. That is 40% more time. There are other factors which are much harder to quantify. For example, how quickly a horse can be classified as unprofitable. If a horse is expected to make a two-year-old and it fails, will it be tried at three? Not if it was bought as a two-year-old type. If it wins at two, and then goes on to make money at three, well and good.

Suffice to say that the type of horse that does not do much until it is a three-year-old, then has to do about 40% better. I doubt if they do that very often. The profitability then, from a business man's point of view - which Wayne and his owners are - lies with two-year-old's.

Personal philosophy

There is in Wayne a combination of the old hard line, uncompromising puritan, with a modern Yuppie. Wayne does not smoke, drink, swear or spit, but he drives like a demon, and loves the symbols of success. Wayne likes expensive cars - Rolls Royce or Mercedes Benz. He has a reputation for driving fast and has had the occasional speeding fine. He probably acquired this taste for fast driving in his college days, while crisscrossing the neighbouring states to go to horse sales, and later as a trainer in the vast stretches of Texas, Oklahoma and New Mexico.

He makes no apologies for his cars or his cash and is not afraid to say that he thinks he is the best. Jim Tunstall of Echelon Magazine asked him if he was successful: "Am I successful?" said Wayne. "More than anyone in the world. We win races and we don't plan to stop. Everything I have in this world, every single thing, is directly related to what I can do with a horse."

Religion

I asked Wayne if he was religious.

"To a degree."

"Was your family religious?"

"Yes. I was very moderate. Not over the board, but on the other hand, we're definitely God-fearing people."

Wayne's business philosophy

Wayne's business style is simple. He knows his strengths lie in selecting and training horses and in organizing and motivating others. He does those things and employs top-notch professionals to do anything else. In the parlance of those who study successful businessmen, 'he sticks to the knitting' i.e. to what he knows he is good at. (The businessman who makes it in knitting but then shifts into banking for example, frequently goes down the drain and is found more often in studies of bankruptcy.)

Without doubt Wayne can run stables all over the country because he can pick horses. While he can choose outstanding horses, he only needs competent management and competent trainers to do the rest.

"I want everything that happens with the horses I train to cross my desk -anything to do with the vet, blacksmith, the feed, whatever. I want to control these horses from the yearling sales to the Breeders' Cup."

He pays people on a higher salary scale than other barns and has a profit-sharing system. "My philosophy is that I teach and motivate my people. Then they will seek to achieve on their own, and their striving for the top will lift the whole D. Wayne Lukas organisation. What I have is 250 people all pulling in the same direction. That has to make a difference. Our employees are motivated to care about their work and see the larger picture. When we achieve something, we don't sit back and enjoy it. We look for the next challenge and set our goals even higher. Let me tell you, at this rate we're going to rewrite it all."

Betting

When the odds are better than they should be in Wayne's estimation, he will have a bet. Some of his staff have a bet. He has no rules about staff betting.

Selling strategies

Wayne is an excellent salesman. His principal strategy now is to use his past results, his proven ability to produce champions and profits, to convince a potential owner, but there must have been a time before there were results to point at. Back then he relied more on the impression he made, with his knowledge, energy and diligence, his neat clothes and neat barns.

Wayne may have been a natural salesman, improved by his teenage horsedealing experiences, but I'd be very surprised if he hasn't read books on selling. I'll bet he knows the importance of qualifying a prospect and the ways of closing. If you are a trainer and you don't know what the terms mean, then you'd best do some reading. Salesmanship is a very misunderstood thing. Many associate it only with the offensive overselling salesman, the very type that gets awful results and who should read a book like Tom Hopkin's 'How to Master the Art of Selling'. Salesmanship comes in two flavors: good and bad.

Good salesmanship consists of finding out what the prospect wants and then selling it to them. Good salesmanship helps the prospect refine and define their desires and needs, and corrects any delusions. Sell them something they want and they will be happy. They will become friends and they'll be back -with their friends.

Bad salesmanship is selling people things they don't want and don't need: icemakers to eskimos. Try to sell anyone something they don't want and they'll be looking for the exits. Sell them something by toe to toe pressure or trickery and they'll hate you. It is OK if you can keep moving along like the traveling snake oil salesman.

The true salesman is not the overzealous pushy person, but the unobtrusive store worker you never even thought of as trying to make a sale. The one you thought of as very helpful, *the one you'll look for next time.* Chances are that little old 'helpful' has been to the salesmanship course and 'pushy' hasn't. One excellent company manual says to its salespeople, "Ask at least 5 questions about what they want before you mention even one plug point for a product." Way back in his most difficult days, Wayne did not hassle Bob Moore to buy a horse. (You could point out that he hustled Albert Yank, but instead Albert sold Wayne a horse. Yet the results were a plus for Wayne.)

Is he a risk-taker?

He'd still be a school teacher if he wasn't a risk-taker.

"All my life I've put my head on the chopping block and it has worked." Wayne is definitely a risk-taker when it comes to buying horses. He has put a lot of his own money into his purchases. Many trainers have shares in horses only because they were given them. Clearly though, when you can choose horses as skillfully as Wayne, it is not a huge risk.

Is he an innovator?

The way Wayne developed his training is typical of his approach to problems. He would rather try to work out his own method. This makes him an innovator. The shoe he sold to Converse was another example.

Time management

(Most time management authorities consider that many people fail to achieve long term goals because they are distracted by less important, but at the time more pressing tasks. Work on long term goals is easily put off. These authorities suggest ways of re-ordering priorities so that some progress is made on the long term goals every day. Do you wash the car or do you

The horse dozes as Wayne concentrates on some of his horses working on the smaller training track behind the barns. He takes everything very seriously.

lay some bricks for the new garage?)

"You used to budget 20 hours in a day - a time management man from way back."

"Right. But the problem is you can overmatch yourself."

!!!

Goal and step setter or day by day?

There is no way someone as thoughtful as Wayne could NOT plan. He sets goals for himself and for his organization. For example, at the beginning of 1985, Lukas said his goal was for the stable to earn $6m in purses and forty stakes.

13.4 Any record of a positive drug test?

Many people on the racetracks believe that Lukas uses drugs. One common story was the one about him having bought someone off in the swabbing boxes in New York and California. Urine from normal horses was swapped for the samples from Lukas horses so that he could then use whatever drugs he liked. At the time, the story went that he had not been able to

win a Kentucky Derby because he couldn't buy off anyone in the system there. Since then he has won with Winning Colors. I always asked if there was anyone that could give me any further information on this. They could not name anyone.

Sometimes cited as evidence of Lukas's use of drugs was the way his horses run at the front. The claim was that they were so souped up on drugs that you couldn't try to rate them. One very thoughtful fellow believed Lukas used his well-known friendships with coaches in basketball to obtain 'the latest undetectable drug'.

Another story said that Wayne had been using cocaine on the tongue ties of his runners. A tongue tie is a loop around the tongue that is tied to the jaw or the bit. This prevents the horse retracting the tongue so it cannot get the tongue over the top of the bit and in some cases it prevents choking. Tongue ties are put on just before the race and that was why laboratories had not been able to pick cocaine up in the pre-race blood sample. The pre-race sample is taken in the detention barn about an hour before the race. Presumably the cocaine is absorbed rapidly enough to affect the horse's performance during the race.

But why wasn't cocaine detected in the postrace samples - the winner's blood and urine? Because the action of Lasix makes the urine sample more dilute, making the drug harder to detect. Lasix effectively masks the cocaine in the tests was the claim. What about his success in New York where Lasix is not allowed? He sends his better horses up there. Keeps his second stringers where he can use the drugs.

This is not a very likely scenario to me. Cocaine is readily detected, even in dilute urine. It would restrict its use to bleeders on Lasix, using tongue ties and would only work if the dose can be so small as to not show in a swab and yet still improve performance.

What was Wayne's position? I asked him in June 1988:

"One of the things that is consistently said, and this was also said about Tommy Smith and Fred Kersley - is that you've got the magic needle. That you've 'got something."

"It's interesting; we went through all those record breaking years in the Quarter Horse industry, and the minute anybody does well, that eventually surfaces. When we went into Thoroughbreds and went into New York, where absolutely no medication is allowed, we got to winning a lot of races. Then, in the second and third year, we dominated New York racing. Stakeswise, if you look at the record books, we dominated the stakes program. Made all that money. So, the natural thing always happens; somebody says to the Racing Board, 'You must investigate this guy, he obviously has got something the rest of us don't.'"

"So they came to us, and they said: 'Look, we get the usual requests, pressure'. So we told them, 'Why don't you take the pressure off yourself and off us - test every horse we run, no matter where it finishes. Even test it beyond what you normally would. Just take 150, 200, 300 of them in a row, and put this to bed.'"

"So they tested, I think 187 of them - just to protect themselves. And then when somebody would call in, they'd say, 'Well, we got 187 in a row, every horse he's run, we have nothing.' Later on, they found a bunch of new sophisticated testing procedures, here in California, and they had frozen a number - thousands - of tests in a refrigerator car out here."

"They were catching all the fellas in New Mexico and some of them over there in the Quarter Horse game and everything. I think it made some trainers nervous. I was talking to one of the Commissioners up here at Hollywood Park at lunch one day, and he happened to be a friend of mine. I said, 'Why don't you do yourself a favor with me? Don't randomly test out of the refrigerator car where I'm concerned. Just go get a hundred of mine and test 'em right now. Just go pick 'em up. I'll take my chances.'"

"Yes, it is one of the things that winning trainers have to contend with."

"That's ridiculous. When you work hard, they always give you that crap."

"Someone said that you had a positive for a morphine-like compound at Bay Meadows at one stage."

"Right. 1973."

"What was the story?"

"1973. I think we had something like eighty-seven wins; the next guy had twelve. They were the standings. We were absolutely dominating the meets. We had a horse that was located two barns over because we had so many horses we couldn't keep them all in the one barn. The cheapest horse we had was a $2000 claimer. He ran third in a claiming race one night, and they came back with the test. That particular test supposedly had a morphine-derivative or something in it. My veterinarian had treated that horse."

"Two things that I look back on, on that thing. They gave me a forty-five day suspension which - I knew I was innocent, but I thought at forty-five days, it would take me that long to prove my innocence plus a lot of money. At the end of forty-three days - or maybe it was about forty days - they were going to review the case, thinking that the penalty was not severe enough."

"At that point I went and got a lawyer. And the first thing my lawyer did was say, 'Did you save a portion of the sample of the test? Is it frozen?' They said, 'Yes'. He said, 'I want that sample tested by an independent lab in Denver, Colorado.' He sent it off and it was negative."

"So now he wanted to build a case of slander, and so forth. I did not. The days had run out. I wanted to get back to work. The Racing Board of California asked me to sign a document that I would not bring any further suit, and that the case'd be dropped."

"The other thing that bothered me, is that the vet that I used on that particular horse, and other horses years before, was eventually ruled off over here. So he might have been a little zealous too. You know, sometimes when you're training horses, you have a tendency to say, 'Okay.' Some of those vets take great pride in being able to run a horse. I never give them that liberty, but when they're in and out of the stalls, I'm not looking at everything. Eventually, I think, he was ruled off over here for getting a little bit beyond the limits. So I look back at that as a learning experience. I'm not ashamed of it. I put it on my record all the time. I think that a) either he took it upon himself, or b) the test was falsely analyzed."

"Well, it depends a bit on the stability of the compound. I would say that if the Denver laboratory knew what the positive was supposed to be on the first one, they would have tested it with whatever that first laboratory had, only better."

"In my own defense, nobody in the United States, nobody in the world, runs more horses or has more tested, than we have. Especially in high class races. Now, Van Berg may run more horses, but nobody has more tested, because we win more than Van Berg, by far. Nobody is tested more in high class races - graded races. Yet at no time, other than that one incident, can anybody even point to 'bute'. We have never, in New York even, had a horse pulled out in a pre-race test or anything, for even any incidental thing."

"To me, people like you have too many employees to hide what you do and too much to lose."

"Oh, gosh yes. By the way, the net worth of my gains on the horse that was tested positive was $26. That was what it meant to me. If I'll put my career on the line for $26, I don't think I'd have got where I am today."

Wayne had not volunteered the information about his drug test in 1973, but he certainly had a plausible explanation, after I brought it up.

In February 1989, Lukas, along with Hall Of Fame trainer Laz Barrera and Barrera's son, were charged with returning a positive swab for cocaine and one of its metabolites in a retest of frozen samples. A metabolite of cocaine is a compound produced from the cocaine when it is broken down in the body. The presence of the metabolite, ecognine, means that cocaine has not simply been added to the sample from the hands of someone collecting the urine nor from a lab worker.

This is important because a cocaine user handling the collection utensils or test vials could possibly leave enough to return a positive on such sensitive tests. However any cross contamination or mixing of samples could end with cocaine plus metabolite in more than one sample. Both these things are known to have happened in forensic labs. Just one failure to change a pipette tip, or any of a number of scenarios, and you have one guilty but many charged. A saboteur could add urine from a drugged horse to the test urine. Who listens when a horse trainer says, "The test must be wrong?"

Swabbing at Santa Anita and Hollywood Park routinely includes all winners, plus seven randoms which cannot include the winner, plus the first three in any stakes race and the first two in exacta races. Occasionally the last horse or any horse the stewards choose will also be swabbed. Anything that is heavily backed but runs poorly, like a beaten favorite, is always swabbed. This typically totals 29 - 31 horses on the day.

These cocaine positives however were from frozen samples reported to have been tested at the request of the California

Horsemans' Benevolent and Protective Association. This implied there were a lot of horsemen who either knew or believed some trainers were using drugs and they wanted them caught. A member of the Association's medication committee told me there was a belief among the horsemen that designer drugs were being used. The Lukas horse was Crown Collection, swabbed after a win some six months before, on the 29th of August 1988.

The feeling among many from the barn area was given voice by George Steinbrenner, best known as a baseball man, but interviewed on his way to a meeting of the Florida Thoroughbred Breeders' Association. He told Dave Goldman from the Thoroughbred Record: "I think we are seeing something happening in California right now that could have far reaching effects . . . I'm talking about horse drugging, the use of illegal drugs on horses in racing . . . I don't know the facts in any of the cases, but if the allegations are proved, and we don't deal with them with a hammer instead of a slap on the wrist, then the whole industry will suffer."

Los Angeles journalists were the first to inform Wayne. His reported response to the charges was, "We've raced in 16 states, had 5,000 or 6,000 [tests] probably more, and we've had no positives. Something is drastically wrong . . . I would not accept any ruling, no matter how minor it was. Jeff and I are paranoid about this thing. We preach it constantly. We never test the system, never push the line. Something's very very wrong." To another journalist: "We take every precaution, we're paranoid about this thing."

Speaking to the press with Barrera, Wayne said, "It's bizarre. I don't even know what the stuff looks like." Barrera called it, " . . . an insult to my career."

International Diagnostic Systems, an independent testing company weighed in with a statement that use of illegal drugs on Californian horses 'apparently is rampant.'

The early part of 1989 was a tough time for Lukas. He went to the 1989 Kentucky Derby under the dark cloud of charged horse doper. On the telecast he looked pale and tired. There seemed to be a lot more gray hair. He was having serious back pain and had to have surgery. His father died.

Then the testing lab shifted its position. Dr Norman Hester, technical director of Truesdail Labs, said he believed the samples, "probably were contaminated. I think the samples do have cocaine, but that none of the trainers involved gave it to the horses. I believe the problem is lax security on the backstretch. People using cocaine are coming into contact with the horses."

Len Foote of the California Horse Racing Board added, " . . . make no mistake, we still have a drug problem in this state."

Wayne however was not sitting around wringing his hands. After the charges were finally dismissed in late July 1989, I asked Wayne his side of the story: "They had enough sample and I had them retest my tests. They sent it to the leading labs in the country - Utah, Cornell, Colorado - the ones that are world renowned. They told them what to look for. They normally take those tests down to 10 nanograms. They took it down to one nanogram. (1/1,000,000,000th of a gram. A gram is about 1/25th of an ounce.) They found nothing."

"So it was a false positive? (A reading that says something is present when it is not.)"

"They either got a false positive or contamination by the guy who did the tests on the day. The consensus was that it was a false positive. The expert at Cornell, Dr Maylin, said he'd bet anything that they didn't have anything. They took it down as far as you can go and it was perfectly clean."

"The statement after the backdown implied, 'Well we can't prove it this time but - no prejudice - if we can improve the sensitivity we want to have another crack at him."

"They did two things wrong. They had a back-up test at a lab in Ohio State. They didn't check with them before they released the statement. Then when they did check with Ohio State, Ohio said, 'Well we can't find anything.' Then they knew they were in trouble. So they took a position, 'We'll further look into this'. In the meantime we subpoenaed enough sample to do four more tests. We asked them who would be the best in the world to do this. They gave us a list. We sent it to the people they most respected. Those people could not find anything."

"They said they found the metabolite as well."

"Maylin had a look at their data and he says that what they found did not go through a horse. He said that if they can prove that that went through a horse they'll get the Nobel Prize for chemistry."

"It is a pity for your position as an example to young racehorse trainers."

"Once they were embarrassed by it they tried to sweep it under the carpet. They said, 'We'll drop charges, we're sorry' and so on. But we're not going to let that happen because we *want* to be an example in the industry. I've put too much of my life into the thing to let some goofy guy who is a cocaine user and handles the beakers in some lab ruin my career."

"So you will be taking it to court?"

"There'll be some apologies issued believe me."

"The other thing that made it look bad was that it said the testing on the frozen samples was done at the request of the Horseman's Association, which looked as though a lot of people thought you were using something and they wanted you caught."

"What we found out there was that they had a whole rash of false positives. They had a new system and they didn't know how to run it. They dismissed that. They don't even want to talk about that. I was tested 1428 times last year in 16 different states and I get one millionth of a milligram in a maiden! Oh no."

"It was only one sample and that was a maiden?"
"Yes."

"Do you think they were out to get you?"

"No I don't think there was any vindictiveness. They thought they really had something. We're going to make them issue the statements, only it'll never make the papers like it did the first time."

The State Attorney General's Department issued a statement in response to pressure from the lawyer representing Lukas and Barrera. " . . . These cases are closed. Not only are they dismissed, but no further investigation is pending as to these cases against your clients. Furthermore no further investigation is contemplated . . . "

If Wayne was the most visible and best ambassador for racing's image, then the affair of the cocaine positives in California was a disaster for the image of Wayne and of racing. Newspapers in some states carried banner headlines: LUKAS, BARRERA IN HORSE DRUGGING SCANDAL. No retraction or vindication ever gets the same headlines. Perhaps 10 or 20 lines buried in the sports section many months later.

Mel Hatley had this to say to me: "I know this man, he's a very dear friend to me. He doesn't use drugs. I'd stake my life on it. I know better than that. You couldn't send horses all over the country and be doing that. That's just jealousy and bar talk."

But this episode, a drug positive for Lukas, was seen by many as confirmation of something they had long believed. The end result is unknown to them or they write it off as the track backing down to Lukas's lawyers. Edward "Ned" Bonnie, a Kentucky lawyer prominent in racing circles was reported to have said, "There are at least 10 drugs being used in every racing jurisdiction - I repeat - in every racing jurisdiction."

So the waters have remained very murky and everyone can have their own opinion about what is lurking in those waters. I was stunned when the charges were announced in early 1989. Now those charges represent one of the great cockups of recent racing history.

A racing journalist had drawn my attention to the National Association of Racing Commissioners in Kentucky. He said they would give the drug testing history on any trainer in America. I phoned up. A lady answered the phone and I asked if Wayne Lukas had any record of drugs in his tests.

"Oh yes he has had them I'm sure." She proceeded to bring his record up on a computer. "March of 1986 he had PEG - Poly Ethylene Glycol. Fined $200." That is a stabilising agent for a lot of drugs used in veterinary medicines. "April 1977, oxymorphone hydrochloride." Then the computer started to give trouble. Then the lady started asking why I wanted the information. I told her - for a book. That threw a spanner in the works. "You better write a letter to the director," she said. The Association's answer, after legal advice, was, 'Sorry, we can't help you'. In this land of litigation, I couldn't blame them, but I knew it would raise cries of 'cover-up'. Eventually I was able ascertain that Wayne had a positive test for a Quarter Horse called Moving Moon, in April 1977. The drug was oxymorphone. D. Wayne Lukas was suspended for 60 days and placed on probation for the balance of 1977.

Unless I had heard the year wrong, Wayne had told me about some other occasion, some other oxymorphone positive. I listened again to the tape. He definitely said 1973. Suspended for 45 days. A man with a very good memory. There was food for thought here.

Oxymorphone Hydrochloride

This is a morphine-like compound, which is marketed as Numorphan and as Oxymorphone. When it was developed it was hoped it would be useful as a painkiller for colic in horses, but other drugs were preferred by vets. Its main use in veterinary practice is for sedating dogs (particularly bitey dogs) for minor procedures like removing a plaster cast, clipping nails etc. Equine vets said they never found any use for it. Since it was a controlled substance, a vet had to have a particularly good reason to carry it. Controlled substances must be kept under lock and key and every dose must be recorded in a special logbook. Most of the morphine group attract drug addicts. If a druggie breaks into a vet's premises and finds *anything* useable, you can guarantee the premises will then be broken into every week for a month. So most vets avoid keeping the stuff. There are other non-narcotic drugs that will do the job. So it's not something likely to be given as part of legitimate medical treatment of a horse.

From what older American vets and trainers tell me, oxymorphone soon acquired a reputation as a drug that would stimulate horses and make them run faster. It was especially used in Quarter Horses. It made Thoroughbreds go too fast too early, and they burnt themselves out instead of winning. Over the years there have been more than a few positive drug tests for oxymorphone in Quarter Horses. Many of those positives were traced back to certain veterinarians in a recent major enquiry.

The timing of Wayne's suspension is interesting. The race was in April 1977, so the test and hearings would take say a month. The two month 'holiday' would probably have run right up to the Keeneland July Yearling Sales at which Wayne bought Terlingua. Did this suspension have something to do with Wayne switching to Thoroughbreds? Did it allow Blane Schvaneveld to get by Wayne in total money won for the first time?

It also explained some peculiar things I had noticed in the Quarter Horse records. For example Little Blue Sheep, winner of many major races, and trained by Wayne for Bob French. Bob French is recorded as her owner for all the wins.

Wins of LITTLE BLUE SHEEP

Year/Race		Trainer Listed
1976		
Vessels Maturity	G1	Wayne Lukas
1977		
Double Bid Handicap	G3	Wayne Lukas
Go Man Go Handicap	G1	Wayne Lukas
Miss Peninsula Handicap	G2	Wayne Lukas
Peninsula Championship	G1	Ken Teutsch
Shue Fly Handicap		Tom MacKenzie
1978		
Kaweah Bar Handicap	G3	Wayne Lukas
Las Damas Handicap	G1	Wayne Lukas
Miss Peninsula Handicap	G2	Wayne Lukas

This kind of thing can of course be due to another trainer taking a horse to faraway tracks to race, but all these races were in California at major meets. Tom MacKenzie was Wayne's right-hand man in 1978.

Kenneth Teutsch was also the trainer of record for the winner of the 1977 Bay Meadows Futurity. If he was just standing in for Wayne while he was suspended it would explain the claim that Lukas won this event four times straight.

When I asked Bob Moore if the suspension for a drug test had anything to do with Wayne changing over, he said, "No, that didn't hurt him. His people were pushing him in that direction."

Bobby Adair, the jockey who was a long-standing friend of Wayne and Blane, also said the drug suspension was not the reason. Said Bobby, "Wayne is ambitious. He wanted to go over there where the big money was and prove something. And he has. He's the most successful trainer in the world. It's all there in the records and no one can take that away from him."

No one can take the records away, but the other trainers are not going to applaud if they think Wayne did it with the help of drugs. If there is one thing harder to explain than a positive for oxymorphone, it's two positives for oxymorphone. Omitting to mention them to me while going on about how the drugging accusations always crop up when a trainer is successful, did not do a lot for Wayne's credibilty in my eyes.

If Wayne *did* use oxymorphone in 1973, it is hard to believe he would use it again after having the first positive. Anyone using it would presumably have to pick their spots because it was detectable. Maybe in smalltime events, because then the labs often don't test so many horses nor analyze for so many drugs. Maybe in a claimer which still won't win, to improve the likelihood of it being claimed by someone who sees the improvement.

Wayne's horse Moving Moon finished second in spite of the oxymorphone, which makes me wonder how the horse came to be swabbed. Was there something that attracted the eye of the stewards? Was Wayne regarded as a trainer who used drugs back then? Was there a tip-off? If you like fancy plots, maybe someone else, someone who didn't like Wayne, gave it and then tipped off the stewards. Around American track stables, there is usually a quiet time of the day when very few staff are about. I found that I could wander into many stables on the tracks and go completely unnoticed.

Of course most trainers believe Wayne uses drugs, and so they would not be surprised he was swabbed.

Two Quarter Horse trainers of Wayne's vintage have told me that going back in time, at some Quarter racing tracks, you could only compete with any great success if you used, "what everyone else was using: Numorphan, Dilaudid, Apomorphine. Later that was all cleared up by better testing." I'm told the same was true of some harness racing and Thoroughbred tracks at that time.

There are a lot of possibilities: -Wayne may have never used illegal drugs, merely been the victim of others, such as a vet, or staff member, or a freelance chemical racing fiend.

-Wayne may have used oxymorphone in Quarter Horses, but after being suspended, decided to make a clean, fresh start in Thoroughbreds.

-Wayne may, as many in racing believe, be using drugs in his Thoroughbreds. Designer drugs or something undetectable. Except if he had such a thing, why would he use cocaine?

After several months of thinking what a sneaky bastard Wayne was, I decided to ask him about it.

"Did you have two positives for Oxymorphone?"

"No."

"You told me about one in 1973, and there is one in the records for 1977."

"1977? Are you sure? Well, whatever it shows in the records, that's the one. There was only one, and I explained that to you. I don't worry about it."

Whatever the truth of the matter, just who gave the oxymorphone, there has been enough smoke for people to talk about fires, and Wayne will have to live with the accusation that he uses drugs in his horses for as long as he is in racing. If he is guilty, it is a sad blemish on an otherwise outstanding career. If he is innocent, it is a tragic blemish, and probably nothing Wayne could do would remove the stain.

Australians reading this will be astonished to read that Wayne was given a 60 day suspension for a narcotic positive. The penalties for drug use in American racing must seem pa-

thetic to Australian trainers. In Australia, for a narcotic or caffeine, a year is on the low side, five years is common and 20 years was the penalty in 1987/1988 for a trainer who returned two positives for etorphine (elephant juice).

The small penalties in America mean that more trainers will take the risk. It does however, mean that even a trainer who is innocent will be reluctant to fight the authorities through the courts.

If Wayne had received a penalty of 15 years in 1977, he would, in 1990, have some other career, in which I have no doubt he would be outstandingly successful. He'd be wondering if he wanted to get back into racing in 1992. Wondering if he should give Thoroughbreds a try.

13.5 Luck and other reasons for success

Wayne certainly doesn't feel that luck had much to do with his rise. If you want to get Wayne mad, tell him he only got to the top because he has wealthy owners who will buy any horse he wants. *"Wayne, when I'm in amongst local horsemen, and I ask how the top trainer made it to the top, they'll often say, 'He's the best because he gets the best horses'. Someone gives them to him is their attitude."*

"How do they think that happens? Do they think that God looked down one day and said, 'We're going to take this farm boy out of Wisconsin - he doesn't even live in horse country - and we'll bring him along and give him all the money and all the horses?' That happens because you EARN that right."

"Their close competition, the other top trainers, usually respect them a great deal."

"See, the people that are critical, that you talk to, are never the people that I've competed with over there. If you go to Blane Schvaneveldt, who is the leading Quarter Horse trainer over at Los Alamitos now, he and I competed head to head, many many years. If you were to take him in a room and say, 'Let's discuss the other guy, Wayne Lukas,' I'd feel confident that he would say good things."

"He did say good things. Also Caesar Dominguez: he's a Quarter Horse trainer; I was asking him, 'Did you know Wayne Lukas?' "

"Sure, he knew me."

"I said, 'What do you think is his secret? Is it his ability to choose horses? Is it his organizing ability? Is it his big-money backers?' and so on. Caesar says, 'All of the above!' He did not say anything like, 'He was lucky. People gave him good horses."

Conclusion: Wayne bought good horses for below average prices in his early days in Quarter Horses and in Thoroughbreds. Even now he buys a horse like Open Mind, champion filly at two-year-old and three-year-old, for $150,000 when the sale average was $297,000. I cannot think of any trainer who's rise was more inevitable: the hours he worked, the pace at which he worked, the single-minded devotion to his objectives etc. Luck had very little to do with Wayne's rise. It is interesting to speculate on his results if he had been born into a horse racing family in a racing state, or had simply gone into training earlier in life.

13.6 What Wayne thinks made him successful

When this question has been asked in interviews, Wayne tends to go into his speech about how good his staff is etc., so exactly what he believes I can only guess. No doubt by the effort he puts into it he would list drive, dedication and hard work. A lot of people who haven't gone very far have those things too, but few have them to the same degree. The real difference is in the intelligent application of that drive, making himself an outstanding yearling judge.

13.7 Trainer, conman or businessman?

Without doubt Wayne is a man with a carefully educated eye for a horse. About his training there could be some argument. He is an excellent organizer and businessman. He is regarded by many as very good with words, some even call him a bull-artist. But that is a very easy refuge for the envious trainer. I well remember in veterinary practice, how the top vets in the eyes of the public were so often described by rival vets and envious academics as conmen and bulldusters.

I had the opportunity to see some of the academics and some of these 'conmen' practitioners at work. There *were* some vets whose crowd pulling ability rested mainly with a golden tongue. But these were not highly respected by other vets and nurses with whom they worked. They didn't fool many breeders. The very best practitioners, on the other hand, knew their theory, knew how to get results, knew how to communicate with the breeders and owners. They ran rings around their arrogant academic critics and their envious suburban rivals.

It has been a similar experience interviewing Wayne Lukas. He is a master of what sounds like high flying hyperbole, except that he *has* done the things he claims to have done. He has an awful lot to boast about. His reasons for doing things are well thought out, probably much better thought out than those of his critics.

His ability to impress people is based on knowledge, a convincing logical argument, and results. It is certainly not built upon a groveling manner or excuses. There is a fine line to be trodden when winning over clients. Extravagant claims or the building of false hopes can only have short term success. Those who write Wayne off as a conman or a doper of horses would do better to look much more closely at his approach and carefully compare it with their own to find ways to improve.

The key to the success of Wayne Lukas is his ability to choose a high proportion of the best racehorses in the yearling sales. Other people can do that too, but they have not achieved anything like his overall success. That tells us that Wayne has some other skills carried to a high level, that in fact he is the 'compleat trainer': one that can choose the best yearlings; attract wealthy clients to pay for them; set up and run a scattered organization which can condition the horses to realise their athletic potential; and a trainer who can make the whole operation profitable for himself and his owners.

Summary: The jury is still out on Wayne's training because it is so different and because the issue is confused by his selection abilities. He is not a conman, but does state his case to its limits. He is very logical and very convincing. He is a superb businessman.

13.8 What drives him?

Wayne has a very powerful ego, a lot of ambition. He wants to rewrite the record books so that they'll be reading about him in a hundred years. Unless there's a nuclear lunacy, they will. I would say Wayne's main drive is for recognition and status, several points ahead of money. His staff management suggests he is not a power tripper. If he was merely trying to be independent, he could easily slacken off. He keeps to himself too much to be socially motivated, in fact he works so hard it severely cramps his social life. But he keeps on driving himself, carving his way through the record books.

He is on record with this comment: " . . . years from now, I don't want people to say, 'Oh, he won an Eclipse Award.' I want them to say, 'He was a good horseman." Ironically that is an accolade that can only be bestowed upon him by other trainers, and I think it reveals a desire for recognition by other trainers. Blane Schvaneveldt, Caesar Dominguez and Kiaran McLaughlin would give him that title, but a lot of his detractors wouldn't. That's now. What about in 20 years time? 100 years time?

13.9 Lessons for beginning trainers

What are the lessons to be learnt from the rise and rise of Wayne Lukas?

a) Learn to select horses.

This is probably the key to Wayne's success, the single most important factor in his success. It is easy to say now that Wayne has good horses because his wealthy owners can afford expensive yearlings. But two things should not be forgotten: First, it is very easy to spend big bucks at a yearling sale and come up with nothing. Over the years some very wealthy people have ventured small fortunes on yearlings, bought a bunch of failures and faded from the scene. Even some of the great yearling selectors have had "off" years. Second, Wayne Lukas had to start at the bottom. He proved his eye by bidding on horses that *ran well for the price paid*. He impressed some owners and it built from there. Then, when he had the backers, he went for the top end of the market.

Wayne has a word with his Hollywood foreman Ruben Perez as he waits with his horse for the start of the next race. In Wayne's rise there are many lessons for other trainers.

Wayne developed his eye by looking for common traits in the winners of everyday races. He started in Quarter Horses where the horses are a lot cheaper to buy and where conformation is a very large determinant of racing ability. This allowed him to train his eye well before he moved into Thoroughbreds in which heart size and ratable temperament are larger hidden factors. He still prefers the short and fast end of Thoroughbreds, possibly because he came from that end, possibly because he has found that there is a greater 'hidden' component in the stayer; most probably because there is more money in the shorter races.

What can an aspiring or new trainer do? Develop an eye for muscling, for joint angles, bone lengths and body types. Start with a long list of factors you think might be important in determining racing talent. Concentrate on the ones you think are the most important. Team up with someone, pool ideas and halve the work.

Let experience over large numbers determine what is ideal. DON'T think something like a short neck can't be a bad trait simply because you see one winner with a short neck. Think in percentages. What percentage of the horses in the sales had short necks? Let's say 20% by your eye. What percentage of the first hundred winners had short necks? 10% by your eye. What percentage of horses coming last had short necks? If it is 25% or 40% you have a trend and a conclusion: short necks are a disadvantage but not a severe one.

Maybe a very short neck could by itself be a severe disadvantage. If you see a winner with some trait you think is a severe impediment to race speed, look for something else in the horse's build that may be a compensation for that weakness.

Assess horses of known ability as often as you can. Assess the winners of every race for conformation. Make notes, take pictures if it will help you. Take measurements and calculate ratios - on the horses or the pictures. Measuring anything improves your eyeballing accuracy. Initially you might find a simple grading system works best. Such as - obviously very long, long if you look hard, average, short if you look hard and obviously short. Five levels to start with, or even three.

Go to the races and assess all the horses entered that day for just one trait e.g. neck length or stifle angle. Compare first and last in each race. This is easier in some parts of the world than others. At some tracks the horses are not seen until just before a brief and distant pre-post parade. Others parade the horses for a full 20 minutes in various parts of the course before the same pre-post parade. Horses that come last in trials are often very educational examples of the worst in gait and non-athletic build.

Go to the yearling sales and look at as many yearlings as possible. Make notes on how they are put together, then come to a conclusion on their athletic rating, probable best distance and how much racing you think they'll stand. See if you can predict their soundness, and if you expect them to go unsound, try to pinpoint their weak link - too fine in the fetlocks, prone to knee chips etc.

You can see the same horses at the track next year. Make notes of the changes in length and height and body type. You may find that one you note in the racebook as too heavy, when you check back in the yearling sales catalogue, appeared just right at that age. At the end of their two and three-year-old years you can track them down in various publications.

You may not find them all, but if you are able to compare one or two hundred track assessments with your yearling assessment, you will learn a lot. Repeat that every year and you'll be a hot shot in no time.

If you are in North America, and you or your owners can afford it, have Equix in Lexington or any similar scientific company do a biomechanical analysis - even if only on 1 or 2 horses. You should learn a lot about your 'eye' from their assessment. If you have your top four selections assessed it would cost you something around $2,000 plus travel expenses. This is not a lot if you intend paying even $20,000 for a yearling, let alone $200,000 or $2m.

You will probably find at least one to be a write-off for some reason you overlooked. This, incidentally, is the horse you would most likely have ended up buying. Why? Because competitors may not have overlooked the same fault, indeed they may have an Equix report on it. They would not bid against you on that one. You would tootle off home delighted with the 'bargain' everyone else missed! Such a 'bargain' is highly likely to end up on the inglorious end of your statistical record as a chooser of champions.

I well remember a trainer at the yearling sales who said to me, "When you are a small-timer like me, practically every bad yearling purchase is another owner lost."

b) Be business-like.

Set goals for yourself and your staff. Have incentive schemes based on results. Work hard and set an example to your staff.

Tell them what you expect. Often. Get rid of people who do not like hard work or who become disheartened easily.

c) Polish-up your image.

Most trainers put a lot of effort into making their horses look good in the parade ring, and they dress well on raceday. However most trainers could start with the barn and make quite a difference without much monetary expenditure. Buy some rugged flower pots or construct some boxes of the type and size that allow you to slip plastic pots of plants in and out easily. Select some hardy long-flowering plants of enough types to cover most of the year. Rotate them through the back yard. If you can't interest one of the staff or the spouse in the intricacies of horticulture, learn a bit about it yourself. It might give you an interest in retirement. (Early, wealthy retirement of course.)

d) Be straightforward with owners.

Many trainers believe Wayne is a great conman, but his owners say Wayne tells them everything - lays it on the line.

Trainers who tell lies and half-truths, who omit any damaging facts, who may even pride themselves on their ability to con people along, usually end up mired in a truckload of their own bulldust. Owners often repeat amazing stories to veterinarians, unbelievable stories spun to them by low level trainers. Confused or unbelieving, these owners phone the vet who is treating the horse.

Sometimes trainers lie to cover up something stupid the trainer did. But surprisingly, some trainers lie about something when the simple truth would satisfy the owner. Why the convoluted lies? Possibly because the trainer perceives any injury as indicating a fault, an error, imagining that the top trainers don't have the same problems at all.

For the lies-and-proud-of-it type, chew on this: Intelligent, business-like people will see through the haze of horseshit and they won't like what they see. They more than likely won't tell you why they are not patronizing you any more. (This is what owners tell me.) They'll simply take up with another trainer or fade right out of racing. The more intelligent, perceptive and business-like they are, the more likely they are to see through you. Unfortunately the more intelligent, perceptive and business-like they are, the wealthier they are likely to be! The conman is more likely to end up with owners who are mugs. Mugs are not famous for the ability to acquire great wealth on a continuing basis.

You don't have to have a degree and a posh accent to deal with the highly educated owner who comes from hereditary money, nor with business-school-trained captains of industry. There will be examples in this series, of trainers with very little schooling, who did very well with these groups, but they did it by being believable.

14. The Future

14.1 Perfect conditions for him would be?

Wayne would like to have the chance to buy every Thoroughbred born in every crop, every year. In practical terms the cream of the crop is concentrated in a half dozen sales around the country. He is confident that over a period of time he can pick a lot of great horses. Horses that go to other trainers without going through the sales are his nemesis.

14.2 Probabilities

With the announcement that Klein would be dramatically shrinking his operation, there was a lot of speculation as to how this would affect Lukas. Wayne, however, said he was inundated with, "a lot of hustle guys with all kinds of schemes". Apart from hustlers there would no doubt be people who wanted to be the next Klein, the next high profile, profit-making king of racing's owners. I'm sure if their bank account checked out, Wayne would sit down and talk.

But Lukas already had a major replacement. William T. Young has amassed a fortune in such disparate lines as Jiffy peanut butter and the Humana hospital chain. It was at the Humana Corporation's flagship hospital in Louisville that the first artificial heart operation was performed in 1982. Young is no stranger to the limelight. He is a member of The Jockey Club, a director of Churchill Downs, and a director of the Breeders' Cup.

Young has Overbrook Farm in Kentucky, and in 1988 he was the major contributor to Wayne's $21m or so expenditure on yearlings. (Klein bought none.) Lukas and Young hit it off after they were introduced a couple of years ago. The only drawback is Young's age. Young is not young, he's 71. But he wants to make a big splash in racing so he's likely to spend big to make his mark quickly. That should suit Wayne.

Wayne almost had a champion for Young at the end of 1989. The horse cost $825,000 and Wayne had a quarter share. Named Grand Canyon, the colt put up some impressive performances but was beaten two lengths by Rhythm in the Breeders' Cup Juvenile for Colts. Then Grand Canyon won the million dollar Hollywood Futurity by 6½ lengths in what is believed to be the fastest time for the mile ever run by a two-year-old in North America - 1:33. The time broke Snow Chief's record by 1 and 1/5 sec. Wayne lobbied hard but Rhythm was voted Champion two-year-old colt.

Grand Canyon became winter book favorite for the 1990 Kentucky Derby. The horse was in line for a $1m bonus if it could add the Kentucky Derby to its win in the Kentucky Jockey Club Stakes. But when early nominations closed in February, Grand Canyon was not one of them. He had damaged a knee when he stumbled pulling up after the Futurity. The horse had already won $1,019,540 and Wayne decided to rest

him and bring him back for the late three-year-old races - and the Breeders' Cup no doubt. Two other horses ran in the Kentucky Derby in the ownership name of Lukas and Overbrook Farm. Neither horse did much, but it showed the depth and quality of the partnership's stock.

If Young wasn't enough, Wayne has Peter Brant, a major money man in publishing and newsprint manufacturing. (Brant's interests include a number of Thoroughbred racing publications, so some journalists might be saying nicer things about Wayne now. Then again , Brant has run afoul of the Internal Revenue Service and may have to curtail his racing activities.) Plus: Wayne has Calumet Farms, one of the most famous names in Thoroughbred breeding. Plus: Wayne has the volatile Daniel Wildenstein giving him top European turf horses like Steinlen. All these are added to his long-standing clients. Wayne has what is called in American sports parlance a deep bench.

A Lukas attack on Europe?

"Do you think you'll have a tilt at England and Europe?"

"I don't think I will, unless it be the major races, because there's no money over there. Even my major clients, like Peter Brant, are very disillusioned. There's no money. It used to be, you could develop those horses over there and they would syndicate or fetch great prices in the sales, but even that's slipping now. It's down to money and there's no purse money there. I don't know how the hell you'd make any money in Europe with a string. If I went over there it would break me."

"You could buy in Europe, if the prices were lower."

"I don't go over there and shop. A lot of these guys do. I haven't pursued that market at all."

Just training his own horses?

It is possible that in time Wayne may become wealthy enough to buy most of the best horses for himself: the eights, the nines and if he ever sees any, the tens. He could have done so towards the end of the 1980's, but preferred to have larger percentages of a larger number of prospects. Besides, it wouldn't look good if a trainer ended up with the plum picks of the yearling crop all to himself. Long-faithful owners would not be impressed. But if Wayne continues to succeed to the extent that he already has, he will reach a transition point in the 1990's, when it will become financially possible for him achieve the 'ultimate dream' of trainers: to train only his own horses.

Should he reach that financial position, there are other options open to Wayne, besides training his own 'top twenty'. He may just continue his present policy, increasing his percentage ownership in each horse and increasing his present training numbers. Or he could simply expand his numbers. Lukas and friends could end up buying a very substantial part of the annual yearling crop. It could force some people to buy weanlings, or yearlings off the farm, to counter Wayne's ability to pick the best prospects and purchase them. It may be better to buy 10 weanlings Lukas hasn't picked over than 10 yearlings he has.

Of course, he may start to invest outside racing. He may even retire, if someone would introduce him to the word, explain its meaning to him, and show him a video about beachfront condominiums. What he would do with all that energy I don't know.

The probabilities are that Wayne will remain at No. 1 for many years and continue to stretch the cumulative records. More than likely he will break many of his own annual records as well. Rumours are that he will take Jeff on as partner, presumably on the way to handing over the business. Only time will tell.

Wayne could not have a higher opinion of Jeff than he has. When I mentioned John Gosden's high opinion of Jeff, Wayne said, "Yes, they all think that he is absolutely going to be the next guy. I do too. He dominates New York too much for him not to. I mean, he's seven or eight in front over there right now, among all the best trainers, Woody and those guys. He handles them left-handed. He's got a great future. He knows more at age thirty than I ever even begin to know at age fifty. He's an extremely good organiser too. His future is so bright it's scary. The thing that I'm proudest of where Jeff is concerned is that a trainer like Laz Bererra - if you go ask Laz to name the top four trainers in America, I think he'll include Jeff."

But even if Wayne retired now, we know that he has reached the top and dominated in two competitive racing worlds. Only Vincent O'Brien of Ireland might be considered by some to have done more in this regard. Certainly Vincent's many fans worldwide will say so.

Vincent made it to the top of Hurdle and Steeplechase racing, collectively known as National Hunt Racing, then went on to international fame in flat racing. In both Ireland and England in the 1940's and 50's, National Hunt racing 'over the jumps' was a national passion. From his base in Ireland, Vincent pillaged the biggest plums England had to offer. He won the Cheltenham Gold Cup three years running from 1948, the Champion Hurdle three years running from 1949, and the Grand National Steelechase three years running from 1953. For Americans, that is the National Hunt equivalent of winning the Kentucky Derby, Preakness and Belmont Stakes, and winning each three times running. Vincent then shifted his focus from National Hunt racing and went on to become the terror of the Irish and English Triple Crown races, the principal plump plum plunderer of flat racing.

Because of differences in era, country and code of racing, closer assessment of the relative achievements of the two begins to compare apples to oranges.

The future - a book? politics?
Early in 1990 Wayne was testing the water in a new area. He had bought some yearlings at the 1989 sales in the name Lukas two-year-old in Training. In January he advertised the original purchase price of these horses and their accumulated training costs, and the Two-year-olds in Training sale at which they would be available. These horses were from the cheap end of the Kentucky sales, ranging from $31,000 to $160,000. The seven or eight months of care and training from July to March was valued at $20,000.

Wayne is offering his eye to help pick a cheap champ which will end up in his barn. No doubt some will say that if Wayne really thought they were champions he would buy them himself. It is a new venture, but he is still sticking to the knitting.

"I hope you're going to write a detailed book before you pass on."

"No. I'm not interested in that. There've been some people who wanted to do a book, because they think I have a lot of humor. I have a lot of stories that I've told to different writers, and they get a kick out of me. They think it'd be a great human-interest story. Maybe some day, but surely not now. I don't think anybody'd buy it, for one thing."

(I find Wayne Lukas fascinating because I am a science junkie and I think he has the answers to some interesting questions. I doubt he'll want to give those answers away, but I hope he writes some kind of book.)

"Do you have any other ambitions beyond horse-racing? Have you ever thought about politics?"

"I've been approached privately by some very powerful people, to get into politics. Not in the last couple of years, but I've had some very serious approaches in this state and in another state, but it's never appealed to me. I'm not into that kind of stuff. I do think I have the ability to motivate people and to get people to follow. Maybe that is what politics is, but I don't have the inclination to ever get into politics."

"I just think I'd like to be good at what I do, or the best at what I do. I would like to personally rewrite all the books, and I'm not intimidated by Charlie and Woody and the people in front of me at all, because I think it's just a matter of time until I swallow those up. I don't see that that's going to be a problem. I mean, Woody's been at it forty-nine years and since '78, we've completely surpassed his earnings, his stakes records and his world champions record."

"Charlie has been at it fifty-one years or something like that, and this year we're going to pass him. Without a doubt we're going to pass him. So over an eleven-year span we are going to become the all-time money-winnings trainer - and the two guys right below us are Woody and Charlie, and they're fifty-one and forty-nine years at it. So - given the fifty years, if I get the fifty years - I think we'll be okay."

"You'd have to live a to a ripe old age to get fifty years. How many Triple Crowns would you like?"

"Well . . . we haven't won any Triple Crowns. We've won those other races. But I don't think that's any big stuff. I think we're going to win."

His interest in Quarter Horses continues. At the 1989 Phillips Ranch Sale, Wayne paid $42,000 for a sorrel filly, a full sister to World Champion Dashingly. Perhaps he bought it for a client, perhaps the All-American still haunts Wayne, still tugs at his subconscious. It's the race a Quarter Horse trainer has to win to die happy.

On Saturday May 12th 1990, Criminal Type caught the lead horse in the stretch and won the $1 million Pimlico Special by a neck. The Overbrook Farm homebred set a track record. In this spectacular fashion, Wayne Lukas became the first trainer in horse racing history to pass $100 million dollars in winnings. In Wayne Lukas, popularity rating notwithstanding, you have seen one of the greatest achievers in racing history in action.

First race on a pleasant Californian evening. Riders wait to lead the competing horses to the starting gates, while the fans put their money on. In America the racehorses are led from another horse out to the starting gate. They seldom go for a warm up canter or gallop. Quarter Horses are much favored for the role of 'Pony', even at Thoroughbred meets. They are very placid, but can usually catch a runaway in a short distance, before it wears itself out and has to be scratched from the race. These 'Pony' riders are free agents, like jockeys, not track employees. They compete for horses and stables, and are paid per horse.

Competitors and 'Pony' horses are paired off for the trip. Caesar's wife was a 'Pony' girl when they met.

CAESAR FRANCISCO DOMINGUEZ

Caesar Francisco Dominguez became the King of the Claimers in Quarter Horse racing before he was 40. He is an example to anyone, but because he is Mexican, he is especially an inspiration to the many Mexicans in the horse racing industry of North America. Starting at the very bottom, 'walking hots' for 50 cents an hour and sleeping on the tack room floor, Caesar became a Quarter Horse trainer and rose steadily up the trainers' list. Most of his wins and money came from claiming races, and he has amassed the second highest number of winners in the history of Quarter Horse racing.

King of the Claimers,
now moving into stakes
Quarter Horse Trainer

LOS ALAMITOS, CALIFORNIA, U.S.A.

He spent many years as one of the top three trainers in California, before finally breaking through to be leading trainer on wins and money in California for 1989. Much of the breakthrough was due to wins in some big-money graded stakes races. He is also interesting because he has had some experience training Thoroughbreds and can compare them with Quarter Horses.

I have tried to retain as much as possible of Caesar's highly enjoyable and very characteristic speech. If at times it is a little hard to follow, that is my fault, not Caesar's, because Caesar himself is very easy to understand. In fact, the transcript makes Caesar sound a little backward, folksy perhaps, when he is really very sharp.

2. What start in life did Caesar have?

The fact that a Mexican is one of America's leading Quarter Horse trainers may come as a surprise to readers in some parts of the world. To those familiar with the history of the Quarter Horse, or of the Mexican people, it will be little or no surprise. Ever since the horse helped the Spaniard Cortés overwhelm the Aztecs in 1521, the horse has been a significant part of the Mexican culture.

The Aztecs and their neighboring rivals had never seen a horse until Cortés rode up. Initially the natives believed the horses were immortal, and the clatter of their hooves on the miles of stone plazas helped to create a powerful impression of invincibility. This, and the Aztec demand for people to use as human sacrifices, caused the neighboring tribes to side with Cortés, a decisive factor in his success.

The Spanish settlers brought more horses to the New World. The best remained in the hands of the colonial elite, a status symbol, but over the centuries the horses bred and spread. By purchase, stealing, or capture from escaped wild herds, these horses became the mounts of the early Mexican settlers and tribal Indians. The horses spread north where they later interbred with those imported into the colonies that later became the United States.

The resulting horsey hodge podge served the American settlers, and ultimately, the cowboy. The main selection pressure on this genetic whirlpool was for a horse that could be ridden all day, but which could outmaneuver cattle in their zigzag attempts to break away. It helped if the horse could overhaul a runaway steer in a matter of yards, not miles. The result of this quest for acceleration was an amazingly tractable, physically stocky sprinter, the breed now known as the Quarter Horse. Not until 1940 was the breed named and a registry formed.

Quarter Horse racing began to blossom at about the same time as the breed society was formed. The racing was mostly over a quarter of a mile. For cow work, the 'best racing distance' was probably 5 to 100 yards. Consequently Quarter Horses were sometimes beaten over the quarter mile dash by Thoroughbreds. The introduction of crosses of Thoroughbred blood were therefore very successful, and eventually the racing Quarter Horse strain so developed would prove superior to both cattle-working strains and Thoroughbreds over the quarter mile distance.

Caesar Dominguez

Even after the second race, the sun is visible thru the Los Angeles haze.

Just as the Spanish horses had a major input into the ancestry of the Quarter Horse, the Spanish settlers had a large influence in the ethnic mix of the region, which was known as New Spain for 300 years. (That was trendy then: the French settling what is now Canada called it New France; the English settling the Boston area called it New England.)

At the time they settled the area, the invading Spanish were from the most advanced country in Europe. The Aztecs were the most advanced culture in North America at that same time. The two groups intermarried and the ethnic mixing has gone on for over 350 years. They became one people, known today as Mexicans.

Over the last two centuries the borders between Mexico and the United States have shifted about and so have the people. The belt from California across to Texas was once part of New Spain. By a series of deliberate provocations, followed by "outraged retaliation", a technique later made famous by Adolf Hitler, the Americans annexed the territory.

As the American standard of living and need for labor rose, more Mexicans shifted into the region. So today there are many millions of people of Mexican ancestry in the United States. However, citizens of Spanish ancestry in today's United States may have come from other parts of the Americas besides Mexico, so the term Hispanic is used to indicate anyone of Spanish-American ancestry. People of Mexican ancestry and people shifting from Mexico to America are usually still called Mexicans, but at census time they are Hispanics. Hispanics make up about 10% of the U.S. population.

Mexico itself has many thousands of Quarter Horses, and modern Mexicans have a great love of horses. Racing is popular in Mexico and varies from legalized pari-mutuel racing i.e.,

at tracks with betting, through non-betting races at fairs, to match races with just two horses and big bets. Such is the cultural place of the horse among Mexicans. Ownership of horses, however, is pretty well restricted to the landed gentry in an increasingly arid land with many many poor people.

Caesar's parents, Francisco and Juliette Dominguez, were some of those poor people. Both came from the Chihuahua area in northern Mexico, where the Rio Grande river forms the border with Texas. They emigrated to El Paso, Texas because there were more jobs and better prospects there. They married in the mid 1940's but did not start a family for several years. Caesar was born on August 1st, 1949, the second born in a family of 5 boys and 2 girls.

At the time of Caesar's birth, the family lived in a very poor area, a *barrio*, the Mexican word for a district or suburb, but usually used to imply a slum. Oldest brother Albert remembers: "It was one bedroom, a living room, a kitchen and a bathroom, and we lived in that, all of us. The boys, we had a twin bed, one on top, one on bottom; and a big bed and three guys sleep sideways in there. The girls sleep in the other room with my Mum and Dad. We were all crowded."

2.1 How much help were his parents?

Father Francisco worked in the construction industry. Mother Juliette was keen to have a large family, and pretty soon she had a large family, so she was very busy raising the children. Albert, as the eldest, had the privilege of growing out of clothes and getting new ones. Caesar had to wear Albert's cast offs. José had to wear them when Caesar had finished with them and so on down the line. There are treasured family photos in which Albert wears new jeans, Caesar wears a smaller pair of worn jeans, José has an even smaller pair of very worn

Caesar rides between his stables and the track to watch his horses work.

jeans, down to Henry's jeans, rolled up to conceal holes.

The kids learned to sell at an early age. Mrs Dominguez would cook Mexican food - Burritos, Tomalis, or a thing like a doughnut called a 'Spudnut' - and the kids would head out around the district selling them. "Sometimes we used to keep the profits and go to the movies," recalls José.

The parents worked and saved and eventually moved the family to a better area. Caesar's parents helped him by moving to an area with better prospects and giving him a solid upbringing, but they certainly couldn't give him a bankroll to start off with.

2.2 Was Caesar's family in racing or horses?

Caesar's parents were neither involved with, nor interested in horses. Caesar's interest in horses developed because several uncles were in the horse business. They were at times trainers themselves, at times working for other trainers. One of these uncles, Pedro 'Pete' Payan was a major factor in switching the youngsters from 'Barrio Boys' to horsemen.

José is a lively, expressive talker, and he explained to me why the boys developed an interest in horses. Pete used to take them to a ranch on the banks of the Rio Grande. At the ranch Pete would break and ride horses for the owner while the boys, around 5 to 9 years old, picked cotton for a well

known radio commentator called Paul Harvey.

"So you picked cotton all day?"

"All God-damn day", said José with great feeling. "He left us there at 5 o'clock in the morning and didn't pick our asses up until 6 in the afternoon. I tell you what - we figured there was an easier way to make money. We used to go and pick onions - we did everything - anything - to make a dollar. But when that racetrack opened (Sunland Park in 1958) - it was a lot easier to make a dollar at the track. We walked horses for 50 cents or a dollar, stood horses in ice for 50 cents."

"Was Pete a trainer at this time?"

"No. He was a rider."

"But he got you all into the racetrack?"

"Yes he took us and he took his sons - our cousins. It was a big family thing."

"So he took you out of the cotton fields and into the racetrack?"

"Yes but he was the one that put us into the cotton fields", says José, still with feeling. He clearly does not relish the memory of picking cotton. "But he took us out of the cotton fields and put us into paper routes. We all had a paper route. When he started taking us to the track, we could make a dollar - plus - we used to fill up popcorn boxes with thrown betting tickets.

CAESAR DOMINGUEZ

Caesar's brother Albert at Ruidoso Downs, New Mexico.

We were required by him to fill up 5 popcorn boxes each, by the end of the day, if you wanted to go to the races again. What you do with those tickets, you get a payoff sheet when the races is over, come home, read'em, and you're going to find tickets that pay. We made extra money. But it was 5 boxes per kid if you wanted to go back next week to the races. And we got it done."

"What was the biggest paying ticket you ever found?"

"You would be surprised. We found combinations, quinellas, I think the biggest paying ticket was 52 dollars. That would have been in the early 1960s."

"That would have been a lot of money then."

"Oh yes. That track made a big difference. The first day Sunland Park opened in 1958 we were all there, all of us, waiting at the gate."

"That was because your uncle took out a training license?"

"Yes, more or less. But you couldn't find a job in the city to make any money, especially if you were kids. I cleaned cars at a Suzuki place but it didn't pay. When I graduated from high school, I could have gone into some government jobs, been a cop, worked for some company, but I just kept coming here."

Albert put it this way: "Working with the horses every sum-

mer, at least we didn't run around and get arrested."

El Paso is a city in the middle of Quarter Horse country. It's population nudging up towards the half million mark, El Paso is at the tip of a horn of Texas that projects in between the country of Mexico and the American state of New Mexico. It is 140 miles south of Ruidoso Downs, the site of what was for several decades the richest horse-race in the world, the All-American Futurity for Quarter Horses.

The influence of the area, and of Caesar's uncles must have been considerable. Caesar and three of his four brothers have ended up in the horse industry. Older brother Albert and younger brother José are successful trainers in New Mexico, racing at Ruidoso Downs, Sunland Park in El Paso, and at the track in Albuquerque. One of Pete Payan's sons, Ruben is also a trainer.

Albert is older and quieter, less ambitious than Caesar. His best horse has been Pat's Phantasy, voted best three-year-old Thoroughbred in New Mexico. He also claimed Shen, a Thoroughbred, for $4,000 and ran it all the way up to allowance class.

José has proven himself a capable trainer from an early age. Before he was 21 years old, he had trained both a Quarter Horse *and* a Thoroughbred to win $100,000.

Younger brother Henry is Caesar's foreman. Even the remaining brother, who works as a mailman in Denver, has a share in a racehorse with Caesar.

2.3 How far did Caesar go at school?

"I went to get by at school. Give me a C, give me a D, pass me and leave me alone. My mind was always in *The Daily Racing Form*. I decided that school was not teaching me what I wanted to learn. I quit when I was 16, in the 9th grade."

Albert told me, "Caesar never cared for school since he was a baby. Since he was in the first grade, he hated school. My Mum used to take him to school to make sure he got in the grade. When she got home he was already back there. He used to beat my Mum back home. I was the oldest so I had to make sure he stayed in school."

2.4 What were Caesar's early ambitions?

"Did you always want to be a horse trainer?"

"Always. From when I was 7 years old. My first dream was to be a jockey, but when I realized I was going to be too big, I decided to be a trainer."

3. How did Caesar get his training skills?

As you have seen, Caesar had uncles who were trainers, so he had role models and he knew it was a realistic dream.

3.1 Any early experience with horses?

"I started from the bottom, working for my uncles. Going to the barns on the weekends, helping them clean stalls, walking hots. (Hots in America are horses cooling down after a race or work.) Then on summer vacations we'd spend the whole 3 months working for one uncle, for 5, maybe 10 dollars a week, and he'd feed us. Gradually learning the ropes from a very young age - 6 or 7 years old, before you know it, you are 16 years old and can get a license of your own. In the 1960s you are making a dollar per half hour for walking hots and that's good money. You are 16 years old and you are making 5 - 6 dollars a day and man you think you are in heaven."

3.2 Experience as a rider or jockey?

Caesar did very little riding.

3.3 Why did Caesar become a trainer?

"There's good money to be made in this business: Not only money but prestige. Its a business, but it's not a job to me. If I was a millionaire, I would train for free, because I enjoy it - the thrill of winning a big race. You meet a lot of good people; doctors, lawyers, judges, movie stars, baseball players. Other people get to meet doctors when they're dying. I meet doctors because they enjoy horse racing. You'd be surprised how many people love horse racing."

"What did your parents think of training as a career choice?"

"They never interfered with us. They raised us good and said, 'If that's what you want to do, that's what you do'. I was 16 years old and in the summer vacation I had broken into making $200 or $300 a week when every one else was making $50 a week. That made it very hard to go back to school. I had made up my mind. I told my parents, 'I want to quit school, go to California and find me a career'. At first they were not very happy about it. But I say to them: 'Even if you make me go back to school, and I finish high school, my heart is in horse racing and school cannot teach me nothing about horses."

Off to California

During the summer vacation Caesar had worked for a trainer named Jerry Fisher at Ruidoso Downs. He had made an impression on Fisher, and he knew he could go with him to California and have a job.

"I left home when I was 16 years old and came right here to California. I lived in the tack room at the stables. Just like in the movies."

"Was that allowed?"

"You are allowed to do it. I let my boys sleep in my barn. You can't just let anyone sleep in there - before you know it you got all the homeless sleeping in your barn." (Today there are grooms rooms at the tracks, adjoining or close to the stables.)

One of the leading jockeys of that era was Bobby Adair. He was also from New Mexico, a veteran of Ruidoso Downs, and he remembered Caesar then. "I knew Caesar when he slept on the tack room floor and didn't have two cents to rub together. But he had an attitude, that he wanted to get on. That was what was different about Caesar."

3.4 Acquiring his training skills

3.4-1 Did he work with a top trainer?

Caesar had worked with Jerry for a year in California when he was approached by Earl Holmes and went to work for him as a groom. Holmes was *the top Quarter Horse man* in California. Why did Holmes offer Caesar a job?

"He was conscientious and he paid attention", Earl told me. Good help was hard to find. Caesar worked for Earl Holmes for 5 years (on and off) at Los Alamitos between 1966 and 1973. Rather than Caesar going and begging for a job with the top man, Earl Holmes came to Caesar and offered him better horses to work with and better money.

All Holmes had was 15 horses but they were almost all stakes horses. This was invaluable experience in the training of good horses and exposure to top level clients. When any stable wins a big race, there is a little extra money spread around. With Holmes that was a regular event. Caesar's cash flow increased as well. Holmes was regarded as a tough man to work for, so Caesar's 5 years was a solid effort.

At one point Caesar and Mr Holmes had a bit of an argument. ("Kids will be kids," was Earl's comment.) The same day Caesar signed up with the military for 2 years from 1968 to 1970. He went to Vietnam for 14 months in the artillery at Pleiku. With shells exploding around him, Caesar had a shift in perspective. Back in California he worked as a groom again, sometimes for Earl Holmes.

While working for Earl Holmes, Caesar was offered a job as a private trainer. Pickwick Stable's trainer had been disqualified for drugging his horses. Although Caesar did not know the people at Pickwick Stable, they knew about him, and approached him in 1973. The fateful contact was jockey Bobby Adair, who knew Caesar and considered he would be a good trainer. Bobby's father-in-law Jim Coffman was the main man behind Pickwick Stable. Coffman owned a western tack and riding equipment store. Said Bobby, "My father-in-law had a lot to do with where Caesar is at right now. Mr Coffman gave Caesar his start."

Another person who recommended him was Earl Holmes: "He was working for me, had been for a long time. He had worked hard and I thought he deserved it. He was ready to become a trainer."

Caesar started at the Bay Meadows track in San Francisco with 20 or 30 head of horses including 4 world champions. Pickwick Stables was a top stable. They took Caesar, untried as a trainer, and put him in charge. A major factor in their decision was the advice of top jockey Robert Adair, that Caesar could handle it.

3.4-2 Did Caesar watch other trainers?

"When you worked for Earl Holmes, did you prepare yourself to be a trainer by asking yourself what you would do with a particular horse and then seeing what Earl did with it?"

"No, that never crossed my mind until it actually happened."

It seems that Caesar was a bit surprised to be offered the position.

"Did you watch other trainers then?"

Caesar said there wasn't time, he had to get on with the job.

3.4-3 Did he try published workouts?

"Were there works of other trainers in something like the Racing Form, that you could look at?"

"No, nothing like that."

3.4-4 Asking questions, reading, seminars.

I asked Earl Holmes if Caesar asked questions.

"He did everything I asked him to do, and he paid attention. He watched what I did, and that's the way he learned from me. He didn't ask a whole lot of questions, but he paid attention, and then he figured out why I did things."

Caesar's early aversion to schooling left him something less than a bookworm. I asked him if he had read *Conditioning To Win* which came out in 1974. He said he knew of the book but had not read it. Practical experience was his principal teacher. Nowadays he reads the Quarter Horse racing magazines and occasionally dips into veterinary books.

3.4-5 Experiments and experience
"So how did you go about training those first horses?"

"The horse was in front of you, so you did what you had to do."

So Caesar did not have an apprenticeship training a small stable, struggling on his own. Rather he had time to learn with one of the best, Earl Holmes, and even when he was training on his own for Pickwick, he could go to Holmes for advice on such things as sore horses. When I asked Caesar who he had learned the most from, he replied, "Earl Holmes, who now runs the Vessels Stallion Farms. Even when we were rivals he would give me advice. He's hard-headed but he's a nice guy." In addition he had the advice and support of Bobby Adair. Nevertheless there was the pressure of having a large stable and top name horses, when Caesar was 23 - 24 years old.

Caesar trained for Pickwick for 12 months starting in 1973, then started his own public stable in 1974. Why did he leave such a large, quality stable? The first time I asked Caesar about it he explained it this way: At Pickwick it became apparent to Caesar that with a number of partners, if you fell foul of any one of the partners you could be sacked and that was that. When other people approached him to train their horses, Caesar asked Pickwick if he could train outside horses but the answer was no. Caesar wanted multiple owners and the security and independence that represented, so he parted company with Pickwick.

At a later date I asked him how well he had done with Pickwick's champions, and he said that although the stable had done very well, the Pickwick partnership was dissolved. That left Caesar on his own as a trainer.

Bobby Adair remembers his father-in-law was getting old and tired, so he got out of the Pickwick tack shop, and dissolved the racing partnership. He did, however, keep a few horses in racing and these he put with Caesar.

4. Starting out on his own

4.1 How he got his first horses

Caesar's first owner was a Mr Davis, one of the Pickwick partnership's friends, but he only had one horse. Caesar went to Ruidoso Downs with just that ONE horse, but within 6 months he had 15 or 20 horses. That was because Caesar did not have to wait long for his first good horse. It was that very first horse he took to Ruidoso. She was a filly called Catchajet, which won a trial of the All-American Futurity at Ruidoso Downs. She was from the first crop of the now legendary sire Easy Jet. Even winning a TRIAL of the All-American is a big deal. She went on to run 5th in the second consolation. Her career record was Speed Index (see glossary) of 96 and winnings of $75,802. Caesar's recollection is that she won about $200,000 and he certainly believes she won more than $75,000. In Caesar's memory Catchajet was regional or track co-champion in one class one year.

4.2 How he got his first clients

After gaining an owner from Pickwick's dissolution, Caesar was also approached by clients because of Catchajet's win and by people who knew him and now wanted to put a horse or two with him. Caesar says he still trains for his first 4 clients - or their descendants!

4.3 Financing the start

Ups and downs are part of a trainer's life, especially in the first years. Unless they are gambling or horse-trading with some success, their income is pretty much the 10% of prizemoney they receive; perhaps a small margin on the daily charge per horse. When Caesar's winnings for his first few years of training are considered, it is hard to see how he survived.

YEAR	WINS	MONEY	
1973	9	$22,995	Part of a year
1974	12	$84,482	
1975	9	$36,657	10% is $3,600!
1976	14	$29,870	How do you live on $2,987?
1977	26	$91,683	Married

I put the question to Caesar: *"Ten percent of your winnings in your first years would hardly keep body and soul together. Was it that tough?"*

"When you first start off you are struggling. You owe the feed man, the groom. You are not making ends meet. You are going further and further in the hole every day. You just hope something breaks."

"How many years did it take until you got out of that hole?"

"Oh it took about 4 or 5 years."

4.3-1 Did Caesar bet?

"In those difficult early years was betting a help or a hindrance?"

"That was what kept you above water. That was how you survived. If you got lucky, that was how you paid the bills."

"What was your biggest payoff in those days?"

"$1500, $1000."

"Considering your stable winnings that was nearly the same as your income-"

"For the year."

4.3-2 Did he borrow money?

"Did you ever borrow money from the bank in a big way?"

"Oh yes! In fact, when I first started, I borrowed in a big way, as you call it. At that time a big way was five hundred dollars. I was audited by the IRS (American Taxation office), and that's what I owed them - $500. I didn't have $500 to pay them. So they threatened cutting it out of my horses; you can't run them, you can't do this, you can't do that. At that time I was just building again, right after I split with Pickwick. I had six or seven horses coming from Ruidoso and I did not have $500. You might as well ask for $50,000, because I didn't have it."

"I went to the Bank of America, the biggest bank in California, for that loan, and they turned me down. They said, 'You've got no collateral, you've got nothing'. I said, 'Well, you've got my name. I'll pay you.' 'No, that's not good enough.' So I come to the racecourse, and I was so depressed. I walked in on this guy by the name of Ruben Perez, and he asked me how come I looked so down. I said, 'I haven't had breakfast today. I'm so down that I'm not even hungry.'"

"So then I sat down and told him the story, that I needed $500, not knowing that this guy owned the bank at Hawaiian Gardens about three miles from here. He says, 'Go to Hawaiian Gardens Bank and tell them who you are, tell them what you want.' I said, 'Well, I already went to the Bank of America and they said no.' He said, 'Well, this is not the Bank of America. You go.' So I did. I went up there. See, this guy was a friend of mine. I always knew him, but I didn't know he owned a bank. I didn't know he owned Los Alamitos - the city of Los Alamitos, not the racetrack. Very wealthy man, but I didn't know he was that wealthy."

Saved from the IRS - By the plumber

"So it was awful funny, because as soon as I walked in that bank, there was the General Manager waiting for me, and the Vice President. He knew my name and everything - and I'm dressed just like I am now - levis, dirty boots. He took me right to his office and said, 'How much do you need?' I said, 'I need five hundred.' He said, 'Will five hundred cover you?' I said, 'That's all I need.' 'No,' he says, 'what about fifteen hundred?' So I said, 'God Almighty, fifteen hundred - how much will my repayments be?' 'How much can you pay?' The guy said, 'We'll give you fifteen hundred to start off and we'll write you out a payment plan, something like $120, or $150 a month.' I said, 'I can handle that.' So I got my credit through there."

"They gave me the $1500. I paid everybody off and I bought some feed. The next year I got everything together, and things started picking up. I got that loan and I paid it off, and then in fact, I went back one time and got a loan for $20,000 just on my signature, from the same bank. I wasn't even married, either. I was single, but that's when you're struggling, you know."

"One of my grooms went off to the Bank of America and asked them for $500. At least the grooms can prove that they've got a job. They can call me, see that he's on the payroll, $250 a week and whatever, but see, me, I was not on the payroll. I was self-employed. Sorry, we can't go by your word."

"But this man Ruben Perez did. He knew me because he took care of all the plumbing around the town of Los Alamitos, and he took care of the plumbing here at the racetrack. He'd come by and we'd talk and bullshit all the time, when I was working."

"He took care of the plumbing?"

"Yes. The way he started owning Los Alamitos way back, he'd buy one house, and then two houses. Before you knew it, he bought everything. But his true job was a plumber."

"And he kept plumbing even though he was into banking and all these other things?"

"Well, he was more like a supervisor. He'd drive up with his truck, with all the plumbing deal, but he wouldn't do nothing. He'd have his field crew. But we'd call him Ruben the plumber. I never knew he was that wealthy. He was an all-time millionaire."

"Amazing. Does he have any horses with you?"

"No. He never bought a horse."

"He collects houses not horses."

4.4 Steady rise or sudden breakthrough

Through the publicity from Catchajet's win and meeting people, Caesar was able to pick up a horse that had run 3rd in the All-American Futurity, called David Capri. (Many of the horses that go to Ruidoso Downs are from states where there is not much racing. After the All-American Futurity meeting most are handed over to trainers with traveling teams, or trainers from California.) When Caesar returned to California he had two horses to train and two babies to break.

4.4-1 How long until first progress?

In spite of his one-horse start, Caesar did not have any long period struggling at the bottom in total anonymity. Things kicked along very quickly from the very start for Caesar. Apart from the clients attracted by his wins, the publicity let others who had met him before know that he was now separate from Pickwick and free to train the horses of others. Caesar was *rolling* and only 25 years old. Not much money, not many horses, but some winners.

4.4-2 Did one horse provide a sudden lift?

Under Caesar's training, David Capri, the horse he got at the All-American, set a track record on his first outing. It then went on to win the Dash For Cash Derby and other races. All this was in 1974 and 1975, right at the start of Caesar's public training career.

4.4-3 Important helpers

Earl Holmes is the man Caesar credits with helping him the most. Bobby Adair and his father-in-law Jim Coffman, the Pickwick man, were also a great help.

4.5 Age married and role of spouse

Caesar's wife is Sherry, who was rubbing (grooming) and ponying horses (leading them to the starting gates) at the track when they met. Her mother was a horse enthusiast and Sherry grew up with horses. She is a keen dressage rider. They married in 1977, when Caesar was 27 or 28 years old. Sherry says it was financially tough in the beginning: "We didn't go out very much, and I was working also."

Caesar and Sherry have three daughters; Krystal, Amanda, and Colleen.

"Caesar, what's that like for your family life, that night-time racing, nearly every night of the week?"

"I never see them, so I don't know."

"How old are your kids?"

"The oldest is ten, and I've got a set of twins that are seven (1988). But see, they stay active. My wife is very active - she's in riding. So while the kids are in school, she's out there riding, and when she comes in from riding, she picks up the kids from school, so it's not that bad, because she knew it when we got married. She used to be in the rodeos. She used to barrel-race, so she's been a horse-woman all her life."

I asked Sherry what it was like having a husband whose work took him away three or four nights a week.

"You mean more like five nights a week." From her tone of voice I expected Sherry to have a gripe about it, but the next sentence surprised me. "For us it's good because we both like the time alone. I don't think nothing of it (I think she learned that phrase from Caesar). It's our life."

"What do the kids think of it?"

"They miss him a lot. But they have their little things - like before he leaves, he hollers, 'OK, I'm leaving, line up for kisses,' and there's a mad dash to line up, including whatever little neighbor girl is in the vicinity. Games like that. And he spoils them. He knows I don't like them to have gum and candy, so he sneaks them gum and candy when I'm not in sight or not around. The kids love it because, 'Oh boy, we get to do something Mom doesn't like us to do."

Caesar's parents visit from New Mexico about every second year, and stay for about half the summer. They speak very little English, so everyone in the family gets to brush up on their Spanish. Sherry did three years of Spanish at high school, so you might think the kids are being brought up bilingual. Not so.

"Caesar thinks it's up to their Mom to teach them Spanish, and I think it's up to their Dad. But I'm going to make sure they do it at high-school."

Sherry reads a lot in the evenings and works her horses

during the day. The kids are also heavily into riding horses. They go to the races about once a month, sometimes more often in the summer. Sherry keeps up with all the results penciled in Caesar's race program and reads any articles in the Quarter Horse magazines.

Bob Baffert amusing two friends. He and Caesar are battling each other and Blane for the training title.

Blane Schvaneveldt with his foreman Joe Orozco, who has been with him for 15 years. Blane has dominated Quarter Horse racing in America for almost that long.

5. Caesar's achievements as a trainer

Caesar is a rising rocket, with perhaps 10, 20 or even 30 of his best years in front of him.

Caesar had big leaps in his annual winnings in 1977 and 1983. When I asked him if those were due to a particular horse or strategy, he said no. The increases were simply due to more wins.

On the all-time total wins, to the end of 1989, Caesar ranked 2nd with 965. Blane Schvaneveld led with a whopping 3,205. Caesar said that an old-timer called John Cooper might have a number up around the same as his own, but a lot of Cooper's racing was 'before they had rails' - and before records were kept. The amazing Wayne Lukas still had 739 Quarter Horse wins on the books.

5.1 Training titles, money, and stakes

Caesar's Results - American Quarter Horse Association National Standings

YEAR	WINS	STARTS	WIN RANK	MONEY	MONEY RANK (national)
1973	9	74	(national)	$22,995	Part of a year
1974	12	82		$84,482	Mainly David Capri
1975	9	74		$36,657	How do you live on $3,600?
1976	14	105		$29,870	Slump then jump
1977	26	235		$91,683	Year he got married
1978	43	235		$107,256	
1979	25	235		$66,295	
1980	27	249		$95,169	
1981	26	225		$147,081	
1982	40	318	27th	$171,426	- Not in top 50
1983	90	411	6th	$496,851	- 12th Caesar's Leap Year
1984	109	655	4th	$533,498	- 10th Beginning of a plateau
1985	110	682	3rd	$567,319	- 11th
1986	121	716	4th	$552,865	- 14th
1987	88	588	6th	$373,092	- 13th
1988	86	584	8th	$430,296	- 12th
1989	130	750	4th	$842,518	- 5th His first Grade 1 wins

Striving to be number one

Caesar has not won the national title - the Quarter Racing Champion Trainer Award - yet, but he's working on it. He has been top trainer at various meets. When I met him in June 1988, his next stepping stone on the path to the national title would be to win the Trainer Of The Year title for California.

June 1988

"On the training score, you're second all-time winning in the nation. That's nearly a thousand wins."

"My expansion started in 1974, but when I first started, I win maybe five, six races a meet. A total of maybe twenty a year. Our periods of racing were less then. We'd race maybe three months, and they'd be off six months. If you won twenty races a meet, you were leading trainer. Now, it takes sixty and seventy wins because there's a lot more racedays. Not only that, there's more races each day. We get ten, eleven races a day. Before, it used to be nine. In the last five or six years, we're winning way over a hundred races a year."

"What's the highest position you've reached?"

"I was leading trainer three years in a row at Orange County meet in '84, '85 and '86, and then I was leading trainer twice in a row right here at Los Alamitos. We're talking about four different meetings per season. I've been second for ever, because I'm behind Blane for the last five years."

Blane Schvaneveldt has dominated the Quarter Horse scene since the departure of Wayne Lukas in 1977/ 78.

"Do you have any plans by which you hope to overtake Blane Schvaneveldt?"

"Well, you're still aiming at him. Right now I got a lot of nice horses. Useful horses. I think I'll overtake him this meet. See, right now he's only like three wins ahead of me, so I'm in the striking position now, because I got a lot of live horses. So I think this is probably the best year that I have to overtake him."

But Caesar didn't beat Blane in California in 1988.

1989

By mid year when the numbers start to mean something, Caesar was leading the trainer's table for California. Arch rival Bob Baffert briefly took the lead in the last months, but Caesar managed enough winners to retake the front position. At

5.2 Important races

G1, G2, G3 = Grade 1 etc. See glossary.

ALL-AMERICAN FUTURITY GI - none. By 1990 Caesar has only taken one horse to the great race. That was Catchajet, his first horse as a public trainer. Caesar says he'll only take a horse with a chance. (The Ruidoso Downs track is some 700 road miles away.) In 1990 he sent Takin On The Cash to his brother Albert, but the horse didn't make the final. Below are some major races by year.

POMONA INVITATIONAL H'CAP	G2	1984	A Zure Hope	Purse $20,000
None in 1985				
ENDURANCE HANDICAP	G3	1986	Truly A Pleasure	32,700
GOLD RUSH 870 DERBY		1986	Truly A Pleasure	82,000
LASSIE HANDICAP	G2	1986	Pines Time	33,250
WAR CHIC HANDICAP	G3	1986	Truly A Pleasure	26,700
1986 must have been a great year for Caesar.				
BARBRA B HANDICAP	G3	1987	Truly A Pleasure	22.250
GOLD RUSH 870 DERBY		1987	Town Native	66,600
870 CHAMPIONSHIP		1988	Truly A Pleasure	won 13,475
EL OCHO SETENTA HANDICAP	G3	1988	Truly A Pleasure	26,900
ENDURANCE HANDICAP	G3	1988	Truly A Pleasure	26,700
MARATHON INVITATIONAL HCP	G2	1988	Truly A Pleasure	30,000
WAR CHIC HANDICAP	G3	1988	Truly A Pleasure	26,850
BAY MEADOWS FUTURITY	G1	1989	Hez Class	288,460

Note: For wins in the $26 - $30,000 range, the winner took home $15 -$16,000

year's end he had taken out his first ever title as Trainer Of The Year in California. He was top of California in wins and money, defeating Blane Schvaneveldt and Bob Baffert.

On the national scene Blane beat Caesar in both money and wins, because of the large contingent of horses he campaigns outside the state, particularly at Ruidoso Downs. Caesar says he does not have enough quality horses to run a block of them at Ruidoso Downs - yet. In addition Blane had good results at the Quarter Horse Breeders' Classics, (similar to the Breeders' Cup in Thoroughbreds) which was run at Sunland Park, New Mexico.

Caesar's win in California was seen by many as well deserved and there was much hearty congratulation and acclaim. There was also some back biting that went with being Numero Uno. Sherry said, "That doesn't worry Caesar one bit. He just says he's glad they aren't bad-mouthing some other poor innocent sucker." Caesar was happy to wear that, because the publicity and recognition as top trainer brought more owners and better horses.

Caesar's first ever Grade 1 race win came in June 1989. Hez Class, bought at the All-American Super Select Sale for Felipé Tiscareno at a cost of $9,500, won the Bay Meadows Futurity. Note the step up in prizemoney compared to the other Grade races. There was a considerable irony in this win. If Caesar had started one week earlier with Pickwick Stables, all those years ago, he'd have had his first Grade 1 win back in 1973. Pickwick's horse Ima On won the same race, the Bay Meadows Futurity, while the arrangements to employ Caesar as trainer were proceeding. John Bassett was the stop-gap trainer.

After his first Grade 1 win Caesar told Ty Wyant of Quarter Week, "I never dreamed we would win, he's been a little green and he's still learning to run." The horse was 0 wins from three starts and broke his maiden in the Futurity Trial. Caesar showed his horsemanship. "When he ran for $20,000 he lost by a nose when he should have won. He waited for that other horse. This time we cut his blinkers a little bit. I wanted him to see that other horse (Strawfly Special)." Strawfly Special, the favorite, drew next to Hez Class and this pleased Caesar.

Surprisingly, after the big win Caesar wasn't getting too excited: "It's just another day at the track. I feel good because it's a Grade 1 win. It means a bigger pay check this month but it's just another day at the job. If the horse gives 100% I feel good. He gave 150%."

After breaking a 15 year drought, Caesar won his second Grade 1 race just 3 weeks later when Games Up Gary won the 1989 VESSELS MATURITY in 21.64 seconds. The purse was $155,000. The horse had been claimed for $5,000 in November by Bonafacio Rayas. In May he moved Games Up Gary to Caesar's stable. Although the horse was only third in his trial, Caesar was confident. He told Richard Chamberlain of *The*

Quarter Racing Journal, "This horse is ready. He should have had the fastest time. He got sandwiched, wiped out - dead last early and came flying late. This is my year. I win the Maturity." The Maturity win was well deserved as Caesar had come second the previous year with April Nine.

5.3 Some major horses

David Capri
This horse was a contender at the All-American when Caesar went with Catchajet. Career record was Speed Index 102 and winnings of $182,396 - a lot of money in the early 1970's.

Truly A Pleasure
Champion Distance Horse at the 1988 American Quarter Horse Association convention in Phoenix. The horse had 4 consecutive wins at 870 yards. All 5 wins for the year were graded stakes. For Caesar, the performances of Truly A Pleasure truly gave him pleasure because he also owned the horse. Truly A Pleasure was retired in 1989 aged six, with winnings in excess of $250,000.

Hez Class
Won the 1989 Bay Meadows Futurity Gr 1 $155,000 total purse.

Games Up Gary
Won the 1989 Vessels Maturity Gr 1 $288,460 total purse.

5.4 Where was Caesar at age -
20 - In Vietnam
30 - Trying to claim his way up the trainer's lists, and making steady progress.
40 - 1989 Building up a Thoroughbred team and trying to get past Blane Schvaneveldt in Quarter Horses.

6. His operation now

6.1 Home
Home was near the Los Alamitos track in the suburb of Cypress. Recently Caesar shifted to La Habra Heights.

6.2 Organization, stables and staff
Caesar has his racing Quarter Horses at the Quarter Horse track, some racing Thoroughbreds at the Thoroughbred track, and a bunch of youngsters, layoffs and leftovers at 'the ranch'. Caesar leases the 110 acre ranch which has a training track, starting gate, pool and stables. There he trains the 'babies' and those coming back from a layoff. The lame and any others in need of a rest also go there.

He has a staff of about 20. His Thoroughbreds are under the direction of his brother Henry. The man in charge of the racing stables when Caesar is away is Jesus Calvilo.

Looking down between the rows of barns. The stands of the track are visible in the distance.

6.3 Number of horses

1988

Caesar had some 60 good clients, 63 Quarter Horses in training at Los Alamitos and 20 Thoroughbreds in training at the Riverside Thoroughbred Farms. A total of 83 horses, but an unknown number at the ranch.

1990

Caesar had 40 horses in racing at Bay Meadows, 90 at the ranch, 35 at Pomona track and 7 Thoroughbreds at Santa Anita. A total of 172.

6.4 His typical day week and year

For non-Americans it will be easier to understand the variations in Caesar's day and week if I outline the Californian Quarter Horse racing year first.

The annual circuit for the year in California has usually begun with a January layoff. Racing starts in February at Bay Meadows outside San Francisco. Since the rest of the year's racing takes place in Los Angeles, this means about 10 weeks of racing that is 450 miles from home. Towards the end of April racing shifts to Los Alamitos. The average daily handle (amount bet) after the first two weeks of Los Alamitos in 1990 was $1,092,800 while the crowd was 6,573, betting $166 per person. In July there is a short two week stint at the Orange County Fair, then on to Hollywood Park for about 9 or 10 weeks. In mid October racing starts again at Los Alamitos, running until late December. Except for Bay Meadows, all the other tracks are within 30 miles of each other in the Los Angeles area.

This circuit varies every year because it is the subject of state government control, which sets the number of weeks for each racing code at each zone and track. Quarter Horse, Thoroughbred and Standardbred interests do battle for the best deal. The circuit means that if you are a Quarter Horse trainer, you have a lot of time away from home and the horses and equipment have to be shifted. Barn phone numbers change every few months.

If you are a horse fan or a punter living near Los Alamitos, it means a very mixed up year. Nothing happens in January, then there is nearly three months of Standardbred racing. Two or three months of Quarter Horse racing follows, then two to four weeks with no racing, unless you make the drive to Orange County and then Hollywood Park. After the drought there is two months of Standardbred racing and then a short gap and about six weeks more of Quarter Horses.

The schedule for Caesar's week usually consists of races every night from Tuesday to Saturday inclusive. That leaves a trainer with Sunday and Monday nights at home with the family if he has one. Sometimes Tuesday night is free too.

Caesar's day is a very long one. He rises at 5:30 - 6am and is at the track by 7am where, he says, he 'works like a dog.' By 11am he has finished with the training and the stables. Most days he then goes to the ranch to attend to the horses out there. Sometimes there are other bits of business, sometimes

Coffee break after the horses have worked. The bright orange of Caesar's stables stands out in the gray of the Los Alamitos barn area.

Under the shedrow verandah.

he gets home in time for a nap. He is back at the stables around 5pm to get his horses ready for the evening's races. The first race is typically at 7.30pm and the whole ten races are usually over by about 11pm. Surprisingly, the stands clear rather slowly considering the hour. Many people stay to chat and re-hash the evening's events. Caesar doesn't usually get to bed until 1.30am.

To an Australian, the changes from month to month seem pretty strange. Most cities in Australia have separate Stan-dardbred and Thoroughbred tracks. Thoroughbreds race dur-ing the day and most Standardbreds at night. The average punter or horse lover follows one or the other and can go to at least one, usually two, and occasionally three race programs a week, but they can go *every* week of the year. The Australian punter would go nuts if he or she couldn't follow the same bunch of horses week in and week out, right through the year.

So Caesar's day and week depend a lot on which track the racing is at. When his Quarter Horse team is racing at Bay Meadows, Caesar is dropped off at the airport in Los Angeles on Wednesday afternoon and he is at the Bay Meadows track that night for the racing. When he finishes his morning train-ing there is no ranch to go to, so he gets some unaccustomed rest. On Sunday morning Sherry or one of his workers collects him from the airport when he returns.

6.5 His car

A Lincoln Continental is Caesar's choice. He also has a Chevy pickup truck for second vehicle come-workhorse.

7. Does he get good horses?

7.1 Where does he get his horses from?

Prior to 1987, Caesar bought very few horses, and got very few from breeders.

(Jan 1988)*"Do you select your own horses or do the owners bring them to you, or a bit of both?"*

"Ninety percent of the horses come to you. You don't have no choice because the owner owns the horse and they bring them to you."

In 1987 he had sufficient money to go to the sales and buy some 'babies' for $4,000 or so each. No doubt the money and the enthusiasm at the sales in September 1987 came from the wins of Truly A Pleasure, but there has been enough money since then to continue, even increase the buying. Caesar is at the transition point between claiming trainer and someone seen as a stakes horse trainer.

"Do you ever buy horses at the sales for yourself or to sell later to clients? Do you ever buy one on spec (specu-lation) that you can find an owner for it?"

"Oh yes. We do that all the time. I always buy a yearling from each sale for myself, because I'm in the business just like any owner, looking for the big horse. What I do, I go out and I'll look for a horse that's cheap, but got the conformation, and maybe got the bloodlines. I'm taking the chance that might be a good horse."

7.2-1 Who Chooses?

"When we go to yearling sales, we select them together - you and the owner. Because they're spending a lot of money, you want them to have the say so."

This is an interesting area. There is no doubt that to get the best results on the track, the person with the most expertise should choose, but for many owners, choosing the horse is part of the joy of being an owner. Trainers like Wayne Lukas and Tommy Smith have a very dominant role in the selection process. Trainers who regard it largely as a lottery anyway, like Fred Kersley, are quite content to let owners have a large role in making the choice.

7.2-2 Can he pick the best yearlings?

As we heard earlier, most of Caesar's horses were sent to him. Like many predominantly claiming trainers, he did not buy many at the yearling sales, but that is changing.

One of Caesar's earliest selections was Truly A Pleasure, which won the inaugural Gold Rush 870 Derby as well as many other stakes races. A beautiful flashy buckskin, he was the first champion by Thoroughbred sire Truly's Easter. Truly A Pleasure had amassed $252,000 by mid 1989. Caesar had bought the youngster in 1984 for $2,200.

A 1988 buy of Caesar's was 1989 Bay Meadows Futurity win-ner Hez Class, for which Felipé Tiscareno paid $9,500. By May 1990 this horse had won over $160,000.

At the Ruidoso Super Select Session of the 1989 All-Ameri-can Sales, Caesar selected a yearling by the mighty Dash For Cash out of an Easy Jet mare, Take You On. Felipé Tiscareno paid $52,000, for it, the fifth highest price of the select sale. Top price was $75,000. This high-priced baby went on to win the 1990 Bay Meadows Futurity. Indeed Caesar had selected 1st, 4th and 9th placegetters. The three cost $52,000, $19,000 and $17,000 and earned $95,988, $12,630 and $8,336.

7.2-3 His methods - type versus pedigree

"Are you mainly a pedigree man or are you a confor-mation man?"

"When I buy, I like to put conformation first. I figure if a horse is pretty and good looking, he's going to run."

"Do you narrow the catalog down by sires or dams?"

"First of all I'll go through the sale catalog every day, for about a week, and I'll circle the horses I like. That's just on pe-digree, because I haven't seen them yet. Once I get all the pe-digrees, then I go to the sale, and I'll try to look at those horses first, to see if they've got the conformation that fits the pedi-gree. I put a price range on each horse: the price that I think the horse is worth. When it comes to the horses, then I start eliminating. This horse don't look like what I'm looking for, so I scratch. At the same time that I'm scratching, I'm looking at the horses that I did not like in the catalog, that I might like through sight, through conformation. So I'll eliminate some, but I'll gain some. And you put it all together slowly. You've got five clients who want to buy horses, so you start deciding your first pick, your second pick, your third pick. And then your highest price on down the line. That's the way I do it."

"Do you look at every horse in the sale?"

"No, it's hard because a lot of sales, when you go, there's a thousand horses. There is no way you can see all thousand unless you sit in front of the arena, and as they walk in, you can see them. You can say actually, yes, you did see them, but you cannot go through them. So what we do: let's say I have got five clients who want to buy horses, and you'd be surprised how each client got different- "

"Do they phone you up and say, 'I want a particular type of horse,' or do you phone them up and say, 'I'm going to this sale?"

"All the clients know the sale's coming up and they'll say, 'Caesar, I want to buy a filly in the price range of $10,000. Okay?' So now you know that Joe Blow wants a filly in the $10,000 range, and this other guy comes out and says, 'You know, we ought to get two or three horses, and we'll spend $50-60,000'. So now you know what another client wants."

"So when you come to the sale, you've got your different categories of owners and you've got your different categories of horses that you know are going to bring that price. So you look at the horses that are going to be that price, and got some bloodlines and got conformation. You go towards the breeders that breed good horses. You go to see their stock first."

"Once in a while you might see a horse walk by that you don't know nothing about, but he catches your eye. I do that a lot. I just wander around and see a lot of people walking their horses, and the horse who catches my eye, I look at his hip number and see; who is he; have I got him marked? And if I don't, but I kind of like his looks, I mark him down to look at him closer, next time around. That's the way you go about it."

"Like, for instance, all this last year (1987), I was looking for Easy Jets. If I went to a sale, I took this one client with me, and for one day that's all we did, look for Easy Jets. Nothing else, just Easy Jets. The next day, another client or two clients got together, and they were looking for a bargain. For those bargain hunters, you look around and you just wander. You don't even go for the big horses, because you know they're not going to get bargains. Big horses, big names. You're not going to get them for a bargain price."

Do you charge your clients to select a horse?
"If you have to go to a sale, do you charge them for your expenses? To get there?"

"No. I figure they're my clients, they're giving me their business all year long - that's part of my job. Now, if you, from Australia, wanted horses to take to Australia, and you wanted my advice, then there'd probably be a fee, because the horses would not be under my name. You want to buy some and take them out of state, it runs between 5 and 10%."

Finding bargains at the yearling sales
"You said you looked for conformation that fit the pedigree."

"Right. See, you might have a horse that's real beautiful. Conformation-wise, it's perfect. If that horse had another kind of breeding, he'd bring $100,000. By being of the breeding he is, and the individual he is, you're lucky if he brings $1500. But he's that kind of horse, and especially if the mother is a young mare, or the daddy is a young stud, then those are the bargain horses. But if his mummy and his daddy have already had five or six full brothers that are no good, then you don't buy him for racing. If he's a good looking horse, then you can actually buy him for a pony horse or for showing, but not for racing, because he's already proved to you that his looks don't mean nothing. His brothers and sisters have never run. But if he's a first-timer, that is the kind of horse that I would buy as a bargain."

"Real speculation?"

"Yes, because they've got good looks. The bloodline are not there, but he might be all right."

Buying yearlings by first season sires
"One of the things in Thoroughbred racing that still amazes me is the price of the offspring of some first season sires. They bring enormous money. First season - when no one knows whether he's good or bad. Then you can have a stallion that's proven - in the bottom end of the top ten, his offspring will not bring as much, and yet the chances of these first season sires getting into that top ten ever, are very small. Does that happen in the Quarter Horses as well?"

"Yes. I like to buy a lot of first-time babies out of mares, or a young stud coming up. See, our industry is not as high-priced as in Thoroughbreds. You can have a horse that's a first-time stud, that made over a million, and you could still buy that baby for an average $10,000. If you try to buy a baby from a horse that's already proven, already got horses on the racetrack that are stakes horses - you can't touch them for less than $50,000."

"So in our industry, first-timers are very good. I look for a lot of first-timers, and even in Thoroughbreds, you'd be surprised. A lot of times, a good horse that showed a lot of run, its babies will bring top money but not as much as a sire that's already proven, because a sire that's already proven, in Thoroughbreds, will bring the millions. A sire that's not proven, of

CAESAR DOMINGUEZ

*One race finishes at Los Alamitos, and the brightly lit saddling
shed awaits the next field of contenders.*

Caesar's night at the races.

Most nights then Caesar had 2 to 4 horses racing. Time to saddle up an entry.

*This horse
has got
a chance*

*Caesar and owner Tony Sedor watch the
race on a monitor at their table in the restaurant. Tony has had horses with Caesar
for over 5 years. No winner this time.*

*A different jacket,
different night, but it's
the winner's circle.
Caesar has been in this
ring more times than
anyone except Blane
Schvaneveldt.*

course, he'll still bring the $200,000 and $300,000, which is still a lot of money, but it's harder for them to bring that million, until that sire has sired at least one offspring that shows that he's a stakes caliber producer. Then the millions come in."

"When you're selecting yearlings, do you put your fist between the jawbones?"

"No. They tell you you're putting your fist between the jawbones, you're looking for a big nostril, a big eye, long ears and on and on. I tried that in the first five years of my training and I went through all that. It don't matter. If a horse is goin' to have the desire at the heart, he's going to be a racehorse."

"How do you pick that horse with desire? Is that in the look"

"You don't. You just hope that when you do pick one out of the ten or twenty babies, that you pick the right one."

Why he selected Truly A Pleasure.
Truly A Pleasure cost only $2,200, but earned over a quarter of a million dollars. The low purchase price was not surprising when the parentage is considered. Sire Truly's Easter had only a few crops running and his Speed Index of 96 was low by sire standards. He went to stud with 9 wins from 27 starts. His winnings were not high - $67,477. From 8 crops Truly's Easter produced only 3 stakes winners from 236 foals. Dam Azure Pleasure had a speed index of 88 but only one win and $1,853. In the year of the sale, she had a two-year-old running which eventually earned a Speed Index of 89.

I asked Caesar what attracted him.

"He was a buckskin, a nice horse. Like the man used to ride in Gunsmoke. I thought, 'If he won't make a racehorse he'll make a good pony horse." Caesar considered the bloodlines good. "Truly Easter was a world champion, he won a Los Alamitos Derby. He was a racehorse. He was out of an Azure Te mare and Azure Te mares are always good mares." (I couldn't find Truly Easter listed as a world champion, nor could I find him listed as a winner of the Los Alamitos Derby. His best result seems to have been a second in the Golden State Derby G1, gross purse $300,000 to $530,000.)

I asked Caesar about the low speed index and he said it was a good figure for those days. I replied that I believed the Speed Index should be fairly constant over the years. Caesar said a lot of things had to be taken into account. He said, "A poor quality horse running on a good track during the day when it is hot, with a tail wind, could get a Speed Index of 110. At night the track is slower, maybe wet, and the same horse might get a 90. I have some cheap horses that got a 100 Speed Index, but that don't mean much."

How he selected Hez Class
Caesar was at the sales with an order for an Easy Jet out of a Thoroughbred mare for $10,000. He liked Hez Class because he looked like his sire, including the short back.

How he selected Special Elan
Special Elan won $70,000 as a two-year-old, and had the fastest qualifying time for the Golden State Derby. Caesar said this horse was by a World Champion, out of a World Champion, and his full brother/full sister was a World Champion. "His daddy won over a million, his mama made over a million, he should have been selling for $100,000." When they saw the bidding hanging at $50,000 he and Felipé jumped in and got the horse for $54,000.

How he selected Takin On The Cash
Caesar told Richard Chamberlain of The Quarter Racing Journal why he paid $52,000 for the 1990 Bay Meadows Futurity winner:

"I thought he was cheap at that price. He's a little buck-kneed, and everybody was shying away from the buck knees. My brothers train at Sunland Park, and they were telling me, 'Oh no, no, no, he's got buck knees! I've had nothing but luck with buck-kneed horses, so it was a fault for everybody but me. I told 'em, 'I know he's got buck knees, but that's one of the reasons we're going to get him cheap, and he's got everything else."

In summary, Caesar, has not bought enough horses to fully assess his buying skills. His purchase of Truly A Pleasure appears to have been a bit of a fluke, but he does have an approach to buying cheapies that gives him the prospect of an occasional 'fluke'. He began to really spend at the sales when he spent $80,000 in 1987. This was because he had a new owner, Felipé Tiscareno.

Their first buy was a $47,000 yearling they called St Louis Beduino, which did not win a race. Caesar says, "Felipé could have just gone back to his house and cried, but he didn't. He bought more horses, so he deserves all the wins he's getting now." Until Felipé came along, Caesar was spending a maximum of $10,000 on any individual purchase because that was the most any of his clients wanted to spend. Caesar considered it too difficult to get owners to go into partnerships to buy more expensive horses. Tiscareno had a lot more to spend, so Caesar says he went from buying yearlings out of winners, to yearlings out of stakes winners. He says this has enabled him to buy horses that became stakes winners.

His 1989 sales spending was $120,000. In the last two years he has bought two Bay Meadows Futurity winners.

8. How he trains
"How different is your training now to what you learnt from Earl Holmes?"

"No different except there is a lot more medication. It used to be you trained them and you used rubbing and Absorbine and ice. It is still the same but there so many drugs you can use for joints, and pain, and bleeding, and whatever. That is now very advanced, but the training stays the same.

"Do you have to geld some of the Quarter Horses?"

"Ninety percent are geldings, because the value as studs is not that good anyway."

"So you're not slow to cut them?"

"No. You might as well cut them as keep them as studs."

Gear and equipment

"Is there much to know about the equipment and saddles in the Quarter Horses? Do bits and bridles and saddles make much difference?"

"No. Bits and bridles and saddles, everything, the same way as you would in the Thoroughbreds. The equipment's all the same. Ninety percent of Quarter Horses wear blinkers for the reason that when they run in a race, they're all in a line, and you want their mind to stay on what's happening. See, you got so many horses on the side, that without blinkers, they get to looking at 'em and they're paying more attention to the other horses. When you're in front, you don't turn back and see who's competition. You keep running. Blinkers keep the horse's mind running forward. In Thoroughbreds it don't matter, because a horse is looking at the horse in front of him, at the horse behind him - it don't really matter. But Quarter Horses, you cover 'em because you don't want 'em to be looking at their fellows."

"Are there any situations when you decide to take blinkers off a horse?"

"Oh yes. There's a lot of times where horses seem to keep turning their head because they want to look back. You take the blinkers off and it's a different world. Let's try him *without* blinkers. Let's try him *with* blinkers. All mine are tried without. They all get started without, and as they go along, we put them on or off, or keep them on."

"Everything starts without blinkers?"

"Without. And some of them never ever need them."

"Going that short distance, are tongue-ties common or important?"

"No. Very seldom do you see a tongue-tie with a Quarter Horse. Thoroughbreds, yes, because they tend to get tired and stick their tongue out, maybe it'll swallow it. But a Quarter Horse - no."

"Breast-plates on the saddles, the strap that goes round the front to hold the saddle, are they used?"

"No, no, we don't never use that."

"No? I thought they might have been useful for Quarter Horses, to stop the saddle slipping back during that burst from the gates."

"No, you never see them. Even at race time you never see a breast collar on a Quarter Horse, and they're not even common in Thoroughbreds. They're more common on jumpers, I guess."

"Do you rug your horses?"

"No blanket. In Southern California you don't have to, because the weather's so nice."

Los Angeles has a mid July average temperature of 72°F (22°C), a mid January average temperature of 55°F (13°C), and an annual average of 13 inches (32.5cm) of rain.

Tapering for a big race

"Do you ever decrease the training coming up to a big event, to get the horse fresh, jumping out of it's skin?"

"Oh yes. Once you get a horse fit and ready to run, you can, without doing too much work with him, keep him in very tip top shape for at least thirty days, without having to go out there and work him, and take that edge off. You want to keep that edge on, but you're still working and you breeze him along to keep that edge, and still keep that fitness. You can gallop that horse, give him no works and keep him fit for about thirty days. I do that a lot: just breezing or gallops, with no works."

"When you're peaking for a stake race, you already know what day that race is, so you can aim him to that peak. If you see that the horse is peaking too early or too fast, then you're going to have to breeze him or back off, one or the other, because you don't want him to peak three or four days before, or three or four days after. Instinct tells you, either you back off or you move up."

Have you tried interval training?

"I was reading about that, but I don't think it works in our deal, because our horses are too fragile. They're talking about training the horse and then bringing them back - training them three or four times a day. I think their legs are too fragile. There's no way they could stand it. I read part of Tom Ivers' book and I didn't believe in it, so I didn't finish it."

"Do you know of anyone that's tried it in Quarter Horses?"

"I think the new people that start training their own horses have tried it and they have been no success at all. If you have a horse that's training three, four times a day - four, five miles a day, and the horse is not eating, that means he's not accepting that training. Yet you're doing it again tomorrow and tomorrow and tomorrow, and before you know it, this horse draws up to nothing and they say well, he might have air to run five miles but he ain't got the strength to go half a mile. So what did you accomplish? You didn't accomplish nothing."

"So you tend to run the Quarter Horses with a lot of weight and well-being in them?"

"You want a lot of power in them. You want a lot of fire, because they're explosions. You want them like a piece of dynamite with a short fuse. Thoroughbreds are like a piece of dynamite with a long fuse, because it takes them forever to come. Quarter Horses, you want them sharp but at the same time you want them calmed down, because the biggest deal in

Caesar's training chart for February 1988 at Bay Meadows. The full charts are sorted into age and sex groups in the tables. The racing and training are shown for 3 from each group in the expanded tables. (See p 196-216)

Quarter Horses is the starting gate."

Spelling (turning out)

"Do you spell horses (turn them out) routinely, or do they race all year through if they'll stand up to it."

"Quarter Horse racing here shuts down for three months, so you have no choice but to shut down yourself unless you want to go out of state. If you want to go out of state, New Mexico runs all year long, and Arizona runs all year long."

"So what do you do?"

"We turn out. We give horses rest."

"Do you try to hold the horse up for the whole nine months?"

"Yes. I try to go the whole nine months with them. When you bring them back up, it takes you forty-five to fifty days to get them ready, so of course if you want to have the horse ready to run on opening day, you bring them up a lot earlier. You can turn them out earlier. If I've got some slow horses or they're quitting on me now, I'm not going to wait until November to turn 'em out. I might start early, give them some time off and be ready to run in October and November. If you have a sore horse, he ain't going to win anyway, so you might as well give him time off. It all depends on the individuals. We race them through. If a horse is running often, then of course you're going to train it more lightly than a horse that's not running. You just can't say we're going to walk 'em and gallop, walk 'em and gallop, because some horses will not accept the walk every other day, or the jog every other day. It's all individual. Some that we've got at the ranch, we swim 'em. Horses that are shin-bucked, go swimming. We do a lot of things."

Quitters

"In Thoroughbreds you get a type of a horse called a quitter. Doesn't put in at the end of the race. Do you get those in the Quarter Horses?"

"Oh yes, but in Quarter Horses you don't notice he's a quitter. See, in Thoroughbreds, you can see a horse break on the lead and he quits heading for home. He's tired. He's hurt. In the Quarter Horse, if he's tired and he's hurting, he just won't break out of the gates as sharp. Them other horses will break ahead of him and he just won't try. And that's how you can tell a sore horse. In our business, if a horse is not breaking, there's something wrong with him."

"Do you have much trouble in the Quarter Horses with them having growth spurts?"

"No, not in the Quarter Horses. You have more of that in Thoroughbreds."

What to do in a slump - "don't change nothing"

"You start doing bad, and if you let your emotions and the stress get to you, you'll fall as quick as you went up. That's one thing that I've learned. It's no different from a ball player: you get in the slumps. I've been in slumps, and what I've learned, I learned from this one man called Henk Wood. Super, super good horseman. He'd be getting on for eighty now, but I trained for him for about five years. We did well together and we worked well together."

"I was the trainer, he was the owner, but at one time he was a trainer, so he knew what it was, and when we come to a slump, we'd sit down and we'd talk about it. He'd always say, 'You're in a slump. Don't change nothing of your training methods. Leave everything alone. The only thing you change is you take a week off, on condition races. (Races limiting the field by conditions e.g., two-year-old non-winners of last 2 races. See glossary.) If you've got horses picked to run, for the next week, forget the condition races. Don't enter nothing for a week. Let the slump go away,' he says, 'but don't change your training.' And that's one thing I don't do. I have slumps like everybody else has slumps, but I don't change my training. My work force, everything stays the same, except that now, instead of me entering say, five or six horses per day we race six days a week, so you're talking an average of thirty horses a week - I might enter five for the week; the ones that need to run, like first time starters, maidens; the ones that, whether you're in a slump or not, they need to race anyway; and of course, you've got to run your stakes horses."

"So effectively what he was saying was not to race so often, when you're in a slump?"

"Yes. If you've got a horse that's just run a week ago, and you're preferring a 350 yards, and there's a 400, forget the 400 and wait for the 350. When you're on a roll, it don't matter if it's 350 or 400, you're gonna win, because you're on a roll."

"It's interesting to wonder what produces some of those rolls and slumps in a stable."

"A lot of timing. Conditions fit your way. The race secretary writes the conditions exactly the way you want 'em. It just happens. The horses, you're working them perfect, everything working perfect. The vet comes, checks the horse, there's nothing wrong with the horse. I mean, things like that, they hit. Last May, I won twelve races in one week. The only person ever to win more than twelve was Blane - he won thirteen. But everything was clicking. I wanted 350, I get 350. I wanted 440, I get 440. Whatever I wanted, it was there."

8.1 Training program and charts

Training the young Quarter Horse

"Our babies are bought in sales in August to December. We start them between 18 and 24 months old. A baby takes from 90 to 150 days to be broke and into a race. Thoroughbreds take 6 months. Quarter Horses are quicker to bring up because you are running in shorter sprints. Thoroughbreds take months to build up stamina, to go 6 furlongs, to go a mile. A Quarter Horse baby is only going to run 220 yards. So that is one eighth the distance."

Continued on p. 217

CAESAR DOMINGUEZ' TRAINING CHART For his stable at Bay Meadows, February and March 1988.

GB = breeze from the gates
Gs = worked out of the gates

w = walk
G = gallop (equivalent of a canter in Australia or England)

B = breeze
Q = qualifying trial
R = race
s = stall only

FEBRUARY

Two-year-old colts & geldings

Date	February	1	2	3	4	5	6 (Sat)	7	8	9	10	11	12	13 (Sat)	14	15	16	17	18	19	20 (Sat)	21	22	23	24	25	26	27 (Sat)	28	29
Dear Little Dash		w	w	w	w	Q	w	w	w	w	G	w	G	Q	w	w	w	w	w	w	G	w	G	w	w	w	G	R	w	w
Sailed		s	w	w	G	w	Q	w	w	w	w	Gs	w	w	Q	w	w	w	w	w	w	G	w	R	w	w	w	w	w	G
Brilliant Light		s	w	w	w	G	Q	w	w	w	w	G	w	w	Q	w	w	w	w	w	w	G	w	G	s	s	s	s	?	?	?
Busy Doctor g		s	w	w	w	G	Gs	w	w	w	G	w	w	Q	w	w	w	w	w	Gs	w	Q	w	w	w	w	w	G	w	w	R
California Time g		w	w	w	w	G	Q	w	w	w	w	G	w	G	w	w	G	w	w	G	w	w	w	G	w	w	w	G	w	w	R
Cold Cash Two g		w	w	w	s	s	s	s																						
Dickens Dandy g		w	w	w	G	Q	w	w	w	w	G	w	w	Gs	G	w	w	G	w	w	G	w	w	w	w	G	w	G	w	R
Luck's Hempen Olene g		w	w	G	w	Q	w	w	w	w	G	w	w	w	G	w	w	w	Gs	w	w	Q	w	w	w	w	w	w	w	w
Distinctive Cash	sent to El Paso																													
Free Special	sent to El Paso																													

Two-year-old fillies

Date	February	1	2	3	4	5	6 (Sat)	7	8	9	10	11	12	13 (Sat)	14	15	16	17	18	19	20 (Sat)	21	22	23	24	25	26	27 (Sat)	28	29
Allred Dancer		w	w	w	G	w	Q	w	w	w	w	G	w	w	G	w	w	G	w	Gs	Gs	R	w	w	w	w	w	G	w	w
Casadys Concept		s	w	w	G	Q	w	w	w	w	G	w	w	Q	w	w	w	w	w	w	Gs	w	G	w	w	G	w	GB	w	w
Going To Be A Star		s	w	G	w	GB	w	w	Gs	w	w	w	G	Q	w	w	w	w	Gs	w	Q	w	w	w	w	G	w	G	w	R
Little Doll Rae		s	w	w	G	Q	w	w	w	w	G	w	w	Q	w	w	w	w	w	Gs	w	Gs	w	w	24	w	w	G	R	w
Sheza Swifty.		s	w	w	w	Q	w	w	w	w	G	w	w	Gs	Q	w	w	w	w	w	G	w	G	w	G	w	w	G	w	w
St Loius Bedouino		w	w	w	w	G	w	Q	w	w	w	w	w	G	w	w	w	G	w	w	Gs	Q	w	w	w	w	G	w	w

Three-year-old colts and geldings

Date	February	1	2	3	4	5	6 (Sat)	7	8	9	10	11	12	13 (Sat)	14	15	16	17	18	19	20 (Sat)	21	22	23	24	25	26	27 (Sat)	28	29
Your Gonna Know Me		s	w	w	w	G	w	GB	w	w	w	G	R	w	w	w	w	G	w	w	R	w	w	w	w	w	w	G	w	Gb
High Tide Rip g		w	w	B	w	w	R	w	w	w	w	w	G	w	R	w	w	w	w	G	w	w	R	w	w	w	w	w	G	w
Sail On A Cloud		s	w	w	w	R	w	R	w	w	w	w	w	G	w	Gs	w	w	w	R	w	w	w	w	w	G	w	w	R
Dandy Solution g										IN	G	w	w	G	Q	w	w	w	w	G	w	Q	w	w	w	w	G	w	R
Fleet Champion g		w	w	G	w	R	w	w	w	w	w	w	w	w	w	w	w	w	w	G	w	w	w	G	w	w	G	w	R	w
Oh what A Charger g			s	w	w	G	w	GB	w	w	w	G	w	w	OUT															
Pick Pocket Jonny g																								IN	w	G	Q	w	w
Spirit De Corps g		w	w	w	G	w	G	w	Gs	w	w	w	R	w	w	w	w	w	Gs	R	w	w	Q	w	w	G	w	G	w	w
Tuffest Bullet g		w	w	w	G	w	R	w	w	w	w	w	w	Gs	R	w	w	w	w	?	R	claimed								

Three-year-old mares

Date	February	1	2	3	4	5	6 (Sat)	7	8	9	10	11	12	13 (Sat)	14	15	16	17	18	19	20 (Sat)	21	22	23	24	25	26	27 (Sat)	28	29
Bandette Miss		w	w	w	G	w	w	Gs	R	w	w	w	w	w	G	w	G	w	w	Gs	w	R	w	w	w	w	w	Gs	w	R
Betsy Y Now		s	w	w	w	G	w	GB	w	w	w	G	w	w	Q	w	w	w	w	G	w	G	w	GB	w	w	w	G	w	w
Bettys Promise		w	w	G	w	R	w	w	w	w	G	w	w	R	w	w	w	w	G	w	w	G	w	w	Gs	w	R	w	w	
Bet Your Bimy		w	w	w	G	w	Gs	R	w	w	w	w	gs	R	w	w	w	w	w	Gs	w	Gs	w	w	w	Gs	w	R	w	w
Casadee Class		w	w	w	G	w	G	R	w	w	w	w	w	Gs	w	w	w	w	Gs	R	w	w	w	w	w	w	w	G	w	w
Heradeck		s	w	w	G	w	Q	w	w	w	w	G	w	R	w	w	w	w	Gs	w	G	w	Gs	w	w	w	Gs	w	G	w
Rythms Little Dream		w	w	G	w	G	w	B	w	w	w	w	w	R	w	Gs	Gs	w	w	w	Gs	Gs	Gs	w	w	w	w	w	GB	w	R
Merridoc Star		w	w	G	w	R	w	w	w	w	w	G	w	w	R	w	w	w	w	w	G	w	Q	w	w	w	w	w	G	w
Dayna Celerity Thoroughbred					IN	w	GB	w	w	w	G	w	w	G	w	w	w	G	w	w	G	w	w	w	w	w	w	s	s	s

Older horses

Date	February	1	2	3	4	5	6 (Sat)	7	8	9	10	11	12	13 (Sat)	14	15	16	17	18	19	20 (Sat)	21	22	23	24	25	26	27 (Sat)	28	29
4yo m April Nine		w	w	w	G	w	GB	w	w	w	G	w	w	R	w	w	w	w	Gs	w	w	G	w	w	G	w	w	G?	w	w
4yo m Elises Ecstasies		w	w	G	w	w	G	w	R	w	w	w	w	w	w	w	w	w	G	w	R	w	w	w	w	w	w	w	w	w
4yo h Boo Coo Trouble		s	w	w	w	G	w	R	claimed																					
4yo h Town Native		w	w	w	G	w	R	w	w	w	w	w	G	w	G	w	w	w	R	w	w	w	w	w	w	w	G	w	w
4yo g Sarawak Wings		w	w	w	G	w	G	w	B	w	w	w	G	R	w	w	w	w	G	w	w	G	w	w	w	R	w	w	w
4yo g Fols Dynasty		s	w	w	G	w	Q	w	w	w	w	w	G	w	w	w	Gs	R	claimed											
4yo g Ta Advantage		w	w	w	G	w	G	w	w	w	w	w	w	G	w	w	Gs	w	R	w	w	w	w	w	w	w	w	G	w
5yo g Truly A Pleasure		w	w	G	w	R	w	w	w	w	w	G	w	w	?	R	w	w	w	w	w	w	w	G	w	R	w
7yo h Little Hubie		s	w	w	G	w	Q	w	w	w	w	Gs	R	w	w	w	w	Gs	w	w	Gs	w	w	w	w	R	w	w

Note: horses listed as geldings may have been entires at the time of this training. Horse's names are spelled as they were on AQHA records. Apostrophe's are not allowed in names.

MARCH

Two-year-old colts & geldings

Date March	1	2	3	4	5	6	7	8	9	10	11	12	13	14	15	16	17	18	19	20	21	22	23	24	25	26	27	28	29	30	31	1
Dear Little Dash	w	w	w	G	w	w	R	w	w	w	w	G	w	w	w	w	G	w	R	w	w	w	w	OUT								
Sailed	w	w	G	w	w	G	w	w	G	w	w	B	w	OUT																		
Brilliant Light	w	w	w	w	w	w	w	w	w	G	w	w	G	w	G	w	w	G	R	w	w	w	OUT									
Busy Doctor g		w	w	OUT																												
California Time g	w	w	w	w	G	w	w	w	w	G	w	w	G	w	G	w	w	B	w	w	w	w	OUT									
Cold Cash Two g																																
Dickens Dandy g		w	w	OUT																												
Luck's Hempen Olene g		w	w	OUT																												
Distinctive Cash																																
Free Special																																

Two-year-old fillies

Date March	1	2	3	4	5	6	7	8	9	10	11	12	13	14	15	16	17	18	19	20	21	22	23	24	25	26	27	28	29	30	31	1
Allred Dancer	w	G	w	w	G	w	G	w	w	G	w	G	w	R	w	w	w	w	w	w	G	w	w	G	w	w	G	w	R	w	w	w
Casadys Concept	w	w	Gs	w	R	w	w	w	w	w	G	w	R	w	w	w	w	w	w	w	R	w	w	w	w	w	Gs	w	w	Gs	w	w	G
Going To Be A Star	w	w	OUT																													
Little Doll Rae	w	w	w	G	w	w	G	w	w	G	w	w	G	w	w	G	w	G	w	R	w	OUT										
Sheza Swifty	w	GB	w	w	w	G	w	w	G	w	G	w	Q	w	w	w	w	w	w	G	w	G	?	?	?	?	Gs	w	w	w	w	?
St Loius Bedouino	w	G	w	G	w	G	w	w	G	w	w	GB	R	w	w	w	w	w	w	G	w	w	w	G	w	w	Gs	R	w	w	w	

Three-year-old colts and geldings

Date March	1	2	3	4	5	6	7	8	9	10	11	12	13	14	15	16	17	18	19	20	21	22	23	24	25	26	27	28	29	30	31	1
Your Gonna Know Me	w	w	w	G	w	G	w	w	G	w	B	w	w	w	w	w	G	w	G	R	w	w	w	w	w	w	G	w	w	G	w	w
High Tide Rip g	w	GB	w	w	w	G	w	w	G	w	R	w	w	w	w	w	R	w	G	R	w	w	w	w	w	w	G	w	G	w	w	GB
Sail On A Cloud	w	w	w	w	Q	w	w	w	w	w	w	R	w	w	w	w	w	w	G	w	R	w	w	w	OUT							
Dandy Solution g	w	w	w	w	G	R	w	w	w	w	Q	w	w	w	w	w	G	w	w	R	w	w	w	w	w	ww	R	w	w	w	w	w
Fleet Champion g	w	w	w	w	w	w	w	w	G	w	w	G	w	w	w	w	w	w	w	OUT												
Oh what A Charger g																																
Pick Pocket Jonny g	w	w	w	w	G	R	w	w	w	w	w	G	w	OUT	w	w	s	s	s	s	s											
Spirit De Corps g	w	G	w	G	w	R	w	w	w	w	w	w	G	R	w	w	w	w	w	w	G	R	w	w	w	w	Gs	OUT				
Tuffest Bullet g																																

Three-year-old mares

Date March	1	2	3	4	5	6	7	8	9	10	11	12	13	14	15	16	17	18	19	20	21	22	23	24	25	26	27	28	29	30	31	1
Bandette Miss	w	w	w	w	w	G	w	w	w	G	w	w	G	R	w	w	w	w	G	w	R	w	w	w	w	w	Gs	R	w	w	w	w
Betsy Y Now	w	G	w	w	Q	w	w	w	w	w	w	G	w	w	R	w	w	w	w	G	w	GB	w	w	w	G	R	w	w	w	w	w
Bettys Promise	w	w	w	G	w	w	w	w	w	w	w	G	w	G	w	G	w	R	w	w	w	w	w	w	w	w	w	R	w	w	w	
Bet Your Bimy	w	w	w	w	w	w	w	G	w	w	G	w	G	w	w	G	w	R	w	w	s	s	s	s	s	s	OUT					
Casadee Class	w	w	w	R	w	w	w	w	w	w	G	w	w	OUT																		
Heradeck	w	GB	w	w	w	G	w	w	G	w	w	G	R	w	w	w	w	w	w	G	w	GB	w	w	w	Gs	?	R	w	w	w	w
Rythms Little Dream	w	OUT	w	s	s?																											
Merridoc Star	w	w	G	w	w	R	w	w	w	w	Q	w	G	w	w	w	w	w	G	R	w	w	OUT									
Dayna Celerity Thoroughbred				IN	w	GB	w	w	w	G	w	w	G	w	w	w	w	w	G	w	w	w	w	w	w	w	s	s	s			

Older horses

Date March	1	2	3	4	5	6	7	8	9	10	11	12	13	14	15	16	17	18	19	20	21	22	23	24	25	26	27	28	29	30	31	1
4yo m April Nine	w	OUT	w	s																												
4yo m Elises Ecstasies	w	w	w	w	w	w	G	w	w	G	w	w	R	w	w	w	w	w	w	w	s	OUT										
4yo h Boo Coo Trouble																																
4yo h Town Native	w	G	w	G	w	w	R	w	w	w	w	w	w	w	w	w	G	w	G	w	s	?	s	s	R	w	w	w	w	w	w	R
4yo g Sarawak Wings	w	w	w	R	w	w	w	w	w	w	G	w	G	w	w	G	w	R	w	w	w	w	w	w	G	w	G	w	?	?	w	G
4yo g Fols Dynasty																																
4yo g Ta Advantage	w	GB	w	w	G	R	w	w	w	w	w	w	G	w	G	w	w	G	R	w	w	w	w	w	w	?	G	w	G	w	w	B
5yo g Truly A Pleasure	w	w	w	w	w	G	w	w	w	G	w	w	G	w	w	G	w	G	w	G	w	s	s	s	s	s	B	w	w	w	w	G
7yo h Little Hubie	w	w	w	w	Gs	w	w	w	w	w	w	G	R	w	w	w	w	w	G	R	w	w	w	w	w	w	w	Gs	w	w	w	G

Caesar's training charts expanded

Training Charts For February and March 1988

In the record sheets for individual horses issued by the American Quarter Horse Association, there is a wonderful wealth of information, but the trainer is not listed. The current owner is listed, and claims after claiming races are indicated by a code, but changes in ownership by sale are not recorded. So the horses listed in Caesar's training tables in February and March may not have been trained by him when the horse raced before or after that training period: Caesar or the owner may have bought the horse before February or sold them after March; the owner may have switched trainers.

All races during February and March were at Bay Meadows track near San Francisco. Horses listed as geldings may have been colts at the time of the training records.

The grade rating for a horse's time in a race is determined the same way as the speed index (see glossary). The speed index is the highest grade rating a horse ever achieved.

We will start with some of Caesar's top money-earners, the older horses TRULY A PLEASURE, which Caesar owned, and TOWN NATIVE.

ABBREVIATIONS:

RACES

10000	Claiming race, any horse entered can be claimed for $10,000
M5000	Maiden claiming, any horse in the field can be claimed for $5,000
A8000	Starter race. Must not have run in a claimer over $8000
AW8000	Allowance race, $8000 purse
Dby Trl	Derby Trial to qualify for a Derby
Fty Trl	Futurity Trial to qualify for a Futurity
Hcap Hcp	A Handicap race
HcpStk	Handicap Stakes (Handicapped by weight)
Inv HS	Invitation Handicap Stake
G1,2,3	Grade 1, Grade 2, Grade 3
SI90	For horses with a Speed Index of 90 or less
L, Len	Length
2yo	Two-year-old
ROM	Register of Merit

Race Records at Bay Meadows for the end of 1987

300 yds 15.43 Set by Just Jim Dandy in 1977.
350 yds 17.49 Set by Pie Runner in 1987.
400 yds 19.66 Set by Countin The Cash 1986.
440 yds 21.39 Set by Tolltac in 1984.
870 yds 44.23 Set by Rise Again in 1987.

TRACKS

BK	East Idaho Fair, Blackfoot, Idaho
BM	Bay Meadows, San Francisco, California
BR	Blue Ribbon Downs, Sallisaw, Oklahoma
CA	Cassia County Fair, Burley, Idaho
FP	Fairplex Park, Pomona, California
HO	Hollywood Park, Los Angeles, California
LA	Los Alamitos, Los Angeles, California
PL	Alameda County Fair, Pleasanton, California
PD	Bannock County Fair, Idaho Falls, Idaho
PR	Prescott Downs, Prescott, Arizona
SJ	San Joaquin County Fair, California
SO	Solano County Fair, Vallejo, California
TE	Teton Racing Ass., Idaho Falls, Idaho
WY	Wyoming Downs, Evanston, Wyoming

Older Horses

TRULY A PLEASURE   Buckskin Gelding foaled in 1983
SIRE Truly's Easter - DAM Azure Pleasure by Azure Te
Best Grade 0118 Register Of Merit
Superior Racing and 1988 World Champion Distance Horse
1985 i.e. 2yo

Date	Track	Dist	Race	Place Margin	Winnings	Time	Grade	Odds
May 5	LA	350	M20000	2nd by a head	$945	18.35 sec	76	Pd 6.30
May 15	LA	350	M20000	3rd by ½ L	$525	18.39 sec	75	Pd 2.50
May 30	LA	350	16000	2nd by ¾ L	$1,125	18.10 sec	84	Pd 6.30
Jun 11	LA	350	M20000	Won by ½ L	$2,310	18.11 sec	83	Pd 0.80

Ended run of near wins. Odds suggest may have been favorite.

| Jun 19 | LA | 350 | 25000 | 5th by ¾ L | $138 | 18.01 sec | 86 | Pd 8.50 |

Good time, must have had tough opposition, as claiming class and odds confirm. Takes a risk and drops to $16,000 claimer.

| Jul 8 | LA | 350 | 16000 | Won by ½ L | $2,640 | 17.93 sec | 88 | Pd 1.00 |

All these close results would be giving Caesar heart attacks. He moves the horse back up into a $25,000 claimer.

| Jul 20 | LA | 350 | 25000 | 7th by 3 ¼ L | $0 | 18.25 sec | 79 | Pd 2.70 |

Outclassed. Back down to a $16,000 claimer - 4 days later!

Jul 24	LA	350	16000	5th by 2 L	$50	18.21 sec	80	Pd 3.70
Aug 7	LA	350	16000	10th by 2 ½ L	$0	18.33 sec	77	Pd 14.00
Sep 13	FP	350	Fut Trl	3rd by a neck	$375	18.14 sec	82	
Sep 22	FP	350	Futurity	5th by 2 L	$11,400	18.05 sec	85	Pd 26.78
Oct 24	LA	350	Fut Trl	3rd by ½ L	$375	17.97 sec	87	Pd 16.10
Nov 9	LA	350	25000	2nd by nose	$1,080	17.96 sec	88	Pd 4.10
Nov 20	LA	400	25000	3rd by ½ L	$538	20.27 sec	86	Pd 1.30
Nov 29	LA	350	20000	Won by ¾ L	$2,255	17.85 sec	91	Pd 1.60
Dec 10	LA	400	20000	2nd by a nose	$922	20.18 sec	89	Pd 1.20
Dec 26	LA	350	20000	2nd by a neck	$922	17.96 sec	88	Pd 2.80

Yes that's the day after Christmas.

1986 i.e. 3yo

Jan 10	LA	400	AW6000	Won by head	$3,300	20.23 sec	87	Pd 5.60
Mar 8	BM	400	AW4600	2nd a neck	$1,034	20.14 sec	94	Pd 1.40
Mar 22	BM	400	AW4600	Won by 1 ¼	$2,530	20.07 sec	95	Pd 0.60
Apr 11	BM	870	Dby Trl	Won by 8 L	$1,650	45.59 sec	88	Pd 0.80
Apr 20	BM	870	Derby	Won by 4 L	$37,720	45.05 sec	102	Pd .50

This was the first running of the Gold Rush 870 Derby

May 9	LA	870	Hcap G3	Won by ½	$15,450	45.68 sec	85	Pd 1.00
May 30	LA	870	Hcap G3	Won 1 ½	$19,200	45.81 sec	82	Pd 2.80
Jun 28	LA	870	Hcap G3	2nd 2 ½ L	$4,500	45.61 sec	87	Pd 1.40
Jul 18	LA	870	HcapStk	Won 1 ¼ L	$5,500	45.13 sec	99	Pd 1.30
Aug 8	HO	870	HcapStk	Won by 2 L	$12,800	46.10 sec		Pd 0.60

Did this horse find its right distance or what!

Date	Track	Dist	Race	Result	Prize	Time	Rating	Odds
Aug 31	HO	870	HcapStk	3rd by 1 L	$3,125	46.03 sec		Pd 0.50
Oct 2	HO	870	InvHS G2	7th by ¾ L	$0	46.47 sec		Pd 1.20

1987 i.e. 4yo

Date	Track	Dist	Race	Result	Prize	Time	Rating	Odds
May 2	LA	870	HcapStk G3	2nd by 1L	$4,500	44.99 sec	99	Pd 1.40
May 23	LA	870	HcapStk G3	3rd ½ L	$3,125	45.05 sec	98	Pd 2.30
Jul 3	LA	870	HcapStk G3	6th by 1 L	$0	45.27 sec	92	Pd 3.90
Jul 21	LA	870	AW7900	3rd by 1 ½	$988	45.84 sec	78	Pd 1.80
Jul 31	HO	870	HcapStk	2nd ½ L	$4,500	44.90 sec	118	Pd 7.20

The Los Alamitos 870 record was 44.42

Date	Track	Dist	Race	Result	Prize	Time	Rating	Odds
Aug 22	LA	870	Inv Hcap Stk	2nd 1 ½	$3,000	45.04 sec		Pd 1.10
Sep 16	HO	550	HcapStk G3	Won ½L	$13,250	27.34 sec		Pd 3.60
Sep 26	FP	870	InvHStk	8th distanced	$0			Pd 4.40
Oct 31	LA	400	HcapStk	4th 1 ¾ L	$1,875	20.43 sec	82	Pd 10.90
Nov 21	LA	400	HcapStk	5th 2 ¼ L	$250	20.18 sec	88	Pd 16.70

1988 i.e. 5yo
February

Day	Activity		Dist	Race	Result	Prize	Time	Rating	Odds
1	w								
2	w								
3	w								
4	Gallop								
5	w								
6		RACE	870	AW7000	2nd by ½ L	$1,575	45.62 sec	83	Pd 1.40
7	w								
8	w								
9	w								
10	w								
11	w								
12	w								
13	Gallop								
14	w								
15	Gallop, Cortisone								
16	w								
17	w								
18	Gallop Gates								
19		RACE	870	HcapStk	7th 3 ¼ L	$0	46.15 sec	70	Pd 2.70
20	w, Eqvalan wormer								
21	w								
22	w								
23									
24	w								
25	w, Shoes changed								
26	Gallop								
27	w								
28		RACE	870	AW7000	4th 4 ¼ L	$525	47.37 sec	39	Pd 2.00
29	w								

March

1	w
2	w
3	w
4	w
5	w
6	w
7	Gallop
8	w
9	w
10	Gallop
11	w
12	w
13	Gallop
14	w
15	w
16	Gallop
17	w
8	Gallop
19	w
20	Gallop
21	w
22	?STALL REST?
23	?
24	?
25	?
26	Strong Breeze, 34.4
27	w, Cortisone
28	w
29	w
30	w
31	w

April

01	Gallop								
Apr 10	BM	870	Champ	Won by 1 L	$13,475	45.33 sec	90	Pd 7.50
May 14	LA	870	HcpStk G3	Won head	$15,600	45.31 sec	88	Pd 2.50
Jun 3	LA	870	HcpStk G3	Won neck	$15,450	45.29 sec	88	Pd 2.20
Jul 2	LA	870	HcpStk G3	Won ½L	$15,650	44.97 sec	96	Pd 1.70
Jul 15	LA	870	HcpStk G3	3rd 3 ½L	$3,125	45.62 sec	80	Pd 0.90
Aug 5	LA	870	InvStk	5th by 2 L	$500	45.43 sec		Pd 2.20
Sep 9	LA	870	InvStk G2	Won 1 ¾	$16,500	45.34 sec	87	Pd 2.50
Oct 14	LA	870	Stk G3	4th 3 ½	$3,612	45.62 sec	80	Pd 0.50

1989 i.e. 6yo

Jul 8	LA	870	HcpStk	3rd 1 ½	$2,500	45.47 sec	82	Pd 8.70

To July 1989, 51 starts,17 wins, 11 seconds, 9 thirds, for $252,409 including 11 stakes wins and 8 stakes places.

TOWN NATIVE Bay Stallion foaled 1984

Fol's Native TB - Up Town Etta

Best Grade 0089   Register Of Merit

1986 i.e. 2yo

Date	Track	Dist	Race	Place Margin	Winnings	Time	Grade	Odds
May 1	LA	350	M10000	Won by nose	$1,595	18.34 sec	76	Pd 12.70
May 15	LA	350	12500	2nd by ½ L	$855	18.21 sec	80	Pd 21.30
Jun 5	LA	350	8000	3rd by 1 Len	$290	18.20 sec	80	Pd 2.50
Jun 12	LA	350	8000	Won by nose	$1,595	18.00 sec	86	Pd 3.10
Jul 3	LA	350	8000	Won by ½ L	$1,595	18.14 sec	82	Pd 1.70
Jul 26	HO	350	8000	7th 7 ¾ L	$0	19.13 sec	63	Pd 1.50

Ran a shocker. Note time and grade. Low odds - probably favorite or second favorite in the betting.

Date	Track	Dist	Race	Place Margin	Winnings	Time	Grade	Odds
Aug 7	HO	350	6250	3rd by ½ L	$363	18.42 sec	83	Pd 1.90
Aug 17	HO	350	6250	3rd by ¾ L	$413	18.50 sec		Pd 1.80
Aug 28	HO	400	6250	2nd by ½ L	$742	20.79 sec	84	Pd 2.10
Sep 7	HO	400	10000	3rd by 1 Len	$488	20.75 sec		Pd 6.10
Sep 24	HO	350	8000	6th 2 ½ L	$0	18.74 sec	74	Pd 9.00
Nov 1	LA	400	16000	2nd by a head	$718	20.34 sec	84	Pd 5.50
Nov 12	LA	400	16000	Won by ¾ L	$2,255	20.24 sec	87	Pd 4.60
Nov 22	LA	400	AW5400	5th 1 ¼ L	$135	20.42 sec	82	Pd 4.60

1987 i.e. 3yo

Date	Track	Dist	Race	Place Margin	Winnings	Time	Grade	Odds
Feb 23	BM	400	AW4600	5th by 2 L	$115	20.54 sec	82	Pd 3.30
Mar 1	BM	400	Hcap Stk	3rd 1 ½ L	$1,250	20.25 sec	89	Pd 14.60
Apr 3	BM	870	Dby Trl	Won by 1 L	$1,650	47.23 sec	44	Pd 0.30

Seems amazing to win with such a low grade. Very low odds.

Date	Track	Dist	Race	Place Margin	Winnings	Time	Grade	Odds
Apr 12	BM	870	Derby	Won 2 ½ L	$30,636	45.94 sec	76	Pd 0.90

Gold Rush Derby - Caesar made it two wins in a row.

Date	Track	Dist	Race	Place Margin	Winnings	Time	Grade	Odds
Oct 23	LA	400	Hcap Stk	5th by 4 L	$375	21.03 sec	67	Pd 12.30
Nov 6	LA	870	Hcap Stk	5th by 7 L	$375	47.22 sec	43	Pd 2.90
Nov 18	LA	870	5000	Won by neck	$1,870	45.94 sec	75	Pd 1.50

This is a marked improvement in time and grade.

Date	Track	Dist	Race	Place Margin	Winnings	Time	Grade	Odds
Dec 8	LA	870	3200	4th by 6 L	$225	45.93 sec	76	Pd 3.30

Seems very risky to drop in class after a win.   Poor result
may indicate problems with the horse and a desire to get rid of it.

1988 i.e. 4yo

February

1	w							
2	w							
3	w							
4	Gallop							
5	w							
6	RACE BM	870	2500	3rd by 1 Len	$300	46.69 sec	56	Pd 2.20
7	w							

w, Eqvalan wormer

9	w							
10	w							
11	w							
12	w							
13	Gallop							
14	w, Shoes changed							
15	Gallop Cortisone							
16	w							
7	w							
18	w							
19	RACE	870	2500	Won by ½ L	$1,320	46.12 sec	70	Pd 0.80
20	w							
21	w							
22	w							
23	w							
24	w							
25	w							
26	w							
27	Gallop							
28	w							
29	w							

March

1	w							
2	Gallop							
3	w							
4	Gallop							
5	w							
6	w							
7	RACE	870	3200	3rd 3 ½ L	$288	45.73 sec	80	Pd 4.00
8	w							
9	w, Cortisone							
10	w							
11	w							
12	w							
13	w							
14	w							
15	w							
16	w							
17	Gallop							
18	w							
19	Gallop							
20	w							
21	?Stall rest?							
22	?							
23	?							
24	?							
25	RACE	870	2000	2nd by 3 ½ L	$472	46.86 sec	52	Pd 0.80
26	w							
27	w							

CAESAR DOMINGUEZ

28	w							
29	w							
30	w							
31	w							

April

1	RACE	870	2000	4th by 3 ½ L	$157	46.90 sec	51	Pd 4.20
May 13	LA	870	2000	7th by 7 ¾ L	$0	46.87 sec	49	Pd 5.50

Presume sold - tracks below are in Idaho and Wyoming.

Jun 17	TE	990	3500	2nd by a neck	$87	54.24 sec		Pd 3.50
Jul 4	TE	870	AW600	2nd by 3 L	$150	47.92 sec	42	Pd 0.80
Jul 13	TE	880	AW450	3rd by 1 L	$68	47.36 sec		Pd 6.00
Jul 30	TE	400	3500	2nd by 2 ½ L	$113	20.62 sec	87	Pd 5.00
Aug 6	WY	870	3200	4th by 1 L	$80	45.72 sec	85	Pd 7.60
Aug 13	TE	400	SI90	4th by 1 ¼ L	$0	20.84 sec	81	Pd 2.50
Aug 19	CA	550	2500	8th by distance	$0			Pd 3.30
Sep 5	BK	575	2500	6th by 6 ¾	$0	33.10 sec		Pd 5.90
Sep 9	BK	575	2500	3rd by ½ L	$90	32.49 sec		Pd 9.10
Sep 17	PD	870	2000	Won by 1 ¼ L	$270	47.41 sec		Pd 9.10

Layout for horses below:

HORSE'S NAME Description Year foaled
Sire - Dam
Best grade. Register Of Merit (if earned)
1988 starts wins 2nds 3rds money

Older Horses continued

TA ADVANTAGE Brown Gelding 1984
Timeto Thinkrich - Kellers Policy
Best Grade 0114 ROM Superior Racing Award

1986 2yo

Date	Track	Dist	Class	Place	Money
Apr 12	BM	300	M6250	8th	$0
Jun 10	LA	350	M6250	3rd	$300
Jun 25	LA	350	M6250	3rd	$300
Jul 3	LA	350	M8000	Won	$1,430
Jul 27	HO	350	6250	Won	$1,595
Aug 10	HO	400	6250	Won	$1,595
Aug 30	HO	350	10000	4th	$277
Sep 10	HO	350	6250	Won	$1,925
Sep 24	HO	350	8000	3rd	$463
Oct 25	LA	400	6250	5th	$78

Claimed by Caesar off Blane Schvaneveldt.

Date	Track	Dist	Class	Place	Money
Nov 17	LA	350	8000	5th	$83
Nov 29	LA	400	5000	4th	$232
Dec 16	LA	350	5000	2nd	$742

1987 3yo

Date	Track	Dist	Class	Place	Money
Feb 20	BM	400	5000	4th	$187
Feb 28	BM	350	4000	Won	$1,320
Mar 28	BM	870	16000	Won	$2,750
Apr 12	BM	870	AW4800	Won	$2,640
May 1	LA	870	AW5100	Won	$2,805
May 12	LA	870	20000	2nd	$1,305
May 23	LA	870	Hcap G3	5th	$625
May 30	LA	870	AW5500	Won	$3,025
Jun 25	LA	870	16000	4th	$420
Jul 29	LA	550	Hcap G3	9th	$0
Aug 7	HO	870	16000	Won	$3,080
Aug 23	HO	870	16000	5th	$140
Sep 5	HO	870	Hcp G2	3rd	$3,750
Sep 19	FP	870	Stk	4th	$750
Oct 23	LA	870	20000	4th	$487
Nov 6	LA	870	Hcap	3rd	$1,875
Dec 10	LA	870	16000	4th	$360
Dec 18	LA	870	Hcap	3rd	$2,500

1988 4yo

February

1 w
2 w
3 w
4 Gallop
5 w
6 RACE 870 AW7000 6th $0 45.94sec 2.5L
7 w
8 w
9 w
10 w
11 Gallop
12 w
13 w
14 Gallop
15 w
16 w
17 Gallop GATES
18 w
19 RACE 870 Hcap Stakes Won $9,875 45.64 sec
20 w Eqvalan wormer
21 w
22 w
23 w
24 w
25 w
26 w
27 w
28 Gallop
29 w

March

1 w
2 Breeze
3 w
4 w Shoes changed
5 Gallop
6 RACE 870 Hcap Stakes 3rd $1,875 45.90 sec 5L
7 w
8 w
9 w
10 w
11 w
12 Gallop
13 w
14 Gallop
15 w
16 w
17 Gallop
18 RACE 870 Hcap Stakes Won $4,895 45.52 sec
19 w
20 w
21 w
22 w
23 w
24 w
25 w
26 Gallop

27 w
28 Gallop
29 w
30 w
31 Strong Breeze ¼
April
1 w

Date	Track					
Apr 10	BM	870	Champ HcapS	6th	$0
May 14	LA	870	G3	6th	$0
May 26	LA	870	AW8000	4th	$600
Jun 25	LA	870	16000	5th	$150
Jul 5	LA	870	20000	7th	$0

9L off the leader

Date	Track					
Sep 3	LA	870	12500	4th	$420

Beaten 2½L but dropped way down and continues down.

Date	Track					
Sep 14	LA	870	5000	3rd	$475
Sep 23	FP	870	5000	2nd	$1,125
Oct 2	FP	870	A5000	4th	$412
Oct 15	LA	870	4000	7th	$0
Oct 26	LA	870	4000	3rd	$500
Nov 5	LA	870	2500	2nd	$765
Nov 11	LA	870	2500	Won	$1,870
Nov 19	LA	870	2500	2nd	$765

1989 5yo

Date	Track					
May 9	LA	870	6250	Won	$2,530

Won by 1¾ lengths.

Date	Track					
May 19	LA	870	12500	5th	$138

Beaten 4½ lengths

Date	Track					
Jun 3	LA	870	8000	6th	$0

6L off leader. Down it goes

Date	Track					
Jun 17	LA	870	4000	2nd	$900

Claimed (Off Caesar?)

Date	Track					
Jun 30	LA	870	6000	8th	by 8L

Two-year-old Colts
CALIFORNIA TIME
Timeto Bed - Sages War Woman
Best grade - 0086   ROM
1988 8 starts 1 win 2 2nds, 2 3rds $3,805
February
1 w
2 w
3 w
4 w
5 Gallop
6 QUALIFYING TRIAL 13.6 sec
7 w
8 w
9 w
10 w
11 Gallop
12 w
13 w
14 Gallop
15 w
16 w
17 Gallop
18 w
19 w
20 Gallop
21 w
22 w
23 w
24 Gallop
25 w
26 w
27 Gallop
28 RACE   300   MdnCl 8000   Won $1,375   16.16 sec
29 w
March
1 w
2 w
3 w
4 w
5 Gallop
6 w
7 w
8 w
9 Gallop
10 w
11 w
12 Gallop
13 w
14 Gallop
15 w

16 w
17 Strong Breeze
18 w
19 w
20 w
21 w
22 OUT

Jun 15	LA	350	12500	10th	$0
Jun 23	LA	350	6250	5th	$90
Jul 19	LA	350	4000	2nd	$720
Aug 19	LA	350	6250	3rd	$450
Aug 30	LA	350	6250	3rd	$360
Sep 9	LA	350	6250	2nd	$810
Oct 18	LA	440	6250	7th	$0

1989 3yo

May 23	LA	350	8000	2nd	$855
			DBY		
Jun 20	LA	870	TRL	4th	$300
Jun 29	LA	870	12500	Won	$2,585
Jul 12	LA	870	AW6500	3rd	$813

Life: 12 starts 2 wins 3 3 $8,358

DEAR LITTLE DASH Sorrel colt
Dash For Cash - Dear Little Me
Best Grade - 0061
1988 3 races 0 wins 0 0 $0
February
1 w
2 w
3 w
4 w
5 QUALIFYING TRIAL 13.7
6 w
7 w
8 w
9 w
10 Gallop
11 w
12 w Shoes changed
13 Gallop GATES
14 QUALIFYING TRIAL 13.7
15 w
16 w
17 w
18 w
19 w
20 Gallop
21 w
22 Gallop
23 w
24 w
25 w
26 Gallop
27 RACE 250 Mdn 7th $0 14.81 by 6¼L
28 w
29 w
March
1 w
2 w
3 w
4 Gallop
5 w
6 w
7 RACE 220 Mdn 9th $0 13.13 by 5¾L
8 w
9 w
10 w
11 w
12 Gallop
13 w Shoes changed
14 w
15 w
16 Gallop

CAESAR DOMINGUEZ

17 w

18 RACE 300 Mdn 6th 16.71 by 3½L

19 w

20 w

21 w

22 OUT No other race to Sep 89

DICKENS DANDY Bay gelding

Total Departure TB - Pay The Bird

(Sire once a Lukas racehorse)

Best grade - 0081 ROM

1988 10 starts 1 win 1 0 $2,610

February

1 w

2 w

3 w

4 Gallop

5 QUALIFYING TRIAL 13.4

6 w

7 w

8 w

9 w

10 Gallop

11 w

12 w

13 Gallop GATES

14 Gallop

15 w

16 w

17 Gallop

18 w

19 w

20 Gallop

21 w

22 w

23 w

24 Gallop

25 w

26 w

27 Gallop

28 w

29 RACE 250 MdnCl 12500 Won $1,485 13.99

March

1 w

2 w

3 OUT

Date	Track				
Sep 6	LA	350	4000	8th	$0
Sep 15	LA	400	4000	7th	$0
Sep 25	FP	350	4000	4th	$270
Oct 5	LA	350	3200	10th	$0
1989					
May 16	LA	350	3200	4th	$225
May 27	LA	400	3200	6th	$0
Jun 3	LA	870	2000	4th	Disq
Jun 17	LA	870	2000	Won	$1,650
Jun 23	LA	870	3200	Won	$1,760
Jul 8	LA	870	5000	7th	$0

Date	Track				
May 11	LA	350	16000	7th	$0
May 17	LA	350	8000	5th	$90
Jun 4	LA	350	6250	6th	$0
Jun 9	LA	350	4000	8th	$0
Aug 25	LA	350	5000	2nd	$765

Two-year-old fillies

ALLRED DANCER   Chesnut
Texas Dancer - Easy Hustler
Best grade - 0085   ROM
1988 11 starts 1 win 1 3 $4,333

February
1 w
2 w
3 w
4 Gallop
5 w
6 QUALIFYING TRIAL 13.4
7 w
8 w
9 w
10 w
11 Gallop
12 w
13 w
14 Gallop
15 w
16 w
17 Gallop
18 w
19 ? GATES?
20 Gallop GATES

| 21 | RACE | 300 | Mdn | 2nd | $855 | 16.08 | | ¾L |

22 w
23 w
24 w
25 w
26 w
27 Gallop
28 w
29 w

March
1 w
2 Gallop
3 w
4 w
5 Gallop
6 w
7 Gallop
8 w
9 w
10 Gallop
11 w
12 Gallop
13 w

| 14 | RACE | 350 | Maiden | 4th | $248 | 16.26 | | 1¼L |

15 w

16 w
17 w
18 w
19 w
20 Gallop
21 w
22 w
23 Gallop
24 w
25 w
26 Gallop GATES
27 w

| 28 | RACE | 350 | Futrty Trl | 5th | $70 | 18.54 | | 2½ |

29 w
30 w
31 w

April
1 w

May 7	LA	350	M8000	3rd	$425
May 24	LA	350	M5000	3rd	$375
Jun 9	LA	350	M5000	Won	$1,650
Jun 28	LA	350	4000	9th	$0
Jul 7	LA	350	5000	3rd	$425
Jul 22	LA	350	8000	4th	$285
Aug 25	LA	350	5000	6th	$0
Sep 9	LA	350	4000	7th	$0

No more races to Sep 89

CASADYS CONCEPT Gray
Casady Casanova- Miss Silky TB
Best grade - 0066
1988 6 races 0 wins 1 0 $667
Feb
1 -
2 w
3 w
4 Gallop
5 QUALIFYING TRIAL 14.3
6 w
7 w
8 w
9 w
10 Gallop
11 w
12 w
13 QUALIFYING TRIAL 14.1
14 w
15 w
16 w
17 w
18 w
19 Gallop GATES Shoes changed
20 w
21 Gallop
22 w
23 w
24 Gallop
25 w
26 w
27 Breeze
28 w
29 w
March
1 w
2 w
3 Gallop GATES
4 w
5 RACE 220 MdnCl 10000 6th $0 13.20 4½
6 w
7 w
8 w
9 w
10 Gallop
11 w
12 RACE 300 MdnCl 5000 2nd $495 16.55 1¼
13 w Equipoise (Anabolic)
14 w
15 w
16 w

17 w Shoes changed
18 w
19 RACE 300 MdnCl 6250 4th $172 16.66 3L
20 w
21 w
22 w
23 w
24 w
25 Gallop GATES
26 w
27 w
28 Gallop GATES
29 w
30 w
31 Gallop
April
1 w
2 RACE 300 MdnCl 12500 7th $0 17.59 10 L
May 6 LA 350 5000 10th $0
Jun 2 LA 350 4000 7th $0

LITTLE DOLL RAE Sorrel
Merridoc - Rae Gosee Bar
Best grade - 0085
1988 14 starts 1 win 1 1 $3,522
February
1 w
2 w
3 Gallop
4 QUALIFYING TRIAL 13.4
5 w
6 w
7 w
8 w
9 w
10 Gallop
11 w
12 w Shoes changed
13 QUALIFYING TRIAL 13.7
14 w
15 w
16 w
17 w
18 w
19 Gallop GATES
20 w
21 Gallop GATES
22 w
23 w
24 Gallop
25 w
26 w
27 Gallop
28 RACE 220 Maiden 7th $0 12.61 1¼
29 w
March
1 w
2 w
3 w
4 Gallop
5 w
6 w
7 Gallop
8 w
9 w
10 Gallop
11 w
12 w
13 Gallop Shoes changed
14 w
15 w
16 Gallop

17 w
18 Gallop
19 w
20 RACE 250 Maiden Won $1,815 13.74
21 w

Date	Track	Dist	Class	Place	Earnings
May 27	LA	350	Hcap	6th	$0
Jun 8	LA	350	Fut Trl	8th	$0
Jun 22	LA	350	8000	5th	$95
Jun 28	LA	350	4000	7th	$0
Jul 19	LA	350	4000	6th	$0
Aug 17	LA	350	4000	5th	$80
Aug 27	LA	400	4000	2nd	$720
Sep 6	LA	350	4000	3rd	$400
Sep 13	LA	350	4000	4th	$202
Sep 30	LA	350	4000	9th	$0
Oct 6	LA	350	3200	4th	$210
Oct 20	LA	350	3200	7th	$0
1989					
May 25	LA	350	4000	5th	$78
Jun 3	LA	350	3200	6th	$0
Jun 9	LA	350	3200	7th	$0
Jun 22	LA	400	4000	6th	$64

Total 18 starts 1 win 1 1 $3,664

CAESAR DOMINGUEZ

Three-year-old colts

DANDY SOLUTION Brown gelding
Advance Solution - Little Dandy Jet
Best grade 0079
1988 14 starts 2 wins 1 2 $2,834
February
9 IN
10 Gallop
11 w TEETH
12 w
13 w Shoes changed
14 QUALIFYING TRIAL 19.1
15 w
16 w
17 w
18 w
19 Gallop
20 w
21 QUALIFYING TRIAL 19.3
22 w
23 w
24 w
25 w
26 Gallop
27 w
28 w
29 RACE 400 MdnCl 3200 7th $0 22.57 10 L
March
1 w
2 w
3 w
4 w
5 Gallop
6 RACE 400 MdnCl 4000 6th $0 20.88 3½
7 w
8 w
9 w
10 w
11 QUALIFYING TRIAL 47.4?
12 w
13 w
14 w
15 w
16 Gallop
17 w Shoes changed
18 w
19 RACE 870 MdnCl 3200 2nd $450 46.52 1L
20 w Cortisone
21 w ?
22 w

23 w
24 w
25 w
26 RACE 870 MdnCl 3200 Won $1,100 47.03
27 w
28 w
29 w
30 w
31 w
May 19 LA 870 4000 3rd $310
Jun 10 LA 870 3200 7th $0
Seemed to go on tour. Sold?

SPIRIT DE CORPS Bay gelding
Timeto Thinkrich - Fishers
Favorite. Best Grade- 0108 ROM
1987 2yo

Sep 9	HO	350	M16000	4th	$277	
Nov 6	LA	350	M12500	7th	$0	
Nov 26	LA	350	M4000	Won	$1,320	
Dec 5	LA	350	4000	4th	$202	

Claimed by Henry Dominguez

Dec 15	LA	550	5000	4th	$240	
Dec 19	LA	350	5000	6th	$0	

1988 3yo
February
1 w
2 w
3 w
4 Gallop
5 w
6 Gallop
7 w
8 Gallop GATES
9 w
10 w
11 w
12 RACE 400 Clmg 2500 4th $157 20.67 1¼
13 w
14 w
15 w
16 w
17 w
18 Gallop GATES Shoes changed
19 RACE 440 Clmg 5000 4th $187 22.60 ¾L
20 w
21 w
22 QUALIFYING TRIAL 48.9
23 w
24 w
25 Gallop
26 w
27 Gallop
28 w
29 w
March
1 w
2 Gallop
3 w
4 Gallop
5 w
6 RACE 400 Clmg 2500 2nd $450 20.26 1½
7 w Eqvalan wormer

8 w Cortisone
9 w
10 w
11 w
12 Gallop
13 RACE 400 Clmg 3200 Won $1,210
14 w
15 w
16 w
17 w
18 w
19 Gallop
20 RACE 400 Clmg 3200 Won $1,210 20.14
21 w Cortisone
22 w
23 w
24 w
25 Gallop GATES
26 RACE 440 Clmg 2500 4th $150 22.54 3¼
CLAIMED off Henry and Caesar

ECONOMICS:
Paid $4000 when claiming the horse.
Cost of 3½ months training approx $3100.
Won $3604, paid $2500 by the claimer.
Loss of $1000 unless betting was successful.

After the claim, the horse was owned by Barney Leard and trained by Rob Ingerbritson. It went on to some big wins of the kind that give claiming trainers nightmares.

Apr 4	BM	400	4000	Won	$1,265
Jun 18	SJ	400	AW8000	Won	$4,400
Jul 2	PL	350	AW9500	2nd	$2,138
Jul 23	SO	440	Derby	Won	$10,050
Aug 13	BM	400	AW9000	2nd	$2,025
Aug 28	SA	350	AW8000	Won	$4,400
Sep 4	SA	350	Stake	2nd	$2,250
Sep 22	FP	350	12500	2nd	$1,575
Oct 1	LA	350	Hcap	8th	$0
1989					
May 12	LA	350	5000	7th	$0
May 24	LA	350	3200	2nd	$765
CLAIMED					
Jun 16	LA	350	5000	8th	$0

TUFFEST BULLET Sorrel gelding
Chick In Command - Tuff Go Flight   Best grade 0107   ROM
Superior Racing - Stakes win
1987 2yo

Date	Track	Dist	Race	Place	Winnings
Mar 7	EN	300	SI49	2nd	$84
Mar 14	EN	330	Fut Trl	2nd	
Mar 21	EN	330	Futurity	3rd	$1.257
Apr 19	GT	350	Mdn	Won	$380
May 9	UD	330	Fut Trl	Won	$343
May 16	UD	330	Futurity	Won	$6,753
Jun 27	EU	350	Fut Trl	2nd	
Jul 18	EU	350	Fut Trl	Won	Disq 2
Aug 14	QD	350	SI79	4th	$33
Sep 12	QD	400	Fut Trl	Won	$120
Sep 19	QD	400	Fut	2nd	$3,048
Sep 26	AD	350	AW8570	3rd	$1,065
Oct 13	BE	400	Fut Trl	Won	
Oct 18	BE	400	Fut	4th	$864
Dec 9	LA	330	10000	5th	$88
Dec 16	LA	350	4000	8th	$0

Claimed by Caesar or one of his owners.
1988 3yo
February
1 w
2 w
3 w
4 Gallop
5 w
6 RACE 350 Clmg 4000 Won $1,320 18.18sec
7 w
8 w
9 w
10 w
11 w
12 w
13 Gallop GATES
14 RACE 350 Clmg 4000 Won $1,320 17.96
15 w Cortisone
16 w
17 w
18 w Shoes changed
19 GATES
20 RACE 350 Clmg 3200 Won $1,265 18.21
Claimed off Caesar

ECONOMICS:
Cost to claim $4,000.
Training 9 weeks @ $30/day, $1,890.
Winnings $3,905.
Paid by claimer $3,200.
Profit $1215.

Trainer Jerry Loveland

Date	Track	Dist	Race	Place	Winnings
Mar 5	BM	350	6250	6th	$0
Mar 14	BM	330	4000	4th	$172
Apr 9	BM	350	4000	4th	$172

Claimed again

BETSY Y KNOW Brown Mare
Last Hurrah - Rulla Time Miss
Best grade 0085   ROM
1987 2yo

Date	Track	Dist	Race	Place	Winnings
Jul 8	LA	350	M10000	6th	$0
Jul 23	LA	350	M10000	9th	$0
Jul 31	HO	350	M6250	3rd	$363
Aug 13	HO	350	M8000	5th	$232
Aug 27	HO	350	M6250	4th	$217
Oct 16	LA	350	M6250	Won	$1,540
Oct 24	LA	400	8000	3rd	$438
Nov 11	LA	400	8000	6th	$0
Nov 28	LA	400	6250	3rd	$413
Dec 4	LA	870	5000	4th	$247

February
2 w
3 w
4 w
5 Gallop
6 w
7 Breeze
8 w
9 w
10 w
11 Gallop
12 w
13 w
14 QUALIFYING TRIAL 19.1
15 w
16 w
17 w
18 w
19 Gallop
20 w Shoes changed
21 Gallop
22 w
23 w
24 Breeze
25 w
26 w
27 w
28 Gallop
29 w

March
1 w
2 Gallop
3 w
4 w
5 QUALIFYING TRIAL
6 w
7 w
8 w
9 w
10 w
11 Gallop
12 w
13 w
14 RACE 330 Clmg 4000 5th $58 17.36 3 L
15 w
16 w
17 w
18 w
19 Gallop
20 w
21 Breeze
22 w
23 w
24 w
25 Gallop
26 RACE 870 Dby Trl 5th $70 49.06 14 L
27 w
28 w
29 w
30 w
31 Gallop
April
1 w

Apr 8	BM	400	2500	8th	$0
May 19	LA	350	3200	3rd	$375
Jun 10	LA	400	4000	7th	$0

HERADECK Brown mare
Hempen TB - Sirius Deck
Best grade - 0100 Reg Of Merit
1987 2yo

Mar 3	BR	300	Mdn	5th	$64
Mar 19	BR	330	FutTrl	3rd	$70
Mar 28	BR	330	FutCon	2nd	$2,982
May 29	BR	400	FutTrl	2nd	$105
Jun 7	BR	400	FutCon	4th	$3,052
Jun 17	RD	400	FutTrl	4th	$68
Oct 7	BR	400	FutTrl	3rd	$100
Nov 5	BR	400	FutTrl	Won	$125
Nov 14	BR	400	FutTrl	3rd	$7,285

I presume this was now sent to Caesar after its Futurity year
in Texas
1988
February
2 w
3 w
4 Gallop GATES
5 w Shoes changed
6 QUALIFYING TRIAL 18.9
7 w
8 w
9 w
10 w
11 Gallop
12 w
13 RACE 350 Allow 4600 Won $2,530 17.81
14 w
15 w
16 w
17 w
18 Gallop GATES
19 w
20 Gallop
21 w
22 Gallop GATES
23 w
24 w
25 w
26 Gallop GATES
27 w
28 Gallop
29 w
March
1 w
2 Breeze
3 w
4 w

5 w
6 Gallop
7 w
8 w
9 Gallop
10 w Shoes changed
11 w
12 Gallop
13 RACE 350 Allow 6000 Won $3,300 17.60
14 w Eqvalan wormer
15 w
16 w
17 w
18 w
19 Gallop
20 w
21 Breeze
22 w
23 w
24 w
25 Gallop GATES
26 w
27 RACE 350 Handicap 4th $562 17.65 neck
28 w
29 w
30 w
31 w

Date	Track	Dist	Class	Pos	Prize	Time	
May 5	LA	350	Hcap G3	10th	$0		
May 18	LA	440	Drby Tr	7th	$0		
Jun 10	LA	400	Hcap G2	8th	$0		
Jul 7	LA	350	AW8000	5th	$200		
Jul 12	LA	350	AW7000	6th	$0		
Jul 23	LA	400	AW8000	7th	$0		

BANDETTE MISS Bay Mare
Band Of Azure - Ramamente TB
Best Grade 0083 Reg. Of Merit
1987 2yo

Date	Track	Dist	Class	Pos	Prize	Time	
Jun 20	PR	330	Mdn	5th	$38		
Jul 11	PR	330	StkTrl	7th	$0		
Jul 18	PR	330	Mdn	4th	$0		
Nov 25	LA	350	M3200	4th	$172		
Dec 8	LA	350	M3200	2nd	$517		
Dec 18	LA	400	M3200	4th	$232		

1988 3yo
February
1 w
2 w
3 w
4 Gallop
5 w Shoes changed
6 w
7 Gallop GATES
8 RACE 400 MdnCl 4000 5th $55 20.59 2L
9 w
10 w
11 w
12 w
13 Gallop
14 w
15 Gallop
16 w
17 w
18 Gallop GATES
19 w
20 RACE 350 MdnCl 4000 2nd $630 18.36 1L
21 w
22 w
23 w
24 w
25 w
26 Gallop GATES
27 w
28 w
29 RACE 400 MdnCl 3200 3rd $250 20.79 2L
March
1 w
2 w
3 w
4 w
5 w
6 Gallop
7 w
8 w

9 w
10 Gallop
11 w Shoes changed
12 w
13 Gallop
14 RACE 440 MdnCl 32003rd $250 22.56 2L
15 w
16 w
17 w
18 w
19 Gallop
20 w
21 RACE 350 MdnCl 3200 2nd $450 18.20½L
22 w
23 w
24 w
25 w
26 w
27 Gallop GATES
28 RACE 350 MdnCl 4000 2nd $473 18.32¾L
29 w
30 w
31 w
April
1 w
2 RACE 400 Claiming 4th $100 20.67 ¾L

May 6	LA	350	M4000	3rd	$350
May 26	LA	350	M5000	6th	$0
Jun 9	LA	350	M4000	6th	$70

Same placing (6th) in a cheaper claiming race - and get more money!

RYTHMS LITTLE DREAM Chesnut Mare (Not my spelling of Rhythm. I include this one for the gate work)

Merridoc - Hot Rythm

Best Grade -0090 Reg Of Merit

1987 2yo

Nov 12	LA	350	M3200	won	$1,595
Nov 28	LA	350	6250	won	$1,705
Dec 17	LA	440	AW8000	7th	$0

1988 3yo
February
1 w
2 w
3 Gallop
4 w
5 Gallop
6 w
7 Strong Breeze
8 w
9 w
10 w
11 w
12 RACE 350 Clmg 10000 3rd $400 18.28 1½
13 w
14 Gallop GATES
15 Gallop GATES
16 w
17 w
18 w
19 Gallop GATES Shoes changed
20 Gallop GATES
21 Gallop GATES
22 w
23 w
24 w
25 w
26 w
27 Breeze
28 w
29 RACE 350 Clmg 10000 5th $0 18.73 2½
March
1 w
2 OUT

May 31	LA	350	8000	Won	$2,035
Jun 10	LA	350	10000	8th	$0
Jun 24	LA	350	8000	4th	$292
Jul 8	LA	350	5000	6th	$0
Jul 15	LA	350	3200	2nd	$720
Aug 1	LA	400	3200	Won	$2,090

Claimed (Note the severe decline in claiming race standard. It went from a win at 8000 down to 3200 before it could win again, in a shade over 2 months.)

CAESAR DOMINGUEZ

ANALYSIS OF TABLES

Looking at the two months of training tables, there are the following intervals:

Race-to-Race interval

6 days	**3 times**
7 days	**13 times**
8	4
9	5
10	2
11	1
12	7
13	6
14	9
15	1
16	**3**

The two peaks at 6 to 9 and 12 to 16 days are partly due to the races only being run on 4 or 5 days a week. The weekly nature of the races for any individual is emphasized by the fact that 7 and 14 days are the two most frequent race-to-race intervals.

Of the 16 instances of 6 or 7 day intervals, four were run by Spirit De Corps, a 3yo male. This horse had probably the toughest campaign during this period, with 6 starts at intervals of 7, 16, 7, 7 and 6 days. It is possible that this was too hard for this horse in view of his wins at higher levels of competition later in the year, with more time between his races. Then again it may have been a horse that was going to hit its top at that age anyway.

Race/Qualifier-to-next-Gallop

2 days	**2 times**
4	1
5	37
6	46
7	12
8	6
9	2
10	1

Rhythm's Little Dream was galloped out of the gates 2 days after a race and then the next day as well. Merridoc Star galloped 2 days after a qualifying trial. These were rare departures from Caesar's usual 5, 6 or 7 days rest after a race or qualifying run.

The average rest period for the 2yo's was 5.5 days, for the 3yo's 5.8 and for the older horses, 7 days.

Gallop-to-Gallop interval

1 day	**4 times**
2	57
3	72
4	37
5	5

Rhythm's Little Dream was responsible for most of the gallops separated by one day and they were gate training sessions.

Gallop-to-Race or Qualifier

1 day	**44 times**
2	44
3	24
4	3
5	2
6	1
7	2

In summary, generalizing, Caesar races his horses every one or two weeks. After a race, the horses are walked for 5 or 6 days before resuming gallops. They are galloped every 2 or 3 days. The last gallop is given 1 or 2 days before the race.

8.1 Training program cont.

"A Quarter Horse that has been raced and rested for roughly 2 or 3 months, you can bring him back within 45 to 60 days. A Thoroughbred will take 90 to 120 days to get him fit for 6 furlongs."

"The babies, 18 months old, they go in a stall and all we do for 30 days is handle them. No tack. Petting them, patting them, picking the legs up. Teach them to back up; how to walk on the hot walker; clip their muzzles; clip their bridle path; play with them; pull their mane and tail. Teach them respect but give them confidence in the human around them."

"Do you cut their feed at that time?"

"No. I've always kept the feed up - the grain and the alfalfa, but no supplements, no vitamins, no iron. In the second 30 days you tack them up and bit them up - let them get used to the bit. You drive them like a buggy but there is no buggy. You teach him to turn left, turn right, stop; and how to relax. He's got a saddle on his back. At the end of the first sixty days, the horse knows many things: the vet can handle the horse, do his teeth or whatever; the horseshoer can come and shoe him. All this is at the ranch. You don't bring him to the racetrack until he's ready to go out of the starting gates."

"Then for the next 30 days, the rider will get on him and all he'll do is walk him or jog him, maybe only around the barn. Then they are going to the track, almost every day, jogging maybe half a mile, galloping maybe a mile. At this stage I teach him to walk in and out through the starting gates. Let them be confident with starting gates. You don't break them out of the gates - just walk them in and out."

Gate training is vital

"After 90 days you start teaching him how to stand inside the gates and how to break out of the gates. And you're doing it with company - 2 or 3 other colts that are doing the same thing. You're still jogging them a lot, you're galloping them, you're giving them short breezes. You breeze them together from about 100 to 120 days - short breezes - about 100 yards. No whip, no urging, just an easy run together, sometimes out of the gates and sometimes from anywhere on the track. Twice a week. By 120 days they're breaking out of the gates pretty good and working an eighth of a mile."

"For the next 30 days you bring them out of the gate a little harder, like 75 - 80% of their ability. Still no whip. After the 150 days he goes to the racetrack, and you do some hard works out of the gates which are timed by an official, for him to be eligible to run. That takes about 15 days. In the rest of that 30 days you put in some more works and at 180 days your horse is ready to race."

"Coming out of the gates is vitally important in Quarter Horses isn't it? At Yakima Meadows I remember going up behind the starting gates and those horses had
their bums right down in the starting gate. How do you teach them to get their hind quarters down like that?"

"A horse will learn to break by himself once you do it. They have to be confident that's why I take them through the gates every time I go to the track. When they are very confident, after 120 days, you lock them up. You let them feel comfortable inside that gate. You make them stand so that they are not fidgeting. They already know how to run. The first few times, they only come out faster than a walk, then a little bit faster, and so on. They learn to put their feet together and they know. They learn. It's not that difficult."

"Thoroughbreds don't do it though, do they?"

"In Thoroughbreds starting is 10%. In our business it's 90%."

How long from last fast work to first race?

"Let's take a baby that has qualified twice over 220 yds - they have to go in under 13.5 seconds, timed from the break of the gates. That's very slow in my opinion, but it is good because you are teaching them. However a good baby should go in 12 seconds. Once I have them fit I like to have my horses breeze at 50% of their ability every 10 days. No whip. The jockey carries it but he virtually never uses it. The baby gets hit in the qualifying trials because he's got to get used to it in the races."

How often do you race them?

"A baby you want to race him every 10 to 15 days. An older horse you can race him every 7 to 10 days. Three times a month is average. In Thoroughbreds if you get two starts a month that's enough, because they lose more weight, more of their condition. Quarter Horses run fat so they can lose 10 or 15 pounds and still come back for another race."

What work do they do between races?

"In between, you take them out and jog them and gallop them, but we don't do it on an every day basis, we do it like every second day. On the days when they don't go to the track, they go on the hotwalker, or by hand. Jog every day just to keep fit. If he's not going to run in 7 to 15 days then you give him a sprint or a breeze just to keep that edge. Once the horse is fit, the training is very common, you walk and you gallop and you walk and you gallop."

"The gallops for my Thoroughbreds go at 18 seconds for an eighth of a mile. A Quarter Horse goes slower, 20 or 22 seconds per eighth of a mile. Some go a half a mile, some go a mile and some go a mile and a half. If you have a horse carrying a lot of weight and always nervous and on the go, you want to settle him down, so you give him a mile and a half. If you got a skinny filly -timid, don't eat good, hates the racetrack - you just want to take them to the track to keep them from getting bored. Bored from the stalls, bored from the walking machine. You might only go a quarter of a mile."

How long do yours walk?

"The reason we walk between 30 and 45 minutes is because that's how long it takes to clean a stall. After they have a race, the next morning they are still sore and tired and they aren't going to walk 45 minutes, maybe only 20 minutes."

Optimal distance

"For an individual horse, how do you work out what is his best distance?"

"By his performance. See, all your Quarter Horse babies are going to start at 220, 300 yards. All of them. Then after they start running a few times you'll eliminate - either they want to go further or shorter. In the Thoroughbred, they all start at five and a half furlongs, six furlongs. From those races, you're deciding either that horse wants more distance or less distance, a router or a sprinter. Nine out of ten times, if he's bred for sprints, that's what he's going to be. If he's bred for a route, you can have both; you can teach him to go sprints, and at the same time, you know he's going to have the routes because of his bloodlines."

"What tells you in a race that a horse needs more distance?"

"The way he's closing. If a horse at 350 yards is in front by two lengths and stops, then of course you know that he wants shorter distance. There's no rating in Quarter Horses."

"So when you shift into Thoroughbreds, you don't take your jockeys with you?"

"No. You use the jockeys at Santa Anita. The jockeys here at Los Alamitos don't know how to rate."

"When you start racing over 660 and 870 yards, do you have to rate them a little then, or do they just go?"

"On them kind of races, you also go a lot by breeding. If a horse has a lot of Thoroughbred in him, then of course you would think that he would go half a mile, which 90% do. But then again, you still want speed, because actually half a mile is not that long of a distance. You want to have speed, at the same time you want to have a horse that will finish the race strong. That's where also it involves a little bit of Thoroughbred and a little bit of Quarter Horse training mixed."

How do you train for a half mile?

"Once I know he is a half a mile horse, he gallops a mile and a half. He'll jog maybe half a mile and gallop a mile, and he'll go to the racetrack more often than he would if he was a 440 or a 400. I try to keep him as lean as a Thoroughbred, but at the same time I want to keep that fitness as a Quarter Horse. I keep his sharpness out of the gates, as if he was a 350 yard horse, but at the same time I keep his length in his training to go the distance of half a mile."

"So he does more of what?"

"He does more of everything. He does more galloping and he does more jogging."

"Your gallop is a canter, isn't it?"

"Yes. And his gallops are a lot longer."

"I saw a horse on the track this morning go - what did he go - three times around. Started at about 22 seconds to the furlong, quickly got up to about 19, 20, and then finished at about 17, 18 a furlong."

"That might have been a Thoroughbred, because Thoroughbreds usually go three turns around this racetrack, because this racetrack is five eighths of a mile. My Thoroughbreds on this racetrack, they'll go four turns."

"At those kinds of speeds?"

"Mine, when they're just galloping, go 36 seconds for the quarter."

Comparing Thoroughbreds and Quarter Horses

"A Thoroughbred I breeze him every 5 days, but a Quarter Horse I breeze like every 10 days."

"Have you had some Quarter Horses that you have spaced out to 15 or 20 days?"

"Oh yes, you have to do that with those bad legged horses. 90% of your claimers are in that bracket because they are lame horses."

"Do you train a cheap horse any different to a good horse?

"You have to train them differently because a stakes horse can take a lot more punishment than a cheap horse. A stakes horse is running for more money, so you want to make sure that stakes horse doesn't come up short on the day. You got to have that stakes horse fit and sharp. A cheap horse, he can come up short and you can drop him in class and make up the difference. If he's not right, you can cheat a little and drop him in class."

"What about those old horses you have that are 7, 8, 9, 10 - do you train them less often?"

"Those horses train themselves. They already know everything, the gates and the routine and so on. They're pro's. You run them every 8 to 15 days. They'll stand in the gates as long as nothing is hurting them."

8.2 Hard or soft trainer?

"Compared to the other trainers, do you work your horses more or less?"

"I don't know if you could say more or less. I give 'em whatever they need. My 870 yard horses, I give them more work. They go to the track more often and they go further. So it's kind of hard to say if I give more or less."

8.3 Best with what category of horse?

Caesar's greatest success has been with 870 yard races and older horses. He has a considerable reputation with claiming horses. Recent wins with futurity horses show he can also win big with two-year-olds.

8.4 Policy on jockeys

"Do you have a particular jockey, or do you try to get different jockeys for different horses."

"We usually have our own jockey, but there are a lot of horses that take different jockeys. You try to use the jockey that actually fits that horse, but 50% of my stable is ridden by one jockey, and the rest - it varies. Some horses like one jockey, and I try to stay with it that way."

"Some jockeys are better out of the gate with different horses?"

"No, I think they're all good out of the gate. It's just that some jockeys hit harder than others. One jockey that might ride a filly will not use a whip as much as another rider, would just hand ride or just tap. That's the main deal. A lot of jockeys, their hands are just too strong, they manhandle the horse. Maybe a jockey is manhandling a horse - a filly will not accept it, but a stud will. We pick jockeys."

"Some of those jockeys, they hit like girls. We get them for the fillies, because although they're making a lot of noise and effort, they 're not really hitting them hard. There's even studs that have very tender skin, and they can't accept a strong rider. A lot of people think just because he's a stud, we're going to whip him. Not necessarily, because they're very tender and they cut too easy, and they won't run as hard as they would with a jockey that handles them right."

"You must have situations where the jockey thinks some other horse in the race is better, and you can't get him."

"Oh, it happens all the time."

"Nothing you can do about that.?"

"There's not that much you can do about it, you just try to pick a rider of the same caliber."

"What do the jockeys get here? 10% of the money won?"

"They get 10% of the win, and their wages are $33 per mount."

"Do you ever offer them, say 15% if they ride your horse."

"No. I've never done that."

"They'll reckon 10% of a win is better than 15% of a third."

"Sometimes owners will like you to give a jockey, if they win, a little extra, besides their 10%."

"Well, sometimes in the Thoroughbred game, they'll offer a guy quite a sizable amount of money in big races. The jockey might say, 'I want to ride so and so, because I think it's got a better chance'. They might say, 'We'll give you $2000, win, lose or draw, to ride ours, and then you still get your 10%." Do you get those sort of deals in Quarter Horses?"

"No. You see, our money's not as big as Thoroughbreds. It's never happened with me."

8.5 Placing horses in races

In England there is a condition book with all the races listed for the year. At American tracks this is not so. There is usually a schedule of stakes races and major races, but the rest of the races are 'designed' by the racing secretary of the track. The races are designed to attract bettors to bet and horses to provide a full field. There are usually more races on offer than will be run. Those with the fullest fields and the most attraction to the gamblers will run. The 'race designer' comes under a lot pressure from trainers who want races tailor-made for their own horses.

The condition book

"At Los Alamitos there isn't a condition book, they just issue lists of possible races a couple of weeks ahead?"

"Every ten days."

"Does that make it difficult to plan a horse's campaign?"

"If the race fills (with a minimum size field), it's not difficult, because you can train that horse to that race. But if the race don't fill, then it's difficult, because you've trained that horse to that one race and now the race is a different one. You've got to come right back and work him. Then maybe two days later, a suitable race pops up. But now you're done, because you've worked your horse and you can't run him in the race. Then it's hard."

"So the conditions for entry in a race come out every ten days, but when they come out, how many days is it till the first race listed?"

"Only about four. That's why it's hard to train on the conditions they give. For a stake race, you know when they're going to run, so you can train your stake horse for that race, but in the claiming race, you can't. You just train them day by day, and then hopefully, you give yourself three to four days in between. Dealing with Quarter Horses, you can do it. You can skip one or two days of training and still be in good shape. Knowing how to read a condition book wins you a lot of races. That's where a good trainer and a bad trainer can make a difference, or a good agent or a bad agent. The jockey's agent accepts mounts for the jockey. If he's got three or four more in the same race, then he's got to pick which one's going to be the best, or which one that rider would prefer to ride. Sometimes he's obligated to the trainer, he's obligated to the owner, or whatever. That's where an agent comes in handy. And they've got to know exactly what horse is the best horse."

"With such detailed conditions in those condition races, do you know which other horses are going to be the main opposition in that race?"

"Yes. I know 90% of the horses that are on the track, and

when I enter a horse in one race, I know what's going to get in, that can beat me. Once the race is filled and comes out, then I can tell you exactly. I can look at the 'overnight' and tell you what horse will be my main threat in the race. On a short-filled race, you can't scratch. Nine out of ten times you're looking at it. But your main threat - he can stumble, he can break slow. There's so many 'if's' in our business, that's why it don't bother me to run my horses against somebody."

Little chance in a big race - or big chance in a little race?

"The problem is that if you put them in the glamor races and they're not up to it, then they don't win money. If they were in a lesser race, they would definitely win money, but a lot less money than if they won in the glamor race. Are the decisions easy or hard?"

"It's easy, because you know exactly what the horse is worth. Sometimes it's a little hard for an owner to realize what their horse is worth, and an owner will want you to run that horse over his head. He wants to see his horse run in the glamor races, but I tell them, 'Hey, why would you want to run in a glamorous race and run ninth and tenth, when you're going to bring up some friends? All you're going to do is get embarrassed. That's all you're doing, because your chances of you winning them races is one in a million.' I tell them, 'Your better chance is to go buy a Lotto ticket. You make more money in the Lotto.'"

"Do you show them a race that you think it can win?"

"No, no. I tell them what race we're going to go in, and after a while, see, I'll lean towards the owner. But if I see that he's not leaning or helping me out, then I won't suggest - I'll tell him: 'Your horse will run for so and so,' and that's the way it stands. No, I'm not the type who like to run in a glamor race just to run ninth or tenth."

8.6 What are his claiming strategies?

Caesar has a considerable reputation on the Californian Quarter Horse circuit as a trainer of claimers. One of the horses in the training tables, Ta Advantage, was claimed by Caesar off Blane Schvaneveldt in a $6,250 claiming race. It went on to win Grade 2 and Grade 3 events and over $50,000 for Caesar.

I asked José Dominguez if any of the trainers Caesar worked with were noted claiming trainers. He said that Earl Holmes was a smart claimer. Earl, since the 1960's, has been better known as a trainer of stakes horses. He joins the long list of stakes trainers who proved themselves in claimers first. Caesar no doubt hopes to follow that path. When I asked Earl, a man of few words and even less drama, what he thought made Caesar a successful claiming trainer he simply said, "He's a horseman, a very good horseman."

Claiming Quarter Horses

"I claim a lot of horses, and I lose a lot of horses. Just this meet alone, I've claimed sixteen. I claimed sixteen off other people, and they've claimed something like five off me. Ninety percent of the horses that we claim, I pick for the client. The other 10%, the client will pick a horse that he likes for some reason or another, and we'll claim."

"What do you look for in a horse before you claim it?"

"We go strictly by past performance. We look at the racing form. We don't look at pedigree, we don't look at bloodline, because we already know how fast the horse is. We're looking at a horse whose past performance tells you everything you want to know about him, so you're not looking for breeding, you're not looking for conformation or nothing."

"Do you look for trainers that can't get the best out of them?"

"Exactly. You look for horses that you think have problems. You got a trainer that you know he's not taking care of that horse. It's a horse that, in your mind, he's running for five thousand, but you think you can run him for ten thousand. You can improve that horse, for one reason or another. And nine out of ten times it's true. You can move 'em up."

"The art of claiming is the condition of the horse. You are taking a chance that the horse is halfway sound, and that it is peaking as well. I just claimed a horse that was running for $2500 and four months later I won a stakes race with him, a horse called Leading Effort. Why does he win a race for me? Maybe that trainer wasn't taking good care of him, maybe I'm a better trainer, maybe it's the feed, maybe he was just peaking. We do a lot of things that your normal claiming trainer does not do. Once a horse is entered for a race, doesn't matter if it's for $5,000 or for $100,000, that horse is treated special. For three days before the race, he is bathed, he is covered in blankets, he is hand walked instead of going on the hot walker (walking machine). Our stakes horses are always walked by hand, all the time."

"When you are looking for horses to claim, do you look for horses that have gone down in class or up in class?"

"I try never to claim a horse coming down in class, unless he's a class horse and I know the horse. They usually have something wrong with them, and I don't want to take a chance. 90% of my claims are horses that are staying the same or going up in class, or young horses. A lot of young horses have not yet reached their potential. Sometimes they have a problem that their trainer has not figured out, but I have."

"Give me an example of something they could not cure and you could."

"Bucked shins. I pin fire them."

"And the other guys don't?"

"Yes. I pin fire them and tell the owner they are going to be out two months.

"So you watch the races for a horse that seems to be having trouble with a shin buck, and claim it?"

"Yes, if I know that trainer is not that good of a caretaker."

"How do owners react when you drop their horse in class and it is claimed?"

"My owners are very good. They know that if someone gets that horse, that was all he was worth. Some horses might go up, but nearly all the horses claimed from me go down. If you go back over the records, you'll find that 95% of the horses claimed from me never did anything."

"Do you have to discuss it with the owner every time you enter a horse in a claiming race - the price etc?"

"Yes, you keep them informed: how the horse is going, if it should go in this class of race or that class of race."

"Do you ever claim a lot off one trainer, and none of them improve, and you think that trainer must have been doping them?"

"No, I really believe our industry is very clean. The technology has improved a lot. If you use drugs in our racing you won't last."

"Do you take a lot of notice of things like trainers standing a horse in ice baths all the time so rival trainers will think it's lame and not claim it?"

"There are trainers that are going to try to throw a curve ball at you, but you get to know who they are."

"How?"

"You're looking, you're thinking, but mostly you hear. You hear talk. The guys to watch are the trainers that need a win, that are dropping a horse to win."

"So the guy who is desperate to win is a good target. He'll drop them to win some money."

"Yes, the guys that are like me when I was starting off."

"If you think back to the last few horses you claimed, what can you tell me about the reasons for those claims?"

"Lots of reasons. You have an owner that wants a horse for that price, or that distance. If the trainer is half and half, and you want a $5,000 horse that can go 870 yards for a client, then you claim."

"Do you find any difference between the people who want to get in by claiming a horse, and those who want to buy one in the sales?"

"The person who wants to claim a horse is just your average raceday person who comes to the races, but the person who wants a stakes horse, who wants to buy at a sale, is usually a business man or a breeder."

Do the top trainers claim off each other?

"Is there a bit of an understanding amongst the top trainers, that they don't claim horses off each other?"

"No, it's not true at all. I claim a lot of horses from Baffert and I claim a lot of horses from Blane. I don't look at the trainer a lot of times, I look at the horse first, his past performance. If I like his past performance, then I look at the trainer. If I can better the horse, if I can move him up, then it don't matter if my brother has got the horse, I'm going to claim him."

"What's it like when a horse is claimed off you? How do you feel?"

"Ninety percent of the times they claim a horse off of me, they're claiming a horse that that's all he's worth. Either at their level or maybe one step below, so they're not getting no bargains. And I know that they're not getting no bargains, because I do all there is to do about horses, and I think I'm one of the top trainers. They're not going to move up a horse that easy from me anyway, and they know it. That's why I don't lose that many horses. Of course, there's going to be one or two horses that they claim from me and it goes up the ladder and wins two, three good races, but that's only normal. You're going to have one or two."

"How do you handle that in your own mind?"

"It don't bother me."

"Do you watch closely what they do, in case you're going to learn something from them?"

"I'll take notice, because I'm there every night. Of course I'm going to watch him run. If a horse wins I just take it like nothing is happening, keep on going. Sometimes you get teased by the other trainers, 'Oh, this guy he's doing good.' But if he claim a horse from me, and he made a winner out of him, that means that tomorrow he'll want to claim another one, see, and there's horses that you want to turn over. So you say, 'Hey that's good, because now he can claim another one.' It don't bother me. Sometimes you hope they'll take 'em."

"One horse that was claimed off you for $2,500 went on to win a Derby four months later. The owner wouldn't like that."

"No, that hasn't happened, I don't remember that."

"His name was Spirit De Corps."

"Well that Derby was not graded, it was a small Derby at a county fair. Spirit De Corps, it was claimed by a trainer called Robert Ingerbritson. That horse got back down to $2500. That happens but that don't bother me none."

It was over two years since Spirit De Corps was claimed off Caesar, but he certainly remembered who claimed it and what Derby it won. Of those claimed in the training charts, all had gone down in class, but the numbers are small. Ta Advantage was his most profitable claim of those in the tables, claimed for $6,250 and winning over $50,000. When I had once asked Caesar to name some horses he'd claimed and done well with, Ta Advantage was not mentioned!

"When you are claiming a horse like Ta Advantage off Blane, what do you look for?"

"When Blane has not had a win for a while, when he's low

in the standings, and he needs a win. Then I watch closely, very closely. He might drop a $10,000 horse down to $5,000 and he hope nobody notices. I do the same thing, Baffert does the same thing. At one time I took horses to the start of Bay Meadows and everyone claimed them off me, because I did well with fresh horses there the previous years. But I learned."

8.7 Injuries and therapies

"Do you pack the area under the hooves with mud?"

"Yes. It's very important. We use Ocean Mud. We mix it with a little Epsom salts and sometimes a little vinegar."

"Does every horse have its feet packed?"

"No, only those that goes to the racetrack or works."

"What happens if you don't pack the sole with mud?"

"The hoof gets real real hard. It is hard for the shoeing, and you get a lot of quarter cracks."

"You use those muds on the leg as well."

"Yes. There are medication muds, cool mud, muds with menthol in them - all types. They might be called a poultice or a tightner. I believe anything you put on a horse's leg is better than nothing."

"In Quarter Horses you go above the knee with those preparations."

"Yes. You want to protect the ankle, the shin, and the knee. Above the knee you might want to sweat the muscles, you might just use Absorbine or rubbing alcohol."

8.7-1 Shinsoreness

"Very common. Ninety percent of your young horses will shin-buck. It's a lameness problem that you will have when you're dealing with young horses."

"So what can you do to avoid that?"

"There is nothing really that you can do to avoid it. If you're going to have a horse in training, getting ready for a race, you just cross your fingers and hope that he does not shin-buck, because you've still got to train him. I've tried both ways. I've tried slower work, slower gallops, and longer periods, and they still shin-buck. I've tried the regular routine of my 120-150 days, and they still shin-buck. I've had some that I've trained, and they never shin-bucked. So it's really up to the individual. If he's going to shin-buck, he's going to shin-buck."

"What do you do with them when they do?"

"I go ahead and pin fire them, turn them out on the farm for six weeks and then bring them back slow. I might swim them for fifteen or twenty days, then put them back in training - a normal every day jog."

"That swimming, is that out of their depth or chest-deep in the water or what?"

"It's an eight-foot-deep swimming pool, but I do that mainly to build up their lungs and it builds up their muscles, without the pounding of the legs."

"At what stage do the horses usually shin-buck?"

"Mainly coming out of the gates. Instead of taking 120 days, I've taken 180 days. Just a gallop, nice and easy, and break them out of the gate, nice and easy. Then when it come to the nitty gritty, to get them really fit to race, and you give them the hard works out of the gate - boom! - they buck. Quite a few horses buck the second time. In fact, I got two right now that bucked the second time after I give them six weeks off. But see, that's where the owners come in and interfere. They want their horses back in training as soon as possible, because of course, they want to make that purse money. They don't realize that by pushing 'em, in the long run, they're going to waste another six weeks. Now we've got to waste another four weeks. Going to be a total of ten weeks because the owner wanted the horse brought up faster than normal."

8.7-2 Tying up

"I don't have that many horses tying up, but the reason for tying up is because a horse is not fit, and you're sending him distance or you're making him do something that he's just not ready for. He's not quite fit for it. That's what causes tying up."

"Does it happen more in the horses that go further?"

"More in Thoroughbreds than in anything, yes."

"But in the Quarter Horses, is it the further they go, the more often you get tying up?"

"No, not normally."

"You can have it in the horses going 200 yards? I guess because that's their first race."

"You could have it in any distance. All my horses before they even do any gallops, I jog them for half an hour, if you want to call that warming up."

"And do you have a warm down?"

"The warm down is mainly when they walk in the walker after. Where they gallop or they work, I jog them at least a quarter of a mile, and then they walk the last quarter of a mile out of the racetrack, and back into the barn. Then they walk in the walker for 35 to 45 minutes, depending on the horse."

8.7-3 His most common lameness

Caesar didn't have to think about that question.

"Knee chips and ankle chips are common injuries in Quarter Horses. In Thoroughbreds its bows, because that extra furlong they have to go, that they're not fit to go, they're already rubber-legged and they're pushing up and that makes 'em bow."

"What do you do with knee chips?"

"It depends on how good a horse he is. If he's a good horse, you operate; if he's a cheap horse, you just drop him in a claiming race and hope somebody claims him - and use cortisone. We use a lot of cortisone for chips and it works."

"Do you find that if you use cortisone repeatedly in the knees, the knees will get a lot worse?"

"They start losing bone tissue and they start losing their

cartilage - that's what they say. But I would have to disagree, because I probably run more cripples than anybody, and I cortisone more than anybody. I've had horses run with me, and I've had them two years old all the way to ten years old. In a period like that, those horses have probably had over a hundred starts each, and at least one third of the time they've been cortisoned, so you're talking about thirty to forty times they've been cortisoned, and their joints are no worse when they were ten years old than when they were five years old. So I would have to say I would disagree with that."

"Well, there are quite a few vets and trainers that do disagree, as you probably know. It is mainly research in rabbit knees that the anti-cortisone vets are going on. Some of the people in vet schools see horses that are gone in the knees and which have had cortisone. Add their desire to believe that private vets are ruining horses and ripping off the public, to what seems like an explanation, and they go for it like utter dumbheads. They refuse to believe that at least some practitioners and trainers are not stupid."

"The probable explanation of the overall picture is that out of say 50 horses that get cortisone, 10 had knees that were already on the way to destruction no matter what happened. Cortisone and pain killers probably make that situation worse but they were unsalvageable anyway. They are the ones that end up at the university, in the hands of zealots who have never been in practice, who sprout the dogma to another generation of vet students. 'See what this unscrupulous practitioner has done with cortisone etc."

"The practitioner and the trainers see the other 40 improve, stand training, maybe win races. There may even be individual genetic differences in response, and the university only sees those that react by degenerating. So you end up with two groups with opposite views, both convinced they are right. It could also be that dose or brand are important. Injection skill matters with the long acting steroids, because injecting around the joint can cause arthritis. Possibly certain case types are damaged by cortisone. There is some explanation that will make sense of it all."

"Those researchers, they say this and that, but no, I got to be against them. I believe in cortisone."

"Have you had horses that have had cortisone four, five, and six times in a row, and held up?"

"Oh yes. I've done it four or five times, and they're still doing it."

"What about hyaluronic acid?"

"I tried it and I don't like it. I tried it and I didn't see any improvement."

"Do Quarter Horses get much in the way of back trouble?"

"Very few, but we do have back problems. The ones that break so fast, sometimes their hind legs give way and the back muscles get pulled, but a Quarter Horse is so muscularly built, they've got so much muscle, that one might rip, but two others would take its place. Thoroughbreds have a lot of stifle problems, talking of the back ends of horses."

"Do you get much navicular disease?"

"I'd say in my thirteen, fourteen years of training, I think I've had like three horses with navicular problems, so it's not that bad."

"Roaring?"

"Roaring is in Thoroughbreds more than in Quarter Horses. Right now I've got one horse, one in the last two, three years that's a roarer."

"Does roaring matter much to a Quarter Horse?"

"Yes, because it's still breathing problems, whether you go 300 yards or three miles, you still got to breathe. But I've had maybe two in the last five, ten years."

"What about bleeders?"

"Bleeders are very common. I think there's just as much in the Quarter Horse as there is in the Thoroughbreds. Bleeding is very very common in our business."

"Have you tried chiropractors or acupuncture?"

"I had three horses done with acupuncture, it helped one and did not help two. I quit that and I've never tried chiropractors."

8.8 Role of the vet: why three vets?
In the short while I was around Caesar's barn, I met three vets. One specialized in horse dentistry.

"Why do you have three vets?"

"Different opinions. I have one vet that's a very very good vet, but there's certain areas that he's better than others, and some are better than he in other areas. I use each one a little bit and I compare notes. Different vets have different strengths and you get multiple opinions and then you can learn from that."

8.8-1 How much does he blood test?
Caesar has blood tests - blood counts he calls them - done on all horses coming in from the ranch, all horses he claims out of claiming races, and any horse that is not doing well. He does not do any as a periodic routine but does a lot on horses that don't look right, and horses that have put in a poor race effort. He finds that a lot of them are anemic and need iron. They respond very well to iron injections.

8.8-2 Jugs (intravenous drips)
"I usually give the horses jugs three days before they run, and a day after they run if a horse comes back knocked out. I give them a lot to horses that are on Lasix. They dehydrate.

You try to give them at least two bottles. Lasix is normally only for my bleeders. My other horses - if a horse comes off the race in good shape, bucking and kicking, then of course, I don't spend money on that horse, because he don't need it. But if a horse is let down a little bit, then I might use jugs. I use it one hundred percent on bleeders, because they use a lot of Lasix and they dehydrate their bodies."

"What's the legal position with drugs and horses in California - it's 24 hours before a race, isn't it?"

"It's 24 hours in California, and the only thing you can administer, the day of the race, is Lasix, if that horse is on Lasix."

Does Lasix make Quarter Horses run better? (1988)

"A lot of Thoroughbreds apparently run so much better on Lasix that you have the trainers trying to have their horses registered as bleeders. The cause of the improvement is unknown. In Quarter Horses, it should reduce their weight by straight water loss, increasing the power to weight ratio, but it might mess up some muscle electrolytes or have some other effects. Does Lasix make Quarter Horses run better?"

"Well, I don't think it makes them run any better or any faster than they can already run, but if a horse is bleeding inside, it will make them perform to their ability. But if they're not bleeding and you administer Lasix, all it does is work against you, because it's dehydrating your horse, and it's not helping. It ain't going to make you win. Before you can put a horse that's a bleeder on Lasix, you've got to prove that he did bleed, and the vets will come out and scope him, and that's the only way that you can prove it."

"That's the private vet or the state vet?"

"A private vet. He can come by and scope it. A lot of times, if a horse bleeds during a race, the state vet in the test barn, the receiving barn, will see that the horse did bleed through the nostril, so he'll put him down as a Lasix horse."

"So you don't try to get them on the Lasix. You'd prefer them not on it?"

"I'd prefer not to, because it's more expense for the owner. If you've got to put them on the Lasix, then after the Lasix you've got to come back and hit them with jugs, to replace all the fluids. I don't care too much for Lasix."

What is in the jugs?

"A lot of electrolytes. 90% of the jugs you can mix yourself, because there's just a lot of salts in it."

"Do you add B vitamins, and do you use the ones that have amino acids in them?"

"Yes. Amino acids, and then the vets add a little bit of whatever - B_1 or B_{12}, into the jug."

Do Quarter Horses need electrolytes?

"With the jugs and the vitamins, and all the minerals you got in your hay and your grains, and a pinch of salt, that's enough electrolytes. Electrolytes are good mainly on Thoroughbreds. They often put them in the water. I've noticed that in Thoroughbreds they do use a lot of electrolytes."

When and how frequently do you use anabolics?

"I use a lot of steroids. I give a lot of my geldings and my mares steroids. Equipoise, or any steroids, you give to build up a horse. I like to give it within thirty to forty days, but there's some horses that you give it within twenty days. These are horses that are more let down, a horse that you're running every seven days. It's still all individual; how you're training the horse; how many times he's running."

"So the more often they run, the more often you give them?"

"Yes."

"And what dose do you use?"

"What I do, I use 10cc's of Equipoise, and usually, a booster of 10cc's iron, 10cc's B_1, 10cc's B_{12}, 10cc's B Complex - to a booster of 50cc, in the jugular vein. The Equipoise and the iron goes in the muscle."

8.9 Shoeing - do you use big toe grabs?

"No. I don't. I use regular grabs on my horses."

"But I've heard of grabs being three-quarters of an inch long."

"Those big grabs are called Louisiana grabs, but a grab like that would do no good in California because our tracks are sandy tracks. It's just like you running at the beach. If you go to the beach in the sand, it don't matter much. Spikes are not going to get a hold of the sand anyway, because it's loose. You get just as much footing if you're jogging barefoot, as with spikes. But you put the spikes on a hard track, then it grips. Our tracks are sandy tracks, so we don't need 'em. We use a lot of rim shoes and I always use an average grab in front, and an average grab behind."

"Does anyone here use those very big grabs?"

"Well, sure there's got to be somebody that uses them, but I don't use them. I use a lot of steel shoes behind, because our horses are so powerful that when they break on their hind legs, they spread them, they spread the aluminum shoe. With the steel, they won't spread. And a lot of times - we've got these brick barns - horses kick a lot, spread the shoe all the time. You've got more protection with steel. Of course, my steel grabs are bigger than the normal aluminum. I use a little bigger grab behind than I do in front, but the reason for that is because it's a steel shoe. I use a lot of steel shoes behind."

"Front aluminum and back steel. How often do you change the shoes?"

"I usually go about twenty to forty-five days. We've got asphalt. It wears out the grab a lot quicker than you would in dirt. The normal time for a horse to grow out of those shoes is thirty days."

Traffic between the barns and the track at Los Alamitos during morning training. Note the dirt track. This functions as a 600 yd chute for races. Caesar's brother Henry leads one back to the barn. At the time this was taken in mid 1988, Henry was at Los Alamitos. In 1990 he was at other tracks running Caesar's Thoroughbred team.

"Do you change shoes on race day?"

"No. I never change shoes on race day, I like to do it at least four to five days before they run. That way, if we get a hot nail or something goes wrong with the foot, we've got time to work with it."

8.10 Has he 'produced' any good trainers?

"Have you had any staff go off and become trainers themselves?"

"Only one has gone and become a trainer, in Arizona, but apparently he must not have learned nothing from me, because he didn't win no races."

8.11 Analysis of Caesar's training

It was hard to get opinions on Caesar's training. Caesar starts his horses more often than most Quarter Horse trainers. This may be because he has fewer youngsters and more older claiming horses. But he considers himself the master of the 870 at Los Alamitos, and his tables should be studied for clues to the training of mature 870 horses.

9. Feeding

"Can you remember any points where there was some breakthrough in your understanding?"

"When I was working for Earl Holmes we fed all the horses breakfast in the morning at five o'clock. Work started at six. I noticed that at six o'clock, when they went up to walk or exercise, 90% of the horses, their grain was still in the bucket. They never ate it. Some of those grooms would throw it out and give them fresh. I'd leave it, and I noticed that after the horse exercised, he'd come back in, he would be hungry and he would eat that grain. So when I started training, I didn't feed our horses at five o'clock. What I do - after they exercise and after they walk, when they come in, inside the stall, that's when they get their grain, and they eat it. I've noticed I'm the only one that does it in the whole racetrack. And the thing is about it, the horses look better, they feel better, and you don't use as much grain as before."

"We start at six o'clock. Nine out of ten times, we're done galloping horses by nine o'clock, so the last horse that goes out at nine o'clock, he's back in his stall at ten o'clock. By eleven o'clock, you walk down the shed, and all my horses have got all their grain eaten. The other way, 90% will not eat. When I wake up in the morning, I don't want to have breakfast. Some people do. I'm not that type. I wake up, give me a cup of coffee and that's it. But now, after I get done, I'm getting hungry. My horses are the same way."

"My boys, they know you're not going to feed a horse at ten o' clock and then come back and feed him eleven o'clock. They know that if this horse went out and he's eaten his grain at eleven o'clock, they know that by the time the barn is done and he has lunch, it'll be twelve-thirty, one o'clock. Then he'll swing by, and if he's still eating, he won't add no more. But if it's gone, then he'll add some more, and then go about his business until four o'clock. We feed our horses by how much they're eating."

9.1 First ration

"Did you get your first ration from someone you were working for?"

"Oh yes. That come in handy, working with some people, seeing how they fed."

9.2 Grains - how many pounds of oats a day?

"The grains, the hay and everything, they're the same, from one trainer to the next because we all go to the same mill to buy. In the mornings we feed -it's a coffee can and it holds a gallon - I think it holds three pounds of oats [A Folgers coffee can is 6.5" high (16.25 cm) and 6" in diameter. It holds about 2 lbs 12 ozs (1.25 kg) of oats when filled to one inch below the brim. 2½ lbs (1.14 kg) might be a more realistic figure]. Then noon it's another three pounds. This is average horses. There are some horses that eat maybe five pounds in the morning. Averaging, I would have to say that - roughly - they eat three pounds in the morning, three pounds at noon and at nighttime they get as high as ten pounds for their dinner. There are some horses that will eat less in the morning and will not eat in the afternoon, and then at nighttime, they will only take six pounds instead of ten pounds. This is whole oats, not rolled. A lot of people like to feed rolled or crimped. I feed whole oats."

"You don't bruise them or anything?"

"No. My babies sometimes, because their teeth are still tender, I'll crimp their oats or give them crimped barley. But 90% of my horses, they get whole oats - untouched, unbroken."

"Total pounds of oats per day on average would be three, three and ten?"

"Three, three and nine."

"How does that compare with Thoroughbreds?"

"I have some Thoroughbreds now. In the morning, they eat as much as six pounds, and ten o'clock, eleven o'clock, they're digging for some more. You could give them another three pounds and they'll eat it. Then at nighttime, they give 'em twelve pounds, and they eat it, and still don't get fat. They keep their weight."

"When I was at Yakima Meadows, there was one guy up there who claimed he was feeding 25 to 30 pounds of grain a day to his Quarter Horses."

"No way."

"I couldn't see how you could stuff so much into them, work them so little and not have them go crazy."

"No. I guarantee you, if you ask five different trainers here, top trainers who win races, they'd say between twelve and fifteen pounds of grain a day."

Other grains

"Besides the barley you mentioned, do you feed any other grains?"

"Oh yes, we use a lot of what we call a sweet feed. It's a mixture of oats, corn, barley - a mix of grains - with molasses."

"Is that in addition to this number of pounds of oats?"

"They just get that at nighttime on their supper. They get six pounds of oats and three pounds of the sweet feed. The sweetfeed is one that everyone uses called Fourways."

"So the total night feed grain is as we were talking about - nine pounds - including a few pounds in the three pounds of sweet feed."

9.3 Hay

"Do you have a preference for a particular type of alfalfa hay, late cut or whatever?"

"First cut, second cut, whatever cut it is they want to sell us, that's what they give us. We feed a lot of alfalfa; it's very rich in protein, it's probably the best hay you can feed. We give a lot of timothy mix because it's got some protein, not as much as alfalfa but it's filling, won't get your horses fat, which alfalfa will. We sometimes feed mixed oat hay, but we feed so much oats that sometimes we eliminate the oat hay. I keep my horses on alfalfa and timothy haynets 24 hours a day. Of course, on the hay and alfalfa, I couldn't tell you how much because I don't weigh it."

9.4 Green pick

None.

9.5 Additives

"I give a lot of my horses vitamins through injections, because they absorb it better when you inject it than when they eat it. But there's two or three vitamins that I feed orally, one brand name is Go Fast vitamin. I feed Calf Manna. I use it mainly on my babies when I'm breaking them, because it's got a lot of calcium. It's good for the bones and the teeth and whatever. But as they get older and come to the racetrack, I quit using it, because it's mainly just for young horses. Mainly I do a lot of injections. I inject a lot of B_1, B_{12}, calcium, iron. I use a lot of iron."

"Is that common in the Quarter Horses, to inject iron?"

"You know, I really don't know. It's common in my barn, and I've been very successful with it. In fact -"

"You could really see a difference?"

"Oh yes. I tell you why I do that. See, I work day and night. We race at night and train in the morning. With all these hours that we work, I take a lot of iron and vitamin E, and it helps me a lot."

"What sort of iron do you take?"

"I take Geritol - it's the strongest. It's for old people, to pick up their blood. I take vitamin E in the capsule. I give my horses vitamin E as a powder. They say it's good for the color of the hair, their brightness, and it's also good for wounds. Sores. I've cut myself and I took a capsule and rubbed it on me, like an ointment on that wound, and you'd be surprised that it does work. I use a lot of vitamin E. I use what I call black iron, it is very dark."

"Did you have any horses drop dead from iron injections?"

"No, but I heard of that when people were using iron for pigs in the mainline, the vein in the neck."

"Maize oil?"

"No."

"Wheat germ?"

"No."

"Do you feed carrots?"

"Some horses liked them, some didn't, so I stopped them."

(This made Caesar the only one who did not feed carrots — out of more than 30 trainers.)

Do you use B$_1$ to calm horses down?

"Yes. We use it a lot to calm horses down, but see, B$_1$ comes up in our tests, so we're not allowed to use it within a period of 48 hours."

"I would have thought that with Quarter Horses you wouldn't want to use it, because you want them as explosive as possible."

"Yes, but you want them to calm down here in the barn. You get horses that are just like any Thoroughbred or Quarter Horse or Standardbred."

"You want them quiet in the barn?"

"You want them quiet because a horse that's weaving and nervous, he's not going to get on, he's not relaxed. You hit him with B$_1$ and you make him relax, you make him lay down. You can walk down my barn and you ain't going to see no horses restless. They're all laying down. Like right now, 11:30, they're all resting, the barn is quiet."

"That's interesting, because I noticed that in the top stables there are a lot of quiet, sleepy horses. But I am surprised you use B$_1$ in your Quarter Horses. Do you give it to all of your horses routinely or just certain horses?"

"You use it only on nervous horses. It's not a routine, oh no. If they need it, fine. Right now in this stable, we're not using it period. We'll use it in a mixture with a vitamin, what we call a booster, after a race, if a horse comes back tired, dehydrated and he's lost a lot of strength, he's lost a lot of fluid. If that race took a lot out of him, then we'll add the B$_1$, the B$_{12}$, the B Complex, the iron, the whole works, in what we call a booster shot. But no, we don't do it on a regular basis."

"Any electrolyte?"

"No but in hot weather I give them extra salt. Usually we give them a pinch of salt."

Caesar's feedstall had only salt and an electrolyte mix called 'Lightning' — a sample? He prefers injectable to oral supplements.

10. His management and how he makes money

10.1 Caesar's business philosophy

The tough start he had shows in Caesar's business. There is no attempt to have everything new and near-new. Plastic buckets and so on are kept until they cannot do the job, they are not discarded because they look a bit tatty.

10.1-1 Ownership of horses and premises

Caesar owns 15 horses outright, including all 7 of his Thoroughbreds at the time. He owned his Champion, Truly A Pleasure. He also has part ownership of about another 20. This, he says, allows him to keep control of the animal. "But," he cautions, "the horses have to pay. If they don't win you can't pay your feed bills."

10.2 Personality and management style

Around Caesar's stables, if his employees came up and asked a question, Caesar gave a short reply and the staff member walked off to get on with the job. There was no long discussion, no emotion, no tension. No outbursts - at least not while I was around.

Caesar is no fire-breathing rule maker. He is tolerant. One practice which I first saw at Caesar's was the consumption of cold beers after the morning work was finished. Around the middle of the day, perhaps an hour after Caesar had left, half a dozen cans of beer would 'appear' in a large bucket of crushed ice. The staff that wanted a beer would take one and sit around talking for a while. Before long the area was deserted.

I later saw this in other stables at Los Alamitos, and at the harness racing stables at The Meadowlands outside New York. I seldom saw it around the Thoroughbred stables, but I believe it is not 'code related', rather it is 'night racing' related. Harness and Quarter Horse racing are at night in both of those places. Grooms are up until 11pm or midnight, then have to be there in the stables at 5 or 6am. Many of them cannot get enough sleep in that time, so an afternoon nap is part of their day. Presumably a beer helps some of them get to sleep. Afternoon racing means there is too much to do to even think about a beer, and there is plenty of time to get sleep at night.

10.2-1 Ruthless with horses - or sentimental?

Caesar says that to be a claiming trainer, you cannot afford to be sentimental about horses. "You have to turn them over."

10.3 Staff selection and delegation

Caesar does his own billing and paperwork at the end of every month. It takes him a couple of days. In other areas he delegates. When he was at Bay Meadows in early 1990, he also had Thoroughbreds at Santa Anita, under the care of his brother Henry and he had horses at the ranch he leases. When he flies from Bay Meadows to Los Angeles to be home for the half of the week when there is no racing, he leaves the day to day training in the hands of jockey Henry Garcia. He talks on the phone to each of his lieutenants every day.

"Is there anyone in the team that's very important to you?"

"Yes. Everybody. All the way down from your foreman, to your gallop boys to your grooms. Your grooms play a big big part, because they're with that horse 24 hours a day. They know if he's eaten, they know why he did not eat; if he's got a swollen leg, what to do with a swollen leg. When you're training fifty, sixty head of horses, you see them every day, but you don't see if he ate last night. If that groom don't tell you he did not eat or he did eat, or he's got a filling on an ankle, it's very hard for you to know. So you depend a lot on your help."

"So you look hard for good grooms?"

"We're always looking for good grooms, but the thing is, we make good grooms. Like right now, 90% of the help that I've got has been with me for five, seven years. The new help that I hire - I make my old help teach them my method. That way is a lot easier, because sometimes I don't even know 'em. Until payday, then they call me and ask me if I hired somebody by the name Joe Blow, and I says you know what, I don't even know. I have to talk to my assistants who'd know if we hired a Joe Blow, because I depend on my assistants to do the hiring and the firing and tell me what's going on."

Like many in racing, Caesar has relatives on the payroll. His brother Henry joined him in 1985 and in 1990 was in charge of Caesar's Thoroughbred string. His nephew Michael, son of Albert, works for him.

10.4 Training arrangements

"Do you syndicate horses or anything like that?"

"I got a syndication started with Thoroughbreds, because in Thoroughbreds, it takes more money to operate, and of course they're more expensive than a Quarter Horse. One syndicate is called the Petty Cash Syndicate. Five owners that have put in $5000 apiece, buying a horse for $25,000. Their expense is only one fifth and so on. People are trying to get into Thoroughbreds, and that's my way of introducing Quarter Horse people. By forming syndicates they know that the intake will not be as much, and the outgoing is not as much either. You spend $5000 average on a Quarter Horse, to run for a purse of $2000, yet you can spend $5000 on Thoroughbreds, and buy a $25,000 horse, and he's running for a purse of $20,000 That's still more like an equivalent to $4000 purse, so you're still doubling your money for less money."

10.4-1 Training rates

"How much do you charge to train a horse?"

"A Quarter Horse would cost you about $1000 a month, roughly. It's more like $30 a day. In Thoroughbreds it's more like $1500 a month. It is more money in Thoroughbreds. The purses are bigger, so the pain is bigger."

10.4-2 Debt collection

"Bad debts are the only drawback in this business. A lot of good clients help you pay the bills because they're good clients. But through the years, I would have to say that I probably got stuck for about $20,000. People that just don't pay, and they go in the hole - $1500 here, $2000 there, in fact, no, it's probably more!"

"I remember one owner now that owes me over $10,000 for the last five years, and he keeps saying that he's going to pay as soon as he gets back on his feet. What hurt him - you remember when the Challenger blew up? Okay, his business is a welder, but he makes bolts for NASA, and that was his job. When that Challenger blew up, there was a big investigation, why did it explode? He made the bolts for the Challenger. His company was also in jeopardy. And I guess after something like that happens, you lose contracts. He was a good client, but he ain't been in the business for the last five years. He was my biggest loss, $10,000. I've got a lot of $1500's, $500 here, $2000 there, and so on."

"What can you do? You just bill them regularly or phone them up?"

"You bill them regularly and hopefully someday they'll pay. In fact, one of mine, I took him to the Small Claims Court. The only way you can get some money out of Small Claims is if they own property or something. They can't sell unless they pay you first. I went to the expense of going to a Small Claims Court for this couple, for the simple reason that they were real snotty the way they treated me. They figured for about six or seven months, I'd train a horse for free."

"When I told them, being honest, their horse could not run, and I did not want to spend their money on a bad horse. Get rid of him, and forget about him. So they were hurt when I told

Caesar with Francis Glowacki (center) owner of April Nine, the night she came second in the Vessel's Maturity. With them is Mark Sellers, who trained her in Oklahoma. Frank Glowacki hails from Pennsylvania. He chose Caesar as his trainer in Los Alamitos after reading an article in a series about trainers, because Caesar's middle name was Francisco, and "he had twins like me." He is now a great admirer of Caesar's abilities.

them that their horse was no good; they were spending good money on a bad horse. They said it was my fault for not making him a good horse. So now they said, 'We're not going to pay you.'"

"I could take all mine to Small Claims and probably collect, but they're nice people, they're good clients. They'd pay me if they had it. They just don't have it."

"This couple, they had it but they weren't going to pay me, because they thought it was my fault that the horse was no good. So I took them to Small Claims, and it took them about a year and a half to pay me. They were not going to pay me, and in Small Claims, they cannot make them pay until, as I say, you can put a lien against the property and when they go to sell their house, they can't because they owe Caesar $1500. So all of a sudden, they call me and they want to pay me, and they want me to sign something. They make me wait a year and a half, so I said, 'You know what, I won't be in town for the next thirty days. See me when I come back.' 'Oh no, we need to do it now.' Now it's my turn, the $1500 isn't going to make me no richer anyway, now it's my turn to be a little snotty, so I did it. And they paid me."

"But you can't get interest, can you?"

"No. You don't get interest. You're lucky to get your money."

10.5 Investments outside racing

None. Other than the house and perhaps later a ranch, all Caesar's income goes into his training business and buying horses. "I like to stick with the business I know."

10.6 What is he worth?

When I asked Caesar if he was a millionaire, he said he didn't have a million dollars in the bank. I said, *"A millionaire is someone with assets worth a million after allowing for any money owed."*

"Well, on assets, I might be a millionaire, but I will call myself a millionaire when I have a million dollars in the bank." His main assets are a house worth around $600,000 plus a lot of horses and shares in horses.

10.7 How did Caesar make his money?

Caesar says he has made most of his money from his 10% of winnings, and a bit from betting. Dealing in horses has been insignificant.

11. How he gets and keeps owners

I asked Caesar how new owners came to him.

"Some they phone and make an appointment, some they come up to me at the races."

"How many new owners would you get each year?"

"Between 8 and 12."

"How many of those would buy only the one horse and then leave racing?"

"A lot. A lot of them think they are going to walk in and claim a horse for $5,000 and have another Ta Advantage and win $50,000. If the horse turns out to be not what they expected, they're out of the business."

11.1 What is Caesar's public image?

Caesar does not have a high profile with the public - yet. When I asked racegoers, they said they had seen his name, but they didn't know anything about him. That is more common among American racegoers, who often know little about horses, and even less about trainers. Nevertheless, some of them felt they 'knew' Blane Schvaneveldt and Bob Baffert. When I asked what they knew, it was very little in terms of information, more a "feeling".

11.1-1 Opinion of other trainers

Caesar is seen as a sound horseman, a good guy, a good talker and a successful claiming trainer.

11.1-2 Relations with the stewards

"What's your attitude to the stewards at the races?"

"There are three stewards, and you know, we've all got our bads and goods and the ones we got now (1988), they're good stewards but they're not consistent stewards. They could disqualify a horse today for taking the path of another horse, and yet tomorrow, another horse might do the same thing, and they won't blink an eye. They need to be more consistent."

"A trainer once said to me, '(At his track) They're idiots who have to be placated,' meaning you have to keep in good with them, but they were idiots."

"Well, you have to keep in good with them."

11.2 Getting publicity

At Los Alamitos, Caesar has two main rivals. One is the gargantuan operation of Blane Schvaneveldt. Rival trainers believe he has more horses than the Hun army. Blane doesn't have to make much effort to get publicity, because since the middle 1970's he has had starters in nearly every race, if not two or three, and he often has the winner. He gets lots of publicity as a result. Battling along behind Blane, we find Caesar and Bob Baffert, two youngsters pushing and shoving each other while watching and waiting for the King's crown to drop. Bob Baffert will frankly admit he's more of a public relations man than a trainer, and scanning the magazines, the results are obvious. Caesar would rate a fraction of the coverage Bob Baffert managed.

11.2-1 Caesar and the press

The press seemed less aware of Caesar than of Bob Baffert, Blane, and Bob Gilbert. In the time I was there I never saw Caesar make any effort to be where the press were. They might be a little shy of him because of the difficulty of capturing the flavor of his speech.

"Do you make any effort to talk to the racing journalists, let them know something about yourself?"

"No, not really."

"It seems to me they pay a lot more attention to guys like Baffert and very little to you."

"Well . . . I get mad because a lot of times, a lot of magazines, they don't give me credit. Last year, 1989, I was the leading trainer in California on the numbers and everything, but none of them wrote a thing. A year ago, Baffert and me were battling for the lead and there was something about it every week. After I won - nothing. Even now, no one here knows that I was leading trainer."

"I remember from sitting up in the press box with those guys, that they were surprised when I said I was going to write about you, and they didn't seem to know very much about you."

"They don't want to know. Their attention is focused on Baffert. The only time they say something good about me is when they want to cut Blane down."

"Why do they want to cut Blane down?"

"They don't like him. They are very prejudiced people."

"I don't know, maybe it would pay you to try to get to know them."

"I just forget about it and get on with my job."

11.3 Getting owners

"Can you go looking for clients?"

"No they come to you. It's like a doctor or lawyer, if you're good and they need your service, they'll call you. They just call you and say they have got a horse they'd like you to train and do you have room. Nine out of ten times I check the horse and also the clients. Like any other business, you have bad paying people and people who aren't worthy of being around you. I'm at a stage where I don't need them kind of people. You meet them, you talk to their ex-trainer. Everybody knows everybody. You don't want the owner who is always changing from one trainer to another, because he will leave you after three months or whatever. He will go to the clubhouse and badmouth you, say you don't know how to train - and you don't need that."

"Sometimes you can say to them, 'I note that you change trainers a lot. If I'm to be your trainer, I am fully in charge of that horse. You don't tell me who to run, how to train, who to ride, you leave it completely to me. If you don't like that, go and get another trainer."

"Sometimes they will say, 'Yes,' but then they get on the phone and say, 'Do this, do that.' I say, 'Come by and pick up your horse.' When you are starting off, you accept that because you need the horse. But now I don't need that kind of clown and I don't need the aggravation."

"Wayne Lukas clearly knew how to find wealthy clients. You've got to work out how he finds those people. He finds a lot too many of them for it to be an accident."

"No. He finds them. Exactly. He does something right, to find those kind of people."

"He gives a lot of talks. Lectures around the place."

"But see the reason he gives a lot of talks and lectures is BECAUSE he's Wayne Lukas."

"But they say it goes back a long way, that he gives talks."

"But like he said one time, 'If I were not Wayne Lukas and doing what I've done, they would not be inviting me to give these speeches.'"

"That's true, but I know from inviting horse trainers to give lectures to students in college it's hard to get them to do it. If a trainer got a reputation as a guy that was easy to get to those things, he'd be asked often. At functions, they tell me Lukas is a good speechmaker and he can handle anything that anyone wants to throw at him from the floor. That's a way to pick up owners, - I don't know if that's how he found his rich people - but if you start getting yourself invited to some of these things like Cadillac dealer's meetings or country clubs, that could be how he met them. No one seems to know how he gets those big money men (this was January 1988)."

"But he gets them."

"He gets them! It can't be an accident. Maybe he joins the right golf club, who knows?"

"No, he don't golf. Wayne Lukas don't do nothing. All he does is train horses. See - it is success. He got Peter Brant, one of the biggest owners in New York - Leroy Jolley was his trainer. Why did Brant switch from Leroy Jolley to Wayne Lukas? He just liked Wayne Lukas's organization better. It's not that Wayne Lukas went out looking for him. Brant come to him. In our business, if I pick up a millionaire tomorrow, he won't pick me because I'm Caesar Dominguez, he'll pick me up because of my record. He'll say, 'Well, I've got some horses, and I think you're the man that can make them win some races.' Not because, 'Oh, I like your looks' or, 'I like your family'. Oh no no no!"

Caesar was right. I later learned that Wayne hardly ever left his barn. He met his clients because they heard of his successes and approached him.

11.3-1 Personality and social skills

I found Caesar very straightforward, very down to earth. There was never any doubt where Caesar stood on any issue, but he would listen to anyone else's point of view. He can be a humorist when things are going well. He had a quality that I can only call 'likability'. Everyone on the backstretch seemed to like him. He does not seem to have upset or irritated anyone.

11.3-2 Social stamina and alcohol

"Do you celebrate your successes?"

"I used to. Not any more. You go out and you celebrate and you get drunk and whatever, and the next day you feel terrible, two, three days, and your mind is not working. I left that behind."

11.3-3 Social class of owners

Caesar does not have any of the big names of Quarter Horse racing, but with his recent Grade 1 successes he is getting better quality stock and clients.

I asked Caesar's outspoken brother José if there were disadvantages to being an Hispanic trainer, knowing he wouldn't gloss over the matter: *"Do you feel that being 'Mexican' holds Caesar back a bit?"*

José: "We - the whole family - have never felt discriminated against. We never had that in our minds. Around the track, since we were kids, we've run into winos and millionaires. There are doctors and professors rubbing horses. We have run into Cubans, Puerto Ricans, blacks, whites, purples. If some person sees you just by color, *that* person has a problem. That is their problem. I can go anywhere in the grandstand and I've got friends that are black, blue, yellow, whatever."

"You start judging yourself by where you come from you've got a problem. We didn't come from high society but I tell you what - our parents raised us to be proud of who we are."

"You look at the top of the Quarter Horses or the Thoroughbreds and you'll find a lot of Latins. We're known to be good horse people. There's Laz Barrera (Hall of Fame trainer), Angel Cordero (leading jockey, winner of over $100m), José Santos (top money winning jockey of 1987 with $12.3m). Patrick Valenzuela (Kentucky Derby winning jockey) was brought up right there in our neighborhood in Sunland Park."

That attitude is a very commendable one, but I have no doubt that the cultural separation of being Hispanic does not help Caesar get horses. Most Quarter Horse owners are from the southern states of America, and they are white. There are many Hispanic owners of course. Some owners of a Hereford cattle ranch in Mexico itself, were leading Quarter Horse owners of 1989. Caesar has many Mexican owners. So many that when Town Policy, the outstanding two-year-old of 1977, disappeared, and the suspicion was that the horse had been taken to Mexico for match racing, Caesar was questioned by the FBI. Caesar ignored the slight and gave the investigators advice on where to look. But it was many months later before Town Policy was found in a cornfield in Mexico and returned to Blane Schvaneveldt's stables where he continued his great performances.

My own impression is that Caesar would do even better if there was no cultural barrier. More power to the Dominguez family however, that they don't use that to make excuses. They just get on with doing the job well.

11.3-4 Does he steal owners?
"In the Quarter Horse game here, is there any stealing of owners? Do trainers approach each other's owners in any way?"

"There is a lot of backstabbing. But there are people that don't do it, there are people that do it. I've never done it for the simple reason that I want an owner to feel confidence with me. I want him to come to me because he wants to come. I don't want to go up there and beg him to come to me. No. I've never done it, but I know people that have done it, because my own clients have called me and said, 'You know what, Joe Blow called me and said that you're doing something with my horse that I don't agree with.'"

"You must see horses that you reckon you could train better."

Oh, I see them all the time. I got owners now that have horses in other stables, that actually have come to me and asked for my opinion. I tell them; "I'll give you my opinion under one condition, that you do not tell your trainer that I said so."

11.3-5 Has Caesar ever advertised?
Quarter Horse magazines carry more advertisements from trainers looking for horses than I have seen in Thoroughbreds or Standardbreds. I believe that is probably due to the huge number of small breeders and owners, scattered across the face of America, many many of them in areas where there is little or no racing. They often want a trainer, and yet have no contact with trainers. The solution for some of these owners is to look through the ads. I hadn't seen any advertisements by Caesar, but I asked if he'd ever tried any.

"No. But we made a TV deal - it wasn't in California, it was mainly in the South West and the Mid West, all except California. They just picked the top three trainers, which was Blane, me and Baffert, and they talked about our good horses and our success and how we're willing to accept horses from out of state. Some company from back east that just wanted to interview top trainers from down here."

"And they didn't charge you for that?"

"So far they haven't. I haven't had no phone calls either, about people wanting their horses trained or anything. But I tell you what, the best advertisement is the win. You win a race and you're in the magazines, you're in the newspaper.

That's advertising, but it's free advertising because they've got to talk about that horse, and if they're talking about that horse, they got to talk about you."

"Have you tried advertising in the newspapers?"

"Well, they asked me if I want to advertise in the Yellow Pages. I've always said no. The way I look at it, you advertise yourself by your performance. Ninety percent of the people that are going to buy a racehorse are people that come to the races and are gamblers. They know a little bit about the business, they'll say, 'Hey, I want to get in the business,' and they'll know what trainers to go to."

11.3-6 Does he give talks?
As we have seen, Caesar doesn't give talks, even if Wayne Lukas does.

11.3-7 Any affiliation with studs?
At this point in time Caesar gets very few horses from studs. Studs usually keep the cream of their own products, so someone else is getting that cream. Of course they also keep some with bent legs and so on, but in general it is a plus to get stock from stud owners. That is something in the future for Caesar.

Earl Holmes considers Caesar capable of training a quality horse as well as anybody. "If he was to get some owner with a lot of broodmares, raising some good horses, he'd train them as well as anyone. He wouldn't have any problem with that."

11.4 Managing owners
"Do you phone your owners or do they phone you?"

"It's both ways. A lot of times the owners will call me, but if I need to tell them that their horse pulled up sore, or their horse is sick and I don't expect it to be in races for the next five or ten days, I call them."

"So if some guy hasn't phoned you in a fair while, you know and you phone him?"

"Oh no. They always call me. If I don't call them, they'll call me."

"Is there a time of day for that?"

"They know the best time to call me. They know that nighttime, if they want to see me in person, they'll always see me at the races."

"Do you ever have parties or barbecues for your owners?"

"I used to do that a lot, but it seemed like the more time you spent with the clients, and the more friendships you had with them, they somehow - it don't work. You get too much friendliness and I've noticed that it don't work at your business, because now they want to tell you how to train. They become too friendly with different jockeys, and jockeys will of course be trying to get the mount on their horses. Before you know it - well let's try this one, and let's try this one. I want to ride Joe Blow because he's my friend. He liked the way the jockey smiled at his wife. Talk like that."

11.5 Main owners

Felipé Tiscareno is a labor contractor from Fresno California. If you have a large acreage you want planted and harvested, Felipé will organize it for a fee. He approached Caesar with a couple of claimers he wanted trained. He chose Caesar because Caesar could speak Spanish. Felipé bought his first Quarter Horse yearling in 1987. That youngster was a $47,000 flop but that didn't stop him. He is reported to have spent $300,000 on horses in 1987 and 1988. Caesar and Felipé have been a very successful combination. They bought Hez Class for $9,500 and it won $130,000 in less than a year. They jumped in and bought Special Elan which won the Jet Deck Stakes and $70,000 as a two-year-old in 1989. They bought Takin On The Cash which won a second Bay Meadows Futurity and $95,988 then won two other Grade 1 races.

11.5-1 How well would Caesar have gone without Felipé?

Tiscareno has provided Caesar with a major breakthrough - the opportunity to demonstrate his selection skills and two-year-old training skills.

11.5-2 Is Felipé losing money?

According to Caesar, Felipé is very much ahead in dollars, and his very talented team of horses is still very young.

12. Caesar and the breeding game

12.1 Caesar as a stallion maker

"Any time you come up with a runner, a super, super runner, you get a share in him when he becomes a stallion. That comes automatically. With mares you don't have no shares, no nothing. A lot of times you get a good horse, let's say you sell him, then you get your 10% on the sale plus you keep shares. For instance, I sold a Dash for Cash stud, named Brown Dasher; I trained him and did everything. When I sold him, I got 30% of what I sold him for, plus I kept two lifetime breedings to him. That's what keeps you for the future. You've got to have something."

"Do you consciously buy for a subsequent stallion market?"

"No, mainly you buy them to race and then if they do race, then they go into the breeding shed."

12.2 Caesar as a breeder

"Is breeding part of your game?"

"Right now, I have a Quarter Horse and a Thoroughbred mare that I bred, but no, my main deal is training."

13. What makes Caesar Dominguez successful?

13.1 How he acquired his skills and knowledge

Although his parents were not into horses, Caesar learnt the ropes from a very early age by working for his uncles. From there he worked with other trainers, notably Earl Holmes. Though only 24 when he first had his own stable to train, he had 8 years full-time experience and nearly 10 years part-time before that.

13.2 Personality traits

Caesar is an outgoing, happy, likable fellow, pleasant to be around. He is a very good talker. In spite of his grammar he gets his message across, in fact when you are with Caesar you don't really notice the, 'don't got nothin' style of his speech because he speaks clearly and confidently. It seems to be normal when he says it. Caesar puts his case in straightforward style.

Intelligence and memory

You quickly see that Caesar's no dummy. One of the keys to any successful claiming is a good memory, especially for horses. Sherry says Caesar can remember things about horses from 20 years ago in great detail. He was a bit off in his recollections of the achievements of the sire of Truly A Pleasure.

Productivity - sleep, energy and health

Caesar is a picture of health and vitality. He moves about with energy but is very relaxed.

"How many hours sleep a night do you need?"

"I don't go to sleep every night till one o'clock, and I get up at six, so I get five hours."

"Do you ever sleep in the afternoon?"

"Sometimes, when we have no races. I usually pick Sundays and Mondays to go to the ranch, because I got twenty Thoroughbreds at the ranch (1988)."

"That is not very much sleep."

"Four to five hours is all I need. When you die you're gonna sleep for ever. Sleeping is for the dead."

Stress management

Halfway through 1989, Caesar led the winners table at the Los Alamitos track with 60 wins, 8 ahead of Bob Baffert. Was he letting the pressure affect him? He told Ty Wyant: "I think I'm leading the standings because my horses are fitting the conditions better than the other trainers right now. That can change. If I make leading trainer, fine, if not, that's fine."

Natural good health and vitality allow Caesar to make a high pressure existence look easy. His attitude after a win or a loss is " . . . just another race. Now for the next race." But he hasn't always had such a relaxed attitude. Earl Holmes remembers Caesar crying when the Holmes stable lost a race.

"Crying! How old was he then?"

"He was just out of military service. It hurt him, that's how much he wanted to win. And a trainer has to have that. But he has started from nothing and worked his way up. He deserves everything he's got."

Workaholic or workaphilic

Caesar is not afraid of work but doesn't go looking for extra work at the Lukas end of the tidiness scale. He loves horses, he loves racing, and he loves training. He says if he was a millionaire he would still do it for fun.

Retire or die on the job?

"Are you going to die on the job, are you going to retire, or are you going to switch to something else?"

"No. I'll never switch to something else. What I want to do as I retire, I want to get me five or ten acres and maybe keep about four to five brood mares, breed four or five babies as your own, maybe sell three in a sale, keep two, raise 'em to see if they're good, and then start over, year after year after year. Retire into breeding."

Celebrates successes

Caesar is not one for a big boozy celebration. Sherry says, "We don't go out and party after a win. It's more, 'Hooray, we can pay the bills now.'"

Scrapbook of race wins

Caesar keeps a scrap book on his horses and one whole wall of his home is taken up with pictures of Truly A Pleasure.

Hobbies and interests

Sherry says Caesar relaxes well at home. I asked Caesar about any outside hobbies or interests.

"None. Nothing. Just horses. I don't play golf. I used to play racquetball. I might pick up racquetball again, or even start going to a health spa, just to do something different."

"Do you take an annual vacation?"

"There is no such thing as a vacation. What is a vacation? No, I don't take vacations. Going to the horse sales is my vacation."

Drive and application

"Did you ever think about being anything besides a horse trainer?"

"Other jobs? Never."

"Did you ever, at any stage, when you were, say, starting off, feel that you'd made a wrong choice, or that you might have to get out of it or anything like that?"

"No, never have. Of course, you get to the stage when you're running five or six a night, and you think you can win five races, and you wind up winning none. You get a little discouraged and you go home and have tea with the wife and say, 'You know what: I think I'm going to quit my job and become a bar-

tender.' But you know that's only because we've had such a bad night."

"Do you want your kids to become horse trainers?"

"Well, they're riding right now. My wife, she's in the dressage, and she's got all my kids doing the same thing, so I would have to say that in the long run, they'll wind up doing something or other with horses, but it's up to them what they want to do."

Optimist or pessimist?

Without question an optimist.

Socializing - loner or outgoing?

Caesar is a very good socializer, but he doesn't let it get in the way of work that has to be done.

Inborn talent or something learned?

Caesar has applied himself, but he does believe the ability to be a good trainer is God-given.

13.3 The formulated approach

Personal philosophy

Caesar enjoys his job and wants to continue to do so. He does not want to drive himself into the ground. *"Wayne Lukas has everything spotless and organized. Are you like that?"*

"No. I like it comfortable, and livable. I don't want it spotless to where you can't step on a carpet."

Religion

Caesar doesn't go to church often but he believes in God.

Business philosophy

"What are the guidelines to making money in Quarter Horses?"

"If you do everything the best, especially for the horses, the money will follow."

Betting

Wagering was an important part of starvation prevention in Caesar's early years. Today he says it is still an important source of income. He bets to win, on his own horses, and he takes exactas. That means selecting first and second in the correct order. He only bets on his own because as the trainer, "You see little things about the horse that can make that horse good value."

Selling strategies

While not in the league that could sell ice-makers to Eskimos, Caesar has a good mix of friendliness and business sense that would make him a good salesman. Caesar is not afraid to say that he is a damn good trainer, and use his claiming results to prove his point.

Innovator

From his observation of the feeding habits of Earl Holmes' horses, and his subsequent adoption of a different feeding routine, we can see that Caesar is an innovator. Some trainers are mortally afraid to do anything different, especially different to what a top name man like Earl Holmes was doing.

Risk-taker
Caesar took his chances leaving home at 16 to go to California. He took his chances when Pickwick offered him the training position. A medium risk-taker would be my estimate.

Time management
Caesar does not waste time, but he is not keyed up, hypertensive, worried he is wasting time. He really has an excellent attitude.

Goal and step setter or day by day?
When you talk to Caesar there are very few things that he doesn't seem to have already thought about, to already have an opinion on. This long range outlook shows in the way he split with Pickwick in 1974 because they would not let him develop a safety net of his own clients. He also has moved into Thoroughbreds in the last few years. With the changes in ownership and policy at Los Alamitos, this was a prudent move.

13.4 Has he ever had a positive drug test?
"Have you ever been disqualified for a positive swab?"

"Oh no. My record is as clean, probably cleaner than Mr Clean when it comes to drugs. Of course they'll give you a hype for giving over the level (of approved medications), and that's only been once in the fifteen years I've been training, and that happened only last year. No, I've been very clean."

13.5 Luck and other reasons for success
Caesar has made his own luck all the way, with the possible exception of the filly that constituted his entire starting string, Catchajet. Even that was not all luck. I asked Caesar if he knew how good she was when he started out his one horse public stable. He said he knew she was exceptional because he broke her in as a baby.

He has not had any advantages in family wealth or position. As a youngster, he learned as his Uncle Pete Payan learned. Then he left home at 16 to go west, paid his dues, and learned the trade.

13.6 What Caesar thinks made him successful
"What are the traits that you see as reasons for your success? What are the things that have gotten you up there?"

"It's got to be hard work for one, and then after the hard work, the intelligence or the gift that God gave me to train a horse, to spot a horse. I think all those who are successful in any sport or business, somehow you're God-gifted to that sport."

"Do you have any personality traits that you wish you could alter a little bit? Like maybe temper or tendency to spend money?"

"Well, I tell you what, I'm very hot tempered, and my boys tell me that all the time. See, they know me. And my wife says that I'm very moody. If things don't go my way, I'm very moody. I get hot-tempered. I get mad. But through your older age, you're more mellowed. You try not to be so snappy at clients, so snappy at your help, so snappy at the wife."

13.7 Trainer, conman or businessman?
Caesar is respected in the barn area as a good horseman, and a man who can put his case well in words. He is also very popular, a likable person.

13.8 What drives Caesar?
Bobby Adair remembers that a long time back Caesar had an attitude that he was going to succeed, an attitude that Bobby says set Caesar apart from most other grooms. Caesar has respect for money, but it doesn't seem to be his focus. He likes the independence, the social aspects, and the status it brings. He loves his work. This 'workaphilia', coupled with his laid back attitude to so many things ("If I win OK. If I don't win that's OK too."), makes Caesar a man of mixed drives, a very balanced person.

13.9 Lessons for beginning trainers
Caesar has the usual ingredients for success - common sense, thinks ahead, works hard etc. Caesar's horsemanship derives from those things and from working with a top trainer like Earl Holmes. But one of Caesar's greatest attributes, one which has been important in his success, is difficult to simply copy: He is very likable. Everyone you talk to in the barn area at the track knows and likes him, in fact he might very well be the most popular person there.

14. The future
When Los Alamitos started, in August 1947, it was a poorly demarcated track on Frank Vessels' farm. There was no parimutuel betting. Mrs Vessels served hot dogs out of her kitchen window. The track was a long way from the urban sprawl of Los Angeles.

Early 1988
Today it is still intact, but surrounded for mile upon mile by housing, like something ingested by a growing amoeba. It is resisting digestion, but for how long? The Los Alamitos track is in constant danger of being closed. The annual profit or loss to the owners is tiny compared to the capital value of such acreage in the giant sardine can that is Los Angeles. The owners want to close the track, subdivide and develop.

Rumors come and go: the owners have permission to subdivide; the track is to be sold for housing; the track is to become a shopping center and a golf course; the track is to be

Inside the Pavilion in Ruidoso at the Super Select session of the 1989 All-American Sales. Note those hats. It is one heck of a lot cheaper to buy a Quarter Horse than a Thoroughbred.

rescued by some wealthy Quarter Horse owners; the track will be sold to Standardbred interests. This does not give the Quarter Horse trainers much hope in the long term. How Caesar would welcome the permanency racing has in those parts of the world where the track cannot be sold simply because the land is now valuable.

June 1988 Testing the water in Thoroughbreds
Caesar has prepared himself for the worst by developing a string of Thoroughbreds.

"Now that you're training Thoroughbreds, do you go around trying to see what the top Thoroughbred trainers do?"

"Yes. I read a lot of *Racing Forms* from back east, and from here. I see how the Thoroughbred trainers train a good horse, how they train a cheap horse. I ask questions. I do a lot, yes."

"You go to the Thoroughbred racing much?"

"Yes, and I watch races every night on TV, from Hollywood Park and Santa Anita. I see a million races. When they're running at Santa Anita, I go at least three or four times a week, just to see how things are running and to talk to trainers. Also, when I train my Thoroughbreds, there's nothing but Thor-

oughbred people there. So I observe how other people train their Thoroughbreds. So yes, I'm learning a lot on Thoroughbreds."

"Do you see yourself becoming a Thoroughbred trainer?"

"Oh, I figure at least within five years. Five years. I want to keep my Quarter Horses, because like I said, I've been very successful in Quarter Horses, and it's been good to me, gave me a good life. But I want to move into Thoroughbreds. I don't want to jump in full bore, I want to go in slowly."

"Was that how Wayne Lukas went, slowly?"

"Ah, well, Wayne started that way, slowly, but he still started with a lot of money. He started with Beal and French, two of the richest men in Texas and with Bob Spreen, one of the wealthiest men in California. So when you start with that kind of money, you're going to come up with something."

I would add, however, that a lot of people have spent amounts like the money Lukas spent to acquire Terlingua and other horses, and come up with nothing you ever heard of, often nothing that even raced.

January 1989

The next time I saw Caesar, he was racing Thoroughbreds at Santa Anita because the management at Bay Meadows was not running Quarter Horses at that time and the future of Los Alamitos was looking somewhat confused. Other Quarter Horse trainers were also at Santa Anita, but they were trying to cobble together a string of horses. Caesar already had his string. Sixteen head. One step ahead of the game. One trainer said it was $27,000 for a maiden win at Santa Anita, compared with $15,000 for a stakes win at Los Alamitos. But then the Thoroughbreds cost about 15 times as much for the same quality of horse.

At the Ruidoso Super Select Sale in 1989, 105 Quarter Horses sold for a *total* of $2,146,900. After taking out 22 buybacks (horses bought by the owner because the price was too low), the average for these elite prospects was $20,447. For 176 sold in the All-American sessions, the average was close to $5,400. The average at the Pacific Quarter Horse Sales at Los Alamitos were also in the $5,000 - $6,000 range. At other sales around the country, $2,500 is often the average. It is a heck of a lot cheaper for an owner to play around in Quarter Horses.

At the Keeneland July Select Sale in 1989, 388 Thoroughbreds sold for an average price of $302,211.

Caesar concentrates on the bidding. The horse he bought raced in 1990 as Takin On The Cash.

At the sale: From left, brothers José, Albert and Caesar Dominguez, with owner Felipé Tiscareno. It was after midnight.

January 1990

Things had improved a great deal. The end of year figures for 1989 showed that Quarter Horse racing at Los Alamitos had reversed a five year downward trend in people and purses. In the dying months of 1989, Bay Meadows scheduled a 38 day season for 1990, beginning February 9th. The spread would be 4 race days a week for 9 weeks and include 4 major Grade 1 races that have usually been run at that track: La Primera del Ano Derby, El Primero del Ano Derby, Golden State Derby and the Bay Meadows Futurity. (In 1989 these races had to be re-scheduled and run at Los Alamitos.)

But there was some bad news from the view of the Quarter Horse boys: the Los Alamitos track had fallen into the hands of Standardbred interests. Perhaps because of that there was talk of a new Quarter Horse track to be built not far away. Ed Allred and R.D. Hubbard, major money men of long standing in Quarter Horses, were the people proposing the new track.

For Caesar's Quarter Horse stable, the snowball effects of winning Grade 1 events and the Trainer Of The Year title for California in 1989 were apparent early in 1990. In Sherry's words, "Everyone wants to be at the top, so there are some calls." She described the quality improvement as, 'real scary', but said it was wonderful having top contenders in so many of the quality races.

I asked Caesar if he had been able to buy a larger number of horses at the sales in 1989.

"Oh yes. I have bought 15 babies."

"How many would you have bought in the previous years?"

"Maybe one or two."

"So a couple of Grade 1 results can make that much difference?"

"Yes. Then people start respecting you."

"Does that mean you'll be running a few in futurities now?"

"Exactly, and when you run them in futurities, then you're talking about big money from one race, instead of having to fight to win 20 races to win $10,000. In futurities, just to be 4th you make $20,000."

Caesar and Sherry were able to enjoy some financial fruits too. They moved from house-plot suburbia to one acre at La Habra Heights. It took Sherry a long time to persuade Caesar to do this, but she is overjoyed with the move. It means they can have their horses at home and not on agistment blocks miles away. The horses are Sherry's dressage horse, the kids' pony and Truly A Pleasure, the retired hero of the whole Dominguez family. Caesar has plenty to occupy him around the new property, but the thing he likes most about it is that it is on a private road. Only the six or seven families who live there can drive into the road. "That means my kids can go out on the street and play with a bat and ball, and they are safe."

And the Thoroughbreds? They had won 5 races from 18 starts at one point, the best win percentage at Santa Anita at that stage of the meet. But the total wins and money are nothing to boast about yet according to Caesar.

"So you are not a threat to Wayne Lukas yet?"

"No, oh no."

14.1 Perfect conditions for him would be ?

Heaven in the 1990's for Caesar would be a string of top quality horses that enabled him to take out the national trainer's title of the American Quarter Horse Association. The man who has had that title since he took it off Wayne Lukas in the mid 1970's is Blane Schvaneveldt. So the perfect conditions for Caesar would be lots of good horses and Blane's retirement. But I don't see Blane retiring, just yet, and maybe Caesar would rather he didn't. I have a feeling Caesar wouldn't want to get the national title by default. He'd much rather win it in pitched battle.

14.2 Probabilities

Caesar has already proven himself among the Quarter Horse claimers in his neck of the woods, but trainers are seldom happy to be known for that title alone. They want to be known as trainers of stakes winners, grade 1 winners, the winners of the premier events, of Champions.

Caesar is no exception, and he is building his reputation as a trainer of class horses. Two interesting things will affect Caesar's chances in this elite realm. One is the rise in the number of quality horses purchased or sent to him, following his Grade 1 wins. From quality stock, since he knows what he is doing, should come more Grade 1 wins, more quality stock etc. and a higher place on the money-won table. This is already happening.

The other is the effect of Quarter Horse racing in Texas. Texas and the surrounding states are the cradle of the Quarter Horse, and yet racing with betting has only just been legalized in Texas. The 1990's should see quite a number of tracks built. If racing were to blossom there, many of the better horses that are sent to Los Alamitos to end up in the hands of rival trainers, would stay in the Texas area. Some of the trainers originally from that region might move back home. Because Caesar's owners are Californian, he would still have the same number of owners and horses. Bob Baffert and Blane Schvaneveldt would receive fewer horses. These changes would increase Caesar's win and money results.

Of course it's difficult to predict accurately the outcome of what is happening in Texas. It may be that it will develop as a an even greater source of quality stock and those Californian trainers with a strong Texas connection will have an even greater advantage. That would be bad news for Caesar.

Still another possibility is that Texas could eclipse California, with more tracks and better prizemoney. This would be a distinct possibility if Los Alamitos were to close. Even without that happening, if oil prices were to recover and Texas rise from its recession, it could conceivably become the center of Quarter Horse racing, with the most tracks and the biggest prizemoney. If Texas were to become the mecca of Quarter Racing, it would spell the end of Caesar's hopes for a national title.

The most likely scenario is that racing in Texas will have a slow beginning, taking much longer for the crowd following to build up than many would expect in such cowboy country. But it will become a major part of the national scene and anyone who wants to be Number One nationally will probably have to have divisions racing in California, New Mexico and Texas - a Wayne Lukas style operation. That will suit Blane Schvaneveldt and other trainers who already have divisions in New Mexico and California, AND have good connections in Texas.

I asked Earl Holmes:

"Is it possible, with all the pari-mutuel tracks opening up in Texas, that a lot of those breeders will keep their horses there?"

"The good horses will go where the money is."

"You think that will still be Los Alamitos?"

"Yes."

When I asked Caesar about the effects of racing in Texas, his view was almost identical to Earl's.

Of course there could be some catastrophe like the permanent closure of Los Alamitos to Quarter Horses, and the collapse of the Quarter Horse circuit in California. It almost happened. In that case Caesar would stay in California and move into Thoroughbreds. But that dark scenario has moved into the realm of the unlikely. Early in 1990, those Quarter Horse Knights Dee Hubbard and Ed Allred purchased a half share of Los Alamitos and they are planning another track at Riverside.

By mid 1990 Los Alamitos had set a number of new wagering records. This allowed the purses to be raised by 12%. Sunland Park and Ruidoso Downs were also setting records, suggesting that a slump in Quarter Horse racing was over.

At the Bay Meadows Futurity in April 1990, three of the ten finalists had been selected at yearling sales and trained by Caesar. The $52,000 Dash For Cash colt Takin On The Cash showed he had that cash in his blood alright by winning the Grade 1 event and $95,988. Later he won the Kindergarten Stakes and took his earnings to $185,000 followed by a win in a third Grade 1 race, the Dash For Cash. This race was named after his sire, and it added $121,000 to his winnings. Takin On The Cash was then aimed at the almighty All-American Futurity.

It may be that in spite of nearly two decades with the older claiming horses, Caesar has what it takes to choose and train futurity champions. Only time will tell, but choosing Hez Class and Takin On The Cash, consecutive winners of the Bay Meadows Futurity, has to be one terrific start. If all goes well, in 5 or 10 years you'll be hearing that Caesar gets the best horses because he has the richest owners - etc.

With the increase in quality stock following his winning performance in 1989, and some big wins in the first half of 1990, Caesar seems very content to push on in Quarter Horses, while keeping his Thoroughbred option open. He has a couple of very exciting decades in front of him. Those around him - Bobby Adair, Earl Holmes, his wife and his brothers - all agree he deserves every bit of his success.

EPILOGUE

In July 1990 Caesar was notified that a horse he ran in early May had returned a positive drug test for cocaine. In August he was suspended for one year. Takin On The Cash ran third in his heat of the All-American Futurity, failing to qualify for the final. The fabric of his success story was unraveling.

The first hints of trouble had come when a steward told Caesar that one of his clients, Bonifacio Rayas, was bad for racing. Rayas was claiming horses with wads of cash, and the steward told Caesar that he had heard the money might be from drug dealing. As far as Caesar was concerned, Bonifacio was a heavy gambler and that was all. The claiming success of Caesar and Rayas was also considered suspicious. Caesar says the steward told him, "We know you must be doing something and we're going to get you."

Rayas kept his horses at the same ranch as Caesar kept his. Caesar supervised the off-track training of the Rayas horses. Early in May, Caesar was at the ranch when it was raided by a horde of 'FBI agents', helicopter and all. Caesar was handcuffed, but the lady who owned the ranch challenged the agents. They checked Caesar's record and quickly let him go. Although nothing was found at the ranch, Bonifacio Rayas was charged with conspiracy to sell drugs. For Caesar it seemed like a bizarre, isolated event, but it was really Day 1 of a nightmare.

That bizarre event didn't stop Caesar and Rayas claiming a horse called Barium in mid May. I asked Caesar why he continued with someone charged with a drug conspiracy. He said, "Because 'Bony' is a great guy, everyone likes him, and I have never seen nothin' that would make me think he was a drug dealer. Even in the big raids on his house and the ranch, they found nothin'. He's a successful gambler, he's a Mexican with money, and they can't stand that."

Eleven days later Caesar ran Barium in a $5,000 maiden race. It was at low odds (6 to 5 in Caesar's recollection), came 2nd, and was tested. The test was positive for cocaine, but since the shambles with the Lukas and Barrera cocaine positives, the authorities have put in place a review system, and Caesar was not told of the positive until July. Perhaps the authorities had doubts about the test, perhaps they hoped for another positive.

Since then there has been a tangle of confusing information. Caesar talked to stewards, vets, lawyers, people from testing labs, and the California Horse Racing Board. Caesar was told that some tests of the horse's sample showed only the metabolites, the end products of processing in the body. He was told by an expert (Dr Maylin) that the amount of cocaine found would not have had an effect on the horse's performance, even if injected into a joint. He was told the drug might have been there from before he claimed the horse, or from a drug user handling the horse.

I asked one equine drug tester how long cocaine might last in a horse's system. He replied that he did not know of any studies, and guessed it would be similar to procaine, which lasts at detectable levels for up to 10 or 11 days. The man who runs the lab for the California Horse Racing Board guessed 10 hours, but when I told him of his colleague's guess, he said that 10 days could well be right. When I mentioned that one source had said that in the U.S. Air Force drug testing, they believed they could detect cocaine up to two months later in humans, he said he could believe that. Indeed he believed the industry would have to look at testing all horses that are claimed.

The horse claimed by Caesar *was* 'tested' the night Caesar and Rayas claimed it, when it also ran second. When Caesar tracked that sample down he was told that because of costs, some samples were discarded without any testing, and that particular sample had been one of them.

When Caesar took his information back to the stewards, he was told that under the rules the trainer is the absolute insurer that the horse is free of drugs, and it was his bad luck.

Meanwhile the horses were racing under Caesar's brother's name, but Caesar's wife said some of the owners were getting anxious about how long this would all go on.

Perhaps the worst aspect of Caesar's position is what appears to be his victimization. The stewards appeared 'delighted' to tell Caesar he had a positive. Another trainer with a positive last November does not have a hearing until December this year, and has been allowed to train his horses and prepare his case until then. There are persistent rumors of another 15 positives about which nothing has been done. When Caesar's lawyer asked the Board vet at Sacramento how many other positives there had been, the vet was not allowed to reply.

Even rival trainers believe Caesar has been treated unfairly, perhaps even set up. The general attitude is that everyone knows cocaine can be easily swabbed, even if it is just rubbed in with DMSO. After the Lukas affair, who wouldn't know? Veteran veterinary practitioner Bart Baker told me, "I've known Caesar for many years, and he wouldn't do anything that stupid."

Caesar's wife, Sherry, says the drugging allegation has aged Caesar 10 years. He has looked into the cost of testing all his own runners before they race, so he can withdraw them if they have been contaminated in some way, but the cost is $30 dollars each for just the cocaine test, let alone other drugs.

The only possible benefit Caesar can see from this catastrophe would be an investigation of the steward situation. At Thoroughbred tracks, the stewards are rotated around the tracks, to avoid relationships between stewards and trainers, be they enmity or cordiality. There are not enough Quarter Horse tracks operating in California to do this. Apparently when it was proposed to rotate the stewards of the Quarter Horse circuit with the Thoroughbred stewards, the reply was that the Thoroughbred tracks would be happy to send in their stewards, but they didn't want to use the Quarter Horse ones. Caesar believes that reflects the industry opinion of the stewards he has to deal with.

Caesar has been approached by many well-wishers. The lawyer thinks the whole business is so unjust he is representing Caesar without charge. Caesar said Lloyd Arnold, the harness racing man who bought the Los Alamitos track, has also declared himself in Caesar's corner. But no matter what the outcome, Caesar's reputation will suffer. It is a no-win situation and he knows it.

Veterinarian Bart Baker has been around the racing game for many decades and he had one observation that may be heartening for Caesar. Bart said, "The good trainers survive these things. Their owners - and everyone around them - they know what sort of person they are."

Los Angeles smog: look carefully and you will see the tall buildings of the city center rising out of the 'mist'.

Tommy 'TJ' Smith leads in his 1988 Golden Slipper winner Star Watch at the Rosehill racecourse. TJ has won this race six times, a trainers record.

TOMMY SMITH

Starting with one horse, which took two years to win its first race, Tommy Smith was not an obvious candidate for success. Many people remember Tommy when he started training. They were appalled by his taste in clothes. He was called a 'lair' (Aussie slang for a loudly dressed layabout) and a 'mug trainer'. Who, they wondered, would be silly enough to give him a horse? How would he make a living?

Tommy Smith, also known as 'TJ', has confounded them all. From a rural childhood in the grinding poverty of the Great Depression, he left home at 13 and has risen by his own efforts to dominate the Sydney racing scene for nearly 40 years. So great was his domination that at one time the controlling body tried to introduce rules to limit him to two entries per race. TJ's flair for getting publicity has carried his name well beyond the racetrack and he has been a living legend in Australia for as long as I can remember. He is almost as well known as the Prime Minister.

Based in Sydney, where the racing is world class in quality and competitiveness, *TJ won the Sydney trainers' premiership for 33 consecutive years.* There was a saying in colonial times: 'It's Sydney or the bush.' It is still true. If you make it in the bush you head off to prove yourself in Sydney. So to stay on top for that long in Sydney, with so many ambitious rivals and challengers, to not have at least one bad year or one year when some contender beat him with an exceptional bunch of horses, TJ Smith had to have some extraordinary talents.

When he eventually lost the training title to Brian Mayfield-Smith in 1985/86, it was seen as the end of an era. Mayfield-Smith had the backing of a megamoney consortium that included international owner Robert Sangster. It would be impossible to beat that kind of money - besides - everyone has to

Tommy Smith, the leading trainer in metropolitan Sydney for 33 consecutive years, a record likely to stand forever.

get old sometime and TJ was somewhere around 70 years old. But the wily TJ came back with a new strategy - a public company and $12 million to spend on yearlings - and took out training title number 34 in 1988/89.

TJ Smith is one of the most successful racehorse trainers that ever lived.

What made TJ Smith great?
Millions of gallons of beer have flowed over this subject, one of the most discussed topics in Australian racing history. Was it the technological advances of his veterinarian Percy Sykes? TJ had already won three premierships before he worked with Percy. Was it some inborn talent for choosing the best horses in the yearling sales? Well there had to be more to it than that because when TJ took over a horse it was reckoned to improve by many lengths. Could it be some breakthrough - something he figured out for himself? Did he break out of the pattern of feeding and training that had been passed from one generation of trainers to another? If it was feeding and training, why have so few of the people who worked for him gone on to any noteworthy level of achievement as trainers? If his ex-employees could imitate his methods but not get his results, was it, as many Australian racegoers firmly believe, the golden needle, some injection that makes his horses go faster?

2. What start in life did Tommy have?
TJ's early years have been a favorite source of stories for many racing writers. One, Bert Lillye, now retired, took the trouble to drive around TJ's childhood stamping grounds and talk to those who had known him. In addition, TJ has always been willing to entertain his owners at his Sunday parties with tales of his early years. So there are many stories about TJ's early days.

TJ has come a long way from his days as a stableboy and trackrider. Here TJ enjoys a lively conversation with the Australian Prime Minister, The Honourable R.J. (Bob) Hawke. At least since the time of Sir Robert Menzies, it has been obligatory for Australian Prime Ministers to be seen at major sporting events. Bob Hawke has excelled in attendance at such events, but it is not only for show: he enjoys himself a great deal at the races.

I found, as one of TJ's closest friends told me I would, that the stories varied somewhat, but the overwhelming impression is of a young boy who refused to be beaten by his harsh circumstances.

TJ was born in a town towards the Snowy Mountains called Jembaicumbene, but as his older sister Gladys fondly tells everyone, he always said he was born in Jindabyne because it was easier to spell. What school child wouldn't want to avoid spelling J-e-m-b-a-i-c-u-m-b-e-n-e?

If there is a little confusion about his birthplace, there is wholesale confusion about his age. TJ Smith makes a bigger secret of his age than any woman I know. Those close to him, including his relatives, either do not know, claim not to know, or admit they know but won't disclose when he was born for fear of incurring his displeasure. Gladys told me he is very sensitive about his age, and she wasn't going to give any clues let alone the year. Tommy's friend Percy Sykes recalled some journalist referring to TJ as the 'veteran' trainer. "Tommy went berserk."

Many articles over the years have given an age for Tommy. From that age and the date of the story, it should be possible to arrive at an approximate year of birth. The day is agreed (September 3rd), but there is a range of possible years from 1913 to 1921, from the articles I have seen. In 1990 Tommy could be anywhere from 69 to 77 years old! Most point to 1916 or 1918.

Former Tatts chairman Tony McSweeney who has had a few classic winners trained by TJ, says he was born the same year as TJ and he was 72 in April 1988. If this is true, TJ would have been born in September 1916, and be 74 in 1990.

TJ was the second of seven children, of which five were boys. The oldest was Gladys. Tommy's father died when TJ was 16, about 1932 or 1934, and I was told that Gladys raised the last kids after their mother died in 1936. After Gladys and Thomas John (hence TJ) came Cecil; then Richard (Dick), with whom Tommy was very close; sister Jessie; Ernest Joseph (Ernie), now his foreman; and last was brother Pat.

Cecil and Pat became businessmen. Gladys still lived in Goolgowi, the tiny town in which Tommy spent most of his first years, when I spoke to her in 1987. Goolgowi is a long 300 miles (500km) straight inland from Sydney, a few hundred people far out on the plains that start behind the coastal mountain range. The plains are dry, west Texas-flat, and a pinky brown that eventually blends into the flat redness that spreads interminably across the dead center. There are rivers on the plains, the Lachlan River to the north, and the Murrumbidgee River to the south, but they are there because of rainfall in the great range hundreds of miles away. Neither river gets closer to Goolgowi than 40 miles.

The area in which Tommy's parents settled was being opened up for stock grazing and later for grain growing. Not until many years later would the water problem be solved by river dams and irrigation schemes that exploited the ankle-high horizon, the very same flatness that allowed water to flow along channels for miles and miles. Water would turn these plains into prime agricultural land, a region that became known as the Riverina.

Tommy grew up there in the pioneer era, an era of candles and kerosene lamps. It's hard to imagine what drew people out there in those days, but it could only have been a hunger for land when all the land further in was taken. Neil and May Smith and their small children started in tents. The first houses were made of split timber, the holes plugged with clay. Beds were bags or sacks split down the sides and slung as a hammock. Floors were bare earth, interior walls were sacks, split and sewn together, perhaps painted with lime or plaster. Roofing was crudely split timber shingles. Then came mill-sawn timber and corrugated iron (Corrugated iron has long been a hallmark of rural Australian dwellings.) Eventually there were 'real homes', a school and a Catholic Church. Living was primitive and improved only very slowly.

2.1 How much help were his parents?
TJ's father was a jack of many trades. He was a butcher, a teamster, and a road-maker. He at one time had a mail run. Tommy's father was a man who tried many things, but always seemed to be struggling.

"Tommy, tell me about your parents."

"We were only battling people, we had all sorts of businesses. Mostly we had horse teams. We were wool carters, tank sinkers, putting dams in for people. It was very dry out there, water was the big problem."

"Was your mother much of an influence on your life?"

"No, not very much. She was flat-out rearing the kids. There were seven of us."

2.2 Was Tommy's family in racing or horses?

Both. TJ's father kept teams of horses for his cartage, road work and bore sinking businesses. Tommy remembers looking after about 80 at one stage. His father was a great teamster and horseman who broke in all the horses himself. Later he raced horses at meetings around the little country towns. Tommy's father was breaking brumbies (wild horses) and, so the story goes, enough of a rodeo buckjumper to be selected to represent Australia at the Calgary Stampede in Canada. But he couldn't raise enough money to go to Canada.

2.3 How far did Tommy go at school?

"Did you have much schooling?"

"No, not a lot, I was taught to work."

Little Tommy was working so hard that school was somewhere to catch up on sleep. The teacher was tired of caning him, and Tommy was tired of being caned. Gladys says one day Tom was called out the front for another whallop, but jumped out the window instead. That was his last day of school!

While he didn't get much formal education, Tommy developed street smarts from an early age. He showed drive and stamina. He was willing to do almost anything for money, small money, because cash was desperately short in the little bush town. Tommy was known as the town 'runner'. He ran bets for the local bookmaker, messages, deliveries. He also, as he got older, cut scrub, carted water and significantly, he broke in bush brumbies. He even stayed up late to put rabbit skins on the night train for trappers - for a fee. No wonder he fell asleep at his school desk.

2.4 What were Tommy's early ambitions?

"I always wanted to be a jockey. We had a few old race-horses or two about the place. Dad always took one or two horses to meetings out there in those depression times."

3. How did Tommy get his training skills?

3.1 Any early experience with horses?

In a battling family during tough times, there was no money to pay hired hands, so from a very early age, TJ, the oldest son, had to help his father Neil with the horses in the cartage teams. TJ sometimes delivered meat or the mail for his father,

on horseback. He also cracked the whip over teams of bullocks. One of his jobs was to collect water twice a week from a nearby rail head. Perhaps most important of all, he helped with his father's racehorses.

"Going to the racemeetings, my job was to lead the racehorses behind a buggy, a wagon. We were at Goolgowi which was 20 mile (32km) out of Griffith and we would go to meetings in Hillston - that was 40 mile away - and Hay - that was 70 mile away. The horses used to just trot behind. It'd take us three days to go to Hay. Going to Carrathool in the middle of summer, you'd get up early in the morning and you'd go along quietly, walk and jig-jog. Then you'd rest them through the middle of the day. You'd do that for two days. It was saltbush plains in the middle of summer. Not a very happy sort of place."

"So you were associated with racing horses from a very early age?"

"Yes, it's a good education for people, teaches you how to ride a horse, how to handle a horse."

3.2 Experience as a rider or jockey

"Did you ride your father's horses in those races?"
"Oh yes."

One of his father's horses, called Desert King, was barred from the pony tracks because it wouldn't start properly. Neil changed its name but not its starting manners. However it was so superior to the country competition it still won numerous races. TJ was winning races on this horse at 13.

TJ could see little future for himself in the environment he was in. Everyone worked hard and long but the battling barely brought comfort, let alone riches or respite. Everyone trapped rabbits, and everyone sold the skins. It was hard, harsh country; pitiless, dry, flat country, where making a living was one long relentless struggle. And no matter how hard anyone struggled, a year without rain could ruin them. One year TJ and his father had to cut scrub and haul it home for the starving stock. For someone as small in stature as TJ in a land of hard physical labor, becoming a jockey in the city, the 'big smoke,' was the obvious way out. He had little education, but a lot of experience with horses.

The big smoke he chose was Melbourne, a major city some 300 miles (500km) to the south. The first thing he needed was the train fare - one pound - which was a lot of money at that time. Whatever money he had earned to that time had usually ended up in the family kitty. (Some stories say his father was partial to a drop, and that was where the cash went.) So the next time TJ came by some money from his horse and stock trading, he kept it. When he was ready he told his family of his plans - unsure how they would take it because he was still very young, just 14 years of age. His father might very well have insisted he stay to help out - but he didn't.

TJ told Bert Lillye that he told his father he wanted to go to Melbourne to try out as a jockey. His father said that was OK but he'd have to find his own fare and keep. The one pound fare was such an obstacle to a thirteen-year-old that his father may have thought that would keep him in Goolgowi. But the resourceful TJ made three pounds selling a lunatic horse out of the local pound to a rodeo. Tommy told Bert, "Dad said, 'Lend me the money and I will give it back when we get home.' I never saw that three quid (three pounds) again. Dad got on the grog and blew the lot." After his next profitable business deal, TJ kept quiet until his mother bought the train ticket.

Then it was off to the town with the railway station to wait for the train, which came through in the small hours of the morning. TJ had been worried about his father's response. Neil would be losing his main helper. In those days many families saw children as cheap labor, had as many as health allowed, and kept them as long as possible. Because of the hard work, the long dry hours, the sweat and the pressure, father and son sometimes hadn't gotten along too well. But at the station, as the train pulled in out of the darkness, his father gave him an extra few pounds to bolster his meager reserves. It was a moment of closeness, about as close as the young TJ and his father would ever get.

The tiny TJ climbed onto the train with a few pounds to help him fend for himself in a strange city at 13 years of age. Depending on Tommy's birthdate, this could have been about 1929, just before the country plunged into the depression, or 1931, when the country was awash with unemployed. Many farmers were forced off their land and workers lost jobs. Great numbers were wandering the roads begging for any kind of work.

TJ started with "Battling" Bill McLaughlin in Mordialloc. The nick-name, TJ found, was very appropriate. McLaughlin could barely feed his staff and certainly couldn't afford wages at the time. To get some cash Tommy ran bets for a bookie. It was more experience with gambling, which would stand him in good stead later.

Tommy was not long in deciding to leave McLaughlin's. One story attributed to Tommy is that when he went up to McLaughlin's house to tell him he was leaving, he found no- one in the back of the house but there was roast chicken on the table. Tommy hadn't seen good food since he'd been there, so he took a leg and scampered.

A second version was that although McLaughlin didn't pay his workers, and expected them to go hunting for their food, he lived quite well himself. In that version, Tommy took the whole chicken for 'revenge'. Yet another version said McLaughlin went so far down the hole he had to sell his stables.

From there Tommy went to work near Mildura, then Sydney, where he worked for five shillings (50 cents) a week and keep. TJ made an impression and was offered better employment by Malcom "Mac" Sawyer, who was just establishing a stable in Sydney. He was the son of a wealthy pastoralist, Matt Sawyer, whose family property was 'Eulomo', a sheep station near Cootamundra. Young Mac was not long married, but his new wife Nancy had been snubbed by *his* parents because *her* parents owned a hotel, the Albion in Cootamundra. (This attitude will surprise many Australians who would view marrying into a hotel family as heaven on earth.) Rather than stay on the property in such unhappy circumstances, Young Mac and his wife had moved to Sydney.

Young Mac, like his father, was very taken with horse racing, and he proceeded to put together a string with the help of one of the auctioneering Inglis family. He rented stables in their Newmarket saleyards (Which Tommy hires these days for his yearling overflow).Tommy was paid 30 shillings a week (a big step up in pay), and his job with Young Mac Sawyer was to prove a vital step in his career. Tommy told Bert Lillye:

"He took me to interstate race meetings, dressed me up like a little king. I was his chauffeur and he always put me up at the best hotels." Indeed there is a photo of a very dapperly dressed 16 year-old Tommy in Bert's book *Backstage of Racing.* Tommy is a picture of confidence, showing his hesitant-looking father and youngest brother Pat around Sydney. The caption says it is 1934.

Young Mac Sawyer's trainer was Harry Darwon, and TJ lived with the Darwons. Harry Darwon became something of a second father to young Tommy. At the time however, TJ was a chauffeur, track rider and strapper, still trying to make it as a jockey. Sawyer allowed him to ride freelance for other trainers. His poor results as a jockey on the flat lead him to try his luck as a hurdle jockey. His luck wasn't good.

Failure as a jockey and a broken hip
During a schooling race at Randwick, Tommy fell and broke his hip. Tommy told racing journalist Bill Whittaker, "I spent four months in St Vincent's Hospital . . . the trainer didn't even come to see me in hospital." The injury left him barely able to get around and he went home to Goolgowi. One account said he was lame for three years. Those who knew and liked his irrepressible, cocky personality remember feeling very sorry for him. Surprisingly there was a "compo" payment of 15 shillings a week, (when his wage was 30 shillings) even in those days. Worker's compensation goes back a long way in Australia.

Anyone familiar with TJ's small size would know he didn't fail as a jockey because of excess weight. I asked TJ why he failed as a jockey.

"I had a lot of rides, but I couldn't ride. I rode over hurdles and everything, but I couldn't ride."

"What do you mean you couldn't ride?"

"Well we used to do a lot of show riding."

The homestead on the sheepstation called 'Eulomo', where the young TJ first learned how to train racehorses. Because of the very high ceilings and wide verandahs, put in for summer cooling, the true size of the building is not apparent. The property is near Cootamundra, New South Wales.

"Does it give you the wrong riding seat or something?"

"Yes. Oh yes. It's a different style altogether to being a jockey. In those little shows in those parts, Hay, Hillston, it was pretty rough in those days. I could ride nearly any kind of horse. If it was a rough horse I could do anything with it, but when it came to being a jockey, something was lacking. Not for want of trying, but I just failed."

One account said Tommy rode in about 30 races, another that he won about 25 races as a jock, another said he didn't win any.

3.3 Why did TJ become a trainer?

Although his dream of becoming a jockey was slipping away, TJ was in no rush to become a trainer instead.

"I never dreamt of being a racehorse trainer. I didn't want to be a trainer."

"What did you have against being a racehorse trainer?"

"Well everyone around the place that was in racing was broke. It was such a hard game, being a trainer, I thought."

"So what turned you in the direction of training?"

"I went up the country, to Cootamundra. Sawyers up there,

he said, 'I'll give you the rides on the horses if you come up and train them for me.' He was very sick at the time. I thought, 'well this'll be a way to get a few rides.' So I went up there."

Life at 'Eulomo' with Matt Sawyer

The homestead building at 'Eulomo' is a veritable weatherboard castle, constructed in 1903. It was built in front of 'Ironbung Run', the original pioneer's homestead. 'Eulomo' is typical of the size and style of the homes of wealthy pastoralists of the time. It is about 100 feet (30m) long by 100 feet wide. At the back there is the frame of what was once a walk-in meatsafe. Seven brick chimneys indicate how many of the rooms had fireplaces. Back when Tommy worked there, the worker's huts and staff numbers created a village atmosphere. Family ownership gave it a somewhat feudal touch. The main source of wealth was sheep farming. One book entry in 1940 was a payment of 30 pounds 4 shillings and tuppence for eight tons of sheep salt! At the time of Tommy's arrival, old Mrs Sawyer, Matt's mother, was chronically ill and for many years two nursing sisters lived on the property to take care of her. In 1987, one of the staff from those days still lived nearby.

Kitty Lloyd nee Owens remembers Tommy

Kitty Owens, 73 years old, and Mrs Lloyd when I met her in 1987, still remembered the day TJ arrived at 'Eulomo'. Her father worked for Matt Sawyer for 50 years and she went to work there as a housemaid after leaving school at 16.

"This day the new boy was coming, I'll never forget it. The mail train from Sydney came in about twenty past seven in the morning. Bill Oddy, the groom -everyone was waiting; and poor little Tommy arrived. There was this little fat fellow. We used to carry everything in four gallon kerosene tins and he couldn't even carry one off the ground, he used to drag it along. He was about 16. We said he'd need jam tins on his heels to carry the tins around. He was short and chubby. Now he's a millionaire."

"He was really good fun to work with. Tommy wasn't above sticking a bag of flour over your bedroom door. In those days, to wait on the Sawyer's table, you had to wear a black dress with a bit of white lace around the collar. Mrs Sawyer was state president of the Country Womens' Association, so you'd go to your mirror to check you didn't have any dandruff or anything. You'd be rushing around getting ready and you'd push the door open, and it'd be nothing for a bag of flour or tin of water to fall on you. Tommy was in it with Jenny and April, two cousins on the place. He was very likable. We used to do some terrible things to him."

Tommy lived in the single men's quarters. There was a big roundyard and a big harness shed. There were eight stables, but according to the people he trained up to 12 horses.

Kitty continued: "Our family lived a short distance from 'the house' (Eulomo), and Tommy being a Catholic he came up to the church every Sunday. He'd tie the horse up in Dad's cow yard and he'd come down and say, 'Well I'm going to Mass now Jimmy. I'll say one for you. Give us two shillings for the plate.' Dad used to give him two shillings every Sunday for the plate."

"The woman over the road had the shop where you'd get the Sunday papers and she was a fussy old girl. Tommy would come back here from Mass and he'd untie the horse, ride it across the road and tie it up in front of the shop. The horse used to mess there and the poor old lady, it'd get her goat (annoy her). Tommy used to say, 'You don't want to go crook, he's been to church this morning.' He never missed church. He was a dedicated Catholic."

"Tommy's job was watering and feeding and grooming the horses. Tommy only looked after the horses. Bill Oddy, a stationhand, helped with the horses when necessary. There was a training track there. They used to go round and round so many times in the morning, and so many times in the afternoon. Young Mac Sawyer (who was mostly away in Sydney) was the one that was really in charge of Tommy. The stationhands and Tommy had their own dining room and they could sit and read there. They had nothing to do with 'the house'."

"Matt Sawyer was the horse trainer but he let his son Mac Sawyer take over and Young Mac became very big in Sydney. Down here at 'Eulomo' he went to the races about once a week. Young Mac had a chauffeur named McDonnell. He used to drive wherever the races were - Wagga, Albury, but not Sydney. The horses went by motor lorry."

"Tommy was here for - oh - five years. He did have a girl-friend here and we thought she would 'bump him off' but he got another one and then in the end neither of them got him."

"Did you think he'd be successful?"

"No. I thought he was a skite. He knew too much about horses. You couldn't argue the point or talk back to him because he used to talk over you all the time. We used to sling off at him, but you couldn't win an argument with him. He'd never give in."

"Did he spend his wages or save them?"

"He'd save them. He didn't go anywhere to spend it. If there was a dance on he'd ride one of the boundary riding horses up to the dance. He didn't go out or muck up much. When Sawyers had guests - often staying over night - Tommy wouldn't mind helping - drying up dishes - he was not afraid of work. He was really good. He used to wear a blue shirt and a big bow tie. He was very neat - spotlessly clean."

Kitty still lived near 'Eulomo' and said she'd like to meet Tommy one day to see if he'd recognize her, to see if he'd talk to her.

3.4 Acquiring his training skills

A taste of training in the bush

Young Mac Sawyer had an old retired Sydney-winning mare named Mafoota. TJ became interested in the mare when he rode her and was impressed by her turn of speed. He persuaded Mr Sawyer to let him train and race the mare. She won at her 3rd start in December 1937. The mare was aged 7yrs and TJ 19, said the report. She went on to win 16 races upto age 10. His successes with Mafoota convinced him that he could make a living as a trainer.

"I became the leading country trainer - in the Riverina - for a couple of seasons, but they were racing in Young Mac Sawyer's name. Mac Sawyer held the license."

3.4-1 Did he work with a top trainer?

Tommy was employed by Young Mac Sawyer and Harry Darwon while in Sydney, and then worked under the direction of Matt and Young Mac Sawyer at 'Eulomo'. This situation was really the making of **trainer** TJ Smith. Matt Sawyer had been known as 'the King of the Country Cups.' (On the walls at 'Eulomo' in 1987 there was still a black and white photo of 'Toohey' winning the 1928 Albury Cup.) Young Mac was up to his eyeballs in the Sydney racing scene and was in frequent

contact with Tommy at the property. Tommy had a sizable string of quality horses to train and race around the country tracks. Supervised by Matt and Young Mac, he was able to learn, to win some big races on the local scene and to realize he had a talent for training.

"I changed. I got a bit of a feeling for it," said Tommy

3.4-2 Did he watch other trainers?
At the time he started training, TJ did not have any opportunity to watch other trainers at 'Eulomo' but had seen the approaches of others when he was an aspiring jockey. At that time however he didn't intend becoming a trainer and may not have paid enough attention.

Later TJ would become a traveler, and a devout watcher of trainers. He has probably watched more trainers in action than anyone alive.

3.4-3 Did he try published workouts?
I doubt if there were any books available then, although work times were published in newspapers.

3.4-4 Asking questions, reading, seminars
In TJ's early days there were questions, but not much reading. I suspect seminars on training would have been unknown then. Nowadays, he told me, he particularly likes to read about old-time horse racing.

3.4-5 Experiments and experience
TJ was at first a product of the Sawyers and the hands on experience he got at 'Eulomo'. TJ had an excellent experimental experience at 'Eulomo', a mix of instruction and minimal supervision that would have made him think before he had been too much indoctrinated into any particular "this is how it's done" approach.

4. Starting out on his own

4.1 How he got his first horses
TJ got his first horses by buying them. One report gave details of TJ's earliest racehorse trading. When he was 20 he won a few pounds and for 40 guineas he bought a gelding called Sleepwalker, his first horse. He leased Sleepwalker to two owners who gave it to a trainer to train. It did not win a race. It was a hurdler which broke down.

The second horse he bought was Bragger. He trained Bragger himself, and Bragger gave Tommy his early breaks.

4.2 How he got his first owners
TJ had to buy his early horses because no-one was going to give him any to train. TJ, as remembered by some who saw him at the racetrack in the early days, and who passed on their recollections to racing journalists, speak of a small, boastful fellow with the most awful taste in clothes. He was described as a 'lair', Australian slang from those days for someone who dresses loudly in the latest, often far-out fashion, and who behaves ostentatiously. The term has an overtone of the layabout and never-do-well. They crop up in every generation, to be adored by the daughters of disapproving parents but eventually, like Tommy, they mostly make good citizens. At the time however, it all contributed to Tommy's difficulties in attracting clients. In their recollections, it was unlikely that TJ would ever be given one horse, let alone a string of them. Clients were some way off.

The real start - Bragger
One of the quality horses the Sawyers had at 'Eulomo', intended for their stables, was a horse by Windbag, a top sire of the day. The horse ended up leaving with the stableboy.

"How did they come to give you Bragger?"

"He was on the list to be shot. I got him because they couldn't handle him. He was running around out in the hills there. So I went out and got him."

Not many people looking at the diminutive TJ would think of him as a rough tough cowboy, but he had broken in brumbies (wild horses) as a boy and his father was a buckjumper. Tiny Tommy was probably able to do the real thing as well as any macho cowboy. He chased the renegade through the hills, lassoed him and choked him down.

"I started to train him and I found out he could run."

"They hadn't been able to do enough with him to find out if he could gallop?"

"No one could ride him, he used to throw them. He was down to be shot. They shoot a lot of horses, old horses and so on down there every year, and he was down to be shot."

"So they gave him to you."

"I decided to leave them. I decided to buy Bragger. They wanted 100 pounds for him. So I thought, 'I'll give you 100 pounds' - that's a service fee -because he was by Windbag."

Where would TJ get 100 pounds you might ask. One magazine story said Tommy won 50 pounds on greyhound races, then bet his bank on Fearless in the Wagga Wagga Gold Cup in May 1941, and ended up with 500 pounds. The win, it said, enabled enabled TJ to pay 200 pounds for Bragger. (By one account TJ prepared Fearless for that Cup and according to an aging photo on the wall at 'Eulomo', Fearless won in the then Australian record time of 2 min. 2 sec.)

So Tommy left 'Eulomo' and set off for Sydney with the renegade horse. The locals thought it was very presumptuous of Tommy to take the horse to Sydney. When he got to Sydney he bought three made-to-order suits in top-of-the-range English material. He was emulating the elegant Young Mac Sawyer, who was rarely seen out of a suit, and was sometimes known as 'Immaculate Mac'. Tommy registered the horse as Bragger, not only because the sire was Windbag but, 'because I was always bragging about him.'

A permit to train

In 1941 Tommy took out his permit to train with the Australian Jockey Club, the controlling body in New South Wales. TJ did not start at Randwick. That, according to Tommy was a very closed shop. He trained at the former pony racetrack at Kensington. It was only across the road from Randwick geographically speaking, but socially speaking it was the other side of the tracks.

Starting out, Tom was joined by his brother Dick as his strapper. TJ rented a single box for five shillings a week in a block that was across the road from the stables he would later buy and and rename Tulloch Lodge. At the outset, still flush

with money, Tommy said he and Dick shared a room at the Doncaster Hotel. But then Dick had to make his contribution to World War II. Things got tough, and TJ rented the box next to Bragger's and moved his bed in there. According to one old-timer he lived in the same stables for some time. The only domestic comfort was one of those hessian covered safes and an ice chest that required a giant block of ice every day. The blocks of ice were sold from trucks on the street. I asked the old-timer what sort of food they kept in the ice chest.

"Food? Food be buggered, that's where Tommy kept his beer."

Bragger's training didn't go well at first.

"After I'd had him about 12 months I couldn't do anything with him - well *I could* - but as soon as I put anyone strange on him he threw them off."

TJ was trying everything to get Bragger under control. He hired a Royal Show buckjumping rider, complete with buckjumping saddle, to take some of the sting out of him. It appeared to work. Bragger bucked madly but the cowboy rode him to a standstill. Nevertheless, next time Bragger ran in a barrier trial he threw the rider.

"One day Sawyer came to see him jump out in a barrier trial. I said, 'Come and have a look at this horse because I think he'll win.' Well Bragger went berserk. He bucked, he jumped, threw the saddle, jumped out of the racecourse and finished out at La Perouse (six miles away, and in those days a wasteland). Sawyer said, 'You can have that bloke, there's your hundred pounds. You can have him.' So that's how I came to get him for nothing." Sawyer probably felt embarrassed to have sold the horse, and wished he'd had it shot. "Get rid of it before it kills someone," he told Tommy. Sawyer even offered to swap the horse for any one of four he had in his own stables, one of which had run second in a race. But TJ had great faith that Bragger was something special.

"What did you do with him then?"

"I had to wait for a couple of days 'til we found him. La Perouse was all just scrub then, very few houses out there. So we brought him back."

After Bragger's spectacular antics it looked like the racing officials would ban the horse. TJ went in and pleaded with them to let the horse continue. Fortunately he was successful.

Ironically, after his two days in the 'wilds' of La Perouse, Bragger was a much more tractable horse. Horses often are like that, like kids who run away, but get lost and miss a few meals. Grateful to be back in familiar surroundings.

4.3 Financing the start

TJ certainly wasn't living off his training fees or 10% of winnings.

"Did you train any other horses?"

"No I only had the one horse."

"So you just went on with his training?"

"Yes but just when I got him going he broke down on me, after 12 months. It was two years after I got him before I raced him. Just when it looked like he might be doing something, he went in the knees and I had to turn him out."

4.3-1 Did Tommy bet?

"What were you doing to keep yourself alive?"

"Round the racetracks. I didn't work for anyone, I just lived off punting. I could live off it. I went to every race meeting - dogs, trots - everything."

"I've always believed a trainer would need to be a good punter to place his horses in the most suitable races. He has to know what his horse can do and what other horses can do. Some trainers are quite surprised when they see the bookies' assessment of their horse. So you certainly got a good grounding in punting."

"Yes I knew the form. I used to go to the track every morning and study the horses. I had a pretty good idea of what could win and what couldn't win. I always had a quick eye for a horse. I only had to see a horse once and I would know him."

Tommy's wife Valerie agreed with that: "He'd pick out a horse anywhere."

While he was out watching everyone else's horses work to pick winners he was also watching how other trainers worked their horses.

"When I started training Bragger I didn't know what I was doing."

He watched dozens of trainers closely, but homed in on Dan Lewis, winner of five Sydney cups and one Melbourne Cup (Foxzami), as a conditioner of stayers, and Fred Cush as a trainer of young horses. Tommy imitated their methods.

"Danny Lewis was the best. He was a very hard trainer." He also watched Jack Holt, a top Melbourne trainer whenever he was in Sydney. Known as 'The Wizard of Mordialloc,' Holt was 14 times premier trainer and twice runner-up in Victoria, in the years 1916 - 32.

Bragger made his first official start at Canterbury on January 31st 1942, by which time he was a five-year-old gelding.

"The first time he ran, he ran last to Billy-Oh. I thought he would nearly win and he ran last. The old bugger bucked for nearly a furlong so I thought, 'dammit he's got a chance.' I thought I'd put him in at Randwick."

One week later Bragger ran at Randwick.

"He was 100 to 1 and he got beat by a head."

""Did you have a bet?""

"I had 10 pounds straight out on him at 200 to 1. I don't bet each way. Very seldom. He got beat a head on the line, run off the track, right on the outside fence."

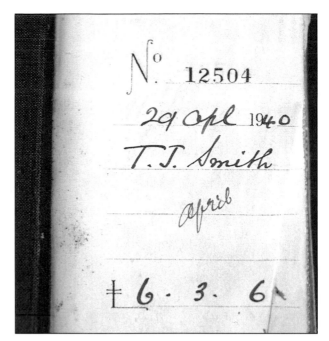

One of the monthly wage entries for TJ in the 'Eulomo' cheque butts, from the year before he left with Bragger for Sydney.

Two weeks later the dogged TJ had raked up another 80 pounds, and he and Bragger were on the train to the races at Newcastle. To conserve money for his betting coup, he'd avoided going anywhere and lived on Sao biscuits (crackers). Bragger ran third at Newcastle. TJ had again bet the lot straight out, and some stories say he had to borrow to get back home. He told Bert Lillye that he got an advance against the two pounds for third place, then plunged it on a horse after he overheard the leading trainer of the day tell an owner his horse had lengths on the rest. TJ said it won, he took Bragger home, then went to a two-up game and ended the night with 40 quid.

TJ rode Bragger in a barrier trial and discovered the horse detested running on the inside of others. Given plenty of room his performance improved dramatically.

Bragger finally broke through to win a Maiden Welter on March 14th 1942 at Rosehill. Jack Thompson, one of the top jockeys of the day, was on board. Bragger went on to win four straight. The fourth win was the Diggers' Cup at Wagga not far from 'Eulomo'. This was apparently to 'rub it in' back in the area he and Bragger had come from, to shove his success under the noses of his critics there, and to show off to someone he wanted to impress.

Did he bet on horses - yes, yes, yes

TJ bet heavily on these races, and Bragger's wins put unbelievable money into his hands. Years later he told racing writer

Bert Lillye that at the end of the four straight wins he had 75,000 pounds, saying that he did not know there was that much money in the world.

This must have required all-up straight-out betting (Putting ALL the winnings from one race on the next, and putting it on to win.) to achieve such a total. Perhaps a bit out for food and reserves. Presuming a first win with 100 pounds at 25/1, he would have 2,500 pounds. The second win at say 6/1 gives him 15,000. After two wins he'd be lucky to get 3/1, which would give him 45,000. I doubt he'd have found any bookie at Wagga who would lay him to pay out 75,000, so the heavy betting would have been on the first three races. An average man's wage was under 10 pound a week then, so it would be the equivalent of winning well over $A1.5 million in 1990, or $US1.2m.

TJ and his wife Valerie put it to me this way:

TJ: "He won four straight and that kicked us off."

Valerie: "That was the first rung of the ladder wasn't it."

TJ: "Yes that was the start."

TJ was unused to having much money, and he did not know much about banks, so he kept it hidden under his bed in the stable!

4.3-2 Did TJ borrow money?

Probably only to get home now and again. He certainly wouldn't have needed to borrow for a while after Bragger's four wins. While he did win a massive amount of money, and it would have meant financial security to the average person, it might have been diminished or even depleted quite rapidly in the hands of an all-up straight-out gambler.

4.4 Steady rise or sudden breakthrough?

Bragger had provided the first major breakthrough, and it was sudden -sudden wealth really. There was also a certain amount of fame because people knew the horse was unmanagable in anyone else's hands.

"Then Bragger broke down again, kept breaking down all the time. They didn't have the things they have nowadays. In those days they used to fire them with a hot iron - oh, cruel sort of thing. They'd have to be out for 8 or 9 months before you could possibly do anything with them."

Although he was now out in the paddock, Bragger had done the job TJ had hoped he would when he took the horse from 'Eulomo'. The four wins brought money and a small number of clients. He also got Tommy into Randwick in the middle of 1942. When the war forced the closure of Kensington pony track, only a few of the trainers were allowed into Randwick. Bragger's wins enabled TJ to be one of them, and he was elevated to a Number 2 license at that time.

Sometime earlier he had seen a filly he liked passed in at the sales at 75 guineas. He had approached the sellers, Widden stud, and leased her. Named Ajixa, she won the Gimcrack

Stakes to give Tommy his first win at Randwick in October 1942. He said he won a packet betting on her as well.

Training at Randwick, Tommy was at first treated as a bit of a joke. There were only 16 trainers allowed to train on the main work tracks. Consequently they all knew each other very well, and they all knew who was new. Tommy was told by one of them, Bayly Payten, to wear a tie at trackwork. He was also told to contribute a bottle of whisky or rum to an unofficial bar the trainers had set up, and from which they watched their horses work. TJ contributed the bottle but declined to join them at the bar.

Later Tommy shifted his viewing position to the middle of the track. From a mound there he could see horses clearly on any part of the track and his horses could be brought to him straight after their fastwork. It was also the best place to accurately clock horses working from any furlong post on the track.

(Eventually, as other trainers and clockers for the papers joined TJ out in the middle, the AJC put a transportable shed there. In 1988 they erected an elegant, permanent, two story viewing structure, with glass all round and heating in winter. It ought to be properly dedicated and called "TJ's Tower.")

TJ bought one yearling in 1942. In 1943 it won at it's 5th start and Bragger also came back into the fray. In the 1943/44 season TJ was doing so well that he was granted a Number 1 license - over older trainers. (The article said he was 23 or 24, but he was more likely 27 or 28) 1945 was a poor year, but Bragger, aged 9, won many races including some big ones, then went on to win at 10. Bragger had to be destroyed after a float (van) fire. They got the other horses out but Bragger became stuck across a partition, and was badly burnt. TJ was joined by a horse lover named Jim Benrodt and a doctor, in a long fight to save Bragger's life. They applied ointments, salves and potions, but as time passed Bragger's suffering was too great to go on and the iron horse was put down. Tommy wept at the loss of the horse he called "Dadda." Bragger's record was 58 starts for 13 wins and 25 places. He bled many many times and under today's rules in Australia would have been banned very early in his career.

TJ's brother Ernie Smith had this to say about Bragger's wins:

"When Bragger won he usually won at 20/1. When he won a big handicap at Newcastle - Athol Mulley rode him - he was 20/1. He broke a track record. Bragger used to do those sort of things. He always put 3 and 4 races together - such a great horse. In those days if you had 2 or 3 pounds to put on him you always got a good dividend back and it lasted a long while."

TJ's early difficulties getting owners

"In the 1940s you were training for yourself?"

"Well the trouble those days was they reckoned I was too young to do any good. You see in those days they reckoned you couldn't get a breakthrough, without you'd been a head man for someone - like the English idea - you had to be a foreman first. Then a trainer had to die or something before you could get a go on." (Fred Kersley would sympathize.)

"But I started with no-one, and everyone was saying, 'What does he know? He doesn't know anything! He's never worked for anyone, he's never been a foreman.' And that's how it was. My way of living was different to everybody else's too. You see in those days I was a nightclub fella, and I came out with all these new suits and things and they couldn't tolerate it because I was dealing with a lot of people. It's different today."

"What did most of them wear then?"

"Plain dress."

"They'd have reckoned you were flashy."

"Oh yes. I came out with all the modern ideas. If a movie star came out with something on, I'd have it on. (TJ popularised a different type of hat -wider brimmed - that is now very common) I changed it around. I thought if they want to talk about me well bugger them. And then in those days everyone was so tight-lipped. You wouldn't say a word to anyone. So when I got hold of a sure horse I told everyone. I said, 'I think my horse can win."

"You preceded Cassius Clay!"

"Yes. I'd say they had a pretty good chance of winning and they used to win too. I went, in three years, from a permit man to a Number 1 trainer. Never been heard of."

"You started with an owner-trainer permit."

"Yes, then they granted me a number two, and that allowed me to have an apprentice and I only had 7 or 8 horses. When I applied for the Number one, 17 people applied for it including the Chairman's trainer - they only granted one and I got it."

"So they were good to you - or you deserved it?"

"Well you see I ran third in the premiership the second year I was training -with no horses. The third year I was second. The fourth year, after I got my number one, I won the premiership. I *won* the premiership with 13 horses."

Can you remember some breakthroughs?

"Before I met Percy (his vet after about 1956), I went away to America. I went around the world. I said to Valerie, 'This is not a holiday. I'm going to concentrate on these trainers.' We went from here to Singapore, where the racing was very limited, then we went to Italy - racing was down. Then we went to France, and that was when I started realizing it was chalk and cheese between the training of horses."

"There was a chap there training for Boussac, (a major French owner and breeder) and the horse was in the Ascot Gold Cup. He galloped him two miles on the Thursday morning before the Cup. He came out in England and he bolted in and

I said, 'Well there's a case in point."

"Then I got to England and I was watching the trainers. I was quite a while at Newmarket, then I went to New York and the training there was altogether different. This was something - just what I wanted to see - in America they train just as they want them - which is how I think horses should be trained. So I got in with a couple of the top trainers there and I was there quite a while and I could see their way of training. It suited me, but I just cut in between English and American ideas - I didn't really go to extremes because in America they pull the whip on the horses. Every morning when they say, 'breeze 'em' they really gallop them so I just cut in between them - I didn't go over the (top). I just came back and that's when I really got firing."

"What year did you go overseas?"

"1946."

"You would have been ahead of your time in having a look at what so many other people did."

"Yes. Nobody ever thought of it."

"Did you look in the feed bins?"

"I used to get there and watch them feed and everything. But no-one from here ever thought of it. If they went away they just went away for a holiday. But I thought I'll just go away and concentrate on trainers, on training horses."

"It was amazing to see the difference in the feeding from America to England and France. There was an old trainer in America, about 80, called 'Sunny Jim' Fitzsimmons - everyone called him "Fitz". He was a genius. He was telling me that when the prohibition (on racing) came in New York, the Americans shifted over to France. The Americans scooped the pool, they won everything, won all the races. Old Fitz was a marvelous trainer. He'd won every classic race in America."

"He went from America to France and beat them because of superior feeding?"

"Yes."

I asked Alec Head about it and he remembered TJ's visit in 1946. He confirmed the story of the domination by the Americans when they moved to France. They fed a lot more grain.

Who was James E. 'Sunny Jim' Fitzsimmons?

He was born in 1874, retired in 1963 and died in 1966 aged 91, so he'd have been around 72 when Tommy first started his friendship with him. 'Mr Fitz' had won TWO Triple Crowns, an astounding feat. The first was in 1930 with Gallant Fox, the second with Omaha in 1935. In addition he had won the Kentucky Derby in 1939 with Johnstown. By the end of his life he had won the Preakness 4 times and the Belmont 6 times. Nashua and Bold Ruler were among many great horses he trained. He won the better known stakes races of New York many times each and his stakes total was 470, from over 2,275 race wins.

He and Tommy would have had a bit in common. 'Mr Fitz' was from farmer stock and broke into racing as a jockey, although he was a bit more successful than Tommy, riding for 16 years and for some good stables before his increasing weight forced him to try training. He scratched and scraped around the 'outlaw' tracks for many years before being employed by a wealthy New York stable in 1901. That was his big start.

In 1911 however, racing was banned in New York. 'Mr Fitz' was forced to race in Canada and Maryland before racing resumed in 1912. Presumably this was the period when some American trainers shifted to France and trained there. I could find no indication that 'Mr Fitz' himself trained in France.

'Mr Fitz' was considered a tough trainer. He demanded a lot from his horses in their morning workouts. The survivors were champions. Sports Illustrated of 1955 gave his preparation of Nashua for his match race with Swaps. Swaps beat Nashua in the Kentucky Derby, but a challenge to a rematch was accepted. The works were over thick heavy mud and were described by 'Mr Fitz' as light because Nashua had run in the Arlington Classic on July 16 and was already seasoned.

Aug 4	3/4 mile	(6f or 1200m)	in 1:17 2/5
Aug 6	7/8 mile	(7f or 1400m)	in 1:37
Aug 9	3/4 mile	(6f or 1200m)	in 1:15
Aug 12	7/8 mile	(7f or 1400m)	in 1:34 4/5
Aug 15	easy 1⅛ mile	(9f or 1800m)	in 2:20 2/5
Aug 24	1¼ mile	(10f or 2000m)	in 2:05

This was the full race distance. Shipped that day from Saratoga to Arlington.

| Aug 28 | Eased up mile | (8f or 1600m) | in 1:39 |

Aug 31 Match raced Swaps 1¼ mile and won

The other trainer to make a big impression on Tommy was Willie Head Junior. The Head racing dynasty in France began when Willie Head Senior and some other English trainers shifted across the Channel in the middle of the 1800s. Willie Head Jr was born in 1889, and like his father was a successful rider before becoming a successful trainer. He married the daughter of another Englishman who had trained successfully in Europe. Willie Head Jr was one of the most distinguished trainers in French racing history, eventually becoming known as 'The first gentleman of the French turf'.

"The present day Alec Head - I got to know his father well over in France -he was telling me, 'We had to change our ideas because they used to feed their horses hard and they used to give them hay which we never used to give but we had to change to compete."

"And old man Head learnt from the French then?"
"Yes."

"What did they feed if they didn't feed hay?"
"Oh I don't know - bit of lucerne or something over there.

They don't give them oaten hay in England and those places - you won't see oaten hay over there."

4.4-1 How long until first progress?
TJ didn't spend a lot of time going nowhere. The nearest would have been his two year spell trying to get Bragger to the track. As a major career goal recedes into impossibility, some people switch careers with almost no effect on their self esteem, while others see themselves as a failure. TJ's eternal optimism was not easily squashed. He switched from hoping to become a jockey, to training, and set his goals straight away - become leading trainer, train a Derby winner. Even when Bragger seemed a hopeless case, TJ was doing well from gambling, which kept bread on the table.

"Times have changed but back then if you did something and you were my age (about 25 - 35) it was a problem. My biggest problem was where to get horses, because everyone was saying I was so successful because I was doing this and doing that. And old people, trainers, wouldn't change. You see in those days if you took a horse off a trainer it would be like committing a crime, because they didn't shift horses around. But when I did get a horse off someone I'd improve it out of sight. And people would say he's doing this, doing that."

"Yes I can remember many stories as to what you were supposed to be doing to them. I think if a rumor had gone out that you were hitting them over the head with a hammer every-night then half the trainers in Australia would have tried it."

"Well that's it. They say you are doing these things but common sense I was using, and I was just lucky enough to be able to see the future quicker than someone else that I was competing against."

"I think the inertia of the other trainers must have been a great help to you - the way they wouldn't change."

"Oh yes - they wouldn't change, they had to die out before there was any change. But the biggest problem was still getting the horse. I was lucky enough to be able to go the the sales and buy them and if I couldn't sell them I'd race them."

4.4-2 Did one horse provide a sudden lift?
"You were greatly improving horses you took over - you would have had a lot of owners knocking your door down wouldn't you?"

"Oh no. My best breakthrough was E.R. Williams. He was the big owner here -he owned Woolworth Stores. I went and bought a horse off him. The horse's name was Kookaburra. Kookaburra was put in the sale ring - he was the highest priced horse in the sale - he wanted 7000 pounds for him. So I rang him up and said, 'I'll give you 5000 pounds for the horse.' He said, 'No I want 7000,' so I said, 'Can I come and see you?' So I walked in and it was like walking in a royal palace - 4 or 5 guards."

"I said, 'I'll give you 5000 pounds cash straight away for him.' I said, 'You didn't get a bid for him on the 5000, because I was out there, I bid 4000 for the horse. After my bid no one else bid on the horse."

"He thought about it for a little while then he said, 'Alright I'll take the 5000 pounds."

"So I just pulled the 5000 out of my pocket and paid him. He went as white as chalk. I said, 'The day he comes out and I think he should win, you should put that 5000 on him."

"Hah!' he said, 'I only put five pound on a horse.' 'Oh that's no good' I said."

"Anyway I had the horse for about three or four months and I rang him up the day he was in and I said, 'I think Kookaburra will win today."

"Oh,' he said, 'he's got no chance, I was looking at the paper, he's 20 to 1."

"I said, 'You come out and put your five pound on."

"Kookaburra was backed from 20s down to favorite and got beat a half a head."

"It was a funny thing with the old fellow. When I was saddling up Kookaburra he was there. Anyway after the race I was walking back to the stall going crook to myself and who should be at the stall but Williams and he says, 'I want to see you Tom Smith. Tomorrow I want you to have lunch with me at Tattersall's Club.' So I went into Tattersall's Club and he said to me, 'I have horses with three trainers, three top trainers in Sydney and no one ever tells me about a horse. But I can't work it out how you come to have that horse 20 to 1 and start favorite, you said he would beat ... and he gets beat a half head. He's never got in the money while I had him."

"He said, 'I want you to go and buy the best horse in Sydney or anywhere in Australia.' And that was my kick. He was the man that packed me off to New Zealand. He said, 'I want you to go to New Zealand and buy some horses for me.' And that was how I first came to go to New Zealand."

"What year was that?"

"Oh I don't know. But that was my first breakthrough, to get a good client. So I did pretty good for him. I bought him Waterlady, Pride of Paris. I bought him a lot of good horses. Well of course as soon as I got him I got other clients." (Kookaburra was a three-year-old in William's name in March 1942, when the horse ran second to Bragger in a welter. TJ may have been impressed by a horse that could run a good second to his Bragger!)

"He was the breakthrough?"

"Because owners wouldn't come to me, but after that, everyone at the racecourse was saying, 'Oh look, Williams with Tommy Smith.' And every horse he took off other trainers and gave to me, I won for him. He was the first man with money to give me a horse."

Sudden lift or slow upward spiral?

Bragger is generally considered to have been all it took to bring TJ fame and fortune, but it would seem that his purchase of Kookaburra and the improvement of that horse in the eyes of E.R. Williams played a very important role, some time after 1942. The important stepping stones in TJ's upward spiral were Bragger, bringing publicity and money, and Williams, bringing money and social acceptability.

1949/50 TJ 3rd on the premiership table with 12 wins. McCarten had 31, Fred Cush had 19. (Another report said TJ was 2nd with 19 wins) Bragger was still winning in 1950, including a cup race.

1950/51 TJ 3rd again but with 18 wins. McCarten scored 38 wins, Frank Dalton 24.

1951/52 TJ 2nd with 26 wins. McCarten's 4th premiership in succession, with 36 wins.

1952/53 TJ 1st. TJ broke through to take the premiership, aged around 36 and just 12 years after setting off from 'Eulomo' with Bragger. One report said he won his 1st premiership with 15 horses in the stable. Two-year-old winners were a major part of his success.

Tommy would go on to break one record after another, often breaking a record he himself had set. He started by breaking Bayly Payten's record of 46 winners in a season by sending out 56 winners (54 in another report).

A factor in TJ's rise was the decline of Maurice McCarten, premier trainer in the years of TJ's blossoming. Why did he go into a decline? One explanation I heard said that Maurice McCarten used caffeine as did many of the trainers in those days and that when they brought in progressively more stringent swabbing around 1950 or 52, his results dropped off and he went into a decline.

But Neville Begg, a leading Sydney trainer who worked with McCarten for many years, says that is untrue, that McCarten's decline was mainly due to plain bad luck. He had good owners die and quite a number of his best owners retired. Neville Sellwood, McCarten's stable jockey, a man of international reputation for his riding skills, began riding in Europe and was killed in a race fall in France in November 1962. Everything just went wrong.

The person who attributed McCarten's decline to caffeine swabbing said it was most successful with overtrained horses, but McCarten's were not overtrained, far from it, according to Bill Whittaker, who was citing Tommy Smith's opinion. Furthermore, according to Bert Lillye in *The Racing Game*, swabbing was introduced in 1947. A more likely scenario is not that McCarten declined, but that TJ elbowed him aside with superior selection and training, and a flair for publicity.

McCarten trained until 1969. One account said he was runner-up to TJ for 10 straight years from 1953 to 1964. McCarten won the title four years before that. If it hadn't been for TJ, McCarten probably would have the record for consecutive titles, and a larger place on the mantlepiece of racing history.

Over the years a number of other trainers have played second fiddle to TJ, trainers who might have been household names themselves in TJ's absence. One was John (Jack) Green, who was granted a permit to train in 1947. By 1952 he was a No 1 licence trainer, a meteoric rise. Four times he was runner-up to TJ (57/8, 58/9, 64/5 65/6 Some of these years conflict with the claims made for McCarten). He was an innovator. Among his breaks with tradition, he ceased walking his horses to the track and floated them in a two-horse van which shuttled back and forth between his stables and the track. Old-timers predicted poor results but Jack Green won even more races.

He was widely respected, campaigning horses like 1958 Melbourne Cup winner Baystone; Sky High, second highest stakeswinner to Tulloch; and Skyline, winner of the 1958 Golden Slipper and AJC Derby. If TJ Smith had not been there hogging the limelight, Jack Green's personality and skill would have become much better known. He was killed in a car smash in 1972.

Jack Denham was second for six consecutive seasons, from 70/71 to 75/76, when he was training for Stan and Millie Fox. Jack has a marvellous reputation as a trainer, but in the charisma stakes he was less than a threat to Tommy.

In recent times Neville Begg has proven an outstanding trainer, but he is a quiet and unassuming fellow, not a contender for TJ's position as Publicity King of the Racing Page.

4.4-3 Important helpers

TJ's brother Dick was his most important helper in the early days. George Moore was another. During the 40s TJ developed a friendship with George, a man who was to become an Australian racing legend in his own right. Born in Mackay, Queensland in 1923, Moore became a top jockey in Brisbane before shifting to Sydney. TJ and George first met on a train to Melbourne in 1939. They were both unknowns but got along very well. By the end of the trip, the ever confident TJ was predicting that George would win a Derby on a horse he trained. By one report George had his first ride for TJ in 1946 - a win on Bragger. By 1949 George was a hard-bitten rider who only rode horses he thought could win. He had once passed up the winning ride to pilot a friend's horse in a race. He had a fall from the lesser chance and vowed from then on to go for the mount with the best prospects.

But George and Tommy became the most livewire, entertaining duo in racing, a magnet for racing writers and owners. Each was good publicity for the other, each telling outrageous stories against the other.

TJ's first derby

E.R. Williams asked TJ to buy a staying colt at the 1948 yearling sales. TJ bought one by The Buzzard (imported as The Bastard from the U.K. but renamed at the request of the registry). But Williams would not take it because The Buzzard's offspring were considered slow maturing. Having paid 1150 guineas, TJ was unable to sell the horse. So he trained it for himself and it started four times without success. Then TJ entered his maiden three-year-old in the 1949 AJC Derby. Moore rode Playboy and the pair took out first place and won 8277 pounds. In addition TJ put 500 pounds on his horse at 100 to one, netting him 50,000 pounds of bookies' money, considered by some the sweetest money of all. (Americans would be interested to know that no tax is taken out of an individual's gambling wins in Australia.) Playboy went on to win the AJC St. Leger in 1950. The wins gave TJ more than monetary satisfaction:

"I had been winning all the two-year old races around the place but people were saying I couldn't train stayers."

It would be the first of many, many Derbies, a world record of Derbies.

Bet you didn't know this . . .

"Did you gradually accumulate more horses and gradually move into training or did you suddenly decide, 'Right I want to be a trainer'?"

"I thought well I'll get in and get some money and get into a business. But when I got the money and I bought a business - well I don't know - I got the bug to go on training."

"What business did you buy?"

"I bought a shop, and a bottle shop over in Rainbow St, a little grocer's shop - you've probably never seen it - I must take you round and show you where it was."

"A grocer's shop and a bottle shop - it sold liquor did it?"

"Yes a good bottle shop. A full bottle shop. Operated on a concession."

Anyone familiar with TJ as the lively focal point of the saddling paddock after a win would find it hard to imagine TJ behind the counter in a liquor store. At the bar with a glass in hand, yes . . .

Staff - any crucial helpers

Racing writer Bill Whittaker: "There was a stable foreman called Happy Rolls. He played a very big part in Smith's rise to success and fame. Happy was a brother of Cecil Rolls, the fellow who trained Eskimo Prince for Perc Galea (the million dollar betting man). They were a magnificent racing family from around Grafton, the Rolls's. The two best known were Cecil -

who was a good Randwick trainer in his own right - and Happy who must have been stable foreman for Tommy Smith for twenty years." I wondered how much Cecil benefited from what Happy learnt at TJ's.

"For TJ's first twenty years?"

"I'd say so. He was there nearly all the time, from I'd say the mid-forties to about the mid-sixties, Happy Rolls."

"Had he worked with other trainers? Was he someone Tommy could learn from - or was he Tommy's age and starting up?"

"I'd say Tommy met him somewhere at a country meeting and offered him the job in the forties when Tommy didn't have many horses. They were about the one age. I don't know quite how he came up with Happy Rolls."

"So what happened - did Happy Rolls die or retire or . . ."

"No, he retired and he's dead now. So is his brother Cecil. I don't know that he and Tommy had a parting of the ways, I think he just retired."

Important clients

"One of the things you hear out in the woods about TJ is that he got his start by getting into the nightclub set . . . because he couldn't get into the pastoralist's and grazier's set."

Bill Whittaker: "That's dead right. His chief clients in the late forties and early fifties were two very well known Sydney bookmakers, Jack Large and John Rogan. Jack Large fell foul of the stewards and got warned off, but John is held in the highest respect by everyone. He's the man who puts Packer's money on now. He's a retired bookmaker; he was mainly a trotting bookmaker, John Rogan. He and Jack Large and two or three others had a syndicate in the early fifties, and I'd say that at any one time they had up to twenty horses in Tulloch Lodge. Well, it wasn't Tulloch Lodge then, it was just Tommy Smith's stables. And as a matter of fact, in 1956 when Smith bought that horse - the Khorassan colt who turned out to be Tulloch - they had first choice but they picked three or four others from that draft and rejected the colt which was Tulloch."

"So they were part of the nightclub set?"

"They were the nightclub set. Tommy's clients largely at that period were the highfliers around Sydney rather than the breeders and pastoralists."

Important horses continued

Tommy's youngest brother Ernie told me he was connected with Tommy in Sydney from the time TJ took out a license and trained Bragger. In Ernie's recollections Tommy's second horse was a hurdler which ran 2nd or 3rd at Randwick. That helped.

"Then there was Kookaburra, which TJ bought from E.R.

Williams, a prominent owner and a director of Woolworths. It had been trained by George Price and they thought the horse was no good. Tommy won 2 or 3 on end with it. E.R. Williams thought, 'Well this young fellow knows how to train,' and he started to send Tommy horses."

In Ernie's memory another major horse was a horse called Two Grand.

"What really got Tommy going - a horse that got Tommy a lot of publicity -was a horse called Two Grand - it was one of the most promising horses in training and the fellow that owned it had a dispute with the trainer at Canterbury."

"Tommy was away in the country but I knew the man. He said: 'I'm taking this horse off this fellow,' so I said, 'Would you like to give it to us,' and he said, 'Yes'. We got the horse and it won, but then it broke down. But Two Grand was going to be one of the favorites for the Derby and the classics and it was tremendous for a young fellow to get so much publicity. Even though it didn't go on, it did win and it was such a good horse, such a promising horse and the guys connected with it were pretty big in the racing game."

"When did Tommy buy Tulloch Lodge?"

"Peter Riddle bought it from Marsden and Tommy got it from him. It was very good in those days, not so much traffic, close to the track. Being right on the track would be alright provided you had your own conditions, provided you weren't on top of one another. The trouble with being right on the track is that everyone is on top of one another."

Ernie on breakthroughs

"Do you go and have a look at racing around the world?"

"Oh yes, I've seen racing everywhere."

"Do you go with TJ?"

"No we go separately. We've been watching races run around the world for 30 years." That would have been 1958 onwards.

"What are some ideas you can remember bringing back?"

"I don't think we've bought any ideas back. The ideas here were just as good as anywhere else in the world. Australians knew how to train horses. What you have to remember is that the Australian was a horseman - brought up pretty hard and pretty tough. When we were kids we had to shoe the horse, be a sort of dentist; we were our own vet - there weren't any vets. You had to do the lot, you had to understand it. My father was just a bushy but there was nothing he couldn't do with a horse. They had to do the feet, do the teeth, do everything possible because there was no one else to do it. They were very knowledgeable people but they never put it together."

"Were there any things that stuck in your mind, as innovations, of Tommy's that got him to the front or kept

him there in the 40's and 50's?"

"Well he's always worked and that was the key to it. You see a lot of horse trainers, they go out of a night - then they don't go to the track. That's not Tommy - he works seven days a week and that's what's kept him together and we've always done it including myself. Seven days a week, and Dick used to be there too, and some of those were pretty rough days."

"So there was quite a team of you really. TJ is the man at the front but there were three of you there in the formative years."

"Dick came into it after he came out of the army."

Bill Whittaker - a leading Sydney racing writer

Bill was on the brink of retiring as racing editor of the Sydney Morning Herald after a lifetime on the track.

"I wrote trotting and racing, but I don't write any trotting now. For the last eight years it's just racing. As a youngster from the bush, growing up around Sydney, I was already keen on racing. I remember Tommy Smith when he trained Bragger. Remember him well. A trainer with one horse, two horses. The first good yearling he ever bought was called Ajixa. That's the first yearling that he trained that won. And he would have leased her in 1941 or 1942. She was by Brueghel, the Italian stallion."

"What's your earliest recollection of TJ Smith?"

"As a brash young trainer in Sydney about 1947, when he wasn't really accepted by the older brigade of trainers. He had different methods to most of them - he gave his horses muscle and bone, whereas most of the trainers of that period had them big and gross-looking; fed them a lot of soft barley and that kind of food, and of course, he was the first trainer - and this is probably the most significant factor about him - to go and buy horses on spec."

"He was the first to do that?"

"The first to do it. All those old trainers like Bayly Payten and George Price and Fred Williams and plenty of others, they always bought yearlings with the owner sitting alongside them, and waited for the owners to send the yearlings to them. Tom Smith used to go and buy twenty or thirty at times -in New Zealand and in Sydney - and then look for owners. Tulloch, the greatest yearling he ever bought, was one of those. The year that he bought Tulloch, 1956, I think it was - he came back with twenty-odd yearlings and the last one to be sold off was Tulloch. He had a sway back."

"What Tommy Smith did differently: a) he bought yearlings on his own and b) he fed them differently. He always told me he copied an old trainer in Sydney, Dan Lewis. Dan Lewis trained five Sydney Cup winners and a Melbourne Cup winner, Foxzami. He was a Randwick trainer - but he wasn't regarded as one of the top ... He wasn't a high profile trainer, Danny Lewis; he'd been a bookmaker earlier in his life. Gave up being a bookmaker to become a horse trainer. 'Canny Danny' they called him. But Smith has said in later years that he copied a lot of Danny Lewis's methods. Not the top trainers. He didn't agree with the top trainers. But of course Tommy was a punter too at that time, a big punter."

"Where did TJ get his earliest owners from? When he was going to these sales and buying these large numbers - would he be ringing up people he already knew?"

"He always had a couple of long-standing clients - their names escape me -who always gave this cheeky brash young kid a horse to train and then ... "

"It wasn't E.R. Williams, was it?"

"No, certainly not. E.R. Williams transferred his horses to TJ Smith when Ted Hush died. Tom Smith was a bit lucky in that respect. A lot of trainers died in Sydney in the 1940's. Notably Bayly Payten, who was the leading trainer of Sydney, who died young. He was only in his late forties, at best early fifties. Bayly Payton came from one of Sydney's most famous training families. His father Thomas Payten had been the leading trainer at Randwick in the early part of the century and in fact, Thomas Payten's stables were what is now Newmarket Sale Ring (beautiful big stables). So Bayly Payten was reared in that atmosphere. He had the upper crust breeders and pastoralists as his clients, and he had a supply of great horses, one after the other. His roots were completely different from TJ Smith's, absolutely and completely different. He was the son of a champion trainer, from a wealthy family."

"Maurice McCarten was another leading trainer in Sydney, in the forties. He was a New Zealander, came here and became one of the champion jockeys, and then in 1942 he retired and became a trainer. In 1943, I think, when Smith was just starting to make his way as a trainer and had maybe seven or eight horses at the most - well, Maurice McCarten at that same time, having retired as one of the most respected jockeys in Sydney, had a stable full of horses at Randwick, all owned by wealthy people such as Harry and George Tancred, Bill Longworth, and Adolf Basser, who owned Delta, a champion horse, with whom he won the Metropolitan and the Melbourne Cup in 1951. McCarten trained Todman and Noholme for the very influential Stanley Wootton (who selected and imported Star Kingdom, foundation of a dynasty of sires)."

"They were the sort of opposition that Tommy had. Nobody would have guessed - if they had run a book on it in 1943 - who the leading trainer was going to be in 1953. He would have been a thousand to one ... but as you know, he won it for the first time in 52-53 and wasn't beaten until 85-86. He won it thirty-three years in a row. But the nineteen- forties, as a chapter of Tommy's life were tremendous. He started them without a horse, in 1940, and he finished them in 1949 by winning the AJC Derby with a maiden, Playboy."

"How did Harry Darwon go? He got the same start as

TJ, perhaps better. He was set up as a trainer in Sydney by the younger Sawyer, Mac, at the time TJ worked for them as a strapper and track rider."

"Until perhaps 1946 Harry Darwon did have more success. He was a bit older than Tommy too, but he did not have Tommy's application. Finished up losing everything. He was just two or three years older than Tommy. He died two or three years ago. I knew him well. They both came from the same area, down there in the Riverina. They both worked for Matt Sawyer. Matt Sawyer was the man who gave Tommy a break, but he also gave Darwon a chance too. He was a good fellow, Sawyer - he was a rich pastoralist."

"Maurice McCarten, what happened to him?"

"Maurice McCarten trained almost to the day he died. He was a wonderful jockey and trainer, having the unique distinction of winning a Jockey's Premiership and four Trainer's Premierships. His clients died or went into retirement; his stable gradually dwindled. He had clients like Adolf Basser, who owned Delta, and Bill Longworth who owned Wenona Girl. One client after another passed on, and then Neville Begg, who was his loyal stable foreman, branched out on his own."

"That tends to weaken a stable for a while."

"Yes, he took some of Maurice McCarten's clients, which was only fair because Neville had been the stable foreman for so long, and he had to eventually make his own way in life. So McCarten finished with hardly any horses, and in the end was training just three or four, and then retired and died."

Contemporary trainer Albert McKenna - memories of what TJ changed

Albert McKenna retired at the age of 72 in 1988. He started training around the same time as TJ, racing horses from the war years onwards. In his opinion Smith revolutionized racing, introducing the big stable concept. Before TJ got wound up, 20 horses was a large string. TJ took that to 50 plus. While many trainers got by on the punt, TJ chased the prizemoney.

Tommy watched his horses work from the center of the track. He had his horses brought to him straight after their fastwork. He could see if they had blown up over the loins, hear their breathing. He learned to do that, according to Albert, by watching the old-time trainers, who would gallop up on a pony to check their horse straight after a workout.

Bobby Thomsen

Bobby Thomsen, now one of the top ten trainers in Sydney, started with TJ when he left school at 14 years of age in 1957. He started as an apprentice jockey just after Tulloch had won the Caulfield Cup.

"I rode as an apprentice jockey for TJ for seven years, until I was 21. I rode for him for a couple of years as a jockey and then I had a contract to ride in Queensland where I got badly smashed up in a track fall. I spent 12 months away from the stable, then I came back and I took the foreman's job. I had the foreman's job for eight years."

"What was TJ like to work for?"

"He was very hard to work for."

"What were the things that were making him the front runner then?"

"Well, I never knew what happened outside Tulloch Lodge. I wouldn't know what any other trainer fed his horses, or how he worked them."

"What were your first impressions when you went to Tulloch Lodge"

"As a 14 year-old, I just couldn't believe it. I just loved horses. But as I got to know him - he's just a genius. He would walk in the front gate and by the time he'd got to the bottom gate he would have looked at every horse, only for a fraction of a second. Not only that but around the stables he'd see things that I wouldn't see. Cobweb here, plants weren't green enough."

"Good manager?"

"Yes a brilliant organizer."

"How many horses did he have in training when you first went to work with him."

"About 58."

Was Percy Sykes important to Tommy's success?

As mentioned in the introduction, TJ had been number one for some three years before Percy became his regular veterinarian. But Percy Sykes was an outstanding vet and no doubt played some part in keeping TJ at the top, particularly when Percy in later years pretty well restricted himself to the work at Tulloch Lodge. Other trainers could get Percy's associates but rarely The Maestro.

In spite of their very close friendship, TJ did not have a mortgage on Percy's nutritional advances, even when TJ helped test them. According to Percy, he would give additives to some of TJ's horses. If TJ could see a difference in performance he would tell Percy. When Percy was convinced of the benefits of the product, he marketed it. At first Percy sold through his practice, but the products were so successful that the mixing and labeling eventually became a headache. Percy's nurses were mixing products in his basement using cement mixers, when he was approached by businessman Gordon Terry. From this meeting a company was formed, Randwick Veterinary Laboratories, later called Ranvet.

According to Percy, whenever some new additive seemed to work, TJ would say to Percy, "You won't tell the others will you?" Percy said he replied that he had to, that it was his duty to tell all his clients.

Percy is adamant that he never foresaw the financial success of Ranvet, that he agreed to form the company to take the mixing out of his basement. "The whole place stank of B vitamins."

Ernie puts a lot more store by Percy's role than Tommy does.

"When Percy Sykes came along, TJ was already number one on the training ladder: how important was Percy to TJ in staying there?"

"Many trainers are number one for two years or five years but they don't stay there and they miss out a few years during their 'reign'."

"Was Percy Sykes important in keeping TJ at the top?"

"Percy Sykes came here with new ideas. The vets that were here were old vets and had no idea. They were living in the past. He was a young bloke who came here with new ideas and the new ideas worked."

"What were some of those new ideas that you can remember?"

"Things like drenching horses and anabolics - he brought that into the country - which improves things as you'd know."

"Was he one of the first to introduce anabolics?"

"Mmm."

"One of the stories I heard years ago, as a vet student or new graduate, was that the first anabolics were used by a Sydney trainer who had some connection - relative or something - who was a pediatrician in a hospital. The pediatrician was using anabolics to build up babies and children. He suggested them and may have supplied them to the trainer."

"Well I don't know about that. I think Percy Sykes put the whole thing into practice, he's a very clever man and he came here as a young bloke, as a clever bloke. The other old blokes didn't graduate up to the top, they were satisfied to just keep doing what they were doing. Some people are just happy to go along."

Percy was certainly at the forefront of some advances in clinical veterinary science in horses, and some nutritional advances. He kept up with the scientific literature. He would have been very valuable to TJ, but TJ did not have exclusive use of Percy's advances or knowledge. Percy still had an astounding knowledge of those fields when I spent several weeks at the practice in 1986 - some ten years after he had 'retired'.

I asked Percy how important he was to TJ.

"I think Tommy would have been a famous trainer, whether I'd been there or not. I doubt I'd have done so well without Tommy."

How important was Tulloch the wonder horse?

TJ bought Tulloch at the Trentham sales in New Zealand in 1956 for 750 guineas 'on spec'. TJ was unable to convince anyone to buy the horse. It was smallish, and by some accounts sway-backed. In desperation he offered the horse for half the amount he had paid, to three of his staff. They declined. Eventually he managed to sell it to one of his elderly clients, Mr E.A. Haley, who turned up one day and asked TJ if he had bought him a horse in New Zealand.

Veterinarian Dr Arthur Sternhell lived near Mr Haley's city residence. Arthur had this to say about the purchase of Tulloch:

"Tommy Smith must have a very special gift, his 'eye', because all the top horsemen saw that horse and it was passed in at something like 6,500 guineas. Tommy asked if they would take 7,000 and they did. The top prices were 30 or 40,000 guineas. So he got a cheap horse. But when the owner saw me he said, 'Tommy Smith has bought me the best horse in the sale. He told me it will be the best horse to come out of that sale."

"Maybe that's what Tommy tells all his owners?"

"Well maybe- but no. No, he doesn't. I knew Tommy, I was doing veterinary work for him, knew some of his owners. He knew that was a special horse."

Tulloch is considered the greatest horse in Australia since World War II, and may have been the equal of Phar Lap, the greatest three-year-old ever in Australia. Tulloch won the 1½ mile AJC Derby by six lengths in 2.29.1 taking over two seconds off Phar Lap's 28 year old record. It is generally accepted he would have walked-in the Melbourne Cup of his three-year-old year, 1957, because Prince Darius, a horse he regularly beat by 4 to 8 lengths, came second by a neck. In the C.B. Fisher Plate he beat Sailor's Guide by five lengths. Sailor's Guide later went to America and won the Washington International against some of the world's best horses.

Tulloch fell ill in early 1958, after a series of dazzling wins at the AJC Autumn carnival. He developed a chronic diarrhea that lasted almost two years and nearly killed him. For the whole of that two years Tulloch was in danger of dying from sheer dehydration and electrolyte imbalances. Vet Percy Sykes was continually testing Tulloch's blood so he could correct developing problems. Tulloch's scours were repeatedly examined under the microscope and cultured in every known medium, but no disease-causing organism could be found. Percy Sykes 'scoured' the medical literature for a possible cure. Many were tried but the one that worked was an antiseptic compound called Brilliant Green, mixed with formalin and given in a gelatin capsule. Unsure how the dose would affect a horse, Percy and Tommy bought one horse just to test the mixture. The test horse survived so the mixture was given to Tulloch. The scours cleared within days. It was during this period of intensive daily nursing of Tulloch that Tommy's relationship with Percy Sykes was cemented.

Tulloch again won big races but had missed two years. Tulloch thrashed others at weight-for-age, hauled huge weights in handicaps, won by huge margins and was usually long odds-on. He was retired after winning the Brisbane Cup for a career record of 36 wins 12 seconds and 4 thirds from 53 starts. He was only out of a place once, in the 1960 Mebourne Cup when he carried a crushing 10st 1lb (64kg)

Turf expert Warwick Hobson did some research and found that if Tulloch ran and won the same races, he would at 87/88 prizemoney, win $5.6m. Very few horses have won over a million in Australia and the record for winnings in 1988 was $1.6m won by Kingston Town, another horse of TJ's. And Tulloch's total was achieved *in spite of nearly two years out of action!*

Tulloch's scratching from the Melbourne Cup in his three-year-old year, when he appeared a certainty, has long been a source of controversy. One report said TJ scratched Tulloch from the Melbourne Cup because everyone thought he was crucifying the horse. Old Haley, the owner, cried but left it up to TJ, the report went on. Yet another report said Haley considered the Melbourne Cup too severe for a three-year-old.

But Bobby Thomsen's recollection was that, "The old man Haley who owned him wouldn't let him run in the Melbourne Cup, which forced TJ to scratch him, and then he took sick and it was 23 months between his last start and his next start."

It is TJ's reputation to be telling the owner what is going to be done with his horse, but then it doesn't sound like TJ to take it easy with a sound horse. Whatever the truth, Tulloch gave TJ a huge boost in credibility and publicity. Ironically, if TJ had run Tulloch in the Melbourne Cup and *then* the horse had taken sick, he would have lost credibility. Tulloch was the kind of horse that every struggling trainer dreams about. TJ chose the horse but had already been leading trainer for some years when he did. Tulloch was a help but not a key to TJ's rise and continued dominance.

By one account TJ wanted to take Tulloch to America, but the owner believed criminals there had poisoned Phar Lap and that they would do the same to Tulloch. He refused to let the horse go. For the same reason Haley later refused a huge offer to stand Tulloch at stud in America for one year. At stud in Australia, Tulloch failed to sire even one good horse!

4.5 Age married and role of wife

"When did you and Valerie get together?"
Tom: "That's the year we got married, 1946, the year when we went away."

Valerie: "Was there any other way of doing that when we were young - except getting married?"

"Have you enjoyed the racing Valerie? Do you get involved?"

"Yes. I've enjoyed it, I've raced horses since we've been married. I didn't want to waste any Saturdays, well I don't mean waste, but with Gai growing up I did what she wanted on a Saturday. When my husband's brother died I started going regularly, and then when Gai came home from England it was the only time to get the two of them together to talk sometimes. So we all go racing on a Saturday - I've got interests in a few horses - I think shares in about four at the moment."

"How did you meet Tommy?"

"Tommy bought a horse from my brother-in-law, and he was also his punter."

They met at the Wagga races. Val was 'horrified' by their first encounter and it took Tommy six years to win her over.

"What attracted you?"

"He was very cheeky. I don't know what attracted him. It's been very good though because Tom had never had a home and I made a nice home for him which he loves and he doesn't like going out a great deal. He loves being in his home."

"He goes to Brisbane or Melbourne or Perth by himself - but if he's going to go any further than that he always says, 'We'll go.' And he's always said that. It's been a really good combination because he's done his thing and I've done my thing but coming together on the home front."

"What are your interests?"

"I love art, I love china, I love music - things like that. Things that are vastly different to what Tommy likes, but I've got him interested in the things I like now."

Tommy's house is nothing spectacular from the outside but very nice inside. When I had first entered the lounge room, I had noticed a Norman Lindsay portrait of a woman, and a Sali Herman scene, having once had a considerable interest in oil painting and art myself. I had thought to myself that they were probably buying them as investments, probably wouldn't be able to pick even the most highly characteristic works of any artist at five paces.

I told Valerie that the Norman portrait of a woman was unlike his usual fierce Amazons. Much softer, very nice. She replied that she had bought it for that very reason and that it was a painting of Norman Lindsay's wife. She and Tommy then took me for a tour of their 'private gallery', a hallway area with 10 or so works of major Australian painters. Many were somewhat atypical of the particular artist's work. That means you can get them for a lower price, but they are usually a poorer investment. That didn't seem to matter to Valerie, who knew some of the artists and bought what pleased her eye. Tommy knew quite a bit about it all and clearly enjoyed the collection, although he no doubt has one eye on the investment side of it all.

Valerie spent the early years of their marriage trying to impart some of what she learned at the Rose Bay Convent to Tommy. She dragged him off to self improvement and speech classes, according to some, who go on to say things like, 'but that's a bit of a secret,' or, 'didn't do much good did it,' or, 'can you imagine what he must have been like before.' They say she suffered some social penalties for choosing a racehorse trainer and such a cocky, working class one. If she did suffer, she must have had the last laugh as fame came and the Smith fortune piled up.

In the early years Valerie hardly went near the racetracks. It didn't attract her. Trainers were not allowed in the Club members area. Social classes didn't mix easily, and she and Tommy must have straddled a few different levels. She devoted herself to raising Gai, their only child. Not until 30 years later, when Gai began going to the races every week in the 1980's, did Valerie too become a regular.

"It's the only time we can all be together. I've got shares in horses, but I like it because I've got Tommy and Gai together."

The Members Club is now relatively easy to join; trainers and some of their staff are members; connections of the horses are given tickets. The whole scene is more relaxed than in the suffocatingly class-conscious 40's and 50's. For the first time, Valerie has some role in TJ's huge training machine. She helps entertain the clients and owners. After each race Valerie and Gai are with the owners and connections, congratulating or commiserating, and enjoying themselves.

5. Tommy's achievements as a trainer

5.1 Training titles, money and stakes

Thirty-three consecutive Sydney metropolitan training premierships is like being leading trainer based in Newmarket or New York Racing Association tracks for a similar period of time. It is a record that stands alone. There are runs of 10 to 13 years in the record books but 33 consecutive premierships is a record likely to stand forever.

That run was brought to an end by another hard-driving battler from the bush, Brain Mayfield-Smith, who had left life as a drover in northern Queensland to try his hand as a trainer. Brian had 103 city wins to TJ's 95½, and won $2,969,160 to TJ's $3,035,750.

Racing in Sydney is world class. New South Wales has five metropolitan tracks, 120 provincial tracks, tens of thousands of registered Thoroughbred racehorses and thousands of trainers. Most Australian trainers are part- timers, but there are hundreds of full time professionals. The part-timers live in outer suburban or rural areas and have a full-time job. Most keep the horses on anything from one quarter to thousands of acres (0.1 to thousands of hectares) which they own. If they start to do well training a few for friends, they may try to become a public trainer. Those that do exceptionally well in the rural towns usually move to the city, just as TJ did - it's Sydney or the bush. One of the incentives is national fame of a degree American trainers can only dream about. So in effect many thousands of Australians try their hands at racehorse training, and it is a very competitive arena.

TJ added another premiership in 1988/89 and still has the organization and ammunition to win more.

In September 1979 the press reported his 3000th winner, and he has since gone past 4000. He also set an Australian season record of 175 winners back in his heyday, 1973/74.

Money

Bart Cummings beat Tommy by two hours to be the first Australian trainer to win $1m in a season, in June 1974. Tommy bounced back to be first to $2m in 1980, and first to $3m in 1985.

The AJC proposes rules to limit TJ's dominance

By the early 70's Tommy Smith had such a reputation, and such a stable full of stars, that many in racing, either through jealousy or through a belief that the degree of his power was bad for the sport, wanted something done to limit him. The Australian Jockey Club, the governing body in Tommy's state, proposed a maximum of two entries per race. This is a rare achievement. That the ruling body should contemplate such rules shows the degree of TJ's dominance. Tommy (and his owners) campaigned vigorously against the rule change, due to come into force at the start of the 1974/75 season.

"I gave away the provincial meetings because I was doing so well and I wanted to leave those smaller meetings to the battling trainers ... Anyway it seems a ridiculous set-up, especially when AJC officials recently telephoned and asked me to leave horses in a race to make up the field."

One of the country's most analytical racing writers, Graeme Clark, examined 447 consecutive metropolitan races that had been run up to that point of the year. TJ had no runners in 131 races, or 29.3%, 1 runner in 207 races (46.3%), 2 in 76 races (17%), 3 in 21 races (4.78%), 4 in 7 races (1.82%), 5 in 4 races and 7 in 1 race. His multiple starters were usually in two-year-old races. At that point TJ had 60 horses in training out of 1059 in Sydney ie 5.6% of the horses in training. From these he managed 8.42% of starters. Many starters come from outside Sydney so it meant his number of starts per horse was even higher compared to the average Sydney trainer, well over double. Kelly's most telling statistic however was that TJ had won over 25% of the prizemoney. One trainer winning over a quarter of the prizemoney!!!

In the end TJ prevailed: no limits were set.

5.2 Important races and awards

The Melbourne Cup

This is a very peculiar horse race, run in Melbourne, the capital of the state of Victoria. It is open to any horse of three years or over, filly, colt or gelding, but it is a handicap event, which means the best horse doesn't necessarily win. It is run over the outlandishly long distance of two miles while the bulk of the races in the country are run over ⅝ to 1 mile (1000 to 1600m). Consequently it has almost no breeding significance. So infrequent are races over two miles that few of the field have ever run the distance before, most of the jockeys have no idea of a suitable pace, and the favorite rarely *rarely* wins. The race is a serious handicapper's nightmare and a bookie's dream.

It wasn't always this way. When the Melbourne Cup was first run and won back in 1861, two miles was middle distance. It was won by a horse that was walked and ridden down from Sydney, about 600 miles (1000km) away. At that time there were many three and four mile races, sometimes with heats on the same day, but there were also those trendy new shorter races, over 1½ miles, called Derbies. The Melbourne Cup had breeding significance then, now it's an historic relic.

The Cup is run *not* on a weekend, but on the first Tuesday in November, when everyone in the country is at work or in school (except Victorians who get the day off so they can contribute to one of the largest traffic jams you could wish to see). Yet it is Australia's most famous horse race and a national festival. It has a grip of the country's people that far exceeds the grip of the English Derby on the English people or the Kentucky Derby on Americans. An extraordinary percentage of Australians listen to the race or watch the direct telecast - my guess would be around 80%. Most bet on the race even though they will never bet on any other race in their life. It is a national ritual. Over perhaps two or three weeks the press coverage steadily increases, until in the last two days the Melbourne Cup is on the front and back page of every newspaper, and on every TV channel.

The newspapers print lists of the horses entered. Each name is cut out, placed in any suitable container, and then pulled out 'blind'. For ten or twenty cents in classrooms and kitchens; one or two dollars in offices, workplaces, station homesteads and hotel bars; all the way up to hundreds or thousands of dollars at the country club, *everyone* gets a horse. In addition to these sweepstakes, many work, family and social groups delegate some lucky individual to go down to the local betting shop, park with great difficulty, and stand in a long queue to place everyone's bets. These are not only the longest queues of the year, but the slowest moving as well.

At the racetrack, Flemington, there is a gigantic crowd of around 100,000. The scene is similar to other famous races.

The infield is taken over by people having 'boot parties' (Australians call the trunk the boot) - eating roast beef or chicken, and drinking beer, wine or champagne from the boot of the car. Everyone dresses to the limits - either to the heights of high fashion or to the remotest reaches of the imagination. There is a carnival atmosphere as everyone cruises around showing off and checking out the creations of others.

During the race the country does literally come to a standstill, as non-Australians may have often read but seldom believed. Congested streets become a trickle of traffic. If you try phoning a government department at this time, an answer is unlikely, but if there is one, you'll very swiftly find yourself on hold. (What's new?, you ask.) At the the front counter of a small business you probably won't find any service but you may hear a lot of shouting and cheering coming from out the back, mingled with the rapid-fire commentary of an Australian racecaller. On the streets the less aware or less prepared scurry to reach some point of hearing or seeing. Shopfronts with TV sets are surrounded. People stand around cars with turned-up radios, in head-down or head-up concentration. The winner is announced on public address systems by supervisors, principals and pilots. Yes, even school classes stop for the broadcast of the race. It is truly a national event.

At the close of nominations in 1988, TJ had entered 21 horses in the Melbourne Cup. The nomination (June) costs $100, first declaration $200, second declaration $300, third declaration $1,000, and the final declaration $7,575. The prizemoney was $2m. The winner receives over $1m. These days 'only' 24 horses start, but as many as 39 have run.

Early in his career TJ Smith put a lot of effort into trying to win this publicity gala, but as a two mile handicap race, won mostly by four or five-year-olds, it has not been TJ's best event. Nevertheless his two wins have only been bettered by a handfull of trainers over the 130 years of its running.

1955

Toparoa - an almost unheard of 7yo, defeating Rising Fast which carried 10 stone (64kg). Toparoa carried 34lbs (15.5kg) less. Neville Sellwood was credited with brilliant riding tactics devised by TJ, but the stewards suspended Sellwood. Toparoa kept the Cup because the owners of the second horse, the mighty Rising Fast, refused to enter a protest.

1981

Just A Dash TJ's comment: 'The vet wouldn't pass him but I did.'

The last seconds of the 1987 Golden Slipper: TJ's face tells the story, his fist and jaw clenched in a despairing hope. Ernie's hands are falling as he gives up. TJ had Lygon Arms bearing down on Marauding, trained by the man who had broken his training title streak, Brian Mayfield-Smith. Marauding hung on to win, Lygon Arms was 2nd, and TJ's other entry, Christmas Tree, was 4th.

The Golden Slipper

The Sydney Turf Club, based at Rosehill Racecourse, started this 1200m (6f) race for two-year-olds in 1957 and since then it has joined a handful of races that are possibly second to the Melbourne Cup as far as public interest goes. However it is the leading race in the country from a breeding point of view. Colts that win this race are now megabuck stud prospects. Breeders in other countries will wonder why a two-year-old race and only 1200m at that.

The reasons are complex. Briefly, the various state Derbies, run over 1½ miles, have failed to prove a source of great sires, whereas this race has. This is due in part to the predominance of sprints in the Australian racing calendar. Another factor has been the prepotency of the Star Kingdom line as sires. Star Kingdom and his sire sons have dominated the stud scene since his importation in 1951. The Golden Slipper has been won by many of Star Kingdom's best sire sons, starting with Todman from his third crop, who won the very first Slipper in 1957. In fact Star Kingdom's offspring won the first five runnings. You can argue until the beer runs out about which helped the other the most. The Golden Slipper might not have achieved its prestigious position without the Star Kingdom line and the Star Kingdom line might not have achieved its towering status without the Golden Slipper.

Whichever way it was, the Star Kingdom line and the Golden Slipper were *both* made for TJ Smith, who has won the Golden Slipper more times than any other trainer - 6 times out of the first 23 runnings, in spite of a poor start.

Today one of the factors that makes the Slipper a great event is its proximity to the premier Easter Yearling Sales. Breeders, buyers and bloodstock agents from all over Australia and New Zealand, and a few from around the world, are in town inspecting the yearlings. The Slipper is run and then the sales start. It is a great social week for those in racing, with much wining dining and divining.

How has TJ won 6 Golden Slippers?
From his first years of training TJ has been known for his success with two-year-old sprinters. Also, large numbers are a big help in this race, and large numbers have been a part of TJ's approach to racing, so it is not surprising that he has qualified the most horses for the Slipper. With a large field of green youngsters going around some sharp turns, anything can happen in this race. It pays to have a lot of entries if you can qualify them. When they lined up for the 1988 Slipper Tommy had qualified 50 starters since the race began in 1957, more than double the number qualified by his nearest rivals, Neville Begg and Bart Cummings, although they hadn't been training in Sydney for as many years.

TJ Smith's record in the Golden Slipper
In spite of his premierships from the 1952/3 season and his reputation with the babies, TJ did not win the Slipper until 1971, by which time he had run 19 starters in 12 Slippers. In 1967 he ran three entries but none did better than 6th. He couldn't seem to win. (Shades of Wayne Lukas and the Kentucky Derby, except the Slipper should have been right up TJ's alley.)

265

1971 Fairy Walk won and broke an embarrassing maiden.

1972 John's Hope won

1973 Imagele, a heavy favorite, fell during the race.

1974 Hartshill won, 2 others unplaced.

1975 Toy Show won, Denise's Joy 2nd, Dizzy Spell 6th. It was a great shame about Imagele - 5 in a row would have been nice, something to discuss with Woody Stephens of 5 consecutive Belmont Stakes fame. However it seemed it wasn't going to matter, as though TJ had suddenly discovered how it was done and he could not lose.

1976 to **1980** he had 11 starters and none could do better than 3rd.

1981 1982 and **1983** Tommy had no starters. None for 3 consecutive years, even though he had run at least one starter every year since 1964.

1985 Four starters, Speed Check 2nd

1986 Won with Bounding Away, becoming the first to breed, own and train a Slipper winner.

1987 Lygon Arms 2nd, Christmas Tree 4th

1988 Star Watch 1st, Comely Girl 2nd, his second quinella.

1989 Paris Opera 2nd. TJ had four starters

1990 No starter

Apart from Imagele's fall, TJ has lost twice in photo finishes and his 1970 runner-up, Royal Show was severely checked by Baguette, the winner. Because of Baguette's winning margin the protest was dismissed.

The first seconds after TJ's Golden Slipper win in 1988: TJ is obscured by a man shaking hands with TJ's veterinarian, John Peatfield. Between John and TJ, Gai has her hand on her hat. Ernie and Valerie Smith are arriving from the left, as rival trainer Bart Cummings and son Anthony exit. From the right, Bloodstock agent Gilpin extends a congratulatory hand. Behind the rail to the rear, Irishman John Magnier is one of many internationals in the picture.

Jockey Larry Olsen wears TJ's famous colors in this victory pic. with the Golden Slipper trophy. Regular jockey Mick Dittman was under suspension at this crucial time. With TJ, on the right, are the Ingham brothers, Jack and Bob, and their wives. The brothers, barons of the poultry industry, had bought a quarter share in Star Watch for $1m with the right to buy another share if the horse won.

Derbys

TJ has won over 30 Derbys. Because all the states have their own Derby, it is a lot easier to win a Derby than it is in England, where the trainers are limited to the Epsom Derby and the Irish Derby.

As in England and Ireland, Derbys in Australia are run over 1½ miles (2400m), rather than the 1¼ miles (2000m) of American Derbys.

TJ has won more than any other Australian trainer. After his Australian Derby win at the Perth summer carnival, late in 1988, TJ thought he had won his 34th. The press however could only find 33. He had won 4 Australian, 9 Australian Jockey Club (NSW), 5 Victoria Racing Club, 11 Queensland, 2 West Australian, 1 South Australian and 1 Tasmanian Derby. There has only been an Australian Derby since 1973.

Doncaster Handicap 8 - a trainer's record

1968 Unpainted
1969 Bye Bye
1972 Gunsynd
1973 Analie
1976 Authentic Heir
1980 Iko
1988 Lygon Arms

Caulfield Cup

1956 Redcraze
1957 Tulloch
1978 Taksan
1979 Mighty Kingdom

W.S. Cox Plate 7

Epsom Handicap 7 - trainer's record

5.3 Notable horses

Some of the many horses associated with Tommy Smith include Bragger, Tulloch, Redcraze, Prince Grant, Imagele, Gunsynd, Black Onyx, Silver Sharpe, Igloo, Taras Bulba, Kingston Town ($1,605,790 a record that stood for many years), Toy Show, Denise's Joy, Red Anchor, Bounding Away, Star Watch.

Medals and honors

TJ has an unusual distinction among racehorse trainers. He has been awarded two medals - the MBE, an imperial award, which stands for Member of the British Empire, and one of the replacement Australian series, the Australian Medal, for which he was recommended by the then Federal Sports Minister and Sydney racing man John Brown. TJ Smith, MBE, AM.

5.4 Where was he at age -

20 - Working horses in the bush for the Sawyers.

30 - Closing in on the leading trainers.

40 - While many of the world's great trainers, especially in the past, didn't break through to the top of the heap until after 40 years of age, TJ, at the end of 1956 already had four premierships to his credit. If he was born in 1920 he had seven.

50, 60, 70 - Piling up the records.

6. His operation now

6.1 Home

TJ has a home in Wentworth St, Point Piper, a very elite harborside suburb. His house is nothing grandiose from the outside, but very nice inside. He can go to and from Randwick without encountering a lot of the dreaded Sydney traffic.

6.2 Organization, stables and staff

Tulloch Lodge, Tommy's office headquarters and stables, are at 16 Bowral Street Kensington, about a hundred meters from the Randwick track in Sydney. There are 800 horses in training at Randwick according to TJ, and he considers it to be the best track in the world to train on. He's looked hard at many tracks around the world, so he would know.

The stables at Tulloch Lodge are not modern or fancy but they are functional and because he owns them, rent free. Considering his financial standing TJ could obviously afford something grand in the manner of many leading stables around the world, but chooses to keep his operation lean and profitable. Recently he did build a fairly elaborate stable that backed onto Randwick, called Bounding Away Lodge. (All the trainers at Randwick, as in many parts of Australia, name their stables after one of their 'best ever' horses.) This new premises holds a dozen or so horses and seems to have become daughter Gai's territory.

There are about 50 horses at the main stables and another dozen at the back of two houses in neighboring streets. TJ rents stables at the nearby Newmarket sales complex to keep some horses when he has an overflow.

Most of the boxes have oaten straw on the bottom but some have sand, presumably for the over-eaters. Oaten hay sheaves stand in the corners. They have small automatic waterers. One time trainers had water buckets and kept careful tally of water consumption. Now the automatic waterers are preferred because of labor costs and because the freshness of the water tempts them to drink more. There are fans in the ceilings of some boxes. The boxes have highly polished brass along the top of the door where windsuckers would chew.

Pretraining and spelling are at "Woodburn", a 1000 acre property, and several associated properties, all near Cootamundra, 400 km from Sydney. "Woodburn" was owned by Joe Manning but was under contract to be sold to Tulloch Lodge Ltd, and presumably was one of the three properties that went with Tulloch Lodge Ltd.

Key personnel - Ernie Smith

One of TJ's younger brothers and now his foreman. Ernie was reportedly born in 1935 in Griffith NSW and went to school in the central rural town of Armidale. However there is a picture in Bert Lillye's book *Backstage of Racing* showing Ernie's younger brother Pat, who looks at least six, and the photo is supposed to be 1934! I asked Ernie when he was born. He thought for a long time and then said he was born in 1930.

Ernie probably had it even tougher than TJ. Their father died when Ernie was, in his recollection, about 10. Their mother died when he was about 13 (in the year 1936 by Tommy's recollections to Bert Lillye). The oldest daughter Gladys looked after the rest of the kids. This was long before Tommy had enough money to help. Tommy was still struggling. The family survived by continuing the mail run.

There was some confusion about when Ernie joined Tommy. Ernie told me he had been involved with TJ from the Bragger days, but that was not how some others remembered it. Bobby Thomsen: "Ernie hasn't always been on the scene by the way."

"When did Ernie turn up on the scene?"

"Oh about 1960, 1962 I suppose."

"I thought he must have been in on it from the word go."

"No his other brother Dick, who died, had always been very close to Tom."

"When did he die?"

"Oh, eight or nine years ago I suppose. Owned the Light Brigade Hotel. He was a partner in a lot of horses with Tommy. He was his right hand man. Then Ernie came on the scene and there were stories that the AJC weren't very keen to register him, but it's all changed today and he is the backbone of the stable now and has been for at least the last 17, 18 years."

An article in Racetrack magazine in April 1982 said Ernie joined TJ at age 17 in 1952, but Ernie told me he was born in 1930, not 1935. If Ernie was going to school in Armidale he probably saw Tommy and Dick as he was going to and from school. Ernie probably was a frequent visitor as a teenager and considers himself to have been in it all the way. He'd have been twelve when TJ was starting out with Bragger.

Ernie and the rumors

On the Australian racing scene you will hear a few derogatory stories about Ernie Smith. There are two frequently encountered stories. The first is that Ernie Smith cannot go to Victoria because he is wanted by the police there (One version has it that Ernie put his hand in a bookie's bag and another that he was wanted for a drink-driving offense). The second frequently encountered story, a favorite with punters, has it that Ernie runs a tipping service. The recipient of the tip has to bet $500 on Ernie's behalf. If it wins, Ernie gets the money. If it loses it doesn't cost Ernie a cent. The story usually adds that by tipping different people different horses, Ernie is virtually assured of a payoff no matter what wins. How much of this is true?

People who should know say that Ernie was a bit of a wild one in his younger days. Ernie was "mixing with the wrong people." TJ, they said, rescued him from some bad company. Because the "Ernie can't go to Victoria" story was so incredibly widespread, I asked Ernie about it.

"One of the things that I wanted to check with you, that continually crops up when researching Tommy, is that you can't go to Victoria because you are wanted by the police down there. You go to Queensland, and Western Australia, but Tommy has to go down to Melbourne because you are wanted by the police."

"Oh no, that's ridiculous. Who put that in?"

"It's a common story."

"I was in Melbourne the other day."

"It's a common rumor, it's all over Australia. Where does it come from?"

"I think they get that from some other bloke, some other Smith."

I had a good contact in the Victorian police force, a very on-the-ball detective. I called him and he checked it all out. No warrants for Ernie's arrest. They'd simply go and get him if there were. His colleagues in the Racing Squad confirmed that Ernie had been down the previous week and that they had no outstanding problems with him either.

A noteworthy example of the inaccuracy of a widely believed rumor. I presume that TJ likes to go to the big races and carnivals in Victoria and Ernie stays in Sydney to run the show. On the tipping story, Ernie may have had his punting friends but if he tipped half the field every time, the punters would have soon lost faith in his tips.

Ernie is to some extent a victim of the Urban Myth. These are, 'weird but credible stories that everyone tells as if they were true,' according to Jan Brunvand, an American professor of English who collects them. Like ethnic jokes they appear around the world in slightly varied form (only the nationality is changed - to slander the innocent). Urban myths differ in that they are told as true stories.

Example: a woman is horrified when her dog brings home a dead rabbit, the beloved pet of the child next door. To avoid telling the child and her neighbors the awful truth, the woman

Tulloch Lodge in 1988. The offices are at the front, and the stables to the rear. The garage door to the right rolls up to allow horses to come and go. TJ's blue Rolls Royce gleams in the foreground as veterinarian John Peatfield records treatments on the horses.

Hectic times in the offices at Tulloch Lodge. On the left is an oil painting of TJ with his medals. At the rear are trophy cupboards, drinks cabinet and a gallery of horse pictures.

Cleanup time at the front end of the stable area. Note high stable doors with brass along top, potted plants, horses initials on feed bins.

Late afternoon view of the stables at the rear. Note grain silo and bird netting to keep out sparrows and starlings.

cleans up the pet rabbit, and in the dead of night returns it to its cage. Next morning she sees a concerned group around the cage in the yard next door, and goes to offer her sympathy. There she learns that the concern is not for an unexpected death, but because the rabbit had died two days before and they had buried it. Now here it is - blow-dried clean and back in its cage.

I would suggest to Professor Brunvand that there is a sub-type of the urban myth. It is a story about some well-known person at the national or local level, typically a movie star, politician or sportsman. The story is believable (sometimes only because of earlier myths), humerous and often derogatory. The greater the number of stories there are about this unfortunate person, the more people want to invent and hear others about them. The basis in truth to these stories varies greatly but in my researches it is usually close to zero. It would probably take a month of interviews to strip away the myths and find the real Ernie Smith.

Ernie's house is in Kensington. When I visited him there it was a pale pink, average-looking home, but the inside was luxurious. The front porch had a locked steel gate which was carefully fitted to the entrance frame. There was a trained Doberman guard dog inside. Ernie was worried it might get me. Strict security.

In 1961 he married Candy Mitchell, a model and state swimming representative. They have three children: Sterling, who at that time was working for Tommy; Melissa, a model whose photo reminded me of Gai; and another daughter who was overseas.

According to the racing press, Ernie does the race nominations and accounts and trains when TJ is away. He works out which horses to work in groups and organises that on the morning. He is at the track every morning the horses go unless he is away as traveling foreman. The press find him very approachable and he deals with a lot of the enquiries from racing journalists. Once a big punter, 5,000 dollars has been his biggest bet. An article in 1982 said he was now a non-bettor. He races some horses in partnership. In 1986 while TJ was on a boat to Honalulu, Ernie had a heart attack and had bypass surgery.

Malcom Johnson, former Tulloch Lodge jockey.

Malcom is not prone to diplomatic drivel. What he believes - he says.

"I can't speak highly enough of Ernie Smith. I think in every leading stable, there's someone behind the scenes who must take a lot of credit for a lot of things. And I think that Ernie Smith is the best back-up Tulloch Lodge could possibly have. Tommy's a champion trainer, champion bloke, but he gets a lot of accolades for things that Ernie does. Like while Tommy's overseas, or when Tommy might be down in Melbourne, or

Brisbane, or Perth. Well, there's still fifty horses that Ernie's got to look after, and they still win plenty of races while Tommy's away."

"Ernie does a lot of traveling."

"You bet he does. He goes all over the place. I think he's an enormous asset."

"The other thing - watching them around the place is that they seem to get on very well. You don't see any real tension between the two of them."

"Well, Tommy's a very highly strung sort of bloke."

"He has said that himself."

"Tommy'll blow his stack and carry on - he's renowned for it - whereas Ernie just sits back sort of subdued and, 'what the heck - it happens,' sort of attitude. But they work well like that. One pacifies the other all the time. The staff are so scared of Tommy they don't do anything wrong when Tommy's around them."

Gai Waterhouse

Tommy's daughter Gai has become an assistant trainer with her father, the aim being to maintain the empire that Tommy started. What seemed a simple objective in 1980, a family succession, has in 1989 taken on all the aspects of a Greek tragedy, an epic suitable for the attention of Homer or Shakespeare.

As Tommy and Valerie's only child, Gai grew up in much greater comfort than her father did. Like so many first and only children, she was a model child, obedient, maturing into a perfectionist, an achiever. She was devoted to her Dad. She grew up to be a rather stunning young lady with sexy legs and a good brain. Acting was her first career choice and she was among the gilded few accepted by NIDA, the National Instute of Dramatic Art. But TJ persuaded her to go to the university rather than acting school. Too many poofters in acting. So she enrolled in the Bachelor of Arts at the University of New South Wales, barely a stone's throw from Tulloch Lodge. NIDA, ironically, is between the two, and she must have been frequently reminded of her urge to the stage. After graduation she went into modeling, but soon decided to risk the poofters and plunged into acting and television. As many Australian girls do, she went to England. After five years and some successes as varied as Shakespearean acting and being 'a Dr Who girl,' she returned to Australia in 1977.

Gai resumed working in television, and at the tail end of the 1970s, she invited a dashing young bookmaker, Robbie Waterhouse, to appear on *Racing's New Faces*. If you believe in The Gods or The Fates, then they were hard at work in the clouds on that day. Gai and Robbie married on December 14th, 1980. Robbie Waterhouse was from a large, wealthy and well established bookmaking family. Head of the clan was Robbie's father, 'Big Bill' Waterhouse, famous for taking bets of a million dollars without so much as a flicker of a face muscle. The bookie with ice in his veins. Bill was something of a hero when his influence with the then Premier Neville Wran helped to have the government 'take' from betting reduced. Young Robbie was a very successful bookmaker in his own right.

Sometime in the 70's Tommy had convinced Gai there was more money to be made in training racehorses, than appearing on television. He told her that if she would go in with him he would show her the ropes. She accepted that offer and has been diligently learning the trade since.

So Robbie and Gai were the Crown Prince and Princess of Sydney's racing scene, heirs-apparent to a bookmaking dynasty *and* a training dynasty. They had two children and things were just a bed of roses - until the ring-in known as the Fine Cotton Affair in 1984. In one of the most blatant and botched-up substitutions in racing history, the better performed Bold Personality was raced as Fine Cotton. So many people knew about it that "Fine Cotton" was backed off the board at the track and around the country. Bold Personality, dyed red with hairdresser's tints, and bandaged where white socks should have been, cruised home a winner, but some people realized that the horse *was* Bold Personality, others that it *was not* Fine Cotton.

After years of subsequent press diggings, a well known TV program implicated some of the Waterhouse clan and especially Robbie, in numerous scams, mostly involving race rigging. Robbie and his father were warned off ie banned from all racetracks, and Gai ran into the problem that she could, under the rules, lose her forewoman's license for living on the same premises as a warned off person. Feelings against some of the Waterhouses ran high among the racing fraternity because the program, which went to air in November 1987, claimed they diddled the estate and children of the dead brother of Bill Waterhouse. 'Robbing your own blood relatives' did not go down well in the family-oriented racing community.

It was an extremely distressing time for Gai, who skipped the Tuesday track work the morning after the program, but fronted two days later with swollen red eyes. She said she had the flu. At the races some former friends cut her dead and one even pushed her physically out of a conversational group. Others took the view that TJ and Gai had 'kept their noses clean.' It was said that TJ had never had anything to do with the Waterhouses, never trained for them or anything, and that it must have aged him 10 years when Gai walked through the door with Robbie. Some people predicted she'd, 'give Robbie the push.'

But she didn't lose her forewoman's license and has "toughed it out" through years of Robbies's court cases. She is a good Catholic and says she admires Robbie's abilities. Robbie spent his new-found spare time studying pedigrees, and at the 1988 sales was a somewhat subdued part of the Tulloch Lodge group selecting yearlings. In 1988, court charges against Rob-

bie in the Fine Cotton ring-in were quashed for lack of evidence. However, in 1989 there were court battles among the Waterhouses over the dead brother's estate, followed by charges of perjury against Robbie in the Fine Cotton case.

Although no one - journalists, owners, trainers or members - has ever expressed any doubt about her honesty or integrity to me, quite the opposite, Gai Waterhouses's future in racing is clouded with question marks. Tommy wants to retire, but Gai cannot be licenced while she lives with Robbie. She and Ernie have had several disagreements and Ernie resigned after one explosion at morning track work. Although Tommy managed to patch it up, most racing journalists seem convinced Ernie Smith will not work with her if Tommy retires.

No one seems to doubt Robbie was involved in many of the scams described on the TV program, but equally, perhaps surprisingly, no one I met doubts Gai's honesty. She is still held in some regard, even though she has plunged from social queen to pariah in some quarters. Gai will likely have to choose between husband and family life on the one hand, and a training licence, as the key to the Smith training empire, on the other. A choice forced on her through no fault of her own except perhaps naivete.

If Robbie Waterhouse did commit some of the many crimes he is accused of, and if Tommy knew as much as 'the voices' say, did Tommy warn her or didn't he? (Gai later maintained that Robbie was the only one of her boyfriends that TJ got along with.) If Tommy did warn her, did she believe it or was she 'blinded by love'? It's been said that TJ was unhappy about the union, but then a lot of fathers are unimpressed with what their little princess wants to bring to a perch on the family tree. With her obvious devotion to 'Dad', it is all the more remarkable that she went ahead if TJ did say something. And how much the stuff of epic tales, that one of the few defiances of this only child should be so much her undoing.

So Gai continues, rising at 3:30am to go to the track, then racing back to the harborside house in Clifton Gardens, just around from the Taronga Park Zoo, to get the two kids off to school. She has a lot of TJ's energy and drive, and in spite of her business commitments, she has put a lot of time and effort into her children, teaching them to read early, and having a live-in teacher tutor them in the Japanese language. But she won't be leaving her future to The Fates. She'll be leaving no stone unturned in her quest to become a trainer and secure her full inheritance. I wish her luck.

Sterling Smith

Ernie's son Sterling Smith has recently become a trainer. He has a Number 2 licence and a sheik from Dubai has bought him some stables. Years before he did that, he "joined the firm" and spent time with TJ. Sterling then put in time with top trainers around the world, came back and took out his licence. He has a good confident manner, and one hell of a good start for a career as a trainer. After three starts he had already had one winner. Will he, like Fred Kersley, struggle with a near impossible act to follow, a name to live up to?

Do they train staff?
One of the staff said, "Other staff show new staff. Nothing special, they pick it up or they leave. It's not brain surgery."

6.3 Number of horses

Generally put at 100 but because of the pre-training center, horses coming and going, and horse trading, it could be any number. TJ certainly has regular stables for about 42 (sometimes stated to be 50 or 55) at Tulloch Lodge, about 10 at the back of two nearby houses, and several years back built Bounding Away Lodge with 10 boxes. To this total he can add boxes he rents at a nearby sales complex. He often rents 10 or so when his two-year-olds are coming into work. One newspaper report in the mid 80's said TJ bought 120 yearlings for the year, of which half break down or are only good enough for the bush. If a horse is no good, it went on, TJ tells the owner to sell and cut any losses. Another report from later years quoted TJ saying, 'I buy 80 every year, and I sell 80."

Tony McSweeney, who had some notable horses chosen and trained by TJ recalls that Tommy's ambition was to train 100 horses as well as one horse. The most he knew TJ to have in training was 85, when a string of 20 from the Foyster stables was added to his usual 65 boxes.

6.4 His typical day

TJ rises before 4am, drives his Rolls Royce to Tulloch Lodge where he arrives between 4:15 and 4:30. Parking is hard to find for a car of normal length, let alone a Rolls Royce, so Tommy parks at any weird angle. There aren't many parking inspectors about at this hour. From the Tulloch Lodge side entrance, horses have been emerging in sporadic clumps of two, three or four since 4am. They hesitate, peer about, then turn with an occasional slip of the hoof, and move off with the clatter of shoes on bitumen. The blackness swallows them up.

TJ quickly goes into the stables, checks any horses with problems, makes rapid decisions about what to do for them, then returns to the street and hops back into the car. He drives 100 yards, crossing one intersection, and is on the grounds of Randwick Racecourse. Driving slowly and smoothly he veers left, around the back of the grandstand. He parks next to Gai's Holden Commodore. He then makes his way on foot across numerous grass, woodfibre and cinder tracks to the center of the infield. By 5 to 5:30am he is watching his horses work. On a Tuesday or Thursday there may be 40 to 60 horses fast worked and it usually takes less than an hour! He is usually leaving the track by 5:40 to 6:30am. He goes back to Tulloch Lodge, unlocks the front door, sorts out any new problems then goes

Gai Smith with TJ in the saddling paddock.

home for breakfast. He usually phones his vet and any early-rising owners around 7am. May have a nap.

On non-race days TJ will go about the city or travel by plane on business, or he may be at the Tulloch Lodge offices. He checks the horses in the afternoon. Until his brother Dick died, he used to leave Tulloch Lodge in the late afternoon and go to the Light Brigade Hotel, which Dick owned, and where a horde of racing connections would meet after work. It was a racing man's hotel. These days he is more likely to go home and open a bottle of Champagne, eat dinner and spend some more time on the phone, speaking with horse traders, his vet, and his owners.

There are city races on Saturday and on one or two weekdays. The prizemoney averaged $24,000 for a Saturday race, and $12,000 for a midweek in 1988/89 when the Australian dollar was worth about 75 cents US. The crowds are about 2,500 at midweeks, and 12,500 on Saturdays. The tote (pari-mutuel) takes $600,000 on course, but the bookmakers handle millions and the off-course Totalistor Agency Board (TAB) handles millions. TJ attends the city meetings. The horses are handled by the staff and TJ is in the Members area, coming and going from the saddling paddock as required. After his races have finished, TJ enjoys an hour or two in the Champagne Bar with his vets and owners and friends. He often dines out with friends but is not the night-owl of his younger days. TJ's year is much the same throughout. Racing does not stop, but TJ does. He usually goes for an overseas trip or cruise after the racing year ends on August 1st.

6.5 His car

In 1976 TJ purchased a $24,000 Rolls Royce Silver Shadow. He has driven one ever since. In a newspaper article he was photographed with two of them, but in 1989 he told me he only has one. TJ drives to and from the morning track work in it. He doesn't drive a small 'everyday' car, he enjoys his Rolls every day.

That's TJ and Gai up in the tower watching their horses work. Randwick grandstands to left and right. Strappers lead horses circling under the light, waiting to swap horses with trackriders.

TJ's tower in the center of Randwick's many tracks, as the sun rises. TJ has already worked about 60 horses and gone home.

I rode in the Rolls with TJ, a number of times, and it certainly is a beautiful car. Tommy was very happy with it. He told me it was the third one he'd had. It cost over $300,000.

"Is that why you train? So you can have one of these?"

"No. But I always thought if I ever have enough money I'd like to buy a Rolls Royce. Why not?"

"It's just an amazing amount of money, that's all. But then I suppose you've got an amazing amount of money."

"They're actually a good investment. The first one I bought cost me - I think - 20,000 pounds. I sold it for 26,000 or 27,000 after four years. The next one cost about a hundred and something thousand, and I turned around and sold it for more than I gave for it. I'll sell this car for more than I paid for it. This car is four year old. They don't go down in value, they go up."

"I know they go up, but maybe also people want to say, 'this belonged to TJ Smith.'"

"No, no. These cars are good value. How many miles has this car done? It's just turned four."

The speedometer read 58,000.

7. Does he get good horses?

Racing writer Bill Whittaker: "A factor in Smith's rise to fame was his natural ability with horses. He has a great eye for a horse. He told me the other day - 'I wouldn't be a great trainer unless I was a good judge of yearlings.' He said, 'That's where it all happens, at the yearling sales. Looking at yearlings in paddocks and then going and buying them at the sale."

7.1 Where does he get his horses from?

Australia and New Zealand have very few 'in training sales,' and virtually no claiming races. Claiming races have been tried but failed because it would seem Australians are too emotionally attached to their horses to risk losing them.

With his ability to improve horses TJ would have loved claiming races.

"If they had selling races like they've got in America, I would have just stepped in and picked the eyes out of the horses that went into those races. (*'Pick the eyes out of'* means 'pick the best of' - like crows picking the eyes out of dead sheep, only they don't eat the eyes because they are a crow delicacy, but rather because they can't break through the skin to eat other things.) But claiming races didn't work. They tried them but they weren't a success."

"They tried that in Perth and it didn't take off."

"It won't take. Part of the reason for its failure is people wouldn't put their horses in, and if they did put some in they put too high a price on them."

TJ will see horses that interest him in races and make an offer for them. However the vast majority of TJ's horses have come from his own selections at yearling sales. The breeders have never been keen to give him horses. In the beginning this may have been because he was an "outsider". But even after he became leading trainer, most of the breeders preferred to send their stock to others.

Bill Whittaker: "The breeders as a whole have never given Tommy Smith horses. The old breeding establishment really went against him - never accepted him. Even in later years they preferred to send their horses to trainers like Phil Alotta and then Neville Begg, but never Tommy Smith. Sydney businessmen such as E.R. Williams, they gave Tommy horses. Williams, who had his horses with Ted Hush, and before that with George Price, he gave horses to Tommy. Trainers like Bayly Payten and Ted Hush died, and George Price, he got old and cut right down on his string. Well, their clients were all looking for a Randwick trainer. And Smith, probably because he was aggressive and went looking for horses, was able to get horses from their clients who were largely city businessmen like E.R. Williams. Williams frequently bought horses by Delville Wood and Midstream, paid top price nearly every year for yearlings, and Smith was able to get him as a client. And he did help. But he wasn't a breeder."

"Breeders say he doesn't make stallions. If this story started to go out that he didn't make stallions, then they wouldn't give him well-bred horses, and it would become a self perpetuating thing."

"Could have been that."

Around racing circles in the 1960s and 70s, the reason given was that TJ breaks down too many horses. Some breeders added that they believed the severity of his training and his use of anabolic steroids reduced a horse's success at stud. It *is* difficult to name any outstanding sires that TJ trained. Is this coincidence, bad luck if you like? Or are the breeders right? See section 12.1.

If TJ did not receive many horses from the old brigade of breeders, he has in recent years been at the center of a very rich, very powerful *new* group of breeders. These include the Ingham brothers, who own a goodly fraction of the Australian poultry industry, and Sir Tristan Antico of Pioneer Concrete fame, who has bought Baramul Stud and spent big on stallions and mares.

Bill Whittaker: "The Widden Stud and Sir Tristan Antico of Baramul Stud have used his services in recent years and I know that has delighted the old Maestro. He is exceptionally proud of his success with fillies and mares. Also, the Kellys of Newhaven have sent him numerous fillies over the years."

7.2-1 Who chooses

TJ chooses his yearlings with some small input from others in his team, which in 1988 included Ernie, Gai, her husband Robbie and vet John Peatfield. Watching TJ at the sales, he operates without clients, as do most of the major Australian trainers. This is a system that TJ brought about. Back when TJ started off, as Bill Whittaker pointed out, the trainer sat with the owner, the owner bid and paid, and the trainer waited for the owner to send the horse. The small, cocky, unproven TJ however couldn't attract *any* clients, let alone wealthy pastoralists. The remedy to this situation was provided by the huge amount of money he won betting on Bragger. TJ had enough to go to the sales and buy a truckload of yearlings, but he proceeded with caution, first buying one then several. In his third year at the sales he bought 13 for himself and clients. His selections were so successful he was able to continue to do this and he never did become a trainer who sat in hope beside a wealthy benefactor at the yearling sales. Instead he changed the course of history as, eventually, other major trainers followed his lead.

These days in Australia, the top trainers choose and buy the horses, many millions of dollars worth, then resell them to their clients. This has given them great experience in selecting yearlings and they have become experts. The level of horsemanship of the people attracted to racehorse ownership however, has shown the opposite trend. Once they were mainly landowners who had been around horses all their lives. Now a typical owner is likely to have grown up in a city suburb and be the owner of a successful panel-beating business or chain of hair-dressing salons. As a result, many present day owners would consider themselves foolish to go to the sales and choose a yearling, when they could operate through someone with all that accumulated expertise.

In retrospect it would seem to be a change that had to come. But there are many alternatives. In the old system, the owner-to-be and the trainer looked together and with input from each, choices were made. The owner-to-be was at the sale and did the bidding. We have seen how TJ extended the role of the trainer to being the one who chooses the horses, bids, buys and resells to a passive owner. The opposite extension of that has been for an owner to seek out experts in the art of yearling selection and use their information to make a choice. The role of the trainer then depends on that trainer's selection expertise, but sometimes the trainer's role approaches zero.

Owner Robert Sangster carried this to the level of a very successful artform. He began with Vincent O'Brien's eye and progressed until he had a team to make the choices while he and to some extent his other trainers waited to see what they came up with. The assembled-team approach is probably the way of the future, but Sangster has not done so well in recent years. Either the team of experts was not as good as Vincent O'Brien's eye, or Sangster was outdone by the Arabs who also assembled teams, but could outbid him. The expert team approach has been impractical for the average owner, let alone the novice owner. They find it easier to have a selection expert and trainer in one.

Russell Smith, TJ's traveling foreman
(Russell is not a relative)

"Does TJ like to go out to the studs and see the yearlings run? Some people like to see them gallop, see their action, see which ones like to lead."

"He just goes anywhere and looks at them. He loves looking at horses. If you've got a horse over there and he's driving past, he'll be looking at your horse, and he'll be checking out everyone's horses. He's on planes, he's up to Scone, he's down to Victoria looking at horses. He's in New Zealand at the moment looking at horses."

"He buys a lot that never even get near the sales?"

"Like any trainer, but no, he basically buys out of the sales. He remembers horses and that. When he comes down to Perth (when he has a horse racing) he's off the plane and straight down to Heytesbury Stud looking at horses."

"Does he see horses at Randwick that he likes, and go after them to buy?"

"Yes. He tried to buy Vo Rogue. He made an offer to buy Vo Rogue, before Vo Rogue was what he is today."

7.2-2 Can he pick the best yearlings?

"When I got Bragger back from La Perouse, I went up and bought Ajixa. (in one report TJ leased Ajixa) She won the classic Gimcrack Stakes (a two-year-old race) in 1942. Ajixa was the grand dam of Nollari Star, grand dam of Kaoru Star. The next horse I bought at the sales was Playboy. He won the AJC Derby. Then I went to the sales and bought 13 two-year-olds. And the 13 of them won. That was the third year I went to the sales. The whole lot of them won."

Bill Whittaker remembers TJ buying many horses between 1942 and 1948 when he bought Playboy. I think TJ means the next *good* horse he bought.

Tommy presumably had the money to buy yearlings from his betting, especially on Bragger. His prizemoney and betting coup on Playboy's Derby could only have accelerated the buying.

Some highlights that hit the papers.
1952 TJ started 6 2yo and all won.
1953 TJ started 11 2yo and 7 won that season.

Percy Sykes on TJ as a yearling judge

"Only twice have I gone into high-priced yearlings, none of which was chosen by Tommy, and none of them was worth a

Robbie Waterhouse (probably pondering his court cases), TJ Smith, John Peatfield and Gai Waterhouse, assessing a three-quarter brother to Golden Slipper winner Star Watch at the Easter Yearling Sales. TJ bid $500,000 for this colt but the vendors wanted more.

penny. However, *with Tommy*, a group of us paid $A30,000 for a bunch of yearlings in New Zealand. They turned out to be Our Shout, Together Again, and Forward Charge. They won $560,000 in prizemoney. Forward Charge won the St Leger here."

"Bill Ritchie used to buy high-priced yearlings and they'd do no good. He worked out he had spent $1.2m, and at that stage his had won $780 and our $30,000 worth had won $65,000. He said he wanted to be in any others we bought."

Owner Tony McSweeney

"For me TJ trained Movie Boy, which won the Canterbury Guineas; Dubbo which won the Oakleigh Plate in Australasian record time; Orient which won the Queensland Oaks and Sandown Guineas; Versailles; and Silver Sharpe, winner of three Derbies. Only three horses have won the three Derbies: The mighty Tulloch, Royal Sovereign and Silver Sharpe. Silver Sharpe was a maiden when he won the Derby, just like Playboy. We used to buy about two horses in each sale. At one time I had about six horses with TJ. I think the hungry Smith, when he really had to buy a yearling, was absolutely phenomenal. As he got on - well . . . "

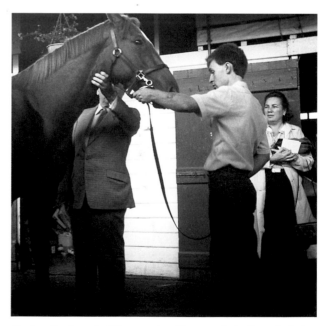

Under the hand of the master. Tommy feels the windpipe and throat area of a yearling at the sales. He seems to do this with every yearling he is interested in, and daughter Gai does the same.

"I remember Jack Green, a great trainer, won the Epsom with a horse called Silver Phantom. A fellow called Malcom Campbell owned the horse. He said to Jack Green, 'I'll reward you handsomely monetarily - or you can go to the yearling sales and buy any two yearlings you like. He went to the sale and bought the brother to Shannon, who was sweeping all before him, and the brother to another good horse. We used to meet in the Light Brigade Hotel every weekday at five if there was no racing. Tommy read this in the papers and he said, 'I've inspected those two yearlings. I wouldn't have paid 500 pounds for either one of them.' It seemed an audacious statement and he was given to audacious statements, but he was right. One won one race, and the other I think didn't win at all. They topped the yearling sales, the first and second highest prices of the sale."

"When the first of the Showdown's came in at the sales, it was a very poor sale, unseasonably cold night, and the yearling that would be called Royal Show was knocked down for 2,500 guineas. Silver Sharpe was next, he brought 3,750 guineas. Dual Choice came in, brought 10,500 guineas, TJ was bidding on him, but they were running him up (pushing up the bidding) so TJ dropped off at 6,500 guineas. They were all outstanding horses."

"I said I wanted the one that turned out to be Royal Show. Next morning I met John Inglis who was staying at the Australian, and he told me TJ had bought two nice horses, meaning Royal Show and Silver Sharpe. He said to me, 'I like the second one because it is better bred on the dam side.' So I went to Tommy and said, 'Do you mind if I switch?' He said, 'No, but you should buy them both."

Instead, Tony found some new owners for Tommy and they took Royal Show with Tommy keeping a share. Royal Show went on to run second in the Golden Slipper, win races at weight for age, win the Canterbury Guineas, win the Rosehill Guineas - while Tony's horse Silver Sharpe was still a maiden well into its third year.

"We were fourth in the Rosehill Guineas coming from last. You can imagine how I felt. I used to put my hands on my hips and think *John Inglis!* In the Derby of 1970, Royal Show was nine-to-four favorite, we were twelve-to-one. Down the outside came Silver Sharpe and he beat Planet Kingdom and Gunsynd. Then we went to Melbourne and beat Gay Icarus and Gunsynd and we beat Gunsynd again in Brisbane. Three Derbies, the AJC, VRC and QTC. And he always had bad legs - that's why we gelded him."

Jack Pollard's book on Australian racing had a list of great horses associated with the name of TJ Smith. To these I have added any Slipper and Caulfield and Melbourne Cup winners not already on the list. As far as I could find out, they are listed

TJ outlines the sales strategy to Ernie, and Ernie's son Sterling, who was working at Tulloch Lodge at the time. Now that Sterling has started his own training stable, he says TJ's attitude is, 'You're on your own.'

as taken over by Tommy or not. Where there is no comment, they were more than likely bought by TJ at yearling sales.

Redcraze	Taken over from NZ
Grand Garry	Taken over from Queensland to win a Sydney Cup
Versailles	
Prince Grant	
Bold Pilot	
Silver Sharpe	Bought as a yearling
Zambesi	
Tulloch	Bought as a yearling
Gunsynd	Taken over
Kingston Town	Sent by the breeder
Blazing Saddles	
Black Onyx	
Analie	Taken over from South Australia
Toy Show	

Jan's Image
Mighty Kingdom
Gurner's Lane
Red Anchor   Taken over
Imagele
Alibhai
Bounding Away   Bred by TJ
Star Watch   Bought as a yearling
Fairy Walk
John's Hope
Toy Show
Toparoa   Taken over from New Zealand
Taksan   Taken over

7.2-3 Does he favor type or pedigree?

Walking around racetracks and yearling sales you will often hear such comments as, 'TJ will like that one,' 'That's a ready-to-run one for Tommy Smith,' 'TJ's horse in the 3rd race is typical of his runners'.

Bill Whittaker on the TJ 'Type':

"Ninety percent of Smith's horses were of a type. They walked around the enclosure usually with their heads down, and a lovely walk, with sloping shoulders. He still buys those sort of horses. The only horses he trains that don't look like that are the ones that someone else might buy and send to him. But the horses he buys in the yearling sales are usually very good walkers, and very sensible types."

Len Morton on TJ's selection criteria

Len left station life and worked for TJ to help prepare himself for a career as a racehorse trainer. He is now a successful trainer in Perth. He worked for TJ in the 1972/3 season. I asked Len if the yearlings TJ bought were of a type, similar in any way.

"No not in any way. It was something I was very conscious of and kept notes on. He was buying 80 to 100 yearlings annually. There were no similarities. There were conformation faults - back at the knee, over at the knee, turned out in front, you name it - but I concluded that he was looking for horses from successful families. It was then that I started reading catalogues and studying pedigrees and trying to put a pattern together."

"You find that he's had a lot of years in the game now and he knows most of the families, he's trained a lot of mares that have gone to stud and there are different branches of those families that he likes to chose from. And I really think that's the only criterion he uses. He likes a good individual but he doesn't have any rubber stamp idea of what they have to look like."

When I mentioned Len's view to Bill he had this to say: "Despite what Len Morton says, the yearlings TJ buys usually have a good low trajectory walk, and shoulders that conform to a certain standard in his eyes. I agree that he does not worry much about turned out legs and off-set knees. Tulloch and Playboy, two of the best yearlings he ever bought certainly were not from families with which TJ had succeeded previously."

It would seem that Bill Whittaker and Len Morton have irreconcilable views of TJ's approach to yearling selection. But there may be an explanation. Back in the 1940's I doubt TJ knew much about mare families. Knowledge of female lines is usually acquired more slowly, years or decades after a knowledge of type and sires.

TJ may have started selecting mainly by type at a time when Bill was watching the new sensation closely. As time passed TJ acquired experience with dam lines, considered the knowledge useful and increasingly took it into account in his selection process. When Len made his observations some twenty years later, TJ may have been selecting by mare family first and type second. Consequently his range of types would have to be wider if he buys the same number of horses.

Bill agrees that TJ has bought into successful families in the last 20 years, but not always. Bill believes it is very important to TJ that they walk right and have good shoulders.

A veterinarian who has observed TJ at work believes he has a freak ability to assess 'muscle quality', by looking and prodding, and so is able to buy horses that will stand his demanding level of hard work. Wayne Lukas also assesses some kind of muscle tone factor.

TJ's approach now

"Do you go for breeding first or conformation first?"

"If you go to buy a yearling, you have to buy the breeding don't you. No good going if you don't concentrate on the breeding."

"So breeding first, then you look at the conformation?"

"Well, I look through the book and there are about 500 horses in the catalogue, but I only look at about 100, the ones that I want to look at."

"So you cut them down to 100 on breeding?"

"Then if they don't have a good head and shoulder they don't gallop. I look at them and I like to see the type of horse I've had success with."

"Are you put off by poor conformation?"

"If their necks don't fit into their shoulders I won't buy them or if they haven't got the proper neck and shoulder. A horse has got to be balanced right. Has to have a good head, that's where he thinks. A horse has to have good eyes, for a start. I've never had a good horse yet that didn't have good eyes."

"What do you mean by good eyes?"

"Big eyes. Not those cunning eyes. I never buy a horse with a cunning eye. You can see that some horses have no will to win by their eyes."

Ernie Smith told me that TJ runs a lot of horses that trace back on their dam's side to fillies he raced. An example would be Christmas Tree, out of Joy And Fun, out of Denise's Joy, both of which he trained. TJ had another Denise's Joy offspring, Record Dash, in his stable at the time.

TJ, in choosing from families he has had success with, would in effect be selecting for families that could not only win, but could stand his hard preparation. If he chose yearlings from families he hasn't trained, their success may have come from light preparations. It is easy to lay out an argument that all trainers should give a high priority to lines they have already had successes with. The argument is not necessary because most trainers do it anyway. Human nature will take anyone back to the well with the sweetest water. However some trainers are apt to go back more to the sires of their better performers than to the dam lines. Tommy Smith goes back to the female side.

TJ's physical examination of yearlings

When he examines yearlings at the sales, TJ will feel the area of the throat latch. It's a little hard to tell whether he is feeling for the thickness of the windpipe or not because he tends to include the couple of muscle layers there. (Not surprisingly, Gai, in her examination, does exactly what TJ does.) TJ will go up to them and have a good look at the shoulder. He will often push the muscle somewhere around the shoulder blade. Some of the "TJ Watchers" say he is testing the muscle tone. When there is some delay and no horses are being trotted up for him, he will go over to look at a horse in a nearby stall. He will undo the door, stand a little inside the doorway and stare at them, particularly at their head, as though evaluating their response to his intrusion. He often watches the head and eyes when he is feeling their throat.

Veterinary examination

Percy Sykes and later John Peatfield, his successor, looked at the horses especially closely if TJ asked. Generally, John was part of the Tulloch Lodge team that moved around and inspected and assessed each yearling on TJ's list. John and TJ would put their heads together and discuss each yearling.

Heart Score

The Heart Score is a value determined for each horse from measurements on its electrocardiograph tracing. The score is considered by many to reflect heart size. Professor Steele, the Australian veterinarian who developed the Heart Score concept, did much of his earliest work on Thoroughbreds in Sydney. Indeed he first concluded there was a relationship between the width of the QRS and racetrack performance using horses from Maurice McCarten's Thoroughbred stable in the 1950s.

As his reputation grew, Steele was asked by more and more owners to score their horses. He scored one for a client of Tommy's and gave the owner a different opinion of the horse's ability to that arrived at by TJ on the track. This did not amuse Tommy and one day when he arrived at his stables to find Steele there scoring a client's horse, they 'had words' and Tommy ordered Steele off his premises.

Tommy, according to Percy Sykes, considers the heart score useless. Percy does not have a high opinion of the usefulness of heart scores himself. But some studs have all their yearlings scored and inform their favorite trainers and clients as to which yearlings have outstanding scores. At the sales one of the managers was of the opinion that TJ was interested in the heart scores, 'but doesn't like to let on.' Of course some horse traders prefer a horse with a high heart score, not because they believe it to be a great guide to performance, but because it may help in a resale.

Does TJ check yearlings on the studs?

TJ spends a lot of time traveling to the major studs looking at yearlings. If you phone Tulloch Lodge on Mondays or Tuesdays in the sales season you are likely to be told he is off at some studs in New Zealand or wherever.

At sales TJ is no easy sell. He seldom looks pleased or impressed. Damien Antico, son of the proprietor of Baramul Stud, pointed to a filly carrying hip number 318 and told Tommy, 'You trained her mother.' TJ's response was to completely ignore the filly and quickly cross her off in his catalogue. On another, Damien said to Tommy, 'This one will come on something terrific in the next eight weeks. 'Yes' replied a dour TJ, 'but the sale is next week'.

At the 1987 Sydney Easter yearling sales, TJ bought quite a few by the first season sires Sir Dapper and Salieri. I asked Gai why he would pay $100,000 for such horses and she replied that they were easier to sell to clients.

I presume that is because clients still remember the stallion's racetrack exploits, especially if they had starred locally, and also because they are untested and could be anything. Sheer optimism.

TJ bought one of two similarly bred Salieri's for something like $100,000. The other went for $16,000. Gai said they were not interested in the cheap one because, 'they have to look like they can run.' A cynical acquaintance suggested that, 'TJ and the other high rollers' cannot buy the cheapies because their millionaire clients don't want to look cheap. I can only say that I don't believe TJ would pass up a good horse because it was too cheap. He is simply very confident he can pick the horses that, 'look like they can run.' The price difference suggested that others agreed with him.

Veterinarian Dr Tony Stewart with a display that includes Tulloch's enormous heart, at Caulfield racetrack. Tulloch had a heart nearly twice the size of the average racehorse's heart, and a heart score of 136. A heart score of 120 is considered high. Dr Stewart worked with Dr Jim Steele, who developed the heart score concept. The heart score appears to be more important in Standardbreds than in Thoroughbreds, probably because they race for longer periods of time, especially in Australia. The role of the heart is greater in longer events.

Most people believe TJ pays above average prices for his horses, to buy top stock. He has paid top price on occasion and at one recent Sydney Easter Yearling Sales he paid second highest price. One reason given for the formation of the public company, Tulloch Lodge Ltd, was that Tommy's individual owners didn't have the money to pay top prices. But at the Trentham (N.Z.) sales in 1987, when he was able to splurge with $12m of the $15m from the Tulloch Lodge share issue, what did Tommy buy?

In round figures he paid $3.8m for 38 head (of 490 head offered) at an average of $100,000 which was a shade under the sale average. Not one of his purchases was in the top twenty lots on price. His top price was $300,000 for a Sir Tristram yearling, when the sale topper, also a Sir Tristram, went for $800,000. The most heavily represented stallions in TJ's selection were new season sire Danzatore with 6, Noble Bijou 5 and Grosvenor and Sir Tristram with 3 each. He bought yearlings by 17 different sires. Perhaps most spectacular on a percent-

age basis was his purchase of 5 of the 13 Noble Bijou's offered. I asked Ernie about the number of Noble Bijou's and he said they needed to build up their number of stayers.

Bidding strategy

An interesting sidelight of major sales is the bidding strategies of the main buyers. At the Sydney Easter Yearling Sales, Bart Cummings bids from a tunnel under the seating, known as 'Bart's Burrow,' so that others cannot see him. TJ, on the other hand, sits out under the magnificent central tree, where all and sundry can see what he's doing. Unlike Wayne Lukas he doesn't go in for a 'pre-arranged secret signal of the session.' Usually he will wave his catalogue, nod to one of the spotters, or nod to Ernie who then signals with a wave of his catalogue. Like Wayne Lukas, TJ has a reputation for picking horses and it must force up the prices he pays. Imagine: You have scouted the sales and want to buy lot 65. You throw in a bid or two and find you are bidding against TJ. Wouldn't that make you even

Star Watch, one of TJ's yearling purchases, just before winning the 1988 Golden Slipper.

more certain you had made a good choice; more inclined to go a few thousand higher? Wayne Lukas clearly thinks so. But some believe competitors give in early when they know the opposition is TJ. And I did find one 'little guy' who said he dropped out when he knew he was up against TJ. 'What chance have I got against his kind of bucks?'

Some recent purchases
STAR WATCH
Cost $400,000, won the 1988 Golden Slipper. Hopefully with his breeding he will prove a top sire. Sold a quarter share for $1m before the Slipper win and another quarter for $1m after, valuing the horse at $4m.

COMELY GIRL
Cost $165,000, second in the 1988 Slipper, winner of the AJC Sires Produce Stakes.

LYGON ARMS
A $90,000 yearling, castrated even after coming second in the 1987 Slipper and even though sired by Bletchingly who was by Biscay, a noted sire of sires. Won the 1988 Doncaster Handicap after the operation.

How did TJ develop his eye for a horse?
"Did you consciously develop your eye for a horse?"

"I think I was born to it. We had a lot of horses because my father and me, we did a lot of wool carting and tank sinking and things like that. We had a lot of horses, we had teams of draft horses and we always had a few racehorses about the place."

"Your father didn't say look at the rump on that one, look at the leg on that one."

"No. I don't think they knew anything about it in those days."

Can Tommy pass his selection talent on?
Wayne Lukas has a clearly enumerated list of 'not negotiables,' and a scoring system. That should make it easy for him to train his son Jeff. What about TJ? If he has a non-specific 'instinctive eye,' it may not be easy for him to pass the talent on.

Tony McSweeney, once one of TJ's clients: "It's something he was born with and I don't think you can teach it to somebody. Jack Green was a great trainer, very intelligent man, but he never had it."

I asked Gai: *"When he's teaching you, does he talk*

TOMMY SMITH

about the overall thing or-"

"The overall thing."

"He must say this has a good hind leg, a good-"

"He likes a good hind leg, likes a good leg."

"So he can break it down into legs, neck etc."

"He hates a horse with a weak hind leg."

"What does he mean by a weak hind leg?"

"He doesn't like a straight hind leg, he likes one with a nice stifle and-"

"A bit of angle in the stifle?"

"Yes."

"So he can make it specific to parts of the horse. How did he develop that ability? Did he look at one thing at a time?"

"No, that's not in his make-up. He always looks at an overall picture. That's very much him. He just got his eye trained."

"If he did it that way he may be doing it by something that is pattern recognition at a level where they can't explain it. Some people can see enough horses and knowing those horse's abilities - after many years, some part of their brain, the right hemisphere, the intuitive, whatever, can start to make connections, make choices. They can choose the best horses alright, but find it difficult to say why they like that horse."

"Well I think a good horseman does that."

"The instinctive horseman."

"Well Dad is an instinctive horseman. Most of them aren't."

"But one of the problems of the instinctive guys is that it is hard for them to vocalise it and give it to someone else."

"He can't."

"But Wayne Lukas, by doing it one thing at a time, he can give it to you in great detail."

"No, Dad can't vocalise it. But because you've been with him so long you become educated. You're looking at all the same things he's looking at after a while. When you pick the wrong thing he'll tell you, 'That's wrong."

"And he can tell you what's wrong with it?"

"Yes. He says, 'That's the wrong thing, I don't like it. (Looking at something else) That's alright."

Interestingly enough, that is how to learn from an intuitive person, keep pushing up examples and ask them if it is OK, and if not why not. Sometimes they can say a specimen is no good but can't say why. Often it is because it involves such a constellation of small factors; sometimes processes at the level of the brain that solves problems for you overnight if you 'sleep on it.' Computer programmers developing expert systems keep running up against the limits of the expert's logic system, long before the expert's full capability has been duplicated. The ex-

pert starts saying, 'I can't tell you how I know this or why I choose that alternative.' Words like 'instinctive', 'intuitive', 'gut feeling' and 'hunch' start to creep into the vocabulary. Many veterinarians in clinical practice, especially the busy ones, exposed to thousands of cases, develop a 'sixth sense', an abilty to know more about some cases, eg the probable outcome, than any textbook knowledge can explain.

As an example of something about which we have an opinion but have difficulty explaining in a logical way, try describing what constitutes beauty in the opposite sex - to a Martian. Especially, try describing why one face shape is better than another. When you have exhausted your verbal rules there will still not be enough to separate the finalists. It is much easier to explain with a gallery of pictures or a bevy of models. If enough examples are compared, eventually you will be able to unearth most of the rules of the previously unexpressed 'expert system' that constitutes *your* idea of beauty in the opposite sex. Even after all that, the Martian will probably be shaking its head as to how you decided the winner.

For the intuitive or instinctive horseman, that is what it can be like trying to describe an ideal type or explaining why they prefer lot 103 to lot 389.

8. How he trains

TJ Smith's name is synonymous with hard training. He changed the approach to training, and with such good results that trainers across the country tried to imitate him.

Bill Whittaker:

"He changed the training methods. Muscle and bone. He worked horses. McCarten (the leading trainer at the time) didn't work his horses as hard. Very light. Ask Tommy himself. Tommy will tell you that Maurice McCarten's horses raced themselves fit. They were magnificently produced, more like the English style - they were always well rounded. They'd come into the enclosure looking a million dollars, bit like show horses - but Tommy Smith's would come in looking, well, looking muscle and bone. No fat on them at all. He altered all that from 1942."

Bill went on to say that McCarten's horses couldn't have been too unfit - McCarten trained Delta to win a Melbourne Cup in 1951, and later Todman to run first-up in an Australasian record time for the 5f (1000m).

Perhaps in the middle 1940's when TJ was watching McCarten's methods, that trainer worked his horses lightly. Perhaps after TJ's early successes, the tables were turned, and McCarten started to pay attention to how the upstart trained, and *perhaps*, put more work into them. On the other hand there are many examples of 'soft' trainers doing well, becoming famous, so 'hard' training may not be as important to TJ's success as many Australians believe.

Did TJ really improve horses?
If so, by how much?

This is another favorite Australian bar room topic. However I had a novel chance to obtain a meaningful answer to this question. A brilliant Dutch immigrant had applied careful mathematical analysis to horse racing in Sydney over the period from the early 60s to the middle 70s. His name was Remy Plante Febure de Villeneuve. He was a very talented man, being at various times a math teacher, naval officer, solicitor, pilot and judge.

Thrown out of Indonesia by Sukarno's revolution, his qualifications unrecognized in Australia, he ended up working for a turf paper in Sydney. He kept tens of thousands of race records and under the name Rem Plante, published a book called *Australian Horse Racing*. This was the bible of Australian punters for 13 years, until Don Scott's book *Winning* appeared. Rem died in 1978 but his son Marcel Plante still runs the *Handicapper's Weight Charts* that his father started. I asked him if his father had studied the question of how much TJ improved a horse from another trainer, and the answer was yes. Did TJ improve horses that came from other trainers? Yes, definitely, although obviously it depended *who* it came from. How much, on average, did Rem allow for improvement

by TJ at their next start? FOUR lengths. Did he improve them that much in a week? Marcel wasn't clear about the time sequence but was fairly sure most of these improvements occurred over a number of weeks or longer. I certainly have not heard of any big improvements in a horse if it raced for TJ soon after he took it over.

It is possible that TJ had an even greater advantage before the sixties, before some of his feeding and other advances became more widely known and used. TJ himself claimed he could improve a horse 10 lengths. What do Marcel's charts suggest TJ's advantage to be today? That is proprietary information only available to subscribers.

8.1 Tommy Smith's training program

Below is the training program of Bounding Away, for which I am grateful to Dr Bert Inglis. Dr Inglis, a vet with an interest in racehorse training and breeding, started a newsletter called Australasian Thoroughbred Science Review (which can be reached at PO Box 199 Benalla, Victoria, Australia 3672).

Dr Inglis pulled all this detail on Bounding Away's training out of months of *The Sportsman* for a reason. While TJ considered that it was a breakthrough for him to fastwork his horses three times a week, Dr Inglis, found something which suggests it has to be used with care. He described his findings in an interesting series of articles called "Not Enough Fuel Left in the Tank." He had long lists of poor performances by favorites which he felt were probably caused by the last workout before the race being too severe.

Perusing the training works of TJ's star filly Bounding Away, as reported in the racing papers, he found that some of her few disappointing performances also followed scorchingly good times in her previous fastwork.

Dr Inglis: "While this filly has not really run a bad race, her three-year-old form has been regarded as a little disappointing. A pattern can be seen in her form. Her best runs are when she had a relatively easy Thursday. When she had a relatively hard Thursday, she ran her worst races. When Tuesday and Thursday are the same she ran average races."

I found the articles very thought-provoking. This problem would be more likely to occur when the last fastwork is two days before the race, as it so often is in Australia. It is less likely when the last fastwork is three, four or more days prior to the race, as with most American trainers.

Bounding Away was a gray filly bred by TJ himself. She was Horse of the Year for 1985/6 and the first female racehorse in Australasia to win a million dollars. In the process she was the first winner of the Golden Slipper-AJC Oaks double, which was TJ's 6th AJC Oaks.

For our purposes it is an example of TJ's training. Here are the details of the filly's preparation.

THE PREPARATION OF CHAMPION FILLY BOUNDING AWAY

Recorded track times, reference *The Sportsman.* Abbreviations: B = best time of the morning. Unless stated to be run on woodfibre (wood), runs are on turf. 'm out' refers to how many meters out from the inside rail the horse had to work.

Note: Ernie tells me that the filly would have worked on the Saturdays that she didn't race, either pace work or sprinted up, typically over 600m. (Those Saturday fast works are not reported in *The Sportsman.*) In other words she was fastworked three times per week. She was also taken swimming.

Two-year-old year 1986

Day	Date		Dist m	Time	Best	Last part	Track	m out
Tues	Jan	7	800	51.5	B49.5		wood	
Thurs		9	800	53.5	B48.5		Good	8m out
Sat		11	probably worked but Sat works not recorded					
Tues		14	800	51.75	B51.25		wood	
Thurs		16	track closed because of bad weather					
Tues		21	600	36	Best		wood	
Thurs		23	track closed because of bad weather					
Sat		**25**	**1000**	**RACE**	**Won by 1½ lengths**			
Tues		28	Not worked fast					
Thurs		30	not worked fast					
Tues	Feb	4	800	49	Best	400 in 24.5	Good	4m out
Thurs		6	800	53.75	B52.75	400 in 25	Good	6m out
Sat		**8**	**1000**	**RACE**	**Won by ½ length**			
Tues		11	Not worked fast					
Thurs		13	800	56.00	B52	400 in 26.75	Dead	10m out
Tues		18	800	54	B50	400 in 26	Dead	14m out
Thurs		20	600	37.25	B36.75		Good	14m out
Tues		25	800	52.5	Best	400 in 24.75	Dead	16m out
Thurs		27	600	38	Best		Dead	8m out
Sat	**Mar**	**1**	**1200**	**RACE**	**Won by 4 lengths**			
Tues		4	not worked fast					
Thurs		6	800	56	B49.75		Dead	2m out
Tues		11	600	36.5	Best		wood	
Thurs		13	600	37.5	Best		Dead	12m out
Sat		**15**	**1200**	**RACE**	**Won by 3 lengths**			
Tues		18	not worked fast					
Thurs		20	600	37.25	B37		Good	15m out
Sat		**22**	**1200**	**RACE**	**Won by a long neck**			
Tues		25	not worked fast					
Thurs		27	Easter: trackwork not reported					
Mon		**31**	**1400**	**RACE**	**Second beaten 3¼ lengths**			
Tues	Apr	1	not worked fast					
Thurs		3	600	39.25	B36.75		Good	12m out
Tues		8	Trackwork not reported					
Thurs		10	600	36.25	no others		after pacework	
Sat		**12**	**1600**	**RACE**	**Won by 1¾ lengths**			

Spelled after accumulating nearly $1m, winning 6 of 7 starts, 3 of them Group 1 including the Golden Slipper. She had certainly lived up to her name.

Three-year-old year

(Aug 1 is Thoroughbred's birthday in Australia.)

Day	Month	Date	Dist	Time				
Tues	Aug	12	600	37.5	B36	Dead	2m out	
Thurs		14	800	49.75	Best		Dead	Rails
Tues		19	800	50.5	Best		Dead	20m out
Thurs		21	800	52.5	B51.5		Good	22m out
Sat		**23**	**1200**	**RACE**	**Second beaten 1¾ lengths**			
Tues		26	Not worked fast					
Thurs		28	1000	1:06	B1:04		Good	10m out
Tues	Sept	2	800	51	B49.75		Good	25m out
Thurs		4	800	51.5	Best		wood	
Tues		**6**	**800**	**TRIAL**	**Won 47.5 Track good**			
Thurs		11	800	56	B49.5	400 in 24.25	Good	15m out
Sat		**13**	**1200**	**RACE**	**Beaten a head**			
Tues		16	Not worked fast					
Thurs		18	800	52		400 in 26	Slow	
Sat		**20**	**1200**	**RACE**	**Second beaten 5 lengths**			
Tues		23	Not worked fast					
Thurs		25	1000	evens				
Tues		30	1000	1:02.75	B1:02		Dead	10m out
Thurs	Oct	2	800	49.75	B48.75		Good	Rails
Sat		**4**	**1600**	**RACE**	**Won by a neck**			
Tues		7	Not worked fast					
Thurs		9	Not worked fast					
Tues		14	1000	1:05.75	Best	200 in 13	Good	18m out
Thurs		16	1000	1:05.5	Best	400 in 25.25	Good	20m out
Sat		18	1600	RACE	Sixth beaten 4¾ lengths			

Spelled

Day	Month	Date	Dist	Time				
Tues	Dec	30	600	41.75	B36.75	wood		
Thurs	Jan	1	New Year's Day Trackwork not reported					
Tues		6	800	53.5	B51.5		wood	
Thurs		8	800	53.5	B49		Good	6m out
Tues		13	800	51	B50.25	600 in 35.5	wood	
Thurs		15	800	48.75	Best		wood	
Tues		20	600	40.75	B37.5	200 in 13	Good	10m out
Thurs		22	800	51	Best	200 in 25.75	good	14m out
Mon		**26**	**1200**	**RACE**	**Fourth beaten 1 length**			
Tues		27	Not worked fast					
Thurs		29	Not worked fast					
Tues	Feb	3	1200	1:27		200 in 13.25	Good	18m out
Thurs		5	1000	1:10.75		400 in 25.5	Good	20m out
Tues		10	Not worked fast					
Thurs		12	1000	1:06	Best	400 in 24	Good	3m out
Sat		**14**	**1600**	**RACE**	**Fifth beaten 5 lengths**			
Tues		17	Not worked fast					
Thurs		19	Not worked fast					
Tues		24	800	56	B54		wood	
Thurs		26	Not worked fast					

Tues	Mar	3	1000	1:08		Heavy	3m out
Thurs		5	600	40	B37.5	Slow	10m out
Tues		10	800	51	B50.75	Good	14m out
Thurs		12	800	51.5	B51.25	Good	20m out
Sat		**14**	**1400**	**RACE**	**Second beaten 1¼ lengths**		
Tues		17	Not worked fast				
Thurs		19	1000	1:06.25	only one	Good	12m out
Tues		24	1000	1:03.5	B1:03.5	good	6m out
Thurs		26	Not worked fast				
Sat		**28**	**1500**	**RACE**	**Won by a long neck**		

In the next month, Bounding Away won the AJC Oaks a matter of days after running 4th in the AJC Derby behind Myocard.

She retired a winner of 9 races, 6 of them Group 1, and $1,464,150 in stakes. She was sent to New Zealand stud Sir Tristram, the Irish-bred sire of more Group 1 winners than any other stallion in the world. Owner Patrick Hogan is said to have refused an American offer of $US50 million for him. Unfortunately Bounding Away didn't like Sir Tristram's accent and stubbornly refused him. Eventually she went for the presumably more appealing American accent of Danzatore. TJ has had success with the offspring of this young sire so he would not have been too unhappy.

It is interesting that TJ should swim Bounding Away. Early in his training career it was well known that he was a believer in swimming horses. Later the various local authorities made it more and more difficult to find a beach at which horses could be taken swimming. Eventually TJ's favorite, Coogee was closed to horses. Some years after that, I heard (several times) that Tommy was reputed to have said, "Swimming is no good for racehorses. I'll swim horses when they have swimming races for them." I mentioned this at a racehorse training seminar and someone stood up and said, "TJ would love to swim his horses; he knows it does them good. But after they closed Coogee he couldn't swim his and he didn't want anyone else swimming theirs if he couldn't swim his."

Ernie said they did very little swimming of their horses. Bounding Away was taken for a swim of only a minute or so on very hot days. Ernie didn't see it as work for the horse, more a freshener.

Russell Smith, TJ's travelling foreman
I interviewed Russell while he was in Perth with one of TJ's horses for the 1988 Australian Derby. He was spoken of very highly by Ernie, but is not related to TJ. At the time Russell was working very hard on his sun tan by the pool at the Ascot Inn. With him was Irishman Bernie McGarrigle who was over with one of Bart Cummings' horses.

RS = Russell Smith and BM = Bernie McGarrigle

Russell was quite proud of TJ's achievements, so I asked him what he thought made TJ so successful.
RS "His eye has been his greatest thing. You win more races at the yearling sales than you do at the track. Training's only the routine. Anyone can train."
BM "Bart is into horses that are going to make three-year-old, staying-type horses. He trains that type of horse for the Cup races and the Derbies and whatnot. TJ - it's a different kettle of fish. He's into sharp two-year-olds, it looks like he likes to have a quick turnaround. Bart wants plenty of time to be able to sit down and train them so they go on. TJ is looking for quick turnover in either return of stake money, or turn the horse over and get another one."
"What does Bart's horse do? (A horse preparing for the 1988 Australian Derby over 1½ miles.)"
BM "He does about ten furlongs trotting, and the same cantering, on a slow morning, and that's it."
"And what's he do on his fast days?"
BM "Up until now he's been working over six furlongs. He'd probably do the first three in even time, and the last three at about 12 seconds a furlong."

"People say that Bart does more long distance, more slow work, than TJ."

BM   "Oh, Bart does in the beginning. Once the horse is fit, it isn't doing an awful lot."

"What sort of distance would Bart's do when they're getting fit?"

BM   "It all depends on the horse. If he thought he needed it, instead of one circuit of the sand, he'd probably do two - about twenty furlongs (4km). The sand is a mile and a quarter per lap - 10 furlongs (2km). But that'd be the most we'd do, for a horse that needed an awful lot of work. Some horses, eight furlongs is all they'll do. It depends on the horse."

"Twenty furlongs would be the maximum?"

BM   "Yes. There's a lot of horses that would never do that. Like Campaign King, he's a sprinter. At the most he'd do about ten furlongs on the sand. Maybe more trotting, you'd do an awful lot more trotting. They might trot him for twenty minutes, twenty-five minutes, before he does any cantering at all.

RS   "Bart's and TJ's, they're different types of horses, you know."

"So what do TJ's do at a comparable stage?"

RS   "Early in the preparation?"

"Yes. Twenty furlongs?"

RS   "Oh, they wouldn't do that much. Long slow steady work, plenty of mileage, plenty of trotting, plenty of cantering."

"How much would TJ's do?"

RS   "Depends. You might have a light filly come in that doesn't require a lot of work. Eight furlongs is all they'll do. You might have a big gross colt come in."

"Would TJ's do that twenty minutes of trotting before they work?"

RS   "Yes, we trot. Our horses will walk before they work."

"How long do they walk for? Legend says it used to be an hour."

RS   "Yes, well I remember when I first went here, we used to walk at least half an hour, but now things have speeded up and I'd say fifteen, twenty minutes."

"I followed them some mornings and some of them barely get over there before they're out on the track, the first ones to go. But always there was this story we used to hear in Perth - Tommy used to do an hour by the clock, minimum."

RS   "Yes, used to, but a long time ago. They're back to fifteen minutes to loosen up."

"How long does he walk them in the afternoon?"

RS   "They walk half an hour in the afternoon, at least. Some of them, the better ones, they walk for longer."

"Puts a bit more into the better ones?"

RS   "Yes. The younger horses - say your two-year-olds that have just come in -they mightn't be with you for too long, so it's pointless to walk them all afternoon, so they only get a short walk."

"Until he knows whether they're any good?"

RS   "Well, not really that. They might only be in the stable three weeks and then they might go sore. Over half of your young horses that come in go sore. They've got to go out and have a rest and come back and have another try."

"What does Bart do with his in the afternoon?"

BM   "Probably fifteen minutes walking, a pick of grass."

"TJ said it is important to get two-year-olds to learn to breathe when they come out of the barrier. I was wondering how he does that."

RS   "That's in the sort of work he gives them at home, all the steady work. It's like people going to aerobics. They're taught to relax and do their work properly, rather than be so uptight coming out of the barriers. There's a two-year-old flying at a hundred miles an hour for two furlongs, three furlongs, but if he doesn't do it the right way, that's as far as he'll go. Someone like TJ knows how to train them to relax and get the distance that he wants them to get, at a certain speed."

"How does he go about relaxing them so they breathe?"

RS   "That comes naturally, teaching the horse in its slow work at home. That's where he teaches them to relax and breathe and do all the things right."

"Does he have any specific instructions coming out of the barriers, about getting them settled or balanced or whatever?"

RS   "That depends on what the horse is up to. If it's going through the barrier the first time, it just goes through. As long as it doesn't get a fright, as long as everything goes nice."

"Does he put them through a lot, or is he one of these people who thinks that gets them uptight?"

RS   "Once they do everything correct, that's it."

"How many times do they go through on average?"

RS   "From the breakers they might have two or three little goes, and then when they come to us, they'll have a jump out. If they do that correctly, then they go to the trials, so really not a lot. But they're not uptight when they go there, they've had plenty of work, it's not all new to them.

"Who does Tommy's breaking?"

RS   "John Drennan. He operates out of the stables in Inglis's. He breaks in thirty or forty at a time."

"What can you do if you have a two-year-old that you think is tending to hold its breath and come out uptight?"

RS   "If they're uptight, they just spend more time on them until they learn to relax, and sometimes it might take a few races to do that. He might run, and mightn't run as well as he could do, but he'll run anyway because he needs the experience, to teach him to relax. You're lucky if you get youngsters that just click, and they do everything right."

"Our horses thrive on company because they're all in together, they work together, they're used to other horses around them. They see another horse do something, they just go. You ride one and you lead one - all the time - in morning exercise, afternoon exercise. They work with partners all the time. That helps relax them, so they're not on their own. They've got another horse to follow or walk around with . . . they're like kids. Sheep."

"How long does it take to get them up to racing?"
RS   "Depending on the horse. Nowadays horses are spelled better than they used to be. They're fed and looked after, whereas before, they'd throw them out in the paddock - like that - fend for yourself! Have a spell! Now most horses don't even see a paddock. They're in a small yard. They're fed twice a day. Before they come in they've done say a fortnight or three weeks of pre-conditioning work, bit of mileage on a treadmill, or they've trotted and cantered. We need a couple of weeks, before we do pace work."

"You start by trotting them?"
RS   "We trot and canter, yeah.

"Then what sort of pace work do you do?"
RS   "Depending on the horse, but you start off after about a fortnight or three weeks, just going three furlongs three quarter pace. After that you build up to half a mile three quarter pace, and then you build up a further half a mile three quarter pace, home your last furlong. Next thing you know, you're going easy half mile and then . . . (indicates a fast finish with a swish of the hands)."

"So they go out and they do a full lap, but how far from home you speed up increases gradually."

"They go a whole lap, but you just canter up to the mark, which is nothing, and then . . . "

"Wind them up."
RS   "Away you go, yes."

"What do Bart's do at the pace work stage?"
BM   "He's got such a varied selection: he's got horses that sprint, right up to two mile Cup horses - 3200 meter horses - and they all do so many different things. We've got a big selection of horses over different distances, where TJ's haven't. They're basically all the same type of horse."

"So what would be the extremes in preparation that you've seen at Bart's? Something that's going a sprint, what would it have done? Just come home three furlongs? And then there'd be some stayer that's come home seven at the other extreme?"
BM   "Nothing ever comes home much more than three, four at the most."

"So the difference between his and TJ's is more in what they do before that?"

BM   "Yes, we do even time a lot more. Some of the stayers, on a gallop morning, will do ten furlongs at even time."
"And the sprinters at the same point?"
BM   "They'll come home three. The sprinters only work over five. Home two, some of them. Horses like Bowie, he's a seven furlong horse, he normally works six, home the last three furlongs."
"So six evens and then home three?"
BM   "Yes."

"I always found it interesting that Bart, with his Melbourne Cup horses, going two miles (3200m), will start them in very short races, which they sometimes win, and then they move out in distance."
BM   "Most of his run over shorter distances. It's something that I've never understood about Australian racing - you get a horse like Beau Zam starting over 1200 or 1400 metres. It would be unheard of, in Europe, to start a champion 2400 metre horse like Beau Zam in a sprint race, because he couldn't win it. There'd be nothing but sprinters in that race, and he is not a sprinter. All we'd end up doing over there is probably degrading him, because he'd be going flat to the boards for the six furlongs or whatever, you'd probably do a lot more damage - structural damage. Here you can do it, because sometimes races over that distance have got stayers in it, old stayers. So therefore they're all doing the same thing over the same distance and therefore it is good for them."

"Back home we do have gallops, and they're just like racecourses, and you can prepare a horse. Like Dancing Brave: he is prepared to win over 2000 metres, first time on the track, after five months off. He'll go through his, maybe six or seven races, near enough unbeaten for a mile and a half."

"He just stays on that distance?"
BM   "Some of them start them over a mile and a quarter (2000m), which is slightly shorter than their best, but then they'll end up running a mile and a half (2400m) and I can guarantee you that 90% of their races are over a mile and a half."

"Does TJ move his out in distance as much?"
BM   "Oh yes. If he got a horse that was capable, and a real Derby-type horse, or a Cox Plate horse (2040m) or a Caulfield Cup horse, he would train it differently. But see, most of his horses that he buys are horses that would never race beyond a mile, would they?
RS   He does buy stayers, but as far as commercial horses, he always says there's no money in older horses. There's only money in young horses, like prize money or turning them over or selling them as yearlings."
BM   "That's what I mean, he's not into that sort of thing, but if he happens to come across one, he'll train it of course."
RS   "He still buys horses with staying pedigrees. They always start off in short races. The good ones always win. The

good stayers always win over short ground."

"What would be the difference in training between Tommy's sprinters and his stayers? What are the extremes of training you get there?"

RS   "Basically his sprinters - everything - they just gallop half a mile. But his stayers, even if he was training a horse for a two-mile race, he'd never work it any more than nine furlongs total, because it had already built up to that distance. It'd be pretty fit. Wouldn't require any more work - work it over six furlongs at three quarter pace, and come home your last three furlongs or your last half mile. That's all he'd do."

"Is there any difference between the three quarters?"

RS   "Well, our three quarters is fourteen (seconds to the furlong)."

BM   "Bart's is seventeen, the first three quarters is seventeen."

"So when you put a new rider on at TJ's, you say go your six three quarter home three, and you've got to say three quarters means fourteen."

BM   "So actually, TJ's go pretty fast in those early stages, and then he really puts the stick on a bit at the end?"

RS   "I don't think he gallops horses as hard as a lot of people have that I've seen. If a horse raced on a Saturday and it was going to back-up on the following Saturday, he would never gallop it on the Tuesday."

BM   "Bart would sometimes."

RS   "I wouldn't say TJ never does, but he doesn't. If they were racing and they were fit and they were going to back-up (race again) on the Saturday, they don't do anything, he just potters around with them on the Tuesday. They have a blowout on Thursday morning, and then go into the race."

"Bert Inglis started a newsletter and he was making the case that TJ's horses sometimes worked so hard on the Thursday that it took a bit of the edge off them. Some would say it sounds a bit crazy when someone thinks they know better than TJ, but Bert had some figures to back his argument."

RS   "I don't know. I see them work on Thursday morning, and they come out Saturday morning and you can't sit on them. So they've got to be doing something right. Come out race day and you can't sit on the buggers."

"How's TJ coping with not using anabolics any more? I know Bart's really protesting. How's TJ taking it all?"

RS   "We've had a lot of geldings at our stables throughout the years and they're the ones that are suffering. Really they are. They don't stand up to the work."

"TJ is considered to be hard on his horses though."

RS   "Some horses come and they don't cop it, and others do. The ones that cop it, they just improve."

"Does he go easy on any of them?"

RS   "Oh yes. He can be tough on horses, but look, he's not as tough as a lot of people have said, not at all."

"A lot of people say that TJ's formula is to just put them under heavy pressure, and if they stand up to it, they'll be the best in a race."

RS   "Not at all. I don't go along with that."

"The thing that always interested me was this - Bonecrusher, an Australasian champion, gets one fast work a week, and thrives on very little work. Would TJ - if he had a horse like that, have worked him that little?"

RS   "Yes. I've seen him, once he's worked a horse out - horses we've had around there for a while - he'll back off them if he finds out that the right formula is not to work him too hard."

"What would be the lightest training of a horse that you've seen there, at Tommy's?"

RS   "I remember a horse a couple of years ago, Our Shout. He used to race him once a month. He would never do any more than, say seven furlongs of three quarter and home one. That's all he'd do with him. Put him in a 2000 metre race once a month and he'd win every time. Didn't have to work him."

"Well, that's interesting, because it's a lot less work and a lot less racing than most people would think TJ would ever put into a horse. So many trainers have hammered hell out of horses trying to be the next TJ."

RS   "Yes. Our Shout was a staying horse that was carrying 58, 59kg over 2000m or 2400m (a mile and a half). He used to start at the same price every month and we loved it. He might be five to two, nine to four every month."

"What's the toughest that you've seen him put a horse through?"

RS   "Hard to say, really. If the horse is gross, and it needs a lot of work, then he'll give it to it."

"If he gives them extra, is it mainly trotting and walking? Or is it pacework?"

RS   "Pacework. The trotting and cantering is only the warming up stage. That's like a day off. Horses are like athletes, you train hard on say, the Tuesday or the Thursday and you play on the Saturday, and all the other nights you might go for a bit of a jog, and that's all that is."

"So if he's putting more pace work into a horse, he puts it into them on their fast work morning?"

RS   "Yes."

"What's the most pace work you've seen him put into a gross horse?"

RS   "That depends on the horse. That depends if he's a sprinting-type horse, or a staying-type horse. If he's a staying horse, he wouldn't work him any more than a mile. Like I say, a two mile horse, about nine furlongs, ten furlongs - about three quarter pace and come home your last half mile or something. Make 'em work a bit quicker. Work two together. That improves them a bit."

Walking across from Tulloch Lodge one morning at about 4.30am, I asked Ernie about training.

"What do you see that tells you that one horse needs more work than another"

Ernie: "That's the trainer's eye. It's very hard to explain. It comes back to the knowledge of horses, knowing everything about them, coming up from the bottom and learning shoeing, everything. You look at the individual and you study him and you know what's required. It's no good just taking them all over there and working them like a factory, working them all the same way, that doesn't work. You'll get some winners but if you want to get the very best out of them, the top results, you can't work them all the same. That's what happens with fellas, and when they get rid of horses, another trainer gets it, makes it a good horse, and everyone says, 'Oh that was with so-and-so, why couldn't he do it?' And it was because he didn't know how to do it."

"So are you looking at the muscling or what?"

"Well once you get them muscled up it doesn't take much work to keep them fit."

"How long does it take you to get them from the paddock to their first race?"

"Six weeks." (I remember in 1970, the first time I heard about TJ getting youngsters from paddock to trials or track in six weeks, because a trainer present at the time - an outer Sydney trainer - declared most vehemently that it had to be absolute codswallop.)

"Are they doing much at the pre-training place"

"We don't do much at the pre-training place. They might trot around for a couple of weeks. But you can get horses to the races in six weeks."

"Obviously some would take longer, for individual reasons."

"Oh yes, bigger, grosser horses, things like that, naturally. Some horses come to hand very quickly. But you take those light framed horses - they don't take much work. The main thing is when you get a horse fit and racing, you haven't got to gallop the guts out of him. Then the horse will train on."

An Australian I interviewed about Charlie Whittingham told me that when he descibed TJ's strenuous training regime to Charlie, Charlie would just shake his head in disbelief. Indeed, during the many months he worked for Charlie, Charlie would ask him about it over and over again, always shaking his head from side to side in amazement.

What else is different about TJ's training?

The first thing everyone lists after the high work load and the rapid preparation for racing, is his early morning use of the track. TJ is famous for taking his horses onto the track around 5am, and for completing the work of his large string in very quick time - around 40 to 60 horses in a about an hour. Why does he do this? When he was starting out he had less reason than most because he only had a small string of horses and did not have another job. Many a trainer in Australia has an ordinary full-time job, has to train the string then get to work by 7am, 8am, 9am. TJ had to be at one track or another for punting purposes but not until the afternoon or evening. But he may have started earlier to have the use of top track riders and jockeys and because many of his early morning workers had full-time jobs.

The reason usually given is that TJ likes to have first use of the track, particularly the grass for fastwork. First use means fewer clods of turf gouged out, and fewer holes for a horse to stumble over - with fewer injuries as a result. But in TJ's heavy gambling days it probably helped to stop the touts seeing his horses' workouts. They would sell the information or bet the horses themselves, lowering the odds for Tommy. It also might have been to allow him to wait around and watch the work of rivals' horses.

The track is considerably more crowded with horses later in the morning. This increases the chances of a collision between horses although there is more light. There are a lot more people watching too, but these days any gambling advantage of TJ's early start is largely lost because there are at least two clockers from racing papers in the center tower of the track (the one I believe should be officially called Tommy's Tower). They are in the same room at the same time as Tommy, Ernie and Gai. They ask Tommy to identify horses or check his team's clockings if they have any doubts. This information comes out in print and is available to all and sundry. So he doesn't train early to hide anything these days. Finishing work so early does fit well with his policy of phoning his clients about the progress of their horses at about 7am - 8am, before they leave for work.

"When did you start these hideously early morning starts?"

"I've always been first."

"Even with Bragger?"

"First here. You get the best of the tracks."

"Is that your reason for doing it?"

"Yes and I think the horses relax better. They go home and they eat. You can go in my yard at half past eight and of my sixty horses, forty will be laying down."

"And you like them like that?"

"Oh you must have them resting. You can't get them fit if they don't rest."

"I thought in the beginning when you were betting a lot, you might not want the bookies to see what they did."

"I tell people what they do."

"You were making your living betting, you would have

wanted to watch the other people's horses working afterwards?"

"I always had my eye on other people's horses."

"Would you see some that you wanted to buy?"

"I would see horses that I liked but I don't try to buy many. I prefer to buy in the yearling sales. I've been successful at that."

"Do you start your morning training at the same time, winter or summer?"

"Yes, winter or summer. With the lights it doesn't make any difference."

"But the lights are in the middle! Not out on the track. When they are going around the back straight there, I wonder how you can tell which horse is what."

"Oh we can pick them out."

"They look like little black things!"

"There's nothing like practice is there."

Percy Sykes attended trackwork with TJ for many years, and he had this to say about TJ's ability to tell horses in the dark: "When it was dark or foggy, Tommy would recognize a horse by its breathing or its footfalls before you could see it well enough as they came to the hut in the center. The other trainers would be over on the side and couldn't see what their horses were doing for half the distance. They'd be chatting and not paying attention at all, some of them. Tommy knew everything about his horses and their work."

"He'd watch every one of his horses go round and everybody else's. He'd have two or three clockers with him and he'd look out in the gloom and recognize a horse that was a rival to his own and he'd say, 'Clock that one.'"

"The horses would come to him in the center after their work, and he could look at the horse's eye and say, 'That hurt him. He felt that.'"

I asked Percy what Tommy looks for.

"He couldn't tell you. He'll tell you, well not deliberate lies, but he'd say something, and he really doesn't know."

I asked TJ about his training paces.

"How many seconds to the furlong do you tell your guys to go for half pace and ¾ pace."

"I don't have any half pace, any evens, I only have ¾ pace at 14 seconds to the furlong. My ¾ pace is about three furlongs in 41, 42 seconds."

"The last week or two before a horse of yours goes into its first race do you put them over the race distance?"

"No. Just the the five (furlongs)."

TJ likes as far as possible to work on the grass. A typical instruction was, "go along seven (furlongs), home the last three," or "bowl along for three."

Training good horses and moderate horses

TJ felt many trainers missed out with their first good horse:

"It is amazing the work a horse can do, especially good horses. Training good horses and training ordinary horses is like chalk and cheese. That's where a lot of people that have never had a good horse get tricked up. They get a good horse and they train that good horse like they trained the moderate horse. You've got to rethink altogether when you get hold of a good horse. They can recuperate quicker than a moderate horse."

"One of the things I was told was that when you started off, everyone did one fast work in the week between races, but you started doing two lots of fast work in the week between races?"

"I never give a horse a rest once I've started, I keep them working every day. When I let up on them I keep them working because you must keep that muscle up on horses. If you lose it, it takes a long time to get it back."

"Were the others only doing a race and one fast work a week when you started?"

"Trainers used to gallop on the Tuesday morning and they'd say, 'Now I've got him fixed,' and then they'd just go easy. Then they couldn't understand why the horse was getting knocked out race day because he wasn't quite fit to stand it."

"So that was a breakthrough for you to give them another hard hit out on the Thursday."

"Yes."

TJ told me he won with the first four horses he trained. He believes Bragger won on sheer ability, in spite of mistakes. By the time TJ started training the later horses he had learnt a lot from watching other trainers.

Former top jockey Athol, 'call me George' Mulley

Quoted in *A Racing Heart*, George remembers TJ as a firm but steady trainer who didn't give them easy work one day and hard work the next.

Bobby Thomsen

Former stable jockey and later foreman at Tulloch Lodge. Now a top ten Sydney metropolitan trainer

"I train only about 30 horses so I can give them a bit more individual attention. I have to be very careful about training my horses and think about what I'm going to do because I don't have the numbers behind me that TJ's got. He tries a lot of different things with horses that other trainers wouldn't try. A lot of different things."

"Part of being the Perfect Trainer - my guess was that they would be very experimental, because they have to find things out and find things when they are very new. But if you're too experimental you could ruin horses."

"He's tried everything. He'll run a horse first up in a 1600m - of course they are good horses too - he'll run a horse in a 1600 first up, 2000m second up, all those sorts of things and they'll win, but a lot of trainers wouldn't do that - can't do it. If you've got a good horse you put them in cotton wool so to speak. He trains his horses to win from Saturday to Saturday, he doesn't train horses to win specific races and that's the difference between him and Bart Cummings. Cummings will train a horse to win a particular race, Tommy will win four races coming up to that race. If the horse is still going it will win the race on that day, but prior to running that race it will have won 3 or 4 whereas Bart's hasn't."

"Trainers have said to me if you're an owner you get a pretty poor deal out of Bart because he may win a Melbourne Cup, but he'll pass up winning a lot of races with 4 or 5 horses to win one Melbourne Cup and the owners of the other 3 or 4 do very poorly out of it because they've been all that time in training. (Some trainers have lost staying horses to Bart so their comments may have some jealousy at the back of them.)"

"Tommy started this getting horses ready to race six weeks from the paddock, pushing horses. Bart's take 90 days (13 weeks) from the paddock until they're ready to race. Tommy started this quick turnover of horses."

"I think that you would have to be a very good trainer and have a very good eye for how the horse is handling it to be doing that - wouldn't you? And you'd need very good track workers, because that's another way you can go wrong."

"He's always had a lot of staff, he never cuts down on staff. No short cuts at TJ's."

"If he sends a track worker out with certain instructions and they go a bit faster than they are supposed to, do they get a rocket?"

"Well he's always had brilliant trackworkers, always the best - I don't know what he's got now, probably uses jockeys now. But in the years I was there we had the best track riders around - not jockeys, trackriders. They had stop watches in their heads, they could judge a pace to the second. That's a big thing. One gallop the wrong day can ruin a horse."

"I think some of these people who think TJ's got some magic formula -they don't realize that at least part of it's because TJ is looking after all the details, all the way. He doesn't have a horse given too much work one day."

"He does train his horses hard, they gallop hard. I've learnt from him, with little variations that's all."

"Do you experiment much yourself?"

"Oh yes, I do. I like to experiment with horses."

"What would be a recent example that you tried?"

"Well I won the Galaxy first up with a horse. That was a Group 1 race."

"How do you get them into a Group race without any previous runs? What are the entry requirements?"

"There are none. You can run a maiden in a Doncaster if he gets a run. You can run a maiden in a Derby. TJ's won two Derbys with maidens. Playboy was a maiden when he won the Derby and so was Silver Sharpe."

"Aren't there a stack of horses trying to get into a race like that?"

"There there might be 190 or something horses nominated for a race, but come Derby day they are flat out getting a full field."

"What's happened to the rest of the horses? They've realized that it's not their distance, or they don't have the class?"

"That's right."

"I guess they don't want the embarrassment of having a horse 14 lengths last, trailing the field. Is that part of it?"

"Probably. There is the cost of running them and that. No - you can get into these races. I've run a maiden in the Brisbane Cup, got a run quite easy. That was a big thing winning the Galaxy first up with Gray Receiver."

"People often comment on how frequently Tommy runs them."

"Yes he does, he runs his horses pretty regular."

"He gets a lot to run weekly. Would that be more so than other trainers? Most of them seem to aim for fortnightly runs."

"Yes"

"With keeping horses up when he's racing them weekly like that, does he expect them to have a shorter campaign or can he keep them up?"

"Most of his horses do have shorter campaigns because he gets the best out of them as quick as he can."

"And then back out to the spelling place and then back in again?"

"A lot of them don't come up the next time and that's the difference. When I get a horse with potential I've got to be very kind to them and think of a long term preparation, and then of course you've long careers with them. He wins what he can, when he can, and if they come back the next time fine, if they don't, out they go."

"Is that part of the pressure on him? He wants that total number of wins?"

"These owners, they pay big money for their yearlings and so they expect quick returns and he suits them because of his style of training. A lot of people now are running them weekly - more so than they used to. But then again I can think of years ago when a horse was raced on a Saturday, then back up on a Wednesday, then back up on the Monday. TJ ran a horse four times in a week once - won three of the four. Saturday, Monday, Wednesday and Saturday. 2000m, 1600m, 1600m and 2000m. He was a tough horse - Regal Rhythm. Won over 20 races."

"A lot of trainers have a big hoodoo on coming back in distance."

"That's TJ. He tries everything. But with good horses."

Keiran Bredin, who rode out with TJ's string

Keiran graduated as a vet in 1965 from Dublin University. Keiran found it difficult to break into equine veterinary practice in Ireland. ("You had to be a 7th son of a 7th son.") So he went out to Australia to see what he could learn from a vet he'd heard a lot about, Percy Sykes. Keiran was a successful equine practitioner on Ireland's famous Curragh when I spoke to him in 1987.

"You went and worked for Percy Sykes from February '73 to February '74."

"I lived on the premises of Percy Sykes's vet practice, and every evening I went into the lab and I fiddled around doing some tests for myself, just so that when I went back to Ireland I knew what it was about. I studied all the blood reports and watched the race form. I used to go to the track every morning with Tommy Smith, riding out, just to get the feel of things and to see exactly what they were doing. Then up with Tommy, watching. Tommy Smith got his horses out first every morning and they were in and out in the cool of the morning. Now, many fellows worked for Tommy Smith, and then set up training -like Gil Ings and several others at the time. They tried to imitate Tommy Smith, but they didn't copy those obvious things. They were plodding out with the second lot at 9:30 and the heat of the day was there at that stage. They hadn't got the staff, the money or the manpower, to give them as much preliminary work as Tommy gave them."

"That's one of the things that has intrigued me, that Tommy can have remained so long at the top when people who worked for him have not done very well. It should be so easy for people that worked for him to just go and imitate."

"Yes, his methods were there for everybody to see. But when they set up they never had the manpower. None of them did the same preliminaries. There was nobody that was giving them that hour in the car park, it must have done a lot for the stamina - and their legs stood up well."

"What sort of surface was that car park?"

"It was kind of bitumen, a rough surface, you'd wonder that they didn't get more stone bruises from it. But no, they didn't mimic him completely."

"Walking on bitumen might have cut down on shinsoreness, might have done a few things. When I talk to students who come out into veterinary practice with me sometimes - about surgical technique or whatever, I say, 'When you watch someone who's getting the best results you have to be careful of thinking you know what parts of their technique get the results. In the beginning what you should do is imitate - exactly."

"Yes."

"He gave a lot of preliminary work?"

"They walked from the old yard across that busy road and into Randwick. An average of one horse a year was killed on that journey at that time, with the early morning traffic. He got into an area there at Randwick at the back of Neville Beggs's yard. There was a big area that looked like a rough old car park, maybe they've built on it now. But Tommy's horses spent an hour walking around there."

"Was that with a rider on the back, or leading them?"

"A rider on the back and an experienced rider leading one, a more experienced rider leading two. The amazing thing about Gunsynd was you could lead two fillies off Gunsynd and it wouldn't make any difference. But they strolled around there with riders half asleep for a full hour."

"That must be from around 4am to 5am, was it?"

"Well it was a full hour anyhow, because I timed it at the time. Then they went on to the track, and they all did a preliminary canter on the side. There were amateur riders and old retired boys - part-timers. Old boys that were maybe lesser jockeys, maybe had a job in town, I could never figure out what they were. They came in and some mornings the whole string could move off."

"He'd have that many riders?"

"He'd have that many riders at times. But certainly half the string could move out there, and they all went around the sand track. Tommy was on the big hump in the center of the field there, and Dick was with him, the brother that had the pub in town. What fascinated me was that there were no secrets there. The Press were up in their little boxes. One or two of those pressmen became trainers afterwards. Well anyway Langby was the jockey at the time, and they all gradually came into the center to Tommy, and they were paraded past him and he saw them and he sent them off to do their bit of work."

"So they did a lap of cantering."

"At least a lap. I mean the stayers and the ones that were not long in from their spell, they did a good bit on the sand. They came in then after working and went straight to the sand roll and then were brought into a hosing area and hosed and then they were brought back. They hosed them down completely in summer and hosed them trace high in winter."

"So they went straight into a sand roll first and everything rolled. That is something they don't practice in Europe. If a horse didn't roll it had to be seen by a vet when it got back to the yard. They considered that to be as good a guide as a high temperature. If he didn't roll there was something wrong. There was a pain from a lameness or he was incubating something."

"On a fast work morning, what did they do?"

"I couldn't tell you exactly in distances or times or anything like that. They always did the canter first."

"Would they ever go around twice?"

"Not the horses in advanced work, not sprinters in advanced work, they did one canter, and then the rider took it into the center. He jumped down and Langby or Quinton, or somebody like that, got on and did the fast work."

"You would hear of the odd horse that came out of Smith's stables - Tommy Smith trained him and let him off - and then some fellow won the Perth Cup with the horse. The machine type training - and it was a machine, Tommy's day at the track was all over in an hour, an hour and a half - it mightn't have suited one or two horses, maybe about 2% of horses. If they happened to be horses with latent ability, well they're the only ones that have improved out, but not many have improved out because that system suited most horses. They got plenty of work, a lot more work than they would get in Europe, and that would account for the fact that colts did very little messing around. Colts are very sensitive animals, but they had no energy left when they came back in from their work. Oh, and another thing they got, that the smaller trainer trying to imitate Tommy Smith couldn't afford, was a little bit of afternoon exercise. They were always taken out, but not necessarily for an hour. They would go into a cul de sac near the main yard and the whole string would go round and round, a lot of yapping and talking, but no horses prancing about or messing about at all."

"For a while that became almost an Australia-wide institution. When I got to Newmarket it amazed me that very few trainers get their horses out in the afternoon. I presumed it would be something everybody did. Afternoon walking is very subject to fashion."

"Tommy came in in the evenings and I always tried to coincide with him in the evenings because I used to pick up a lot from him. I'd go round with Tommy and just note his observations and whatever. But he left a good bit to Percy. Tommy never came down to re-look at a leg or anything like that, he left a lot to Sykes and they got on well together."

"But Tommy has changed. He was here in Ireland this year (1987) and he came out, a lovely day it was, in June I think, and he looked around. You could hear the birds and everything was lush and green. And he said, 'Keiran you've a lovely country here.' He wouldn't say that the last time he was here. 'Oh can't wait to go home, we've been to Ascot and it rained and it poured and the prizemoney is miserable. Give me the Melbourne Cup.' But this time it was different. 'Ahh Ascot,' he said, 'there's no place like Ascot.' 'Oh what is it, what is it Tommy? Haven't you got Melbourne?' 'No' he says, 'You've got tradition here,' he says. 'The Queen coming down . . . ' But he's mellowed, he's mellowed. A likable man. An amazing character."

Len Morton

Len remembers that the horses had to be ready to leave the stables at 5 am, and the first of them had to go out to the middle at 6:05. He considered the walking morning and night had a very settling, calming effect on the horses. If horses went off their food slightly, TJ keep up the training, and over a 2 to 4 week period, they would become fit enough to cope with it and resume eating well. TJ didn't usually hold them at one point, like Charlie Whittingham, he pushed on with the speed and distance of their fastwork.

The times I have watched Tommy's horses, in 1987, 1988, and 1989, the horses didn't seem to go round under the trees for anything like an hour, many in fact came over from Tulloch Lodge and disappeared out into the middle within 10 minutes. With horses coming and going it was hard to be certain but 20 minutes might have been average. In September 1989 I asked Ernie about it as we walked through the dawn light and the horses circled under the gloom of the trees. He said twenty minutes was the aim. The old hour-a-day had gone because labour costs were so high.

That led to an interesting story. Ernie told me how one of the staff had been hungover so often he was useless, and after several warnings, they had sacked him. Next thing, the union man had appeared, demanding that the sacked man be reinstated. They didn't want to do that but the union man threatened to close them down if they didn't. Tommy had had union strife before. Anyone familiar with the power and bloody-minded arrogance of Australia's unions in the 1970s would know that the best thing for an individual business to do was avoid confrontation with the unions. So Tommy put the hangover man back on. Two days later, the union man appeared again. 'What now?', asked Ernie. 'The man is not a member of the union, you gotta sack the bastard,' says the union man. 'What! You sack him, you made us put him back on.' Out went the hangover man.

8.2 Hard or soft trainer?

TJ has a reputation as a very hard trainer, THE hardest. "He's a butcher." "He just trains the hell out of them all and races the survivors." But as we saw in the previous section, Russell Smith could give examples of horses that TJ trained lightly.

Vet John Peatfield: "He'll push a horse to a level, and then hold it there until it adapts. It might be off its food or have some filling in its legs, but he'll just decide to keep it at that level. After another run or two it'll suddenly start eating, or the filling will go down. Sometimes it doesn't and he has to back right off or send it to the paddock, but he's a genius at knowing which ones to push. He's not often wrong."

"Tommy calls it the sound barrier. He pushes them and if they take it and eat up and go on, they're the ones that might

At Randwick track a horse enters the sand yard where all TJ's horses are taken for a roll after a work. When Keirin Bredin was there 1973, any horse that did not roll was examined later by the veterinarian.

be champions. You can tell in June or July of their yearling year (which ends on Aug 1st). So they're not yet two-year-olds. If they go off their feed but do OK in a barrier trial, then they might be a useful horse. If they fall away, you might as well get rid of them."

I have often wondered how TJ could test Thoroughbreds so young and apparently not let any top horses escape him. I had heard many years ago of a trainer who had a time for a young horse's last furlong, which he used as a cut-off point. He only kept those that could cover the last furlong in some certain time. This sounded good to a vet student, but years later I would learn that many horses don't achieve their best racing conformation until three or four years of age. It would be like selecting human mile runners of the future by sprinting teen-agers over 400 yards and timing their last 100 yards. What that trainer was doing was probably more suited to Quarter Horses.

TJ was apparently more interested in whether or not they kept eating. TJ pushes all his new youngsters. Only later does he back off the ones he believes need less work. I wonder if a strong appetite is a sufficiently important feature of champions that any horses with a weak appetite can be safely discarded. More likely it is just a matter of percentages, that very few champions have a weak appetite.

When I spoke to Dave Johnson, a veterinarian who worked for Percy for many years, about the horses that were tried out at TJ's, he said, "They come, and some of them are only there for a matter of weeks. They go, and they seem to disappear off the face of the earth."

Two strappers who have worked for both TJ and Bart Cummings

"It's a totally different atmosphere at Bart's, the people and horses are more relaxed. At TJ's it's very well organized, very clockwork. They come to the track, they get their horses worked and they move home straight away. Bart's horses work, they have a pick of the grass, and they walk home. You take your time. There's no rushing."

"And what about the work? Bart's horses are said to do more slow work."

"Bart's horses take their time, they just go out, they're worked a lot slower and longer."

"So how far would they go compared to TJ's? How many laps?"

"Depends on the horses. The horses are brought up slower than they are at TJ's."

"How many weeks?"

"Well you see that's the difference, TJ's are all pre-trained before they come in the stables, but they're not at Bart's so it's a slower pace. Some of the horses at Bart's are ready to gallop, but they don't because they just keep them going, and they're

TOMMY SMITH

brought along gradually because they might be a little bit nervous sometimes. TJ's just go on - it doesn't matter."

"If TJ is supposed to take six or eight weeks - pretraining included - to get to the races, how long would it take Bart on average?"

"I don't know, 2 even 4 weeks longer - depends on how the horses react to it. At TJ's there are a lot of sprinters, ready made race horses. Bart's, they're late developers so they take longer to mature than TJ's because they're a completely different breeding. If there's a little bit of a problem with a horse, they're inclined to go on with them at TJ's and take the chance, but Bart's inclined not to. He'd rather put it straight back into the paddock and give it a bit of a rest."

"Of all the trainers I've come across around the world, TJ is the greatest one for pushing on. Bit of filling in the legs, a bit off food, and he keeps going."

"Yes he is very intensive. He's got the vet there practically 24 hours. John Peatfield was there every morning, every afternoon - the slightest thing and they would bring him out. If a horse has a nick at Bart's you bandage it yourself and keep an eye on it, but at Tommy's the vet there looks at it straight away. They come out instantly and check them. Bart's, you do it yourself, you check it and hose it."

"TJ's horses go faster in their fastwork don't they?"

"Yes. Bart's horses work and gallop a lot further, and then they don't run home as far as TJ's. TJ's come home 3 furlongs after they've worked 9."

"What would Bart's do?"

"Only the last couple after 9. They would come home 3 after 9 but not as hard. TJ pushes his a bit - maybe 1 second per furlong and it makes a big difference. TJ gallops his 12 or 13 to the furlong whereas Bart's might be a bit slower. But Bart's are bred to stay and not rushed up to their work. I've found a lot of Bart's horses race different to TJ's. They learn to race in with the field and then get to the line. TJ's are up on the pace and then they've still got to get to the line."

Malcom Johnson

Ex-stable jockey for TJ - now with Paul Sutherland

As an apprentice to the legendary jockey-maker Theo Green, Malcom Johnson set the Sydney racing scene on fire. It wasn't long before TJ Smith was putting him up and then wanting him as stable jockey. Malcom shifted to Tulloch Lodge for six stormy years. Things became so heated between Malcom, TJ and the stewards that Malcom couldn't stand it any longer and he took time out to ride in Singapore. Then he returned to ride for Paul Sutherland, one of TJ's main rival's, a man who makes no secret of his desire to take TJ's crown. At the time of the interview, Malcom had been with Paul 12 months. He had topped the jockey premiership in his first full year back, his 4th title.

"Malcolm, could you compare Paul Sutherland and TJ Smith: their training methods, what they actually ask you to do on horses."

"Paul's a very hard working guy, same as Tommy. Tommy is probably a little bit harder on his horses than Paul is. I think Paul's a great trainer and I think in years to come he's undoubtedly going to be the leading trainer. He is a young guy, and I can't give Paul any bigger wrap than saying that I think Paul Sutherland is the Tommy Smith of Sydney racing, as Tommy was twenty or thirty years ago when he was just starting off."

"So in terms of training their horses, they both fast work three times a week?"

"Yes."

"They both send their sprinters mainly over six hundred fast?"

"Yes. It varies, though, they're both individual trainers and they've both got a great eye for a horse. They train to suit those horses. We've got a little filly which can go five furlongs, and very very quick, called Mother Duck - and a trainer without the eye that Paul Sutherland has got wouldn't work her the way he does. He's done a very good job with her. Slow morning, she goes twice around the sand. (At the Rosehill track.) Well, for a horse that can only go five furlongs, that is unheard of. But he's got such a great eye for a horse. They've got a sort of a special sense that can tell what the horse needs - and that's what makes them the great trainers they are."

"Is there any difference in the way they train their stayers?"

"Not really, not really. Paul hasn't got experience on his side whereas Tommy has. The main difference is Tommy's probably a little bit harder."

"When you say a little bit harder, what is it that he's harder on? He makes them go a bit faster over the same distance?"

"No, a bit faster probably over a bit further. Tommy is a great believer in his horses being the fittest horses on the racecourse. And if his horses can stand the preparation he gives them, they *are* the fittest horses on the racecourse, whereas Paul just - he loves to give them just that little bit of a cuddle - which is not a bad idea also - he tends to go just that little bit easier on them and then let them become the fittest horses on the racecourse *after* they've had a few runs."

"So when they go into their first race, there's perhaps a second or two difference in six hundred meters in what those horses are doing?"

"Yes. I think that's pretty right. Paul's sent a horse - say a stayer -worked him over seven furlongs and brush home the last three. He'd probably come home in thirty nine, whereas Tommy would want his stayer to come home in thirty seven. That's the difference - whereas Paul just loves to give them that little bit of a cuddle, which I think suits a lot of horses."

"It is often said that if other people try to train as hard as TJ that the horses won't stand it at all. Lots of people try to train as hard as TJ but they can't seem to. Have you any idea of why that is?"

"Well, I think the main reason ... Tommy can afford to do it. Tommy'll either make them or break them. If they can stand his training methods, they *are* the fittest horses on a racecourse. Human hands can't get 'em any fitter. But by the same token, if they don't make the racecourse, they go out to the paddock that afternoon. Tommy will have something in its box to take its place, so he can afford to do it. Young trainers can't afford to adopt that policy because if they do break 'em down, where are they going to get another one from? So it's a no-win situation for them. They've got to try to cuddle, and nurse, and look after them. Because it's their livelihood. They've got to try and hold them together whereas Tommy says, 'Well, I want to get them fit and if it breaks down, well, I've got the numbers.'"

"Another thing that's a difference with TJ is that if a horse leaves one lot of feed, he'll usually push on with it, whereas most trainers will usually back off at that point."

"Yes, that's the difference between TJ Smith and anyone else. At Paul Sutherland's if a horse left a little bit of feed, we won't go as hard with him that morning. Whereas TJ Smith - 'I'll make him eat, I'll make him work - make him hungry.' But that's his method. That's the way he's survived, and he's been leading trainer for umpteen years. Who can say its wrong? You can't."

"Do they find out what you think about the horse after its track work?"

"Paul does more than Tommy. After each fast work morning we have a chat -what I rode, what worked good, what felt good and what didn't feel good, whereas Tommy was different. You'd come off the track and if he was happy with what it did on the clock, your opinion didn't matter anyway. That's Tommy, though. There was no sit down and have a chat about it, whereas Paul if he was happy with something I'd still have to make it even better for him. I have to confirm what he already believes."

"What if a horse performs poorly? Does Tommy want to know all about it then?"

"If a horse doesn't perform on the track like he expects it to, then he'll come to you and he'll say, 'What happened, was there anything wrong with it?'"

How hard does TJ train?

Riding for the TJ Smith stable in 1990 was Mick Dittman, one of Australia's top jockeys, who took out the 1988/89 Sydney Jockey's Premiership and was the country's leading rider of feature race winners.

"Mick you've ridden horses for a lot of trainers, are TJ's horses a little bit fitter, a lot fitter or no different?" (This is a difficult question for any jockey, because they have to avoid insulting other trainers for whom they have ridden horses. Most jockeys, to be diplomatic, effectively say nothing. Some tell you their opinion and then say, 'But don't use that,' which is frustrating, but at least it's informative.)

"Well, he starts out to train them very hard. If you can train horses harder then naturally they're going to be fitter. He has a lot of problems with some horses when he trains them hard but the way he feeds them and the way he cares for them off the track, they seem to be able to cope with the harder yakka (work) and of course on a majority and percentage basis, that makes a better horse."

"What about the trainers that have tried to imitate that?"

"Yes, I'm sure they have. But it isn't just one thing. He isn't just a hard worker of his horses, he is also a very hard feeder. Not much soft stuff, a lot of hard grain. He can't afford to go easy on them because if he does, with the hard feeding, then they start to get above themselves, problems in the legs, things like that."

"Going out doing track work for him, does he get you to do the last 600m one second, two seconds or three seconds faster than the average trainer around?"

"He works his horses a lot with mates, and gets them very competitive. Basically the only difference with his fast work would be that if you had to go three-quarter pace say six or three-quarter pace a mile and one, his three-quarter pace is not really three-quarter pace, but just under the working gallop, so he likes them to do a bit of work."

"How many seconds to the furlong is that?"
"I'd say TJ's run along at about 15.5 with a three-quarter pace, whereas most of them would run 16.5 - 17."

"So is there much difference in his last 600m, or is the difference in the early work?"

"Well, I think it is the overall work. A lot of trainers getting a horse ready for a mile race, might only go three- quarter pace for 600m, then home the last three furlongs twice a week. He might gallop them three times a week, depending on the individual. But he isn't afraid to stick the yakka into them, and if they are not copping it they seem to get to the stage where the body learns to cope. That is his theory anyway: 'No good having a soft horse because the majority of them get beat.'"

"Does he ever tell you to take it easy with some horse because it is starting to train off?"

"Oh yes, plenty of times. He has a great eye for looking at horses. A perfect example was this horse he won the Golden

Slipper with - Star Watch. He trained him very hard in the early stages. Galloping him three times a week, hard, with mates, because he was a little round fatty. I thought he was doing too much with him but he proved me wrong - came out and won his first three starts. And the last fortnight before the Slipper, Tommy came right back off him. Going into a big race, worth a million dollars to win, you'd think he would want to keep him up to the mark. But that's the difference, he knew the horse was fit, knew he didn't need it, had all that hard yakka behind him and at the last little bit, came right off him."

"After trackwork each morning, does TJ want to know in detail what you think about each horse you have ridden?"

"He is always pretty keen to ask you about everything you've ridden and galloped. He's the same as all the big trainers, he's got a lot of horses in the stables. I mainly ride the good horses in the morning and he wants to know all about them."

"If you were ever going to attempt training yourself, would you be trying to do exactly what TJ does?"

"Well I think if you couldn't learn something from him, you would have to be pretty dumb. Training horses hard, you do seem to go through a lot of horses. There are a few that fall by the wayside, but I think you'd find that even if you trained them soft, sometime or another, they would fall by the wayside anyway. You must teach them to be a little bit hardy. It's a tough, competitive world out there, and you have to have a fit horse with the ability. If you have a fit horse without the ability, you've got some chance of winning, but if you've got a soft horse without the ability, then you've got no hope."

The problem for a trainer is to convince an owner when the horse goes lame, that it was going to go lame anyway. I have talked to owners who say they would rather have a trainer like TJ, who finds out very quickly if the horse is any good, and tells you, than a trainer who keeps on with a horse because he doesn't know if the horse is any good, or doesn't want to tell you its no good.

When did TJ start training hard?

Whenever the matter of TJ's hard training comes up, trainers will say, 'That's OK for TJ, he's got a battalion of horses waiting to replace those that break down.' That would suggest that TJ must have started with soft training and wound up the work as his numbers grew. I also wondered if he had to perfect his feeding first, so they could stand up to it.

"Tommy, when did you first start training HARD?"
"I was training hard all me life."
"So even Bragger you trained hard?"
"Oh yes."
"Did you learn that from watching the other trainers at Randwick?"

"I just watched a few fellas that I thought could train, and I found the hard trainers were always better than the soft trainers. When I was trying to be a jockey, the horses that were trained hard would always be in the finish. Better than the soft-trained horses."

"So even though you only had one horse you trained it hard?"

"Mmm. I trained Bragger hard. I might have trained him a little bit *too* hard because I didn't know enough about it."

What is the toughest horse TJ has trained?
"I think Redcraze."
"You could really put some work into him?"
"Oh yes, but he could stand racing too. He'd thrive on racing. You could work him hard and run him hard - I ran him on a Saturday in a mile and a half, came out on the Monday in a mile and five here in the Metropolitan; won by six lengths pulling up. Then he went to Melbourne, ran in a weight for age, which he won, on the Wednesday. The following Saturday he came out in the Caulfield Cup and carried nine stone thirteen pounds and won by six lengths."
"Would you train a horse like that pretty hard?"
"He was trained hard all his life, but he just thrived on it."

Can other trainers win with TJ's cast-offs?

The image of TJ Smith is that he trains everything hard and I have long wondered if some champion like Bonecrusher, which needs very little work mightn't have been rejected by TJ and thrived in some other trainer's hands. But in all the years he's been training, that does not seem to have happened. His rejects have won on rural tracks and had the occasional city win. But no one has taken a TJ Smith reject and had big wins with it - not that I've heard of and his critics would surely broadcast it if it had happened. This would suggest the popular image is wrong, and as Russell Smith says, TJ works the softies out and trains them - softly.

Tommy Smith sees himself more as a horse dealer than a trainer, and he says the idea is to sell a horse while it still has a win in it, otherwise no one is ever going to offer you money for a horse. Larry Pickering, the cartoonist famous for his calender of naked dignitaries, and now also a trainer says, "Look, I've bought horses off TJ Smith and won with them, but they win once or twice a year and that's not enough for TJ Smith. I'm not enough of a mug that I think I'm the greatest trainer in history because I can win with something TJ Smith finished with."

Many of the horses TJ sells are horses he knows can win in the country, but he doesn't want to race at country tracks, so he sells them. TJ's reasons and strategy notwithstanding, in some country towns a trainer's reputation has been based on the fact that they won with a horse when TJ couldn't. Never mind that TJ couldn't win with it at Warwick Farm in town, and the gloating country boy cleaned up at the annual Widgiemooltha picnic meeting.

TJ can train harder for a number of reasons. One is that he has better stock, and as he says himself, you can't put as much work into a lesser horse - as a generalisation. The battlers in Torrowangee and along the Willandra Billabong hear how hard TJ pushes his youngsters and try to emulate him with stock that would not even get into the Sydney sales. Another reason is that TJ has more replacements available. His owners accept and possibly encourage his high pressure culling. Anabolics, additives and protein levels would also have contributed.

8.3 Best with what category of horse?

TJ's name is inevitably linked to his success with the juveniles. It is not that TJ can't train any particular category of horse. Two Melbourne Cups -a two-mile event - is a rare achievement, bettered only by a handful of trainers in history. His extraordinary cleanup of the various state Derbys -over 30 of them - proves he can train for one and a half miles. He has won with older horses, male and female horses, handicaps and weight-for-age horses, but he is exceptional when it comes to winning with the youngsters. He buys a ready-to-run type at the sales, indeed it is difficult to separate his success into sales selection and training components. As a tough trainer it might be asked what his results have been with fillies. He has had many more famous colts and geldings than famous fillies, but most trainers do.

TJ on training two-year-olds

TJ told Bill Whittaker just before the 1988 Slipper that he fed and worked his two-year-olds much the same as he did 30 years ago.

"I started working them harder and feeding them harder because I found that they can cop more work than older horses. They develop muscle and don't fall away like older horses. I train them all the same and if at first they don't conform I set about teaching them. Yes I changed feeding and training patterns in Australia, and horses are going better and faster for it."

TJ on training stayers

I asked TJ about his big buy-up of Noble Bijous: five of the thirteen offered in the sale:

"Well he's a staying sort of horse and I had no stayers in the place. But you gotta buy a lot of staying horses to get one that can stay. By the time you get them going they either break down or they can't gallop."

"You get a lower percentage of stayers to the starting line?"

"Of course you do. First you have to get the horse that can

gallop, then he's got to go through a lot more work than a sprinter."

TJ on training older horses

According to TJ, "Age never seems to worry true stayers." TJ trained Bragger to win a Rosehill Cup at 10 years of age. He resurrected Lancelotto at eight years of age, after inspecting him at Sir Tristan Antico's Baramul Stud. Lancelotto was a 'minder' for the weanlings and had been out of racing for 18 months. Lancelotto became TJ's best hope for the Melbourne Cup of 1986. To get into the field the tough old stayer had to win the Werribee Cup and receive a 1kg penalty. No one except TJ expected it to have a showing.

Lancelotto went out and not only won, he took 0.7 sec off the track record for 2600m. When the Werribee Cup broadcast finished, the astonished fellow next to me in Melbourne said, "It's a wonder the horse doesn't drop dead: TJ must have had to dose that horse to the eyeballs with whatever he's got, to get it to win that race." Handicapper Jim Bowler however, did not give the penalty because it was Lancelotto's first start in two years. (Reasoning I find hard to follow.)

8.4 Policy on jockeys

At some point very early in his career, TJ decided that he would always have the best jockey.

"It's no good getting up at 4am and you don't use the best jockeys. I discovered this early in my career." Not the best available but the very best. That often means flying jockeys around and getting into arguments about prior engagements and the like. TJ employed the top jockey of his day, Jack Thompson, to ride Bragger after just a few starts under relatively unknown riders. Later, when his stable grew, he offered Jack Thompson the position as his stable jockey, but Thompson had his choice of mounts in Sydney and he preferred to retain his independence. Then TJ formed a relationship with the magnificent George Moore. Since that time TJ has almost always had the best jockey in New South Wales, if not Australia, riding for his stable. Because he has so many winners, only races in the city, and wins so many big races, TJ is an attractive proposition to jockeys. TJ does not vary his jockeys much for reasons of individual horses or tactics.

Bill Whittaker: "TJ and George Moore met on a train. They were sleeping on trains going to Melbourne with horses and things like that. They had met long before they got together. Moore came to Sydney as a successful Brisbane apprentice. I took a keen interest in George Moore. I know a lot about his career and I got to know him very well. He and Smith were two of the brightest characters you could ever meet anywhere, in any sphere."

"Brightest as in intelligent?"

"Yes, they're bright, they're intelligent, but they're also

bright personalities. Anyone can be intelligent. Some of the dumbest people you know are intelligent if you get what I mean."

"George Moore is a live wire."

"Oh marvelous. A marvelous character, full of stories and quick on the uptake. He's had to be, to be the great jockey that he was."

"So when did he get mixed up with TJ then?"

"He came to Sydney, and he was apprenticed to Peter Riddle. Peter Riddle had been the champion trotting driver of Sydney just after the First World War, and when trotting went bad, he switched to galloping and became a great success as a gallops trainer. His best horse was Shannon, one of the best horses that I ever watched at Randwick. George was apprenticed to Riddle in 1943 and it would have been at that time that he would have had a ride or two with Smith. Even at that stage, Smith only had one or two horses; Smith was nothing; Smith had to take his horses to places like Wagga."

"Part of TJ's formula is to have the best jockey - he says that - and I'm trying to work out at what point he might have been able to afford the best jockey - it sounds like it might have been from the beginning."

"Even when TJ was a youthful trainer in his twenties he always had top jockeys. Darby Munro, for example, was on Playboy in that 1950 Melbourne Cup, and Jack Thompson did a lot of riding for him. If you look at Bragger's record you'll find that Jack Thompson rode it quite a bit, George Mulley rode it and Bill Cook rode it. I'm not quite sure about Cook, but certainly Jack Thompson. Smith has told me that he did offer Thompson a job to ride all his horses, but Thompson was attached to other stables and he didn't really accept the job. But when TJ got stronger and stronger with more and more horses, Thompson still had the offer of that job, but Moore got it, because Moore was just the right man in the right place at the right time. I'd say that would have been about 1946 or 47, just after the war, when Moore was flying in the city. He was going great. He broke an arm or a leg in a fall, otherwise he would have won one of the premierships in Sydney as far back as 46 or 47. He fell from a little horse, and when he came back from that accident he had a different attitude."

"He seemed to get attached to Smith. They would have been out together. They were both young single fellas. They were both going to racing meetings interstate and in the country. Moore always rode at the big interstate meetings and Tommy Smith took horses all over the place, on trains, even then. No aeroplanes then."

"So how then did Darby Munro come to be riding Playboy in Melbourne?"

"Because he was the best jockey. Smith always liked to have the best jockey. Smith would have regarded Munro as the best for Melbourne. See, Moore hadn't ridden a winner in Mel-

bourne. It took Moore about ten years to ride a winner there. It was a coincidence, a little bit of history that until the day that Playboy started favorite in the 1950 Melbourne Cup ridden by Darby Munroe, Moore hadn't ridden a winner in Melbourne. His first Melbourne winner was a horse called Commentator on 1950 that Cup Day. Later he would become very effective in Melbourne, winning the Victoria Derby in 1971 on Classic Mission, the last ride of his wonderful career."

"He was only riding a few days a year down there wasn't he?"

"Oh, well, you'd be surprised how many rides he did have. I'd say that before Moore rode a winner in Melbourne, he probably had twenty or thirty rides there. Which is a very poor percentage. In fact, he won a weight-for-age race on Playboy - first past the post - and lost it on protest. I remember him saying at the time that he didn't think he'd ever be able to win a race, having won a race and having it taken from him on protest. Even at that time, the Melbourne stewards weren't too keen on Sydney jockeys."

TJ outlined his policy on jockeys to a newsman. He engages risk-taking jocks for his horses because those who take the easier outside running cost his horse ground. Top jocks have reflexes that allow them to be in tight situations with less risk and have the nerve to stay there.

John Peatfield said TJ preferred his horses up near the lead or on the lead because his were fit enough to set the pace, they get into less trouble, and the owners get a show.

TJ's instructions to Bobby Thomsen

Bobby: "TJ's known for his horses to be just bone and muscle, they are so fit. Very rarely would you see a TJ Smith horse hit the front and get beaten, they can just run and run."

"His strategy is to have his runners at the front because his are fitter than the others, so the others have to run his down?"

"That's been his outlook from the word go - even when I was riding for him. His horses would hit the front and just keep going."

"What were his usual instructions? Get to the front?"

"Oh no, his instructions weren't to get to the front. His horses are always raced up near the lead, but not necessarily on the lead. His strategy was to have them ready to hit the front when they straightened up. So you'd have them running in the first three or four. If you are watching two-year-old races, most of his do lead nearly all the way. But nearly any two-year-old winner does lead all the way."

TJ's instructions to Malcom Johnson

"Compare the racing instructions of TJ and Paul Sutherland."

"Well, that's probably a major difference between Tommy

Smith and Paul. Paul - I've got to give credit where credit's due - I think he's a great guy to ride for. He doesn't put any added pressure on his jockey, which is very important because we can't go out there and perform at our best when there is that added pressure. I think trainer/jockey combinations are probably one of the most important things in getting results. Going back to the training methods again - Tommy is a great believer in being on the speed. 'My horses are fit, put 'em on the speed, let them beat us.' Tommy loves 'em - one, two, three, four - ideal spot for Tommy Smith horses. That's his theory and that's the way he loves horses ridden: right on the speed."

"Does he make a point of getting them balanced or settled or anything like that?"

"No, not Tommy - stuff that getting balanced and settled. Just have them one, two, three or four."

"And as a jockey, what would you say about that? There must be some horses that you'd like to get back, and settled, and balanced."

"Oh yes, sure, sure there is."

"That's the pressure on you as a jockey, you might have a horse where you disagree with TJ on what's to be done with it?"

"Well, yes, but I love 'em one, two, three, four. That suits me because I consider myself a great speed rider and that's my gift. Every jockey's got their gift, and my gift is being able to get horses to run. To ping out of that box and have 'em in that spot. That's my forte, just having them on that speed."

"Well, if Tommy gets one that likes to stay at the back, obviously that isn't going to suit him. Does he try to change that in the horse; does he tell you to have it up the front?"

"Well, yes and no. I can only keep giving you examples. There are a lot of horses that I've ridden for Tommy that I would have loved to have jumped out and just given a cuddle, but because of my instructions - you can't, you've got to have 'em on the speed. There are times when horses - I feel - should be ridden further back in the field, but because of your instructions you've got to be on the speed and it doesn't suit them and they race accordingly."

"Would you be adventurous enough to say that there were some horses that TJ insists on racing up on the pace that might have won more races if they had been raced further back?"

"I'm not game enough to say it. (Laughs loudly) When I retire I can comment on things like that. (Laughs loudly again) But I do think that by the same token there undoubtedly have been horses of Tommy's that I've ridden up near the speed that should have been ridden back, and vice versa with Paul. I've ridden horses back in the field that I feel should have been on the speed and they've got beat, but you learn by your mistakes. But the only thing is - see, I'm put on them to do a job -

and if I ride them the way they want them ridden, they can't whinge, can they?"

"I can imagine what it's like with the crowd plus the stables. Someone as forceful as TJ - if you didn't ride according to instructions and the horse lost-"

"Ooohh boy!!!!! Well, if you win, no problem. I've ridden some of the worst races in me life and won, and people just pat you on the back. You ride a horse and it gets beat a head and you ride the race of your life, there's never any congratulations or, 'What a great ride.'"

"What about gear? Is there any sort of equipment that TJ uses on horses that's different?"

"Tommy Smith was the person that introduced breastplates - compulsory on all his horses. Paul has adopted that approach and I think it's a good thing to adopt because there are so many ways to get beaten in a race, and you should minimize the chances of anything going wrong. It's no extra weight at all, but it's just a precautionary measure." (To stop the saddle slipping back.)

"What was it like socially, with TJ? He used to have that Sunday morning session, didn't he?"

"Yes, I used to go to those, but socially, what people don't seem to realize is that I was only twenty one years of age when I was at Tommy Smith's - and I was a little bit young to handle the pressure that he put me under. I was only a kid. I really thought I could handle it and I did my best to handle it, but in the long run, I was a zombie. Didn't enjoy going to the races and I just got pissed off with it. But socially, you never mixed with Tommy very much. You saw him at the track in the morning and it was just all business. Whereas with Paul - I'm a lot older now - but with Paul there is a social aspect to it. I go out for dinner with Paul a lot and we go out with his owners a lot; it's a completely different thing."

"Did Tommy ever try to give you advice on how to handle it all, or were you left pretty much to your own devices?"

"Yeah." (enigmatic pause)

"Another thing that's legendary about TJ is how tight he is with money."

"Well, one thing I will say about TJ Smith. It is legendary that he is tight with money, but I've never ridden for a better trainer to pay than Tommy. Exactly the extra five percent, but it is there every time. At the end of the month, it's there. Every winner you rode. Five percent by the AJC and the extra five percent he charges the owners - it's there, at the end of the month, every month. Paul is good, but Tommy was spot on. Absolutely spot on."

"The difference between me now and when I was riding for Tommy - I was scared of Tommy then because he was the boss, although I was leading jockey at the time. If Tommy 'give me a pay' about riding a bad race or something, I wasn't game enough to answer him back and I'd go home and kick shit out of the dog or something. I wasn't man enough to stand up to him and say, 'No, you're wrong,' whereas today, if Paul 'gives me a pay' and I deserve it, I'll cop it, but if I don't deserve it, I'll speak up for myself. But Mick Dittman handles Tommy very well. He's a genius in how he handles Tommy. I don't know how he does it. I really don't. If Mick don't want to ride something, he says, 'I'm not riding it,' or he goes away on holidays. When I was there, I couldn't get a holiday at all. I had to be there every morning. Mick doesn't ride work, only fast mornings. And that's unbelievable. But you know I had a ride for TJ yesterday and I reckon if I went back to Randwick today, I'd still get a lot of rides out of Tulloch Lodge."

Will TJ run horses off the pace?

A leading jockey, Shane Dye, rode TJ's horse Lygon Arms in the 1988 Doncaster Handicap. The horse was 40 to 1.

"TJ and I worked out a plan to ride Lygon Arms quietly and give him a chance to get home. The horse had never been ridden quiet before, apart from in the Slipper . . . He'd been going up to win and just dying on his run over the last bit . . . His freshness from a three week race spell made him a good chance . . . The horse has a habit of hanging in badly, which suited me because I'm a natural right-handed whip rider . . . (Sydney is a clockwise course) We jumped and settled down back in the field." 800m from the finish Lygon Arms was second last. "I didn't hit him with the whip. After watching the videos he didn't seem to give much when hit with the whip . . ."

The horse went on to win the $400,000 event.

8.5 Placing horses in races

A racing writer stated that it has always been TJ's policy to push promising restricted class horses into higher grade races. TJ has won a lot of cup races with lightweights near the limit. As an example, in 1953, Castillo won a restricted class race at Canterbury and in October won the Queensland Derby. It is worth noting that Bragger's first race was about three levels above the lowest he could have raced in.

TJ is not afraid to 'have a go.' Some trainers have had a very good horse early in their career and not realized it's high class until too late. One trainer told me he had a real contender early in his career but was too over-awed to enter it in big races for the first year he had it. Not TJ. Very early in his career he was aiming at Derbies and stakes races. He put Ajixa in the 1942 Gimcrack Stakes, very early in the two-year-old season, and Playboy, still a maiden, in the AJC Derby. The fact that Playboy won indicates TJ did not belong to another group, the "erroneous optimists", who enter horses in big races, with not a hope in hell of winning. These erroneous optimists don't enter their horse as a calculated publicity exercise but be-

cause they think the horse can win. When it comes in a tired, flagging 15 lengths off the winner, they are shocked. According to the betting boys you rarely see TJ's finish that far off the leader.

8.7 Injuries and therapies

"TJ, have any injuries become less common or more common over the time you have been training?"

"Well I don't think it's much different - the vets treat them differently to what they used to. But horses do the same, they still go sore, they go shinsore, they go muscle sore."

TJ was an advocate of standing horses with leg problems in salt water. Bert Lillye's book *Backstage of Racing* has a 1945 shot of TJ with a bunch of horses, out in the water at a beach on Botany Bay. TJ is mounted on a small pony, and holding two racehorses. The water comes up to just below their knees and hocks. The horses are showing interest in the cameraman, but the bored look on TJ's face suggests it was a lengthy business.

8.7-1 Shinsoreness

"Can racehorses go shinsore on one run?"

"I've had horses go shinsore cantering. A horse can go shinsore on one piece of work - just a bit of work."

8.7-2 Tying up

Horses prone to tying-up are exercised on Sundays, whereas the other horses aren't.

Firing then and now

"In those days - when Bragger went lame - they used to fire them with a hot iron - oh, cruel thing. They'd have to be out 8 or 9 months before you could possibly do anything with them. Percy introduced this modern type of firing (small point and local anaesthetic) which is the best thing that ever came into racing. When Percy came in and fired a horse they all looked and said it couldn't possibly be right."

"Percy told me the old-timers used a full-size soldering iron, burning right through to the bone."

"When I was over in America I watched them firing, and Percy was a mile in front of them. They didn't know what struck them out here when I got this horse fired by Percy. I had a couple of other vets who used to work in the yard. They said, 'Oh no, this cannot possibly be fired.' I said, 'It is fired.' They used to put a big iron in a fire and get it really hot, push it into them, burn the horse's leg. Oh it was cruel, it was murder."

"Percy said they had to tie them up to do it."

"Yes and they used to be tied up for at least a month after. Walk them and then tie them up. It was murder."

"Did any of them get bone infections or anything like that?"

"No, no. But I tell you what - they wouldn't break down after that."

"Percy said he did not know if his method would work or not, but he just thought the other way was so barbaric."

"Yes I only ever let them fire one or two. I couldn't let them fire any more. After they fired Bragger I said to them I couldn't put up with it. It was too cruel."

Oxygen for racehorses

Many years ago I heard that TJ was giving his horses oxygen on the way to the racetrack to improve their chances of winning. A cylinder was carried in the truck or float, and the gas was administered through a tube into the bottom of a mask like a nosebag feeder. A lot of trainers tried it. It was all the rage in human athletics and football at the time. It all passed into disuse. The body, it was said, could not store enough extra oxygen for long enough to make any difference. Many years later when I had a chance to look around TJ's stables - there were the oxygen cylinders still, and obviously in use.

I asked Percy about them. He told me that many many years ago TJ had a horse that would become very distressed after it's races. It thrashed around and fell over. It breathed rapidly and deeply like it was starving for oxygen. Percy decided to try oxygen after its races. A cylinder and a mask were set up and the horse was given oxygen after its next race. The horse appeared to settle. It was kept and used for any horses that seemed to be distressed after their races. The strappers say that the distressed horses still get the oxygen treatment for about a minute when they first get back home.

The oxygen flow rate used when the mask was put on a horse was such that the mask may have acted as a carbon dioxide rebreathing bag. After they race, horses have a very high lactic acid level in the blood. Carbon dioxide in the blood is mildly acidic. To rapidly decrease the acidity of the blood the horse breathes out a lot of carbon dioxide. About one hour later, the lactic acid having been removed, the blood is alkaline due to a low carbon dioxide level. This condition, called alkalosis, makes the brain very excitable.

In old-time asylums for the insane, nutcases would talk so rapidly and loudly, and breathe so excitedly, that they would breathe off their carbon dioxide and become even more excited and deranged. This was a vicious circle. To break it the attendants would put a bag over the lunatic's head to trap the carbon dioxide and calm them down. This is probably the origin of the derogatory expression "Go bag your head" - implying that someone who talks too much is pathologically excitable or insane.

In summary, the horses may have been calmed down by the carbon dioxide accumulating in the mask. The oxygen flow prevented any oxygen starvation rather than being the therapeutic agent itself. It's a possibility anyway, but I think it would only work if any really over-excited horse got more than a minute in the mask.

Oxygen cylinders and nose bag attachment. Horses are given oxygen after races, rather than before, as in some sports. Oxygen was first used on a horse that was distressed after its races.

The only other place I have seen oxygen used in racehorses was at Ruidoso Downs for Quarter Horses. A number of trainers there used it *before* a race.

Tommy's quick eye for a horse's action

Vet John Peatfield had told me how astonishingly quick TJ's eye was when it came to assessing a horse. I was with John at Tulloch Lodge one morning when a horse was brought forward to be checked because it's morning rider had reported that it had a 'scratchy action.' TJ, John and myself lined up to watch the horse trotted up. I kept one eye on TJ and one on the horse. It took 3, at most 4 steps, and had not yet gotten into even stride, when TJ turned away saying, 'there's nothing wrong with that horse.' John and I watched it go up and back twice before we could agree.

Bobby Thomsen: "He's a genius with a horse, Tom - he can look at a horse for one minute-"

"And tell you more about it than most people can after half an hour."

"Yes."

Percy told he me he had seen and heard of numerous instances of TJ recognizing horses. One example was TJ's recognition of a mare he had trained many years before when he drove onto a stud. "All Tommy could see was her head and shoulders." She was older, out of racing condition and so on. When they met up with the stud's manager, they were able to check the mare's identity and TJ was right. "Not a special mare, no reason for her to stick in his mind."

8.8 Role of the veterinarian

Probably no vet's name has been so intertwined with a trainer's success as has the name Percy Sykes with the success of

TJ Smith. Stanley Dancer, one of the all-time great Standardbred trainers was closely linked with Dr Churchill, and the great Irish Thoroughbred trainer Vincent O'Brien relied heavily on Dr Bob Griffin, but the racing public and other trainers knew little of those vets. The name Percy Sykes is well known among the racegoers of Australia.

Percy developed a lot of feed additives and sold them. The demand became so great, as mentioned in an earlier section, that he formed a company, Ranvet, which was very successful. The knowledge that TJ used these products was a great plus for the company's sales.

"Tommy, how did you start up with Percy Sykes?"

"Well I'd heard about Percy Sykes. I had a horse with a broken sesamoid. In those days we used to shoot them. I was driving up the High Street and I spotted this fellow coming down in this old car. I saw it was Percy Sykes, so I turned round and got up alongside him. I said, 'Come and have a look at this horse.' He looked at it and he said, 'I can fix that.' So I said, 'Well you fix it.' So he came back and he X-rayed it - we never used to X-ray horses in those days - and he came back and started talking about it. I said, 'I don't want to hear about it, it's your baby, you fix it. You said you can fix it, so fix it.'"

"So he put a shoe on it himself, or rather he designed it himself and got the blacksmith to put it on - but he's a very good blacksmith Percy Sykes - he can do anything. Then he put it in a cast - I'd never seen anything like it. I spent four months in St Vincent's Hospital with a broken hip and they couldn't put one on my leg as good. We had this old vet Roy Stewart, and we took him down and showed it to him."

"'Oh that's no good' he said, 'that leg'll get gangrene in it.' Anyway Percy said to me, 'I'll change that shoe every eight days.' You know three months later that horse came out at Randwick and won - first up. So old Roy went - we dissolved the partnerships and Percy moved in and he's been here until he retired."

"Some trainers have different vets for different jobs - like one for lamenesses and one better for wind or heart problems. Did you have any preferences according to what was wrong with the horse?"

"No. I'd never have two vets. I have one vet. I do say trainers have to work with vets. Without a good vet you're . . . (shrugs)."

"Percy was there at the stable every morning?"

"Yes. Percy was there in the morning, and then he'd call in during the afternoon. Now John Peatfield does the same. It's no good them coming when you've finished. They've got to be there when the work is going on. It's better and it's quicker for everyone."

Percy Sykes went to trackwork ever morning for years as part of his efforts to win more clients, and to sort out the meaning of the blood tests. Percy describes TJ as very demanding of a vet's time. "If you're gone for half an hour, or half a week, he always says, 'Where've you been. I've been looking for you." John Peatfield has been TJ's vet for most of the years since Percy's retirement. John Peatfield had a very nearly full-time job at TJ Smith's, although I never saw him at trackwork. John said he was usually having trouble waking up when TJ phoned him at 7am to discuss the horses' works. Once, after John took a well-earned two day rest at Percy's urging, TJ said to him, "Where've you been? Have you retired?"

Percy told me that Tommy would not know most of the time exactly what the vet did. TJ expected his vet to do whatever was necessary, but not to break any rules. Percy claimed that even when a survey showed that 60 - 80% of all trainers (I think that was starters) were using dexadresin or similar corticosteroids, Tommy would not allow Percy to use it.

In the anabolic days there was a round of injections every three weeks or so, with different anabolics for geldings, fillies and colts. Most, but not all, were given anabolics. According to the Sydney vets of those days like Percy and Arthur Sternhell, anabolics were allowed as hormones, but somewhere in my training I was given the impression they were illegal, and a lot of other people thought so. There was a lot of confusion.

In his work at Tulloch Lodge John Peatfield used some products developed by Percy but not commercially available because of things like insufficient shelf life. Thiamine and kalaemic (potassium) syrups, and a powder containing an extract of Derris root were amongst these. The thiamine was fed to all the horses at tranquilizer doses and along with the hard and frequent workouts may contribute to the extreme quiet around TJ's stables. The horses hardly move in their boxes. Not many bucking their brands off around Tulloch Lodge. No energy left for weaving and nodding.

Some horses receive saline drenches. As far as I can determine saline drenches are an Australian racing practice. I never found anyone in other parts of the world using them. These drenches contain various salts of sodium and potassium as well as other compounds. The preparation has a bright yellow color due to a compound Percy added which was variously described to me as a mild laxative and as a digestive stimulant. I asked Percy about saline drenches:

"Saline drenches were an old army habit (Percy had been a British Army vet in colonial India). The horse was starved for 24 hours, then drenched with one pound of plain salt and one pound of Glauber's salts. It was pumped in with a stomach pump. During the starvation period the horse had to be muzzled, otherwise they'd pick at their bedding and get colicky. If you were doing 10 -12 horses, the first would be squirting diarrhoea by the time you did the last. But it definitely freshened them up. Sometimes it knocked them flat, and they'd fall away,

Two of TJ's vets. Percy Sykes is in the center of the picture, in conversation with Ernie Smith on the right. To the left, behind Percy, John Peatfield is in conversation with his wife, who is wearing a red hat.

especially if they were on pasture. They were OK if they were on concentrates. People thought they were fat, but it was all just water, and it knocked it out of them." Percy later tried drenching horses with alkaline salts which were a mild diuretic, and liked the results. The alkaline salts became Ranvet products.

Pre-race intravenous drips (jugs to Americans) were given to most horses. Occasionally drips were also given to horses that had signs of a poor recovery after a race. Percy said that he started out by giving drips to horses that were dehydrated. The first was Laing's Solution, a 5% saline. 5% is a very concentrated (hypertonic) solution - the saline concentration equivalent to the salts in blood is 0.9%. This would seem to be disastrous, to aggravate the problem, but according to Percy, " . . . It made them urinate so much they flooded their box, and it *made* them drink. It caused some breakdown of the red cells, but it corrected the dehydration. Their skin elasticity the next day was wonderfully improved. Later I used a 2.5% solution."

The Laing's solution probably worked by giving the regulatory system a jolt. Later Percy acquired a flame photometer and this revealed that many poorly-performing horses had low blood potassium. "Especially after losses with the urination caused by Laing's solution, or the saline drench." To counteract this, up close to a race, Percy used Darrow's Solution (rich in potassium), given intravenously. He was so impressed with the results he gave it to other horses which had not had Laing's or a saline drench, and again considered the results good. Later still, Percy tried balanced solutions like Hartman's or Ringer's. When I was there in later years, John Peatfield was using 'normal' isotonic sodium chloride with three grams of potassium chloride added to the litre of solution.

Years ago the vets would give the drip on the morning of the race. This meant Saturday morning was a very busy time. They would insert the cannula into the jugular vein. The bottle would be hung at full armstretch on the wall - hooked over a nail driven into the woodwork for the purpose. The strapper or groom would stay with the horse until the drip ran in while the vet raced around setting up drips for the number of horses requiring them. In later years the pre-race drips were moved back to Friday morning for a Saturday race as the new rules required.

One wag told me that originally the drips at TJ's were only given to the horses that TJ thought had a chance in a race. Later the stableboys caught on to this, and started to bet and tip accordingly. That led to a stage where half the drips were given to mislead the stableboys!

8.8-1 How much does TJ blood test?
TJ's horses are probably the most blood-tested in the world. In the late 1960's and 1970's any Smith horse in racing was tested weekly. Horses with problems were treated and another sample taken before raceday to see if the treatment was effective. The samples were processed at Percy's lab, in his practice about a mile from TJ's stable.

Percy Sykes is generally credited with being the first to use blood tests as a part of racetrack practice. Some workers at Sydney Uni (now retired) have claimed they were the first to use blood tests to monitor racehorses. After some research, I concluded neither of them was first.

As far as I could determine, Randwick trainer Pat Murray, trainer of Tails, was the first to use blood testing as a training aid in racehorses in Australia, possibly the first in the world.

TOMMY SMITH

He started training at Randwick in 1951. From the start he had a special interest in the scientific side of training.

"I was interested in anything that would improve the horse or be beneficial to a horse."

That same year he linked up with Mark Percival, laboratory man for a Macquarie St specialist, a pathologist named Dr Neville Davis.

"Mark did all the blood tests. We tried to get the normal values from Sydney Uni, from the United States, but they didn't do blood counts at that time. We had some horses, so we did hundreds of counts - some horses every day - until we arrived at our own set of normals," Pat told me.

Percival the lab man did the tests in trainer Pat's garage. Dr Arthur Sternhell was Pat's vet. (Arthur says he first met Tommy Smith when Tommy asked him, through a friend to come around and talk about the blood tests, so Tommy certainly had an ear out for any new developments.) Arthur says he employed Percy Sykes, after Percy split with Roy Stewart. Percy saw the equipment and the normals and the results at Pat's. When Percy split with Arthur, he set up practice in the Western suburbs where he worked a lot with trotters, and he set up his own lab. Later he shifted back closer to Randwick. (Percy never mentions Arthur or his time in the Western suburbs.)

Percy began using intensive blood testing of racehorses to improve their performance. What began as a scientific approach to horses that were clearly racing a long way below their best was gradually extended over decades into a search for the ideal or truly optimal blood values.

People at Sydney Uni, now retired, have claimed they pioneered blood testing in racehorses. However Percy's claim to me was that he started first - in the middle 1950s - and found a lot of exciting cases. Initially the cases were mostly anemic horses that raced streets better after correction. Percy says he gave a talk at Sydney Uni to a veterinary group, wanting to share his stimulating findings. To his amazement his presentation was torn apart and ridiculed by the academics. (Having spent some time with academics and with Percy, I believe the problem may have been that Percy relies more on deductions from small numbers of cases, even single cases, while most academics rely on large numbers and statistics.)

Percy was further amazed when the same academics started doing the same hematology and very soon were behaving, "as though they were the experts." Later there were accusations that Percy commercialized their ideas. Percy had not had any experience of academics then and had believed they would welcome his contributions. He had looked forward to lots of warm applause and constructive criticism.

While he was aware that ripping into other peoples' ideas is part of testing them, he was unprepared for their attitudes to him. He was unaware that holier-than-thou stances (often hypocritical), and arrogant assumptions of superiority (frequently incorrect) are things that characterize a segment of the academic population.

As I have said, Pat Murray and Mark Percival were probably first to do blood tests on racehorses, but I had an opportunity to settle the argument about who might have been second, in Sydney at least. Percy had thrown out most of his old blood test records from the 50's, 60's and 70's, but a few survived in a bound book. They were not Percy's oldest records but they were the oldest still left with dates. One of the people retired from Sydney Uni had said that he left his books recording his work in the department. I went over to Sydney Uni and found the books recording blood test methods, as well as those listing the dates of blood samples from racehorses. The first of these were several years after Percy's. I took photos of both lots.

How could so many people claim to have started blood testing in racehorses? Well Pat Murray was the first to think of it and organize the expertise to do it. Mark Percival was the first technician to do blood counts on racehorses. Dr Arthur Sternhell was the first vet to offer it as a service to clients. Percy was the first vet to have a full scale lab in his practice. Sydney Uni academics may have been the first to publish. That, as far as I can determine, is the Sydney story.

Once Percy had learnt what to expect from academics, he forgot about them and went on his merry way. He was happy to be judged by trainers on his results. Percy visited other racing countries a number of times. His observations on the overseas scene back then were as follows:

"In America, pre-race 'jugging' as they call it, consisted mainly of various B vitamin concoctions." In racing technology, he believed that England had stood still for 20 years; the French were more progressive; but the Americans were always looking for the miracle single-measurement guide to fitness. "They just didn't understand how many factors had to be considered."

How useful was Percy's blood testing to TJ? Without a doubt it was very useful in the 50's and 60's. (But don't forget: TJ was already at the top.) There were many horses with correctable blood and electrolyte disorders. However, as the standard of nutrition increased, and more preventative supplements appeared, including many developed by Percy himself, such curable cases decreased. Worms, a prime cause of anemia, were beaten back with better and more frequent treatments. Today, the number of simple cases that can be dramatically improved has diminished. The usefulness of routine blood tests in racehorses which are not displaying any signs of problems has become a matter of debate amongst trainers and amongst exercise scientists.

TJ on the usefulness of anabolics

I first asked TJ about anabolics in 1987.

"What was racing like before anabolics and after anabolics?"

"I don't think it's much different. A lot of the anabolics we have today -people get carried away with it. The main thing is to get the horse fit."

"Some people reckon they hold up a lot longer, you get a much longer campaign with a Thoroughbred on anabolics."

"It all depends on the horse - some of them react to it better than others. Before, when they used to go doping or stinging horses, they used to say, 'We'll get it and sting it,' but the main thing is to get it fit. The biggest trouble for most fellas is that they can't get the damn things fit. People say horses are dishonest and things like that - but the poor horse is not really fit. It's not dishonest at all. They just haven't worked out what's wrong with the horse - they've got to study the horse - that way you can improve a horse out of sight."

Ernie, as mentioned earlier, remembers Percy introducing anabolics to TJ's stable and appeared to consider them a fairly important advance.

Bill Whittaker: "Percy Sykes was always going around the stables. You know, trotting stables as well as galloping stables. Friends of mine who had trotters swore by him, and that was in about 1952, 53 - in that period. Long time ago."

"Anabolics came on the scene a bit after that, didn't they?"

"No, anabolics were being used in the late forties - in dogs. Racing greyhounds."

"Was that testosterone? It's confusing because it's hard to work out quite which things people are talking about. I understand that testosterone was available from the mid-thirties or even earlier. Somebody in the swabbing game at some place in the world has told me that the first anabolic was not manufactured until about 1950 and I suppose it wouldn't have been much more than an experimental thing in its first couple of years."

"People were using something they referred to as 'hormones' in 1950,"

Testosterone is a male hormone with powerful anabolic effects, but it also makes the horse's behaviour very stallionish.

When did TJ start using anabolics?

When the Australian Conference of Principal Racing Clubs banned anabolic steroids in March 1988, to take affect from August 1988, TJ was loud and long in his criticism of the decision. He certainly did not sound as though he believed anabolics were over-rated as he had told me the year before.

"I reckon I was one of the first in the country to use anabolic steroids more than 30 years ago," he proudly told pressmen.

8.9 Shoeing

I've never heard of anything different about TJ's shoeing.

8.10 Has he 'produced' any good trainers?

In spite of Tommy's ability to improve horses, there are very few of his ex-employees who have made it to the top of the training ranks. Bobby Thomsen, usually in the top ten in Tommy's own territory has the best record. Len Morton, usually in the top five in Perth is the only other city success I could find. A contributing factor may have been Tommy's use of family members as main training confidantes and help. Paid staff at TJ's don't learn as much about the system, the strategy, as assistant trainers do elsewhere. And Tommy would not be keen to train up a potential rival.

I talked to Bobby Thomsen:

"What about your own success as a trainer, what are some of the best horses you've had, and your best wins?"

"My best horse would be Gray Receiver, he won a Galaxy (Group 1) first up after 13 weeks of training and went on to win the Elder's handicap. Got beat a head by one of TJ's in the Rothman's. The first race I won was a Group race, a mile and a half stakes. My first winner I trained was a cast- off. Bought him for $5000. The bloke had never trained him to run beyond 1400 meters. I won the 2400 meter Winter Stakes."

"So the other guy just picked the wrong distance for that horse?"

"Oh yes, if they cut out all 1200 meter races that bloke wouldn't train a winner - the bloke that I bought it off."

"Why do you think that guy couldn't realize that the horse's best distance was a lot further out?"

"A lot of trainers win a 1200 or 1400m race with a horse so that's all they do with them. They find 1200 or 1400m races. They win one, they get beaten in half a dozen. Then they might win another and then they'll get beaten in another 8 or 9. They'll keep it at the distance but I don't believe in that. I look at the horse's breeding, and the horse as an individual. I think well geez he should go further than 1400m. This horse is by Capricorno, who is by Never Say Die, out of a Snark mare. He's a big, slummocky, long barreled horse, long rein on him. He'd have to run a mile and a half - which he did, and we had a lot of fun."

"Sounds like it. What year was that - your first win?"

"I'm not really sure, I got my trainer's license in January and he won the winter stakes in June - I think it must have been about 1976. Had a very good horse - Bianco Lady. She was a great staying mare. She run 5th in the Melbourne Cup Kingston Town got beaten in - Gurner's Lane won. She won the Sandown Cup, then we took her to Perth and won the Perth Cup, in about 1983 I think it was. That was a great thrill, Tommy was there for that."

"Does Tommy enjoy seeing your success? - as a protege?"

"I feel he does now. He never used to - he wouldn't talk to me. But when I won the Perth Cup he paid me one of the greatest compliments that a trainer could ever be paid by another trainer. He said, 'I didn't see a good horse win today but I saw a very good trainer.' To me - they put that in print - and that was the best compliment. That was the first time he acknowledged me, and it was a big thrill for me 'cos I'd spent 18 years of my life there from the time I was 14 till I was 32 - it's a long time."

8.11 Analysis of his training

"A lot of people say that he's successful because he gets so many horses in and he breaks a lot down-"
Bobby Thomsen: "Oh yes. He works quantity and quality."

Sterling Smith, after spending one month with Charlie Whittingham, probably the trainer most admired by trainers in the USA; and two months with Alec Head, leading trainer for 15 years in France. I asked Sterling about Alec and Charlie.

"Both take their time with their horses. If they don't think a horse needs a run, they won't give it a run."

"When you start training yourself, are you going to go that direction or TJ's direction?"

"I think I'll go TJ's direction because you don't want to break a formula that's been going for forty years with so much success. I have ideas and I'll weigh it up."

"A lot of people - if they try to train as hard as Tommy, the horses get screwed up white-cell counts, they train off - and so a lot of them just turn around and say Tommy's using something."

"He's not using anything at all. I think it's a case of TJ's so popular, and so much of a trainer, that if the horse breaks down, he's got another one to bring up. So it really doesn't matter, whereas these other trainers haven't, so-"

"They've got to coddle them along."

"Exactly. If one goes out, bring another one in. It's like a factory."

How did TJ improve other trainer's horses four lengths?

One factor would have been his realisation that, 'training good horses and bad horses was like chalk and cheese,' that better horses could stand and benefit from harder training. TJ may have seen horses winning top races, even though to him they had signs they could be made fitter. He may have targeted lesser trainers, (like Caesar Dominguez targeting trainers in the Quarter Horse claiming races) or trainers not using anabolics. He would not want to make the mistake of taking a horse over and have it perform poorly. A big part of TJ's success was his proven ability to improve horses, and the bait that represented to an owner. Even if an owner didn't switch a horse, they often put their next one with TJ, or asked him to buy one.

9. His feeding

9.1 Where did TJ get his first ration?

TJ's first ration would have been based on what the Sawyers fed, but he was on the alert for any possible improvement.

"You went and watched what the four top trainers were doing, and picked up the best of their ideas. That seems like a pretty smart move."

"I realized horses were not being fed. We used to feed four times a day you know. Everyone gave them great big tubs of feed. Seven o'clock at night you'd be running around feeding and haying them up. I cut all that out. I thought: I'll cut them right back; I'll feed them half; I'll feed them twice a day, but I'll feed them hard. Everyone said they'd get foundered and that they couldn't stand it. It was too hot and the horses wouldn't stand it, they said."

TJ further modified his feeding after his 1946 tour of major racing centers of the world. It was probably a very big factor in his abilty to train hard before anabolics appeared.

9.2 Grains and 9.3 Hays

This was the feeding of TJ's champion Kingston Town, as reported in 1985.

Morning meal:
    4 pints oats
    2 pints corn
    2 pints beans (Tick beans)
    4 pints lucerne and oaten chaff
(The last is ambiguous and I don't know if that means four pints total or each.)

Second meal:
    8 pints oats
    4 pints corn
    2 pints beans
    4 pints lucerne and oaten chaff

The article said the usual glucose and vitamin additives were given. Tuesday, Thursday and Saturday were work days. Extra feeds such as boiled feeds were given to supplement the diet.

Len Morton's recollection of TJ's feeding was 8-10 pounds of oats. 3 pounds of corn (maize), 1½-2 pounds of Tick beans, little bit of chaff and not much in the way of additives. Len remembers the diet made the horses loose. Their droppings were like a cow's. (Percy preferred that to 'pebbly' dung.)

Percy Sykes on TJ's feeding

"When I first met Tommy, everyone fed two of chaff to one of oats. They fed hay ad lib and a bit of bran. The chaff was oaten, wheaten and lucerne chaff -a mixture. It's hard to say how much grain they fed because they all used dippers, but I'd say about eight to ten pounds. They fed more often because labor was cheap." (Tommy fed more grain and less hay and chaff.)

"Tommy fed differently to Jack Green and all the others. Theirs were mostly first-up winners, and then their bloods would go wrong. Tommy realised the significance of protein, and I remember how we discovered that. Jack Kramer the tennis promoter, and George Ryder, bred some foals by Newtown Wonder to Northern Hemisphere time. (To race them in the Northern Hemisphere if they turned out OK) They gave them tennis names like Smash Hit, Drop Volley and so on. We tried an experiment on the stud. We put half the Northern Hemisphere time and half the Southern Hemisphere time foals on cottonseed meal. The Northern Hemisphere time foals on the cottonseed grew so much better they caught up and passed the Southern Hemisphere time foals which were not getting the cottonseed - even though they were older."

"Tommy's horses at this time had a reputation for splitting the jockeys. They complained they needed a cushion under the saddle. We put a pound of cottonseed per day in each of Tommy's racehorse's feed and they really came on. Jack Green didn't miss much and he asked me, 'What have you done with Tommy's horses? They used to be so poor the jockeys complained, but now they're muscled, they look great."

"Cottonseed meal was used as a fertiliser at one time, because of the dangers of something in it called gossypol. Then it was found it could be de-gossypolled by adding one pound of ferrous sulphate per ton. It could also be destroyed by heat during extraction."

"They were feeding it to pigs in Queensland. Anything new you know you're going to be knocked. They came out with all the dangers of gossypol. Anything that went wrong with a horse that was on cottonseed meal, they'd blame the gossypol. But so much of it was coming down to New South Wales that the authorities in Queensland restricted it."

"When soybean first started here, it used to be very expensive. It had already been in use in the USA for many years and they were very experienced with it. Tommy tried it but he said that some of the horses had stopped eating, and he stopped feeding it. He's very quick to decide."

"When I researched the matter, I found that soybean meal contained an anemic factor and an appetite depressant factor. These could be destroyed by heating. But even after changes were made, Tommy wouldn't try it, he'd lost all faith in it."

Dozing horse in a box. Note lucerne and oaten hay in hay net, and netting on window. Boxes have automatic waterers and fans.

Mick Dittman, TJ's stable jock

Mick's wife trains a few racehorses, so you can bet Mick has his eyes open at Tulloch Lodge.

"What's the main difference in TJ's feeding?"

"I don't think he's much of a bran mash man, it's mostly grain - oats and corn. Not much lucerne, a very small amount of lucerne. All pretty hard feed."

"They don't get much hay?"

"No, they eat oaten hay which is a hard type of feed itself. And a lot of high protein food."

TJ's oats were 44.7 pounds to the bushel, a reading identical to Bart Cumming's oats, but TJ's are supposed to come from a property near the Cootamundra pre-training property. Apart from oats there were bins of lucerne chaff, sunflower seed, cracked corn and some things that looked like peanuts. Ernie said they were called Tick beans.

There was a 44 gallon drum of maize oil. (Maize is the word

used in Australia for what is called corn in America. Corn is a word to be used carefully. It is an ancient word originally meaning any small hard fruit or grain. It has come to mean different things in different countries: wheat in England, oats in Scotland, maize in Australia. In America, the word corn is used to designate agricultural strains of the plant derived from native Mexican or Indian maize. Maize was one of the native American names for the plant and the cobs. Nevertheless, around stables in America you will find an occasional person to whom corn is wheat. The word maize in America usually refers to the native strains of corn. So be careful with the word corn.)

TJ's horses were fed a cupful (200 ml) of the corn/maize oil each day. This was in 1987. The feeding of oil was widespread and spreading in Australia at that time. When asked why they fed corn oil, a few trainers said it put a gloss on the coat but nearly all trainers said that horses stood more work or stood their work better.

This was something to think about. There is a disadvantage to burning fats in a short race, certainly any race of less than five minutes duration: the animal gets less energy from each unit of oxygen taken in and burnt with fat -and the oxygen supply is limited.

If the extra work in training sessions was their own observation and they were correct - not simply seeing something they expected to see because another trainer saw some improvement - one possible explanation was the sheer caloric density of oil. A cup of oil would contain something like four times as many calories as a cup of soaked oats. I say soaked because oats take up stomach fluids after they enter the stomach and it is the volume that seems to count. Racehorse trainers have long tried to encourage horses to eat more so they could train them more. The extra energy in the oil meant they could do more work.

But there was a theoretical possibility that these same horses might burn more fat during a race and lose a length or two. It depended how good the horse's system was at shutting off the burning of fat during a race. Perhaps the extra training made up the lost length? I asked a few trainers if there was any sign of decreased race performance? No, better, definitely better. I was skeptical. Some trainers are easily sucked in by glossy coats and harder training. I was not convinced either way about its effectiveness on raceday. More evidence was required.

An interesting sidelight was the issue of oil feeding in racing Greyhounds. Greyhound trainers are very careful to trim all the excess fat off any meat fed to their dogs and have done for many years. (Oils are a type of fat - unsaturated fats in chemical terms.) Total energy intake is less of a limitation in Greyhounds, and any fat fed was likely to become weight to carry. Yet veterinarian Dr Alex Hauler, a very keen observer of the Greyhound scene had been telling me how the top trainers in his practice fed a sizable dollop of oil, and that they were very sure it benefited the dog's racing performance. Again I was skeptical. Many Greyhound trainers of my own acquaintance not only trimmed off any fat, they then boiled the meat and skimmed off any oil. This led to dry scaly coats. Adding an oil to the feed of these dogs certainly made them look a lot better, but no-one had mentioned better race times.

In 1989 a study showed that horses receiving oil every day replenished the glycogen in their muscle fibers more rapidly, and to a higher level, after fast work. The study showed that oil-fed horses broke down more glycogen during a race, and broke it down at a more rapid rate. They had faster five furlong times by a second or two. This result was not statistically significant, in other words may have happened by chance. This landmark piece of research opens up a lot of interesting avenues for more research when it is considered with other information.

At present the view is that the benefit of the oil is mainly a glucose-sparing effect, which is to say the horse uses the oil for its resting energy needs instead of using the glucose coming into its bloodstream from the digestion of starch in the oats. This glucose is then available to make glycogen in the muscle. Oil feeding in effect promotes glycogen loading during recovery and this in turn promotes glycogen unloading in a race.

This research will cast more light on the role of feeding practices in tying-up. Some trainers have told me they had more tying up when they fed maize, or fed 'too much' maize. Maize of course contains maize oil, as well as starch. The more maize is fed instead of oats, the more starch is converted to glycogen. Higher levels of muscle glycogen are generally presumed to predispose to Monday Morning Disease (Azoturia) and tying up. Perhaps alteration of the level of corn and oil feeding will be important in the management of horses that tie up.

This work also backs up the claims of trainers like Howard Wilson from the Gold Coast, who trained Come On Eileen to win the Golden Nugget, that the more maize he can feed, the better his results.

Cod liver oil, linseed and linseed oil were used a lot by old-time trainers and are still used by some trainers. It would be interesting to know how effective these, and flax seed, and sunflower seed are in delivering oil. There may be a difference in the effectiveness of different oils and fats in glycogen boosting.

Grain quality and grain weight

Percy told me of a problem Tommy had many years ago that shows the importance of grain quality. Tommy sends his horses down to Melbourne with instructions on how much to feed. On this occasion he sent some horses down, but when he followed three weeks later he found they were 'skeletons'.

They were getting the same work, and they were getting the same feed and they were eating it all up. After an analysis it turned out that there was a one-third difference in the quality of the oats even though they weighed the same. The bad batch of oats apparently had a thick seed coat, which meant less protein and less carbohydrate. Large poultry producers have a protein and carbohydrate analysis done on every new source of grain because the quality varies so much.

Ernie on Tommy's feeding

"Percy said one of the first advances or improvements Tommy made was that he fed differently - the others fed a lot of hay and chaff and roughage."

"Well Tommy fed hard - fed corn and oats. Most of the others were feeding a lot of bran and chaff in those days. They were light feeders. But you have to remember there were a lot of amateurs around in those days. For someone to look at it in a professional light was a different proposition."

"Where did Tommy get that professional outlook from?"

"Well I think if you are broke, you become a professional very quickly."

Bobby Thomsen:

"He was the first one to use high-protein feed. They get hardly any roughage at all. The roughage they get is oaten hay and lucerne hay - they don't get any real roughage in their feed. You get onto high protein content, and if you feed them hard you can work them hard."

"Well it's interesting because the people who try to do the same, what they believe is the same anyway, if they feed that they get horses that get excitable, get fat, get tied up and everything else - I think you really have to be an excellent trainer as well to feed that much. How many pounds of grain is the maximum Tommy gets into a horse?"

"About 28 pounds."

I asked Bobby about the sequence of the changes. *"Percy's explanation of Tommy's progression was that the first thing Tommy got into was cutting the roughage and increasing the oats, then they got onto cotton-seed meal and then I think mixed grain, then amino acid supplements."*

"Yes TJ's a very high protein feeder, very little roughage, they get their roughage through oats and hay and straw. Feed them like that you can work them hard.

"With Tommy's success there would have been a lot of other trainers asking you about his feeding?"

"No. They didn't ask. And I can't speak for a lot of trainers 'cos you can't go into their feed room and see what they're feeding their horses."

"It amazes me that other trainers didn't ask."

"I fed the horses for eight years at Tulloch Lodge. Tommy wouldn't have fed a horse himself for twenty years."

"But I gather he has all the feed bins brought to one spot before the next feeding, and looks in them (Bobby's head wag was saying no) - or used to? - no?"

"Of an afternoon he would, not of a morning. Of an afternoon he would have all the feed bins brought up to the one stable, but he's only told how much a horse has left by the person looking after it."

"Someone many moons ago told me all the feed bins were brought to one area and Tommy looked in them to see which horses left what. Must have changed. How many feeds a day does he give them?"

"Only twice. As far as I know most of the stables in Sydney only feed twice a day."

"The other thing is that TJ feeds so that they clean up doesn't he?"

"Yes."

"Some people feed them so they leave a handful to try to get the most into them."

"I think to keep a horse eating, keep them a little bit hungry. I don't mean cut them back, but you have to know how much to feed them so they'll lick the tin. Then they keep looking for the bottom of the tin. Never cut a horse back on its feed, doesn't matter how big and gross it is - never cut it back. But you have to know how much to feed them so they'll just lick the tin out."

"Just put more work in?"

"Yes - but of course you've got to have sound horses."

Bill Whittaker

"McCarten was one of those that Smith - while he probably admired McCarten as a man and as a jockey, he didn't admire his feeding methods. Tommy's is the absolute reverse to the methods of Bayly Payten, George Price and Maurice McCarten, who were the leading trainers in the city in the thirties and the forties. They always believed in having their horses big, and Tommy Smith worked it out that that wasn't the way to have horses at all."

"Someone told me that the going thing then was that they tended to overtrain the horses and they used to have these tonics that had caffeine in them. He said they used caffeine a lot, and overtrained horses would run well on caffeine. He said that when swabbing for caffeine came in, that's when Tommy really came to the fore because his horses were actually better-trained in the fitness department and not overtrained."

"I agree they used caffeine, some of the old trainers, and cocaine also. Cocaine was used a lot on horses that were sore. At least two Melbourne Cup winners that I know of had cocaine injections, to deaden pain in their legs."

"The horses were big - was that because they were big in the stomach -because of the bulky food?"

"Yes, they kept them big due to the different diet. Smith changed the diet of horses; he fed them harder grain, more grain and of course was able to somehow or other - I think it's a bit of a secret exactly how and why he can feed them so much of this hard grain, full of protein and get away with it. A lot of trainers wouldn't be able to get away with it."

"That's the experience in Perth. A lot of trainers try it and it doesn't work for them."

"No. He's got something. It's one of the secrets of his success, but not entirely. People will say that Percy Sykes the vet was the man, but Smith would have survived and thrived."

"Smith was already up there before Percy came along."

"A lot of the success is in the feeding: that mystery of how he can feed them all that hard grain, more oats than anyone else."

"Well, I think that for a long time he had the advantage of anabolics when very few did. He's prepared to admit that now."

"Yes, he did, through Percy Sykes."

"When I asked Percy about it, Percy said, 'Oh, I don't think anabolics were that important.' He didn't say much about it, but Ernie said that it was Percy who introduced the anabolics. That must have been something they had to do rather carefully."

"Anabolic steroids were considered to be completely safe. They were hormones. Horses manufacture their own hormones. But many trainers would like to know how TJ can feed the horses that hard grain and get away with it. Because places that he goes and stays, such as Grafton - he might go up there for the Grafton Cup - and he'll have his horses stabled at some old country trainer's place. They're amazed at how he just hits them with so much hard grain. They suspect that some injections or something else are given that helps the horse digest it, because given normally, the horse couldn't possibly digest it. It'd twist up their bowels or something."

"The other thing is that on blood counts, TJ pushes his horses until they get these blood changes, high neutrophil to lymphocyte ratios, and other people can't push them that far: they fall apart."

"You'd understand that being a vet, but there is something which is his secret. Good luck to him. But the secret is that he can give them this hard feed and then work them harder and they don't fold up, they thrive on it."

9.4 Cut green grass or grazing

I never saw any Tulloch Lodge horses grazing at the track nor any freshly cut green grass at Tulloch Lodge. Some other trainers graze their horses at Randwick, including Bart Cummings.

9.5 What additives does he use?

TJ's feed room looks like an advertising spread for Ranvet products. This is not surprising since Percy Sykes, his veterinarian and friend of long standing, was the developer of the products of this company. Percy began by mixing the ingredients at his practice. As demand grew, he was approached by a businessman and they started a company. Randwick Veterinary Laboratories (later Ranvet) was formed in the middle 1960s. The company was an immediate success.

There has always been a chicken and egg story in the success of Ranvet. Some believe it was successful because Percy developed many useful, effective products for the stud and racing stable. A more skeptical group said the products were at worst useless placebos, at best no better than the similar products of other companies. The skeptics believed the success of Ranvet was due to the widespread belief that the company's products played an important part in TJ's phenomenal success. The obvious financial health of Ranvet would suggest there are plenty in the horse industry who think the products work. It no longer concerns Percy - he has sold his interest in the company, although he continues as a consultant developing new products.

TJ's feedroom contained:

Folactin Blue - contains vitamins A and D, calcium and phosphorus, folic acid and inositol.

Salkavite - vitamin B group and electrolyte replacer

Neutrolene - body acid neutralizer and alkali reserve replacer

Thiatone - large amounts of B vitamins, particularly B_1, plus magnesium, for nervous horses

Hoof Food - biotin, zinc and amino acid supplement to aid hoof growth

Supplement "C" - amino acids aimed at boosting protein quality

Blud - there were sachets of Blud, an iron supplement that is not a Ranvet product. Blud is made by Sterivet in Canada, and I saw it in stables around the world. Even Bart Cummings, then a major shareholder in Ranvet, used large amounts of it.

Feromel - an iron supplement that *is* made by Ranvet.

Containers of Syke's practice products that have too short a shelf life to be registered for commercial sale.

A Ranvet employee told me that TJ feeds his horses a very high energy diet and works his horses to the limit. He said all the horses get B_1, B_2, B_6 and (in?) thiatone.

I had been told by Percy that TJ never had shares in Ranvet. I wondered if there was some secret arrangement. Afterall, Tommy's use of the products was a major selling point, and if it was known TJ made money out of Ranvet sales, some trainers would probably stop buying. Maybe Tommy got his Ranvet products free or at a cut rate?

One of the feed rooms at Tulloch Lodge. TJ had most of Ranvet's products, as well as some non-commercial Sykes Practice products, all developed by Percy, except for an iron tonic called Blud.

"Tommy, you were so involved with Percy in all the experimentation to develop products for Ranvet, why didn't you get into the company itself?"

"I always said to Percy, 'You should get into that,' because the old fella before Percy was Roy Stewart, and Roy Stewart made his money from making tonics and things for horses. In those days they didn't have many. Percy decided, but he never put me into it."

"Apparently Bart Cummings (One of TJ's main training rivals) insisted on being in it."

Valerie: "A lot of it was Tom's ideas that he brought back from America."

"I thought you might have decided not to be in the company because you wanted to use products from whoever you felt had the best."

Valerie: "They used Tommy's picture, his name and everything."

Tommy turned to Valerie: "Oh that's nothing." Turning back to me he said, "You should get into that. Especially those fellows on farms with mares and foals. Especially through the summer time." (Summer in most of the southern half of Australia consists of a six month drought. The paddock feed consists of dried, weather-beaten leftovers, since the horses eat the best fodder first. Mid summer and especially late summer, supplementation is essential for good foal growth.)

"Well Folactin for the stud market has apparently been one of Ranvet's best sellers."

"Yes well all the other times you might as well throw them out the window."

"From a profit point of view, or because they don't do anything?"

"I don't think they do much."

(TJ's offhandedness about anabolics when I spoke to him, contrasted with his strong criticism of the ban on anabolics, gives cause for suspicion about his offhandedness on the usefulness of additives, particularly since Ranvet at the time was principally owned by his arch rival Bart Cummings. Ranvet product sales would be putting money in a rival's pocket, yet TJ continued using them.)

"What about Darrow's solution?"

"Well I reckon its hard to tell just what is the best. I don't know if it does them good. Percy reckons it does."

"Laing's solution?"

"Well that seems to keep them loose and so on. I'm not really mad on a lot of the stuff myself. I've only kept it up because Percy has put it there, especially that iron and things like that."

"Did iron make a big difference?"

"Well I don't know. See I won all the races before all this. But they do last longer when the horse is tuned up. You must keep horses tuned up to keep them racing hard."

Len Morton's recollection was that when he was there in the 1972/73 season, TJ did not feed many additives, did not feed iron. This would surprise me because Percy advocates iron.

At one point in a discussion, Percy said the main anemias (in the days when they saw a lot of horses with anemia) were large-cell anemias due to nutritional deficiencies. The widespread use of vitamins, minerals and wormers, on studs and in stables, had made such things uncommon today. Nevertheless, Percy's practice still gives many horses vitamin injections because of the results of the blood tests. About B vitamins, he had this to say about 'the old days': "With some of the horses, they were very overtrained, and they needed a rest. But the trainers wouldn't take any notice of your instructions, so as much for psychological reasons I'd give them a course of B complex, and say that while the horse was on this course, the horse could only do pacework; then after a week, one sprint; then race one week later. Lots won that race two or three weeks later. It was so successful it looked like you had a sting. Even some of the trainers thought so, and used to ask if it would show on a swab.

10. His management and how he makes money

TJ has clearly shown himself to be a good business and money manager. His tough start in life meant that although he was no trained accountant, he knew how to make a dollar and how to keep a dollar. This sounds rather incongruous in a man who used to bet so ferociously, but TJ bets to make money, and I'm sure if it failed to do so for any prolonged period of time he would stop betting.

Although very successful at choosing yearlings, TJ has never gone heavily into buying and racing horses with large amounts of his own money. He did start without clients and raced Bragger, which he owned, then Ajixa which he leased or owned, then Playboy which he owned because the client rejected it. Once he had made his name he let others pay, while owning a small number and shares in some himself. His own money largely went into bricks and mortar rental properties. Wayne Lukas on the other hand apparently invests all his own money in buying horses.

10.1 Tommy's business philosophy

TJ has been described as concise, direct and positive. One of his nicknames is 'The Little General.' He believes in having the best people and he believes in giving orders. In support of being dictatorial he cites the success of Bob Menzies (a former Australian Prime Minister) and Henry Ford the car maker. He believes if you are to control any business, an individual should have the strength to stand by his own opinions and judgments, even in the face of the severest opposition.

Len Morton, now a successful trainer in Perth, spent some time working with TJ expressly to prepare himself as a trainer. TJ's advice to him was to, "do whatever he had to do for the horse, and don't give a damn about what other people think. Don't listen to critics." Things like leading a horse miles to the races if it races poorly after vanning.

I asked Bobby Thomsen if TJ ever turned up in his nightclub gear at four in the morning to start work.

"No"

"Did TJ ever say something like, 'Look people will come and ask you and you are not to tell them' - I mean other trainers would have been asking you all the time what TJ was doing - wouldn't they?"

"No, I never got asked. Trainers are creatures of habit like their horses, they stick to the same thing. That's why he's gone ahead because he's tried different things and TJ can cop advice off people. He's not one to shun advice. His trips to America and Europe he would pick up things all the time."

"It sounded to me like there weren't too many trainers of any significance in the world that he hadn't visited."

"No I think he's been to them all."

"He's not only visited them, he says, 'I've watched them work their horses and looked in their feed bins.'"

"Well, that's exactly what he's done."

"I'm surprised that other trainers didn't try to find out from you."

"Well they certainly never approached me when I was foreman."

TJ's integrity came into question in the 'Galway Bay Affair.' An Irish lady had put a well-bred horse called Galway Bay with TJ and at some point TJ had been instructed to sell it or he had advised her to sell it. The horse was duly sold to a New Zealander for stud duty. By coincidence the Irish lady and the New Zealander met somewhere in the world, as racing people often do. They discovered there was a sizable discrepancy in the amount TJ paid to the Irish lady and the amount the New Zealander paid to TJ. Much more than a trainer's commission in such deals.

The Irish lady hired lawyers and filed suit against TJ in the courts of Sydney. The time for the case arrived, the Irish lady moved into the Hilton with her lawyers, and the press looked forward to watching TJ squirm. Then to their acute disappointment, TJ settled out of court.

Bill Whittaker: "He doesn't tell anybody about it but he is very generous. I don't know whether you'd describe him as a philanthropist but he's certainly extremely benevolent."

"Is that within the church or in general?"

"In general. He gives to a lot of charities. You'd be surprised, but he doesn't seek any publicity, doesn't get it, doesn't want it."

"He and Gai and Valerie go to church don't they?"

"They go to church, yes, they do. They're regular church-goers."

10.1-1 Ownership of horses and premises

TJ is too much the dictator to tolerate business partnerships well. He prefers to own things like his premises outright, by himself. He would no doubt subscribe to the business dictum that you don't invest without control.

He will engage in partnerships in horses. Again, he has control. TJ started by owning horses and has always owned a few. He has had shares in many racehorses. Now he is a significant breeder, and in the case of Bounding Away he bred and kept a champion. Because of her efforts he topped the money-winning owners list in the 1985/86 season.

10.2 Personality and management style

TJ is a forward planner, an innovative thinker and a very determined man. He does not wait for things to go wrong. His willingness to work hard and long are well known, as is his attention to detail. His mind is very active, continuously alert. He misses nothing, not the smallest detail, especially where horses are concerned.

10.3 Staff selection and delegation

I wondered if the thoroughness of TJ Smith extended to careful selection of staff so I asked Percy Sykes about it. He recalled how in times of full employment in the early 70s, TJ had been so hard up for any kind of employee that he had tried the government employment service and put advertisements in newspapers. Things got so desperate that TJ walked out onto the road in front of his stables and was asking young men on the street if they would come and work for him. There was not much chance of picking and choosing, even in times of high unemployment.

Delegation

TJ doesn't try to do it all. He delegates and lets people get on with the job but he keeps an absolutely all-seeing eye on the operation. A bawling out, if warranted, is immediate, but he does explain what is required.

10.4 Training arrangements

It is often claimed around the tracks in Australia that TJ has offered free training to the owners of some top horses. This means no daily charge, just the standard trainer's 10% of prizemoney. In the eyes of other trainers, this is one of TJ's most heinous sins. I asked Ernie about it and he denied it, saying that every horse in the stable pays its daily rate. Bill Whittaker must have asked TJ at some time because he said TJ would deny it emphatically.

Naturally this is cheaper for the owners and an attractive proposition, but if TJ does do it, it is no act of generosity on his part. Ten percent of an outstanding racehorse's winnings would still leave TJ well in front financially and bring in a lot of publicity.

I was surprised to learn from Ernie that for clients of Tulloch Lodge there were no fees or percentages taken on the buying or selling of horses. Ernie said this was because training was so competitive in Australia. I don't know if TJ marks up horses he buys and sells.

10.4-1 Training rates

In 1989 Tulloch Lodge charged $60 per horse per day but according to Ernie, the books showed a loss of $15,000 for a full year, on that fee. Clearly the profits have to come from winners. In 1990 the rate was $62 per day. The extra $2 per horse per day will bring in an extra $100 per day on 50 boxes, or $36,500 for the year, so like Wayne Lukas, it would seem TJ is not trying to make his money on the daily rate.

10.4-2 Debt collection

I for one would not like to owe TJ money. I've no doubt he would be a persistent collector.

10.5 Investments outside racing

TJ owned the hotel in the tiny country town of Bethungra for a time. Bethungra was near 'Eulomo'. He bought the hotel in the early 1960s. Built in 1886, it was at one time a Cobb and Co Staging Station. In Tommy's youth it was no doubt a local financial plum, probably the main watering hole for the district around 'Eulomo', without competition for many miles. But the Australian rural areas, like others in the developed world, have been steadily losing population. Presumably TJ found it to be a fading shadow of the crowded meeting place of his younger days, and moved his money elsewhere.

TJ's brother Dick owned a hotel, The Light Brigade. Percy Sykes said TJ had a financial interest in it. For many years Tommy could be found there after every working day unless it was raceday. Tommy's presence did a lot to help patronage.

TJ's main investment outside of racing has been in houses and flats, of which he owns many.

10.6 How wealthy is TJ Smith?

Business Review Weekly of May 1989 estimated TJ's personal

wealth at a minimum of $35m.

TJ's maintenance man was at the stables one day, re-painting some of the dark green walls of Tulloch Lodge. (They obviously don't wait for the paint to fade or peel.) He said TJ would own over 200 units and houses and also some shops at what's called 'Peter's Corner' at the junction of Allison and Avoca streets. He said Tommy would get an average of $170 a week from the units and they would cost you something of the order of $200,000 to buy - "some of the better ones." I had the feeling he is proud of TJ's accomplishments.

It doesn't take much arithmetic to arrive at a total value of about 40 million dollars, bringing in a gross of $34,000 a week or more than $1.7m per year. But that presumes 100% occupancy rate and is gross, not net, and anyone who has owned rental houses knows the net can be negligible after costs - especially if he borrows money and has a mortgage on each one. The *gross* return at $170 per week is only a pathetic 4.4% on $200,000. TJ does not appear to buy and sell houses like he does horses, so he must simply accumulate them, and expect capital gain to make up for the low return on capital. Capital gain was tax free in Australia until recently, and still is on property bought before the law was changed. Tax-free capital gain investments are very useful to someone with a high taxable income from other sources.

According to the handyman, TJ looks at them and buys them himself. At one stage he did have a bit of a hook-up with a real estate agent who may have bought some of them for him but usually the real estate agent lets TJ know they are for sale and TJ has a look at them. The handyman says they are mostly in the Randwick, Coogee, Bondi area, and he'd know.

10.7 How did TJ make his money?

In his early days TJ made most of his money from betting. Later that was supplemented by income from training, and he became a major horse trader. Eventually he had so much money he had to think about investments outside racing.

Bobby Thomsen: "He's made more money out of buying and selling (horses) than he has out of training. Any money he got went straight into bricks and mortar. He has a handyman, and all he and his son do is go round fixing up the places he's bought, converting them into flats and whatever. St Peters, Erskineville, Paddington, Randwick."

I asked TJ what he saw himself as - a horse trainer, manager, businessman or what?

"I see myself as a horse dealer."

He told another interviewer; "My success is turning horses over. I buy about 80 yearlings a year and sell about 80. Some horses I've bought and sold and bought again. One horse I bought and sold three times."

TJ's 10% of prizemoney would be around $400,000 per year for most recent years.

11) How he gets and keeps owners

After his early difficulties getting owners, TJ Smith's success eventually brought him many many clients. One article said TJ had 600 clients. He held Sunday champagne parties at Tulloch Lodge for his patrons. He and his clients usually had plenty to celebrate. It created a social scene of its own, which many people wanted to be a part of. Being able to have a social ale with Tommy and talk later with friends about what TJ said and did was like being able to dine with the Prime Minister. The ticket to membership of this exciting club was a horse with TJ. "You can't be around Tommy if you don't have a horse," I was told. For some ambitious souls it was a way to meet other go-getters with a bit of money, even if it wasn't the entree to the upper crust North Shore set.

Peter Alidenes

Peter is a lawyer, owner of Kincay, which TJ trained to win the 1989 Gimcrack Stakes: "He's not totally a man without guile because he's had to deal in his life with a lot of smarties. He doesn't say a great deal but if he tells you something it's the truth. He'd rather not say anything than mislead you."

"He has to deal with businessmen quite a lot. Yet the public image is that TJ is good at bulldusting people. I've often thought that businessmen aren't mugs, surely they'd wake up if all he had going for him was bulldusting."

"TJ Smith is one of the most alert, smartest men that I've ever met."

"Was TJ your first trainer?"

"I've had horses with Neville Begg, Brian Mayfield-Smith and Bart Cummings, and I find all of them gentlemen, they all have their different qualities, but as an all round professional businessman, I'd say I find TJ Smith the best."

"Out of that group that's something."

"He has a great team. His family is part of that team. He's got a great secretary. Tommy is a great communicator, he takes the time although very briefly, to talk to his clients. He's just my style of person. He deals with the thing: not a lot of frills."

"Do you ring TJ or does TJ ring you?"

"He rings me all the time; once a fortnight, twice a week, it depends what's happening. Gai rings me mostly: reports on trackwork, entries in a race - I have interests in other horses there. Their telephone communication is fantastic, do credit to any business."

"They phone you at work and let you know what's happening."

"They phone you in the car, they phone you at work, they phone you at home. Tommy likes to start early, he rings early in the morning or seven o'clock at night."

"Do you go and watch your horses work at the track?"

"No. I got into racing as a gambler, which was singularly un-succesful I can tell you. But I love the feel of racecourses, the horses. I gave up gambling and started breeding racehorses."

Bill Ritchie is another of TJ's owners. He is a breeder, and has been with TJ for 30 or 40 years. He had great praise for TJ.

At the other extreme is one ex-TJ owner who calls him a thief, but who doesn't want to amplify, nor get on the wrong side of TJ because he has to see him in the members area all the time.

11.1 TJ's public image

There would be very few Australians who have not heard of Tommy Smith. Those who have not heard of him might be politely described as outside the cultural mainstream: ethnic, insular or lobotomized. The public regard TJ as an amazing phenomenon, a living legend. Some, mostly those a little older, know he started with nothing and admire him greatly for his success. To them he epitomizes the 'little Aussie battler' who makes good, the Australian equivalent of The American Dream. Others say he is only the best because he gets the best horses, that he breaks horses down, that he uses drugs, etc. Even these detractors however, are apt to say, 'but the others do the same, so good luck to him'.

11.1-1 Opinion of other trainers

The opinions of other trainers have a considerable influence on potential owners. Other trainers have a very healthy respect for TJ. They fear his ability to 'steal' horses and improve them. Many have tried to imitate him and every one of them, successful or desperate, will turn an ear to the latest rumor about what TJ is doing. But they are in competition with him so they will often say derogatory things about him. Some of them rubbish TJ's optimistic statements (as reported in the press) whenever an owner brings up his name. Many will tell you TJ, 'must use something,' but if you ask they don't have any idea what.

In fact, as I found with the American trainer's opinions of Wayne Lukas, most trainers have a strong dislike of TJ, in spite of knowing very little about him. There is a great willingness to believe anything nasty about both these trainers, and a reluctance to believe anything positive.

It seems as though each 'world' of trainers has a trainer they love to hate, and one they like to praise. In Austalia, TJ is the trainer they love to hear put down. But they have a healthy, respectful fear of him as well.

11.1-2 Relations with stewards

In his early big-betting days TJ had some heat from the stewards, particularly in Melbourne. In 1968 TJ was suspended for a month for failing to report that one of his horses had bled after a race. Usually when a trainer is suspended, the owners

Tommy holds up the Golden Slipper trophy for the press to take photos. TJ has this special smile for photographers, which he can turn on and off like a tap. It is one of many components of his outstanding ability to get himself into the newspapers.

transfer their horses to another trainer - temporarily or permanently. TJ's owners decided unanimously to leave their horses with Tommy. Not allowed on any Thoroughbred tracks, TJ trained his string at a trotting track.

These days, in the reign of Chief Steward Schreck, known as "The Sheriff", TJ makes public statements about the track that seem to carefully curry favor with the powers that rule Randwick.

11.2 Getting publicity

In the period from the 1950's onward, TJ Smith has had, at a guess, more press coverage than the next three trainers put together. When I have discussed this with young trainers, they often say he gets the publicity because he has the best horses. It is another 'which came first: the chicken or the egg,' argument. But TJ got publicity when he was a one-horse trainer. He played up the Bragger story then and now. He quickly realized that publicity brought owners, which brought more opportunities to buy yearlings, and the more yearlings you buy, the more you learn and the more winners you produce. Those wins provide the soapbox, the megaphone, etc.

Bobby Thomsen: "I learnt at Tommy Smith's that one of the main things is *publicity*. You have to get publicity. He said to me a long, long time ago -'Never turn your back on a reporter."

"He is so co-operative for reporters and photographers in the saddling area. It's unbelievable."

"I have followed that to the 'T'. See, the publicity we get - you can't buy it - you can't go to a reporter and say I want $1000 or $2000 worth or publicity. These reporters are after any little snippets for the paper and things like that. Tommy would say - 'Tell them anything as long as your name's there, that's stopping someone else's name from being there. There is only certain limited space."

"I was out there taking photos on Saturday and he might be in a conversation with someone, but if he sees you're trying to get a photo - he'll just turn slightly and give you the picture - and then turns back into the conversation. He's immensely co-operative."

"He said, 'Never turn your back on a reporter!' I've been lucky enough to always have a horse that could get me publicity. Little things that people want to know about a horse. Little things have always got me publicity, all through the 10 or 11 years I've been training."

"TJ is well known for his love of publicity. There were two guys - I don't know whether they were reporters or trainers or officials or what - at the races on Saturday, and when Christmas Tree won his race, one said, 'Oh God. You've got to hand it to TJ, I thought he was playing all this Christmas Tree stuff for the publicity, I thought it was going to fall in a hole today.' They had obviously bet on something else. They thought that press about the horse's injury and treatment was for publicity - TJ keeping the sore horse in the big race for the publicity."

An example of TJ's knack for getting headlines when the press spotlight is turned towards opposition horses and trainers, occurred when everyone's attention was on the rematch of Bonecrusher and Our Waverley Star. Previously, these two champions had put in the "race of the decade," battling each other head and head for over 600 meters at the end of the Cox Plate, usually about 2040m. Everyone awaited the rematch, and the papers were filled with stories on these two horses and their connections. TJ got sick of that. He jumped in and claimed that his champion filly Bounding Away could beat them both!

TJ's calculated outrageous streak, his natural super- optimism, (or his stupidity, depending on how you see it) - while it does bring him headlines, also brings him ridicule and disbelief. Even that however, is publicity. For example the Toorak Times regularly rubbishes Tommy's proclamations. At the time of Tommy's claim that Bounding Away could beat Bonecrusher and Our Waverley Star, the Toorak Times said, 'Tommy Smith must have two of them. You couldn't go that silly playing with one of them.' (The Toorak Times' own claim to fame was that its registered publisher was a dog!!!! This was to discourage potential libel suits.)

Tommy's unequalled ability to get onto the pages of the newspapers began in the 1940's with his policy of speaking to the press when most trainers wouldn't. It was easier for TJ because at first he had no owners and later he had a large number, so offending one didn't matter too much. Tommy's rivals in the 1940's and early 50's had a small number of very wealthy patrons who were all part of one elite social class. They did not like their trainers 'showing orf.' Some owners were heavy betting men and the last thing they wanted to see was their trainer declaring a horse a certainty for Saturday's race, as TJ often did.

Incidentally, Maurice McCarten, TJ's main rival for nearly 15 years, had two of Sydney's newspaper barons, Sir Frank Packer and Ezra Norton as owners. That might have helped the attitudes of journalists to McCarten, but the two barons were feuding types and they drove him mad.

Having discovered how easy it was to get free publicity by talking freely to the press, and how much it benefited his search for owners outside the elite, TJ made a vocation of starring on the racing pages. George Moore helped, and ironically so did TJ's riots and ructions with a succession of other jockeys. While outrageous statements have been his hallmark in the major papers, pressmen will tell you that TJ is accessible, and frank and detailed, and loves to talk. Ernie's the same.

What does TJ talk about? Anything and everything, including routine stable stuff. When Christmas Tree was troubled by some mysterious hip problem in the run up to the Golden Slipper, TJ made no attempt to hide the fact. Instead he told all and sundry, let the press talk to vet John Peatfield, and allowed photographers in during the horse's long ultrasound treatment sessions. Neither TJ nor John was afraid to admit some uncertainty as to the exact problem. When the horse won next out, John and TJ looked like geniuses, and TJ had been in a dozen press articles.

Many trainers would not have the confidence to do what TJ did in that situation. In that same week I heard a reporter ask a trainer if he was having leg problems with his candidate in a major upcoming race. The trainer was very worried, and practically begged the reporter not to write anything about it, much less come around and take pictures.

Trainers worry that they may not appear to know what the problem is, that their vet might say the wrong thing, that if the horse breaks down, pulls up sore, or just simply loses - they will not look good. Reporters **will** ask difficult questions, but TJ has all the lines for those situations and it would pay a young trainer to listen to TJ. Think up all the tricky questions and work out the answers in advance.

Next in importance to *what* TJ says, is *how* he says it. When TJ wins his 4,038th race, he seems as enthusiastic as if it was the first race win in his life. That enthusiasm rubs off onto pressmen and owners and staff. It makes everyone happy.

That enthusiasm has great importance for television. There are a lot of on-course interviews in racing in Australia, and some of those from big races make it onto the evening TV news. I'm sure everyone has seen the interview where the trainer being interviewed, the winner of this great and exciting event, replies in dull serious monosyllables. It looks like the interviewer is ten times as excited as the trainer! This can be such a negative thing, that at the Harness Racing Expo at the 1990 Hambletonian, a firm of publicity consultants screened one as an example to be avoided. It is a miserable non-advertisement for the trainer (and for the sport).

I don't know if TJ is just naturally that enthusiastic, or if he cultivated it as he learned its beneficial effects. He certainly has cultivated a smile for photographers, and will do almost anything the photographers ask in the way of posing with horses or people.

11.2-1 TJ and the press

All the racing pressmen I know have great, if at times cynical respect for TJ Smith. Bill Whittaker has great admiration for TJ, but even pressmen who dislike TJ seem to end up writing about him. One very cynical young fellow in the press area, who definitely disliked TJ, said the other trainers brought it on themselves. "Even if they will talk, they talk such uninteresting rubbish. They're so afraid they'll offend someone, or let something out. Bart Cummings is funny, Doc Chapman is controversial, but after that, who besides TJ is going to give you a story every time?" Most trainers have no idea what would make a good press story, but TJ does.

I was standing with a contingent of the press when a big race was won by one of the less charismatic Sydney trainers. The press herd wandered off to surround the winners. Two hung back. One said, "I think we'll get a better story if we ask TJ why he lost," and off they went to see TJ.

A Victorian trainer told me that once, when TJ was down at Flemington racetrack in Victoria, and hadn't had a winner in several weeks of the carnival, TJ had pulled a lovely new hundred dollar note out of his pocket and given it to the racing journalists. 'There you are boys, go and buy yourselves a drink.' The Victorian trainer didn't think that was very fair. "I can't afford to do that. How am I supposed to compete with that?"

TJ has had many articles written about him that could have soured him against the press, but he hasn't let that happen. If TJ has a low opinion of pressmen, as so many trainers do, he keeps it well hidden and never loses sight of their importance to his career. That there is another side to the relationship there can be no doubt.

Ernie Smith: "Big race days are always good because you get all the critics giving opinions and criticizing you. In the Herald a well known bookmaker said that Tommy Smith and Ernie Smith were imbeciles - didn't know what they were talking about. I really got the shock of my life to see a guy like him say it. Well, along comes the horse and wins, but I don't see him writing in the paper that we were right and he was wrong. That's what racing is like. The press like to pick you when you're wrong, but they don't say anything when you win."

There *are* some racing writers who don't like Tommy, love to have a dig at him, even write him up as a buffoon, but TJ doesn't seem to care. He doesn't appear to have a 'hate list', and I didn't hear of any feuds between him and particular journalists.

In summary, publicity is hard to get without wins, but every opportunity should be taken, because it will bring more owners, more horses, more winners. It is an important part of the upward spiral to success. To mumble at the press after a win, to ignore or hurry the picture takers, is to climb three rungs of the ladder, then step down two.

11.3 Getting owners and horses

TJ offers owners a horse chosen by one of the best judges of a horse in the country, one of the best trainers in the country, and a very quick and reliable appraisal once training is started. The quick appraisal saves money. Other trainers might take several sessions of many months - "Let's put him away and see if he'll make it as a three-year-old." TJ also offers entry into a social club consisting of his owners. It is a very attractive package.

Tommy keeps a record of all his clients and possible clients. In some cases he knows when someone is having a profitable time and might be able to afford a horse. He might not phone for years if he knows they are having a tough time financially. Tommy is always recruiting new owners. Bill Whittaker: "Tommy loves to be where there might be someone who'll buy a horse for him. Even now."

"Even now?"

"Even now. Sixty-nine years old (1987 - Bill believes TJ was born in 1918), and even now his life is to be where someone might buy a horse for a million dollars for him."

TJ believes in making his horses a walking advertisement. Bill Whittaker: "TJ introduced white surcingles and bridles and breastplates. He was the first to do that too." (A Wayne Lukas feature many years later.)

"Was that leather or plastic in those days?"

"I'm not sure if it was plastic or leather but it was white anyway, and his horses would come into the enclosure; always first. Always. Particularly at the big carnivals, so that the owners and the breeders could see the Smith horses. They were always first into the enclosure. He was a great organizer. Some of the trainers would have them come in just when the jockeys were ready to mount."

I guess some of them used to try to keep nervous horses out or keep them out to preserve their odds, all sorts of malarkey going on.

"Yes. But not Smith horses - first into the enclosure with immaculate white gear. That was another change, a very important change too, I think."

11.3-1 Personality and social skills

Tommy has always had an enthusiastic, energetic personality. He has always been serious in the workplace where he can be gruff and abrupt with staff or anyone else, but socially he is funny and serious by turns. Tommy can be anything the situation demands, although the dedicated manager and money maker are never far below the surface. He has a very quick wit and can hold his own with anyone in verbal jousts.

In spite of his humble origins, TJ has never grovelled to owners, even in the beginning. I asked Bill Ritchie, one of TJ's owners, if TJ was more polite when he was starting off. He, among others remembers, TJ always being, "just the same as he is now."

If TJ has a peculiarity it is his somewhat high-pitched voice and his characteristic delivery pattern - staccato bursts of words, like a Tommy gun. The combination makes his speech easily recognizable, and nearly every second person around him has a servicable TJ imitation.

Valerie Smith, schooled at the Rose Bay Convent, is said to have dragged TJ off to elocution lessons and various other self-improvement courses. Her connections were said to be aghast at her choice of husband and no doubt she was intent on making him more socially acceptable.

11.3-2 Social stamina and alcohol

Tommy can handle alcohol very well. Vet Percy Sykes could match Tommy on sleep deprivation but not beer consumption, and could not keep up when the French champagne started flowing. "It goes to my head," says Percy. In fact TJ's stamina and ability to drink until the small hours of the morning, yet still front at 4am for trackwork are legendary. Percy Sykes told me that on occasion at the carnivals in Melbourne TJ would not actually go to bed. He'd party til late, wash and change and go straight to the track to watch his horses work. In spite of having much to celebrate and a partiality for beer and later champagne, I have never heard of TJ being drunk or disorderly.

Percy recounted this about Tommy's drinking history: "Tommy and his crowd used to go down to his pub, The Light Brigade, which he had an interest in with his brother Dick. They used to drink pony beers, which are small, but if you drink enough of them, they still affect you. This was in the days of the six o'clock swill - everyone drinking to beat the six o'clock closing. I used to get home stupid, so I stopped going."

"Then Tommy developed some mysterious illness. At a sale he just keeled over and they thought he was dead. The other trainers were just starting to think about dividing up his horses, when he started breathing again. Well it went on for about three years, but he couldn't get a diagnosis. He went to everyone, even the Mayo Clinic in the United States. He became nauseatingly sanctimonious, telling everyone he'd given up beer, given up this, given up that, and so on."

"He found this Harley St specialist in London who said it would be OK for him to drink champagne. Well! He became a champagne drunk overnight. He always drank Great Western. Tommy popularised champagne in this country. When he started, the Champagne Bar at Randwick was the size of a small room. Now it's huge, it's very long, it's upstairs and downstairs. He had everyone drinking it."

"One day we were with George Moore and George ordered Moet - a French champagne. Ever since, Tommy has been drinking French champagne, but it's so expensive, it's too strong and it dehydrates you."

Tommy's ability to handle alcohol is all the more surprising when it is a proven fact that greater size and a large percentage body fat help to decrease the effects of alcohol. Tommy is the very opposite of large and fat. He must have a champion liver.

11.3-3 Social class of owners

TJ can claim to have made a lot of progress on the social scale. When he won the 1949 AJC Derby with Playboy, which he owned and trained, the Committee members ignored him and invited the connections of Delta, the runner-up, up to the inner sanctum for a drink. McCarten, Adolph Basser and Neville Sellwood got a free drink with the doddering aristocrats: TJ got a snub. Trainers were not allowed into the Members area.

TJ fought this stuffiness (as did many others) and nowadays he has the run of the Members area. The Members clubs in Australian raceclubs have become very egalitarian. The diminishing attendance forced the abandonment of rules and a lowering of the fees. They are now very pleasant places, a surprisingly classless society, with stable staff rubbing shoulders with owners.

In the last years of the 80's, win, lose or draw, TJ and his crowd would get into the French champagne at the Champagne Bar at Randwick. Tommy's bunch included Sir Tristan Antico, vets John Peatfield and Percy Sykes, the Ingham brothers and of course Gai and Valerie, and miscellaneous other owners. There were usually about 10 or 20 of them by the end of the day's racing.

The Moet makers (about 40 dollars a bottle) should erect a monument to him for the sales boost he must have given them. (Even if it was cheap I refuse to buy anything French while they continue arrogantly detonating nuclear bombs in the Pacific, blowing up Greenpeace boats and killing protestors.)

While TJ never really made it with the multi-generation megabuck brigade, he has made it with the self-made set, who have eventually become some of the wealthiest and most influential people in racing. As a self-made man himself, TJ readily identifies with these people, and they with him. TJ cannot understand the genteel people who didn't have to struggle, who have had money on tap as far back as they can remember. They in turn can't understand TJ's 'hungriness', his 'greedy grasping' ways.

TJ's success at socialising is exemplified by the way journalists love to say TJ mixes with everyone from touts, tipsters and conmen to bank managers, captains of industry and prime ministers. (There's not much difference I hear you say!)

11.3-4 Does TJ steal owners?

A Perth trainer and some of his clients had a few social drinks with TJ on two occasions when TJ was over for a Perth Cup meeting. Some months later, one of the ladies was phoned up by TJ, who told her he had bought a horse for her. The lady was flattered and would have taken the horse but her husband said no. The husband had to hope and pray it didn't turn out to be another Tulloch. Some trainers call this 'white anting', others call it stealing clients, still other say it's fair game. TJ obviously ranks racehorse training with love and war.

Ask other trainers what they think has made TJ successful and more than a few will say it's because he steals good horses off other trainers. Listening to trainers, it has happened right around Australia, but TJ may be getting the blame for some shifts the owners initiated. Below are a some of the better known examples:

Redcraze

Racetrack May 81: Subheading, "One of the first proven horses to be improved by TJ Smith." In 1955 TJ won the Melbourne Cup with Toparoa, a horse from New Zealand. Redcraze, also from N.Z. was fourth. Redcraze was regarded as a very good horse. TJ could see something he wanted and he made a special trip to N.Z. to see Mrs Bradley, the owner, with an offer of purchase. She refused but later sent it to him to train as a five and six-year-old.

Redcraze went on to win the Brisbane Cup, and be second to Evening Peal in the Melbourne Cup in 1956. Before TJ trained him, Redcraze's record was 53 starts for 17 wins and 12 placings. Under TJ his record was 8 starts for 7 wins, according to the article. The solitary loss was expected because he was coming back from an injury. But Bill Whittaker says it was 23 starts for 15 wins 5 seconds and 2 thirds.

Bill Whittaker: "Redcraze was a champion horse but I think that Tommy improved it. The horse came here and he was the

champion of Australia, whereas when he was in New Zealand under Syd Brown, he was a very good horse, but he wasn't a dominant horse. After Smith had had him for about a month, he became dominant. Redcraze won a fortune in bets for the followers of the TJ Smith stable. And there were plenty of others. Very good with secondhand horses."

Gunsynd, the Goondiwindi Gray

Racetrack Annual of 1973 ran a story on TJ's acquisition of this popular horse. Trainer Bill Wehlow took Gunsynd as a yearling and won 12 races with him including five first up. He took the horse to Sydney and beat TJ's horses. Jim Coorey, one of the owners, said Ernie Smith approached them to buy the horse even though Gunsynd had bled. Then the horse was taken by the owners and given to TJ just before the Epsom Handicap in 1971. Gunsynd was later sold to a syndicate headed by major Sydney racing identity Mr George Ryder. Bill Wehlow was very bitter.

TJ has trained horses for Robert Sangster, seen here with his wife Susan, Ernie Smith, and jockey Jim Cassidy. Good picture for a caption contest.

TOMMY SMITH

Taras Bulba

Turf Monthly ran a story on this horse in January 1979. The background was as follows: In 1974, Taras Bulba, trained in Melbourne by George Hanlon, won the Rosehill Guineas, the AJC Derby, and the 2nd Australian Derby. Coming back in 1975 he won the Australian Champion Stakes, VRC St Leger and the Underwood Stakes, setting a record for three-year-old prizemoney. Towards the end of 1975, and to the astonishment of everyone, the owners switched the horse to TJ.

Hanlon was not a famous trainer at that time but neither was he an unknown. Many people consider George a training genius. Hanlon had his first Melbourne winner in 1952 and had gone on to win numerous top events with a small string, often with patched-up crocks. He had won the Melbourne Cup in 1972 with Piping Lane. The same year he had won the Sydney Cup with Dark Suit, a very rare double. He had every reason to consider himself a very talented trainer. George was very bitter at the loss of Taras Bulba but had a measure of revenge when he won the Melbourne Cup with Arwon, a horse Smith turned down. Hanlon is now better known and highly respected by other trainers - and less likely to lose horses to TJ.

TJ had offered the owners $500,000 for the horse, but Percy Sykes failed the horse on a veterinary examination. The owners then put the horse with TJ. One observer said TJ did not improve this horse, that Taras Bulba was a horse that won off his brilliance, and didn't like TJ's hard work.

Red Anchor

Sterling Smith: "Dad (Ernie) got Red Anchor after he saw the horse get beaten in Brisbane. The jockey hit it with the whip about forty-five times down the straight. Dad said, 'I've never said a horse was a champion but this one IS a champion.' Went to Melbourne; won the Guineas, won the Cox Plate, won the Derby."

"It's interesting to speculate, whether it would have done all those things if Paul Sutherland had kept it. It had already done a lot."

(Trainer Paul Sutherland was involved in the sale of this horse, but it is often cited as a horse TJ stole.)

TJ's reply on stealing horses

"Your critics would say that one reason you did well was because you stole horses, that you phone people up and say, 'I could put five lengths on your horse,' and by that means you stole the best horses."

"I never phoned anyone up in my life for a horse."

"No!"

"I never phoned anyone up in my life for a horse."

"Really!"

"I never phoned anyone up in my life for a horse."

"Is that trainer claiming that you phoned up his owner, when in fact the owners had simply buggered off with the horse because they wanted to put it with you?"

"I never rang them up in my life. And the buggers wouldn't give them to you anyhow for a start. They'd give them to someone else, because when I'd buy one off someone, I'd improve it 10 lengths."

Bobby Thomsen: "Years ago, many of TJ's good horses - that he won major races with - were horses that he acquired off other stables."

"When I said to him, 'A lot of people will say that a part of your success is due to the fact that you steal other people's horses,' He said, 'I don't steal horses."

"Naturally he wouldn't say he did it. Many of his horses are horses that he's improved off other trainers. But you hear all sorts of stories: He'll offer to train them for nothing."

"Yes that's another thing. I was told he made that offer to the people connected with Our Waverly Star."

"He'll train them for nothing. But he's done that all his life. Still, many of his best horses have been horses he got off other people; however he's got them I don't know; it's immaterial; but he certainly has improved them."

I discussed it with Ernie Smith:

"Tommy is accused of stealing horses from other trainers. I asked him about that, and he said he'd never phoned up to steal a horse in his life: He phones up to buy them perhaps?"

Ernie: "He buys them off people, of course he does. I don't know any horse trainer that won't take a horse off anybody."

I think TJ *does* try to buy a lot of horses that are performing well. Horse dealing is a big part of his life. This must have a very unsettling effect on owners, because it implies that TJ feels he could do a lot better than the present trainer. If he ends up training it for the same owners then he simply regards it as the second best possible outcome. Owners are well aware of TJ's reputation for improving horses and must be sorely tempted to switch a good horse.

A few trainers I know have refused the horse when an owner has wanted to switch one from another trainer. But lots of trainers take horses off other trainers. TJ is simply more successful at taking good horses off other trainers. Having a good horse trained FREE by TJ Smith would be a very severe temptation to an owner. Ernie and TJ deny it, but if TJ does do it, it wouldn't be his first choice - it'd be the third best outcome. The ethics of these tactics will be argued amongst trainers but there are no rules against it and it's a tough game.

Some hard-bitten trainers will say that a trainer who refuses an owner's request to take a horse the owner has with another trainer is just afraid the horse will go backwards in their hands. But I do believe that in some parts of the world, some trainers refuse for the simple reason they believe it is not ethical. Much depends on the local customs and ethics.

With his ability to improve a horse, it was an obvious tactic for TJ to chase proven horses. The very fact that he had improved so many meant that for other trainers, having their stable star switched to TJ was their worst nightmare. His tactics made him as popular among trainers as a shark among fish.

11.3-5 Has Tommy ever advertised?
In 1970/71 TJ wrote a column for a monthly racing magazine. The arrangement presumably didn't work too well for one party or the other because it didn't last long. Many years ago TJ was featured in ads for Ranvet products, as 'Champion Trainer.' I have never heard of TJ advertising, it virtually isn't done in Australian Thoroughbred racing, but as the probable all-time champion of free publicity, he hasn't needed to.

11.3-6 Does he give talks?
TJ is not a speech-maker, but he has never needed this approach because of his ability to generate large amounts of free publicity in the daily papers and racing magazines.

11.3-7 Any affiliation with studs?
In his first years the studs were not important contributors to TJ's success story, a few giving him horses *after* he was at the top. They have not given him many horses for reasons discussed in sections 7.1-1 and 12.1.

11.4 Managing owners
For Tony McSweeney TJ chose and trained many good horses including Dubbo, which set an Australasian record in the Oakleigh Plate; Versaille, which won a VRC St Leger and a Canterbury Cup; and Silver Sharpe which won three Derbies.

"What made you put horses with TJ?"
I'd known him. My wife Molly, her father was a leading trainer. One of his clients was E. R. Williams. They sold TJ a horse called Brightspot. My wife's father died in the early 1950s. TJ always had the 'get up and go' and I suppose the cheek, the confidence, the brashness. It was infectious. But I always thought that he'd make it.

"What was TJ like to deal with - for you as an owner?"
"Well he was a dominant force; owners had no say really. He said, 'You've given me the horse. You must have confidence in me.' But that is one of the criticisms I'd have of him, that he took a lot of the joy from the owner. He argued that he had to go through it all, engaging the best jockeys etc. He said, 'I'm an expert in it. It would be too time consuming (to consult with the owners)' So John Rogan and I, if, say, we wanted Moore on a horse instead of an apprentice - TJ had a leading apprentice, Frankie Leman, a good rider -we'd say the opposite thing, we'd say, 'Put Leman on him.' They used to call him Little Caesar,

and he'd say, 'No no no.' If we wanted Leman we'd ask for Moore - always vice versa. And that way we got our way."

"What is he like when he is talking to owners?"
Bobby Thomsen: "He lets them know who's the boss. He says, 'Jump!' they say, 'How high?' If they don't toe the line they're out. Take the horse away."

I was told of an instance when an owner told TJ he did not want Mick Dittman riding his horse. TJ told the owner to take his horse away. The owner changed his mind: it was OK for Dittman to ride the horse. But Tommy didn't change *his* mind. He still made the owner take the horse away. (Can't have been much of a horse.)

Far from grovelling to owners, even though he has to persuade many of them to buy a horse, TJ is quite firmly in charge.

11.5 Main owners
After his start with E.R. Williams, then with Jack Large, John Rogan, and Tony McSweeney, TJ has never been heavily reliant on one owner. Legendary bookmaker Tom Powell was another early client although they were to fall out later. TJ got most owners from press publicity and race wins, rather than by one owner arm-twisting for him. This meant he was less reliant on any one owner and less indebted to any individual owner, than were most trainers.

Tulloch Lodge - TJ's public company buying and racing horses
In February 1987 Tommy Smith and some business associates brought out a prospectus for the issue of shares by a public company. This was the first time anyone had been allowed to issue shares and raise money on a public stock exchange for the purpose of racing horses - to the best of my knowledge. I would imagine it has been tried before - sometime, somewhere. Apparently other major Australian trainers applied to follow suit but were told to wait. The controlling authorities at the stock exchange wanted to see if the trial balloon went up or down.

Meanwhile Vincent O'Brien in Ireland also formed a public company, called Classic Thoroughbreds. Wayne Lukas, I found, had one which was formed just months after Tommy's. Lukas said he was not impressed with the amount of hassle involved in running a public company. I told him how Tulloch Lodge had a phone number that shareholders could ring for information on any horses that were running, including their race chances, but that wasn't the kind of hassle he meant. In 1989 Wayne was facing court action by dissatisfied shareholders.

Early in 1988 I asked Ernie Smith about the origins of the company concept. I thought it might have been TJ's idea to enable him to compete with Brian Mayfield-Smith for the training premiership. The initial publicity quoted TJ as saying the scheme would put him, "back where I used to be. Last season I had the lowest number of horses in about 20 years." TJ said that although he would still have 60 horses in work, "the difference will be that instead of having only 30 in pre-training at Cootamundra as I did last season, there will always be 60 waiting to come in." There was certainly a lot of public skepticism that it could ever make a profit, so it seemed unlikely to me that the idea would have come from the corporate sector.

"The idea to go public with Tulloch Lodge - where did that come from?"

Ernie: "That was a set-up by other people really. Brian Yuill, who was the chairman of Tulloch Lodge - it was his idea - he said, 'You should be able to make it go, you win all the races and you're the top trainers every year so why can't you make it go?' He said, 'I can produce the money and put the thing together. Why can't it go?' They've tried to make stud farms go, and there's not much in stud farms as you'd know. At least in the business we're running, you are turning over money every day."

"It has a cash flow."

"Cash flow, yes."

"Was it partly brought on by the fact that Tommy was having to compete with Mayfield-Smith and Mayfield-Smith having all that money behind him - Robert Sangster and also Bob Lapointe, the take-away food chain king?"

"Well that was one of the big factors - that group formed a company didn't they, but they didn't float it. But they did have the A.R.A.B.S. (Australian Racing And Breeding Stables) and its been hard to compete with people like that. If you're going to be at the top you've got to have the numbers, if you haven't got the numbers you can't get there."

The prospectus for Tommy's company, to be named Tulloch Lodge Ltd., was for the issue of 30 million fully paid shares at 40 cents, to be issued at a premium of 10 cents plus 15 million free options. In other words 50 cents per share, which would raise $15m. The company was to acquire the horse training and bloodstock dealing activities of TJ Smith for $2.45m over four years and lease Tulloch Lodge and his other training facilities round the country for a little over $100,000 per year. TJ was to be paid $150,000 per year and $35,000 for each $1m in net profit. Ernie Smith was to be paid $50,000 per year. In addition it would acquire the spelling and pre-training properties at Cootamundra.

Tommy was able to spend $12 million on yearlings at sales in Australia and New Zealand in 1987. Things were looking bleak when the company filed a return on its first six months of operation in March 1988. It had a loss of $308,000. A lot of questions were being asked in the press about how the company could ever show a profit. How could anyone expect to recoup $12m from prizemoney, when few Australian horses ever top $1m in prizemoney? How would you make it from sire prospects unless you had a colt by Sir Tristram or Bletchingly or Biscay win the Slipper? Share prices waned. 50 cent shares went as low as 32 cents.

At the Randwick track one morning, early in 1988, I asked TJ how the company could make a profit.

"We will buy about 80 horses and some of them we'll share with Tulloch Lodge and some of them they will own outright, and if you feel like you want to buy a share in a horse you can, and that's how it will be run. If I can buy a horse as good as Bounding Away, well naturally the company's going to have some fun. Ever since I've been training horses I have had a good two-year-old, and I can't see why I can't buy one this year."

Then came Golden Slipper time 1988, one week after I talked to Tommy, and everything changed. Tulloch Lodge's Star Watch, by Bletchingly, won the Slipper. Comely girl was second, giving him the quinella. Another Smith horse, Wonder Dancer, won a major breeding race, the VRC Sires' Produce Stakes, down in Melbourne on the same day. Gai cried and hugged Tommy in a way that suggested a crisis had been turned to ultimate victory. The wins were worth $1,409,900 in cash, $15,000 in trophies and somewhere around 4 to 8 million dollars in stud value. The shares, which had risen steadily with Star Watch's earlier wins, had dipped with his loss in the leadup race, but rose another 10 cents in the week after these wins. From a year's low of 32 cents they had climbed back up to 45 cents.

Brian Yuill the merchant banker who came up with the scheme gave an interview explaining why the company had been started. He believed Tommy had an edge on other trainers, but insufficient cash to get the young horses he wanted.

"He is (a) a tremendous judge of yearlings and (b) a tremendous dealer in horses ... only last week Tommy sold Sir Tris three fillies in a deal which will realize the thick end of $2 million." He had TJ insured for $2 million. (TJ's age was given as 69 at this time, March 1988, but journalists were skeptical.)

Comely Girl went on to win the AJC Sires Produce shortly after, giving Tommy his 29th two-year-old win for the season. The very next day TJ was out at the Sydney Easter yearling sales, where he paid $700,000 for a Bletchingly - Gelsomino colt, "to win the Golden Slipper, just like I bought Star Watch last year." Later the same day TJ offered $500,000 for Star Watch's three-quarter brother, but the vendors had a higher reserve and it was passed in. TJ seemed very annoyed, and declined to go and negotiate further.

Interestingly, a knowledgeable breeding consultant's estimate of the value of this horse was given to me the evening before the sale. As a breeding proposition, should it fail at the racetrack, his estimate was $500,000. In other words that was

Sir Tristan Antico is one of the most important owners and breeders in New South Wales. Here TJ poses with Sir Tristan and Comely Girl after she won the AJC Sires Produce Stakes for them, in 1988.

ble to such a horse at the time. In the breeding game you have to make a profit on the stallion in three years because if it fails at stud, as the majority do, it will begin to show when the first crop reaches sales age and be confirmed when the first crop races. Unless there are a lot of winners in that first crop, there is little money to be made after three years.

At the close of the first day of the sale Tulloch Lodge had bought 21 yearlings for more than $3 million. I asked TJ if the successful money-raising of Tulloch Lodge would cause a rush of trainers to start companies.

"There should be quite a few people interested in companies. To compete in the top bracket these days you have got to be able to go to the sales and buy quite a few horses. The horse markets have jumped up about 50 or 60% in the last twelve months. Horses I used to be buying for $50,000 - now they're bringing in $80 or $90,000."

"To the person buying shares, the company owns mainly the horses do they?"

"Yes"

"So the profits of the company will come from training and then one or two good horses?"

"And a property running agistment up there. We spell horses there and we train them there. It's the first time anyone's put a proper trainer in to pretrain the horses."

"Some of those pre-trainers do more damage than good don't they."

"Well that's why I put a professional trainer there, I didn't just go and pick someone up who had just worked on a farm, I've got a professional trainer."

TJ went on to win a few million dollars, but not the trainer's premiership for 1987/88. If Star Watch and others could be sold for over $10m it seemed that TJ would have as much to spend in 1989 as he'd had in 1987. Was 1988 an unusually good year or could TJ pull off a similar result every year if he had this much money to spend? If the cash boost could be recycled year after year, Tommy could regain the top trainer title for many years.

That would be especially likely to happen if TJ were to produce a top sire, something many breeders didn't believe he could do. The crunch would come if he failed to produce a good stallion prospect for several consecutive years. The commonly predicted outcomes were dramatically different: a steady frittering away of the company's assets, as predicted by the skeptics and critics, or a continued domination of racing with spectacular profits from plundered prizemoney and the sale of breeding plums - the Tulloch Lodge 'official portrait'.

The whole thing had the aura of a test match in cricket. There were 'sides': TJ versus his critics. In the first innings, his critics predicted a batting collapse, a rapid wipe-out of Tulloch Lodge funds. TJ however, astounded the critics with the results of his selections. The spectators sat up and took notice. This was not the expected one-sided walkover for the critics. This was an exciting battle between equals. The second innings was anticipated with great interest. 'He cannot expect to be that lucky again,' said the critics. Barely had the next innings begun however, than there were rumors of financial problems. Then, suddenly, Tulloch Lodge Ltd was gone from the field. The watchers were left with that feeling you have when a match between the two top teams is ballyhooed for weeks and then cancelled because of the weather; a gut filled

TOMMY SMITH

with disappointment and chagrin and a touch of 'I wonder what . . .'

In May 1989 Tulloch Lodge shares were suspended from trading because Brian Yuill's group of companies had run into financial difficulties. Yuill owned 38% of the shares which were trading at 34c. This share price put the company's value at $10m, which was fairly accurate: the book value was $23m with liabilities of $11.5m. TJ had already signed for 11 million dollars worth of yearlings at auctions in Australia and New Zealand.

Unable to pay, Tulloch Lodge began to look for buyers for its horses, and there was talk of an auction. Gai and Tommy were scouring the international world of racing for a buyer and found one in the United States. A mystery buyer, rumored to be American billionaire John Werner Kluge, a friend of Robert Sangster's, bought Tulloch Lodge for a sum believed to be 10 to 12 million dollars. Kluge is worth over $5 billion.

Later the papers would say it *was* Kluge, and that he paid $7.5m for 105 racehorses and three country properties. Tulloch Lodge the company was gone, but Tulloch Lodge the training premises was still owned by TJ, and TJ was now training the horses for Kluge, one of the richest men in the world.

11.5-1 Are his main owners winning or losing?

TJ has not had a single major patron, but as far as I could determine most of his major owners are ahead. That is probably why they are major woners and still with TJ. Many smaller owners have lost, which is normal, the luck of the draw. The fact that TJ puts so much into real estate rather than investing all his own money in horses, as Wayne Lukas does, suggests that it's not profitable overall. Tulloch Lodge started with $15m and was sold for $7.5m in spite of selling Star Watch for a good price.

11.5-2 How well without his main owners?

TJ initially made his own luck with horses he owned. He has never been reliant on one main owner or owners. E.R. Williams, who opened the doors to some level of patronage was important, but only sped up TJ's inevitable rise.

12. TJ and the breeding game.

In the breeding arena TJ is as controversial a figure as he is in the field of racing.

12.1 TJ as a stallion maker

One of the things you hear most often about TJ is that he can't produce stallions. When you ask why this is so, they say it's because he trains males and females so hard they can't produce winners; he gives them anabolics and (they say) horses that have had anabolics never make top stallions.

New Zealanders are particularly interested in breeding (they produce an inordinate number of Australia's top horses) and they are particularly critical of TJ.

"You Australians rave about your TJ Smith over there, but he doesn't turn horses into stallions, so he must be giving them something that ruins them, or something that makes them perform better than they are. Name horses he's turned into stallions! He's been at the top for so long, he should have had a bundle turned into stallions."

When I asked around, the only significant stallion trained by TJ seemed to be Imposing, a 1975 foal by Todman. Imposing was 8th in the 1988/89 General Sire List. I asked Ernie and he couldn't think of any.

Always mentioned in the 'anabolics ruin stallions' argument is the success of Angus Armanasco, who trained a number of racehorses which later were among Australia's greatest sires, notably Bletchingly and Biscay. Angus says he has never used anabolics. He is sent many well bred yearlings because of that.

It is a very interesting but difficult issue, complicated by widespread beliefs of unproven and improbable scientific basis. For example, geneticists would find it hard to even *hypothesize* a scientific basis for the belief that anabolic injections would lower the racing quality of a horse's offspring. But let me tell you a cautionary tale. I remember savvy old breeders telling me that as a generalisation, first foals, and old mare's foals did not do well on the track. (Some stupid ones told me too, but what counts is the intelligence, the shrewdness, the judgement, of those who say they saw it for themselves. If ten fools, three liars and one wise man tell you something, it's probably true, simply because of that one good observer. It is a sucker-trap to discard the information because the fools and liars outnumber the good observers. Percentages and trends are data, not democratic judgements.) Many breeders sold all mares except top producers when they hit 12 or 13, or 14 years of age.

Geneticists and vets said that was garbage. "Good grief, they don't understand do they? They spend their whole lives breeding horses and they believe something like that! How can the age of the dam affect the genes of the offspring? Do older women have runts, dumb kids? I tell you, these people will believe anything."

Well, older women *don't* have children, they have menopause. Ever heard of a 60 or 70 year old woman giving birth? Older Greyhound bitches *do* have litters, and after I graduated I would see some 'perfectly awful,' small, runty, sickly litters from nine and ten-year-old bitches, which were still being bred because they were champions, or had produced champions. I saw some good litters too, but we're talking percentages, and it was obviously a greater risk with older bitches.

I remember discussing this with a horse breeder, who had been surprised when I did not dismiss the aged-mare effect out of hand. He said something like: "Young vets, they come out of vet school, and they think they know it all. If you mention the effect of the mare's age on race performance, they give you that look like they're sympathetic because you're so dumb. Then they tell you some things they learned in vet school that *are* dumb." This always reminds me of the way Christians and Buddhists and Moslems are always incredulous at some of the others' beliefs.

Then I found Peter Pring's marvellous study of champion Australian racehorses, and it made a very convincing argument that relatively few of them were the foals of older mares. There were of course some champions among the offspring of older mares, but fewer, as a percentage. About a decade later, someone analysed American breeding and racing results and showed *statistically* significant differences. First foals *weren't* as successful as second and third foals, and the foals of mares over 12 *were* even less successful. Once it was *in print* and *statistically* proven, it was necessary to *explain* it. Well, it was obvious (afterwards). The uterine arteries supplying nutrients are small, and lag behind the development of the first foal. Later foals have the benefit of the enlarged arteries from the word go. After 12 years of age, the mare is just getting too old to give the foal the best of everything. The dogma had engulfed and rationalised the previously unacceptable belief, indeed it was now *holy writ*.

So, can anabolics or hard racing lower the racetrack quality of a horse's offspring? I know of no scientific evidence to support either belief, nor can I think of any convincing hypothetical explanations. Since one of the main arguments FOR these beliefs seems to be TJ's failure to produce famous stallions, I would prefer to start by seeing how much can be explained by what is already known. What are some other possible explanations for TJ's failure to produce top stallions?

(1) Were the horses improved or benefited by TJ's training and therefore not as good as their race record indicated? Certainly, if TJ could improve horses four or more lengths by his feeding, training, use of anabolics and whatever, then they would win a lot more races and money than a horse of comparable ability that went to another trainer. As a group, TJ's horses would then be disappointing at stud, but some should still have been stars.

(2) Did TJ fail to make stallions because he was never given that select blue blood that the breeders usually keep for themselves? ("Only blue blood can make blue blood.") This was an interesting issue because most of the stallions that made Angus Armanasco's reputation were sent to him by Stanley Wootton. Most people believe TJ was never on the list of trainers used by the breeders of stallion prospects. But this is not entirely true. While TJ was not the darling of the horse-breeding grazier set, Tony McSweeney told me that TJ was sent horses by some major breeders. These included George Ryder, chairman of the Sydney Turf Club and originator of the Golden Slipper. Ryder stood the outstanding sprint sire Newtown Wonder, and he gave TJ a lot of help. TJ was sensational with the Newtown Wonder horses, having hundreds of wins. John Kelly, who stood prominent stallions including Wilkes at his stud, Newhaven Park, also sent TJ horses, as did some other breeders. Bill Ritchie describes himself as a breeder and he's been putting horses with TJ for 30 years. So TJ did get *some* well-bred horses.

(3) Did TJ choose a physical type that is unsuccessful at stud? An internationally known mathematician, Paul Mostert, has analysed the relationship of stud success and physical type. He found that some 'types' are successful on the track, but not at stud. He started a company, Equix Biomechanics, in Lexington, Kentucky, which measures horses to predict their track success, and to assess their breeding potential and devise matings. His work is described in the section on Wayne Lukas's selection skills. From Paul's very general description of the unsuccessful body type and comparison with TJ's purchases, it seems unlikely.

In addition, it was TJ who recommended that George Ryder buy Showdown after seeing the horse in England. When Ryder didn't, TJ advised Ken Cox, Treaurer of the VRC, to do so. Cox bought Showdown and the horse went on to become one of the most successful stallions in Australian breeding history. Was this a fluke? Or could TJ pick a stallion type if that was what was required? One example is not enough to decide either way.

(4) Was he choosing on type, and consequently buying horses with poor pedigree? It is well known that even horses with dazzling race performances are seldom a success at stud if they have a poor pedigree. Certainly TJ does buy a type, according to most people, but these days he buys type *after* cutting the list by pedigree. His pedigree buying, however, is not with sire prospects in mind, rather it is with the previous success of the female family in mind, especially success in his own hands.

(5) Was he simply not buying offspring of sires from sire-making lines? Certain sires rapidly become known as sires capable of producing successful sire sons. Buyers who have stallion syndication in mind go after their yearlings. Northern Dancer was a famous example in Thoroughbreds, Meadow Skipper was an example in the Standardbreds, Easy Jet has the same reputation in Quarter Horses. The Vincent O'Brien/ Robert Sangster team paid big money for Northern Dancer yearlings *because* resale as sire prospects was an important part of their profits. In England and Ireland, prizemoney is pathetic, but yearling prices and stud fees are high. There is also a ready world-wide market for English and Irish racehorses as potential studs.

TJ's buying pattern did not show any preponderance of sires who were sires of sires, almost the opposite. He bought many yearlings by first season sires, who's ability to sire *anything* was unknown. He bought many by sires who had been around for years without having a notable sire son. It may even be that when he fancied the yearling sons of known sires of sires on the Australian scene, like Biscay or Sir Tristram, he was often outbid by those who buy to make sires. With the public money he got from Tulloch Lodge Ltd, and encouraged by the money he got for Star Watch as a stallion prospect, I think TJ started to bid a bit higher on sire prospects he liked as types.

Why *wouldn't* TJ go after sire prospects? TJ is very much profit motivated. Profit seeking is a capital sin in the eyes of some (at least in public), but it does keep owners solvent, happy, and in the game. So how much money is there in syndicating or standing Thoroughbred horses at stud in Australia? Answer: nothing like as much as in England, Ireland or America. For a start, although Australian prizemoney is probably second only to America, and is commented upon by many foreign visitors, yearling prices and stud fees are lower. At the most expensive sale of 1988, the Inglis Easter Yearling Sale, 399 sold at an average of $61,308 - about $46,000 US, or about one sixth of the top US sale's average price. (At the 1989 Inglis Easter sales the average was $106,832 - an aberration caused by Bart Cummings spending millions he didn't have, for a syndication scheme that fell through. He had to sell them off again in a 'fire' sale.) In 1988 you could buy at the best sale in Victoria for an average of $40,000, in South Australia, for $13,500.

In addition, many stallion prospects are imported every year from overseas. In the years when TJ was starting out, imported sires absolutely dominated the scene. It was as if they had to grow up on ye olde Englishe soile to have sperme. Then in the 1960s, the success at stud of 'colonial' stallions like Todman, Biscay, Planet Kingdom, Manihi and Vain shifted the equilibrium.

But imported stallions still do very well in Australia today. Of the top 20 in the 1988/89 General Sires List, 11 were from Europe or America - USA(3), Ireland(3), Great Britain(2), France(2), Canada(1) - and two from New Zealand. That left seven out of twenty from Australian breeding. Many of the most successful stallions in that list of 20 stand at stud in New Zealand, to the delight of New Zealanders and perpetual chagrin of Aussies. The stallion export market from Australia is almost negligible. As a result of these things, the prices of horses leaving racing as stallion prospects is low.

Hunting for sire prospects dramatically narrows the available list of yearlings - to perhaps one tenth. This narrowing of the list means accepting a lower standard of 'type', and adds a lot to the average cost. No - TJ goes for the horse that can win the prizemoney on the track - and a quick return.

When I asked TJ about his failure to get stallions, he replied, "I'm not interested in stallions. I go and pick'em, and when they come along they're winners. I'm a horse trainer, not a stallion man. Helps to get so many winners."

Nevertheless, TJ Smith has had an enormous number of horses go through his stables, probably more than any Australian trainer, living or dead. Some of the horses were well bred, including some by sires of sires like Star Kingdom and Biscay. He has not produced many top stallions. It should be said however, that of Australian trainers, only Angus Armansasco seems to *have* a reputation as a stallion maker. Many other well known Australian trainers have had similar numbers of horses through their hands, some more than Angus Armanasco, without producing well known stallions. Perhaps the stallion-maker claim could be made for the man Tommy pushed out of the training title, Maurice McCarten. Mc Carten trained Todman and also Noholme which went on to success as a sire in America. But like Armanasco, these sires of McCarten's were Star Kingdom horses sent to him by Stanley Wootton. Perhaps the key was the genius of Stanley Wootton, a very successful man in every aspect of racing.

Perhaps the points above, plus luck, are a sufficient explanation, but many will feel there has to be something more to it.

12.2 Record as a breeder

TJ has bred many horses, and been successful enough to sometimes be the leading breeder in the country - not bad going for an anabolic fiend. Recent examples of his breeding are Bounding Away which he kept, and Doncaster winner Lygon Arms which he sold. Over the years he has bred three derby winners -Denise's Joy, Great Lover and Brewery Boy.

Ernie Smith: "Dick was a good horseman and he bred a lot of good horses, he bought Luna Park as a yearling and bred from her. From that breeding have come all these good horses including Bounding Away - they've all come from the one line or family."

"Tommy places great emphasis on the female line?"

"When you're on a good thing stick to it."

At the sales I saw TJ buy several yearlings that traced back to that same family.

13. What makes Tommy Smith successful?

Probably the most debated bar-room topic in Australian racing history. By now I hope you have something more than bar talk to go on.

13.1 How he acquired his skills and knowledge

TJ spent a lot of his early life with horses, on a daily, hour by hour basis. He raced horses as a kid and rode as a professional jockey. TJ did not work for any notable trainers in the city but he did work for 'The King of the Country Cups.' He made up for the lack of experience with top trainers by looking at Sydney's best:

"Was there anything you can remember that you saw as giving you a breakthrough, an advantage over other trainers?"

"When I got this idea on going into training, old Bragger went lame. (It took TJ two years to win with Bragger.) I went and concentrated on the four top trainers because I had nothing to do. I thought: I'll go and watch how these fellows train. I didn't work for them, I just helped them. I thought, 'I'll just watch how they work these horses then I'll work it out myself.' I thought Dan Lewis was the best trainer I watched. He was a very hard trainer and a wizard. He won about 6 or 7 Sydney Cups."

Later TJ would tour the world to see what he could learn from other trainers. TJ served a very solid apprenticeship, but he never became bogged down in a routine he learned from working with one trainer. He watched different trainers feed and work their horses, and no doubt modified his own 'experimental' training as he went along. He took it a step further than most by traveling the world to do the same thing, funded by his gambling wins.

13.2 Personality traits

Intelligence

Everyone up close to TJ has great respect for his rapid and correct decision making. He rarely has to change his choice. He makes a considerable impression. In short he has a very good, very fast computer. Percy Sykes, a very smart fellow himself, believes TJ has a kind of genius all his own. But he likes to annoy Tommy by telling him, 'You're not intelligent, you just have low animal cunning.'

"What does he say when you insult him like that?"

"He says, 'That's alright Percy, you have all the brains but I have all the money.' Tommy's not short of an answer."

Perhaps the most important thing about TJ's intelligence was that it allowed him survive then thrive as a gambler, then to pick winners out of the yearling sales. He was able to pull together the best from the local and overseas trainers and come up with his own training and feeding regime which was immensely succesful. Not bad for someone who left school through a window at a very early age.

Memory

"You must have good concentration to run such a large business and keep so much detail. Do you write anything down?"

TJ: "I don't write anything down. I can walk off the track after working 60 horses and I can tell you everything about a horse and someone else's horses if I concentrate on them."

"What about the track times? Do you write them down?"

"Gai writes them down, that's her job. I never time a horse."

"You just watch them."

"Yes. I've never timed a horse in my life. I just give orders and just watch them."

Sleep

"How many hours sleep do you need?"

"I can live on very little sleep but I can sleep if I really want to."

Valerie: "That's what I envy Tommy, his great ability to sleep, to relax. He can switch off."

TJ: "I can go to sleep anywhere."

"How many hours per night would you have averaged in your heyday."

"Three hours. I still get up at 4 o'clock in the morning."

Ernie: "I don't mind the getting up. It doesn't worry me. It doesn't worry me getting up because you can always come home and have a sleep."

"How many hours sleep a night do you need?"

"I suppose I need 7 hours - 6 or 7 hours."

"Tommy doesn't seem to need much-"

"Oh yes he does, he's telling lies, telling lies."

"-from what Percy Sykes tells me."

"Oh yes he does. I don't know anyone that can survive if they don't sleep. But see the beautiful part is you can come back from the track - we've finished working our horses by half past six - and you can come back home and have a couple of hours sleep before the average person is out of bed."

"Strangely enough with broken sleep, I think you can get more 'sleep' in an hour and not need as much sleep in total. An afternoon nap of an hour can take two hours off your night sleep."

"Yes."

Ernie's views notwithstanding, it would seem that TJ in his younger days was able to manage with very little sleep, at least a few nights a week. His ability to 'catnap' meant he could easily catch up.

Health and energy

TJ's main health concern has been his hip, which was broken in a fall during his jockey days and has given him trouble ever since. In addition he had a leg or hip broken by a kick from a horse in 1980. One of the sympathy cards was from Bob Hawke, the present Prime Minister, which read, 'Next time pick on someone your own size.'

At that time TJ had the great champion Kingston Town and in no time TJ was getting around on two elbow-gripping canes, then one, then none. The injury caused TJ pain for two years.

Following him as he got through and under fences at Randwick in the late 1980's, TJ has a very definite limp but never complains and moves pretty fast for a 'pensioner'.

TJ is legendary for his drive and stamina. Even in 1989 his stamina during the sales season - flying around, looking at yearlings, bidding at sales, and supervising his empire - is quite considerable for a man of his age. He is climbing out of bed at 4am, going to the track, making major decisions, handling millions of dollars and watching every detail when many people of his vintage are content to let the youngsters run the show - if they're not already shuffling around a retirement village.

Stress management

TJ often describes himself as highly strung. His manner is not laid back, more grumpy and gruff. He seems constantly alert. In an interview in New Idea in 1985, TJ admitted losing a lot of money in a gambling binge and at one point suffering a nervous breakdown through overwork. He said he could 'flare up' because he was highly strung like his horses.

Bill Whittaker felt the gambling was a stress on TJ but not the only one: "Gambling, that's how he really got his start. He was never short of money; he was a good judge and a good punter, and if you're a good judge and a good punter you survive in the racing game. Yes, he was a very keen punter but he doesn't punt much at all now."

"In an article in a women's magazine a while back, the way it was phrased made it sound like he really blew a bit of money."

"Maybe, but I doubt that. I'd say that the strain of betting might have been getting too much for him; the strain of spending big money on yearlings, having to off-load them to owners, that creates stress."

Celebrates successes

TJ enjoys his big wins as much as anyone, they certainly don't seem to have become a bore to him. In the paddock after a good win, TJ is as delighted and enthusiastic as if it was his first. He may be carrying on for the benefit of pressmen and owners but I doubt it. It is part of his character and his enthusiasm and optimism.

Scrapbook

Tommy has a collection of trophies at Tulloch Lodge and another at his home. He has enough for both sets to be impressive. He also has many photos and articles from his career in the limelight. Because of the widespread interest in racing in Australia, TJ's genius for publicity, and his dominance over many years, TJ has probably had more general press exposure than any racehorse trainer in history. His main rivals would be trotting trainers in the heyday of that sport.

Hobbies and interests

TJ was based a stone's throw from the Sydney Cricket Ground but until a few years ago he'd never been there. (In his days as a strapper he trained a dog to retrieve golf balls that flew about the area as golfers practiced in the open space. He re-sold the balls.)

"Do you have any hobbies?"
"No."
Valerie: "Horses are his hobby."
"We do take a holiday - every year - we've been doing it for how long? 33? 34 years? Every year we take a holiday."

"Do you still go and look at what the trainers are doing oversees?"
"Yes! I'm going over next year and I'll go around and see what's going on."
Valerie: "He's been everywhere."

"So you still go and check up on them?"
"Yes."
Valerie: "Well the last few years we've been mixing it up - round the world one year and Honalulu the next. Last year we went to Alaska but we went to the racetracks on the way down when we got to America. There are racetracks everywhere. Where did you say you saw a racetrack the other day - when we were in Poland?"

No golf, no movies, no stamp collecting for TJ.

Retire?

1986: "I haven't got time to think of retirement. You'll have to come back in a few years for the answer to that one. Why should I retire? I've never even had a thought in my mind of retirement. It drives me mad when people keep asking about my age." TJ's age was given as 66.

Drive and application

TJ is unrelenting in his drive to better his knowledge. He lives and breathes horses and racing. He has accumulated a lot of information, but knows how to give interesting but useless answers when someone wants to know some of it.

Valerie: "We went to Moscow about 8 or 9 years ago to look at the horses there. The racetrack was difficult to find but we found it."

"Did you learn anything in Moscow?"
TJ: "It was amazing how tall their horses were. They were in pretty good condition too."

"Trotters or gallopers?"
"Gallopers."

"You'd never think of looking for new clues in Russia would you?"
Valerie: "A Russian horse ran third in the Washington DC International about 10 or 12 years ago and that's what took us there. Tom said, 'I'll go and have a look at what they're doing over there - *for a horse to run 3rd in the International it must be worth looking into*'.

"The old General at the Russian Equestrian School had

gone to America with this horse and he knew about Tulloch. And the man that did everything for us was the Irish Trade Commissioner and he wanted a picture of Tulloch sent back to him."

TJ: "You wouldn't credit it would you? They'd heard of Tulloch in Russia." (Russia had its first starter in the Washington International in 1958. It ran 6th. They ran another dozen over the next eight years. The best results were a third behind the mighty Kelso in 1964 and a second two years later, both placings achieved by a Russian horse called Analine. I presume this is the horse TJ was referring to. These were impressive results considering the size of the racing industry in Russia. TJ might have gone later, after the 1972 Olympic Games, at which East Germany and Russia stunned the world with the results of their scientific approach. Western exercise scientists were crawling everywhere they were allowed to go behind the iron curtain after that.)

TJ leaves no stone unturned. I don't know what, if anything, TJ learned in Moscow about training or feeding, but it does show the lengths he will go to to unearth new leads.

Willingness to travel

In the 1940s TJ went wherever necessary with his horses, Newcastle, Melbourne, Brisbane, and all over rural New South Wales. The longer trips were by rail car. Later he would cut down on the trips around the rural circuit but expand his interstate campaigns to the point where he bought stables in Melbourne and Brisbane.

Optimist or pessimist?

TJ's history oozes optimism. He left the security of home and tried out as a flat jockey and a jumps jockey, and when he failed at these he decided to become a trainer. TJ always had great self confidence. Not just in the sense of how he carried himself but in the sense that he firmly believed he could make it to the top. He told people, "call me TJ," while with Matt Sawyer at Randwick aged 21 or 22. 'TJ' has a lot more individuality than 'Tommy'. Even then he was saying he would be the leading trainer. He 'bet his bag' on Bragger. He bought horses where no one would give him any. At an age when most would give the fight away he formed a public company to race horses.

Percy Sykes described Tommy as, "an unbelievable optimist."

Valerie Smith: "In all the bad periods, the dull periods, Tom will see something good. He sees good in everything."

Socializing - loner or homebody?

TJ could function well by himself but he was no loner. For most of his life he has had a family-based team. Socializing came naturally, it was good for developing owner loyalty, and he did plenty of it.

Inborn talent or something learned?

When I asked TJ if his abilities as a trainer and chooser of yearlings were a gift, Valerie was first to speak.
Valerie: "It is not a gift. He worked at it."
TJ: "I thought, 'I'll only know as much as the next man if I stay here.' So I went to see trainers feed and train - even to Germany, Greece, Belgium, Lebanon, the Phillipines, Hong Kong, Japan, Singapore, South Africa, Mexico, Venezuela." (Would this make the trips tax-deductable?)

13.3 The formulated approach

Planning and method

The evidence is there from the very early stages of his life that TJ was a planner. The physically-small 13 year-old Tommy Smith not only worked out for himself that he had little future in Goolgowi, he took the necessary steps to try out as a jockey in faraway Melbourne. He ran bets for bookies and became a successful gambler. He didn't plunge into training until he knew he had a flair for it. Even then he learnt all he could from watching the top Sydney trainers, then the trainers of the world.

A prominent American racing writer visited Sydney and spent some time with TJ. He found he could not mention a track anywhere without Tommy had been there, could name trainers and tell him how they fed and worked their horses. TJ is a constantly thinking, constantly learning trainer. Even at 70 + years of age, he doesn't consider he has no more to learn. He's still looking at trainers around the world. That's at least one reason why he didn't fade after a while at the top. He didn't become complacent, never started to think he knew it all.

Personal philosophy

TJ spent his formative years caring for himself while still a teenager in The Great Depression. He absorbed the ethics and attitudes of the people at the racetracks in very tough times, as much as those of his parents.

Religion

TJ has been a practising Catholic all his life.

TJ's business philosophy

Looking after business is never far from TJ's mind. He is keen to do deals and he plays the game hard. He goes after proven horses and does whatever is necessary - within the official rules - to stay at the top.

Betting

Being able to make a living as a bettor while he struggled with Bragger made betting essential to TJ's success, but I believe the knowledge acquired in betting helps a trainer in many ways. Things like assessing the opposition for placing horses in races, recognising when a horse has improved markedly, learning what is a normal form cycle. It also helps a trainer to deal with and win betting owners. Some trainers have survived on their ability to bet, more than their ability to train.

Of course betting can be the undoing of a trainer, either by losses or because it leads to the trainer not letting his horses always run on their merits. In Australia the penalty for holding a horse back to get better odds in later races can be a lengthy disqualification.

TJ made many monster bets in the 1940s, especially in relation to his stake or net worth, and was broke more than once. Bragger gave TJ his start at least partly by allowing TJ to bet and win. He won a pile on Playboy's Derby win.

Did TJ play 'the quick and the dead', did he hold horses back? Down in Melbourne, in 1950, Playboy ran very poorly in the Melbourne Cup, with Darby Munro riding. Shortly after, in it's next race, it was backed right in to very low odds. The word went around that the 'Sydney boys' were behind the plunge. The crowd became so ugly that Munro refused to ride the horse, saying he'd be lynched if he won. TJ put Jack Purtell up, Playboy won, and someone collected a bundle. The Melbourne stewards investigated, but did not take any action. However they never looked too kindly on the boys from Sydney after that.

Percy remembers Tommy had big bettors who used to travel with Tommy to Melbourne and Brisbane. However his reputation with punters in the 1960's and onwards was very high. Their view was that TJ chased the prizemoney, not the better odds, that his horses ran their best in every race. Even so, he told an interviewer in the 1980's he had to gamble to make money. But he doesn't win all the time. When I was interviewing TJ he took a phone call. He told the caller he'd 'had a blackout' - never picked a winner. Had four bets - four losers. He should have called it a 'redout'!

TJ recognizes the Melbourne Cup is a mug's bet. When he was asked in 1985 if he bet on the Cup, he said, "No. I bet on something easier." He told another interviewer that he'd had to stop gambling for a while for the sake of his health.

Ernie was reported to have stopped betting in the early 80s but at one meeting in 1988 he was standing in the crowd around the bookies looking very interested in comparing the odds.

Selling strategies
TJ has long been able to claim he has a proven eye for horses in the sales, and that he can improve a horse. TJ claimed 10 lengths, and off some trainers, at some times in the 1950's, that was probably correct. He could point to examples of both skills. Before he had those to point to he was unable to win clients, and had to buy or lease his own horses. His success at gambling financed those purchases.

Is he a risk-taker?
TJ's gambling habits would mark him as belonging at the risk-taking end of the spectrum. But I doubt he has 'bet the ranch' since those early Bragger days. Although he bought or leased a lot of his early horses himself, once he was established he mostly bought them with other people's money. The gamble with Tulloch Lodge Ltd was not much of a financial risk for Tommy. He stood to gain from it win lose or draw. His investment policy - buying a suburb or two of houses - is very conservative, almost a classic feature of depression survivors, who trust neither paper money nor high finance.

Is he an innovator?
The image of trainers as people who use the methods of some old-time trainer for whom they strapped or groomed, does not apply to TJ. He changed training, feeding, how yearlings were bought, and he floated a public company. He broke out of the secretive mold and told the racing writers his horse was going to win. He dressed differently. TJ is an innovator par excellence.

Time management
Anyone who has seen TJ at work knows he hates to waste time. Everything is hustle and bustle, everything is done with speed and efficiency - or someone incurs Tommy's wrath.

Goal and step setter, or day by day?
Formal goal setting sessions are not part of TJ's style but he is a long term planner and an innovator with long term strategies. TJ doesn't sit and wait for Opportunity to knock on his door, he goes and knocks on *Opportunity's* door. The most promising new source of wealthy owners on the Australian horizon is Japan. One day when I was there, TJ and Gai were shooting a promotion video for the Japanese market. (Gai's television experience came in handy.) Gai's children have been taught Japanese at home by an au pair girl. Think about the future, make plans, take steps. That's how you end up *in* the headlines instead of *reading* the headlines.

13.4 Has Tommy ever had a positive drug test?
Drug testing was introduced in Sydney in 1947 when a lab was set up. Initially it mainly tested for caffeine, and for a while only two swabs per raceday were taken. Later every winner was swabbed.

TJ was disqualified for five years, after a horse called Sunshine Express won the Maltine Stakes at Randwick in 1950. The horse was positive for morphine or a morphine-like compound. However a rash of positives occurred, and there was a suspicion that the new technology was inaccurate. Because of that, TJ's ban was converted to a reprimand. However Jean Kimble, the lady who analyzed the swabs never retracted her results.

In 1953 TJ won the Doncaster with Tarien but the horse returned a positive swab. On the same day a horse called Cromis, owned by E.A. Underwood, Vice-Chairman of the Victoria

Gai uses her experience in television to make a video to publicise Tulloch Lodge among the Japanese. Forward planning, goal setting.

Racing Club, won the AJC Sire's Produce, and also returned a positive swab. Cromis was trained in Melbourne. The circumstances and other results suggested a 'doper' had operated and there was no penalty.

13.5 Luck and other reasons for success

One of the long term factors in TJ's success has been the decline of the pastoralists over the past 50 years. The pioneers had started with cattle sheep and horses. Their offspring however, had less and less to do with the livestock with each generation, preferring the bright lights of Sydney society. They did, however, retain an interest in the horses. In the period between 1870 and 1955 they were the main owners of Thoroughbred racehorses. This long- established grazier elite have never been great patrons of 'new people' or 'crass people' so the more money they had, the better the horses TJ's older rivals had. Fortunately for TJ, the pastoralists, after a last golden shower of money from the demand for wool during the Korean War in the early 1950s, have been in steady decline, while the wealthy city slickers -his patrons - have been on the rise.

TJ also benefited from being too small for the army. He was able to get on with Bragger at a time of reduced racing but even more reduced competition.

Was TJ's purchase of Bragger good luck? Certainly he was lucky to have the chance to race such a good horse right at the start of his training career, but TJ recognised the ability of the horse and showed great perseverance. Tulloch was something of a fluke but he came after TJ was well into his reign. TJ

bought good horses at yearling sales by skillful selection. He also got proven horses from other trainers. There is some disagreement about whether this is ethical, but some would consider it a skill.

In 1990 TJ had some luck when a disgruntled employee tried to burn down TJ's stables. TJ only lost one horse, but the trainer next door lost ten of his best horses.

13.6 What TJ thinks made him successful

"Why were you more successful than other trainers - what would you put it down to?"

"I don't know. People often ask me that. I often wonder why I was so successful for so long because no way in the world do trainers stay long at the top. The average trainer at the top stays for six years and the only trainer who went 13 years was a fellow called Smith in New York. He's the only fellow since they've been keeping records - that's been leading trainer for more than a dozen years - nobody else has ever kept going."

"Do you think of yourself as a person who is always looking out for new ways and new methods."

"Oh yes. I'm always watching out for things."

"Do you read a lot of stuff about the racing game."

"Not much. I like to read about the things that happened 30 or 50 years ago. It's amazing how horses could run over two miles and then they'd saddle them up again."

In an interview with Bill Whittaker just before the 1988 Slipper, TJ had this to say: "Selecting the right yearling is a gift of God with thousands of factors involved such as many many physical technicalities. But having an eye for a horse is critical. Yearling buying is different to training. I'm good at both. I would not be a good trainer if I wasn't a good judge of a yearling."

Over the years TJ has told a number of journalists that without Bragger he would never have been heard of. He told me: "When I started with Bragger I knew nothing about training."

He told racing writer Bert Lillye, "I learned by constantly experimenting with Bragger. He was so good and so honest that he overcame the many mistakes I made early and was still able to win."

While I have no doubt Tommy had more to learn when he arrived in Sydney, I think he possibly underestimates how much he learned about training at the Sawyers' property. It is also the opinion of everyone, *everyone*, who works closely with him that he would have gotten to the top sooner or later, if not in horse racing then in some other field.

Can Tommy smell a good horse?

Valerie: "In Japan they asked Tommy, 'Why you smell horses - what's your secret to success?' Tommy said, 'I don't smell horses.' 'Something magic because you always smell horses.' Now Tommy's nose is a certain height so that's why when he looks at a horse he always puts his nose near a horse. They reckoned he smelt the horses."

"So the Japanese were trying to find out TJ Smith's secrets too?"

"Yes, they sent some reporters to the hotel to see what magic charms he had, and what makes his horses win. Tom said, 'Yes I have got a magic charm - hard work. Dedication, that's the magic charm."

George Moore, Tommy's jockey and close friend from the early years, attributes TJ's success to dedication, ability to judge a horse, get it super-fit, and to his use of the best people to help him.

13.7 Trainer, conman or businessman?

Tommy Smith introduced some revolutionary changes in the buying, feeding and training of Thoroughbred racehorses in Australia. Yet he did it all in the name of making a dollar. Tommy is a businessman first and foremost, but his horsemanship, his careful scrutiny of feeding and training around the world and his willingness to try new ideas have carried him to the fore as a trainer. As for his ability to attract the owners, TJ is often painted as a conman, but he hasn't really bothered too much about charm school. Owners come to him because he can choose a high percentage of winners as yearlings, because he can determine quickly if it has potential, because he can improve horses many lengths. Owners toe the TJ line or they are out.

Analysis of TJ's training success

To many racegoers in Australia the burning question is whether or not TJ's harder track workouts are possible because of the number of horses he can afford to break down; to the supplements, additives, anabolics and treatments etc.; or to some secret drug.

The evidence that TJ has something secret may be summarized:

FOR

He dramatically improves horses from other trainers.
Few of his employees have gone on to become top trainers.
He has had two positive swabs in the 1950s.
When other trainers try to train as hard, their horses train off. This happens even if they use anabolics and most of the same additives.

AGAINST

When TJ improved horses it may have been because he targeted horses with subtle signs of unfitness that he felt he could remedy, horses that looked as though they could stand more work, or horses of trainers whose methods he knew were outdated.
The ex-employees have not exactly duplicated his training, could not afford the best trackriders in the morning, the best jockeys in races, etc.
Imitators may not have TJ's eye for conditioning. They may have overtrained or trained inconsistently.
They may not have been able to pick the talented stock at the sales.
You have to have good horses to be able to train hard.
Other trainers usually don't have the Sykes practice additives. (They have Ranvet products but not the unmarketed things.)
Other trainers can't compete with TJ to buy from the same tough families.
TJ's horses don't usually improve overnight, more like a month.

There have been examples of trainers dramatically improving horses with great regularity, who have lost their magic touch with improved swabbing, close surveillance, or because their secret got out, etc. This particularly happens to those trainers who can improve a horse "overnight". This suggests a trainer can have years at the top with some secret drug.

How easy would it be for TJ Smith to have some wonder drug or series of them, in regular use? If he has, he must have operated in great secrecy and have kept his secret for over 40 years. The mechanics of this involve being there when the employees are not around, behavior which would make the staff suspicious, or else swearing some of them to secrecy, which risks blackmail. If the vet or some member of the organization was injecting or dosing the runners regularly, the pattern would be noticed by other employees. If it differed from the raceday pattern of other trainers, it would become a matter of gossip. TJ's organization is rather big for secret injections. Surely the secret would have come out sometime in all those years. In spite of the regularity with which the drugging allegation is made by racegoers in Australia, I personally have never heard convincing evidence that TJ has something the others don't.

When other trainers suspect such a situation they watch like hawks. They practically mount their own investigation. They watch for overseas trips by the suspect or relatives or staff. They watch for visits to the stable by people from overseas. They grill the stable employees at a cabaret after getting them suitably pie-eyed. They tip-off the analysts, the stewards, the track security - that something stinks in so-and-so's stable success. Horses from the suspect stable are scrutinized at starting time for tell-tale signs.

The natural progression of a wonder drug is usually this: The drug is one of many existing compounds or a newly invented one. Tens of thousands of new compounds are synthesized *every year*. It may be a human pain killer, something for arthritis or something out of the New York narcotics market. The drug is tested in horses by the ever- active "chemical racing fraternity" and found to improve performance. They test it to see how "swabable" it is. That determines what tracks it can be used at. If it is highly detectable it will be used at some backblocks track that only swabs two races a night, and then only after two winners have been swabbed. Even then it will have to be better than caffeine and a host of other compounds.

If it is difficult to detect it will go via some individual to a "chemical vet" or "chemical trainer". Someone's horses, somewhere, begin to improve. Rarely, I would guess, does it stop there. Good news travels fast. "Can I have some for cousin Freddie?" "I know you've got something good, and I have this good horse in a stakes race, I'll give you $2,000 for one hit, just one dose." "I know you're using something that works and I want some or I'll . . . "

The pusher or the "chemical vet" has every reason to increase the number using it. Soon anyone NOT using it feels foolish. Win rate plummets, owners get restless or may even buy the stuff and give it to the trainer. Human nature decrees that more than likely the bubble will expand and inevitably burst.

Once the stewards get wind of the new "zinger", the analysts start looking harder. A name can cut their work to a tiny fraction. A sample bought by an undercover agent, or donated by a trainer who does not want to use drugs but also is sick of being beaten by those using them, can also cut the time and work. Pretty soon there is a either a rash of positive swabs, or an example is made of some poor sucker, or the word goes out from the stewards, "We know what you are using so quit it." That depends on the attitude and policy of the controlling body. Suffice to say another hot drug bites the dust.

I believe that many different factors combine to give TJ his ability to improve horses. He uses whatever can be used at the appropriate time before a race. Naturally with the rule changes there is less that can be given and it has to be done further and further in advance of the race. He provides every possible additive and feed ingredient that might help a horse. He trains them very hard and because of his training skill and feeding, many of them stand up to it. If a horse needs less work, TJ will see that and give it less work. Those that don't stand up, or are too slow, are quickly moved out of the main stables and sold off.

Tommy Smith has developed a system of hard but careful training, good nutritional and veterinary backup to help his horses with stress, and a supply of horses to replace those that are too slow or can't stand up to his program. By buying from the families that have performed well for him in the past, he has an increased chance of finding his kind of tough horse. TJ doesn't like weak horses. He told Perth trainer Bill Fell, "I can't stand those poofter horses."

Most other trainers lack the quality and numbers of horses. Ironically, TJ gets both because of his ability to choose top yearlings. Owners take their money to TJ.

13.8 What drives TJ Smith?
A word that is often used in reference to TJ is hungry. Former Tatts Chairman Tony McSweeney, who had many classic winners trained by TJ, told Nick Yardley in an interview, "He has always been extraordinarily hungry - he loves money and has been very successful at getting it too."

In interviews with newspapers and magazines TJ has said his ambition was to have the best home, the best car. "The biggest thrill I ever got out of racing was buying a home at Point Piper - trainers used to live next door to their stables." "I've been a money-making man all my life," he told another. TJ has not been so concerned about power, independence or social standing.

People will argue whether that hunger is unadulterated greed, or a deep seated need for financial security, born of a very tough start in life.

13.9 Lessons for beginning trainers
What would TJ do if he were starting out today? One clue is the advice he gave his nephew, which came out in this interview with Sterling Smith:

"How old are you now?"
Sterling Smith: "Twenty three."
"Have you always wanted to be a trainer?"
"Always. All my life. Even when I was twelve, thirteen, fourteen. I've always gone to the stables and helped out, mucking

the boxes out, doing the feed, things like that."

"It's good to be in the position where you know what you're going to do and you can start working on it straight away."

"When I went overseas last year, first stop I went to Charlie Whittingham. Probably that and Alec Head in France were the greatest experiences of my life. Working with them and learning the different methods. I think you have to go overseas to see the different changes.... what it's all about. And *TJ thought it was a good idea as well."*

"Did he recommend that?"

"Oh yes, he said, 'Go to Whittingham and go to Alec Head,' - because TJ and Alec Head and my father are all good friends, and Alec was leading trainer for the last 15 years."

In mid 1989 Sterling was with Wayne Lukas, then went on to spend time with Shug McGauhey, Eclipse Award winning trainer of 1988, and trainer of Easy Goer.

The second lesson from the career of TJ smith was to experiment with all that you learnt by watching other trainers. TJ was constantly changing things.

The third lesson is to become a publicity machine. Learn how to make yourself, your horses, your wins, your losses, your preparations, your problems NEWSWORTHY, INTERESTING. Think like a journalist. Get into the papers and magazines. Have a ready summary of your life and any interesting information printed up and give copies to all the working press. Make sure it has your phone number and make it clear you'll be willing to talk. Ideally have it on a word processing program on a computer, and update it with new wins etc. Take copies with you on days when you might win. Give them to any journalist who is interested.

Don't get 'an attitude' because the journalists don't pay you much attention, or because they made the story too short, or not how you would have liked it. Pressmen will avoid like the plague someone who seems hostile.

Cooperate with photographers, no matter how much you think you are not photogenic. Get your teeth fixed if they're too gross, or half have been punched out. Study yourself in pictures. Improve your smile, choose clothing that shows you up well, learn where to put your hands. Aim to look happy and confident, because that attracts owners.

But the main lesson from TJ's rise is to learn how to select yearlings. This was a major lesson from the life story of Wayne Lukas, and I have expanded on acquiring selection skills in section 13.9 of Lukas. TJ has a better reputation than Wayne as a trainer: where the Americans say Wayne can't train, the Australian trainers *fear* TJ's ability to improve a horse.

Gai Smith after Star Watch's win in 1988. Gai cried then laughed, then cried and then laughed some more. The win seemed to retrieve the financial position of Tulloch Lodge at the time.

14. The future

"What are your plans for the future?"

"I don't know - just keep working and just hope the Lord gives us more time. But I've enjoyed it."

14.1 Perfect conditions for him would be ?

Perfect conditions for TJ now would mean lots of two-year-old races, all youngsters going through the yearling sales so he can pick the best, and owners flocking to him to ask him to buy yearlings. It would be a great help to him if he could produce a top class sire or two. This would help his public company (now gone private) to make money.

14.2 Probabilities

"Who do you see taking the title off TJ? Will Paul Sutherland eventually get up there?"

Bill Whittaker: "Paul Sutherland still doesn't really have the money or the owners to take on the top money that Bart and Tommy divide up, practically between them."

A well dressed duo: Ernie Smith with son Sterling, who was back from overseas and looking to start his own training stable, which he has since done. Ernie is very proud of Sterling and behind him all the way: "You haven't heard the last of the name Smith in racing," he told reporters.

"That's true. But he's making his way. He's only 41 or 42, twenty years younger than Bart, nearly thirty years younger than Tommy."

"I guess if he paces himself right, he should get it."

"Neville Begg would have to be the guy who's been up there for ages but never won the title."

"He nearly got there one year but Neville's great clients have either died or gone broke. He's had a bit of very bad luck with some clients."

Brain Mayfield-Smith has had less to spend because Lapointe has been expanding his businesses and Sangster has been strapped for cash until he sold Vernon's Pools. That gave him 69 million pounds or dollars and he's apparently putting that into horses. Brian may see some of that. Even so Brian has done very well with cheaper horses and now is buying for outside clients of his own.

Ernie smith in 1989

"Have you ever felt that you'd like to go out on your own Ernie?"

"No, not really, I've never really wanted to because this has been a good combination. Why ruin a good thing?"

"In the future do you see your son Sterling taking a role at Tulloch Lodge?"

"Sterling has been away, he's been overseas for 12 months. He's been with us for just on four years. He's going to apply for a license probably at the end of this year."

"As I understand it Gai would have a problem getting a license because of her husband Robbie Waterhouse being a warned off person."

"Yes, probably so, but Sterling is going to go out on his own."

"That would probably be a good thing for him even if he was intending eventually to go with Tulloch Lodge."

"Yes. He's young and he's keen and thats the time to take these things on."

"Yes, it's a hard life. You'd want to get in the habit early because you wouldn't be able to do it later would you? What do you feel like when you get back from holidays and you have to keep getting up at that un-Godly hour?"

"Well I think it's like everything else, you're used to it."

"Are there some directions or goals that you and Tommy have, that you'd really like to achieve in the next few years?"

TOMMY SMITH

"I don't know - you can't win anymore races than what we've won - we've won every race on the program. But it's like everything else, all the big races are important aren't they? See, along comes a race like the Golden Slipper, been going for only 30 years, but it's a real thing when it comes up. It's the same as the Melbourne Cup. Everyone wants to win the Melbourne Cup."

Valerie: "Other fields are greener - but there is no field that is richer and greener than Australia with less work. In America they work very hard and they're all breathing down your neck and waiting for you to make a mistake. Tom could have had top jobs in England, America - anywhere in the world, but he said, 'What I've got in Australia I own. I'm not a boss for anybody." (meaning he doesn't run stables for someone else - this was well before Tommy started Tulloch Lodge Ltd, but even today TJ still owns his stables.)

TJ: "Sydney has everything. If you are interested in boats, speedways - you name it they got it. It's got the best weather in Australia - I think anywhere in the world. But I've been offered some great jobs."

"Yes I'm sure some of those wealthy American owners would have offered you some good jobs."

"Yes, but I love living in Australia."

Valerie: "In Australia you can have a home life. In England they are on the road all the time. In America they are on the racetrack all the time. You know 6 days here and 30 days there. Racing every day of the week."

TJ: "It's the same group of people that you meet. Practically the same people. I couldn't put up with it."

Valerie: "They move from San Francisco right down the coast of California."

"Yes it'd be pretty dreadful for family life. They find it hard to believe the Australian system. When you say the trainers just stay in the one city all year round, they say, 'Well don't they starve in the off season?' They don't realize we have racing all year round in each city. But I must admit when I first read about the 'season' at American tracks I thought it was like our carnivals - bigger prize money and better races. In Melbourne they race all year but there is a spring carnival, with richer races. Sydney has an autumn carnival; Perth has a summer carnival. But in America when the season ends, that's it, the tracks shut - no more racing. Some of them are shut for 10 or 11 months of the year. That's inconceivable to Australians."

TJ: "Hollywood Park use to be shut for eight months of the year until they brought on the trotting. Just idle for eight months of the year."

"You wouldn't believe things could be done so differently."

TJ: "I don't know why. They wanted me to go to America - but if I went to America I would have got hold of two or three fellows and said, 'Look we'll put 3, 4 or 5 million together and just buy the good horses out of the claiming races and make a small fortune."

"Would you like to take one away to the Japan Cup?"

"When I go to Japan I'll take the winner. I won't go there just for the sake of having a run. I could have been there a couple of times. Only horse I've had good enough for that in the last few years was Kingston Town, but he wasn't quite sound enough. He would never have stood what it would take. The English horses can really stay. They're the ones to beat. They're trained to stay. They get more races - you see they run during the week over a mile and a half, a mile and six. But our horses don't get that."

In the latter half of 1989 it became public knowledge that TJ wanted to retire and divide the stable between Ernie and Gai, but it also became public knowledge that Ernie and Gai could not get along. Gai applied for a trainer's licence but on September 7th, 1989, the AJC refused her application with no reason given. You didn't have to be a genius to work out that it was because she was married to wound-off bookmaker Robbie Waterhouse.

A week or two later the AJC was giving a gourmet "Breakfast With The Stars", at which Randwick trainers were to meet the racing press. TJ had driven up at 7:30am, but left before the meal started, to go to a meeting. Ernie Smith arrived and took a seat. Some of the press then began to speculate on where Gai would sit. But another reporter arrived who said Gai had told him she wouldn't be there because, "the AJC doesn't like the color of my husband's hair." She obviously still had a sense of humor.

A further irony was that Gai was reportedly the one who found and convinced John Werner Kluge to bail Tulloch Lodge out of its difficulties. Kluge and his wife soon became grist to the media circus, more larger-than-life people crowding into the already incredible life of TJ Smith. Patricia Kluge had grown up in Baghdad, and graduated to soft porn queen in London. Managing to let that past slide by, she had married American entrepreneur John Kluge, and the two set about building lavish estates and ingratiating themselves with high society and even royalty. When Patricia's feather and tassle days were brought to light by the English press, their progress slipped back about ten notches, but neither is the type to let that stop them. TJ has already won the $500,000 Australian Derby for Kluge.

Considering Kluge's connections to Colin Hayes and the family of former international jockey Ray Hutchinson, it may be a question of who found who. When the Hutchinsons lived in England, Tommy used to stay them with whenever he visited that country. If it was Gai who found Kluge, she may have helped preserve an empire she cannot inherit.

Gai's resilience under pressure has won her some admirers among those who previously considered she'd had everything handed to her on a silver platter. Gai has proven to be a chip off the old block, but she will need some extraordinary strength and extraordinary luck if she is to pursue a career as a licenced trainer. In interviews she quickly says that she expects the AJC will eventually forgive Robbie and she will get a licence. Many feel that is an extraordinarily naive view, that the AJC cannot licence her, and when TJ retires the stable clientele will pass into the hands of Ernie and Sterling Smith.

The story of TJ Smith has enough drama - success against the odds, human failings and tragedy - for a Shakespearian tale. I am sure the story of TJ Smith will be told and retold, written and re-examined for many years to come. It is surely one of the greatest stories in the history of racing.

Tommy 'TJ' Smith, the little Aussie battler: he had a tough start in tough times, but struggled up through the touts, louts and layabouts to win it all.

Tommy Smith speaking to a reporter from New Idea:
"You have to be confident in yourself. A lot of people see opportunities along the way and they say, 'Gee I should have taken advantage of that.' Well what good is that? *The world is full of people who could have but didn't.*"

GLOUCESTER PARK on an average Friday night. Fred is in the pack passing the winning post. At the time of completion in 1929, Gloucester Park was considered the equal of any harness racing venue in the world. More modern stands are out of sight to the left.

Fred gets another horse ready with some help from daughter Kellie and son Greg. Fred says there was no foul play involved in his 'red eye', just a burst blood vessel.

FRED KERSLEY

Fred Kersley was King of the harness racing scene in Perth for 15 years. He first trained the most winners in the 1971/72 season, when he was 33 years old. He then went on to be leading trainer seven times straight, came second once, then led another seven times before again coming second in 1986/87.

Fred is a third generation harness horse trainer. His grandfather was a widely respected horseman and trainer. His father and uncle won 15 training premierships (titles) between them. With this background it might be thought that getting to the top would have been easy for Fred. But he did not make a good start, had severe doubts he could make a living at it, and would have given up if he had been, 'trained for any good job'. A few years after starting out on his own he was suspected of having a chronic ulcer, caused by the stress of doing so poorly. It was bad enough doing poorly, but it was a sheer disgrace if your name was Kersley. Friends told him, out of kindness, to give up harness racing.

What made it so difficult? Surely all he had to do was to apply the proven methods of his illustrious father and uncle. How did he finally get off the bottom rung? If Fred was so slow making headway in the beginning, how did he maintain such a grip once he reached the top?

The man who took the title off Fred in 1987 was Trevor Warwick. He had been second or third to Fred many times, but had eventually won out with a strategy of promoting and organizing public syndicates. Syndication allowed numerous small investors to buy a horse between them. Building up syndicates gave Trevor horses in large numbers and high quality.

Fred Kersley did not want to fight back with a similar public syndication scheme. But he did fight back with his own strategy, and he did win in 1987/88 - his 15th training premiership - at the age of forty

nine. The next year it was Trevor's turn again.

What are the weapons and tactics of this see-saw battle? Who, in the long term, is going to win this struggle for the title of top trainer?

A Model of Perseverance
Standardbred Trainer
PERTH, WESTERN AUSTRALIA

2. What start in life did he have?

First a brief history of trotting in Australia to put the Kersley's in perspective. Australia was founded in 1788 and made a very slow start because of its isolation, and because the soil needed trace elements and other discoveries before it could become really productive. However there was mention in a newssheet of a "famous" trotting mare racing at a fair in 1818. Her performances were compared with those of trotters in England, where trotting is now virtually extinct.

During the gold rushes of the 1850s, many Americans settled in Australia, providing a link to trotting in America. From 1869 American trotting blood was imported and the sport grew steadily throughout Australia. The various states formed trotting associations, beginning with New South Wales in 1902, about the time Lou Dillon and Dan Patch were making the sport famous in America.

Over on the isolated western side of the continent of Australia there was sufficient interest in pacing and trotting for the citizens to form the West Australian Trotting Association (WATA) in 1910. The WATA has been something of a pacesetter in Australian harness racing. The country's first night race meeting was held there in 1914. Patronized by over 2000 people, it was the start of a long era of dominance of the evening entertainment scene in Perth, the state capital. This was followed by the first club tote (pari mutuel) in Australia in 1916 and then in 1925 by the first Australasian Championship, with horses from all over Australia and New Zealand.

Fred Kersley after a morning in the sulky.

The great harness racing administrator J.P. Stratton went on to mold a similar event into the biggest on the Australian and New Zealand calenders, known from the first running in 1936 as the Interdominion Championship. It thrives today in spite of the great distances the competing horses have to travel over sea and land. Australia is some 2,500 miles (4000km) across and New Zealand is separated by 1,200 miles (1,900km) of ocean. In the era before air travel, some horses covered more than 7,000 miles by sea and road to compete.

Western Australia's reputation as a pacesetter was furthered in 1929 by the construction of a magnificent new track. Later named Gloucester Park, it was the main track in the state, and was considered by many to be the finest harness racing venue in the world at the time. Of course 1929 was the start of The Great Depression, but even during the depression, harness racing in Perth did well.

One who was attracted to this glittering mecca was a South Australian who had a horse drawn transport business and trained part-time. His name was Fred J. Kersley (son of a Fred), later better known as Pop Kersley. Pop had driven horses to set South Australian records over the flying half mile and over the mile. At that time South Australian trotting was restricted by a law that prohibited betting after dark. (Love to know how they justified that. Were they afraid it would lower the birth rate?) A friend, who had gone over to Perth, sent glowing letters that convinced Pop he should move his horses and family there and train full-time. So in 1929 he upped stakes and moved nearly 2000 miles to Perth. The three horses went by sea with eldest son Frank while the family traveled overland.

Pop went into full-time training in Perth, but was soon having problems. He had been disqualified in the state of New South Wales in 1927. He had moved to Tasmania and then South Australia, both of which allowed him to train and race. WA had initially given him his license but under pressure from NSW, withdrew it. There was a great deal of controversy and politicking. In the end Pop served a six month suspension. He then went on to train very successfully, until around 1955, although he never topped the list of winning trainers. However two of his four sons went on to dominate the training and driving scene for several decades.

Oldest son Frank E. Kersley (born 1908) first topped the training premiership in the 1933/34 season and went on to win it 11 times before his first 'retirement' as a steward in 1954. Frank won the 1954 Interdominion with Tennessee Sky. He was famous for his ice-cool driving and became well-known in the eastern states driving the great Caduceus to wins in heats of the Interdominion in 1957 and 1959. Frank is the only harness racing identity inducted into the Western Australian Hall of Champions. He eventually retired in 1973 and lives in Perth.

Pop's second son, also called Fred (born 1911), worked for his father for a few years then started out on his own. He was called Ned, I suppose to distinguish him from his father, and I will call him Ned because the name Fred Kersley has no meaning in a family history with lots of them. Ned can remember racing on trotting tracks with four laps to the mile. When the field became strung out, it could be hard to tell who was last. On one occasion a prominent driver, in the confusion, was declared the winner when he was actually coming last. Ned was in races where some trotters were driven in a sulky and some were trotted under saddle. In South Australia he had tried out as an apprentice jockey in the gallops, coming third one year.

In Perth Ned Kersley worked full-time with his father on trotters and pacers. In 1933 he started out as a full-time professional trainer with two horses. It was an era of shotgun starts and elastic starting wires. Trotting races were still run, but there were many more races for pacers. Ned made leading trainer in 1937/38 aged 26, the youngest trainer to win the training premiership, then or since. During World War II, he spent three years with the remount squadron, then returned to training. The racing then was over one and a half miles to two miles. The two-mile events were mainly the big Cups. There was only one mile race per year, the Sprint Championship, later called the Mount Eden Mile.

Ned had been the first reinsman to win four races at a Gloucester Park meeting. He started the 1950s by becoming the first driver to win five races in succession.

When Queen Elizabeth II visited Australia in 1954, she went to her first trotting meeting. 50,000 people packed into Gloucester Park to see the Queen, and, as it turned out, they also saw one of Ned Kersley's finest hours. He won the Queen Elizabeth Stakes, which had a huge prize of five thousand pounds for the occasion, and the Queen herself presented the trophy to him.

But the fabulous 1950s were to have a bitter end for Ned. One of his main clients was Dr Tom Early for whom he had trained an Easter Cup winner called Magic Flute. Magic Flute was a prospect to win the Easter Cup again in 1958. Some time before the race Dr Early had beaten the main power in harness racing, J.P. Stratton, in the Committee elections. Dr Early boasted that he was going to take over from Stratton.

When Easter Cup time rolled around and Magic Flute won, there was a big demonstration from the crowd. Stratton seized his opportunity to strike a blow against Dr Early: Magic Flute was disqualified for inconsistent running. In the process, Ned was disqualified for a year. Dr Early responded by suing Ned Kersley for breach of contract; the contract said the trainer was to let all horses run on their merits at all times. This appeared to be an effort by Dr Early to distance himself from the affair and keep his political ambitions alive, although he later claimed it was merely a way to get the matter out of the closed

stewards' inquiry and into an open court. The judge found that Ned had no case to answer, but by then J. P. Stratton had achieved his goal: Dr Early was disqualified for five years on the grounds he had improperly tried to influence the stewards in the matter.

Ned was told by a connection to Stratton that if he was to appeal he would be allowed to return to training. Traumatized, unsure who to trust in the treacherous maelstrom of Committee politics, and to some extent disgusted with the lot of them, Ned told the go-between he'd rather finish out the year, which he did. Easter 1959 he returned to training, but he never got back into it in a big way.

Ned had won four training premierships, and his older brother Frank eleven, the last in the middle 1950s. Most of the years Frank won, Ned came second.

If 1958 was the bitter, disillusioning end of an almost fairy-tale era for Ned Kersley, it was also to be the disillusioning start to a wonderful-but-disappointing era for his son Fred. (In the USA this story would be about Fred Kersley IV, but I will, from here on in this account give him exclusive use of the name Fred. When you read 'Fred' it means brother of Bill, son of Ned, nephew of Frank and grandson of Pop.)

Fred Kersley fought his way to the top of a sport that was King in Perth when he was growing up. He had seen his father and uncle parade in the glowing popularity and prestige of trotting as top trainers and drivers. It was a time when to be at the top at the trots was to be one of the most written about, most photographed, best known people, not just in sport, but in the state. It brought popularity and respect from all ages and all social levels. It was a time when the trots at Gloucester Park was the most fashionable and prestigious sporting event on Perth's weekend social menu. The crowds crammed the grounds like fish in a shoal for big events like the Cups or an Interdominion. Trotting outranked the gallops in Perth by a large margin in crowds, atmosphere, turnover and prizemoney. It had national status and interstate stars when the gallops in Perth had no national status and few stars.

But it was an era that flourished before television started in Perth in September 1959. Harness racing in Perth, like all forms of racing in many parts of the world, has been in a decline for several decades. In common with other parts of the world, a large part of this downward trend has been attributed to competition from other nighttime entertainment, notably television. In Perth there have been four other new and noteworthy nighttime competitors: Greyhound racing, football, cricket, and basketball. Besides these there is increased competition for the gambling dollar from numerous lotteries and recently a casino.

There has also been another factor at work in Perth: due to the peculiarities of the money distribution from a government controlled wagering system, the gallops receive much more money than harness racing. Why?

With the introduction of the state-run Totalisator Agency Board (TAB) in March 1961, most of the funding for harness racing and the gallops came under government control. The formula for dividing up this monetary plum became a large factor in the relative funding of these two groups. On the basis that galloping races in the eastern states generated much of the turnover, the galloping brigade was given a much larger share of the TAB money - 60%. Trotting had larger attendances and turnover at its meetings but received only two-thirds as much money.

In 1988 the state parliament extended this trend by even further reducing harness racing's share of TAB income. Thoroughbred racing, in addition to this government blessing, has not had such an increase in competition as trotting because of it's afternoon timeslot. So the Thoroughbred fraternity, while also concerned by falling crowds and increased gambling competition, has had less to complain about.

For the trainer-driver the TAB has had some other effects. The extensive network of off-course betting premises means the punters can bet without traveling more than a few miles from their home. This, with of course the help of TV and other factors, has greatly diminished the size of the attending crowds. Where once there was a full-throated sustained roar, no single word discernible as the horses charged down the straight, there is now a collection of individually heard shouts.

As in other parts of the world, the Association, in an effort to bring back the crowds, has tried everything it can think of: free entry, various nights of the week, standing starts, increased prizemoney, a different distribution of prizemoney, claiming and condition races, many parallel attractions, and lotteries. Most recently, local meetings have been held during the late afternoon to coincide with evening harness race meetings in the eastern states to boost betting turnover. To open up the betting, the superior horses were put on the outside at the start. This gives the lesser horse a better chance, a system called a preferential draw. But the overall trend - a steady decline - continues.

Fred had the talent and dedication to be the leading trainer for a long period, but he had the bad luck to do so in a period of steep decline in the industry. He had watched as a youngster as his father and uncle were crowned Kings before large adoring crowds, saw their pictures on the front pages of the papers. He knew these men, knew they were not superhuman, knew he could do what they could do. He left school as soon as possible. It proved a longer, harder struggle than anticipated, but he made it to the top. Sadly, by the time he made it, two-thirds of the crowd had left. The King of Trotting was lucky to appear on the back page of the newspaper.

It was as though he had stood with an immense gathering of excited people, stared at the magnificent glittering prize up there on the bright center stage, then turned his eyes down to concentrate on the long hard task, only to find that when he finally lifted his eyes, the work completed, the prize had been swapped for something much smaller, duller; the stage had shrunk, the lights had dimmed; the people had drifted away.

There was an unspoken belief around Perth that this decline was world-wide and unstoppable, that trotting was losing out to other night entertainment and to the gallopers. In fact, there was a decline due to competing attractions, but there was nothing invincible about the gallops. At Scarborough Downs, Maine, in the north-eastern USA, after the gallops had withered, harness racing took the same track and thrived.

It was against this background that I first interviewed Fred Kersley and Trevor Warwick in 1987. Fred Kersley had dominated pacing in Perth for many years although still surprisingly young. Now, in the year in which I set out to look at great racehorse trainers, it looked as though a new king was emerging in Trevor Warwick. Trevor was winning clients with a new approach - public syndication. His syndicates often had large numbers of small shareholders. The Western Australian Trotting Association welcomed syndicates because they brought many new people into the ownership ranks: people to fill the dining facilities and the beautiful grass terrace of Gloucester Park on warm, clear-skied Perth evenings.

But Fred Kersley was too young and too competitive to settle for the role of ex-king. Competitive is Fred's middle name.

2.1 How much help were his parents?

Frederick Ross Kersley was born in Perth on January 7th, 1939. He grew up in the suburb of Carlisle where his father stabled his horses. Today it would be nearly impossible because of the traffic, but back then they drove or led the horses across the river on the Causeway Bridge, trained at Gloucester Park, then returned home the same way. In that manner, his father, uncle and grandfather trained from Carlisle. Later, because of the steadily increasing traffic problem, Ned Kersley moved to Cannington, an area with a growing band of trotting trainers who used a track on the grounds of the Canning Agricultural Society. It was no high society area, an area of mostly small, mostly asbestos houses. In spite of Perth's searing summer heat, most of the houses in Cannington had roofs of corrugated iron sheeting. A privileged few had the superior insulation of tiles.

As far as I can determine Fred is the older of two brothers. Each tells people the other is the older. They call each other young'un. Fred certainly has a personality more like a first born: driven to succeed, a perfectionist, an organizer. Bill says he prefers to keep his stable numbers at 14 or 15 so he can manage it with his family and not have to employ staff.

Fred's Mum thought Fred was a bit of a wild youngster, always running off with his friends. Both parents considered Bill a model child (well closer to it anyway) while Fred was argumentative. Fred and his father were both strong-willed individuals and they disagreed about many things. But Ned Kersley was a very good example for Fred to follow, and follow he undoubtedly did: in dedication, in calmness, and in thoroughness. Fred also resembles his father in his quiet, thoughtful and deliberate way of speaking. They focus on their differences, but by far they are similar rather than different.

While Fred was growing up, his father and uncle dominated the sport in WA - ruled it until Fred was 15 years old. He had their example, their success, to fuel his hopes and dreams in his most impressionable years.

2.2 Was Fred's family in racing?

"Your family has been into pacing for many years.

After a morning workout this horse gives Fred's helmet a lick. In this book I have given Fred exclusive use of the name Fred, even though in the U.S. he would be called Fred IV. His father is Ned, his uncle is Frank, and his grandfather is "Pop."

How far back does it go?

"Since day one, really. Certainly my grandfather, Pop Kersley kicked off in South Australia with horses - Thoroughbreds and pacers - and then he came overland to Perth in 1929 and brought the family with him. That was in the days when they raced at the Western Australian Cricket Association ground, so it was before Gloucester Park was built. He did mix it up a bit, he did train Thoroughbreds and pacers. When I knew him he was training pacers all the time. My dad did a bit of both too. He was with the gallopers for a season or two. Sir Ernest Lee-Steere (well known Thoroughbred breeder and owner in Perth) was one of his clients in those days. When Pop came back to the trots, we just stayed with the trotters. Pop Kersley was recognized as being a great horseman, he was a home-made vet if you like and he was much respected."

"Qualified vets would have been almost non-existent then."

"There were almost no vets. There was one old guy, Bradley, who I don't think was a qualified vet, but he was the most popular guy in those times. He did all the veterinary work for the trainers. Doctor Stein was one of the first registered vets I remember of that era."

"How successful was your father?"

"Very successful. He was leading trainer and driver for four seasons. His brother Frank had an even better driving and training record - won a record eleven premierships to my dad's four. But Frank cared more about being a leading trainer than my dad did, and I don't think that was a measure of their ability as horsemen - I don't think there was very much difference. It was more of a different attitude about being there. But my father - he was top in his field."

Fred's father was wealthy enough to choose to retire early and to help his sons financially. Carlisle was a middle class, built-up suburb. Cannington was less populous, close to some bush and open land. Fred and Bill attended school and grew up when trotting was picking up steadily after the war, reaching its peak in the 1950s when Fred was in his late teens.

Fred worked for his father but had the typical differences that commonly occur between a father and a strong-willed teenage son. I asked Fred's wife Judy about it.

"Fred seems to have had a bit of strife with his father from what he was saying. His father was telling him he was a bonehead (my word). Was that just normal late-teenage argument?"

"No. There were two brothers, Bill and Fred. There's only about eighteen months difference. Naturewise they're very different. Bill was always fairly quiet. Bill wouldn't argue with you, even if he didn't agree with what you said. The only time Bill will argue is if he's had a couple of beers."

"Which was the older of the two?"

"Fred, but he'll tell everybody Bill is."

"Is that right? I thought Bill looked older."

"Fred is the oldest, and they call each other 'young'un, so you don't know. People think Bill is the oldest. Bill's nature was always very gentle and he wasn't interested in horses really, until much later. He turned to it - only as an alternative - because there was nothing else. But Fred, he won't accept something as right just because you told him it was right. And whereas Bill would stay home - he never went out very much as a young kid and a teenager - Fred always had a mob of kids around him and he had a horse and he'd be off and about. So Fred's father used to think that Bill was the perfect child and

Fred and his mates were ratbags. When they first started, everybody said Bill had a lot more ability than Fred."

(In Fred's debut race in 1957 he was driving a fancied horse from his father's stable. He led early then faded to second last. Bill's first drive was an effortless win with a 12/1 chance at Gloucester Park in January 1959. He was 18 years old. Later that year Bill won the August Cup, the Royal Show Cup and the State Sprint Championship.)

"Bill was steady, they'd all reckon."

"Yes, and they'd say Fred would never be as good as his father. Cringe! In fact, somebody even made a comment the other week. Fred went to a meeting: 'You wouldn't believe it,' he said, 'somebody there said, "Bill is still a better driver than Fred."'

"To Fred, they said that?"

"Yes. They made the comment at the meeting. Where Fred had problems with his father was that his father, I'd say, was very much traditional whereas Fred questioned things. Just because everyone else did it, to him it wasn't necessarily correct."

2.3 How far did Fred go at school?

"How well did you do at school?"

"I had average ability, but I was a terrible clockwatcher. I really didn't have the interest, although I could do it. The subjects never bothered me so much, but I just didn't want to do it: I just wanted to go home."

"So how far did you go at school?"

"I left school in first year high."

"That was as early as you could leave!"

"I was thirteen. I turned fourteen before the holidays were over and I went straight into the stables. Today I think that was a bad decision because I'd have been a better person if I'd learnt more. But I was lucky that in those days, a lot of my competitors also left school for financial reasons or whatever else, so I have been able to compete with them through my life. However I feel that younger kids today, with the generally higher level of education, shouldn't be so silly as to drop out like I did."

"It's a bit tricky, to say what should be the schooling strategy for someone coming up and wanting to get to the top as a trainer. If you get into stables at a young age, you're going to pick up a lot of expertise and experience you need. On paper the ideal thing would be to complete some kind of degree at the same time - for example many people who want to be trainers are trying to do a vet degree - but it is rarely feasible to do both. If you do the degree first, I think the hours of study required to get results good enough for university entrance, especially to get into the vet course - and then the time required to get through university - by the time they get out - they might

not have been able to pick up the horsemanship skills, and it's a bit late to start at the bottom."

2.4 What were Fred's early ambitions?

"Did you ever want to be anything else - other than a trainer?"

"No, it just wasn't programmed."

"So as early as you can remember, you were going to be a pacing trainer. Would you say you wanted to be number one or was it expected you would be number one? Was it a pressure on you - or something you decided for yourself?"

"It was a pressure."

"Did your father want you to be number one?"

"No, no. In fact, he advised that it wasn't the best occupation, that it would have been much better to study a little at school. To fall back to trots if you wanted to, but to have a profession."

3. How did Fred get his training skills?

"In general, there's more of this 'hereditary' father-to-son apprenticeship in Standardbred training than in gallopers. That's one of the things I wanted to analyze. I've tended to put it down to the fact that training a pacer is a hell of a lot more technological than training a galloper."

"Sure. Bit like rigging twelve-metre yachts, I think."

"Rigging and fine-tuning all that gear and the shoeing - but there is no school in it, and there's probably not enough in books, so it's a lifetime apprenticeship. You're better off to be born into it."

"Experience is great, but it worries me, the statement that it's an advantage to be born into a racing family, because I think all those inhibitions in there can hold you back."

"Well, it has its pluses and its minuses, obviously."

"I just think a bright young fellow that came from another country where they didn't have racehorses, who wanted to learn, would probably be better off."

"But - I tell you what I think would happen to him. No doubt a few people have come in from outside galloping, Quarter Horse racing and pacing, and they have come up with an innovation or two, but as soon as it shows - if you take this person who's new and he makes some innovation but his general horsemanship is weak - as soon as the guys who've got a strong background in horsemanship apply the innovation, they just go to the front again, if they ever did lose their overall lead."

"I do agree with that."

"So sure; they do bring innovations but they don't get to the top because their grounding is weak."

"I don't think the guy should come in at the top. I think he should come in with a fresh mind and work through. Then pro-

That is Fred in his purple and gold colors at the rear and his arch-rival, Trevor Warwick, in front as they come out for a race. They both have a horse in almost every race so the battle between them has no let-up.

vided he could keep his mind open - give you an instance: when I decided to stop putting rugs (blankets) on my horses, my dad - and everyone's dad has some influence over you - he says, 'I always thought you were mad and now I know.' See, for me to have confidence enough to think I was right - it was a big dent to me right there. Those type of things. He criticizes me for working them too hard, and that's oppressive to you. I believe it's not right - people say you can't do well in horses unless you've been born into it - family tradition. A lot of people use that as an excuse. For me, the excuse doesn't work. Any kid can come to my place and work alongside my children and learn just as much. There's no favoritism. If you want to learn, you can learn. How much do you want to learn? In fact, kids that are born into it, it seems to me that they have subconsciously developed an attitude that they don't need to learn as much."

"Don't try as hard, yes, possibly. One fellow I see as up and coming, in New Zealand, was quite interesting. He had exactly that attitude you mentioned. He was working in Dave O'Sullivan's stables - top galloping trainer over there - and he was working alongside Dave's son Paul.

His attitude was: Paul's already going to have the stables, the name, this, that and the other; so I've got to try twice as hard. So it wasn't the sort of thing that held him back. Paul's own attitude is, 'I've got a great start, I'm really enjoying this'. I don't think it weakened Paul's resolve. He wasn't one to say, 'Oh well, I'm set'. His attitude was, 'What a fantastic start, I should really do something with it."

"It doesn't have to hold you back, but it doesn't have to work for you either. I just think it's up for grabs."

"Yes perhaps it is."

3.1 Any early experience with horses?

Fred worked in his father's stables from a very early age. He was the third successive generation of Kersleys to grow up with horses in the back yard.

"Did you ever work for stables outside your father's or your grandfather's?"

"No."

"You were a totally home-grown product."

"Yes."

3.2 Driving experience

As a youngster, Fred had plenty of experience on the training track, then drove a few in races for his father. The very first was Rocklee Lass, a well-fancied runner from his father's stable, at Gloucester park in 1957. The mare faced the breeze early, put her head in front with a lap to go then faded to 16th in a 17 horse field. It was an inglorious start and it was not until his 11th race that he had a win. His younger brother Bill was considered a more talented driver and Bill won the big races while Ned was banned in 1959.

Initially Fred got the bulk of his race experience behind horses his father trained, then behind horses he was training himself. As a trainer he drove all his horses in their races unless of course he had more than one entry per race, in which case brother Bill usually drove the other horse.

3.3 Why did Fred become a trainer?

It was Fred's goal from an early age to be a trainer of harness horses, presumably because of the role models around him. He could not see anyone more successful in terms of fame and fortune than his father, his uncle, and his grandfather.

3.4 Acquiring his training skills

Fred first took out a trainer's license in 1958 when his father was disqualified for one year. His father had won the Easter Cup but had been disqualified for inconsistent running. There were considerable forces at work and the disqualification was more political than just. It took much of the gloss off the training life for Fred's father.

Fred was 19 years old at the time, and he was helped by his younger brother Bill. Most of the horses, probably the best, were taken away by the owners and put with other trainers, but even so it would have been very good training experience. Fred had some winners and felt that for the quality of the stock he did OK.

When his father resumed, Fred returned to being one of his father's employees, but kept one or two in work for himself. His father did not want to go back into training in a big way. In the first years of the 1960s, aged about 21, Fred went out on his own. A few years later his father retired, although he always trained a few horses for his best clients. These horses were driven by Bill. That might have been because Ned considered Bill a better driver, because Fred had his own horses, or because as a father, Ned felt Bill needed more help to establish himself.

3.4-1 Did he work with a top trainer?

Yes his father - 4 times leading trainer. He did not work with any other trainers.

3.4-2 Did he watch other trainers?

"I observed everyone very very carefully and I still do." That would have been very educational when he was training at Gloucester Park and later at Cannington, where many other trainers used the tracks.

3.4-3 Did he try published workouts?

There is no Australian equivalent of America's *Daily Racing Form* (at least not with Standardbred statistics), nor are trackwork times published in the daily paper, probably because so many horses are trained on private tracks. So the first published workouts Fred ever saw were those in *The Care and Training of the Trotter and Pacer*, published in 1968, by which time he was doing well and happy with his own training.

3.4-4 Reading, seminars, asking questions

Fred's wife Judy: "His uncle Frank Kersley was the most successful of the elder generation of brothers. He had gone to Melbourne when Fred and I started to go together, so I didn't know him very well. But Frank, during the time he was in Melbourne and I was going with Fred, came across, I think twice, and stayed with Fred's mother and father. I remember Fred thought that was something else - he was about nineteen or twenty at the time. He just picked Frank's brains. I know we went to the airport and met him because Fred just wanted to spend every minute of Frank's visit with him, to ask him his views, his ideas, and just pick his brains. He thought that was enormous to be able to talk to Frank, because when Frank went to Melbourne, Fred still hadn't started to go out in his own right."

Fred has quite a library and reads a lot about his sport. He also consulted with the trainer he felt he could learn the most from, Phil Coulson.

"Do you ask other trainers questions? Is that possible for you?"

"Oh yes, I was a big question-asker in the early days. Through teenage into early twenties, I did ask so many people so many things. I was very curious about things. Of course in racing there is a saying that if you ask a question you're entitled to be told a lie. But I really didn't ever leave home or do any work outside of home in terms of developing that horsemanship."

"Did you look at contrasting styles, different to your father's?"

"Yes."

"Probably went through the teenage rebellion bit where you told father he didn't know what he was doing?"

"Yes, I did, and I really thought his methods were wrong on the conditioning side of it, and yet I never found it easy to fault the actual horsemanship, the care and attention to horses. His motto, and I think it's really a family motto, is - *the horse's comfort comes first*. We've always fed the horses before we fed ourselves, and the whole routine has to be done before you even think about what suits you. That seemed right. I thought the amount of work and the actual conditioning of horses was questionable, and I guess I've altered that over the years. I think there are a lot of tricks in that too: to some extent I modeled myself on Phil Coulson - he was the achiever when I was trying to be, and he was doing the things I wanted to do - so I was influenced by that."

"Phil was widely admired."

"I honestly felt he conned the people a little bit. He put in place that he was a Percy Cerutty type trainer." (Athletics coach Percy Cerutty trained Herb Elliott to dominate the world in the mile. Elliott retired undefeated in international competition. Cerutty trained his athletes in sandhills, and a major component of his success was an attitude that you COULD NOT train too hard. He blew away worries that you could permanently harm yourself by running up sandhills until he burst small blood vessels in his eyes. When he was hale and hearty next day, a man in his 50s or 60s, the athletes dropped any reservations they had about a strained heart.)

"There were photographs of Phil galloping his horses up and down sandhills. Pretty much the same as Cerutty's athletes."

"I remember pictures in the paper. I think the press loved that."

"Oh yes, yes, and he kept it going pretty well too. If the horse could gallop to the top of the sandhill then you could bet on it. If it had to slow down to a trot then it wasn't quite fit. But then I'd look at his horses and none were bigger in condition than his. None of the horses presented at the races were bigger, and none of them blew more after a race than his either. I still to this day don't know, but I think he didn't do as much hard yakka (work) as he wanted people to believe."

"It would depend how many times he went up the sandhill."

"I don't know whether racehorses went up that sandhill. I think some of the others did."

"The ones he was racing stayed home?"

"The ones that weren't winning or that he didn't care about went up the sandhill. Of course he had every trainer in Western Australia running around the sandhills. I'm sure that if people followed that philosophy right through, they wouldn't be producing many winners, and whilst he was the model - I was trying to get where he was at - I worked out that I couldn't do it his way, that it wasn't going to work."

"So when you were in that questioning stage, did you go and watch Phil Coulson work his horses?"

"No, I didn't. You can't really do that, with private trainers. I suppose you could, if you asked him if you could come down, spend time with him. Most of them would let you, but it's almost an unwritten rule that you can't, you can't bludge that information (have it for nothing). That is personal to the people. But when we worked at Gloucester Park, and there could be up to two hundred horses there on a fastwork morning, you would know a certain trainer's horses were running, and if you didn't, somebody else did, and so it wasn't hard to get the information."

"One of the things I advise young people when they ask me, is 'Your best chance, if you really want to go and have someone tell you heaps, is to go interstate because then you're not really a rival.'"

"I think ultimately - having been there, seen it, learnt it - that ultimately it won't necessarily matter much at the end of the day. I think when you get to the stage that you're on your own, then it'll be your attitude, how careful you are and how clever you are. By going and being a strapper working for a top trainer - it doesn't guarantee you anything. Only that you've done a little bit of learning."

The Care and Training of the Trotter and Pacer was printed in 1968. It was over 1000 pages long, a magnificent collection of advice on all aspects of training the harness horse, pulled together by the U.S. Trotting Association, with sections by the greatest names in the game at that time.

"When it came out was it useful to you? You had a lot of experience and experienced people to draw on, perhaps it was more useful to your competition?"

"It is a book I like, because it is an easy-to-read reference to the ideas of people who have had a lot of experience. I think essentially nothing has changed. The logic in that book is still very true today. The horses go quicker today, but in basic horsemanship, nothing has changed. Did it help me? Perhaps not, but it is a bit of a comfort zone when you've been doing something, and then you read where people who have been very successful are doing things similar to you. I was already doing pretty well when it came out, but I read it and it reinforces how I see things. It is a great book to have around."

Seminars

I first met Fred when I gave a talk at a seminar around 1976. There were three or four other speakers and the place was packed, because one speaker was the government analyst, the man who processed the drug tests from race winners. I gave a talk on how lactic acid production related to race pace and race tactics. When the talks ended the analyst was cornered by the chemical racing brigade. Most of the audience made for the drinks. Fred came over, and after some keen questioners had asked me about a point or two and left, he proceeded to ask about another hundred and three questions.

He wanted to fit together in his mind how muscle worked, what the role of lactic acid was in a race, and particularly how it fitted with race driving tactics. (It is a complicated matter, but in a nutshell, acceleration is very costly and generates much more lactic acid per meter than a steady speed. Lactic acid interferes with muscle, making it less efficient, so it should be generated at as even a rate as possible and as late in the race as possible.) Fred impressed me tremendously. It was the first long conversation I had ever had with a top level horse trainer. I realized that as a vet student I had unconsciously been afflicted with the belief of many vet school academics, that all racehorse trainers were fools. It was about this time I was learning that there were some fools in the vet schools. I drove home with a new perspective.

3.4-5 Experiments and experience
This piece of an interview with Judy casts some light on how Fred developed his own methods.

"I got the impression that at one stage he was trying to learn a lot from Phil Coulson. He believed Coulson was extremely good."

"He would never have gone and talked to Schrader, Lindau, Sweetman, any of those guys, but he would go and talk to Phil and ask Phil his opinion. When he decided he wasn't going to rug his horses, that nearly started World War Three, because at that time Fred's father was semi-retired and he just had a couple of horses, and he had them at our stables. Fred put a lot of thought into it and asked a lot of questions. When I say a lot of questions, he probably asked his father, and Frank, and I know he discussed it with Phil. I think they all told him he'd taken leave of his senses."

"This was the bit where his father was calling him a bonehead."

"Oh yes, his father just reckoned he'd flipped. Anyhow, he decided to put it into practice. His dad had about three horses at our place, so it was quite funny, because our horses would all be there with no rugs, and his father's would have double rugs and hoods and all the rest."

"I've got to say it might have been an easy compromise to take the blankets off half of them for a couple of seasons and compare the results."

"He got that almost, because his father didn't want his unrugged."

Fred's unrugged horses thrived in Perth's warm climate, which is classified as Mediterranean. The average mid-winter month temperature is 55°F (13°C), while the mid-summer month average is 74°F (23°C). Los Angeles has temperatures of 55°F in winter and 72°F in summer. This affair of the rugs will no doubt amuse many North Americans who regularly see unrugged horses in snow- covered paddocks.

4. Starting out on his own
Fred first trained on his own when his father was disqualified. After a year's experience he then went back to working for his father, but it was not long before he was training for himself. He had some idea what he was in for, and the experience may have made him keen to be his own boss. But I also I wondered how much the tension between Fred and his father had to do with his branching out. I asked Judy.

"Did Fred go out on his own because he thought it was now time, or because he was having differences with his father? Did he need the money or the separate identity?"

"He didn't do it for the money because he couldn't really survive to start with. No, I think what happened - now I'm probably testing my memory - his father was disqualified for twelve months, and Fred took the trainer's license. He was, I think, eighteen at the time. When his father came back and took up his license up again, I think Fred decided he would like to try. He had a couple of guys who had old horses that were prepared to give him a go. He only had a couple."

"Do you think if that hadn't happened to his father, he would have stayed as a lieutenant to his father?"

"Not for very long, no. Because as you noticed, he is a learner and even now he's still prepared to learn and he still wants information."

What held Fred back?
"When you started into harness racing, were you mainly into driving or training?"

"When you started, you got drives through reinsman's school, (Run by the Association) before you became a trainer, because you had to have the horses to train - and who was going to give you a horse? Nobody. There was an attitude in those days that if you weren't experienced you couldn't drive. And by experienced it seemed to me you had to be forty. They just didn't accept that young kids ought to be driving. This was a field for the more experienced horsemen - that was their area. 'You'll just have to wait until you grow old.' That has changed, I'm pleased to say, and they've put in place junior drivers. But that's only a recent innovation in harness racing. There was never any advantage for young drivers like there is for apprentices in Thoroughbred racing, where they take weight off the horse's back."

"So what do they allow junior drivers now?"

"They give them a lift of one assessment, or in the old terms, where they used to handicap them - put them in rows every ten metres - they get moved ten metres forward in the standing start. In a mobile start they'd go forward one class."

"Until they have a certain number of wins?"

"Til they've won twenty drives in this state, I think."

"So you had to break through a thick crust without that help?"

"Well, I couldn't be successful. What happened, when I look back, is that I got to the top ultimately because I trained well, and that allowed me to drive well. But at first I couldn't drive well because I had nothing to drive. It took me a fair while to climb up the ladder too. People didn't want to give horses to young trainers."

Judy spoke of the same problem:

"Nowadays young people are accepted a lot better. Nowadays, junior reinsmen and the young people get a lot of opportunities. But when Fred was starting off, they didn't. One night his father had qualified two horses for the Pacing Cup, two horses his father trained. Fred was party to the training setup and was helping him. The owner wouldn't put Fred on, wouldn't let Fred drive the other horse. Fred *thought* he was driving it right up until the Saturday night, and that hurt him bad."

"How old was he then?"

"Probably around the twenty mark."

"Who did he blame for that? His father?"

"No, he was cross on the owner because his father - actually they lost the horse - his father told the owner to take the horse away from his stable."

"That's a fair bit of backing."

"Yes, but young people - you never had the experience to drive in those sort of races."

4.1 How he got his first horses

"What age were you when you got your first horse to train?"

"When Dad was disqualified for twelve months, and my brother and I had to shift out of home and rent stables in Cannington. We trained some of the horses people had left in Dad's stables. A lot of them went; probably the best of them went, and what was left, we tried to hold together for that twelve months. And you know, I trained them fairly successfully; I think we won about eight or ten races that season, which was good. I thought it was good to be able to win with those horses at that stage, but when Dad came back, the horses went back to him."

4.2 How he got his first clients

"I trained one or two for my mates - three or four or five of them would just pay the bills. I worked in the stables and just trained one or two. Then I got a couple of other clients, just crept in. I'm pleased to say the first two are still with me. They were not big owners."

"So you were primarily working for your father at the beginning."

"Yes. Then I branched out with a couple of horses."

4.3 Financing the start

Money was very scarce for a man with very few horses to train. Although Fred started to train around 1962, he and Judy did not get married until 1966, and delayed having children for a further year because they needed her income.

"Even Judy, before we got married, would contribute training fees towards a horse we had leased."

Fred's first set of colors was yellow with blue armbands, some he got off one of his father's owners to save money. Later he switched to the yellow and purple colors he has now, colors that had been very successful for another of his father's owners, Walter "Wattie" Clarke. Superstition? Fred didn't exactly want to be considered superstitious: "But there is a belief that you should carry on with what has been successful."

To buy a house *and* start a family was out of the question. So they continued to rent and started a family.

Later Ned Kersley had a financial windfall and was able to help. He had bought a twenty-acre block of land for 10,000 pounds. In the sixties the government bought it for 54,000 pounds as part of the acreage for a new railway yard. He bought Bill a house in Cannington and gave Fred the same amount of money towards his house in James St, Cannington. He also bought a milk round for Bill and built stables for Fred.

But life was still tough. Fred and Judy now had children and relied upon Fred's earnings as a trainer. They had mortgage repayments to make and barely had enough at times.

4.3-1 Did Fred bet?

"Did you find betting any use in trying to make money?"

"I think you can bet and you can win. In saying that I'm not particularly a gambler."

"Would you see yourself as having had a betting phase?"

"No."

"It was ever important in getting yourself established financially?"

"No. I was always too logical. I always reckoned bookmakers had to win if they were to keep standing up, that the state took out 18-20%, whatever, and you couldn't beat it. Now, in saying that, I didn't mean you were never going to have a bet and that you wouldn't make some money, but I don't think you should rely on that."

"Would you say that as a bettor you're in front?"

"Oh yes, yes, sure, no doubt about that - because I'm not a compulsive bettor. I don't feel the need to bet. I only feel the need to win."

4.3-2 Did Fred borrow money?

Ned gave Fred and Judy money, but they still had to borrow to buy their premises in Cannington. Fred insisted on paying his father's gift back when he got on his feet, so that was - well - kind of a loan. Later they also borrowed to buy the Forrestdale property they now live and train on.

"What about the money handling side of things? Did you feel you had to get some expertise in things like debt collecting and money management? You probably don't think it's a big factor, but I see it as a thing that ruins some people who are trying to become trainers. They don't collect the debts, or they over-expand in a period of

success or optimism."

"Well, like most things I try to do, I try to keep it simple. I have a simple logic about money and Judith usually puts that in place. She does all the collecting and banking and that sort of thing, but when it comes to, 'What are we going to do with our money?' then it's a joint decision."

"In decisions like shifting from Cannington to your own track here, did you do that when you could comfortably afford this place, or was it a bit of a gamble? See, one of the things that amazes me with some trainers: if they've had a couple of years where they've improved their income by thirty percent, they're prepared to go and do something that requires that to happen for the next two or three years."

"We delayed it awhile, until we thought we could do it somewhat comfortably, but we did have to stretch. It was a large commitment, and we were a bit unlucky, because when we did it we could have managed it okay, but then along came that interest rate blowout, which gave us a nice kick in the seat, and we had to work pretty hard to get out of it."

"What was the interest rate when you got the Forestdale place and what did it peak at?"

"It was around 10% and it nearly doubled. It just went through the roof. We were people that got hurt by it and it put a lot of pressure on us. I think because we had delayed it and didn't make that move too soon, we were able to trade out of it. But I easily understand how someone could have been hurt by it. Now I'm a naturally cautious guy, and I had a philosophy initially, that I didn't want to borrow money to buy cars, fridges, lounge suites, things like that. I just didn't like the logic of little bit down and pay it off, and that's worked very well for me, in my business. You see, I don't really think that as a horse trainer, you need to load yourself with outside pressures. If you ever start responding to those financial pressures, you will train worse. In saying that, I'm conscious of these instant millionaires that have gone into investment, taken huge risks, and turned up trumps. I wouldn't be so bold as to even comment on that, but if you're asking a horse trainer what he thought about managing the finances, I think steady as he goes, don't be wasteful and don't be too outgoing, because I think that pressure will cause you to train badly."

"I believe a lot in the subconscious - the same reason as why do trainers, drivers, or whatever get on a winning streak? Now you can never pinpoint it. You can't say because of this, that and the other, but clearly there are winning streaks, and you do better when you're going confidently and without outside pressures."

4.4 Steady rise or sudden breakthrough?

The sudden rocket-propelled lift-off of a top horse is what many on the track are waiting for, and dreaming of. Anyone

training horses has that hope, but what is the reality?

4.4-1 How long until first progress?

"What happened was I left school at thirteen, and I didn't become successful until I was thirty, so there was a long time of being no good at it, and a lot of frustration. I think I might have been wiser to spend a couple more years at school. You couldn't drive in races until you were eighteen, so I had four years before I could even get to the races. You learned how to look after horses but you didn't need to take two or three years to do that. At that age too, you don't think about it enough."

"One of the things that emerges as a pattern from talking with trainers, is that the guys who have the lifelong experience don't value it very highly as a factor in their success. The guys who don't have that kind of experience - the group that have come into it as bright young men with almost no horse background - they complain about their lack of expertise in horsemanship."

"It's an excuse. We were leasing or buying rejects, that's all we could get. We just chipped away, just kept chip-chipping away. Then my dad gave it away, retired, and that sort of left me on my own, which was good because I was able to expand in numbers and it seemed - I believe when you win, the phone rings. When you're not winning a race the phone never rings. It's still true today. When I won, then the phone would ring, and gradually I accumulated horses, and climbed up the ladder."

"So it was a gradual climb?"

"Oh, too slow, it was terrible."

"Were there ever times when you felt you weren't going to get up there?"

"Yes. Heaps of frustration to the point of being sick. Gutsaches, couldn't eat, laying in the bed."

"You sound like a classic type A. Worry too much, work too hard and too long."

"Yes well, I was worse than most blokes."

"Did you worry that it was a lack of ability, or did you think it was circumstances?"

"Well, you had to worry that it was your own ability. If you'd never had success, how did you know if the ability was there? How do you measure it? If you weren't winning races, you weren't successful. Everyone knew you were no good because you weren't doing any good. So yes, you did worry, you had those doubts. They were always there because there were never any positive comments; there were never any good feelings; there was never any money. So whatever the yardsticks you use, you felt bad, really, really bad."

"The only thing that kept me going was I was no good at anything else. I went to a football match one day, on my own, and I drove in there. It took me half an hour to find a parking spot. I was running late for the game because I was working horses in the morning. I got to the game halfway through the first quarter and it was the wrong ground, *the wrong bloody ground!* I said, 'You useless bastard, you'd better stay at the trots because at least they go around in circles and you know where the trotting track is'. It was the frustration of it, just being such a ——— dill, you know. I had to be good at the trots because I couldn't do anything else. I didn't enjoy people much, I've always liked animals better than people and I wasn't a good mixer - I didn't have the education. I'd go to a party and be too shy to eat, couldn't dance, not much good at anything."

"You don't know how many budding trainers will be encouraged to read this."

"Well mate, no one felt worse than me, I've got to tell you."

"Did you have problems with things like pre-race nerves or-"

"Yes, yes. But I'd look at the other bloke and say, 'Hell, he's older than me but I don't reckon he's better than me.' But I was nervous and I had to fight that off. You know, you got nervous because you needed to win and you couldn't win and you'd think, 'Is that you? What are you doing? What are you doing wrong?' I used to pick blokes and say, 'Well, that bastard's no better than me, I can beat him.' I had to keep telling myself that, I had to. I am still scared of losing. I still can't take defeat too easy. But I try to logic it out afterwards, and if the horse has raced its best and I've driven it well, then I can't expect any more than that. I know that now."

"That's the only attribute I have in common with champions: I hate losing."

Fred didn't laugh. He was very intent on what were clearly painful memories.

"Mind you, opportunity is another thing that must come along for everyone."

"Did you start to win because you became a better trainer, or because you got better horses?"

"There was a learning curve. I got better at my job. To get to be a trainer you have to be able to win with bad horses, and I did that eventually. I got some bad ones to run and I got some recognition and some better stock, which I did all right with and so on."

"Winning with those bad horses, was that a matter of patching them up or was it training them better?"

"I caused some bad horses to run better. In those days I got a reputation for my horses being a bit tougher - they could sit on the outside and still win from there."

"Do you still have that reputation?"

"Ahhm. It's getting harder. The competition is getting more condensed. It is easier to be a well-informed trainer these days. You didn't have any vets who knew anything about performance in those days. They were cat and dog vets. Today ev-eryone can go to these seminars, there are books, magazines: information coming in. So anyone can become a trainer quicker these days. I don't think they can become a horseman any quicker. But in becoming a good trainer there is more to it - there is an attitude, a lifestyle. You've got to manage yourself, you've got to manage the horse, you've got to manage people. You have to put all those things in place before you can train effectively. It came about slowly, slowly, slowly, and I did some things differently. I'd been training 15 or 20 years and blokes were still saying how easy I was on my horses; how lightly they were trained. I wondered how they knew what I did: because they didn't. I had changed many things and I did many things I wasn't supposed to be doing, and that I was told I was mad to be doing."

"I can see now in hindsight what made me keep going when I shouldn't have, when I kept going against all the logic and all the best advice of the people who knew I couldn't drive and knew I couldn't train - and that was just accepted as being definitely right - was that I had a fierce desire to do this. In my frustration I'd be crook (sick) for days."

"People were giving you a bit of friendly advice and telling you to get out of the game."

"Do the right thing son and give up."

4.4-2 Did one horse provide a sudden lift?

"I asked you before if the climb up the ladder was a gradual thing. For some people, it's a particular horse that lifts them up - a great logarithmic leap."

"Well, there was one horse that did help me make a leap. He was a horse called Willow Rack, a giant of a horse, about 17 hands. He hadn't raced for a couple of years, he smashed carts and did everything wrong. The horse was offered to me after being out of racing for a couple of years. The guy gave me one contract: he says, 'I want him to win first up, and I want to bet on him. I want to have a good bet on him. I don't care how long it takes you or what it costs. I just want that to happen."

"So I set about the task. I did like this horse and I think he got to like me a bit too, because he wasn't all that much trouble. We got along pretty well: I went along with him and didn't drive him mad. He did win first up and he was backed from twenties to five to two or something - a sensational plunge - and there was just a bit more magic in it because he was such a giant of a horse. That win seemed to help me a lot because people did recognize the merit in that. That was fifteen years ago. That was the horse that caused me to become *recognized* as a trainer, that turned it around in the recognition stakes."

"How many horses did you have in training before he came along, and how many did you have a year later?"

"Strangely enough, the numbers don't alter very much, because battling trainers usually have a stable full of some sort of horses. But he caused people to give me better quality horses and therefore it became a little easier. I had better stock to deal with. He wasn't the first horse I won with or anything like that. In 1961 I'd won the Pacing Cup, as a driver. I didn't train that horse, a horse called Beau Travis, and this is against the story I tell of Willow Rack. I did expect, after winning the Pacing Cup, which was the race to win - and I was twenty-two or twenty-three - that it would have a good effect, but I never won another race for thirteen months. It seemed to have the reverse effect. It just didn't do one thing for my career. And yet, it was quite significant - one of the highlights - and should have guaranteed me something. But it didn't work that way - it went the other way."

"Why did Willow Rack's win bring recognition but not Beau Travis's?"

"Well, Willow Rack wasn't a good horse. He was a bad horse, in real terms. He couldn't stay at all. But it just happened, and there was a little bit of magic about it, a fairy tale sort of thing. He'd been out of racing for so long and then raced first up. Also the way he raced. He ran away to the front and opened up a break and hung on. All that sort of thing."

"Was that an unconventional way of driving for its time?"

"Yes but that was him though, he had to do it. He couldn't come home, so it was no good holding him up. You just had to let him go. He used to take giant strides that'd get shorter and shorter as they went all the way back. That is one of the things that gained me recognition."

"Training horses is a bit like that. The number of hours you put in doesn't necessarily reflect in the number of races you win, whereas if you're a bricklayer, each brick you lay, you get paid for. If you're a hard working fella, there's something wrong about training horses, because there isn't a reward for effort."

4.4-3 Important helpers

The driver Fred went to for advice was Phil Coulson. Coulson is regarded by many as one of the greatest trainers and drivers Australia has ever produced. He went rapidly to the top, becoming premiership trainer and driver in his early thirties and looked set to dominate West Australian harness racing for decades. An interesting sidelight is that Phil's hero was his tutor at the Reinsmen's School - none other than Ned Kersley. Both were front-running drivers. After winning the training premierships a few times however, Phil made a decision that helped Fred, who was about six years younger. Fred remembers:

"They held a presentation for the Leading Horseman of the Year, down at the WA Cricket Ground. I was just bumbling around on the edge of the crowd. There I was: unable to get drives or do any good, full of ambition. Phil got up and accepted the award, and said it would be the last one he would be getting because he was choosing not to be there. Phil Coulson made a conscious decision to opt out, to train fewer horses.

I couldn't believe it. He's up there and he doesn't want to be; I'm down here and I can't get up there - and I wanted it that much. I couldn't believe you could get there and then say no. It was just amazing to me."

"Did you corner him and ask him to hand over the secret?"

"Well he was good Phil, he would always talk: we nearly got run over by a road sweeper at 3am, with me driving him mad wanting to know about training horses. It was after a trot meeting and we were still there talking in the street at 3am."

Phil Coulson

"What is your earliest recollection of Fred Kersley?"

"Fred was just a boy when I was going along. He always had ability, but he had the problem of living up to his father's reputation, and his uncle's. His uncle Frank was possibly one of the greatest horsemen and reinsmen we've ever seen here. It was pretty tough to follow that sort of reputation. I think he had a few personality problems until he had matured enough to handle it. The ability was always there."

"Did he come and ask you questions?"

"We've sat down many times and had some real good talks. I'd like to think I helped him a little bit along the way. I certainly gave him encouragement as a boy, and as a young lad, to get out there and do it. When I retired in the late 60s, he took over possibly my best horse at the time, with my blessing, in Colour Glo. He kicked on and won a lot of races with her. She was a top race performer, she'd won heats of the Interdominion for me and the Trotting Cup and so on."

"Fred told me of an occasion when they were presenting you with the Horseman of the Year award. Fred was there and it was at a stage of his career when he could not get off the bottom rung. So he could not believe it when you announced you were going to retire - could not believe that someone who had made it and was up there - was going to give it all away. It was incomprehensible to him and the disbelief, the astonishment in his voice made it very funny."

"It's a true story. I'm that sort of person: I set out with goals. I had achieved all my goals."

"How many times were you leading trainer?"

"Oh - three, four, five. I had difficulty being leading driver because I got too many suspensions to get the wins up. I had pressures - I had one of the biggest betting owners of the time in Bonnie Sweetapple. He used to put undue pressure on you. Because he'd paid a lot for a horse, it had to be good. You'd win a race for him on Saturday night and he'd bet it, and the very next race he's wanting to bet on something else. That was the sort of pressure I was under. I assessed the situation: I had gotten myself into a secure financial situation and I no longer wished to put myself under that pressure."

Fred gained a good horse and some good advice - and there was one less talented trainer fighting for the top position. It would be an interesting topic for the bars of Gloucester Park: if Phil hadn't gone into semi-retirement, would Fred have been able to get past him?

Some breakthroughs - the introduction of routine swabbing Fred believes he was aided in his rise by something besides horses and helpers.

"Caffeine and so on were used widely in that post-war era weren't they?"

"It used to be called Brown Powder, and I think every trainer used it. It had a bit of nux (nux vomica - active ingredient strychnine, a central nervous system stimulant, and some other alkaloids) and cola nut which was for caffeine apparently. When they started to get a little sophisticated with the swabs, many trainers were getting caught, and didn't know why, because it had been almost a family tradition to feed this Brown Powder. That's all we ever knew it as: Brown Powder. Several chemists (A pharmacist or druggist) had the formula and you would just go into a chemist's shop around Perth and ask for some Brown Powder for a tonic. It was used only as a tonic, and it was very good for getting them to eat, especially finicky doers (poor eaters), in those days."

"Caffeine usage was common around the start of the 1950's and it allowed people to overtrain to some extent. The horses could win with the stuff, and their appetites kept up. So when swabbing came in, that was actually to the benefit of the more careful observer of the horses - people who got them fit without overtraining them."

"I think it would be almost a matter of record too that until they routinely swabbed I was unsuccessful."

"Is that right?"

"Yes, it seemed to coincide. It never bothered me when they started to swab but it did hurt a lot of other people. I think when the trots swabbed every winner is about when I started to make it as a trainer."

"So what year did they start to swab routinely?"

"Well, probably about fifteen years ago. They used to hit and miss a bit. They might swab one or two, but guys would always take risks. And they still do, they still do take that risk. But I always welcomed - and I still welcome - as much blood testing, swabs and everything as they want to do. It's never been a hindrance to me, it's been a help."

FRED'S RISE TO THE TRAINER'S PREMIERSHIP

1939 Born in January (with but one destiny in Fred's mind).

1952 Left school at year's end, a few months before turning fourteen.

1958 Fred took out a trainer's license when his father was disqualified. He was 19 years old, and trained for one year. Branched out on his own within a few years - about 1962. He made very little progress initially and had serious doubts that he would ever make it. His health suffered. Friends took him aside out of kindness and told him to give it away. But then he began to rise up the ladder.

1969/70 Lyle Lindau won the trainer's premiership with 31 wins. Fred was fourth with 24 wins, one less than Phil Coulson, the trainer he considered he could learn most from. Phil had 'retired', but still trained a small string of top horses. It was over 10 years since Fred had first taken out a license. Many trainers would consider this good progress, but Fred considered it very slow.

1970/71 Fred was second. The goal was within reach.

1971/72 Fred had the most wins - 37 to Lyle Lindau's 33. However the rules had been changed at the start of the season, and under the new points system Fred came second to Lyle Lindau, 203.5 points to 203.

It must have been hard to take for someone as ambitious, as driven as Fred Kersley. In the uproar, the rules for the following season were changed and the training premiership went back to total wins.

1972/73 Fred finally broke through with 30 wins to Lindau's 27.5. Finally crowned aged 34. Over the next 4 seasons Fred widened the margin every year until in the 76/77 season he won with 54.5 wins - second was Kevin Batt with 27.5!

1978/79 A trainer named Jim Schrader came out of the blue with 3 exceptional horses in the one year and took the title 52 to Fred's 35. The next year Fred took the title back and again went on to establish a wide margin and great dominance over the next 7 years.

1984/85 Fred had 113 wins and the trainer who came second on the ladder had 53. That's domination. It must have seemed to some people that Fred had taken over the game.

4.5 Age married and role of wife

Fred and Judy married in 1966, when Fred was 27, but she was an important part of his life for many years before that.

"How did you meet Fred?"

"Through the local football club, netball club. In those days people stayed within their boundaries."

"Yes, I remember those years. Every district had a Progress Association Hall and everybody knew everyone

else in the district. When you first got to know Fred, what were his attitudes? Was he mainly interested in football, was he interested in being a trainer or a reinsman?"

"He was always interested in his horses. The football had to fit around the horses."

"How old was he then?"

"Probably about seventeen. In the beginning they played B grade, and then they would watch the A grade game. At half time, Fred and some of his mates - we'd all jump in the car and race home to the stables to feed up. You'd miss the third quarter but you'd be back there for the final quarter. Everything had to fit in with the horses."

"What was your background in horses"

"None"

"What did your parents think of your getting involved with someone in horses?"

"Well, we had no background in horses, but my dad was a two- and-six punter at that stage (literally equivalent to betting 25 cents, but more like betting $2 now). He used to follow horses and be interested from a punter's point of view, but he never went to the races or trots or anything. But my oldest sister - she married Russell Roberts - 'Pure Steel Roberts'. (Pure Steel was one of the greatest, gutsiest pacers Australia has ever seen, owned by bookmaker Russell Roberts.) Betty, another sister, married Russell's brother. They were a galloping family."

"Pacing was a very big deal in Western Australia at that time, wasn't it? Not only was it probably bigger than the gallops, but both of those things were bigger to society than they are now."

"Yes, yes - there were no other interests or diversions were there? I mean, your diversions were the trots, the races, and the local picture theater. It was a completely different lifestyle then. I hear them talking about the past - like when they lived in Carlisle and raced at Gloucester Park - they used to drive their horses to the trots, over the Causeway, with a lantern, because they never had motor vehicles. You didn't have horse floats and things, so you all had to live close to where you were racing. You never had country venues, so your opportunities to race weren't as great. They never raced their horses so often. You might only give them one run a month, because they trained them differently. It was a whole different era."

"That stuff about racing once a month fascinates me — how racing has changed and why. How much it's the horse's genes, the trainer's expectations, the training program, the worms, and whatever else it is."

"A lot of those kids were brought up with horses. Like, instead of bikes, some of them would have a horse to ride around the streets. Even the baker's cart was drawn by a horse and the milkman had a horse."

"And as a result of that, not only was horsemanship

more widespread, but there was also more respect for it. It was a very useful everyday thing. If you were good with horses, you were a respected person in the community for that alone. But the 1950s was the end of that era. So did you get into the horses at the level of working in the stables or driving?"*

"Not driving. I worked - I was a shorthand typist and I had a job, but on Friday nights I'd come and spend the weekend at Fred's place. I very much enjoyed being a part of it, because I think all kids enjoy horses. There was a magic about it."

"There's an excitement in racing."

"Yes, and any long weekends or any time really, I practically lived at Fred's place with his mum and dad and that, and did get involved."

"At that time would you have described Fred as ambitious?"

"Yes, he was, always. He was determined."

"Did he have any sort of typical teenage arrogance or didn't he go through that phase?"

"A lot of people who didn't know him thought he was arrogant. He wasn't a public person and he was a fairly shy person, would always stand in the background unless he was with his circle of close friends."

"Did you ever worry when you were lining up to get married that it was a bit of a dicey game, or were you sure of Fred's ability?"

"No, to be honest, he came from a successful family and they were a public family, weren't they. No, I never had any worries, I suppose. When I first met him it was a struggle and when we got married, we didn't really have anything. In fact, before we got married, I had a couple of horses I raced, that Fred was training, because he couldn't get owners. One I shared with two other fellows. Things were tight, and three of us leased it. I had to pay my training fees too. He'd give me the bill every month and I paid."

"People who stay at the top for a long time must have an especially strong drive because it is very easy to become a social lion after a few training premiership wins: go to more parties, drink a bit more, stay at the parties longer, leave a bit more to the lieutenants. Tell a few difficult owners to get stuffed. It has its pressures and sacrifices to stay up there."

"Yes. It is hard work and it's harder work than people appreciate, over the years. I'm not sorry because I've enjoyed it, and I've been there and everything, but you go without, which doesn't worry me. There might be a social function - I mean, we've missed family weddings because it was Saturday night and Fred had a drive. If Fred is driving I am there. The only time I haven't been there is when I've been in hospital having children and then I've had a fight with my doctor because he wouldn't let me out to go to the trots."

"Even you don't go to the wedding?"

"No. I don't go without Fred. If he's driving I'm there. Things like the kids' birthdays - they would have to be held another day, because it was race day, whereas other people aren't prepared to do that."

When the kids were young and money was too short to afford a baby-sitter, the whole family went to the racetrack. The children went to sleep in the truck.

"Particularly after they've been to the top once or twice, I think many trainers swing over to the social side, because by then they're a social entity, even a celebrity. It becomes very easy to stay a bit later at parties, go to more parties and all that sort of thing."

"Well, New Year's Eve when we were just going together, was a big deal - New Year's Eve parties, a teenager and all that. Well New Year's Day would always be Trotting Cup Day - a big trot meeting. We'd always be home in bed asleep by half past nine because it was trots the next day. I mean, you just never saw a New Year's Eve in. We might go to a family party or something and be gone before the other people got there."

"See, Fred's brother Bill's son turned twenty-one today. They had a big party on Saturday night which was a race night. Now how anybody in harness racing - see, they think different to us. To us, you just would not organize a party on a race night. Now, young Brian, as I say, has just turned twenty-one and he's struggling to get drives and make a living. He gave up what turned out to be a winning drive on Saturday night."

"Different priorities, obviously."

"Now, there's no way Fred would do that. He would even have left his own party - if that had to happen."

"Driven the horse and come back?"

"Well we did. He was best man at his brother's wedding and he had one drive that night, and he was battling to get horses and drives were important. It was somebody who had a few horses and was giving him drives and they were good drives. We left the reception, went to Gloucester Park and he drove his race and we came back. He felt if he didn't drive, some other person may have driven it and he might not have got back on those horses. Like young Brian on Saturday night - now that horse has won, he might not get that drive back."

"You are less likely to get it back if it wins. You'll probably only get it back if it runs like a crab. When you were first getting started, how hard did it get economically?"

"Very hard. When we got married, Fred was renting a house. His father had sold his house and stables, and shifted to suburbia, and Fred was renting the house and stables off the real-estate company."

"So he never really got started from his father's place?"

"No, no. We were battling. I was still working. We got married in April and I worked for probably twelve months, be-cause I had Greg in the June. I was about five or six months pregnant when I left work, and my wages paid the rent and kept us, because we didn't have enough. Then we bought the place in James Street. Fred's father had bought a house for Bill in Cannington, and gave us the same - two thousand five hundred pound, and that was our deposit on our place. We had to pay $42 a month to the bank, and it was very hard to find. I mean, some months I'd be raiding the kids' money boxes to make up to the $42. We got married just as it changed over from pounds to dollars, and he had $2 a week. That was his spending money. If he wanted to go and spend it on Thursday night with the boys, well, that was it for the week. Our kids laugh at that, they think that's all a joke, because they think you get your money and you spend it. But we've battled."

"At that stage, did he ever think about changing into another occupation?"

"Never. And when you talk about how determined he was, how he wanted to stand on his own two feet: the first thing he did when we started to be successful and get some money in the bank - do you know what he did? He gave his father back his two thousand five hundred, and his father said he didn't want it, but Fred insisted. Because he wanted to - nobody could ever say he got any leg up because of his father."

"But there must have been stages there, from what he was saying, when he wasn't doing at all well, when he would be wondering what he was doing."

"Well, he got a job as a bread-slicer and all sorts of things. That was before we got married. When he won the Trotting Cup, he was working as a bread-slicer at Tiptop Bakery."

"And he was a long time getting lift-off?"

"Oh, a long time."

"How many years do you think it was, before you felt you were on the way?"

"Well, I suppose it begins when he starts to be recognized. He never ever gave up. He never ever thought he wouldn't get there."

"He always believed he'd get to be number one, did he?"

"I think he did, yes. I don't think he ever talked about not being there. But at one stage they thought he had an ulcer. He would have terrible stomach pains and his stomach - you could knock on it like wood. He used to go to the doctor regularly because they thought he had an ulcer."

"This was when we were going together and then just after we got married, and he would just be in so much pain. As time went on - he didn't have an ulcer at all. I think it was just straight-out nerves and determination and frustration that was causing it. When we look back, I'm convinced it was just his frustration at wanting to be there, and not being able to do it, or not getting there quick enough."

As you can see, Judy was a very important part of Fred's

success. She has been very much a participant in spite of being a mother. She put Fred's career in front of family occasions, which many mothers hate to do. She was just as ambitious as he was, and she was prepared to make the same sacrifices. She may even have had more faith in Fred than he did: Fred at times had doubts about himself, but Judy didn't seem to have those doubts. She is known to be fiercely proud of "my Fred". Whenever he races she is there. She helps by recording the results, times, and recovery heart rates of the horses that race. Judy and Fred are nearly always together, a close knit couple, and a very successful team.

5. Achievements as a trainer

5.1 Training titles, money, and races

Based on number of wins, Fred has taken out 15 training premierships in Western Australia, arguably as tough as any part of Australia or New Zealand in harness racing. He achieved this by the age of fifty. The Kersleys as a trio at this point have 30 between them, which may be some kind of record in harness racing.

Fred's best year for money was the 1985/86 season when his winnings exceeded $800,000.

5.2 Important races and awards

INTERDOMINION CHAMPIONSHIPS The most prestigious harness race in Australia and New Zealand. Fred has been second twice (once with Pure Steel), but a win has eluded him.

TROTTING CUP The major race in WA. This is a race for pacers! Fred won driving Beau Travis in 1961. The race is now called the Benson and Hedges Cup. Under that name Fred has won it with Local Product.

DERBIES Pure Steel, Nixon Adios, OAKS twice. MOUNT EDEN MILE three times.

Fred has also won dozens of other Cups and feature races, in fact the Interdominion is the only significant race to have eluded him in WA.

I found Fred unusual in his inability and unwillingness to recall details of his most glorious moments in the sport. Most trainers are more than willing to recite their triumphs. I had to get information from *The Kersley Dynasty* an excellent article by Ken Casellas. Casellas states that Fred has driven more metropolitan winners than anyone else in Australian harness racing history - over 1100. It remained for journalist Gino de Mori to tell me that Fred had won a record four Australian City Driving Championships.

5.3 Some major horses

Gino de Mori, who covers pacing for the main daily paper, considers Fred has seldom been given good stock, so the list of top horses he has had is not a long one.

Pure Steel would be the best known name, and the best horse Fred trained, although he loathes comparing horses, especially if they never raced against each other. Fred trained Pure Steel until he was four and won a Derby with him. Although related to owner Russell Roberts by marriage, the horse was moved to another trainer. When I asked Fred about it, he said there was no big argument, he and Russell had simply 'grown in different directions.'

Paavo was chosen by Fred in the yearling sales and is half-owned by Fred and Judy. Fred trained Paavo to be Champion Two-Year-Old of his year in Australia. He told Gino in an interview that Paavo is the best he's ever driven. He loves the horse but knows the knee problems will probably prevent a win in a series event like the Interdominion Championship. At the time of that interview, September 1988, Paavo was a five-year-old with 16 wins from 21 starts and stake money of $235,138. Not being able to race frequently nor go for the big events with a series of heats greatly limits a Standardbred horse. This is shown by comparing Paavo's winnings with those of Village Kid, $574,561 in one year, or Our Maestro, over $400,000 the same year.

5.4 Where was Fred at age ?

20 - Finishing up a year of training while his father was disqualified.

30 - Moving up the table into the top ten.

40 - Having his first run of training titles stopped by Jim Schrader.

50 - (1989) Losing out to Trevor Warwick, but still avoiding syndication.

6. His operation now

6.1 Home

Fred and Judy live on 80 acres (32 hectares) on Nicholson Rd in Forrestdale. They moved there from Cannington in 1979. Although the property has roads on three sides, there is a great sense of peace and solitude. About half the property is still bush (native forest). The surrounding bush and the spacing of the buildings down the curve of the central hill gives each building a privacy of its own without isolation. From the houses and stables little or no traffic is seen and none heard. You could be out in the bush a thousand miles from any where, but Fred is only about 12 miles (19km) from Perth and Gloucester Park. The entrance is on a side road off Nicholson Rd.

The surrounding area is open paddocks or swampy bush rising into an area of low sandy hillocks. "Gutless" white sand, agriculturally speaking, but great for wildflowers. The 80 acres is the site of the training track and stables, and Fred's father and mother also have a house on the block. Drivers in the traffic on Nicholson road catch glimpses of the horses and sulkies going their many rounds of the track, a look from the frenzied modern world into what seems like a world apart.

Fred and Judy's house is set down from the top of the hill so they cannot see the road and the traffic, but they do have a commanding view of their track and the surrounding bush. It is a peaceful view to me but it is too close to the workplace for Fred to fully enjoy it. The house is yellow brick and has to one side a very tall aviary, full of parrots. Breeding Australian parrots is an interest of Fred's.

The half-mile track has two straights and two curves. If he ever builds another one, Fred says he will make it circular. The track has a limestone road-base with half an inch (1.25cm) of hot-mix asphalt over that. On top of the hot-mix is two and a half inches (6.25cm) of crushed granite, also called blue-metal. The track is watered every morning before use to soften it.

"It changes from time to time; we add to it and take away for winter or summer. Summers we've just introduced a thin layer of sand to soften it up and take the jar out, but that tends to be played with. The thing is, we've got a very firm base with about two inches to two and a half inches of cushioning material over the top."

"You don't have any trouble with the wind or the rain blowing the cushion away and exposing the hot-mix?"

"No. You would if you had the wrong material."

"This is too heavy for wind and it lets the water through, presumably."

"That's right, if you have too fine a material, you've got too much dust and it will blow away or wash away, so you need a mix, and that's not too difficult."

6.2 Organization, stables and staff

Fred has a small staff of around 10, nearly half of which is family: Judy does the accounts and books; Ned, a pensioner these days, looks after the track, helps out in whatever areas he's needed; son Greg drives and grooms; and daughter Kellie drives and grooms.

Fred's staff have their tea breaks and meal breaks with the family.

JUDY:"As far as helping him to keep contact with the horses, he tries to do that on a personal basis. He found that for him to keep the finger on the pulse, to keep the horse up to where it should be - like he might have one particular staff member that has their favorite horse, so he lets them work that a bit. But every now and again he needs to get on that horse himself. Having the staff in the house for their meals, quite often at lunchtime - he'll ask them how a certain horse went and if there were any problems."

"That's an interesting point too - eating with the staff."

"It doesn't thrill us, but still-"

"No, but there's a syndrome I was aware of even before I really got into this business of analyzing the top fellows,
and that's trainers who seem to do well until they got to perhaps ten or fifteen horses and then they'd go for a big nosedive. Some of the good observers around could name quite a few of them. I used to think it was as simple as the fact that they kept everything in their head, and then when they got to a certain point they simply couldn't keep enough information in their head. They were not recording anything, and it all got beyond them. But I find there are a whole stack of other things that change when people get up in the horse numbers. One of them is that the staff become a separate entity, whereas before they ate and coffeed with the staff. They go from being the entire staff themselves to 2 or 3 staff that they are still communicating with-"

"Yes, yes, very closely."

"Then all of a sudden the trainer has enough money to increase the staff and live off the premises, or further from the premises, and all of a sudden they go bad."

"When we first started off and had no kids, or had babies and the kids were little, it wasn't quite so bad. I'm not complaining but it's always been a lot of work, and you've been tied down. The kids grew up, and now it has a lot of disadvantages because our kids might walk in and they'll go to the fridge and they'll want to grab something, which is okay because it's their house, but then we can't give that to all of them and you can't sit and eat that in front of them."

"And talking at the table: like, you might sit down as a family and chat about things. Now you don't want to talk about things in front of the staff. Sometimes our kids want to have a punch up with each other at the table and you say, 'Don't do it in front of the others, we don't need to bring our family arguments out like that.' So it definitely has some big disadvantages. Lots of times I'll be sitting there and I'll think of something I want to tell Fred and it's not the time to say it, then he'll get up and go up to the room and by the time I've cleaned up, he's asleep and you forget about it. So it has a lot of disadvantages as far as family and home life go, but it probably has advantages as far as keeping contact with your staff."

"One guy was saying to me, that when he went well for a while he lived off the place and so on, then he went so bad he had to shift back to living in the house at the stables. He said, 'You know, I'd only been off the place about two years and when I shifted back, I realized a couple of the guys I'd been employing were real useless.' He hadn't seen it because he didn't see enough of them. Disloyalty and not telling the boss how he really is - those things are more likely to grow up with greater separation."

"Truly I think it's a very personal business, and one in which you can't afford to delegate all the authority. You very much have to be in contact with the animals, and the staff, and what is happening."

The training track and houses are set on 80 acres. That's Ned Kersley's house in the center background and the main stableblock on the right. Fred's house is out of sight at left rear behind the orange-flowered Christmas Tree. Newer stables also out-of-sight to left.

Another lap later and the horses are going a lot faster and showing a lot more sweat. Fred's house is visible on the top of the hill, and the new stable roof below it.

"When we first started off and we were very young, the first staff we had living in called us Judy and Fred, and that was it. That's how we were. He lived in, and my sister only lived down the next street, and Bill and Judy only lived across in the next street too. We were all friends. Our kids all grew up together, more like brothers and sisters, and we might go to one of our places for lunch, or it'll be someone's birthday - and that staff member would come with us. He was sort of part of our family, but very quickly, they didn't have respect for you. They knew too much of your personal and private life and there was no respect, so we had a bit of a problem. After about the second one - he was a bit of a troublemaker and whatnot - we just felt that respect was lacking. So Fred said they had to call us Mr and Mrs Kersley. I felt terrible, like an old grandma - these kids calling me Mrs Kersley, but for sure it's the correct way to go."

"I think ironically, once people have been up there and get into near-legend status, it doesn't matter what they're called or if they have the staff round the place all the time, they sometimes get respect even if they do stupid things."

"Still respected. Yes, I think now we're respected. But while you climb up the ladder you had to-"

"You had to manufacture respect."

"You had to separate it, yes, otherwise you were just one of the boys and they very quickly take liberties."

"I was told a funny story about this fellow - his wife told me this - said he reached the stage where he had two employees but they were so socially dominant to him because of the type of person he was, that he'd go down and do work rather than ask them. They'd sit in the house drinking tea, talking with one another; he'd be down the stables working!"

"Some of the kids working here now, they just call him The Boss, which is probably a bit respectful. But no, it's not as important now; but I think then it was. As it turned out, we learned. I mean, it wasn't that we said, 'OK, you're going to call us Mr and Mrs Kersley.' We tried it the other way first and felt it had failed. They even now get treated a bit like part of the family."

6.3 Number of horses

Fred has stables for 40 horses after recently adding more boxes. Previously he had about 30. Of the Standardbred trainers in Perth, only Trevor Warwick has more, according to Fred.

6.4 His typical day week and year

Fred rises at 5am. By 5.30am he is down with the horses. He works his horses in the morning and likes to have them all worked before 11am. In summer he may rise even earlier, because it can get pretty hot by 10am at that time of year. In the afternoons he gets some odd jobs done, has a nap if at all possible. Almost every evening of the week he is at trots or trials. If he's racing in the country, the main tracks are 60 to 80 miles (100 to 130km) away. There may be one or two hours on the road. The two evenings he's not racing, he dines out to get off the place. He seldom gets to bed before midnight. The year is pretty much the same right through. There is a little more racing in summer than in winter, but there is no stop to the racing.

In Perth there are two meetings a week, one with an average purse of $10,957 per race, and the other about $2,200. The average crowd is 4,000. Typically the betting handle is $115,000 on the on- course tote, $200,000 with on-course bookies, and $440,000 on the off course tote. There are nine races per evening, of which in recent times one per night has been a standing start. A recent winner off the 50 metre mark paid very good odds and had the crowd roaring.

6.5 His car
Fred has a slightly aged gold Mercedes Benz and there was a sparkling new Nissan Skyline alongside it.

7. Does he get good horses?

7.1 Where does he get his horses from?
Claiming races have not taken root in Australia because Australians have a great personal attachment to their horses, and consequently will rarely enter them in such races. When they do, they put unrealistically high prices on them.

The average price for a yearling at the 1988 sales in Western Australia was $6,042. Fred helps clients select a few at the yearling sales. Breeders have not been significant suppliers of yearlings. Most of Fred's horse's come from owners phoning him up to say they have a horse they want him to train.

7.2-1 Who chooses?
"Do you buy horses and place them with clients, do you leave them to choose, or do you prefer to advise them and then they bid?"

"I am mostly just the public trainer that the public ring up and say, 'I've got this sort of horse, would you be interested in training him?' I haven't been a salesman as such - as most of the leading trainers are - that go out and meet, strike deals and do deals and get owners."

Judy cast some more light on the process when we were discussing the role of the trainer in the selection process.

"One outlook on it that is realistic for a trainer, is simply: 'I buy the horses because half these people that want to buy horses, know nothing about horses, and they KNOW they know nothing about horses. So they'd rather I bought it, and if it failed after I bought it, then it was

still a better chance than if they bought one."
JUDY:"Yes if you want a horse, you'd be better to pick your trainer and then say, 'I would like a horse,' rather than you go and buy a horse and come to the trainer and say, 'I've just bought this horse, will you train it?' - and the trainer thinks, 'Ooh, it's a terrible horse. I know its history,' or, 'I hate the breed,' or something."

"Another way some trainers do it is to give the owner a list of horses they like - or the trainer looks at a list of horses the owner likes."

"Well, if it's a yearling sale and somebody rings up and says, 'I'd like to buy a yearling at the sales, would you pick one out?' - well, that's what Fred does. He looks through the catalog and he says, 'You look through the catalog too and pick out what you like, and I'll look through, and then I'll put them together'. If they happen to fluke a couple they both like, then he'll say, 'Well, let's go and look at them'. Then it's a process of elimination, and he might say, 'Well, there's nothing visibly wrong with either of those, so whatever one you think."

"But these guys that want to buy a horse, they want going horses. Now it's not easy to just go and snap one up, and I've rung them a couple of times and I said, 'Look, we haven't forgotten you. It's just that you don't pick up good horses anywhere and it's no good getting one that's not going to -,' and they said, 'Look, don't worry about it. We appreciate the fact that we still haven't got a horse,' they said, 'because we know many trainers that would've had a horse the next day.' So these guys have had horses before, around the track, and one of them, who has been somewhere else, he said, 'It's all right, because I know if I had told someone else to get me a horse, I would've had it a maximum of three days later if not before. And it was just a horse."

"Buy it before they change their mind is the maxim of some trainers. Fred does seem to be the furthest out of the horse selection process, of all the trainers I've talked to in detail so far. He's the one who has least to do with the selection of the horses. It's obviously because he doesn't want to feel responsible for the failures."

"As I just said, he's not a seller. He doesn't go ring up people and say, 'I can buy this horse,' or, 'We should go buy that horse.' Most of the horses we've trained over the years have been brought by people that have come to us."

"And they've already got the horse?"

"Yes. There'd be an odd one that we got for friends, or an owner. Fred'll say, 'There's a horse for sale. I think it could be all right,'or it might be advertised and we've taken it on."

7.2-2 Can Fred pick the best yearlings?
Fred, as you can see, prefers to stay out of the selection process, but has had a great success in his choice of Paavo, Australian Champion Two-year-old.

7.2-3 Does he favor type or pedigree?

Fred didn't want to burden others with his approach. He said to me, "I don't believe I'm any better than anyone else at picking them, and I think the people who think they are better are kidding themselves - because it is a lottery".

8. How he trains

Changes over the last 20 to 40 years

"What changes have there been in your training since you trained your first horses? Do you train them any harder?"

"Yes, training is increasingly demanding. You train horses to win, and you tend to train them to run fast enough to win. As the standard improves, you need to train them harder. Generally, all the horses are now trained harder than they were two years ago, and going back five years ago, that was a lot softer again. But immediately you try to train them soft like that today, you lose. You're always stretching them a little bit, and if you try to compromise, to be a little easier on them, then your horses are not fit."

"Do you ever try psyching yourself into believing that all the times being run are two seconds faster than they are, and you're training like you probably will in ten years time? Or are you really limited in some way by the technology?"

"If you had that attitude, maybe you could do that, but another way of training them as hard is trying to break them down, and I really think there is a limit to what you can do. There are stress factors, whether it's in the horse's condition or in the damage you're doing to him."

"Do you think the horses of fifteen years ago would have stood the training program you're giving now, and would they have given the same faster speeds we have now?"

"I think we could have trained them harder than we thought we could then, and I think they would have given you something, but today's horses are better than yesterday's horses. There *is* that mental barrier. I kept thinking back to a man trying to break through the four minute barrier for the mile, and it seemed they couldn't, until a couple did, and then they all did. I think that in all things, we do have these mental barriers. What you just asked me to do was to try to take that mental barrier out and go faster still."

"Yes. Imagine it's back a couple of seconds from where it is."

"I guess a guy should try really hard to do that, but I guess I'm trying to keep them too. I'm trying to keep them not only for next week, but for next month and so on. If I had a single job to do, getting a horse to win the Derby or something, and that was the end of the story, I'm not sure I wouldn't be more inclined to stretch him harder."

"The Interdominion this year is conducted on a preferential draw, on stake money earned (ie the lowest earners get the best mobile positions). So naturally the trainers will not want to have too high a stake earnings going into that race. They're already putting that in place. The decision's made six months to a year before you go, as to how much racing your horse is going to do - if your horse is good enough. You've got to think in the first place that he's got that potential, and you've got to be bold enough to throw all your eggs into that one basket. But you don't have very many horses fit that category. Still, some of the horses in West Australia are aiming already toward that, and that necessarily means they won't try to win high stake races between now and then. If you're an administrator of racing, that should be of some concern to you."

"That is reminiscent of trainers trying to keep a horse's weight down in the Melbourne Cup - bypassing winnings in the hope of taking out the big one. Would you be able to give me an idea of how much harder, and just exactly what form the harder training takes, compared to what it used to?"

"Well, in the broader sense, from the time when I first came in as a stable hand, a young fellow just leaving school (around 1950) - an acceptable mile-and-a-half time for a training run was 3:12, 3:30. These days I don't think any of us would be happy to run much slower than 3.10 for the mile and a half. Horses then could work 3:30 and go to the races and win. Now they could go to the races off 3:10 and probably not win. It's become more intense. The racing has become more demanding in that there's more of it. The runs are tougher, all the way, whereas in the early days they were easier, softly run for a mile and then sprint home the last quarter mile or a little more. Another difference has come from changing over from standing starts to mobiles. The fastest part of your race in the mobiles is the first hundred metres. So in real terms what we're doing is we're putting a lot more stress on them, a lot more demand on them."

"How differently do you train now - compared to when you started off?"

"You know the gear changes and the shoeing and the different work: how many things can you do to a horse? Millions of things. Different little ways of working, gearing him and that. It never occurred to me until quite some time after I was successful, the main difference is you seem to make the right decisions a lot quicker now. It's not a better decision you eventually get to, it's the same decision, but you get there by the shortest route. And that seems to be the biggest single difference. I see it with some of the younger kids: you put them on a horse and they'll say, 'Oh, it's not going to do this, it's doing that'; and I know they're wrong. I know that's not right. I don't know how I know - I just know that's not right."

A mix of crushed granite several inches thick covers a road blacktop on the half mile (800m) track. Note the moisture content of lower layers. Note water truck to keep it damp.

"You get a lot of trainers of a horse that'll start lugging or something, so they'll put a burr on him, and that's a bad decision, because although he is hanging, and putting a pole on him might get his neck straight, it hasn't fixed the problem. I suppose it's experience and a little bit of intuition. Vets seem as part of their training to be very methodical in their mental processing, but I might jump over all of that and just say, 'Damn, I haven't let his gear out'. And most times, I'll be close to right. Maybe I'll let it out too far, but I'll have changed it, I'll have caused a big change in the stats. It is very educational to go wrong as a trainer, to do something wrong."

Changes in the quality of lower ranks of horses
"Do you think fields are now more equal in terms of ability because there are more horses, a more uniform standard of training, or because of a genetically higher standard?"

"What's happened in my business is quite clear - well I be-lieve it's quite clear. At the top end of our range there's been only marginal improvement in the speed of the horses. At the bottom end of the range, the younger horses - they've just got out of the ground - they are so much better than they used to be, which means you are pushing up the bottom end of your group of horses to your top group and you've condensed it all. If you look at the times the free-for-allers were running fifteen years ago, the finals were going about the same, given that there's improved racetracks and probably veterinary science has lifted a bit and things like that. We've trained maybe better. Maybe better - question mark. But with the youngsters, they just come into your stables and within a few weeks, they're just running. They've improved-"

"Genetically improved?"

"Yes."

"Where has that improvement in the lower grades come from?"

"Whether it's a good analogy or not I don't know, but I think it's like the meat chickens, you know. You've got them to a stage where they develop young, and they kill them at six weeks or something now or perhaps younger. You never used to be able to do that. They've genetically manufactured an early developer, and where all the money has been put in by racing authorities, in my lifetime, has been into the two-year-olds and three-year-olds, so genetically we've manufactured horses that go early. I once read where an American said - he seemed to make a bold statement, even a mad statement - that he believed two-year-olds would be the fastest horses in the land. I thought that had to be wrong. From where I stood then, the two-year-olds were battling to hold their gait. But he's right. I believe right now that the two-year-olds are as fast: for one thing, they're usually sounder; they haven't learned to lose so much; they've grown well; they've got fewer complications in terms of damage that's been done to them - and I think they've got the capacity to run as fast as your old horses."

Changes in the quality of two-year-olds
"How far are they off the older horses' times now?"
"Nothing - in Australia this year."
"And how far were they, say, fifteen years ago?"
"Fifteen seconds. The first two-year-old race that was run in Western Australia, I think they rated 2.16 for the mile. Now the two-year-olds go under two minutes any time you like."
"What year did they run that first two-year-old race?"
"In Sydney they ran about 35 years ago. Here it might be 20. I'm hopeless on dates. I think the horse's name was Prince Melbourne and it was at Pinjarra, and I think the mile rate was 2:16. To be conservative I'd say they've improved 10 seconds in the last 20 years. I'm talking about Australian horses."
"Is that to some extent due to importation of American lines? They've been heavily into two-year-old stuff longer than we have."

Paavo, Fred's best selection in a sale ring, after winning the Kersley Stakes in 1988. His youngest daughter Catherine makes it a complete family affair by leading the horse in.

"One thing is a change of attitude by trainers. We were very much bound by our own inhibitions, as in all other athletic fields. I believe that's been a limiting factor and we were limited by our attitudes, which were given to us by our parents and everyone else. If you raced a two-year-old or worked a two-year-old too hard you were killing him. That has slowly changed around. Some of the newer guys have an advantage there because they haven't had it stuck in their head, and they come in and race the two-year-olds as fast as they can. I believe that's why Mount Eden was so great, because Jack Miles, a milkman and dairy farmer, was one of those guys who wasn't bound by any tradition, and he simply believed the horse should run as fast as it could."

Undertraining and overtraining

"Are there some things you could point to that you consider were errors you were making in your training early in your career? Overtraining or undertraining."

"Undertraining. The attitude of the old-time trainer was that a horse should train conservatively and save his best for race day. As though some magical thing would happen and allow him to race twice as well as he really could. I grew up on that and it was a mistake, I think. That logic doesn't sit comfortably any more. Mind you, it might have worked for them because they carried an enormous worm burden in those days - all horses did - and they were difficult to maintain in good flesh, so it probably did help them a bit. Also I'm not saying they should be overtrained either. I don't think that works well. That was probably one of the attitudes I had to break out of."

"Did you find you oscillated, that you undertrained for a while and then you'd gone the opposite way - you'd

heard that heavy training was the go, and perhaps pushed a lot of horses to the point where they trained off."

"Yes, I went through that stage."

"Was that educational, though, in that you got to see what were the earlier signs of overtraining and undertraining and so on?"

"Yes, and you don't have to be very smart to work it out either. It's so bloody simple."

"What would you summarize as the signs of overtraining?"

"Well, you bugger the horse up."

"Not a very specific term. In what sort of ways? It just won't eat or it's sore?"

I think understanding the horse - the first sign I think will come out of the tucker box. If he's starting to get too picky on his food, you feed him and he doesn't want to look at it, and you look at him and he's got a sort of dull look in his eye. It's really quite simple to see there's something wrong. He's so tired he doesn't want to eat and he can't run anyhow. Within a week of overtraining, he goes to the races and he can't run. I mean, he tells you pretty quick if you're only going to listen. But some of the trainers go harder still, and then the horse could be buggered up for life, and I've seen that."

"They show it first by what - fading in the races?"

"Yes."

"And does that precede things like not eating up at home?"

"Come in at about the same time."

"Are you a skin pincher? To test for dehydration."

"No, not really. I think if you turn the head towards you and pinch the skin, it'll stay up, if you turn it away, it goes back. I'm not really too strong on that. I think it is gut feeling to some extent, but there are some very obvious signs when a horse is overtrained. One of the first things you see is the horse just doesn't want to eat, almost to the stage where he almost won't eat anything at all. That's a sure sign, a surefire sign he's either sick or he's overtrained, which doesn't matter, they're both the same."

"So you'd hop in with a thermometer at that point?"

"Well, I'm not even big on the thermometers because I don't get to that stage now, I see it happening and I start to handle it before I make him sick."

Does it show much on the track before they get to that failure to eat?

"No. A horse can work brilliantly and come off the track, and then you find you've done too much. It's a very fine line we tread in overtraining. One of the other signs, I often think, is a horse that blows too much. I mean, if he was tired before he started, no wonder he's blowing. You've made him really really tired."

"See, some people advocate that for the horse that blows, you train it harder."

"Yes, I know - it blew so I trained him longer. I'm a bit scared of that. It's something I wouldn't do."

"And undertraining, what would you see happening there?"

"It's probably better to undertrain to some extent. The horse is nice and fresh, he will want to run a little bit, he can go okay. He's not going to run at his best but he's going to make a pretty good effort at it. You're probably setting up some shin soreness factors and that type of thing, though it's going to take a little while to surface. But I still think, if you're going to make a mistake, you may as well undertrain because it's easier to go on to a higher level of fitness than to pick up something that's stressed."

"The racing is eventually going to bring it to some level of fitness."

"Sure. All of your logic ought to be that you stay just this side of where you're heading. Because if you get to the other side of where you're heading, it's not good. No good for anyone."

"I think the art of training is to be able to have a horse at the level where he is that tiny bit undertrained and you don't have to push him to a little bit of overtraining to tell you you're near the edge."

"Right. Agreed."

Peaking for a major race

"What about peaking a horse for a big race? Do you consciously try to peak horses for big events?"

"Yes, I try to, but you tread a very fine line: you never never know. I don't think a trainer is entitled to say he can, do that.

He is entitled to say he tries, but if he says he can, then I think he is bullshitting. It is like - I've heard guys say they can pick yearlings, and I say they can't. When you say you peak the horse, that suggests it is the best it is ever going to be, and after that it can only go down. So when you try to peak a horse you are sailing very close to the wind; close to having an overtrained horse. I'm more comfortable not peaking them."

"It would seem trotters are more able to go on and on, at very close to their best, and therefore why try to peak them. I often think it is an invention of journalists more than a training device. I have asked journalists why they said such-and-such a horse was 'trained to the minute,' and they have made very lame replies."

"I often think that in the big races I've been in, and won some of, a hell of a lot of the horses raced below their best."

"The big horses in the big races?"

"Yes, in the big races, when the big money and the big pressure is on, we all try our very best, but we mostly stuff it up. The horses run below their best. I've been in races where good horses have performed at a high level in their lead-up races, but in the big one, they have raced down."

"I know how a lot of that happens: the excitement, the crowds and so on, especially in the Melbourne Cup; it makes the trainer train differently, feed differently; the jockeys ride differently, usually way over pace. Another thing is that in many big races, the horse is having its first go at a new distance. Many of the glamor races are over distances some trainers have never had to train a horse for previously, especially the two mile races. The horses are sometimes entered in a race that is not its best distance; they want some ideas on how to get 2400m out of a 1600m horse."

"I think that's the danger of it - particularly with Cup horses, where they go the longer journey. When you try to condition them to get the longer distance, there is a very real danger you will overtrain them. There are other factors too, like the wind in the last two or three days before that race may favor one horse more than another horse."

"I know from my own running, that sometimes I have gone out and run well, run extraordinarily well, but not been able to explain why I felt so good on that run. Other times I have run like a dog without being able to explain it. If I was a racehorse, my trainer would have been in trouble. But while there is usually a reason you can point to for a poor run, those runs where you went fast and felt so strong - no explanation at all."

"I think one of the reasons for a good performance is which way the wind blows. It can influence how a particular horse goes on the next Friday night."

"Do you mean that as a joke?"

"No. If it's an Easterly wind, loaded with pollen, it can affect the performance of some horses. If it is a cool Southerly wind, some horses will benefit from that. Some stables, in general, will be better off in cooler weather than in hot weather."

"There are syndromes in the human related to persistent hot dry winds. Humans, like horses, sweat to keep cool, and adrenaline is used up in the process. Some of the human population in places like Israel, where these winds can go on for weeks, get a degree of adrenal depletion and cease to be able to sweat properly. They become irritable, and especially lethargic, lazy. Now horses can become unable to sweat, a condition called anhydrosis, and they are useless for racing. It really showed up in horses in the tropics, that is why Hong Kong and Singapore keep their horses in air conditioned stables. But it is still a problem up north near the equator in Darwin and the like. Perhaps the dreaded Easterly produces a low level problem. Racehorses are very adrenal dependent in races. Trainers that have hot stables, will tend to make their horses sweat a lot. Athletes certainly seem to desert the hot areas, dry or humid. They tend to accumulate in cool climates."

"Well I think the wind can muck-up your efforts to peak horses. I similarly believe there are areas where you ought-not to train horses. Byford is one of them. I just would not attempt to be a professional trainer from Byford."

"What made you choose to train from here in Forrestdale?"

"It was the only place we could afford at the time. I was looking at a place in Armadale and was going past here one day, and saw it was for sale. When I found out the price, and that the vendor would carry the finance, I couldn't NOT buy. I am very happy about being here, because it has been good here. The horses run well and the training environment is comfortable. But I had a place that was equally as good and even arguably better in Cannington, a place in a suburban area that you would never have thought would be any good. Greg Harper bought the place from me and he's done very well. Horses trained at Cannington under difficult conditions race better than horses at Byford with all the conditions laid on for them. It doesn't matter who the people are, Cannington trained horses outperform horses trained in Byford or Orange Grove, where the facilities are laid on."

"Why was Cannington selected as training area all those years ago?"

"Because no one else wanted to go there. It was low swampy ground. Couldn't get drains to run, or toilets to work. If you went off the road in the sulky you disappeared from sight. The Canning Agricultural Society owned a lot of the land around there. A few trainers located themselves there. Once the track was put in, and an area of land designated for

stables, a lot of trainers went there. We used to fast work horses there from Carlisle. We had a choice of Gloucester Park or Cannington. Cannington had fewer shadows."

"Joe Petricevich was a trainer in Osborne Park when I was growing up, and he was regarded by some as the best trainer in the state. He did very well with some cheap horses. Joe had dairy farming interests in Byford and he eventually relocated his stables down there. He said to me, 'I'm tellin' you you can't train horses down there - you can't'. And 15 years later he still can't train down there like he could in Osborne Park."

"Do you vary your horses very much in the workload; in the most you give and the least you give to different horses? Ever had a horse that needed very little work?"

"No, but the differences are there and they are real."

"They might all go a mile and a half, but is there a lot of difference in how hard they go? Do some go really hard and some easy?"

"It is a gut feeling and it is a bit haphazard really. I will sit down in the afternoon and work out, for tomorrow, which horses I'll fast work and which I'll slow work. That depends on what they have done, how hard I want to work them, what races are coming up for them. So there are two groups. Having done that, I then go through the fast work group and match up the ones I think ought to work together that day. These two will go together, those two will be OK, they'll go slower together; this one will be best on his own. Then the next morning I'll go out there and depending on how I feel and what I think on that day, I might tell whoever is going to drive the lead horse to take it through in 2:10, 11, 12 or 15, and to let them come home together. Depends if I want to get to the bottom of him or give him an easy day. There is variation, but it isn't dramatic."

Making changes

"I see some trainers who get so angry and frustrated they change everything, and I can't see the point in doing that."

"It is a real trap as far as working out what change was useful."

"You would not know what worked"

Growth spurts

"How can you tell if a horse is having a growth spurt?"

"They look like a yearling, great big long legs, lean, hungry, don't seem to be ready."

"Some trainers say the give-away sign is that they sleep a lot."

"The relaxed ones lay down and the nervous ones stand up. The younger horses lay down more than older horses. They eat a bit more too." (This is typical of Fred - he has his own observations, and they are different to the commonly spouted 'wisdom'.)

"Do you have any problems with horses having a

growth spurt? Do you back off them at that time?"

"A luxury. But I don't think I see a lot of it. There is a colt down there now, and he was headed for a race at Christmas (this was December 22nd). My first logic was not to go for it, however the financial situation, the need to press on, overcame that. He's still growing I think, but he's coped very well with his training. For the wrong reasons the right decision was made. He has continued to grow and eat and get fat. He has developed beautifully, probably better than if I had put him away."

"Did you ever Xray the legs to check for closure of the growth plates, the epiphyses. Do you remember when that was being done?"

"Yes, but it was too expensive. I never got into that."

Optimum race distance

"Some trainers march their horses rapidly out over longer distances - they race them over more and more ground. The classic was galloper Think Big. Bart Cummings trained him and he won a race over 1000 or 1200 meters, in a campaign that marched out to a win in the Melbourne Cup over 3200 meters. Yet there are other trainers whose horses seem to stand still, to keep racing at the same distance. Charlie Whittingham, once his horses are racing at a mile, mile-and-a-quarter, they seem to stay on that."

"I think you can train that in. When I look at Paavo in hindsight I can see that. He was an unfashionably bred, cheap colt that went to the races and went . . . too good. He was unbeaten as a two-year-old, the best in Australia. He was so quick you couldn't believe it, but he went lame at the end of the year. I think he damaged his bone structure because he was undertrained for the speed at which he ran. He races now, and he's racehorse sound and doesn't limp, but the damage is still there."

"Can you use cortisone in the joint?"

"No and I don't want him broken-kneed anyhow. We can document the problem in his knees with Xrays now. So he was a horse who was very very quick with undertraining. He was able to keep his speed as he went through the classes. Now he has to race against the best horses in the land, and I'm having to put more depth and more miles into him. He's able to stand it because he's a little sounder. On Friday night I got beat, because I drove him to sprint and the one thing he can't do now is sprint. I drove to sprint at the end and I lost, but I think if I had reversed my driving tactics I'd have won. So now he has more stamina and less speed."

"But what is it that keeps a horse at one distance?"

"I think it would be undertraining."

"That might work but there must be other ways. You could hardly accuse Charlie Whittingham of undertrain-

The bit board - quite an array of types for a man who likes to keep it simple.

ing. He takes months and months to get them ready. Maybe he has taken them to some static optimum distance."

"Training gallopers, I would have to rethink my training for sprinters, because by comparison sprinting trotters are middle distance. I would have to give them a lot less miles. In the gallopers, it seems to me sprinters are basically undertrained."

"A leading Thoroughbred trainer once said to me, 'A stayer is just a sprinter that can relax'. You can argue about that, but there are certainly some trainers that can't get a horse to relax. They have two types of horse: horses that bolt or horses that are sour. After a half dozen races where they career off to a 5 length lead, are overhauled by the field and have to hang on with their lungs burning and legs like glue, they are stressed. They go mentally sour on the deal or train off."

"Yes, definitely, that is one of the things in training: being able to have the mental attitude right. Once they are sprinting, the demand is there and they are hurting themselves."

Pure steel - naturally fit

"One of the best stayers was Pure Steel, but he was so relaxed, unbelievably relaxed. That was why he could stay so well. Even when he went at his top speed, and he never had a high top speed, but when he went close to it, he did it so easily."

"Was that something to do with his biomechanics, or was it his stamina, his heart size?"

"I don't know, there is so much misinformation about him - stories that he had a low heart score. But I do know he had a small girth, the smallest girth in the whole stable. He was not a big horse. But I always think of him as like a fish - a bloody great trout. Whether you worked him or not, he just seemed to be naturally fit. He healed quick. If he hurt or cut himself he'd heal quicker than other horses. The unusual things about him were: his quick healing; his ignorance - he'd walk all over you; and his natural fitness. He seemed always to be fit whether you worked him or not. It didn't matter who trained him. He had five or six trainers but he went the same for us all. Trainers had less influence on him than on most other horses."

"Are there, in a big group of horses, some that stay fit by themselves?"

"Some horses do. Some horses, the first time you put the straps on them, can get over a mile and a half pretty quick, and not do themselves a whole lot of harm either - not outwardly anyway. Others, after a mile of jog and pace work, they've got to go back to the stable again. But that doesn't mean that after three or four months the one that was naturally fit will be any better. In fact the one that was naturally able to go again, he doesn't seem to get any better - just seems to hang about and even train off."

"Studies in humans generally find that the order of natural ability in an untrained group will be pretty well maintained at the end of a training period. The best will still be the best and the worst will still be the worst. Could it be that some of these horses are kept on a big property where they run a lot and just naturally keep themselves fit?"

"I'd say that is a factor, but not the whole explanation. Horses can come off grass and blow like hell. Others can come off being fed grain, but it doesn't seem to be the only factor. Sometimes you'll have a horse in for his first fast workout after a spell and you'll have one of the younger kids on him, who are not good judges of speed. That horse will get over a mile fairly quick - so quick you'll want to rush out and stop them before they stuff it - and it comes off the track with a low heart rate and everything. Now I'm not sure you shouldn't let them do that. I tell the kids that know how quick they are going, to go a mile in 2:20. Maybe if I was perceptive enough he'd be better off going a mile in 2:15 or 2:10. Save my clients a bit of money."

"I've always been interested in that: does the horse lead the training rate of improvement or does the trainer have a pre-ordained rate of improvement. A lot of the harness trainers do have a set number of seconds per week by which they go down."

"Going back a few years it was almost a sin to carry a stopwatch. According to the old trainers you were training to the stopwatch and that was unforgivable. You must never do that. It was a bad thing to have a stopwatch."

"You were meant to train by the horse then, let the horse set the pace."

"As I got up to be a trainer of raceway horses, the one thing that was constant was time, and I relate very strongly to it. I would not want to train without knowing exactly what they can do at the track and at home. Everything I do relates to that."

"Do you have a predetermined idea of how many seconds per week they should go down by?"

"No not especially."

"So you train by the feel of the horse, what he wants to do?"

"A gut feeling: if he's a horse that likes to get down a little quicker; what he does in the feed box. You tend to know the horses very well. I don't think you can know them if you don't feed them and drive them. I can't drive every one of them every day, but I share myself around as much as I can, and I believe you MUST do that. Also if you don't drive, you must have an input - what you want that horse to do. I get very angry when a horse goes too slow or too fast, because that is what causes problems.

"Do you space their first races more widely, say three weeks?"

"Mostly the program and the horse dictates that. You have three races here and you think he can stand two: which one do you drop off? Can this horse stand three races in a month, four races in a month? Barring problems and ballots you tend to have a pattern about it. The horse that disappoints, I might spend a bit more time with him. If he disappoints again, I will keep him going, put plenty of races in him, and see if that won't improve him or make him go the other way - in which case he is most probably eliminated. The ones that are going pretty well, I tend to spare them a little, spread their runs."

"I had one on Friday night though, that made me look at my training logic. There is a decent race two weeks ahead. I had run him this last Friday and had not intended to go back with him next Friday night. Give him the two weeks between the races. Last week made me change my mind. Although he went pretty well, he just weakened a touch. He had a high heart rate after the run. I thought, 'I can't do enough in two weeks on the track to maximize his chances.' So I made the decision to run him in between. Now I may have made the wrong decision, and we'll find out on Friday night or two weeks time. There are a lot of decisions like that."

"The high heart rate after the race you consider shows he's unfit and therefore needs extra racing?"

"It could mean he was overtrained, but picking him, he was pretty fresh, he was feeling good and he raced pretty good, but he weakened at the end. He came home very well, but if he'd carried his speed another 20 meters he'd have won. He only got beat a meter. He had the other horses done everywhere except the last 10 meters. He can't stay good (hang on at the end), he's not a top class colt, only a handy horse, and if he's going to win this race with three or four better horses, he needs more work. I can't tiptoe around with him. He's a placid colt so the extra race won't take too much out of him. It's easier to train him with a race. Trackwork then becomes less critical. If however he was the kind of horse that nerves up, becomes fierce, worries about the run, comes home and doesn't want to eat - you can't get back with him very often."

"Wider spacing of races for the more nervous horses?"

"Yes. The one that shakes himself to pieces before the race, races right up and pulls himself to bits. Some of them will be a bit nervy when they start racing and settle down a bit later. But if a horse is not hurting with his racing, it is probably the best form of training."

"Were there any particular ways you learned about the gear? Pacing is a very technological form of racing."

"It certainly is. I think what I learned very early in the piece, which is still true today, is that it's trial and error and there's no other way. I suppose you develop a bit better intuition as you get older. You might get to the answer quicker, but still the same comment - it's just trial and error. The other logic I used is that I wanted to put as little gear on as possible, and I think that's important. I don't think horses - pacers - should wear any more gear than they need. A lot of fellows had the idea head checks were a must, for different reasons. Some thought they'd fall over if they didn't have a head check on, and others thought it made them better gaited and all that sort of thing, but in real terms I don't believe that either of those things are important. I think if a horse won't race with his head relatively in the right position, that you can assist him by putting a head check on him where he can't get his head too far down, but he becomes more difficult to steer."

"So you're a minimum gear man."

"Oh Yes. Very much so."

"Were you able to learn much, say, by watching what other people were doing at the track, or from books?"

"No, I don't think books or people helped me there. If you understood the horse and you wanted him to be comfortable when he ran, you could read that from him. When I put extra gear on, I just knew it was annoying him, that he didn't like it. I thought, 'Well, if he doesn't like it that's not going to help him run,' and I still think that's right. For the horse to run to the best of his potential, then he ought to feel good about it. A tight head check - essentially what you do is you put pressure on the roof of the mouth and their tail and push them towards each other! Now how can that help him run?"

"You don't like head checks - how about shadow rolls?"

"There's been some prejudice against shadow rolls, and I don't really have much time for trainers who take the shadow roll off a horse that needs one, because they place every other horse and driver in the race at risk, if the horse should jump. I think they're a great safety thing. They don't weigh anything."

"Hobble length?"

"Well, hobbles are like what size shoe you take. If I need a size seven shoe, I'll wear it. It won't be as good if I've got a size eight on, or a size six."

"Do you do these things like letting them out one hole on race night, or on a big race night?"

"What can that do?"

"To some people it's a magic formula. If I say, 'Well, if that makes it race faster, why don't you do it in training and all its races?' they'll say, 'It doesn't work then.' So I just wonder if they're actually hindering it all the time, and then they suddenly let it out to the length it ought to have been all the time. The claim by one fellow was that on a big race night, the horses sense the excitement, the atmosphere, and they stride longer."

"Balls. How can they? See, a pacing race is about coming out of the barrier fast, checking into a position, maneuvering, taking short strides sometimes just to get back in. When you observe a race, you don't see the subtle speed changes, it looks like they're running around there, but there's a lot of shunting and sprinting and checking off and checking out. The stride length is going to change throughout the race, and I'm sure the hobble length is not related to the length of stride. It's related to the length of the horse, and the way he goes."

"Some smaller horses wear a bit longer hobble because when he's in his pacing gait, that's where he's comfortable, and that doesn't change essentially from time to time. Now you can gear him shorter or you can gear him longer. If you gear him too short he's going to rub all the hair off his legs. If you gear him too long he's going to try to make breaks or he won't do what he's supposed to do, which is keep in one gait. Now we would like them to stay on gait in as long a hobble as they can, given the interference factor and the degree of difficulty of actually running in races."

"A lot of these horses could work around the tracks without any hobbles, but they couldn't with the intensity and difficulty of racing. They need the hobbles to assist them, and that's really all they are."

"One of the things I thought would be an interesting experiment, is to get some horses and deliberately run them, say one inch short, two inches long, one inch long

*With this 'trailer'
(parked at left), hooked
behind a tractor or
other vehicle, Fred or
Ned can exercise a large
number of horses in one
group.*

*etc. - randomize them. You'd work out what you think is
its best and then go up one, two, down one, two, send it
around and see what it does to the times. See how critical
one hole is."*

"You could do that. If you had the hobbles too tight, I'd think
you'd slow him up. I think he'd get tired. He'd be working
against the hobbles. I've read quite a few comments that
shoulder lameness is from pacers wearing hobbles too tight.
The front leg is pulling forward against the back leg, which
may have hit the ground fractionally sooner, causing sore
shoulders. Some bad-mannered horses, we put hobble shorte-
ners on to get them even in mobile races, to get them out of the
gate, to keep them on their pacing gait. You've got to tighten
them a little bit just to keep them balanced in that initial
burst, but after they've settled you can let the hobble go back
to their best length. If you shorten them too much, they cannot reach their full speed. There's no question of that."

*"Do you ever give a horse a hit out, a bit of fastwork, on
the morning of a race? The so-called pipe-opener?"*

"No." (I would later watch Ray Remmen at the Meadowlands take Beach Towel out for some fast works, twice in the
hours before a qualifying heat for a race, and still later the
same in The Little Brown Jug.)

*"A lot of Thoroughbred trainers will do it with what
they call thick-winded horses."*

"Some of the Standardbred trainers do. Some of the old timers would take them out and step them a free-legged mile."

*"Maybe the length and intensity of the warm-up in har-
ness horses is enough to counter any thick-windedness
(wheezing). What is your warm-up routine."*

"We're on the track seven minutes before the race. I
wouldn't be happy to go to the barrier with less than a mile-
and-a-half, and if I could get it, I might go another lap. They do
at least a half a mile going along a little bit. They would do that
half mile in 1:15 or 1:30. Some of them might step out over a
mile. Some of them might sprint a furlong. The horse that is
going to go away from the barrier pretty fast, you might give
him a fast furlong."

Psychological aspects

*"There's quite a strong general belief that the horse
loses something by racing against very strong opposition, and yet a lot of horses will come tenth, ninth, in various classes in their career, but as long as it's happening
in their class, no one seems concerned. No one seems to
consider that losing is having any effect on the horse."*

"Yes. I don't like to do it. If he runs often enough, as hard as
he can, that doesn't necessarily mean he hurts, but he is losing. Essentially you are in the process of teaching him to lose."

"He thinks that's all that's required?"

"Well, he's a creature of habit and he's not the brightest
specimen in the world, and yet I honestly feel like he's learnt,
'this is my usual finishing position,' and he's content with that."

*"Do you believe horses make the connection that if
they're up near the front they get whipped more than if
they're at the rear. They are so far out of it that no one's
going to thrash them because you don't push a horse
that's so far off winning."*

"No, no I don't. I feel almost the opposite to that. I think the
whip has very little influence on them. If I were to walk down
to the stable with a whip in my hand and whack the horse two
or three times, the next time I walked in the stable he would
try to jump out of the stable. But I can whip him in the race

and straight after the race I walk up and he'll put his head on my shoulder. He really doesn't relate. All he relates that to is the intensity of the competition. Their adrenaline's flowing and there's no offense from horse to driver. But if you give him a backhander or slap him a couple of times with a whip at home, well, he'll remember that. He doesn't remember the race, it doesn't hurt him. I don't think the whip essentially hurts him much and makes him go on. It's almost a display that he expects as part of the whole scene of what racing's all about. But there are some others that if you do hit them they're offended by it and they don't go on."

"I feel horses are braver at the front than they are at the back of the field. I don't think they can cope with that many bums in front of them when they're tired."

"So if you were going to try to explain that phenomenon, you've really got to counter the argument that the horse who gets near the front probably gets pushed out harder, gets whipped more than the horse that's at the back, so why do they still want to be at the front? I can only understand it as a primeval instinct - if they were originally being chased by wolves, or something, then the front of the herd was the place to be. Somewhere in their psyche there's a powerful urge to be at the front."

"With most horses I think so, yes. I read a little recently about that herd instinct, and it did bring back my pony club days where you'd be walking in a trail ride or something, and some horses would walk to the front and some wouldn't. When we're developing horses, babies, they don't really know why they're being exercised, or worked, or why the other one's there, and they might sort of look at it, or whinny at it and play with it, but somewhere soon the decent ones are going to look at the other horse and try and beat it. There's a change in mental attitude - the ears go back and they look at the other horse and try to beat it, and that's a beautiful feeling when that starts to happen to a colt or a filly. Some take longer than others, but some display this 'I want to beat you' expression on their face. You can see the penny dropping. They usually want to do that, the ones that try harder to win."

"A trainer has said to me that he likes to keep a few lesser horses about to let other horses beat them - to train them to win."

"From where I sit, dealing with bad, average, and very few good ones, there are so many variations. I mean, I've got some quite game horses that want to win at the races, but are quite happy to run second on the track. They seem to get to the stage of, 'Well, I don't have to, really'. I understand that and I don't want to make him either, because I think he's doing enough. He's keeping fit enough and he's run up to the other horse and he's just parked alongside him. If I get the stick out and make him go past, I can sour him a little. Or if I leave him alone and he's in good form, and goes to races and races

gamely, I'll leave that in place. I'm talking about seven and eight-year-old stallions. Why do I want to drive him mad on the track to do that? Now he might even be hurting a little in the joints and if I'm going to bust him on the track, I think I might come back worse a couple of days later in a race. So I'm happy to leave that, but I don't like to see horses being asked to do more than they can, because that is only teaching them to lose, and they lose hard."

"Some horses that I think are not strong on the competitive spirit, I will keep on their own, trying to save that for the race night. A lot of trainers have kept horses that they use as chopping blocks on the track. Some horse will go out and run through the mile in the required time, and then the better horse will come, blow his brains out and go to the line. It's bad for the chopping block, but it's good for the other horse."

"Yes, that's what this trainer said: he didn't mind keeping some duds in the stable. Some trainers keep horses on and they do that sort of thing with them, and they get money from the owners of those slow horses when that's what they're using them for."

"Well, the client won't put up with that for very long. If the horse has been racing for two months and hasn't earned a cheque, I think the best of clients is going to say, 'Hey, why?' But some New Zealanders have a pretty good idea. Say they've got a colt that's bred to be okay and he's gotten to be two-and-a-half to three- years-old and he's not making it: you can shoot him, or as a last resort you can wait a bit. And you can make him useful. What they do with those horses is they take the hobbles off them and they use them as a galloping pacemaker for the racehorses."

"So he'll lead them through their workouts on the gallop and he'll be very competitive at the gallop too, because he'll bring them on home, and it's easier for him to gallop than it is for him to stay in his hobbles. They might work him three, four, six months in that manner, then throw the hobbles back on him and just see if he hasn't made himself a bit better. And quite often they do, quite often they do. I might even work them two heats. It doesn't matter about him because he's not heading anywhere, but you're keeping him fit and he's becoming competitive, he's working and he was no good anyhow. He might just turn around and be okay."

It was reported by Ross Dunstan in mid-1988 that trainer Judy Gibbons credits the Kersleys - Ned and sons Bill and Fred - with the rapid conversion of her rogue pacer Luv You Perth from a tiger to a lamb. She approached them after the chronically troublesome horse played up so much it got out of its gear and failed to finish.

Race Distance

"My impression is that there's not a huge difference between racing one mile and racing two miles for a pacer."

"No. I don't believe there is. Just from the horses I drive and train, I can't differentiate too much. I think there are some horses that are better suited at the two mile just simply because they haven't got that high speed to call on. They still can win the mile so long as the mile's run for them, but probably if you said, 'What's his better journey?' you could say, 'I think he's better over the two mile.' Basically, the horses that were good at a mile can be pretty good at the two mile."

"When Bonecrusher, the champion New Zealand galloper was trained conventionally, he did poorly, and then more or less through accident, he had almost a fortnight off before a race and won it. Now, he does one little bit of fast work a week and wins on that. If that horse went into a hard trainer's stables, say TJ Smith's stables, it might simply do nothing, or TJ might wake up to what it requires: he's a very good horseman."

"I think that's what successful trainers generally do. They generally pick it, or get it right, the workload or whatever. But you know, some of the horses that have left Australia and raced in America - that we thought when they left would do quite well - have failed. Some of the pigs I've seen go away from here, that I've wondered why they even spent the airfare on - they've been winning races and kept winning."

"Also horses brought to Western Australia from South Australia: the guys over there will tell you they didn't expect some of the horses to do well and they've done marvelously well; others there's been a bit of a wrap on (rated highly) have been disappointing. I believe there is something in them that just the fact of changing the environment has suited, or the different training logic has helped."

"Well just look at some of the experiences people have told me about, within a stable, when they've shifted a horse from one end of the stable to another, or some of these horses that do like to be out in an acre and so on. Mostly by accident, they have changed something, and the horse has improved dramatically. How do people - when they've got fourteen or forty horses in a stable, realize that this one wants to be out in a yard?"

"Not too hard. You get to know your horses as individuals, and I do believe no matter how many horses you've got you really have to take notice of them as individuals. One of the things that'll show up early is that he might not be doing quite as well as he should. That means either you're offending him with the workload, or he's not happy and needs a change of stable. For instance, a lot of horses won't do well locked up. Just put them out in a yard, do no more than that, and they'll eat."

"So that's a very simple thing and very easy to pick. Blind Freddy would see that one. But weaving and all those stable vices - I think that's an environmental drive-the-horse-mad scene. Just change that and he's a happier horse. We've also had conflict between horses: a couple of older stallions that have hated each other and been at each other. Mental stress has been there on a daily basis, and I've shifted one of them from one stable block to another to separate them. Both of them have been better for that."

"As a vet I had been in and out of stables around Perth for years and seen weavers and nodders and horses that stand in corners kicking the fence, horses that are squealing at each other through mesh and going on and on. Lots in one stable - not just the odd one - and I'd never thought a lot about that until one day a trainer said to me, 'If you see stables where they're all weaving and kicking and squealing and so on, and no one's done anything about it, someone needs a kick up the rear.'"

"I think horses are touchy animals too. Some of your aggressive stallions, and horses that at first sight would seem to be aggressive and bad-natured - if you let them go up to another horse, they don't want to bite it, they just want to touch it. They make a bit of a squeal and everything, but those horses are better to be able to touch horses from their stable."

"Well in behavioral terms that's sometimes described as resolving the conflict. With dogs if you keep them apart they'll growl and carry on at each other forever and a day. If you remove the fence between them, one of them will usually give in by body signals. It allows the other one to sniff it in a certain way, and that says, 'All right, you're higher up the ladder than I am,' and the whole relationship changes. But it's unresolved until they touch and find out whether there's going to be a scrap (fight), and even if there has to be a scrap, it is usually sorted out. Do you think with the horses, that touching seems to resolve it?"

"Well, short of letting them have the confrontation, we can't take the risk. Some of those horses I'm talking about, the aggressive one - I'll stable him between two other horses and pick my mark with them, perhaps with a stallion and a gelding each side of him and he will very soon settle down - for the first hour or so there's a bit of bravado, but then they get to be quite good friends. They can reach around the corner of the yard and nuzzle each other, and they don't ever bite. I've had just the odd mean one that's taken a little bit of a nip of the other horse - what you'd describe as mean or vicious - in the short term, but generally speaking, even the most aggressive horse doesn't ever bite the other one."

"Most species have a method of sorting out hierarchy squabbles that falls short of doing actual damage. When I was telling people with dogs to let them get together under supervision and hope they'd sort it out, I used to have my heart in my mouth and one or two people extracted promises of free stitch-ups if this turned into a classic dog fight. Once it did turn into a dog fight, but what surprised me was that very little damage was done. Tremen-

dous amount of noise and scuffle though."

"Dogs are pack killers. They need every able-bodied member to help bring down a deer or whatever, so they need a non-damaging way of sorting out their hierarchy. But in the horse, one stallion will not tolerate another. If you put two stallions that have had mare bands together in a paddock, they'll fight until one is killed. However, stallions that have not had matings or mare bands are often quite tolerant."

"I remember when those two great champions Satinover and Pure Steel had their match race. (This was a match race in 1980 with the whole city's eyes on it, complete with bumper stickers like, 'It's all over Satinover' and 'It's a steal - Pure Steel'.) When they were going out to get ready - I often wondered whether it was intentional or accidental - but Coulson, who was driving Pure Steel, turned him around to great advantage. The two stallions had a screaming match, and at that point, Pure Steel's head was at right angles to and in biting range of the shoulder and neck area of Satinover. Now Satinover could hardly move anywhere, because of the cart. It put Satinover in a submission position at the time of the screeching match. I wondered how much effect that had on the outcome of the race. (Satinover lost.)"

"I've thought about that too, because that was just about the finish of Satinover's winning run. Although he had his moments after that, a lot of people said he lost his heart that night; it was taken out of him, if you like, by Pure Steel. Whether that's correct or not - it may just be a circumstance of time - but the other thing that came into that little bout they had is that Satinover's driver, Max Johnson, tried to avoid the confrontation, which would be your first reaction as a driver. You'd never place two aggressive stallions nose to nose in that sort of situation because they're hyped up for the race. I think Max just tried to get Satinover away from it, which once again put him in a difficult position. You would have been better to let them start at dueling positions and walk towards each other and see which one would have become the aggressor and what would have been the reaction, but as it happened, as they circled around, Pure Steel had all the cards and Satinover had his head turned away by the driver - to move him out of the way - to avoid any confrontation. Whether that left any scars on Satinover I don't know, but it wasn't a fair thing to start with."

"How important is the relationship between horses when they go out to the start, do you think they are trying to sort each other out?"

"I go the other way. I quite like the timid horse as a racehorse, and I think we're talking about the masculine aggressive horse which is into the domination, herd instinct thing. What we're really wanting to do with runners is to get them to break out of that herd instinct. Run away from the others if you like - beat the others. Now, I admire a lot of frail, timid, frightened horses because when they get in a race they seem to feel like they're on even terms and they become good competitors. I don't think a chicken-hearted horse in a fighting contest is necessarily a chicken-hearted horse in a race, so I don't consciously work on trying to get them aggressive. In fact, I try to keep them as nice horses, or 'nice people,' as I like to put it. I just think of them as people."

"Yes, I guess once they get too bullying and aggressive, you've got to castrate some horses to get their mind back on the race."

"That's the other thing too: I'm very happy to race geldings. I think they're courageous. That's something people will always argue about, whether geldings are better racehorses than stallions. Most people think stallions are better. I can't say I believe that. I don't believe their aggressiveness necessarily goes to the racetrack and works for you. Sometimes I'm sure it works against you, because an angry old stallion, he can get real dirty on the world and give up, and if you hit him, he doesn't like it. I'm not one for that."

"There's more to consider with a stallion than a gelding?"

"One of the other things I think you can overdo is the competitive aspect. If you keep putting him down in track work with other horses and essentially he's not a brave horse - in terms of running or racing - it seems to sap his confidence or take out whatever little bit of instinct he has to win. I've had a bit of success working them alone. That horse has gone to the races and shown just a touch more heart in the finish. Some others NEED to go against each other in training to get them mind-right. The lazy fellas and the ones that seem to have a good attitude about beating other horses, those you can train in groups."

"Part of the 'art' of training: knowing which to work by themselves and which to work in a group."

"Sure."

8.1 Fred's training program

"What age do you like to start with young horses?"

"Well, generally speaking, I feel that about one year to eighteen months of age is a good time to start on them. Out of the yearling sales to the breaker. I believe you can start earlier, but there's no special advantage in that. I get some that have been bred on a farm by the farmer. I often start those at one year of age. Also, the sales are in October and some of them are late foals." (The birthday for Standardbreds has been moved from August 1st to September 1st in Australia.)

"So some of these are about one calendar year old?"

"Mm. Can be. The breaker takes them home and then six weeks later he's done his first stint with them and you rest

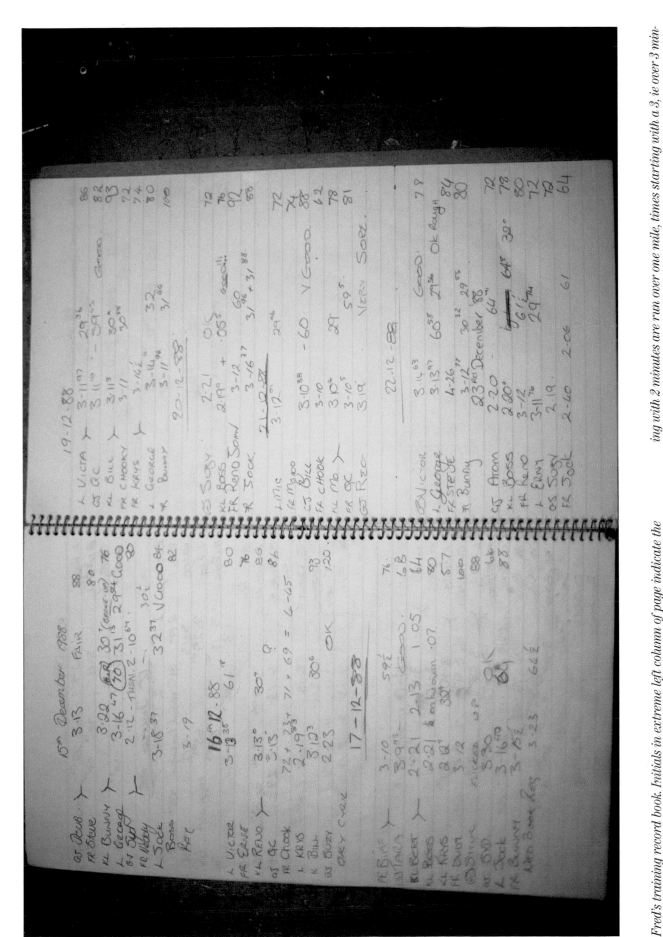

Fred's training record book. Initials in extreme left column of page indicate the driver: GJ is Greg, FR is Fred, KL is Fred, KL is Kellie, L is Lisle. Next column is names of horses. Chook is the stable name for Paavo, the stable star. Lazy Y symbol indicates horses that worked together. The next column is a list of times:- times start-ing with 2 minutes are run over one mile, times starting with a 3, ie over 3 minutes, are run over 1½ miles. The next column contains comments and/or times for the last half or quarter. The extreme right hand column lists the recovery heart rate, taken 8 to 10 minutes after the workout.

them a while."

"What sort of procedures do you like them to be taught at that stage?"

"To be nice and quiet, broken into the cart well. I don't really care if they pace or not."

"Is the next priority the gait?"

"Yes."

"What sort of distances and times would this young horse do over the next few months? Is it entirely a matter of jogging, or does it do some sort of speed?"

"We don't search for any speed at all at this stage. It's just a matter of education, getting him comfortable with his work routine, settled into stable life, learning all the things he will need to do in everyday stable management. Particularly he needs to be good mannered in the sulky, and we'll also get him to the stage where he's starting to establish his pacing gait. That's about all we're going to do in the first month of the preparation."

"When does this young horse first start to put some miles into its legs?"

"Through that first month. He will gradually build his jogging period up to about five miles, and he'll reach that stage after about three weeks and settle into it. At that stage we start to put the hobbles on him so he becomes adjusted to the pacing. Most of them these days are quite natural at that, so it's not very difficult for them."

"They're doing five miles at a jog. How long, roughly, would they take to do that five miles?"

"Just over thirty minutes. You might take thirty-five minutes, might take a little less, just depending on the attitude of the horse. Some are just a little more bold than others."

"How many days a week?"

"They work six days a week, which they would handle very comfortably. They get a rest Sundays. Having put the foundation into them, and starting to go into the hobble work, which is where we're going to look for the speed, we will then bring the work load down a little bit in terms of distance. We go over to the track and work, say, two miles at the jog, and let the horse move over a half mile at the speed he's comfortable at. Now, some of them really don't have any special ability to go much faster than a jog at this stage, and others are more inclined to want to go a little bit. So around that time you see the development of different horses' different abilities and attitudes. But we work from that slightly quicker half mile and repeat it and let him come along as comfortably as he can work without any pressure or any stress on him. Let him make his own way down and break down his times fairly quickly if he can."

"At this stage, do you have much of a problem with horses that want to go faster than you want them to go?"

"Not at this stage, generally speaking, because they haven't learnt about speed. All they've learnt up to this stage is to go slow, but from here on in, we start to see some getting a little speed crazy, and others that are just naturally lazy."

"Does the rate of progress at this stage give you much of a guide to ability, or is that separate from ability?"

"I think it's separate. It's linked to attitude more than ability. Some seem to have a nicer style than others, and they're the sort of horses you start getting a bit more interested in because they're more natural at it. With these younger horses, they're the ones that are going to make it through to the two-year-old racing, because they need to be natural - I guess only 10% of them are going to make it to the two-year-old races. So they need to be natural at it if they're going to be worthwhile."

"In the second preparation you start to wonder whether you should be spending more time with this horse or if you're putting him on the sack list. You really want to know if he can go a little bit."

"So even as early as that second preparation you're getting some idea of what his speed is?"

"The owner's demands mean you've just got to."

"Do you see at this stage of their training, any horses you can cull because of their gait or their sheer lack of speed? "

"Yes, in the next few weeks, that's one of our objectives: to look at the ones that are not as good as the others, and make commercial decisions on them. If they're especially bad-gaited or they're especially bad tempered, it can start to show up around there. I'll give those horses special attention to see if I can train through it. If I can't, I have to talk to the owner along the lines of, 'Well, we look like we've got problems here. Now we've got to make decisions."

"On the gait side of it, is it only a matter of interference type problems, or do some of them step so high or have such a low action you can say, 'that is a very inefficient action'?"

"At this age, it's more of a coordination problem, which is reflected in the gait. They're not interfering much, although they show the tendencies, even in this early stage. I find that most of these horses are not natural. It's a coordination problem, which they may overcome in a year or two, but we're not prepared to wait that long for them these days. A commercial decision has to be made, and it comes back to the owner. Does he want to wait or does he want to sack?"

"Do you sack many horses out of that second preparation group?"

"Oh yes. About half of them."

"Your criterion for sacking - is speed over the last furlongs important?"

"The way they go, their attitude; they start to develop their little traits; also they're becoming good-gaited or they're not. They're a little bit nicer horses. Some are nicer than others.

Gut feeling a little bit. After you get the gut feeling one's no good, then you do start to put some real effort into getting him to prove he's no good. If he can turn around and show me a couple of signs I don't like, I will advise the owner he could quit the horse with a real good chance of not being wrong."

"And this is about eighteen months old?"

"Yes. Now, some of those horses are going to win when they're four and five, but we really can't stay in there that long, and it's OK if you're right - I like to think I'm 80 to 90% right about that time. I think if you're only half right you shouldn't."

"They're probably easier to sell at that age and stage?"

"Yes, there is a chance they're going to make it, because you could quite clearly and fairly advertise that this horse has had twelve weeks education - been broken and had six weeks training and that's where he is. But there isn't a big demand for this type of horse anyhow."

"Because everyone knows they really **have** *been tried?"*

"Well, there's just not a big demand for horses. We've got an oversupply of horses. I often advise at a professional level that the fellow stop spending money on his horse. Now he might choose to lease it out, or if he really was keen on the horse - liked the way it was bred and had some emotional involvement - I might say to him, 'Right, if you can find a cheap way of keeping it for six months or so, then do that and then we'll give it another six weeks and see if it may have improved."

"Things like learning driving tactics - to sit and to pull out - who teaches them that?"

"Usually me, and the whole training process is developed around just that. Once we know the horses we think have the potential to go to the races - we've established that they're good-gaited enough and they're nice enough horses and they've got enough speed - then we teach them that. And they do that by just working on their own."

"So you don't have a time that is a minimum over some distance as a cut-off point in determining which horses to keep?"

"No, I don't."

"I've met people who do have something like that."

"I think my answer to the question is no, I don't. I can tell you what times some horse has run, but that didn't mean I was going to keep him or sack him. I've seen some pretty fast ones over a couple of furlongs very early that I still didn't like much, and I've kept some others that just had a little more of a laid-back attitude that went nearly as quick, but went to the line a little more convincing."

"Here in Perth they'll run some two-year-old races in October. But I don't want to race them before they've had their second birthday. I really never want to do that. If I can get a couple of months after that before I take them to the races, I'll be very happy to do that too. There is one feature race for two-year-olds in December, so they will have been in pretty solid work from August. But I'm not really looking to race them until January if I can have it that soft. There'll be some owner pressures and some demands to get there earlier than that, but I resist that and I won't be tuning them right up until perhaps January."

"They are all doing six weeks in and six weeks out, but as you go along the lesser ones start to spend more time out. Some of them might be put aside for later. But once we've got the better ones and we like them and we think they're going to the races, then we start to be very careful about their manners, and we teach them to go slowly before we teach them to go fast. We don't want them to just come out crazy. We want them to come out and be off the bit and to enjoy what they're doing, to get a good attitude about their work, and we come off the track knowing they could do a bit more."

"Perhaps we should clarify the meaning of 'on the bit' to you?"

"Communication from the driver to the horse is through the reins to the bit. Now, I often think one of the disadvantages of driving horses rather than riding them is you can't touch them. So it's a little like phoning up and asking them. It is a request at all times. Would you move left, would you move right, would you go faster, would you go slower? That's all it can ever be, because you can't have any more influence than that. I'm not sure there isn't even a little bit of mental telepathy in there somewhere. I'm not sure. There is sometimes. And some of them don't tune in either. Some tune in better than others. So what you're really wanting the horse to do is respond very kindly to what you're asking. Now some of them get just a little bit speed crazy by nature and they just fire up on to the bit and want to go. Then you've got a wrestle on your hands. He's on the bit and you're trying to get him back.   It's when the horse is going against what the driver wants. He's trying to tell you what to do, he's on the bit and he's starting to pull you along. That's what I mean by on the bit."

"Can they actually grab the bit in their teeth or is it just an expression, saying it took the bit between its teeth?"

"I think they get the bit under their first molar, down under the gum, and they pull against their molar."

"Which wouldn't worry them."

"Well, it does hurt the gum a little bit. You'll get a horse a bit sore in the mouth, on the gums just where the first molar's coming, and usually one side more than the other, because he'll start shifting his head a little bit to help himself. Once he gets a little sorer on one side, he'll try to take the weight on the other side."

"But they don't actually get it between their teeth?"

"No, if they get the bit between their teeth, you can't steer them."

"Do they ever do that?"

"I've had a couple of pigs in races that have been clever enough to do it, and you knock their head off."

"You can pull and their head doesn't even turn around?"

"No. The bit's too high in their mouth. They've pulled their bloody mouth right up tight, and they're uncomfortable, but so are you because you've lost a bit of control, and it's damn hard to get them to drop it down lower. It's infrequent. More often than not, they carry the bit down, but when I say on the bit, it means he's got more weight on the bit than he should have and he's wanting to go more than he should do."

"It's pretty nice though, turning for home if he's on the bit. Most of them are off the bit by that stage and calling on all of their resources. So turning around the home corner it still means the same thing, but you'd be happy enough about it if they're on the bit. But in training we would prefer they didn't. We deal with some terrible 'mules' at different times. They come out of different stables and some of them are so ignorant you can't believe it. But you've still got to work at those horses in different ways to try to get them to be kinder, because as a driver, for me to win races with horses, it's a team effort. It's not much good him fighting me or me fighting him. We really have to get together in this thing and try to get home first."

"So you try to keep them off the bit in training?"

"Yes. Off the bit to the point where the horse will do exactly what I want him to do, and will rate within half a second at any given time without any effort, of the rate I want him to run."

"What sort of speed would these young horses get up to?"

"Depending on the breaker and of course, the horse. Myself, I don't look for any speed. As I said, if it doesn't want to pace I don't care. But I think it's important he becomes very tractable and he's confident about being in the cart and handles well. Then I think he shouldn't have too long off, about a month to six weeks, then try him again for six weeks. If you had lots of money to spend you could train him softly for an extended period, maybe keeping him in work for six months. But trying to keep the owners' costs down, I think you could quite effectively work for six weeks and then stand him down - then giving him six weeks more concentrated training. You'll get to about where you were going anyhow, because we're not really trying to get them super fit, we're just increasing the speed over short distances."

"What sort of speed over what sort of distances?"

"A lot of them just feel their own way. You let them go the best they can go which might be a half mile in 75 seconds. Some of them are slower than that: might go in 80 seconds. Some of the ones that aren't natural gaited could be even slower: 85 seconds. But even the one's that can go a bit, you

wouldn't want them to go in less than 70, 72. You go a couple of half miles a day and they start to bring the times down. Some of them realize they can run but I don't let them - I suppose I bring them down two or three seconds a week. Once I've got them down to 65 second halves, I might hold them there for some time; like leggy ones and so on, there is no point going any harder. Others tell me they can go a little faster."

"At this stage they are doing how many fast days a week?"

"A slow learning colt, I'll put the gear on every day, until he starts to work hard, then I feel like I ought to make the next day a bit easier so that will be a jog day. One that is natural gaited and can go a bit, as soon as he goes under 70 seconds I'll work him three times a week; every second day and Sunday off."

"So what would that horse do on the fast work day? Start with a warm up?"

"Jog two miles, then work a half mile; jog a mile; work another half mile; jog a lap and come off. At the stage of wanting to get him fitter, I just stick another half on that, to put some legs under him."

"That's interval training."

"I use it until I get near the first trial."

Interval training

"Intervals have been quite a subject in the racing fraternity since Tom Ivers brought his book out. Did you read Tom Ivers' book?"

"Yes, I did."

"And you tried interval training."

"Yes, along with most other people I tried it, and I've got to say right here and now that perhaps it's a training method of the future, but for me, that's where it is. It's pretty much in the future. I have done a little bit of it, and where I think it's got special value is in the development of younger horses. They're receptive to it because they've not known any other way. They do come to hand a little quicker which is good from the owner's point of view, and if he can do it, and do it easily, why not? So I think it's good value in that respect. However I'm not sure that after I've got that initial advantage, that there's any special advantage for me to train by interval work over the methods that I've used for perhaps the last thirteen or fourteen years."

"So, Fred, in your conventional program, on a fast work morning, what would your horse do? How many miles at what sort of speed?"

"Well, if we're talking about our raceway horses, which by and large are called on to race about 2400 to 2500 metres (1½ miles), we'll race and work that distance, and we'd work very close to the intensity of the race, depending on the class of the horse. If he was one of the best horses in the State, that needed to rate two minutes in the 2500, he'd need to work close to that. I don't think you could stretch out the gross time for his training runs any more than five seconds away from what he'd need to win the race."

"Would he train once, twice, in the week between races?"

"All a little different. If they race on a weekly basis, most horses will get away with one hit out in between. Some of them will race a little better doing it twice. I've got a feeling most horses will race better not locked into a seven day time frame. I think the seven day week is not always in the best interest of horses, and I think they could handle six or eight or maybe ten days. Training could be a lot better than having to just get locked into this seven day time frame."

"What sort of intervals did you try?"

"I guess I got stuck on the half miles, because of the half mile track, and the horse would do five of those half miles, starting off relatively slowly and then letting them build up. I've found that about their third heat, they are wanting to get on their way a little bit, and they go just a little quicker than you want them to. The fourth one's okay, but the fifth one, lots of times, was too much."

"What were you using for a rest interval? Was that a fixed time or did you have a heartrate meter on them."

"I had heartrate meters, and found that essentially, a fit horse gets back pretty quick to an acceptable heartrate of something around the 80's and 90's. He comes back within two to three minutes, but there are other factors with heartrate meters, such as the attitude of the horse, other horses on the track with him - that flares up the heart rate. So it's not an accurate guide, though I do think it's a good guide if you can measure it accurately. Our difficulty is in being able to do that."

"So you've had problems with the heartrate meters?"

"Yes, but it depends on what you expect from a heartrate meter. I think if you expect too much, you'll have lots of problems."

"Well, they're usually reliable at the lower heartrates. Their weakness is in telling you accurately what the heartrate is once it is over 200 beats per minute. So, did you find any horses that you think you improved with intervals?"

"I can't think of one that I could say to you, this definitely improved him."

"Did you have any problems with horses becoming lame or so called speed crazy?"

"There were some that started to get speed crazy, and there were some that you wouldn't even attempt to do it with, because those horses had been trained under a different method and they couldn't change. That's why I began to use it on the youngsters. They didn't know anything else, they were more receptive to it. That's where I really thought I got my value, from the youngsters. Certainly interval training has the potential to drive them mad. I think it's probably got value for the old horse that is sluggish and almost determined not to run. He seems to become a better athlete, if you like, but in saying that, I'm still not convinced it makes him any better than he was."

"So what was your time between heats, your relief period?"

"I tried it with the younger horses to start with and basically they were doing half miles with the time for the relief period about double whatever the work period was. They went three half mile heats, if they could cope. If they started to rev up, I'd put a mile in and give them a relief period of twice whatever a mile took, then finish with a half."

"But I found that as I got close to the race I kept going back to what I knew. Today, I'm fairly convinced the future of training will be in interval training. The benefit will come with a new wave of trainers, not inhibited by what has happened before. They will have a bit more confidence, and more of an open mind. See, I find it a bit more difficult: the pressure is on you to perform; you cannot afford to make mistakes; there is owner pressure; the pressure you put on yourself; the horse is valuable. As the race approaches you are not confident enough to experiment. That is about where I get to."

"I see very good value in it for developing horses fairly quickly. They want to do it; they can do it easily; so they do it. They log a lot more miles without hurting themselves."

"Why didn't you take interval training closer to the race? Wasn't it getting them fit enough, or was there some problem?"

"Two things happened. Once you get into your last month before racing, you are into trials and those trials tend to get harder, and become the distances they're racing. So they trial once a week: what are you going to do in the middle? You could continue with the intervals or you could just go the mile and a quarter or mile and a half or whatever. They are young horses and the trialing is stretching them to their limits. Then they are into races. I'm not comfortable hitting horses up for hundred thousand dollar races a month or two after their second birthday - and yet we have to do it. I have the feeling those runs hurt them, so I'm looking for something that will be kind to them in the time I have between races."

"If I was in your boots I'd be more daring with the ones that are too slow or have already reached their mark (Gone as far as its ability will take it)."

"Yes I guess I could be a little more daring and experimental with some of them and take it further."

"I would think the average owner whose horse is too slow or failing to improve would be pleased if you tried something different with it."

"There would be a problem if you bugger it up, because once you get out of the ballots to get into a race - if you haven't got race form with the horse you go out of the computer ballot - that extends the time between runs and the costs of a horse you don't like very much anyhow."

"Most trainers at the Meadowlands apparently go two or three heats in a morning. They go say three-quarters of a mile, or a mile, take the gear off, cool the horse out to some degree and maybe even put it away. Later they bring it out for the next heat, and so on."

"That must increase the degree of difficulty, taking the gear off, putting them away, putting the gear back on. In a hot climate like ours in summer, you'd spend all morning and you still wouldn't be halfway through your team. You'd start to wonder why you were doing it. They might be staffed better than us, perhaps have one staff person for two horses."

"How many do you have?"

"One per three or four, but some of them cannot help you much with the driving."

"How many weeks would you say - from the time you get it back from the breaker - is about average for this new young horse before it gets to its first trial race?"

"He'd probably have two goes at it. He'll do about six to eight weeks training, depending on how naturally he runs, and then he'll go for perhaps another month in agistment, then he'll come back and repeat this development but at a quicker rate. So after two or three weeks, we're letting him run a quarter mile fairly fast, and he's also starting to want to run, and that's important. He starts to develop that natural competitive attitude, and the good ones make very quick progress in the second of their six week training stints."

"So they've had two blocks of six weeks. Are they ready to trial?"

"They are starting to show now that they're the horses that ought to be trained to a level of fitness you can trial on. See, what we've really done is to find out which are more likely to run well. Having done that, we set about conditioning them physically. Until then, not much conditioning goes into them. By the third time round they've got a pretty good idea what training is about, and we start building up some legs, developing the muscle and the bone structure."

"Okay. In the third stint, you're down to the group that you think has a chance of winning. What percentage of the horses you started with, is left?"

"It alters from year to year. You just seem to get a batch of yearlings that are nice, and then the next year you wonder what happened. They're just not as good. I suppose no more than about 10% look like they're going to be money-earners. I think another 15% could race, but race unsuccessfully, and I say to the owners, 'There's no point in trying to race a horse that can't win any money. You're only teaching him to lose.'

"On the slow days, how far in how long?"

"They would work up to six or seven miles in about 35 minutes average, around the outside of the track. I work my babies as far as my older horses. Initially I kept them back. They did a couple of miles less than the racehorses. I have an attitude that young horses are like young people: they are naturally fit. I think they handle the jogging miles. They tend to get a bit above themselves, get a bit cheeky, but I don't find they get tired or leg weary."

"Have you tried going further?"

"I haven't tried more, I've thought about it but I have the view that jogging is not increasing the fitness. I don't think it helps you in a race. But I put together some fairly frequent fast days in this training stint until they get to the stage where a horse could work, say a half mile in 65 seconds. I won't ask him to do that every day: I'll give him easier days in between. If he can get down from 65 to about 62 or 61 seconds, which the nice ones want to do, then we don't go any faster at this stage, but we start to extend the distance. So from the half mile we start getting him up to the miles."

"How many fast days a week, in this stage?"

"He would be doing four days initially, perhaps, and then the faster, the more intense the work gets, and the harder it is on them, the less often they get it. We get back to three, and by the time we go to the trials, I'd say no more than three and probably back to two fast days in the week. I like to run them in at least five simulated races, trials, and that's going to take six or seven weeks. We have night trials under simulated race conditions. You've got the lights and the mobile starting gate."

"What is your approach to their trial races?"

"I like simulated race conditions, under lights. I like to go about five times. A lot of trainers don't; if their horses have got the speed they will go once or twice and go into races. I don't. I like them to learn to go slow in those races, and not to rush out of the gate."

"So you like them to have five outings under those conditions?"

"Yes I do, before I think they are ready to go to the races, where there's money and where it's more intense and they're expected to perform at their highest level. The great advantage of trials is that there's no money bet, and you can give the horse an easy run. If he gets a little frightened in a tight situation, you can back him out; he's got a lot of flexibility and so have you, and I think that's important. I've seen a lot of horses go to the races off one or two trials and then when they get into a difficult situation, they panic. I like them to build confidence. So I go to the trials fairly soon, and I don't mind if he runs behind the field. He's allowed to go there, under-conditioned if you like, but well- mannered; not really competitive with some of the other horses that could be more forward. I'm not disappointed if he just keeps up. I don't expect him to win. I don't even want him to win the trial."

"What do they have to show you to go to the racetrack?"

"He'll answer those questions by his trial performance, which as I said, simulates as near as you can the racing conditions. He'll start to look pretty clever at the trials and he'll start to be more than competitive with the other batch of horses, bearing in mind that he only runs in his own age group. So he's starting to show you he can handle the class quite easily, and in terms of times, I guess he's got to have the capacity to run miles in 2 minutes 5 seconds. If he couldn't do that, there wouldn't be very much point in taking him to the races."

"At this stage, are you experimenting with the horse's gear? Are you trying different hobble lengths?"

"Yes, we're getting to the stage where we need him to be set up very well in his gear, so he can race in the intense competition of the racetrack. Whereas he can bowl around the training track without any pressure on him and he won't make mistakes, under the intense competition of races, he's got a lot of demand on him and the gearing becomes very important. His gear is a very good aid to him under race conditions. We like to get the right hobble length and that's the time when you should be experimenting with that, which only means you're going out a little in the gear and coming up a little to find out where he just feels a little better. The head gear is very important; what are you going to put on his head? Is he going to wear blinkers or shadow rolls and different bits and head checks and all that sort of thing? I don't like to make it any harder than it is, and if he can go without all of these things, that's good, and I'll only add to it if I see a special need."

"Now, horses for courses. How do you select which horses you're going to send to the country and which you're going to race in the city? Do you work that out principally from the times they're delivering to you in the trials?"

"Yes. By the time you've got through the trial standard, you are not only measuring your own horse, but you've been able to measure the other horses you've got to compete with. So where we go is where we've got a chance of winning. If he's not able to win in the city, and the standard's a little less down the line, then he could win some money in the country, so it works itself out."

"Are there certain sorts of races that you go for as their first race?"

"The horses that I'm beginning to like a bit, I'm very careful with. I tend to take my time and look for races that I like, tracks that I like. I don't want to put him in over his depth. Those better horses - even in their training I like them to feel like they can do it, that they can win. I like them to keep a winning attitude."

"So which ones do you have lose in a race between horses at home?"

"I don't think it's a matter of losing although some are smart enough to get up and try to win. If he can get up alongside of the other horse, and he still hasn't quite got to his top, he's not unhappy with that. If you press him hard and it's hurting and he can't get up alongside, and you keep doing that - then he learns, 'What is the point? It's just hurting me'. I will often work these babies with good horses, because they are better mannered, can pull me out and so on, but I don't get to the bottom of him. He's always able to go on home with something left. How much left I never know, but I'm hoping there is more and more and more. The really good horses you take longer to get to the bottom. Some you thought had it but you only get halfway. You really find out how good the horse is when you put him in a stakes race and everyone else puts in their best horses. But the place money in the stakes race is better than first money in a non-stakes race."

"When you start them in racing, do you start them in shorter events or do you already know their best distance?"

"Two-year-olds don't go beyond 1700 meters until later in the season so you are pretty well locked into that. I don't hold the view that a 2100m race is necessarily harder than a 1700m race. A 1700m race is more intense and the pressure is on a lot earlier. So I'm not concerned about letting them go the extra distance as long as the first half is not too quick. But the babies do tend to come out of the gate with a lot of speed and enthusiasm and not much else. They can lay down a 30 second quarter as easily as the free-for-all horses."

"So many of them are bred from American stallions and American horses are bred for an excitement level suitable for racing one mile."

"It is critical that you don't press them for too much speed at that stage because you'll hurt them, and their bones are still developing and you do strain them."

"Okay, the horse is racing, what do you do with it for the week between races?"

"He wouldn't work the next day."

"What does that mean? Does he stay in his stall or does he get walked or-"

"My stalls are walk-in walk-out, they're not boxed. The horse is taken out and put in a large roll yard for a roll and a look around. He's bandaged, medicated on any cuts or scratches and put back. Basically he does nothing. It is remarkable that on Sunday which is our non-work day, a large percentage of the horses lay down and rest, whereas on other days they don't. They seem to know it's Sunday and they seem to like Sunday. They must know from the routine, and more of them lay down at mid-morning than on any other day. They are more contented than on any other day. So: one or two easy days following the race. Then there are only two options in my book: one fast work in between or two. When you are searching for improvement you go the two, and when you are happy, you go the one. You can go none but for me it never works."

"Why? Do they get too fresh to hold? Do they lack punch at the finish next time out?"

"No they don't get too fresh, they don't seem too different; they just don't do as well."

"They don't have it at the end in particular?"

"Mmmmm, yes."

"So say they go out twice, what will they do?"

"Simulated race conditions, 2400 (1½ miles) to 2600 meters, with a mile rate of around 2:08, the last half as quick as they want to go without busting. A last half in 59 and a fast last quarter."

"If you are going to run them twice at home during the week between races, do you make the two runs equal, or the first one harder, or the second one harder?"

"I don't have a routine there. If he raced Friday say, and I was concerned that he hadn't gotten over the run still, I'd soften up that run on the Monday, but on Wednesday he'd have to go good. I can't see any reason to be hard on them on a Monday after a Friday race, so I might let that one go by a couple of seconds slower. You could throw in a couple of miles pace work, just to put some legs on him."

"When you work a two-year-old, how many seconds slower than it's best would you work it? If you think it's best effort would be, say, a two minutes two second mile, would you work it 3 seconds slower, 6 seconds slower?"

"I think a two-year-old can race ten seconds better than his track work at a mile, and if he could get away with it, I'd let him do that."

"You don't think he suffers a bit after the race?"

"No, because he's a juvenile, he's fit. Say he's going to run in two minutes and I train him in two-ten, but his last quarter mile or even his last six hundred would be at race speed. It's not as though he hasn't reached that speed, but do I want him to carry on and run another quarter mile at that speed? No, because then I start hurting him a little bit, he's going to say, 'Ouch. Do I need to do that?" (Note: I don't want any editor-types writing to tell me horses can't speak. Any other advice I'll be pleased to accept.)

"It's been put to me that anything that hurts them on race day - they don't remember, but they'll remember it if it's on a training track. It may relate to the level of effort and the release of endorphins which are natural pain killers."

"Interesting point."

Comparing younger and older horses

"What do you do differently with two-year-olds compared to older horses?"

"Well, just as I believe that kids and young people are basically fit, I think it's the same with young horses. Older horses, like older people, have to work harder at it."

"As kids we used to ride our bikes everywhere. We used to run up and down sandhills at the beach on Sunday, throw balls and wrestle each other halfway to death. When you got too hot, you'd jump in the water, get dumped by a wave, come back out - and that went on almost all our waking hours. As an adult you don't do those things. I take the attitude that young horses are basically fit and don't need to be drilled as much. They need to be worked enough to keep them sensible, they don't want to be too much above themselves. But old horses have to be drilled - not shorter, not less frequent, but not as hard."

"So they do it just as often but at a lower percentage of their top?"

"If you give the young horse short, sharp work, you'll be driving him speed mad. He'll think all he has to do is sprint like a Quarter Horse, and that's not what we need. If I was training a sprinter at the gallops and he only had to race a thousand metres, I might do that, but my horses have to race at least a mile. That is middle distance; he's got to conserve his energy, so I'm not wanting to sharpen him up too much; I've got to keep enough legs in him. But the old grinders, they're getting a bit of age on them. I think four-year-olds are harder to train than three-year-olds, and I've noticed this for quite a few years now. I've had nice three-year-olds, easy to train, and they came in as four-year-olds, the same nice horse, but more difficult to train. It is easier to make errors in their training."

"Do you find they are more frequently sour or disinterested in running?"

"Less fit more than anything else. I also think that some horses, some of the champion horses, retain that young horse level of fitness. Pure Steel was a great example. He was like a bloody trout. You know, you didn't have to get him fit, he just WAS fit. He was trained by seven or eight different people and went just the same for all of them. So the trainer really had a negative input into that horse. Pure Steel was just great. And I feel that some of the super athletes - the elite of the horse world - probably had a characteristic where they retained that youthful fitness level. Some of the others were nice horses too, but it was harder to keep them fit, and it may be that one of the things that makes some of those super horses great is that they had an inherited ability to be fit. There are some families that have juveniles that don't train on. We quite often take the attitude that this horse won't get any better; may as well maximize him now. There are some others that are slow to come for various reasons."

"I would have thought that if there was a group that could do something at two and at three, they would have to swamp stallions whose offspring could only do some-

thing at two. So, to my way of thinking, there must be some advantage to that group that are only good as two-year-olds, just for them to be still in the population. Is it simply that they win more, total, when they're two than that group that comes a bit later? That's the only reason I can think of that they're still in the racing population."

"One of the things we don't do is race our horses to find out who's the best: what you do is you run in and out of classes. The competition at the tail end of the two-year-old season is very intense. Then, beginning your three-year-old season, the higher quality stock are being rested a bit. Now your second-rate two-year-old, which has become an early three-year-old, can win some money. You can have a field that is all non-winners. Something's going to win. You do see that happen. They bring themselves together as classes of horses. A trainer's expertise is to try to get one of his good ones in with the bad ones. You don't keep banging your head against the top ones if you've got a mediocre group."

"There is quite a problem for the trainer in that group where you think they might be top class but it's not really clear that they are. You've got to make the choice: if you put them aside, first of all you lose some time, then you put them in with the top class and they may get thrashed

five races in a row. If you'd left them in a lower grade or started earlier and so on, they may have cleaned up some money. Difficult decision to make."

"Placing horses is an art. It's also fair to say that you could have a lovely horse this season, say a three-year-old colt, that last year or next year, could have won the Derby, but if a couple of blokes have got one the same year as you, that's a little faster than yours, that's just very bad luck. The following year you turn up with a horse that's not as good as him, and he's a standout in his year. These things happen. There's a luck factor and that's racing."

"You've got a better temperament for that than I have. I hate anything where luck is a major factor. In racing you can do everything right and carefully, and you can still lose."

"Well, the glorious uncertainty of racing is a phrase that's stood the test of time. It's true and never becomes less true."

Race frequency

"The frequency with which you race a horse - do you try them weekly to see if they can stand it, or is there something that tells you they need more space between their races?"

"When he first comes into competition, I think it's a bit dan-

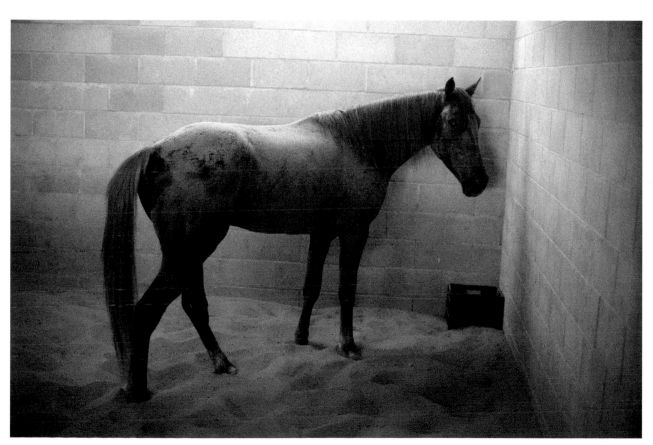

Horse in the sandroll. The concrete bricks are the same throughout the stable and the sand floor is the same in all stalls, but the sandroll is larger.

gerous to go back week after week. I would give him a fort-night and go back again. If he was racing well at that, I might hold him there for a time. If he started to disappoint, or wasn't quite measuring up, then I might put two or three weekly runs together, on the basis that maybe I can get a him little fitter by racing more often. I also have to keep in mind that I can always overdo that, that I am stretching him, and if I stretch too far I'll break him: so it's a judgment that you have to make. I don't like to go to the races and just program him to race every week. I think there's a little more finesse needed."

"What percentage of your horses would you race once a week and what percentage would you race once every two weeks? (Pacing in metropolitan Perth is on Mondays and Fridays, with country races on other nights.)"

"Neither, really. It's harder than that. I reckon the seven day week is a pain to trainers. It would be much better if it was eight days and you raced once every eight days."

"A lot of gallopers are on a ten day cycle or two week cycle. So for your pacers - sometimes it'd be once a week, sometimes might be every two weeks, sometimes in between?"

"I might make it a couple of times in the week, because there were two better races and I would miss the next one which I thought he couldn't win anyhow. That would give him a fortnight off in between. So I'm a bit inclined to run one, two, three runs - miss one and go again, but I won't just say this horse likes racing every fortnight, and religiously bang him in every fortnight. I don't think you should do that. I don't think that he can race every week for a year or anything like that. But he can do quite a bit of racing - you can put thirty to forty starts in him in a campaign, without too much demand on him. It can happen. It's possible to do a lot more, and there are a lot of horses that are doing that."

"In certain situations you could let them race at least once a week, and probably even more often, and get away with it: if he was a horse that had that sort of disposition, that sort of constitution, and preferably ran less than his top. That's not such a bad thing if he's earning. See, I often feel that if you peak a horse, you climb the mountain; there's only one way to go; you've got to come down. I think if they just plateau somewhere up near that peak, and if they're being effective in earning, then it's nice and you can let that horse run often."

"It must be useful when he goes up a grade, to know that there's a bit more."

"When it's really necessary and you try for a little bit more, that's when you're going to run into a bit of a problem, because if he can do more he will, but if he can't he's going to hurt - he's going to get worse."

"What do you do when a horse's next win or two is going to put it into another grade, and that's probably going to be too much for it? You've got to sell it, I guess."

"Yes, I suppose you live in hope a little bit. Now is the time to start to sell him, if you can. You trade out of him depending on where the moneys are and where the emotions are, or else acknowledge the situation and then downgrade him. Run him back into claimers for less money - still being fairly nice to him, but you've dropped him down where he can earn."

"Pacers can go backwards in Australia can they?"
"Claiming races are down grades."

"But are they running many of those, or just a few?"
"We're at the stage here of about one a week and it should be more. I really feel half our program ought to be claimers."

"A lot of people have wanted to bring them into the gallopers in Australia, but it's been a big failure because the owners either won't risk them at all, or want unrealistic prices for them."

"Well, the owners and the administrators can't cope, that's what it means. But the logic is there for claimers. It's a handicap system and it's the most effective and accurate handicap system ever invented."

"The English have selling plates. We seem to be one of the countries without any of that kind of racing. It's well and truly in place in America."

Spelling a horse (Turning it out)
"What brings you to the point of deciding a horse needs a spell?"

"In these very hard economic times: when he stops earning."

"Only then!"

"Yes, that's the only reason to spell. Even if he's gone lame, that will cause him to stop earning anyhow. Generally when he stops earning. But if he's a top horse, and he comes through his classics, then you've got to look at the next season's classics, you've got to logically program where he ought to be and we're locked in then, to dates. When you're training your best group of horses, which are heading for feature races, you need to program your horse. A nice two-year-old, when he breaks off at the end of his two-year-old season, he's got to start looking at the Derby, or if it's a filly, the Oaks, and that timespan will then say look, we've got six weeks here that we could spend effectively by resting him, and then build his training up."

"I think one of the mistakes that you can make with your best horses is try to win every big race: then you might win hardly any of them. But if you cover your best races and the time frame, and then spell your horse accordingly, you can give him the maximum chance of taking part, and racing well when the big run is there."

"From a trainer's point of view that's the hardest thing to do - to get him back in great shape on the day they've allocated the race. That's really testing you a little bit. You can't be wrong. You've got to be right. If he gets a cold halfway through his preparation, you didn't want that but you've still got to arrive. They're not going to put the race back a fortnight because your horse had a cold. So they are the demands on your special horses, and I think that is where we make most of our mistakes. I think that is where good trainers are better than some other trainers, being able to consistently and repeatedly do that."

"Fewer setbacks in training? Better able to catch up?"

"Well, make less mistakes. But with your raceway horses and the economic situation we're dealing with, why rest him if he's earning? There's no point."

"So the others - you just keep them going and then spell them if they have a patch when they're not earning?"

"I have one now, he's in his fifth year of training and he hasn't been out of the stable. In his third year he was racing as good as, or better than ever. But give him six, eight weeks off - there's not a great cost there - but then it's going to take me twelve weeks more to get him back to the races. What have I done? I've wasted five months out of a horse's year. How many years will he race anyhow? With gallopers it's still good logic too. If you get a horse that's basically fit - let's say he's 90% fit and he's running quite well - because I don't know whether you ever get to the 100%, that's pretty magic up there - but just say 90% of fitness, and you put him in the paddock and he drops down to 20% of fitness. Then you've got to pick him up. There are some demands being made. You're trying to get him back up there."

"So it's less stressful to hold him there, than to let him down and then try and pull him up again?"

"For you and me, wouldn't it be? So why not for him? You do stress them on the way up. Now once they're there you don't have to stress them nearly as much. They get used to most things, it's just the change that worries them."

"Sorin Nordin, who is approaching God status in harness racing in Sweden and America, hardly lets up on his youngsters once they go into work, whereas most other trainers ease up or turn them out periodically, like you do. He pushes his very hard, but he's apparently one hell of a legs man. He can fix a lot of things other people can't fix in the legs."

"I've not kept stats, but I have a gut feeling that most breakdowns occur in the prep. So I think there is a lot of logic in keeping your horses in work once you've reached that level. There is one old bugger here that I mentioned to you before, he came into work in March 1984, and he is still in work (November 1988). I'm scared to spell the old bugger now because I guess he wouldn't come back. But he maintains himself very well and he races quite consistently."

"Not all horses are good enough to race all year. The lesser stock have got to be programmed into the weaker races, which in Western Australia is winter time. It's not as though there is a lesser track you can drop them off onto. In the summer months the good horses race everywhere, and the best thing you can do with your lesser horses is spell them then."

Assessing the workload -
Using the recovery heart rate

When heart rate meters became the rage, Fred and his vet gave them a try but eventually Fred retained only the recovery heart rate. After track work, and after races, a stethoscope is used to take the heart rate 8 to 10 minutes after the finish. Fred finds, as have many other people, that in general the best horses have the lowest heart rates. I asked Fred if he had any particular uses for these recovery heart rates, such as a guide to a particular horse's level of fitness, but he could not name any particular cut-off points or heart rates he aims for. The recovery heart rate seems to go into his general summation with a lot of other information about how the horse is going.

"I would be interested to know if the heart rate of the same horse over a period of years goes down. Some of the old retired champions, when you listen to them, have very slow resting heart rates - 19 or 20 beats a minute. Do you see a slow decline in the recovery heart rate over a number of years?"

"I couldn't answer that. One of the difficulties in addressing that is that generally speaking we are training two-year-olds very conservatively, three-year-olds do a bit more and four-year-olds are given a harder task when they become raceway horses."

Blood electrolytes

"Williamson in New Zealand, wrote about blood electrolytes and how much a horse blows. There's enough evidence around to convince me, both from my own exercise efforts, and from talking to trainers and vets, that there's more than just how much work the horse has done and how fit it is, to how much it blows. Do you, occasionally see some horses that are flattened but they don't blow much after a race, or conversely, some horses that blow like hell yet they should be fit and ready?"

"I'm not sure about Williamson's work. As an old guy said to me, 'Son, if they don't blow, they have more work to do.' I think that's a fair comment. I think if you want to stop them blowing, you make them cooler."

"Interesting in this sense - why would we warm them up before a race? We should bring them out of a refrigerator."

"To stop them blowing, but would you improve performance? See, what I'm saying there is I don't care how much they blow. I mean, I often have staff come to me and say, 'Gee, this horse is blowing a lot,' and I say, 'No, that's okay.' I don't even want to look at it. It's not an indicator to me. It doesn't influence me at all."

"So what do you use as the main indicators of how much work a horse has done? To decide if you're going to give him more next time, or the same or less?"

"Well, I use just a logical work loading program to bring him through from being unfit to being ready to go to the races, and I load them how I assess they should be loaded. That's a judgment I make, away from the horse. I come up to the house and make that decision. Having got there, then my judgment's influenced by his performance. I suppose the tricky bit, because you can't afford to be wrong too much, is if you load him with more work and he didn't need it - terrible decision."

"That puts the horse back in its program, off its food?"

"Well, he'd race worse, wouldn't he? He'd go worse if you picked the wrong way to go, and I think that they're all different around about that stage. It's a program through to basic fitness, but from there on, it's judgment about how he raced. Some will race good fresh and some can't. Some of them are not good enough and they're getting beaten, so you have to raise their fitness level, so that they become competitive. It's easy to train good horses because they cover up for bad training. They go to the races and win and you think, 'How clever am I,' but he's a trick and he's a bad horse for you, because you become complacent."

"Deciding what work you're going to do, you come back to the house and you sit down with lists, do you?"

"Yes. Each horse, each day, has a program, it's work for the following day."

"How do you make that decision? You fast work on a particular day and then it does jog work the next day, and the next time it goes out to fast work you've already decided from the previous fastwork what it's going to do?"

"Yes. There's a logical progression of two to three fast runs per week."

"Do you keep records of the times each horse runs?"

"Yes. They're all listed, so we know them all. I only fall back on that when I'm in real trouble and I say, 'What have you done? Have you messed him up that way?' If I've gotten into trouble with a horse I backtrack and say, 'Where did you go wrong?' Strangely enough, I've had horses that have come into work and disappointed me, in this preparation, and I thought well, you know, I can't fault him, I can't think of a reason why he shouldn't run better, so I say, 'Well, what did you do last time you trained him?' So you go back six months to a year: What was your work? How were the times comparing? How frequently did you work him? You'll be amazed how similar the work and times are. Half a second difference in workouts over a mile and a half."

"So each horse comes up very similarly each time."

"Well, I have programs that come up similarly; after that, the variations will start. But I don't think there's anything clever about starting a horse off in slow miles and getting quicker miles, and then blowing out the miles to a mile and a half, depending on where you're heading. I think that's all very logical, and I'd be surprised if other people didn't do that. There doesn't seem to be any other way, to me. I often put myself in the position of the horse. If I was going to train myself to run a mile and a half, I know I'd be a lot more comfortable if I did it in easy stages, and I would do that so that I didn't hurt myself; same thing - I don't want my horses to hurt themselves."

Training Aids

"In spite of all these hills, and all this sand, you only use the track?"

"I don't use the sand or the hills."

"Do you have anything special in your training programs like, say, hill-work, galloping, beach work?"

"No. I am not into that type of training, and I think that the location I'm at, as well as my attitude toward it, just debars most of those things. I think that training is specific, and as far as I'm concerned, my best results are by training them the way they're going to race."

"Have you tried sandhills or the deep sand track?"

"Not since I've been training in my own right. There was no shortage of sand tracks when I started. More sand tracks than roads. Back then we did sand work. We did think it made them a bit leg weary."

"When you ask the other trainers what Sorin Nordin does, they say he works his horses very hard. When you ask them, 'Why don't you work your horses that hard?' they say, 'Ours go in the legs or they fine off'. Now Nordin uses a drag bike, a sulky with a brake - it is harder to pull and he can adjust the resistance - and the other trainers say his horses have big bums. It may be that he is able to strengthen their legs without so much lameness."

"I've heard a similar thing about horses working on treadmills: that they develop a stronger back; more muscle in the lumbar area of the back, and that it is a very noticeable trait. But I think: how the hell is that going to help him in a race? Afterall, in all the miles he puts down on the training track he doesn't develop those muscles. So what is the point of developing that muscle for that purpose? I can only logic it out, and I'm not saying I'm right, that training is specific."

"Specificity of training: I introduced that term into animal training when I wrote an article for a veterinary text book, Current Veterinary Therapy VII, in 1979. It took on like wildfire. People used it in articles all over the world, about training racehorses, greyhounds, sled dogs, bird dogs - even Afghan hounds. So I know what you

mean by specificity. But there is more to it than that. It may be that deep sand, hills and drag bikes (sulkies with a brake) allow the trainer to put a bit more cardiovascular conditioning into the horse without putting a high force or load on the bones and joints."

"Right. But is that the limiting factor to performance?"

"Limiting factors are a very complex ball game and very interesting, but the easy way to put it is this: any extra ability to take in and use oxygen will usually improve performance, even in a sprint, but especially over a distance. More so in harness horses than gallopers. But the two fascinating problems in trying to increase the cardiovascular fitness, the aerobic fitness of horses are: one, that the extra work risks breaking them down; two, that it is hard to increase their fitness without losing some speed."

"Oh you're not wrong. It happens all the time."

"Also if you are not careful, the horse can develop kilograms of muscle it doesn't need, just extra weight, as you observed. But Vincent O'Brien, the most successful and revered Thoroughbred trainer in Europe, uses hill work. He started out on a property with a considerable slope, then deliberately bought another with a big hill and set up his training center there. He called it Ballydoyle, and he has there a steep hill with about six different racing surfaces on it, all beautifully maintained. Only a lunatic or a genius would have that many different tracks up the same slope, and his record definitely says genius."

"What would you say about treadmills with a gradient?"

"There are some traps in treadmills. There is already a lot to know, and yet a lot we still don't understand about them. The gait of the horse determines the main mechanics of its breathing. At a flat gallop the galloping action helps compress and expand the chest cavity, particularly by moving the guts back and forth against the diaphragm. Obviously there is much less assistance to the diaphragm at the trot or pace. Things like shortening stride will alter intake of oxygen."

"When, at a constant speed, you raise a treadmill from horizontal to say five degrees (10% gradient or rising 1 meter in 10 meters covered), you dramatically increase the amount of work the horse has to do per minute; at the same time you shorten and slow it's stride slightly. It is doing more work but its breathing is slower and shallower. Naturally the horse will run out of puff sooner."

"Usually people use hill slopes that effectively prevent the horse stretching out to the same extent it does on the track. It works as hard or nearly as hard as on the track but cannot put in the same number of strides per minute - consequently it cannot take as many breaths per minute. The strides are not of the same length either, so they

may not even get as much per breath. I showed with Greyhounds, which gallop like a horse, that when you raise the angle too much, you can easily decrease the maximal oxygen uptake by 30% - which is a huge reduction."

"I would expect the amount of blood pumped by the heart would be less than maximal too, but possibly not; the rate of heat accumulation is increased because of the decreased air turnover in the lungs and the lack of air going past to cool the body - unless you have a fan capable of generating a force seven gale. At steep angles, things like the fetlock angle are altered, the strain on the bones and tendons and so on are affected. So there are a lot of things to consider about treadmills - so many that sheer experiment and experience by trainers will be very important in discovering the best ways to use them."

"Some trainers see treadmills mainly as an extra bit of variety. Some people have said it alters a horse's action. There may be ways of using them to increase cardiovascular fitness without leg damage, without losing some speed, and without producing leg weariness. There may be ways to cushion them so that sore-legged horses can keep fit."

"There are very few trainers using treadmills and then going straight to the track with the horse, but there are a few. Trevor Warwick uses one with considerable slope, and he gives his horses quite a workout on it. Mostly treadmills are used on youngsters being prepared for the yearling sales, on yearlings early in their race preparation, on other horses being legged up, on lame horses. Some use them on jog day."

"But there are some traps with treadmills, especially in relation to the slope and how long you leave them on. You will hear of athletes, greyhound trainers, and horse trainers who have introduced them and gone worse. The classic is when someone starts a horse on a treadmill when it is already racing. They are amazed how little it takes to make the horse leg weary. There is a lot to learn about surface, slope, duration; where it fits in the overall campaign and the weekly schedule. But they are here to stay and will become more useful as more expertise is acquired."

Swimming

"Do you ever swim your horses?"

"If you have a property near the beach and you develop swimming as part of your training, then I think you should. But I can't see the rationale in transporting the horses for three-quarters of an hour to the beach, swimming them and then transporting them for three-quarters of an hour back again - as many trainers do. Subjecting them to that traveling stress. They tend to want to do it in summer because of the beach conditions. It's lovely while you are at the beach, but then you've got that hot trip home."

"Greg Harper has gotten into it, been fairly successful, believes in it now - believes particularly that it helps stand horses up, but just in the last few months he's broken down quite a few. I fell into it last year with Paavo (Fred's best horse), because Kellie, my daughter, was keen to go and Greg was driving past. I was training him my way anyhow, so the beach work was just something extra. But he didn't go any better, in fact he ran his best times when we dropped the beach work off. Of course I don't know if that was going to happen anyway. See, I'm not comfortable with it, I haven't learnt about it. I think you develop your training along lines you are familiar with, that work for you - and when you start to get off that is when you start to mess them up a bit. I've said it to you before: as trainers, the less we stuff-up the better off we're going to be."

8.2 Hard or soft trainer

The track opinion of how hard Fred trained was patchy, but most said he was a soft trainer. Very few know how he trains so their views are not very useful.

Ned Kersley
"How different is your son Fred's training to yours?"

"He works his horses a lot harder than I did. Young Fred hobbles up more often than I did. His program for a horse not racing is Monday, Wednesday, Friday. I never carried a whip on the track. His horses go faster on the track. He goes about six and a half miles on a slow day, that's about the same as I did."

"Fred races his about every week."

"I raced mine every two weeks but now you have to race more often, you have to take the races you can get."

"How hard is Fred's training compared to your father's?"

"He's probably not quite as hard. My father used to jog at least 10 mile per day in sand." Frank Kersley agrees: "Our father trained a lot harder than we did. I found that you had to be very careful not to push them over the top, to peak them too early. I preferred them a bit underdone. But they can work them a lot harder these days because of the anabolics and the additives and things."

8.3 Best with what category of horse?

JUDY:"I think if you went back and classified all Fred's winners for each year, I think you'd find that there was very rarely one main winner."

"Yes, his name's not generally associated with one horse in particular."

"The other thing he has a reputation for is old horses. Not necessarily picked them up when they're old, but they can go right through, like old Indian Chant. He raced until he was

thirteen. He seems to get on well with the old timers."

PHIL COULSON: "Fred has a very good technique to train short distance horses. I don't think he is a trainer of a true staying horse. He certainly hasn't got the record on the board of being able to produce two-mile horses. But the sprint-type racing that we run over the mile, 1700m stuff - there is no better trainer. He's perfected that."

GINO DE MORI: Gino's view is that Fred has won every type of race and is quite simply, 'good at everything'.

Why should Fred do best with older horses and sprinters? We will have a better idea when more trainers have been covered, because comparison brings these things out best. Suffice to say his formula for the older horses is: not shorter, not less frequent, but not as hard.

8.4 Driving

"In pacing in Australia, most trainers are also drivers, so they have a double barrel income."

"Yes. One of the advantages we do have."

"But it's an added pressure."

"Sure is."

"You don't have to waste. I think that's a big difference. That really wrecks some of those jockeys."

"Yes. I guess that if you can train okay, you're assuring yourself of the drives as well, whereas the jockey's pressures are that he's not guaranteed anything, unless he's negotiated a retainer or a contract."

"The papers publish their sequence of losing rides. So they can easily become flavor of the minute or just as easily have everyone avoiding them."

"You see it far too often and you wonder if it's always a measurement of ability or is it a measurement of some other factors."

"The winning and losing streaks usually start a long way short of statistical significance; they haven't actually gone bad, just the roll of the dice. It is like having one number on a dice with 10 or 15 faces on it; you must have some long losing streaks. But once they have what they consider a bad streak all sorts of things change: they get less rides so they get longer gaps between the rides."

"Essentially what we're doing in race riding or driving is reacting to an instinct. We're not able to make a judgment, a value judgment. You are reacting instinctively to situations. When you're on a winning run you seem to instinctively do everything right."

"When you're hot, you're hot, the old saying."

"That's right, and when you're on the wrong tram, a bad streak - hell it's hard to get a drive."

"I think that business where part of you is thinking, 'Am I doing the right things?' is one of the things that pro-

duces the real or abnormally long losing streak. In golf, in jockeys, drivers."

"I would agree with that, from my experience driving in races. The harder you try at it - it doesn't make it any better."

"When people say, 'I tried harder and did worse,' I think it's because they use a part of the brain to try to alter things. You rarely use that part of the brain in rapid-response things; it's a policy-making area. When you use it, a lot of automatic things take a lot longer to do, and it introduces this element of confusion. Its a part of the brain that when you're hot you don't even use, you're so confident, you shut that section down."

"One of my strategies as a driver, when I seem to be getting into trouble, is I won't make any decisions, I just go to the inside rail."

"Well, that saves you from that business of over-analyzing."

"Might be your horse is a part of your problem, and if that's the case you're better on the rail anyhow. The fact that you know you don't have to make any decisions means you've released a bit of the pressure, and they can run some pretty nice races. If there is such a thing as just purely and simply bad luck, you can't change that anyhow, and you might as well get on the rail. If your luck changes, well then, that will win you a race."

"When you're out of form, you drive worse and you look worse, and everyone says, 'People that get caught wide have gone too soon.' Oh jeez, and you know yourself. You're embarrassed: I wish I'd wake up, this is a bad drive and everyone knows it. And you go the other way: 'Well, it's not so much your fault' - but you know, it is. I haven't found myself going to the rail so much in recent times, but it was a strategy that I used to put in place."

"Well, it'd be very useful if it prevented conscious interference with successful automatic responses."

"If it was becoming too hard, look, just get to the rail and let it happen for you."

"My guess with that losing sequence business in the jockeys, is that they have what is actually a quite a statistically acceptable losing streak, but they get into this mental state, and that's what actually prolongs it; that in fact the less attention they pay to that losing streak the better.

"One of the things that perpetually amazes me is how swiftly you guys can get a horse and sulky to duck out into what amounts to a fairly small opening. The whole apparatus of a rider and cart and horse, always looks to me like it's so cumbersome. It always amazes me when a horse flashes out off the fence like they sometimes do."

"They've got the ability to do it. A horse shies very quickly - almost goes at right angles if a bird frightens him or something. Just seems to be built like that. To maintain a pacing or a trotting gait, and do that, is very demanding on them, and I don't think trotters could do it quite as easily as the pacers, because once again the hobbles aid the pacer. Gallopers, they can almost just lift their weight, front end off, and just put it over there. I have the utmost admiration for the pacers running on half-mile tracks with the demands on them. It's in-

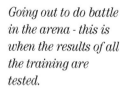

Going out to do battle in the arena - this is when the results of all the training are tested.

credible, and they're not given the credit they deserve. It's absolutely demanding. They hit wheels, blokes tip them over, you pull them around, you're at them, you're trying to back them off, and the pressure, the excitement, the sweat - that's all there - the hurt is in their guts and they just do it. They're beautiful animals to do that."

"Yes, I'm always amazed that with all the equipment that's there, and all the excitement, that there aren't more legs placed in paths of sulkies, for example."

"We used to get a lot of feet in wheels and the spokes would sort of drag them in and bring them down. Now, one of the big safety factors are wheel disks. They hit the disc and bounce off and as a safety measure that's just been unbelievable. It's documented through our spider insurance that we don't have the same number of smashes we used to have. But it's made some drivers a little more careless. Before they didn't want to put their wheel out in case another horse put his foot through it. Now they put it out there anyhow. I think a horse has the ability to maneuver in a short distance, but it's not good driving tactics to be shifting them sideways, you should be making your movements more gradual - and fairly quick."

"It'd cost them a bit of ground to make that sideways step."

Driving tactics

Some statistics were given for races at Gloucester Park and Richmond Raceway, in a newspaper article by Rod White back in 1981. He headed the article 'Sit-and-sprint days in trotting are over'. Of 422 races, 339 or 80% were won by horses in the first four at the start of the last lap, ie the last five-eighths of a mile. Of Fred's 42 city winners in the analysis, 78% led or raced outside of the leader. Of Phil Coulson's 29 winners, 82% led or raced outside the leader. The article credits Phil with introducing this style of driving in the 1960s. Phil was quoted as saying, "If a driver can control a race for one lap and his horse has any ability he is nearly unbeatable." Fred Kersley was quoted too: "I am conscious of the fact that a horse must be near the lead if he is to win. I would rather one of my horses race wide all the way, with a clear run, than go to the line blocked for a run. Whenever possible I try to dictate the terms of a race to my rivals. When they allow me to dictate for long enough they cannot beat me."

"With timid horses, would you try to sit back in the field, tail the field or go to the front?"

"Go to the front."

"One fellow's rationalization of that approach is that they're field shy, and if they hear the thunder of hooves behind them, they'll try to stay in front, but if they can see all the horses in front of them then they won't want to go past them."

"It's my belief that towards the end of a race, they all should be pretty tired. We're two hundred metres out and all the horses should be getting close to fatigue. When they see a lot of bums in front of them, they don't seem to be able to get round them. It seems too hard and I always forgive horses. You'll often read: 'He was disappointing; he failed to run on.' He's fatigued and all those bums look like a wall. But that same horse, if you could have him turning for home alongside of, or in front of, I'm sure he'll run to the line with just a little bit more heart. It'd be a special horse that will come home just as hard when he's got all those bums in front of him and he is tired. My driving attitude works on that: when he's getting tired, I'd rather they had to get past him than I had to get past them. It is a thing that I've believed for a long time. I'm critical of some driving; I've felt that the horse has been given too hard a task, and that I wouldn't expect it to show heart under those circumstances. Quite often they'll say he didn't put in, he didn't try, he gave up."

"Now - a comparison of two of the main strategies: keeping horses at the front, and bringing them off the back somewhere."

"The business of bringing them off the back - they'll enjoy accelerating away if the pace has been overly fast, and the leaders are tired and they're fresh. But statistically what tends to happen is that probably two-thirds of races are sufficiently close to the correct pace for the horse coming from the back to have a hell of a hard job in front of him, and he's already a little bit tired. So within three or four of those kind of races, the horse loses interest."

"If the money is on, he may also get the bum whipped off him too, because one of the failings with the strategy of coming off the back, is that people really don't know if the pace is going to be over or under or correct; they can only guess. The driver or jockey is given those instructions to come from behind late in the race - and for some horses it's the only way they can run - and he is told the money is already on. The driver hopes the pace will be fast and burn the leaders up. In the race, the pace may be right, or worse, it might be slow, but even if the situation tends to look hopeless coming out of the turn the driver feels obliged to beat the hell out of the horse to show the punters and connections he tried. So some horses get a very negative experience out of it. One fellow claimed you can actually pick those horses up for a song when they've had about ten starts - he said you can rejuvenate them by managing them differently in the race."

"I think talking percentages you could expect to. I don't think it'll always work."

"Well I used to be quite sold on the idea that horses that came off the back, if the pace was wrong for them ie too slow, then they had an easy outing because the jockey could sit at the back and say, 'We didn't have a hope' - un-

til I was at the races with a few people in situations where we were trying to alter their horse's tactics. Then you realize that the money is already on and the jockey is frequently in a situation where the race has been run the wrong way for that horse. It doesn't have a hope in hell, but he knows there's a couple of thousand dollars on it, so he's going to whip it pretty hard because he feels obliged to."

"Usually - talking as a driver, and I imagine as a rider it'd be the same - you've got poor options. Most options on how to ride or drive are poor. It's very seldom that you get a good option to exercise, so what you tend to do is pick the least bad, as a driving tactic. With the way our racing's gone, horses are grouped together so closely there isn't even a second between the best and worst in a field. Given that and the dimensions of the racetrack (5/8 mile), we've got an enormous problem in driving well."

"For a horse to come from behind in the field, what he needs is for the other drivers to stuff their charges up. They need to overdo them and have them out on their feet two hundred or four hundred metres from home. Then you can look clever, flashing home late, and they say, 'He timed his run to perfection'. But all he's done is make less mistakes than the drivers who burnt too much fuel early. In the old days that was a copybook drive or ride, the classic - just swooping on them late and getting up to win. Still looks pretty, still looks nice, but it's not effective. What they'd say if it was a copybook drive was: 'He saved his horse for the last burst.' I worked that out a long time ago; I wasn't going to get much money trying to drive like that. Sometimes you've got to drive badly to get money. I gave away trying to be a pretty driver a long time ago. I'd rather be effective."

"I think particularly on a 5/8 mile track you've really got the job ahead of you from the back."

"Racing on the tracks that we have and going as many laps as we are - the advantage is always with the inside runner. To give them a start and then cover more ground to try to catch them, is very hard to do. You used to be able to do it because there was a vast difference between the best and the worst horses in the field. What has happened today is that sometimes it takes three or four years for these horses to classify themselves into a field. It's taken them three years of racing their guts out to arrive in a certain race. They've had eighty starts over three or four years and you've found out exactly how good or bad they are, and they're all in the same race together. They've done the barrier draw, and said go and do your best. One of us is going to win and I think the driver who makes the least mistakes on one of those horses is the one that might win."

When I asked around as to Fred's reputation as a driver, no-one seemed to have strong opinions. There were the usual 'he wins because he gets the best horses' type. There was one 'never will be as good as his father or his uncle,' from an old-timer, who on questioning had never seen either of those drive! The opinion I now believe sums it up best was this one: Fred Kersley is a much better driver than he is given credit for because he is not flamboyant in manner or tactics.

One of the reasons for the re-introduction of standing starts was to lessen the dominance of Fred Kersley and Trevor Warwick. The view was that from 20 or 40 meters behind scratch they wouldn't be able to burn to the front and control the race. But they have continued to dominate.

Fred believes driving helps him a great deal as a trainer, but realizes the trend to catch drivers will continue because it usually means a better drive. However he believes trainers should at least drive the horse in its track work so that they learn about the horse. "If you are not driving, you are just not as well informed about that horse."

Lately he has had to try to give his son and daughter some experience and opportunities, but then Fred doesn't want to keep driving until he is a handicap to his horses anyway.

8.5 Placing horses in races

"You have to learn to classify your horses. You tend as a younger trainer to want to believe they're good, you overrate them and you tend to get caught."

"Does that mean you kept putting them in races where they weren't going to win?"

"Yes, I think that was a tendency."

"I see that as a marked thing with up-and-comings, particularly the guys in the country that are trying to make it in the city."

"Well, I keep being reminded of it, because the new owners have all those attitudes, and it's really hard to talk them down to where they ought to be. So that would be something to be careful of."

8.6 Claiming strategies

There hasn't been enough of this in Perth to develop strategies.

8.7 Injuries and therapies

8.7-1 Shinsoreness

"You mentioned how much harder a horse has to work these days to be competitive. Are you getting more shin soreness out of that?"

"No, I've never had a shin sore horse in all my life. Never had one. And I think the thing is that we do a lot of foundation work. We get a lot of other lamenesses, and I feel like their hooves give them as much trouble as anything. But touch wood, I've got to say I've never had a shin sore horse."

"There are a lot of people who wish they could say that."

"I think they could say it if they trained differently. I think if you put the foundation in and keep that high speed work out of them long enough, then you won't get shin sore horses."

"My own belief is that it relates to the rate at which they go up in fast work, that it only takes a sudden step up somewhere that's just too big a step."

"That's what I was trying to say to you. If you can keep that fast work out of them long enough, or introduce it gradually enough, then you shouldn't cause shinsoreness. You would reduce the incidence of it greatly, by just doing that."

"With some of the galloper trainers, just the consciousness that it is the step up that is too large, or getting through to a track worker that they've got to be going up in these steps, can produce a dramatic drop in their rate of shin soreness."

"Galloping trainers have got a harder problem inasmuchas the horse has got that natural speed from day one, whereas the pacer hasn't. He's got to learn about and develop his speed, and so it's much easier for a galloping trainer to be in error, than for a pacing trainer to be in error."

"They certainly get a lot more shinsoreness. "

8.7-2 Tying up

"Do you get much tying up?"

"Well I can get it if I want it."

"How?"

"Underwork and overfeed them. If you don't want tying up, go the other way. I've had it when you've had quite a number of horses tying up. For me, it usually happens after slow work, and it's usually the old-fashioned 'Mondayitis'. A little bit of an easy time Sunday, come out Monday and tie up. That's my normal pattern with tie-ups."

"More fillies than anything else?"

"Not especially. One thing I have noticed that is common is an excitement factor. A horse that comes up fresh, bucks, kicks, feels really good for ten to fifteen minutes, and the next thing - you wonder what happened; he's just seizing up. That excitement seems to trigger off a tie-up. Not in all cases, but enough of them for me to recognize it."

"You have a day off on Sunday, do you do anything with their feed, or with those particular problem horses on that Sunday?"

"Yes, I cut their feed down. The grain ration ought to be reduced. They still shouldn't be made hungry; I like to feed quite a bit of hay and that sort of thing on a Sunday, on their easy days, but I don't think just one day does it. I think it's a series of two, three, four days. Horses that are especially fit and have been working at a high level of intensity - you drop them down and then I think something starts to happen there; that you're asking for trouble."

"Those that are a bit inclined to tie-up, do you ever take them out and work them on the Sunday, as a preventative?"

"Well, I try to not get into the situation where that's going to happen, but some of the old trainers who never really knew why they were doing it - with the bad tie-up horses, they just had to make him sweat every day."

8.7-3 Most common lameness

"Are there any particular lamenesses that you have found with your horses?"

"Lameness is one of those things that I just can't get a logic to. It seems there are patterns: you seem to get groups of lamenesses at any one time, and yet, when you go back and ask yourself why? - you're unable to come up with a sensible answer. The most common lameness that I, along with most trainers, am dealing with, is foot bruising."

"Foot bruising?"

"Yes, just straight out foot bruising. It comes through the quarter crack, heel crack situation, but it starts off with bruising. Corns, if you like, call it whatever you will, I don't really care, it's bruising of the feet."

"Has that always been there or is that a recent phenomenon?"

"There's a lot more of it now than there used to be. Our tracks are tending to be a little hard, although you could wonder about that, because people have trained on softer tracks in certain areas, and still had similar problems. But I think the intensity with which we train, and the demand we're placing on the horse - his foot is not quite able to cope."

"Does it get to that stage where you have to cut through the sole and drain it?"

"Oh yes, it does. Sometimes you cut through and it bursts out. Hoof pads have been used a lot, and if you get in early enough, hoof pads are great for a horse, because it'll take him from the stage where he's going to be non-raceable to being productive; he can race."

"What about things like, say, navicular disease? Any problem with that?"

"No. Not to speak of."

"Bowed tendons, I think you were complaining of at one stage."

"Yes, bowed tendons. They've been with us from day one and I don't fancy we've gotten especially better at fixing them up. Sometimes we seem to win with them and most times we don't, but once again you seem to get a rash of them, you get a spate of bowed tendons. Not especially tied into high intensity work either; I've seen some horses bow tendons working up, at about the midway point. It's not necessarily going to come off the track broken down. Bowed tendons don't always seem to happen like that. I've seen it happen with horses that have raced two seasons very hard, had a rest, come back into training and just been doing pace work - and they pop a bowed tendon, a genuine bow."

"What do you think is the future for a horse when it bows a tendon? Do you get many of them back and win with them, or is it a bad prospect?"

"I think most trainers these days are having a more positive approach to bowed tendons. We used to rest them. We'd give them twelve months off and then bring them back, and they'd break down. These days we tend to keep training anyhow."

"Keep them going?"

"Yes. Maybe just an easy couple of weeks, there are lots of variations. You can go six weeks, two weeks or not at all if you like, and I think the success rate's about the same. I wouldn't spell a horse for twelve months with a bowed tendon now, because I don't think they've got as good a chance, if you like, as training through it. Being very careful with him and just hoping. All of the lamenesses that they used to get in America ten years ago, we're getting now. Our attitude to lameness once was to rest them, and Americans worked them; now we're working them."

"Are you freezing arthritic legs pre-race yet?"

"They're starting to do that, yes. I'm still a little bit the old fashioned trainer. But you know, we can't afford *not* to work through lameness. Obviously some of the lamenesses you can't do that with, but we're getting all of the stress lamenesses that we've heard about; they're here now."

"Some of those being?"

"We're getting problems in tendons, hocks, knees, feet. My most common - the initial soreness will come into my horses in their front feet. That's a big problem for me, that I have to work around. It seems to be patchy and I often wonder why. You might run into two or three bowed tendons in two or three months in training, and then you mightn't get another one for nine months. You go back and try to work out why, and you can never find a single reason: the track didn't seem to be any different; it didn't have to be that time of year; that horse didn't have to be working hard - and he's popped a tendon. So I don't know the logic of it, but we get a lot of that. Suspensories come in frequently. Flavor-of-the-month for me in lameness is hocks. You know, from three through to eight-year-olds, they just get hocks. Now, I'm not sure that the vets aren't finding hocks that they couldn't have found before."

"Yes, that could be a factor."

"You X-ray them and they've got little spurs or whatever in the hock, and they have varying degrees of lameness, and we have varying degrees of success in propping them up."

"Maybe vets are going to go through a hocks period like they went through a knees period."

"Well, Yanks were getting knees and we weren't, and now I get some knees as well. We're breeding from some of the same horses too, and I thought it wasn't a bad comment that one fellow made: he observed that the most common lameness coming into the Standardbred was knees, and he said that he thought that it was the greater demand plus the most precocious breeds in America had a predisposition towards knee lameness. So maybe we caused some of this problem for ourselves."

"Flavor-of-the-month, perhaps decade in the States, is the osteochondrosis group of bone and joint problems. Apart from being diagnosed more because vets are looking for them more, they now know better how to recognize them. They are generally more common in horses that grow faster and bigger and start earlier and so on."

"Are they the ones on anabolics, or does it just so happen that they're there anyhow?"

"They seem to be there anyhow, in the developing yearling, even where anabolics aren't used. These are abnormalities in bone development that sit there and lead to lameness or even fracture when the horse gets into hard work. Some breeding farms have much more of it than other breeding farms. Many vets believe it is trace element related: perhaps actual levels, relative levels; some say copper deficiency; some say calcium excess; so that's another factor in it. It is a hot spot in research right now."

"I guess that the ones that we are now calling hock-lame, probably when they went lame twenty years ago, in the back end somewhere, we might have thought it was a pulled muscle. So it's really hard to know, but I am getting some back end lameness as well. All of our lamenesses used to be up the front."

"Have you tried any of these American things like clay on the legs or under the hooves?"

"I hate bandages on the horses legs, in any way shape or form. They can give you so much trouble - blistering, rubbing, chafing. They are more problems than they are worth. I had one horse, when he came he had some condition that they had been treating and treating. All I did was leave the bandages off and it got all right. All it had was bandage sores. But it might just be me. When I was a kid, we bandaged just about every bloody horse - wrapped them up in cotton wool every bloody night. I guess in summary I would say it does very little good, it has the potential to do some harm, and I believe it is unnecessary."

"Have you tried things like the mud on the sole that the Americans use?"

"I believe in the 'no foot no horse' rule, and I think the foot is an area we have neglected, but the things that are sold for the hoof don't seem to do what you want them to do."

"What do you want them to do?"

"Keep the foot really healthy."

"You don't use hoof dressing?"

"I am at the moment using paraffin oil, that's the fashion for this year, and I really don't think it does any good except that it makes the staff pick the horse's foot up, clean it up, and look at it."

"What about Reducine and all those hoof dressings?"

"Trainers have been making up their own different concoctions of all different things from lanoline through to Stockholm tar, to sump oil, lard, mutton fat - 100 different varieties of the best hoof dressing ever manufactured; guaranteed to make it grow, keep it healthy, fix seedy toe, corns and anything else with the feet; and I honestly haven't found one yet that I think helps. I've used kerosene and I feel that is no better or worse than any of the others."

"Have you tried any of the things that are supposed to stimulate hoof growth?"

"You should feed them to the ants. The stuff you put in the feed doesn't work; the stuff you put on their hooves doesn't work. A lot of my recommended supplements I've fed to ants. I think it's doing harm so I put it on the ground for the ants. We do things for horses but not always because the horse needs it."

"You should have a good look at it in America. They have all those paints and alcohol rubs."

"I have had a look, but what I would say is, 'What happens if you don't do those things? From my experience, nothing.'"

"With, for example, the hoof preparations, one explanation given is that the dirt tracks in America dry out the hoof wall."

"Well why not hose the hoof? Some of the old farriers, when the feet were hard in summer, would wet the feet to soften them for shoeing. It acted fairly quickly."

"Well the track itself is often quite moist. The full explanation is supposed to be that the dirt track - presumably by abrasion - removes the natural shiny wax coating on the hoof. That coating is meant to partially trap moisture coming from the inside of the hoof, and so keep the hoof wall pliable. The waxes are secreted up near the coronet and creep down the hoof wall. When the waxy coating is gone, the hoof wall can be moistened rapidly but it also dries out rapidly. There is a good logic to the idea of putting a waxy coating on the hoof each day after trackwork. Many of the trainers tape some mud underneath the sole as a slow release moistener. It sounds good but that doesn't mean it works."

"Someone somewhere might know the answer, but no one has been able to tell me something to use that works. I believe - although my farrier disagrees - that some hoof conditions occur in different stables, at different tracks and under different conditions - at the same time. You seem to get a run of quarter cracks, a run of corns, abscesses, of bruised soles-"

"Bruised soles do seem to occur as outbreaks in the opinion of one American vet I was talking to."

"The farrier will say, 'I've seen a lot of these this week'. He will name trainers at different tracks, under different conditions. You will go to the trots and in a six month span, you won't see a horse wearing bumper bandages (to protect the fetlock if it hits the ground). Then all of a sudden they are all wearing them; horses from different stables; it's like an epidemic. Why? I'd like the veterinary profession to explain to me why there should be an outbreak of horses getting down on their bumpers."

"In the opinion of that same American vet, the sole bruises and possibly the sole abscesses, they might sometimes be caused by viruses. That was his guess when it occurred in a lot of the horses in his practice, on a number of occasions. Other possible causes are seasonal factors, shipments of feed from the same feed merchants, batches of additives, fashion changes in feeding and training. Any of those and no doubt a few other things could also be factors. It would take careful record keeping to confirm it, and then detective work to backtrack. You'd need years of records to look for relationships to season and weather and crops."

8.8 Role of the vet

Dr Charlie Stewart is Fred's vet. Charlie has had an intense interest in exercise science for many years. His early interests were in blood testing and heart scoring. Charlie is an archskeptic, one who doesn't readily accept the beliefs of other vets without testing it for himself. Any worthwhile vet will do the same, but Charlie usually takes it a step further than most vets. Most vets will keep an eye on the cases going through and see if the theory fits. This can be very misleading, because the first say three or even ten cases may support the theory or discredit the theory, and people have a very definite tendency to make up their mind before enough cases are in.

Not Charlie.

8.8-1 How much does he blood test?

When Charlie wanted to look at the validity of blood testing as a guide to racing readiness, he took bloods from 60 horses at weekly intervals for six months. When he wanted to determine the usefulness or otherwise of the heart score, he collected hundreds of recorded heart scores from previous years and went to work chasing up the winnings of those horses. He took up driving at the training track to increase his practical knowledge, and plunged into interval training after reading *The Fit Racehorse* by Tom Ivers.

Charlie's findings in the late 1970s and early 1980s were that blood tests were "bullshit" when it came to using them for assessing a horse's race fitness. He found it difficult to establish a normal range - there was a very wide "don't know" area on either side of the accepted normal range. He sent two samples from the same syringe of blood to the same lab or one each to two different labs. The error factor was large. There were too many exceptions:- horses that had low red cell counts that won races; horses with neutrophil to lymphocyte ratios that suggested they were in serious need of a spell that won races; horses with low potassium that won races.

Nevertheless Charlie had some interesting and useful results, such as the horse which had a blood picture (mainly the neutrophil to lymphocyte ratio), which was suggestive of stress, which he decided must be due to being stabled next to the wrong horse. After the horse was moved its blood picture improved dramatically. Charlie's attitude on blood tests in racing breeds could be summarized as: hardly worth doing - he talks most of his clients out of doing them. He believes you should almost never decide what to do with a horse on the basis of a blood test when there was no reason to do the test ie. there were no clinical signs. This is quite the opposite approach to Percy Sykes, TJ Smith's vet.

8.8-2 Jugs (Intravenous drips)
Charlie Stewart did a lot of testing in this area, and the last time I spoke to him, he regarded them as a waste of time.

Charlie Stewart on the heart score
The heart score is a reading of the width of a wave of the electrocardiogram that is held to be proportional to the size of the heart. When the skeptical Charlie compared winnings with heart score, he found that there was indeed a relationship that made the bother of the reading worthwhile, in Standardbreds at least.

Fred on the heart score
"The documentation I've seen seems to indicate that the better performers have the higher scores, however I don't like to take a horse just on the heart score, and I tend not to think there is a heap of value in it. I prefer to go on whether or not they could run. I suppose if you had a young horse you could not make up your mind about, then if it had a poor score you would be pretty safe to sack him."

Charlie's skepticism has found a natural partner in Fred's careful questioning approach to the accepted beliefs and they have a good relationship. However it should be remembered that Fred had made it to the top long before Charlie came on the scene.

Vitamin injections
Fred:"The trainer is not comfortable unless the horse has been injected; the drenches; the drips and all those sort of things. I don't reckon it helps the horse at all. It helps the person."

"I tell you how I think some of that stuff might work - for example a saline drench. I think that there are horses, trained by what I would call the middle level and especially the bad level of trainers, where they have a horse going into a race dehydrated or with an electrolyte problem, and they are unaware of that problem. So in a stable where they do saline drenches, I think that it probably mops up those horses - some of them anyway. Now, to a top trainer that might only be one in a hundred. To some of these middle level trainers it might be one in ten. There are supposedly examples of trainers who have gone on to saline drenches and improved their strike rate, gone off them and gone backwards again, so they can't be without them. But it probably comes back to something in their feeding or their training - for example where they push the horses too far and they need that kind of stuff."

"I could only agree with that. I haven't seen that happening, but if it is happening, they're obviously making mistakes and this is helping them a bit."

"Percy Sykes, a Sydney vet and something of a pioneer, says he was finding anemias in the fifties. He's being crucified by the academics, on the grounds that anemia doesn't really exist or is very rare. But you have to remember that nowadays the quality of feed is better and they're just about all getting supplements of some kind. Anyway he's progressed miles past the anemia thing, he's on to things that are much more subtle. He's ahead of them in a lot of ways. He has been running trials with copper in foals and yearlings when most Australian academics didn't even know it was a factor in the osteochondrosis story. But they're punishing him for the fact that a lot of horsemen and vets are doing things that he did ten and twenty years ago, when he thought they were necessary. He probably wouldn't make a big deal of them now."

"That's right. We had - I don't know whether they were just anemic or if they were sick horses - but we were training quite weak horses, back in the early days, and I think the most significant reason for that was the worm; the parasite loading."

"Better worming has improved the anemia situation out of sight."

"When I was a lad in the stables, every horse had lots of worms. Our only way of ridding them of worms in the very early days was to physic them."

"Just practically shake the worms out of them?"

"Just physic them; flush the worms out of their gut. The manure would hit the ground and it'd walk away. Bloody worms. Then we got on to the phenothiazines, which was the only known drug that trainers used in those days, and that would do some harm as well if you used too much of it - this was before other wormers came into use - we had significant problems with horses because as soon as they got into the stress of their training they would stop eating, and then we had a double-barrelled effect. What we were doing was propping up horses. We had poor-doers which were carrying too little condition, which we were trying to race. Now I think in those days the things that did help were the anabolics and the vitamins, because that made them feel a little bit better and it did help them significantly."

"The anabolics were probably successful because worms cause protein loss and anabolics conserve protein in the body."

"Right. Now the trainers that first went into the usage of those drugs had a big advantage, and history will show the periods of successful trainers who are not there anymore. Then you got the worming programs. How effective the wormers are and how much resistance there is, I couldn't measure, but we don't get a result. The most frequent comment I get from people I talk to is, 'We never see a worm anymore. We keep worming these horses but I don't think the wormer is working because we never see any worms.' Back then we got used to seeing lots and lots of worms."

"Yes, because the purging action threw the worms out alive. Modern wormers don't purge, so usually, if the worms are killed, they disintegrate before they come out. I've had some interesting experiences with wormers. One time by mistake we gave Telmin (Merbendazole) twice about two days apart. We hadn't seen a worm in a year or two, and then we gave this doubled-up dose of Telmin and we got worms everywhere, which really told us that they were resistant, but two days close up was enough to kill them. Also, I used to teach a night course subject called Equine Veterinary Science, and I used to get the whole class to bring in fecal samples from every horse they had - 20 to 40 jars of horse feces - and after they collected the fecal sample they were to give the horse their normal wormer. Then in the class a week later we would do an egg count on another fecal sample. You could virtually divide the class up: the ones that had zero egg count one week later were almost invariably on Equiban (Morantel) or Equigard (Dichlorvos). The ones that were on any of the Benzimidazole derivatives, generally started with higher egg counts and after worming - in some of them there was almost no change! We had one or two spectacular cases where these horses had horrendously high worm counts and I'd say, 'Obviously, this horse is not on a worming program.' They'd say, 'Like Hell. I give it this *@*@* stuff every six weeks!' Usually it was Rintal (Febantel) or Telmin (Merbendazole) they were resistant to."

"Well, where does Panacur (Fenbendazole) fit into that?"

"It is in another group, and it is fairly effective, but its cost was its main problem, but it's still one of the best for killing larvae in the tissues. I remember Doctor Waddell, one of our vet course lecturers, showing us the intestines of a wormy horse. When you looked at it you could see hundreds of visible worms IN the lining of the gut, waiting to come out when the time was right. Then you put it under a low-powered microscope and you could see another hundred smaller ones. That was in a piece of gut wall twice the area of the palm of your hand. Then you start to multiply that bit by the gut length. But the thing that I think mattered as much as the presence of the worm, was that around each one of those parasites there's a lot of damaged tissue and that has to come down to things like little ulcers, and decreased ability to absorb food. I think that the very wormy yearling is like the very wormy poddy calf or sheep: that possibly they can never be brought up to compete with the top end."

"When the damage is done, that's semi-permanent."

"Exactly. And then there are all these other effects that they're only just working out. A lot of those worms suppress the immune system to help themselves. They zap out bits of the immune system so they're not under so much pressure, and of course the host is then more vulnerable to other parasites and diseases."

"So what would be your wormer of choice, given what you know now?"

"I would be using Ivermectin if it was available (At the time it was not available for horses in Australia), especially on the breeding farm. That's where it's most crucial. At present, if I was buying at the sales, I'd be wanting to ask the studmaster or phone up the stud and say, 'What is your worming program? What do you use?' And it would mean nearly as much to me as its conformation."

"Equiban: would you be using it?"

"At present in Australia I think I would probably alternate Equiban and Equigard. Unless I had chooks (Australian for chickens) round the place. Equigard can be eaten out of the horse's droppings and kill chooks. If Ivermectin use becomes widespread we may even move to truly worm-free lines of horses. Think of the money and hassles that would save. You would have to have a stud on new soil or find some way to treat the pasture, but it would be a useful selling point, worm-free yearlings. It would be great to render these worms extinct but they will hang on in zebras, wild horses and poorly managed stock. Have you seen any performance depression with any of the wormers."

"I don't find much problem with wormers slowing them down. No, I really can't think of one that I thought hurt them. Occasionally a horse will seem to be affected by it and that hasn't even bothered me much, because I've felt as though in some cases those horses may have had a lot of worms."

"Interesting you should think the wormy horses got

sick. Before Ivermectin, new horses coming on to studs were sometimes given that ten times dose of Panacur. If the animal had a bit of a setback from it, it was usually presumed it had heaps of migrating larvae. On occasion the horse died - I remember a vet doing a postmortem on one that died. That may just have been bad luck: killing a worm big enough to block a major artery for example; but then maybe you had a horse that was so damn ridden with dormant and migrating worms that you haven't really lost anything."

"It would have been in big trouble anyway."

"Some vets and trainers have commented on a depression that some horses got after Panacur and I first used to ask, 'Does it look like a wormy horse?' In some cases they'd say no. But later on, when I got into doing egg counts and looking at resistance, I came to the conclusion that a lot of wormy-looking horses were not wormy, and a lot of horses that looked to be in good condition were quite wormy. An older vet said to me one time, 'The worms don't show up til the horse is under pressure, sonny,' and I think that was true. I think some of the horses that I used to think were wormy, had some other reason for not thriving. When you're a new graduate, you don't know an awful lot, and you tend to drop things in obvious slots. Then I started to acquire a bit more knowledge, and I would see things like a horse that was doing poorly just because it was so far down the peck order it could never get a decent crack at the feed bins, and other horses that were borderline malabsorbers etc."

"You've still got those. With the worming routine, basically what happens with us is they come into the stable and they're wormed straight away, that day or the next day. Well, with one reservation: horses coming off grass and then getting a change of food; I'm careful about doing it at that particular time, so it could be three or four days later. We'll follow up six weeks later and then six weeks later. That's twelve weeks and that's about where I stop."

"You use what?"

"Well, I've used them all, but just a stomach tube initially. With improvement in the paste, I'm a bit more inclined to stomach tube the first time and then go into the paste on the second or third occasion, but when we've got to that second lot of the six weeks, we're at about the stage where the horse will be going to the races, so from there on I might go into an eight week span or even a twelve week if I'm pretty happy with the horse, and at twelve weeks I will do them anyhow."

"So you do them, say Saturday after they've raced Friday?"

"Yes, Saturday's a good day because Sunday's an easy day and there's downtime, so Saturday midday, when I've finished the work, that's my worm day, and they have the day off on Sunday and go back in full training. Over the years I've altered my opinion. Worming a horse in the early days, you might not hobble (fastwork) him for five to seven days after you've wormed him, and yet I find these days I could hobble him the following day if I wanted to."

"One of the things that used to be a real pain was sanding them - purging them or oiling them to get rid of sand in the gut. I notice you've got yours on sand in their stalls. Do you have any problems with sand?"

"I never give a damn about sand. I really never have. They pass sand, and I think they should. I think that sick horses have problems with sand."

"Some of the postmortems I've done on horses that died 'sanded', you could see that the classic disaster has occurred - blockage of a major artery to the gut by a worm. The gut can no longer contract properly because it is not getting its oxygen supply, and that is why the sand is there. But the other thing I've seen around Perth are cases where the cecum (a sack-like part of the gut) has split through the sheer weight of the sand in it. Wet sand has enormous weight."

"I think the horse probably got crook (sick) first, somewhere along the line. You see, I was just as paranoid as anyone else in the early days, and if a horse would be scratching in the sand or digging a hole and licking the sand I'd just go ape. These days I walk past him. I mean, if he wants to stand there and lick the sand or dig a hole-"

"Interesting to know how many extra kilos on average they're carrying."

"It's hard to find out."

"Yes, I had hopes that ultrasound would enable us to look at the sand content of the gut."

"Has it?"

"No. Not yet."

Anabolics

Fred has gone public with a strong stand against anabolics. In Australia anabolics are currently allowed in harness horses but were recently banned in gallopers. Fred would like anabolics banned in harness horses. He is afraid trainers are being lumped with drug- users.

"I don't use anabolics routinely, but you will find people who say that I do. I do use anabolics occasionally. I've got one horse down there now, which came in awful condition and not wanting to eat. I couldn't see any reason not to give her an anabolic, but that is the last time she will get it. That's when anabolics are useful."

"Did you ever try anabolics routinely?"

"When I was quite a deal younger, and they were becoming popular and people were saying they did this and that, then I tried them. I didn't like them. You can make horses squeal and look better and run slower."

"Run slower?"

"Yes, and there were some very basic trainers said that."

"I had an experimental greyhound running on a treadmill that seemed to go slower on anabolics. He was a very good dog banned at the track for fighting. I was told by a greyhound trainer that he believed it was the better greyhounds that were adversely affected by anabolics. The poor condition greyhounds I ran on the treadmill, they certainly benefited, especially in condition, but they still wouldn't have been racing propositions."

"The better stock may have been naturally more genuine. The lesser ones might have been less genuine and benefited from being more aggressive."

"I have wondered along those lines, if the better racehorses and greyhounds have a higher natural production of anabolics, or a better spectrum of anabolics. No two anabolics are exactly the same in their actions in the body, and the body produces a lot of different anabolics. Probably no two animals have the same levels and ratios of all these slightly different anabolics. Then there are differences in receptors where the anabolics act. If you give an anabolic to a top performer that hasn't had them before, its natural production is cut back and the spectrum may not be as good as its own was."

"How would you know what was best for each of 40 horses in your stable?"

"As a vet I ran across an old trainer who claimed he was one of the first to realize fillies and geldings needed different types of whatever anabolics were available in those days."

"Well my comments on something like that would be useless because I haven't had the experience. But what I would say is that horse trainers need not use anabolics at all. You can get by without it."

"With anabolics banned in Thoroughbreds in Australia now, it should benefit the trainers who are not high grain feeders, rather than the high grain and high additive feeders who work their horses very hard."

"I'm not sure it won't benefit everyone because if you eliminate something, it is one more thing that you can or cannot do. It comes back to simplifying everything. It is one more thing you don't have to consider. I think all that publicity about how we won't be able to train them, the owners will get hurt, the punters will get hurt - it's all bullshit. It will save us all a lot of money - some more than others."

"Some trainers will be pretty desperate without anabolics, their whole training method has evolved with it."

"They'll learn."

"Yes I suppose they'll drop down for a year or two."

"You chop a bloke's leg off - he still get's around."

"But he doesn't win races. It does fall into a bit of a pattern. The trainers who feed high levels of grain and protein use a lot of additives and anabolics, and generally train their horses a lot harder."

"Which came first though - the anabolic needle or the high grain? See if you inject anabolics, you can feed more grain. So which did they do first - feed more grain or use anabolics."

"The trainers I have spoken to who don't use anabolics, if you ask them, 'Did you try them?' will mostly say, 'Yes'. When you ask them why they didn't continue using them, they often say, 'Because it gave me horses I could hardly handle'. Some of the stories these guys tell make me laugh - like throwing the feed at the horse from six feet away; drawing straws to see who went into the box to get the horse; or, 'I didn't get into training to risk life and limb,' 'made bricklaying in winter look attractive again'. Anyway, that would suggest to me that these trainers either already undertrained, or didn't increase the amount of work enough when they started using anabolics."

"I asked one fellow exactly that: 'Did you give the horses more work?' 'More work! - my boys were afraid to get on the bastards.' I'm thinking of the teenage girl whose family hardly knows which end of the horse eats, and she has been given the big tip for whatever she does with her horse - jumping, showing, dressage - give it five ccs of this anabolic. They call you out because it has cut itself rushing about the yard in frustrated stallion fashion. The whole family is terrified of it. You arrive and say, 'Well someone better get a halter on it and bring it over here.' You should have seen their faces. It was like asking a villager to arrest Attila the Hun."

"But all over Australia there were trainers who were trying to 'do a Tommy Smith' - feed high and train hard. They wanted to train harder or had horses that were over trained - flattened. When they tried an anabolic, it helped the horse stand up to the work and the feed and they thought it was marvelous stuff. So they were locked into that cycle."

Fred suggested that using all those things was a state of mind that some trainers get into. I would agree that some trainers do use anything that *might* work or anything in fashion.

"A horse on anabolics is very impressive. He develops a bit of character, his coat looks shiny, he eats well, fights other horses. They're all positive signs. It is one of the most noticeable things you can do to a horse: he looks entirely different, his behavior is entirely different; but he doesn't necessarily race any better."

8.9 Shoeing

"Fred what is your policy with regard to shoeing? This is regarded as a very important part of training pacers and trotters."

"Yes it is very important, and it's one of the things that's changed dramatically over the years. Whereas in days gone by horses were harder to gait and needed all sorts of fancy shoes and that sort of thing, the horses we have right now are pretty natural, and most of them go shod very plainly."

"So you are not into a lot of alterations to shoeing and alterations to the foot?"

"I'm almost totally opposed to that. I just think that the average pacer can be shod the same as the average hack, and I think that his foot is put there by nature, should not be interfered with, and the shoe is only there to stop the foot wearing away."

"So you prefer the farrier to do nothing more than maintain the existing shape of the young horse's foot, and not to really try to do much with it?"

"I fit a plain set of shoes and I want him to trim the feet according to the growth of the foot. I just want him to take the wall off as it grows, not too much and not too little, just dress the natural foot and put the shoe on and don't try to be clever."

"So if the young horse has a long toe or a short toe, or a short inside wall, you don't try to correct that?"

"No I don't. There's not too much that can be done at this stage, in my view. You can start to play with the angles and that sort of thing with little effect, in my opinion. It's more likely to result in sore joints and that sort of thing than to do him any special good. I think if you want to start to manufacture a better looking foot, or a better conformation, then you should have done it before you sent him to me to train him to race."

"Yes, I couldn't agree more. What is needed is more work on the feet of growing horses when they're out on the stud. The business of suddenly altering the joint angles by two and three and especially five or seven degrees, when they're about to go into work, is just dreadful. It may take a few months or even six months for the problem to reach the point where it stops the horse, but they're asking for trouble to make big alterations."

"I think so. I just don't like to see any alterations at all, and what we're essentially talking about is a horse being shod once every four weeks. That's about the average life of the shoes before they start becoming loose and shifting around. I like to get in just before that happens, so somewhere from about 25 to 28 days, the average horse is going to need his shoes replaced. If he's grown a quarter of an inch of foot in that time span, he's done very well."

"So you don't have different shoes for race day; they work in the one set and you take them off after a month."

"Yes. I get a lot of sore-footed horses because of the banging away that we do."

"You put hoof testers on and they're sore all over the foot?"

"They get real sore. They get so sore you don't have to put a hoof tester on; they're going to show you pretty quick; limp like hell and hurt like buggery. And I've got a few. You've got us pressing them too hard and you've got the curators making the tracks too hard to hold them together, because they've got to keep racing week after week. I still don't think we've worked out what sort of shoes we should put on horses, which surprises me in this day and age. The old steel shoe is the best of what we've got, but it's not right, it's still not right."

"Your expertise in shoeing, did you get that mainly from farriers?"

"I suppose I went the whole circle there. When I started off, horses were, generally speaking, bad-gaited and a great deal of importance was put on the correct weighting, balancing and dressing of feet. I guess you could say it was important in those days to get heavily involved in that."

"How much could you rely on the farrier? Was it a case of the farriers knew it all?"

"That's a good question. There are still a lot of people who believe that the farrier is God and can fix this, that, and the other. They send the horse to the farrier with the strapper and tell him it's hitting its knees and leave it to the farrier to fix it up. Now, I think that's wrong. I don't think you ought to do that. I've often heard the comment, 'Oh, the farrier buggered it up. It was going right but the farrier's buggered it up.' That's another way of saying that the trainer didn't take enough interest, because I believe that when you want a horse shod, you should be there, with the farrier, and have him shoe it the way you want it. Farriers shoeing as many horses as they must to make a living - I don't think you can expect him to remember your special horse and get it right every time. So I always accept full responsibility for the way they're shod."

"So who did you get - the legendary Alby Mollet?"

"No. He was a Fremantle man and he had a big reputation but I can't comment on him because he never shod for me. Over the years I've used a lot of farriers. I stayed with my farriers because if I'm there when they put the shoe on then I accept the rest of responsibility, so it's never his fault. If I get it wrong, then I can only blame myself. I just want him to do a neat job. In these days of machine-made shoes, they don't have much influence over what they're going to do, and I don't try to do too much, because I think by and large, when we get the horses, from two years and older, that it's too late to change anything."

"I'm pleased to hear you say that you don't try to change angles."

"I think their conformation's set and I won't be so bold as

Fred's farrier at work. Fred does not want a farrier to do anything more than take off the growth since the last shoeing, an unusual outlook in the Standardbred world.

to try and change anything."

"If you look at the architecture of the fetlock joint and below, to change something by even two or three degrees, let alone five degrees, is asking for problems. The hoof is suddenly level but there is abnormal wear and tear from changes in the distribution of forces. There is a lot of pressure on the studmaster and the farrier as sales time approaches. But the farrier who levels and corrects everything to the textbook picture on his first visit to the horse, in one hit, is a potential cause of lameness."

"If you put a new pair of shoes on your own feet, with just a little bit of a low heel, they're not as comfortable and you can get sore ankles. My biggest criticism of farriers, is that they all tend to want to play God, and the better recognized they get, the more they believe they must have an influence. Then I run into trouble. I want the blacksmith to believe he's no more important than causing the horse not to wear his feet off. I just want to put a shoe on there to stop him wearing his foot away."

"So if you leave the horse alone and replace the shoe only when you have to, then you're going to run into less problems and so's the horse. What we're finding with the workload we put on them is that between three and four weeks the shoe's going to wear out. It has to be replaced, but if you keep taking off more foot than he's grown in that three to four weeks, and you've kept him at work six months, then you've got a problem."

"So I want them to be natural. I don't want to try to change the shape of his feet or the angle of his feet or anything like that. I look at a horse's foot, and where I think it's grown, I think it should be taken away. That's all I want to do."

"Occasionally we run into some horses that have genuine gait problems that you can alter a little bit by putting a heavier shoe on or leaving a longer toe on. You will influence their gait to a small degree by doing that. You've just got a little bit of input. You can't expect too much from it, but you can maximize the horse's gait. He's just a little happier. If a horse needed a little bit of toe in front, and you kept him short in the toes in front, he wouldn't be quite as happy. And that's about all you can take from that. You won't make him a lot faster, he'll just be a little happier and that might make him faster."

"A lot of people in the harness racing game DO regard the farriers as Gods - makers and breakers of a horse's potential."

"Yes, but a long time ago I learnt that I shouldn't do that. I was like everyone else - go off to the blacksmith and say, 'He's touching his knees or he's cross-firing' or something. Now I am careful to avoid making that comment."

"You don't tell farriers about the horses gait problems, because that makes them do things to the foot?"

"Well, the first thing they do is rack the horse's foot over, turn their foot over and make some hit them worse."

"Rack the horse's foot over?"

"Lower them on the outside of their front feet if they're hitting their knees. That's the first thing the farrier's going to go to, and he's going to try very hard to get that to work. If that doesn't work, well, then he'll use reverse psychology and lower the insides. For crossfiring they used to raise them on the outside of their feet behind, but I found those things didn't work like they're supposed to. Your horse might be going okay but just flicking his knee a little bit, and you go off to the farrier and say, 'He's touching his knees, can you just do something about it?' So, trying to please, the farrier would make an alteration, and I usually found that he hit his knees a damn sight harder, so I learnt there and then that it was better if I didn't mention it."

"So what do you do for a horse that is hitting his knees?"

"I like it if he can hit his knees faster. That's all I try to do. Get him to hit them quicker."

"A lot of people - that's their obsession - it's hitting its knees, and they don't seem to really look at the training until they can get it to stop hitting its knees."

"I don't want him to stop hitting his knees. Let him hit them quicker."

"What if he gets sore?"

"If that were the case you should put a better protection on there. A better boot. I'm sure they can hit them hard enough to get sore, but all you're really going to do, if you shoe him away from his knee - you're altering the stats in a way that could cause him to be slower, you're mechanically going to shift him away from where his bones want to go. I'm sure you can do that, but I don't think it's a better result in the end. And what about the old saying the Yanks had - if you got a knee-knocker, swap the horse for a dog and sell the dog: if he's that bad a knee-knocker he can't run, get rid of him. But we've had some pretty good knee-knockers like Paleface Adios and Pure Steel. They never stopped hitting their knees, they just kept banging them away and running very fast for a long time. I'm pretty happy to go along with that."

8.10 Has Fred 'produced' any good trainers?

Geoff O'Neill worked for Fred and went on to train successfully in Macau. Fred's son Greg won the Australian Junior Driver's Championship in 1988. Daughter Kellie wins her share of drives and in that same year tied for Most Improved Reinsperson. One day we could see a race in Perth in which all the drivers were Kersleys or Warwicks.

8.11 Analysis of his training

Because Fred trains on his own track, other trainer's opinions of his methods are not very well informed. Fred is considered somewhat methodical and plodding, but I think that is because he is not a talker and he concentrates on the job in hand.

By steady and thoughtful experimentation, Fred has arrived at his own training program and will probably continue to experiment. Certainly he is not an anabolics and additives trainer. More analysis will be possible when more trainers have been covered and comparisons can be made.

It is perhaps of interest that Fred's brother Bill has a similar program, using intervals at an early stage - in the second of the 6 to 8 week preps - but not close to the race. Bill's intervals however consist of 3 or 4 bursts of 400m with a jog lap in between. Typically the first lap would be a slow 37 to 40 seconds. In the second run, good ones would go in 34 seconds, then do

the third in 32 or 33 seconds. They do a fourth lap if Bill considers it necessary. At the end of the second prep they should be able to do a quarter in 32 or better. He may use intervals in the third prep if the horse is sluggish. The relief jog is at a slow rate. The slow day work is 10 to 12 km (6 to 7.2 miles) at 18 to 20km/hr (11 to 12 miles/hr).

Pacing writer Gino de Mori considers Fred has the ability to have a horse cherry ripe on the night that counts. I asked Gino what his evidence was for that statement and he explained that in his opinion Fred has seldom had outstanding stock and yet has done very well; has taken 'crabs' and won heats of the Interdominion with them.

9. Fred's feeding and additives

Fred talked about watering when he was a lad: "Horses were out in the yards without water until they were brought back in at feed time around 5pm. We'd hold them at the water trough and they would drink their fill. That was all they got until the following morning. They were fed three times a day and they were offered water before each meal. There was a hay-up late at night. They seemed to cope."

"But you'd often get some stupid stallion that would be looking down the paddock at a mare and though you knew he should have had a drink he didn't; that was just bad luck. Of course a lot of trainers then, and a few still today, take the horse's water away the day of the race. Whenever we put the water buckets in the stall and the horse went bad, all the buckets got thrown out again."

"How much did they drink?"

"A couple of hundred swallows."

"That is quite a long drink. What made you change to putting water in the stall? Did you see other people doing that?"

"I think I was worried about the horse that was locked up all night and that you knew had not had a drink. You bring the stallions in and they all lair up when they are coming in from the paddocks. Prancing and dancing. You get to the trough and he's got other things on his mind. So he doesn't drink."

Fred leaned forward and his expression became somewhat intense: "Then on a freezing cold morning they used to hang their heads over the half doors - you had to stand there and offer them a bucket of water. When they are nearly finished they splash the freezing water all over you. You were battling to hold the bucket. You used to feel like drowning the bastard."

Ned Kersley's feeding

Ned: "My brother Frank and I fed a lot different to our father Pop Kersley."

"What was the difference?"

"We were great believers in wet feeds. We used to feed a lot of bran; flaky bran in every feed. Wet feeds with boiled barley, plus oats, oaten hay, and we used oaten chaff in the early days. Later I had to go to wheaten chaff because oaten chaff was very hard to come by. I never fed dry."

"How many pounds of grain would you feed?"

"I didn't go by weight, I went by measure but between three and four pints per feed, on a ratio of approximately one of oats, two of chaff and one of lucerne chaff."

"How many times a day did you feed them?"

"Four when I first started, but I cut it back to three. In the beginning I wasn't a very heavy oat feeder. I only used to feed two pints of oats, four times a day. But the quality of feed has changed. We used to feed oaten chaff, and that had a fair bit of oats in it. We also used to get good oaten hay. It was cut later, when the grain formed."

"Did your father feed salt?"

"Yes and I used to feed salt in their feed every night, about a tablespoonful; I don't know why. They had brown rock salt available to them in their boxes. They also had a bit of clay in their boxes to. It was brown clay from Serpentine. I read about it in some veterinary book, it was supposed to be good for their digestion, so I got some. Some horses would eat it and others wouldn't."

"Does Fred feed clay?"

"Yes he has clay in his sand rolls, and some of the horses when they go in will tear into it."

(For those who think feeding clay sounds weird, studies have shown improved metabolic efficiency when certain types of clay are fed. Such clays are marketed in Australia and fed to cattle, sheep, and horses.)

"Salt?"

"Fred puts salt in their feed."

I asked Fred about his feeding.

"Fred what's your attitude to feeding at the start of training? Do you increase it steadily as the work increases?"

"I don't have a special policy other than I like to feed them what they'll eat and as much as they'll eat. Most horses fit in a very tight range. I'm not into heavy protein supplements or any other supplements for that matter. I just like to feed them a natural diet. There are differences in the horse's capacity to handle food. Some eat a lot more and don't seem to do any better than the one that eats an average amount of food. I'm a bit frightened of bad doers at this stage, because he's obviously a horse that's not going to train on; he's going to start to weaken in his constitution. He's a problem horse and you recognize that. It seems to me the fitter they get, the better they become at assimilating the nutrient from their food. So they all tend to eat less, the closer you get to the races. Because I know this is going to happen, I'm always ready for it."

"It's an interesting thing, it happens with human athletes as well; though they eat more their stomach shrinks and yet they seem to also get more from their food when they are doing more work. An interesting phenomenon."

"I don't know why it happens, but the horses come into the stable and go through volumes of food, and the fitter they get, the tighter they become and the demand for food decreases."

"One of the possibilities is that it is due to a greater natural anabolic secretion. Anabolics improve the efficiency with which the animal takes up the protein compounds from its food, and holds on to the ones that are in the system as well."

"I feel that racehorses don't have the ability to handle great volumes of food and they do better on a smaller volume of food."

"I'm surprised to hear you say that when you have chaff out there."

"I would never go the other way and reduce the roughage content, because I do think that horses need quite a bit of roughage. They seem happier with it, less cribbing and less vices. I like to feed quite a deal of roughage. When they get close to races, they don't tend to eat more grain. You would think they would, but so far as I'm concerned, it doesn't happen that way. They reduce their grain intake and yet stay in good flesh and seem to have enough energy anyhow. I don't know why, but that's what I see."

9.1 Where did he get his first ration?

NED KERSLEY: "I was with Fred for a short time when he first started and we discussed feeding. He wanted to feed harder and at one stage he decided to feed equal parts oats, chaff and lucerne chaff. He has fed bran, but then he cut bran out. He has tried other things like sunflower seeds, peas, beans. But he has come back now to basically where he feeds one of oats, two chaff and one lucerne chaff."

9.2 Grains - how many pounds of oats a day?

"How many pounds of grain do you feed per day?"
FRED: "I don't know. Probably eight to ten pounds."

"Do you feed any grains besides oats?"

"At the moment I'm feeding a little bit of corn and some sunflower seed. The horses like the sunflower seed and I'm always happy to feed that. I've tried all those things like protein supplements and so on and I don't honestly believe that they do anything, I don't see any benefit. I do sometimes wonder, when a horse trains off, if one of these things may have prevented that. But I do prefer to keep everything as simple as possible. The more complications you introduce, the more difficult it becomes."

9.3 Hays

"You give them lots of chaff?"
"I'm big on chaff and I feed them hay as well."

9.4 Cut green grass or grazing

None.

9.5 What additives does he use?

As you saw in the shoeing section, Fred Kersley is a very skeptical man. When I asked him about additives to make hooves grow, he said he had fed a lot of additives to the ants because he could not see any response in his horses. His view may be summarized as, 'If in doubt leave it out,' whereas many trainers take the insurance outlook, 'If in doubt still give it'. Fred's view is part of his 'keep it simple' philosophy.

In addition Fred's veterinarian, Charlie Stewart, is very much a non-believer in additives. Charlie told me, "I won't let my trainers use iron supplements." I asked Charlie what his reasons were. "Because I believe what is in the books, the literature, which says they don't need extra iron."

Fred does however use Minavit Red Band, made by Soutar Rural, which contains a range of minerals and vitamins, including iron. There was some Cal Plus but it was a sample. Fred has just tried one horse on maize oil, and while it improved the coat, he couldn't see any improvement on the track, but he intends to try more horses.

Fred had one bottle each of Robacyl, Coforta and Hemo-15. These are all widely used in Australia. Some trainers give them to weak, anemic animals to build them up, a few trainers give them to every horse in their stable, and some give them to horses close to racing.

Robacyl is an injectable arsenic compound. Arsenic compounds have long been used in horses in Australia, especially Standardbreds. There was a white powder (given orally), as well as injectable forms. When I have asked trainers why they use (or used) arsenic the reason usually given was that it allows the horse to stand more work. For perhaps a century, men working in the mining industry took daily amounts so they could shift more rock.

Arsenic is poisonous in large amounts and horses have died when dosages have been increased or duplicated. The classic story is of a trainer who gives it in the feed; some of the horses don't like it and the bulk of it ends up in the bottom of the feed bin with some 'leftover' grain. The grooms tip the leftovers into the feed bin of the stable 'glutton', which is often the best horse in the stable, and the arsenic kills it.

It is widely stated that horses that have been on arsenicals for any period of months will 'fall in a big hole' when taken off. The hair coat becomes dull, the animal loses muscle and condition - and it seems NOTHING can reverse this. Trainers told me of horses that had been switched to them from arsenic-users, that took six months or a year of time off, before they could stand hard work. One elderly trainer said his vet had told him he believed part or all of its value was that it was a weak worm killer. He believed it was much less effective when decent wormers appeared in the 1960's.

Arsenic spreads into the tissues and stays there for very long periods - months or years. Blood levels are low, but easily detected in tests. The reason you never hear of bans for a positive arsenic test is because it is present in feeds, and consequently in the blood of all horses, at low levels.

Coforta 10% is an injectable containing a phosphate compound and vitamin B_{12}. Vitamin B_{12} was the original 'sting'. If you inject it into a cat as an appetite stimulant, you will find out in about 20 thousandths of one second why it became known as 'the sting'. Vets and academics of the type who like to comfort themselves with the beliefs that nothing increases the performance of horses, and that trainers are idiots, love to point to the use of B_{12}. They say that B_{12} acts to increase the hemoglobin production, but that it takes months for the new red cells to appear in the blood stream. Anyone who gave it hours or days before a race was kidding themselves. The doses used are ridiculously high, and anyway, it could only help if the horses were anemic - low in red cell numbers.

Unfortunately, all these learned people are showing is their ignorance and lack of imagination. Even before a lot of other actions of B_{12} were discovered, it was easy to guess from the complexity of all things biological that there might be other reasons for the effects some trainers described, namely 'fizzed up,' 'up on its toes,' 'healthier coat,' 'faster'. Over the last 20 years many other actions of B_{12} have been discovered. Some of these involve neurotransmitters in the brain. The effects on the horse's nervous system, long observed by trainers of the 'chemical racing fraternity,' will eventually have an explanation. I once gave a dose to a horse to see for myself and it certainly stirred the horse up for several hours.

B_{12} is easily detected in tests but the problem is that normal horses have blood levels of it too. The authorities have the problem of showing that the level in the blood could not have occurred naturally, the same problem that curses the control of arsenic, and hormones like cortisone.

Hemo-15 is an injectable mixture of some vitamins, including B_{12}; some iron and copper; inositol, pantothenol and the amino acids lysine, methionine and glycine.

I had been led to believe by a man in pharmaceutical marketing that Fred was a heavy user of such things, but all three bottles looked a bit aged. In some Standardbred stables I have seen dozens of bottles of one or several of these, all looking new. I told Fred how widespread they seemed to be.

"The old standby isn't it. You always have some on hand, but I don't know how much you put through them. The Hemo-15, it's good logic when you read the label, and yet I don't think I've seen it help a horse."

"Some trainers swear by it. The thing with additives is that the improvement, if there is any, is so small. Anything that improves a horse more than three lengths will probably be noticed but less than that it would need an astute handicapping brain to see it. Statistical analysis would need large numbers and then it still might be missed."

10. His management and how he makes money

10.1 Fred's business philosophy

"My philosophy has been, 'Trust me, let me alone and let me do it for you. I don't want to make a million dollars out of training fees. I will do well as long as you do well. We need to win races. If I can win for you, then pay me, but if I haven't won - we've had bad luck or it was a bad judgment or whatever else - then you haven't been hurt so bad that you're going to give up and go away. You're going to appreciate what's happened and stay involved."

10.1-1 Ownership of horses and premises

"Do you own many horses yourself?"

"Yes, we have done in more recent times."

"Would you describe that as a successful, profitable strategy or not profitable?"

"No, it's not profitable but it did give me flexibility in training a number of horses. You see, when horses of a similar class were obliged to race next week, I could always scratch my entry without a great deal of argument. But if I have two separate owners starting horses with equal chances, and you can only drive one of them, the other fellow feels disadvantaged no matter what you say to him. You can't convince him that you know his horse is as good as the other one, will race as well nor that you've trained it as well as the other."

"But that would tend to make it unprofitable in that you've got to keep scratching your own."

"That's what I said, it is not profitable. It is a luxury, if you like, that I needed. With the number of horses I have for the number of racing opportunities I've got, I need to have that flexibility, so I can keep the owners I have happy. Now I couldn't have done it if every horse had a different owner."

"What about you being part-owner?"

"It's got a little security in there. They really can't take the horse off you even if you don't please them."

"So do you part-own some of them?"

"Yes."

As mentioned earlier, Fred and Judy own their 80 acres. Fred is not the type to rent.

10.2 Personality and management style

Having so many of his family working for him complicates matters in some ways. His son and daughter have their normal rebellious phase superimposed upon their first employment experiences, an ironic rerun of Fred's experiences with his own father.

10.2-1 Ruthless with horses - or sentimental?

"Is Fred one of those people who gets emotionally involved with his horses or is he towards the other extreme,
more interested in turning them over and testing numbers?"

JUDY:"No, he's not interested in turning them over and finding numbers. Not at all. Some horses he gets a little more emotionally involved with, but he gets to understand his horses, he gets to know his horses, and he respects that they're each individuals and have their individual personalities."

"Has he ever had one that was his greatest favorite?"

"There have been a few over the years that he had special feelings for. We had Binshaw who won an Interdominion late in his career. His last campaign, Fred had him. I think he would say Binshaw was the most intelligent horse he ever trained. He practically spoke to you. When people say horses are intelligent - Fred believes horses are not."

"I like stirring the horsy girls by saying that amongst all the mammals, horses have got one of the most reptilian brains outside of the rhinoceros."

"But Binnie was different. He was a funny old horse. He loved his roll in the sand yard, and if he wasn't ready to get out, there's no way you could make him stand up. You'd just walk away and when Binnie was ready to go, he'd stand up and whinny to you. Sort of say, here I am, I'm ready to go now. We saw him yesterday. He's twenty-five or twenty-seven, and he's in our paddock at Byford. It is a 12 acre paddock and he was over the far side with a youngster. When we called out to him, he looked up and came straight across to us; put his head over the fence. They've all got their different personalities. I don't know if I could say what horse Fred felt was his favorite."

FRED:"I have to train myself not to care so much about the horse. I have to make a mental decision not to care so much."

"Some of the top trainers are pretty ruthless, they have to be. I can imagine trainers becoming attached to horses and not training them hard enough. I've known trainers who couldn't train hard enough because of the fear of breaking them down. TJ Smith hates a type of horse he calls 'poofters', horses that can't take a lot of work."

"I can relate to trainers becoming too attached to their horses. I made a comment to Greg Harper about Jaybee's Fella, a horse he had entered in all the Grand Circuit events. He was real keen on the horse and being real nice to him. Greg is a tough trainer, very demanding on the ones he doesn't like. This horse was hanging a little bit and getting to the left. I said to Greg, 'If this horse wasn't a good horse you'd have a pole on him.' He thought about it, said, 'You're right,' and put a pole on him. Jaybee's fella went a lot better. That's just an instance where you can get a bit soft on 'em."

10.3 Staff selection and delegation

Fred is painstaking, careful, methodical and a worrier. Consequently he does not readily delegate decision-making.

It is difficult to attract young people into stablework, so selection between applicants is seldom an issue.

10.4 Training arrangements

Fred will do deals. He will train a horse in return for a share in the horse. He has found this arrangement more necessary as trotting and the general economy declined. The risk is that you can end up with some bad horses, but he is still happy to make such arrangements.

"It would sharpen your eye for a horse. Would you say that owning horses was a factor in your financial side of things?"

"Apart from the flexibility in training, I know it hasn't been an important factor. (Paavo must have made a healthy contribution.)

"So in the main you've made your money with the training fees and percent of prize money?"

"Yes, and of the two, the percentage of prize money is always the dominant one, because I always structure my training fees on the basis that I've covered my costs. For me to make money it had to be out of percentages, and I've always kept a relatively low training fee and asked for a little more percentage. That demand is on me to win."

"Is that allowed by the Trotting Association?"

"The Trotting Association doesn't care who gets what. What they say is they take 5% for the driver and 5% for the trainer. Now I say to clients of mine that I want 15% of stakes won, which means I put on another 5%. In the country trots where they don't take out the percentages, then I take the 15%. There's no mystery, no secret."

10.4-1 Training rates

"So what do you charge per week per horse? (1987)"

"I charge per calendar month and at the moment it's $675."

"How does that compare with other trainers around Perth?"

"Less than most, more than some others."

"So that's a strategy to attract owners, to have the lower training fee. In the gallopers in some places it's a rule of racing - supposedly - that the trainer shall not take nor expect more than 10% of prize money."

"I didn't know that, but it couldn't be enforced in any case. There are slings or presents, call them what you will, that come into it. Slings are not what they used to be. They used to be almost expected and nearly always happened, but these days, trying to make it work with falling stakes and rising inflation, increased costs, more and more what we're doing is just running it according to the book. You're just trading on an agreed basis. Slings are almost a dying art. When we went from pounds to dollars (Australia went decimal about 1966), you might have got a hundred pounds for winning, but when we changed you got a hundred dollars." (There were two dollars to the pound, so in effect slings halved.)

10.4-2 Debt collection

In his early days Fred had no bad debts but 'in modern times' that has changed.

"Did you try calling in debt collectors or selling the debts?"

"We've had the bailiff go round at different times but people are too clever today, there's nothing to take when they get there."

"That's what vets find, the people who leave debts are professionals at it."

"There are certainly more bad debts. You'd have more of it if you advertised, but I tend to sit and wait. I get the more established owner, the one who has been in it a while, or who has friends with me, so I know them."

10.5 Investments outside racing

"Does Fred have to continue training or has he made enough out of it that he could relax a bit. Is the financial pressure off him to keep striving?"

JUDY:"Well, I do think he has won a bit. The financial pressure now isn't as difficult as it was. Regardless of what people think, we're not rich. We've never lived beyond our means."

"Has he been one for buying blocks of land or putting money into investments?"

"No, no. The only things we've ever bought that we couldn't pay for were our property in James Street, Carlisle, and then this Forrestdale property. Anything else - if we wanted a car - you only buy what you can afford, and when you can afford a bit better one, you buy a bit better one. The same with everything. We've never bought anything until we could pay for it. Because of the nature of the industry, you didn't know what was ahead and you couldn't afford to have debts. Even now we're still very cautious. We paid our property off about a month ago. We gathered up what we had and said, 'Well, that's it. We own it'. Because you look at your statement, and what you're paying in interest is unbelievable (interest rates hit 15 to 20%). All that money you've paid and very little of it has gone off the principal. We bought a block at Byford, near the training complex, which hasn't been a good investment."

10.6 What is Fred worth?

JUDY:"I suppose we find we are rich in assets, if you look at the Forrestdale property and the Byford property and add horse floats-"

"But he hasn't geared himself so that if he wanted it there's a fixed income coming in?"

"No. We've been very careful with our money, because we

did start off with nothing, but there's not as much money within the industry as some people think. There probably is if you're a punter, but he's not a punter."

The land zoned rural in Forrestdale used to be $1,000 an acre for many years but lately some major roads have made the area more accessible. Industrial development and housing, once creeping closer are now closing in rapidly. It has recently become possible to subdivide into lots as small as five acres (two hectares). These sell for as much as $60,000 each. Fred has 80 acres and made this comment: "It's a good thing about training. You tend to acquire land and that becomes your superannuation scheme."

10.7 How did Fred make his money?
Resales of horses that are finished with racing, or not good enough to go on with, make very little money in Standardbreds. They generally don't make good saddle horses, so a lot become dog food. Trading in horses can be a large part of some trainers incomes, particularly if they mark up the value of the horses, but Fred and Judy are not into that.

Markup on horses
JUDY: "Some trainers say the markup on horses is fair game. There have been debates about it and some people say, 'You're mad,' that we should do it, and others say, 'No, you're right'. Say Fred flew to New Zealand and bought a horse for $30,000 and then came back here and sold it to one of our owners for $60,000 or $70,000 and that's what some of them do - now, some people say that's fair game."

"I could understand if Fred got on a plane off his own bat, and we both went to New Zealand and we spent a bit of time there, and we used our money to buy three or four horses and brought them home and started to work them, and then somebody said to us, 'We'd like to buy a horse,' and we said, 'These are the three horses that we've bought as youngsters and put some work in'. I can say, 'This is what they're worth. If you want to buy them, okay, if not, we'll just keep them, we're happy to go along with them.' I think we could mark one up that we bought for $20,000 and say it's now $40,000. But if our owners - or a syndicate we put together - said, 'Now go to New Zealand and buy these horses'; the syndicate pay your expenses and everything. I don't morally believe you can come back and mark up those horses."

"I think the guys that do the most marking up are the ones that don't buy through the sales. They go out to the farms."

"Or they have an agent."

"An agent or whatever. But they do the deal privately and no one can check up easily what the price was. Some trainers have done it and some have overdone it, but they may not get their owners back because eventually the rumors have spread that they're ripping everyone off."

"While the horse is successful they'll get away with it, but all of a sudden they're going to turn up a couple of $70,000 horses that are duds. But Fred's not a salesman and he won't go out looking for owners to spend a lot of money. We've had a couple of people that have asked if we could look out for a horse for them - must be three months now. Now we still haven't bought any horses, because it's not easy."

So Fred's bundle has been made by winning a lot of races and taking 15% of the prizemoney. In his best year that would have been 15% of $800,000 - $120,000. No great profit from training fees (although it paid the bills), nor from punting, trading in horses, or outside investments. The Kersleys have been very careful how they spent their money too. The jump in land prices has given Fred and Judy very secure long term prospects and Paavo's winnings have been icing on the cake.

11. How he gets and keeps owners
11.1 What is Fred's public image
Fred has a reputation as a very good and very honest trainer. This is reflected in the short odds at which his horses start.

11.1-1 Opinion of other trainers
Some trainers are in awe of Fred Kersley but others are slower to acknowledge Fred's abilities and are inclined to attribute his success to the Kersley name. His longstanding nickname among the fraternity is "Chook" or "Chooky". That is his stable name for Paavo too. That came about because brother Bill handled Paavo as a youngster, and he named the horse 'Chook'.

11.1-2 Relations with the stewards
I asked Fred if he had any problems with the stewards in his early days. He responded with a long slow sigh.

"Yes. One of the problems we have is that the stewards keep changing every 5 years or so. That is a strategy of control, so they don't become too familiar with the drivers and trainers. Each steward brings his own point of view, his own idiosyncrasies, his own highs and lows. The pressure points change. So it is a continuous adjustment."

"A lot of drivers and jockeys when they are just starting off, find it hard to cope with the stewards when they come down on them. It is easy to feel picked on, victimized."

"I think that would have been true of me and now my son Greg is in a heap of trouble. When you are young you are more aggressive and you think you have a clear understanding of right from wrong, but you get a little older and you begin to see the shades of gray. You see, stewards are not always right, and in Australia they are a bit too domineering. The way the rules of racing are written, especially as regards interference when driving, the pressure is to sail as close to the wind as possible

Warming up the horse for the next race. Having a horse in each race and having to gear it up, warm it up, then drive it and take the gear off - doesn't leave Fred with much time for socialising with the owners.

but don't get caught. Last night, after the meeting, 20% of the drivers were suspended, which is incredible. I'm critical of that, and I think stewards here over- control our racing. At the gallops the stewards don't have that same attitude. I think it is a small-track attitude."

11.2 Getting publicity

"How would you rate yourself at getting publicity? Were there ways to get publicity? I've seen a lot of trainers who were quiet people, shy even. I would consider you one of them, and I wonder how easily you'd get on with racing writers."

"It was important, I think, in the early days. I don't have an outgoing personality and I'm not the sort of bloke that can dress outlandishly (we had been discussing TJ Smith) or do things like that."

11.2-1 Fred and the press

"I used to have a good working relationship with the journos. I've lost it a bit these days - I suppose because lately I've felt the need for publicity a bit less; I've been over publicized and it's made my job harder. Horses have been written up as being better than they are."

"Your horses are always at short odds."

"Short odds and it's made my job a lot harder. A couple of blokes I think have been just unfair and very bloody ordinary at their jobs."

"There's a glint in your eye when you say that. There is a bit of feeling there."

"There's a couple that are bloody impostors. Some of them have a lot of shit in their heads too. If they ring me up, I don't talk to them. That's bad for my career but at this stage I can take that luxury. So a couple of the media outlets, I bar them completely. They're just bad for me in the long term. The blokes I am friendly with write about me, but the blokes that don't like me - they refuse to write about me. If I felt the need, I'd have a look at that; make sure I talk to the blokes that don't like me."

"I'd have thought, with your competitive nature, and Trevor Warwick having beaten you, that you might be reversing that."

"It's a principle I had to shake off there. Yes, there's no question about it, if you wanted to get back there and do it, that's what you should do. I think it is important to get good press. At the moment I'm getting a bad press. If I were to be entirely positive about it, I would try to change that round. I'm probably showing my age a little bit here because it doesn't bother me so much. I just feel like I can cop the bad press and it isn't going to hurt me all that much. That may be a wrong judgment on my part, but just for the moment I'm going to stick to my principles and hope those particular journos get sacked, which they should anyhow. I think I can live through it."

Fred subsequently took legal action against that publication and over the next year or so the people concerned 'disappeared' from its pages.

11.3 Getting owners and horses

"Are stable numbers a limitation?"

"Oh yes."

"I'm surprised you just don't build more - you have plenty of room."

"The temptation is always there, and I think you've got to fight that off. I could train a hundred horses, but I wouldn't train the hundred as well as I can train thirty. I keep around thirty to thirty-five. Now, I think it's fair to say too that I could train twenty better than I could thirty or thirty-five."

"The other thing is - how much racing opportunity do you have? Are you going to race against yourself in some of the classes? Certainly you can't get owner satisfaction when you have a lot of horses in my situation, training and driving them. The temptation is there, because you are offered some nice horses you'd like to take, and you've got to draw the line. Sometimes you get locked in with owners who will give you one or two good horses, but along with them comes four or five that have to be developed or aren't so smart, that you really didn't need."

"Might be time to give your son Greg a section down there of his own."

"Horses should go where they can win. If they can't win at Gloucester Park, then they should race at Richmond. If they can't win there they should go down the line a little, and if they can't win there, they should go further down the line. Now, I stay at the top two tracks - as much as ninety percent of the time. But having spent three months with the horse and found out he's not quite up to that, instead of just passing him by, you're entitled perhaps to send him down the line with a junior trainer-driver, and pull some stake money out of him."

"There is a family in America, the name escapes me, but they have an attitude that if a horse hasn't earned in three starts, he gets downgraded. They race at the top tracks down through to the lowest stake tracks, and eventually back to the agistment farm. So a horse has only got three chances to not earn before he's downgraded and if he's downgraded from there, he goes right out of the system or he goes to the farm for a rest. Then he's worked up at the farm by one of the brothers, passed through the system. That's pretty good logic."

"Henry Cecil is the dominant trainer in English racing.
What's keeping him up at the top in wins according to some people, is that horses that Vincent O'Brien or some other guys would say, 'Sorry, this horse is not up to my standard.'- it just goes down to his bottom level foreman and is still winning low level races, but in Henry Cecil's name. He has about 200 horses. They say that's keeping him at the top, and also it's keeping the owners happy."

"Well, that's the important thing. You're not losing the owner. When you lose the horse you lose the owner. He's keeping them in the system. They're there and one of the owners might turn up a good horse. It's never completely cut and dried. I can't say to some of my owners, 'Look, I just don't want that horse.' At a point in time you're going to get the message through, but you can't just cut it off today and say, 'Look, I'm sick of this horse, get it out of the stable. I want it out tonight, because I want to move one in.' You have to condition him over a period of time, say things like, 'Look, I think we're going to be battling to make it pay; it's not showing me enough to guarantee you a return for your costs. So we'll take it through to the end of the month and I'll talk to you again. We'll see what we've got.' He's usually going to come in and say, 'Give it a little bit more time, because I have got a bit of faith in this horse.' And you've got to do that; you've got to do that."

"I had one last week that was starting to worry me, and I felt like the owner didn't have too much money to spend on horses. I had freshened him up and brought him back, and he wasn't pleasing me in his training. He had his first run after being freshened up, and ran third. Most of the tipsters had marked him down as one to watch, because he was locked up and got out late and ran on a little bit. But my judgment was that the horse was going to cause him problems. I didn't think it was going to get any better than that run, and so I said to him that his options to cut his costs included training it himself - he's done that before - and he was happy to do that. So the horse didn't go home from the trots with me, it went home with him, and I feel I did the right thing there. I could have kept him for next week and seen what happened, but it was my judgment of the horse, that he was not going to get any better, he was only going to get worse in this training preparation. The cost of spelling him, bringing him back - what have you got - five months downtime. Three or four thousand dollars. I couldn't see that I was going to make a little profit from him."

11.3-1 Personality and social skills

Fred walks with the smooth controlled strut that was popular with young men of his era that fancied themselves a bit. The chronic pull of the reins has given him something of the wide shoulders and tapered body of the iron pumping brigade. He seems aloof and is not given to social chatter. Judy comments: "I don't suppose this carries much weight coming from me, but he is a particularly honest person and he doesn't talk unless he's got something to say. He doesn't make small talk. A lot of people might think he's ignorant and rude. A lot of people in harness racing who haven't really known him, and then we've been mixed up with socially - they'll say, 'You're quite a different person. I can't believe this is you."

Not gregarious by nature, Fred spends most of his time at the races attending to the horses, warming them up and driving them in the race. He usually has at least one in each race. In the stabling area Fred is more likely to be found giving close attention to his horses rather than talking to people over the security rail. Even now, when he has son Greg and daughter Kellie to help with the horses, he seldom ducks off to the various bars and lounges.

Away from the track, the horses still dominate his hours. That is not to say he is devoid of social skills. Ask Fred a question and you will - as you have already seen - get a long and interesting answer. He is not a monosyllabic non-talker. His serious nature and focus on his sport impress many. That doesn't mean he is serious to the point of being stuffy. He enjoys a joke but he is no wisecracking joke collector; he doesn't go in for banter and ribbing for the sheer joy of humorous exchanges. He keeps his mind on the job.

11.3-2 Social stamina and alcohol

"Did Fred avoid alcohol or did he drink it a bit socially?"

JUDY:"As young kids you drink it at the football club, socially. Normally when he has a drink he's a happy person."

"I imagine he wouldn't drink very much because he's got to get up so early in the morning."

"Yes."

11.3-3 Social class of owners

Fred told me his owners span the whole spectrum from the working man - who can be quite well off in Australia - through to successful businessmen. Fred finds the businessmen can be the most difficult to please, especially if they want business plans and profit projections.

11.3-4 Does he steal owners?

Fred is more likely to have owners stolen from him than vice versa. Fred is not into the, 'I'm your best buddy, we're mates' approach. The smooth talker he is not - but that is not to say he is not persuasive; he can be very persuasive through the sheer force of his logic.

11.3-5 Has Fred ever advertised?

Advertising has only recently been used by trotting trainers in Perth. Fred said he would consider it if he felt the need.

11.3-6 Does he give talks?

He used to give talks to sporting clubs, and, on occasional interstate trips, to people at harness racing seminars. When he receives awards at presentation nights he makes careful speeches, makes observations on the trends in trotting and gives a good account of himself.

11.3-7 Any affiliation with studs?

Breeding is a poorly developed side of harness racing in Western Australia. Most of the better class stock is bought from New Zealand and the eastern states. Fred has not received any significant number of horses from breeders.

11.4 Managing owners

"How does Fred manage his owners? Is he one of those people that manages them socially with a few beers - or does he do it from a distance?"

JUDY:"That's changed over the years: how you manage them now compared to when you first started off. When you first started off, the couple of clients you had were friends as well, so it was a little bit more social. They'd come around and come in the house and have coffee or a can of beer or something. Nowadays, so many owners you don't know very well at all, they've just been people who've rung up and asked you to take their horse. Some of them are still friends, but very few of them come out - because times have changed."

"Does he report to them every week or get them to phone him once a week?"

"No, no. Most of them have enough confidence to know that if there's a problem he'll ring them up and say so. There are a couple of new owners who ring up, not on a regular basis, but might ring up once or twice a month - their horse isn't racing yet - just to see how it's going. But once a horse starts racing, you see them regularly at the track and they see their horse regularly. Mick Lombardo (Probably the largest owner in WA) - we've had one or two horses for him - and he evidently finds it very hard to cope with Fred, because as I say, if there's nothing to say, Fred doesn't want to talk, and Mick seems to think you should ring up at least once a week and give a report on his horses."

"Fred's stable may be getting to the size where he needs to ritualize something like that."

"He probably does. Early in their training, say in the first three months when the horse doesn't trial or race or anything, then, quite often when I do the account for that particular horse, I'll say to Fred, 'Do you want to say anything?' On the bottom of it I might say, 'It's coming along well - anticipate that he'll trial in two or three weeks'. That just gives them something once a month. He probably still has very much a personal contact with his owners. We've got some owned by two brothers in Bunbury and Collie. I suppose once or twice a month - they're also family friends - he'll get on the phone and give them a rundown on what's happening with their horses."

I asked Fred about his relations with clients.

"What about expertise in client management?"

FRED:"Wrong trainer. I firmly believe it's harder to train owners than horses. That is one of the most difficult areas we come into. Broadly, what I do is throw my hands up in the air and say, 'Trust me.' The owners that can't do that, I don't have a long-term association with. The ones that do, we get a good result. I think you come back to the personality of the people. I'm not a person who's big on the talk and the bullshit like, 'Let me influence you to buy this $100,000 yearling'. I don't feel comfortable about that, I don't want to do it."

"However, I think they're important people and what they deserve is a hundred percent of your effort. You need to be completely honest with them. Sometimes I am honest to the point where they can't cope - it offends them in some way if I tell them the horse is no good. But that has to be said, and it's in their best interests not to try to influence me about where and when the horse should race. I have some owners that want to do that, and I will endeavor to please them, but ultimately it works against them, because the end result is not as good."

"Yes, I was going to ask you about a couple of what I would see as syndromes amongst owners. The first is the owner who wants to feel he's having a big input into where and when it races. The other is the owner who wants the horse to run in glamour races, races it's possibly not up to in your opinion."

"They're both problems we run into a lot. I think carefully chosen words about, say, the horse that's out of his depth; 'I feel at this stage he hasn't shown he could compete at that level and it may even be bad for him, because you're throwing him in out of his depth; it can only hurt him.'"

On one visit Fred told me he'd been having some aggravation from some owners.

"I've had more owner trouble than usual for this part of the year, so I've sacked (fired) a couple of owners. But I'm happy to do that."

"What do you sack an owner for?"

"Driving me mad. Being unfair. Once, when I was younger, I would have stood the crap. There was a guy, and I'd asked him for some programming logic - there was a feature race coming up. There were four of them in a syndicate and I said I'd like to know how they felt about next week's race, because: one - the track doesn't suit the horse; two - the other horses will be too tough. I said I'd understand if they wanted to run him in a high stake race - although - I said, I won't be able to drive him because I have a better horse that I'm going to enter in the race. Discuss it among yourselves and let me know if you want him entered. A bit of anger set in I think, because one of the partners said to me, 'What do you mean you aren't going to drive him?' I said you must understand, I have another horse pointed in the same direction and I can't drive them both. 'Oh! How long is this going to go on?' 'Oh! I can't put up with this,' and so on."

"I tried my best but in the end I just said, 'Look, you know the situation as well as I do, I've done my best, I can't please you. I don't want anyone unhappy, you'd be better off to shift your horses.' So they did. Once upon a time I would have tried to compromise a bit more, found the right words but now-."

"What would you have done? Alternated driving the two horses?"

"I probably would have done that, or waited until the barrier draw and then one horse might get such a bad barrier draw that the other owner would understand. I might have promised to drive it next time or something."

On racenight

Fred is so tied down preparing, warming up and driving his numerous horses he does not have much chance to talk to owners over the rail, let alone spend time in the members or the other bars with them. That probably suits Fred.

11.5 Main owners

Fred's name has never been associated with any main owner or owners. He has a lot of smaller owners. The question, 'Where would he be without his main owner(s)?' is therefore not applicable.

Is his main owner winning or losing? Because of Fred's preoccupation with getting value for his clients, they wouldn't be losing too much, but there is no high profile major client to do a balance of accounts on.

12. Fred and the breeding game

Selling mares and stallions off the racetrack into breeding is not a very fruitful avenue for owners and trainers in harness racing in Western Australia. The Australian breeding industry does not have high expectations from retired local track heroes.

"Do you think in Western Australian pacing there's a good system for finding out which are the best horses to breed from?"

"I think the Americans have been fairly clever. They've only bred from their fastest horses, and they've sent the rest of them to Australia."

"It's a monetary thing. Slow ones are all we can afford."

"Well, their attitude, as I understand, is to breed from the fast stallions, and I think with the mares they lean a little more on bloodlines, but it seems to have been quite successful because their times have kept improving."

"So even if the horse was regarded as a poorly-bred special from the back-blocks, if it set a record time on a particular occasion-"

"If he's especially good, they'll take a risk with him as a sire, rather than a very well-bred horse that couldn't run. Now, the very well-bred horses that couldn't run, that are full brothers to champions, they usually find their way out here and don't make it as stallions. There seems to me to be a pattern there."

"That happens in the gallopers as well. But it surprises me, since Australian harness horses go over more ground, that Australian sires don't do better against the American imports than they do. It might support the view that stamina comes from the dam."

"The people here buy from New Zealand, Victoria, South Australia - anywhere but here. There are a few sires from the Globe Derby line still doing well but they're not in Western Australia."

"What about well-performed fillies and mares?"

"There was a time when the New Zealanders used to buy all the Oaks winners, but the companies there have fallen on hard times. A few get through to America."

12.1 Fred as a stallion maker

Fred has not produced any stallions, but so few local horses go to stud it is almost a non-issue.

12.2 Record as a breeder

Fred has bred a few, but he really wonders why he does so. None of the products have been good enough to stop him wondering.

13. What makes Fred Kersley successful?

13.1 How he acquired his skills and knowledge

Fred paid his dues. He learnt from the bottom up in his father's stables, and his father was at the very top in his day. He also watched and questioned other trainers, especially Phil Coulson and his uncle Frank. Striking out on his own he experimented and improved steadily. He also read everything he could find and attended many seminars - still does.

13.2 Personality traits

Intelligence

Fred's low opinion of his own intelligence, which first bottomed when he went to the wrong football ground and again when he could not make progress as a trainer, is probably not justified. Fred has things carefully worked out, has his own ideas about everything. His questioning reveals him to be an astute individual. Nevertheless, he does not make an immediate impact because he hangs back a little and is not into repartee or witticisms. He speaks rather slowly, and, in terms of his voice, in something of a monotone.

However the ultimate effectiveness of a computer is not determined by its speed and the color range of its monitor, but rather by the programs it holds. If Fred lacks anything in sheer brilliance, he has compensated for it with sheer appli-

cation. Pacing writer Gino de Mori reports that at presentation nights Fred always impresses with his well thought out statements, and that people who meet Fred for the first time come away saying, 'Gee - he's a smart fellow'.

Fred uses his computer to assess everyone and everything he sees connected with trotting. When you talk to Fred about other trainers he repeatedly uses one of his favorite phrases: "I 'logicked' him out ... " His off the record observations of what other trainers do and why make interesting listening. They indicate how closely he watches and how much he thinks. He never spews out the track cliches, the popular one line view of that trainer: he always has an outlook of his own. You have to be an observer and a thinker to do that.

Memory

Fred is not very good at remembering which year things happened but he can relate events to each other. He can remember some things from so long back that when his father starts to tell him about horses from years ago, he knows what Ned is going to say about the shoeing, the gear, how it was trained and so on.

Sleep

JUDY:"He seems to need less now, I think. He's never really had a problem getting up in the morning, even if he's had a night out and might not get to sleep till three o'clock. Getting up is not a problem. Probably was harder before."

"How many hours would he average?"

"Probably the best sleep he has is in the afternoon."

"He's a catnapper?"

"That probably becomes a habit because before we shifted out here and he had to go into Gloucester Park to fast work, they'd have to be up at 4am to work the horses. Then they'd work through until lunchtime and then that night, you might have to go to country trots, or trials, or the trots, so you couldn't do it. You had to sleep after lunch - well, they all do. They all go down and have a nap. He's not a good sleeper any more. At nighttime he might be up and down two or three times, but in the afternoon he usually sleeps better."

"I've never seen him looking fatigued though. How long does he sleep in the afternoon?"

"Oh, probably about an hour and a half."

"How long does he sleep at night?"

"He doesn't have a lot of sleep at night; we go out nearly every night. It's changed of late, but before we had Monday night trots, the twilight meetings, and afterwards we'd go and have a meal just the two of us, and come home. Tuesday night'd be trials. Wednesday night used to be country trots. We don't always go to country trots. Thursday night is when we're home. Our youngest daughter, Fred and I will go into town for a meal. Friday night trots, Saturday night trots, and we go out on Sunday night for a meal with friends - it's just been a long standing thing that we all go out. But when you work at home, you need to go away to relax."

"Everything is there reminding you it needs doing."

"A lot of people come away from work to their home to relax. Sometimes I'll say, 'Do you need to go out?' He just feels he needs to get off the place, because if he's home he's usually reading a vet book, working out a worklist or what he's going to do with his horses, or programs for the week. He just doesn't relax properly. I suppose they'd say like a farmer or even a housewife. I find it hard just to sit down and relax properly, because you think, oh, I should be putting that washing on the line, or I could be doing something. So when we go out, there are a couple of restaurants we frequent, that we feel are friendly."

Energy

Although he is not a talkative, hyperactive dynamo, Fred does not suffer from laziness. He moves very deliberately, without rush, but he doesn't stop until the horses are completely fed, washed, watered and whatever needs to be done is done.

Health

Apart from the stomach condition, brought on by the stress of his own unrequited desire to succeed in the early part of his career, Fred has enjoyed good health.

Stress management

FRED:"My brother Bill didn't feel the need to be a top trainer/driver like I did; I mean, for me there was nothing else; it just had to happen and for a long time it wasn't going to happen. But I was a fairly empty person because of that. I didn't feel worthy until I made it. It was a comfortable feeling to get there."

"It took a lot of weight off your shoulders, did it?"

"Yes, I only now feel comfortable about my career. I really think I would never have felt like I'd done enough."

"A classic type A. Do you know about the type A's and type B's?"

"No."

"It comes out of heart disease studies in relation to personality type. There is a type A, who can never do enough, never achieve enough. They never stop and enjoy what they've done, they're always worrying about the next target. The type B is a laid-back person, who believes tomorrow will look after itself."

"The type A's, of course, are the ones that have the most heart attacks. But there's an interesting subdivision of A's in recent years. You can divide the type A's into people who are workaholics and people who are workaphilics - an American has recently made this distinction, and I'm hoping he's correct. The workaphilics love their work, they enjoy it, and it is really no stress to them. They work hard

and long because they really do enjoy it."

"The workaholics are the people who do the work for an objective that is actually on the other side of the work. They do it for the money, the status, the power, to please the wife or some reason like that. Frequently they hate the work. Now I can name vets who hate the dogs, hate the people, hate their colleagues and their partners and everything else. You think, 'Why does this guy go to work every day?"

"Now sometimes, in veterinary practice, my boss used to have to come and throw me out of the hospital, because if some animal was really sick, I used to want to stay there all night working on it and so on, but the money and that sort of stuff never mattered much. My criterion still is that when I get up in the morning, I have to WANT go and do what I have to do; it's got to be interesting. I'm hoping what this guy postulates is correct: that a lot of type A people not only don't have heart attacks, they live to a ripe old age because they are workaphilics. I hope he's right."

"I hope with you, I hope with you. But I've got to say that to me at times it was just like life or death. I had to succeed."

JUDY:"After the trots nowadays, we go out and have a meal and a couple of beers."

"This is after all the races - say 11pm?"

"On the same Friday or Saturday night. The boys take the horses home. Fred needs to unwind. Before, when we didn't have the staff, we came home from the trots and it might be three or four o'clock in the morning before he could get to sleep."

"How has he taken his loss to Trevor Warwick last year? Was that training and driving?"

"Yes, training and driving. Actually he handled it better than I did, to start with. When I could see the writing on the wall, which was very early in the season, it took me a while to accept it. Not for me personally, just for Fred, but he surprised me how well he handled it."

"He didn't go through stomach pains and lack of sleep?"

"No. I always wondered what would happen. It had to happen one day, and he took it a lot better than I had anticipated."

Celebrates successes

"I don't think Fred would be a great one for champagne for three days after, a big win would he?"

"Oh no. I think he enjoys the feeling that he's done the job well."

Scrapbook

Yes, he keeps a scrapbook.

Hobbies and interests

JUDY:"None really."

"So he's pretty obsessed with the pacing game?"

"Well everything - EVERYTHING - revolves around the trots- he enjoys football."

"Does he go to the football or is he a TV football fan?"

"We always go to the Finals. Through the year we don't go a lot. We very much enjoy football; don't get to go as often as we'd like, but the Sunday games we've really enjoyed. He enjoys the cricket on TV and we became members of the WA Cricket Association. We went to a couple of one-day games this year, which we both enjoyed."

"No golf?"

"No, no."

"Does he do anything to keep fit?"

"No, he's terribly unfit at the moment. Time is the big thing. The last twelve months is the worst he's ever been. He likes tennis and when we first shifted here, we nearly did put a tennis court in, but we didn't have the money. He would still like to put a tennis court down there. I'm a bit of a fly in the ointment there: I just think for the amount of money it would cost, it wouldn't get used much. But we probably should, because the kids and staff - it would do them all good, so I might weaken. We used to play social tennis once a week, and once again time gets to be the thing. He's often saying we should organize to get that going again."

Will he retire?

"I guess I'll always keep a horse or two in the back yard. My father potters around here with the horses. I can't think of a better way to keep active."

Drive and application

"Competitiveness: what were you like as a youngster? You weren't interested in schooling so you never competed academically."

"No, but I was competitive in sport. I always admired sportsmen and tried my hardest: busted my gut."

"Were you much of a sportsman?"

"I don't think I had enough fast twitch fibers. I could run all day. We used to run around the inside of the water sprinkler arms until the last one was left standing. I wouldn't stop running and it hurt like hell but I'd just keep going. I won the 'Most Improved' at football all the time. I just kept trying and trying and trying. I wasn't ever really good, but I did my best and I could hold down a game in the league side - not the big League."

"I just believe in being fiercely competitive."

"A thing that used to irritate me in those days, talking about school football now, was this: We never trained for football. We'd play the first match and I'd run like a bloody chook with its head chopped off. I'd run as hard as I could for the whole match; didn't know how to pace myself. I'd get home from the match absolutely stuffed, and all these other kids would get out and start kicking the footy up and down the street! I thought, 'How can they do that if they'd played the match as hard as they can?' You can't, you shouldn't have any energy left. I thought that was poor, that they had any energy left to kick a football. You almost had to put me in a wheel-chair and wheel me back in the house. I thought that was how it should be, you should bust your guts."

"Your brother Bill?"

"He's driven successfully, trained successfully. Once again, I think there's a difference in attitude. He didn't feel the need to be a top driver/trainer like I did."

Judy added to the perspective on Fred: "Determination he always had. He always wanted to be number one, and he would try very hard to do it. It was a long hard climb. Very hard."

"A lot of people start into it and they don't even think about being number one. But some people seem to have that determination from day one."

"Well, Bill came from the same family and everything-"

"But is just unambitious in that field?"

"Unambitious. Bill's just happy to be an also-ran. I mean, he enjoys winning, naturally. But a lot of people said to Fred, 'You know, you were born with a silver spoon in your mouth and you got there because it was in the family."

"That bugs him, doesn't it?"

"It does bug him, because it wasn't like that at all. In fact, I think it made it harder."

"Was Fred's father an ambitious person?"

"I'm probably not qualified to answer that, not knowing him when he was in full swing and on top of the tree. But I would say he has nowhere near the drive or determination Fred has."

"Was one of the things that produced that drive in Fred the fact that he was held in less regard by his father than Bill. I mean, his father seems to have thought Bill was the shining light."

"No, I don't think so. From stories Fred has told me of his childhood, they'd go down to the local park and the sprinkler would be on and they'd run around and you had to miss the sprinkler, and the last one out was the winner. He would have pains in his legs, he'd be nearly dead, but he had to hang in there. The same running up and down the sandhills. Evidently as a kid even, he would drive himself beyond endurance just to be the winner, and I don't think that had anything to do with harness racing. I think it was just the nature of the person."

"There are a lot of people who seem happy to get to the top once or twice, but then the willingness to continue the hard work drops greatly. The fact that Fred was up there for so many years would suggest there's something dif-

---

FRED KERSLEY

ferent about him and those people that will go after it year after year after year. After all, it is hard work and it's taking on pressures. And he doesn't sound like he considers himself out of the race in future either."

"What would you say gave him the most satisfaction when he was at the top? Was it something he wanted to do or does he enjoy those presentation ceremonies? I imagine he'd be a bit embarrassed."

"No, he doesn't enjoy them. This is what he's like: He's not a handyman, at all, but if he does do anything, he has to do it properly. Now when the kids were little, we had a couple of incidents; you buy the assemble-it-yourself swing. Well, putting this ruddy thing together, there'd always be one or two screws that didn't quite fit where they should. Truly, it turned into a national crisis. It took hours, and he's got a thing that happens to him every now and again: his face, his lip swells up, and it's due to frustration. I'd say, 'Look, that'll do, it doesn't matter'. He says, 'If it's not done properly it won't do'. So no matter what he does, he does set out to do it right."

"A lot of perfectionists narrow their field, because if they get into a wide field it is very frustrating. It's an awful feeling to do it half right."

Fred's brother Bill is a very relaxed character. After a question he pauses for a very long time, longer than Fred even. He has a straight-faced dry humor that made for an entertaining interview.

"What was Fred like growing up?"

"Mongrel." Just the trace of a smile on his face. I probably looked a little shocked, so he amplified and softened that. "I suppose he was the same as every older brother."

"There is some dispute about who is the older brother."

"Yes. He keeps telling fibs about that."

"He was the older brother was he?"

"He is."

"I think I'll need birth certificates to settle this. Where does he get his driving ambition from? I'll rephrase that. Where does he get that powerful ambition from?"

"I really don't know."

"Was your father an ambitious man?"

"No, I don't think so. I could be wrong, but I don't think Dad was terribly ambitious. He was satisfied to just do-"

"Fred says Ned was not as ambitious as his own brother - your uncle Frank. What about your mother? Was she ambitious? Did she want you to achieve things?"

"No more than any other mother I wouldn't think. She wasn't a driving force."

"Fred says you are nowhere near as ambitious as he is, and he doesn't know why that is."

"I can only say that I agree with that. My answer is that it's my nature. I relate back to Dad and his brother. Dad was a bit

like me and Fred was a bit like Frank."

"What was the earliest he ever talked about wanting to be number one?"

"I don't remember any discussions like that. But even before he started to train in his own right, one of the things he had to live down was the name that had gone before him. His uncle and father were both very successful. All the critics - I guess it happens in every walk of life - but everyone said, 'You'll never be as good as your uncle or your father'. I accepted that as just a normal reaction, just something people say. But it seemed to spur Fred, it drove him mad. He never said it to me but I think he said to himself, 'I'll prove they're all wrong.'"

"I think he still has that attitude. I think he gets annoyed that he still has to prove himself."

"Yes I believe that."

"Maybe it never cures."

"In Fred's case he doesn't have anything to prove because he's set all the records and it's going to be a long time before anyone beats them."

"Pity about losing that one in the middle, otherwise he'd have 14 or 15 in a row."

"He holds the title for most consecutive and the most overall so he's still got nothing to prove."

I asked Frank Kersley why he had been more ambitious than his brother Ned.

"I am a bit like young Fred I suppose. I didn't get along too well with my dad. For years my dad was always telling me I wasn't any good or some damn thing, and that used to make me all the more determined that I would be. I wanted to be a top driver, I used to dream about it. I always had that ambition."

"So your brother was the one with good prospects according to your father?"

"Oh yes. He was a leading apprentice jockey at one stage."

If Fred needed an example of how he would be overshadowed by his father and uncle if he did not make it to the top, he only had to look at his two 'other' uncles. Ned and Frank had two other brothers, Ron and Keith. They were competent reinsmen who drove many winners, but they were virtually unknown.

I asked Fred if the reason he had called his son Greg, rather than Fred, was because he had found the name Fred a burden, with all its connotations as something to live upto.

"It's a funny thing that. That was the reason I didn't, initially, but as time went by I changed and I hoped there might be another opportunity. As it turns out there wasn't. (The Kersleys had two more children, both daughters.) I'm a little bit sorry in a way that I couldn't keep it going, and yet I thought it was a bit old fashioned and would be a bit of a burden to a

That's another one done. Fred trains in peaceful bush surroundings, but to him it is still the workplace, a place of irritations, decisions and naturally a bit of stress.

bloke living today. But it would have been worthwhile for being the fifth generation."

"What was it like when you finally had the most wins of all the trainers but they had brought in a points system and someone else was named leading trainer? - what should have been YOUR first premiership."

"It was very frustrating. Very frustrating. I thought it was a very low trick. I was very unhappy. I didn't cop it too sweet at all. But what were you going to do: have a whinge?"

"I would have said something a lot stronger than: 'I'm unhappy.'"

"Well as time went by it mattered less, but if I had never been able to reach that point again it probably would have bugged me for the rest of my life."

Readers would at this time have the impression that Fred and his father don't get along. But today, every day, Ned is at Fred's stables, quietly picking up gear, cleaning harness, taking care of horses and grooming the track. Their father-son relationship had one of its greatest moments in 1972. Fred persuaded his father to come out of retirement to drive a horse called Stitchintime in a big race. Father did that so success-

fully Fred asked him to drive the horse in the heats of the Benson and Hedges Cup. Stitchintime failed by one point to qualify for the final. Fred, however, had qualified two other horses. After much thought Fred decided to drive frontmarker Local Product himself, and offer the drive on James Eden to his father. Ned had driven in this race 18 times without success, one of the few major races to elude him. It would be his last race, but he was more than willing to make it 19 tries.

Ned drove a brilliant race behind James Eden to win easily. The crowd of 34,000 gave him one of the greatest receptions ever heard at Gloucester Park. In his speech after the race, Ned said it was one of the proudest moments of his life. He touched the hearts of the crowd when he paid tribute to his son Fred, saying he was a better trainer than himself. Let me tell you - that is something you rarely hear one trainer say about another.

Willingness to travel

"Have you had a look at harness racing in America - at their shoeing and their training techniques? Do you do that periodically?"

"No. It's one of the things I wish I had done, but being locked in a bit here I haven't. I read a lot about America - their racing

- and listen to any comments I can pick up from trainers there. I don't think essentially that they're all that much different from us except that they are at least five to ten years ahead of us in the demands they're placing on the horses."

Fred had visited America in 1981, but because of work pressures at home was unable to spend much time over there. He visited Stanley Dancer's property in New Egypt and The Meadowlands track, but the visits were too brief to be learning experiences.

JUDY:"He hates flying. He hates traveling. He went to Kalgoorlie for a few days, but if he has to go as far as Adelaide - he won't go. I mean, I go with him because I want to go, and I'm happy to go, and he wants me to go. But he wouldn't go away on his own. He's a terrible traveler, and he hates it. But Roy Annear and Mick Lombardo (probably the two largest owners in WA) have both asked just recently - if they had a horse they wanted to shoot across to Melbourne, would he be prepared to travel, and he said he would. But it would be a short term thing. He'd just fly over for that race and come back."

Trevor Warwick, by contrast, readily campaigns his top horses in the eastern states, and at one stage maintained a stable in Melbourne and flew there to drive every Saturday night.

Optimist or pessimist?

"Fred has a lot of characteristics that would mark him as a pessimist-"
JUDY: "Yes, yes, yes."

"-Or cautious might be a better word, and yet a lot of the people who have been successful are what I would call over-optimists. That's what makes them. However I think what happens is a lot of the over-optimists fail. Some are very successful and you hear about those."

"They do come and go. He's very much a realist and no race is won until it's run. I mean, it doesn't matter if there's a horse that's a ten-to-one on favorite."

Socializing - loner or outgoing?
The dominant feature of Fred's social life is his close relationship with his wife Judy. They are a very integrated unit and to some extent are content with their own company or small gatherings, rather than large or public groups. Fred tends to be rather reserved in the presence of people he doesn't know.

Inborn talent or something learned?
Fred may have had an inborn affinity with animals, but the major feature of his rise has been his ambition to reach the top, which led to a lot of hard work, sacrifice and time spent thinking. Fred did not go to the top because he was super smart and the task easy. He got there through relentless applied ambition. The key feature was the strength of his drive.

As a generalization, a strong desire to succeed is considered a first child trait, which Fred was, but how much it can be due to a person's genes and how much to other environmental influences is hard to say. Maybe when they finish mapping the human genes there will be one with the description 'burning ambition'.

An interesting factor in Fred's case is his very name. He was the fourth Kersley to bear the name Fred. The last two before him had carried it to new heights. Children with grand names usually fantasize about living up to that name. The black civil rights leader, Martin Luther King is believed to have been influenced by his name - combining the name of a great religious leader, Martin Luther, with the regal surname of King. It was in part the name that led him to become a leader of his people, to have a sense of personal destiny that is unlikely to come to a child called Joey Nerk.

Add to this the uncommon situation in which the second born, Bill, was considered by the parents as more likely to achieve something and fulfill parental hopes. Parents seldom make their attitude obvious, but children will form their own view of parental opinions of relative worth, and what children perceive is what forms them. First borns are generally more aware of the wishes and hopes of parents and are more 'conditioned' by them in the direction of those dreams than later children. Fred's experience of finding himself, in terms of parental hopes and approval, pushed aside by his parents and dethroned by his younger brother, may have provided the emotional flame to harden his ambition and make it resistant to opposing and discouraging forces later in life. Interesting that his uncle Frank had a parallel experience and also became very ambitious.

That Fred's hunger continues in spite of considerable achievements may simply reflect the size of the hunger, but there are other factors worth considering. The first is that although his achievements would make him stand out like a beacon in the average family, in the Kersley family his achievements have only made him one of three bright lights. If you consider Pop Kersley's high standing, one of four bright lights.

Added to this is the perception of the public - and worse still, many trainers - that Fred had an easy start. Corporate psychologist Srully Blotnick has studied the public definition of success, and it is very clear that those who inherit their wealth, renown, social status or power are not considered successful. Fred sees himself as a man who made his own way to the top, a man who paid his dues. Many however see him as a man who had a big start. The result is a sizable gap between the level of respect Fred feels he has earned, and the level he gets. The idea that he was born with a silver spoon in his mouth galls him. It cannot be easy to have worked hard, made sacrifices and taken risks for a large and precious prize but then to be presented with something small and ordinary. Not being given the respect he feels he is due may be the reason

Fred doesn't slacken off but instead keeps piling on the achievements.

13.3 The formulated approach

Personal philosophy
Fred obviously believes dedication and hard work can win. He gets up early, no matter what time he went to bed, he does everything necessary for the horses before looking to his own needs.

Religion
When I asked Fred about religion he had to think. It seems Judy is a sporadic Catholic while Fred might be described as a lapsed bush Baptist.

Business philosophy
Fred believes in being very cautious so he is not under any financial pressure. He believes financial pressures can cause the trainer to make bad decisions. Avoid risk, minimize borrowing, and keep it simple are Fred's guiding rules. He tries to keep training inexpensive for the client and has it geared so those winning the most pay him the most.

Betting
JUDY:"He's not a betting person. We do have an odd bet here and there, but he's a very cautious punter. I'll say to Fred, 'Do you think this could win?,' and he'll say, 'Yes, it should win, bet if it's value,' and I'll say, 'What do you think is value?' He'll say, 'Four or five to one,' and I'll say, 'But you're not going to get four or five to one,' and he says, 'Well, it's not worth it.' That's his idea of value because he knows all the things that can go wrong."

"He'd be a bit of a frustration for some of the betting owners."

"Yes, because he's very cautious, and I'm not saying he's mean with his money or anything, but he has a lot of respect for how hard it is to get. He doesn't think anybody should throw it away. I mean, when people go to the casino and just throw it away."

"Have you been inside the Burswood Casino here?"

"We haven't been to the casino only because it did so much damage to the trotting industry. On principle he said he would not be a part of it, so we've never been. We've been to other casinos. When we've gone away, we've always gone to the casino."

"Burswood Casino's not going to get any of his dollars?"

"No. We went to Las Vegas one year, and that's just something else. I like to have a gamble; I'm a punter, and the poker machines and that there; I set alight for two days. Then he said, 'Right, that's it. Finish."

In summary, betting had no major role in the Kersley's finances.

Selling strategies
The Art of the Deal by Donald Trump, and *How to Master the Art of Selling* by Tom Hopkins have probably never made it into Fred's reading list. Yet Fred and people like him, who lack a natural flair for wheeling and dealing, are the ones who should read them. But Fred has not had to sell himself to clients, he has let his results do that. He hasn't wanted to sell horses to the clients, he prefers they buy their own. Horse trading has not been a big part of his income.

Is he a risk-taker?
In describing Fred, cautious and careful would be the words that spring to mind. Calculated risk-taking rather than spur of the moment stuff.

Is he an innovator?
The experiment with the rugs was an early example of Fred's willingness to try something new or different even against opposition. Someone as questioning as Fred usually ends up an innovator.

Time management
"Does he think, 'I should be doing something' or can he sit and just watch the TV. Can he sit and just do nothing in particular."
JUDY:"Very rarely can he sit and just watch the telly."

"Is that because he's in the workaholic bracket?"

"I'd say so, yes. When he watches the telly, he only watches documentary shows like Four Corners or Sixty Minutes. Any nature show. But he doesn't watch any soapies."

Ideally someone can be time-management conscious and still be able to relax during the allotted leisure time.

Goal and step setter or day by day?
Being number one was Fred's goal for a long time. He doesn't necessarily set intermediate steps, but he works out the details of each piece of the puzzle as far as he can, and he certainly sets long term goals.

13.4 Any record of a positive drug test?
"Since I've been studying the successful trainers, I've listened more to what other people think are the reasons certain trainers are successful. One reason usually given for TJ Smith, and often about you Fred, is that you must have something really good - because very few horses win after Fred Kersley's finished with them."

"That's one of the measurements they make on trainers: whether or not the horses go better when they leave. I think it's a bad measurement. I could name horses that left my stable and improved, and I believe that will go on. I guess there are horses that left Smith and Cummings and those trainers - and won. I think if a horse left your stables and never went any good, *that* would be an indictment of the trainer because he might have damaged the horse."

Boards are part of Fred's management. Clearly written instructions remind staff of the holes for the hopple carrier straps as well as any medications. There are similar boards in the feed room.

"TJ Smith sees himself more as a horse dealer than a trainer, and says the idea is to sell a horse while it still has a win in it, otherwise no one is ever going to offer you money for a horse. Larry Pickering (well-known cartoonist and lately horse trainer), says, 'Look, I've bought horses off TJ Smith and won with them, but they win once or twice a year or in the country, and that's not enough for TJ Smith. I'm not enough of a mug that I think I'm the greatest trainer in history because I can win with something TJ Smith finished with."

"The other side of that coin - I was asked to do an ECG (Electrocardiogram) on a horse that an owner had recently swapped between trainers. There had been some bitterness involved. This horse did nothing like as well as it had done previously, and it's T- waves were horrific (generally accepted as a sign of heart "strain"). It looked as though the second trainer had messed it up."

"Some months later I was at another stable, and this young fellow walked up to me and said, 'I believe you did an ECG on-,' and he named the horse. 'And you said its heart was probably buggered'. He seemed to already know what was in my report, so I said, 'Yes, it had one of the worst collections of T-wave changes I've ever seen.' He said, 'I know what happened to that horse. When the owner phoned up and said someone was going to collect it in the afternoon, the boss got it out and he thrashed it about eight laps around his track. It was sickening. The horse was really buggered."

"A trainer doing that deliberately is shooting himself in the foot. What do you get for your ex-horses? Who

would give you a horse in the first place, if they knew that should they wanted to take it off you, you were going to do that kind of thing?"*

"Those attitudes have been around. I think there's less of it today. People have grown up a bit in that respect. There used to be an old saying that if it was leaving a trainer, and if the trainer didn't want it to leave, he'd stick a penny in its stomach and it'd never be any good."

"They'd throw a penny down its throat?"

"Yes, and they reckon it wouldn't be any good afterwards. I really don't know. I think horses change stables more easily these days. Old blokes used to go down a bit hard. I feel that if you haven't got a good working relationship with the owner, it's *better* that his horse goes."

"I've always been a non-needle man - I have never been into that, and yet my opposition, I believe, think we are successful because we have access to this and that. They couldn't be further wrong. But that's good for me, because while they're driving themselves mad trying to find out what I'm using, they're not a threat. They're going down the wrong track, and that's good."

"One trainer claimed to me: 'I use nothing, but to be quite honest, at times I deliberately mislead some of my colleagues into thinking I do, because as long as they're dragging stuff into syringes, they're making nervous wrecks of themselves."

"When they tell me, they're often half joking, and they're half meaning it. I let them believe it. I can't change it. I used to argue with them about it and they'd think, 'That fellow is lying as well,' so now I'm just happy to leave it lay there."

"Now they think you're using something but you're not lying."

"Well, jungle juice or whatever. Blokes ring me up and say, 'Don't know if you know or not but they're able to find such and such' - thinking I know what the stuff is. I can't show my ignorance, so I say, 'Is that right?' 'Yep, just thought I'd give you the tip'. Then friends hear talk - they talk to several trainers - and the other trainers say, 'That stuff Kersley's using, they can detect that now, so tell your mate.' It's unbelievable, the attitude that's been there ever since."

"One old guy had a saying about it. He was just an average knockabout bloke; real desperate; do anything. When I was a small boy he said, 'Son, never do 'em up. All it'll cause you to do is bet more on them, and they'll still lose.' And it stood the test of time. You know how comments stand the test of time."

"Every time somebody's given a horse something - they'll bet on it, and it only causes you to lose more money. It doesn't cause them to win. Saying you are using something - that's probably as good a compliment as the guys can pay you when they think along those lines. I've had horses in the stables that have been disappointing, and I've been at the stage of sacking it. Usually I persevere a bit longer than I ought to. Anyhow some of those horses have turned right round and become good. Now if it had changed stables or something, then it would have looked like he- "

"Had a better training method for that horse?"

"Or better dope than someone else. Yet that same horse has stayed with me, and I've done nothing really clever. It's just developed, and molded itself, and made itself better. Some of them do just get better. But we've often remarked, 'Just think, if we had quit that horse, it really would have made you look very silly.' But other people wouldn't read it that way."

"Many people attribute TJ Smith's success to drugs. Yet if he had some REALLY magic drug, employees would have seen something, and someone would have blabbed. I mean, he's been at it a long time. But then if his success was feed and work, ex-employees would be training successfully everywhere, yet the only person anyone could point to that's of any significance, that's worked with TJ, is a fellow called Bobby Thompson from Randwick. He generally gets into the bottom of the top ten."

"I really don't think you can work in a stable, and not know exactly what went on. I certainly have no secrets from my staff. There's no intention to."

"Even the golden needle argument: you'd have to get up pretty early in the morning, or very be secretive, to be giving it without the staff ever knowing."

"I heard that some of my staff got to the stage of waking every hour just to see if there were any footprints overnight."

"Is that right? They wanted to see if you were getting in there at night?"

"One of my staff didn't believe I wasn't treating the horses pre-race, and he's a suspicious type of a character, so the last thing he would do at night would be rake around the stall, then get there first thing in the morning to see if anyone had walked in."

"But you'd already re-raked it?"(I thought I was pretty funny but Fred didn't laugh.)

"I couldn't be bothered. But you know, on the occasions that we may inject a horse for whatever the reason is, I encourage my staff to ask me what it is, because-"

"If they don't know, the rumors will start."

"Yes. We do very little injecting anyhow, but whatever it may be, I think it's better they know. You say you're going to give anabolics or antibiotics or a vitamin. If you're going to give that, you're better to tell them that. I don't see the point in not telling them. The logic is that we're held responsible for stable security, but we can't be really - it's the staff that falls back on. So if I ever get caught for a positive drug test or something, it will be a staff-administered thing or a staff problem."

"Yes, I think trainers are in a very weak position in that regard."

"There's no defense. If the horse is swabbed and it's a positive, you are the trainer and you are guilty. You're charged with that responsibility. You are the trainer of the horse that turned up with a positive swab. Now, I know I'm not going to do it, but I don't know if somebody else might."

"Well, particularly the people with large numbers of employees. If you've got someone who's nursing a grudge or anything. But I'm sure in some cases it's staff negligence, particularly the people who used caffeine to pick up appetite or whatever in the training, and then somebody forgets to leave it out for the race."

"Vets are very good at prescribing those butazolidin sachets for horses with injuries. Number 17 and number 18 are alongside each other. The boy gives it to number 18 and he's racing. Then the trainer is guilty."

"Well, that's happened to major trainers and they won't have it on the place."

"No, I won't either. I will not have it on the place. None of those things that are fed to horses, which contain any drugs - they can't be on the property. That's my only defense. I'm just not confident that if I'm not there the mistake won't be made, and I don't have a defense against it."

"I would have thought you'd almost be obliged to use butazolidin with some of the borderline lameness horses - just to keep them in work. You can afford to get rid of those horses?"

"No, you can't. You've got them in there. But what's the rule now - a week off the drug before a race? Funnily enough, I haven't had all that much success with the horses that we've had gait problems with where we couldn't pinpoint anything and thought; is it hurting somewhere? Let's put it on a bit of 'bute' or Finadyne (banamine) or something like that and just see. It never seems to work for me."

"One fellow in the United States said to me - 'Butazolidin becomes a psychological prop to some trainers.' Over there they're allowed to slop it around, so they get that way they don't want the horse to be without it."

"They're not as confident if the horse isn't getting the drug. That is a mentality that exists in all things."

Fred says he has not had a positive drug test. I suppose the trauma of his father's disqualification, would have been ample discouragement. Then there is the difficulty obtaining any other work himself if he was penalized, and repayments due etc.

"I think its fair to say that when they started to swab every winner, I started to become a force as a trainer. They always did spot swab a bit but everyone was doing them up and getting away with it anyway. It seemed to me that it got easier for me when they swabbed every winner. So I've never been too shy about having horses swabbed. Apart from the inconvenience I think it is the best thing that has ever happened at a racetrack."

"I have been really cheesed off lately with the general attitude that all horses are doped, and the impression the press gives a lot of times, that all horses need to be doped by vets and trainers. I've tried to come out publicly and say, 'No that's wrong,' but that didn't make the phone ring. You would have thought that caring owners or breeders would be ringing you up. But I don't think the phone rang at all. I think they want their horses doped. I don't think it benefits a trainer to come out and say, 'I'm not up with it, don't use these kind of things'. I think what he should say is, 'Look I'm right up with the times-'"

"I've had owners say to me, 'Which trainer do you think has the best stuff?'"

"Yes. I think it would get you more horses than you would lose. I think you ought to say or have said about you 'He's got the latest and the best."

Fred may have unintentionally succeeded in that without using any drugs.

13.5 Luck and other reasons for success
Fred doesn't like to hear it, but having a father and an uncle to learn from, both people at the top of the game, and a name that was recognized in the industry, would have to have been a considerable help, especially as the elder Kersley's retired.

He had this to say about Lady Luck:

"You can breed or train a good horse very well, but if somebody else in the same year lobs a badly-trained champion in the same age group, and beats you every time, that has an effect; a huge effect on you, over which you don't have any con-

trol. When you turn up with two-year-olds, three-year-olds, it's just as important what the other guys have got. Some of those big-money-earning juveniles aren't much good. I mean, the press say they're good, and they look good, but if you measured it in real terms, they're not especially good. They're just better than the other horses that raced that year. That's all it means."

I can't point to anything outstandingly lucky that contributed to Fred's rise.

13.6 What Fred thinks made him successful
Hard work and a questioning of things considered gospel.

13.7 Trainer, conman or businessman?
No-one could claim Fred's success has been due to a silver tongue and overflowing charm. Gino De Mori recounted to me how someone who went to Fred with the idea of spending big at sales in New Zealand would probably be talked out of it by Fred! I believe he is a careful businessman and driver, and a great trainer.

13.8 What drives Fred?
Fred seems driven by a need to prove himself TO HIS FATHER. He is also driven by a need to prove to others that he measures up AGAINST his father and uncle. These are forms of a desire for recognition and status. He has a healthy respect for money. Independence, uniqueness, and social rating are all well down the list for Fred.

13.9 Lessons for beginning trainers
Fred Kersley's success is a triumph for persistence and dedication -even in the face of self doubt. In spite of discouraging early results he kept trying and eventually succeeded - not only in making a living but rising to be number one for an all-time record number of times in West Australian harness racing.

He also provides a stark contrast to Wayne Lukas and TJ Smith in his approach to buying yearlings. They believe they can choose the best and use it as a big selling point. They are, because of their self confidence in this arena, more than happy to spend big money for a yearling. Probably the most encouraging thing for a beginning trainer is that Fred is living proof that you can be Number One without being a yearling sales hotshot.

14. The future
In the 1984/85 season Fred won the training and driving premierships with 113 wins. The trainer who came second had 53 wins. That is domination, and it must have seemed to some people that Fred was set for another decade at the top.

But his future chief adversary was making progress. Trevor Warwick had been third in the 81/82 season. From that year onward he was in the top three every year until with a concerted and calculated effort, paying more attention to wins and less to money, he finally broke Fred's run in the 86/87 season. In that 1986/87 season Trevor Warwick won with 125 wins to Fred's 95.

Fred Kersley had notched up the most wins each year for 14 years with only the one loss to Schrader in the middle, breaking it into two 7 year winning streaks. What was it that had enabled Fred Kersley to so solidly dominate a strong harness racing state for 14 out of 15 years?

As we have seen, neither an apprenticeship with his father, nor the name Kersley were enough to give him an easy start. Perseverance, application and some of his own ideas eventually lifted Fred to the top. Because he had the right formula, the right skills, once he got the numbers and made it to the top, it became self-perpetuating.

So what was it that broke Fred's grip? Fred certainly hadn't lost the crown through disinterest, distractions or growing old: Fred went down still in his prime, concentrating, fighting hard. Trevor Warwick's most publicized weapon was syndication - enabling groups of people with small amounts of money to band together to buy a horse. People who could not afford to buy and campaign a pacer by themselves, could get into the act with partners. What is very important is that the amounts of money involved allowed Trevor to buy some very good horses, and a lot of horses: quantity and quality -every trainer's dream. Trevor was building new stables, dramatically increasing his numbers, and numbers were probably his main weapon.

But was syndication the ONLY tactic that had enabled Trevor Warwick to take the trainer's title from Fred? Trevor Warwick is very experimental, and his training is very different to Fred's. He uses deep sand work, bush work under saddle, interval training, swimming, and a computerized treadmill: how important was all of that?

Whatever the relative merit of the components contributing to Trevor's success, would the same tactics keep him at the top? At least part of the answer depended on what Fred did. Would Fred stick with his proven but now beaten formula, adopt the same syndication strategy as Trevor, or develop some new counter-tactics? The most obvious direction would be to follow the syndication route and put in more stables. Could Fred make changes rapidly enough to win the crown back or did Trevor now have the upper hand for some time?

"Do you think Fred will regain the trainer's premiership? (start of 1987/88)"
JUDY:"To be honest, I start to doubt it. In the short term, Trevor is the only person capable of keeping him out. The way Trevor is set up now and continuing to improve his chances - we're not in a position to, and really don't want to compete at that level. Trevor's just putting up another block of stables, which is going to give him over sixty horses on his property. He also has contract trainers."

"That train under his name?
"No, not so much under his name, but there are quite a few guys that are bringing the horses up to trial and race standards for him, so he's probably going to finish up controlling about 80 horses in work (I asked Trevor how many he had in work and how many stalls and he said 35 in work and 52 stalls). Well, I've no ambition to do that. Trevor's fired up with his syndicates. Fred has never been a big spender. Some people say he still has the first dollar he ever earned. He won't buy really expensive horses unless he can see there is a chance you can get your money back. Whereas with the syndication and some of the owners Trevor's got behind him, they're jumping on planes and they're buying. It has happened for the last few years, not just this season. They've spent big money on some horses that have never made it. Well, see, that would worry the hell out of Fred. If he got somebody to spend $70,000 or $80,000 on a horse, and it was a blue (error), he would feel he'd let that person down and it would hurt him as much as if he had've paid for the horse himself."

"So far he's the first person I've come across among the top trainers who does worry much about that. Some of them would say quite ruthlessly, 'I don't care,' and others justify it: 'They know what they're getting into.' Fred might have to change his mental attitude there."

"Well, if he wants to get back on top, maybe. If you've got a Laurie Connell, (Wealthy Perth businessman who bought millions of dollars worth of Thoroughbreds) who seems to me to just throw money away, maybe if you had him as an owner, and he said, 'Look, go and buy the thing. If it's no good it doesn't matter,' then you'd do it. But we've never come across any owners that can just throw money away. Some of them never had much. Those who have got money seem to respect their money. They've got it because they have worked. They'll spend if Fred says there is a horse worth buying. But see, Trevor jumped on a plane recently and went to New Zealand, and I think he bought eight horses - anything from $50,000 to $120,000. That's a lot of money. Now, at this stage the way harness racing is, there's no way you can get your money back. I mean, harness racing has got to turn the corner and start picking up before you could even ask - well, that's how we feel, morally and with a clear conscience -before we could say to somebody, 'Buy that horse: it's a lot of money but if it goes up to expectations, it'll be all right."

"What is regarded as part of the success formula by some of the top guys, especially in the galloping side of it, is that you have to find those owners who'll put out the big 'bickies', and the main way it is justifiable is that you might buy ten colts, but you buy them with good breeding, so that if one of them fires, it goes from a hundred thousand dollar yearling, to a three million dollar stallion

just for its stud value. Maybe $15m even $50m in America. That's the carrot they dangle in front of the owners."

"I think we're talking about two different industries, though, because there is money in the gallops. The stakes are enormous."

"I'm told that figures the Harness Racing Board in Melbourne have, show the average return on a dollar in galloping is vastly lower."

"Is it?"

"Yes, lower than it is in Standardbred racing. You can actually make a much better case to the person in the street to go and invest in Standardbreds than you can in Thoroughbreds. I said, 'Why don't you go and publicize that?' He said, 'Because they'd be embarrassed to put up the figures for either lot."

I asked Fred:

"Do you think you'll get back to be Number One?"

"Yes, I can. I could, but for me there are some problems. Harness racing at the moment is at a very low ebb, and I've always tried to be a very realistic person in a realistic relationship with my owners. To be successful right now I'd have to go into the area of paying far too much for the horses for what they're possibly going to earn here. Now that worries me, but I know I can't compete with Trevor Warwick unless I do that. So I've got to struggle with that one. The only other way to go is into syndication, where you spread the payment, but you bring in a lot of problems: dealing with the large number of new owners and that sort of thing."

Fred may have been formulating strategy before his losing season ended. According to Trevor, Fred could see in the last months of the 86/87 season that he was going to lose, so he set some horses aside, held them back in their work or whatever. By the time Trevor got over his celebrations, took a holiday and came back, he found Fred had stolen off to a very sizable lead in the new 87/88 season. He also believed Fred was running horses capable of winning at Gloucester Park at the less lucrative Richmond Raceway instead -simply to make sure he won more races - to get the numbers to win the training premiership.

However, one month into the season, in September 1987, Trevor Warwick got the go-ahead to raise $2.5 million on the stock exchange by means of a public company called Globetrotting International Ltd, the first listed harness racing company in Australia. Fred's slender lead now looked even more fragile.

By the end of February, with 5 months to go, Trevor had raced up alongside Fred, and the scores were tied. Fred led by 5 at Richmond while Trevor led by 5 at the Gloucester Park where the prizemoney was higher. On any kind of projection,

it looked like Trevor's second win coming up, but at the end of the 1987/88 season, Fred, without going down the syndication road, led with 123 to Trevor's 102. The extent to which it was a two man tussle shows in the gap to 3rd place. Chris Lewis was third with 38.

It was Fred's 15th title and he was 49 years old.

I asked Judy how she felt about that win.
JUDY:"That was a bit of a surprise for us. We had a very ordinary team, we didn't go out and spend a lot of money on horses. A surprise and a bonus."

FRED: "I shouldn't have beaten him because I had poor quality horses. But I guess the raceway attitude helped -putting horses in the right races, consistently being there, not damaging or losing too many. Trevor had a stable full of stars that fell by the wayside. He had heaps of high-priced replacements which didn't make it for one reason or another."

"After that year when he beat you, Judy said your only chance was if his high-priced horses didn't come up with the goods. Is that what happened?" "I think the year he beat me was a big year for him. Luck -how do you talk about luck? That year things went right for him. It's a very important ingredient."

"Colin (Trevor Warwick's brother) told me that prior to their win they had been receiving some flack about not being able to beat you for the trainer's premiership. So although they had beaten you on money, they made a decision to make a deliberate concerted effort to win on numbers, and get the training premiership for Trevor. To see if it would help in syndication publicity I suppose."

"Yeh?" Fred looked skeptical. "That's a mental attitude thing with them. Trevor's always had those - comfort zones. Once he couldn't beat me because of numbers. Then when he had the number of horses, he couldn't beat me because he was only concentrating on feature races. Then in that year he won them all - big races and little races."

He gave another skeptical sigh. He wasn't buying the idea that Trevor could step over and win the training title when it suited him.

"How do you really know?"

"Maybe he concentrated on little races to get numbers?"

"The little races you win with your cheap horses; you win with the horses that are eligible. The program stays the same. If you have a horse that can go to the races and win, you should. There's no point in leaving them home fit and ready. I mean, how do you keep them right without racing them? I can't speak for anyone else but when a horse is fit and ready to go to the races you might just as well go."

"*Trevor said that at the end of that season when he was beating you, you must have conceded about six weeks before the end of the season because your horses just disappeared. Then in the first weeks of the new season your horses were everywhere, and you ran off to a 21 race lead or something like that.*"

"Yes, ahhm, it did work like that. I didn't plan it to happen that way. He was fired up and in form and everything was going well for him, and he went right through to the end of the year. I was in trouble, my horses were worn out, not doing much - and I just had to start to rebuild, keep working at finding new horses. Then that year fell into place for me. Now this year (1988/89), is being more difficult for me. I'm not being quite as lucky, and I think you make your own luck, but things are not quite falling into place."

"The Warwick camp tend to develop these attitudes and change their style. Like this year they have been bringing back good horses undertrained, running them home last a few times, and saying, 'I want them later on'. Just a different method to what they had last season, and I don't know why they do that. But they are entitled to go their own way. Me, I wouldn't want to be racing my best horses underdone. But he's doing it now. He never used to do that, so it's a new tactic. There have been some new tactics: like he's let them go all the way; ripped a couple up; horses that have been banned for poor performance, like - they've led and given up. I don't know what the logic is there, but they're driving and enthusiastic, and new at the top, and new to big numbers of horses. They're trying different things. I'm the other way, I'm going down hill."

"*You've been through all that.*"

"Yes. I don't feel the need to be too daring, to come up with new ideas. In all things I try to keep it as uncomplicated as it can be. I think training horses is very basic. I don't think trainers have to be all that intelligent, they don't have to have good academic skills."

1988/89 season

Trevor Warwick wins his second Leading Trainer award.

1989/90 season

After just a few months of the season, Fred does not hold out much hope of making a comeback for that year. As the season progresses Trevor looks set for his third title and perhaps a reign of his own. Fred can't beat him, but he is not going to join him in syndication either. For several years Fred has been checking out a different game.

A license to train gallopers

"*You were interested in getting a license to train gallopers? Was that because it might be financially more rewarding? (This was 1987)*"

"Well, my kids want to become drivers. At some stage I've

Kellie Kersley adds a bit of glamor as well as driving skill to the night-time trotting scene.

got to leave a bit of room for them. That won't necessarily help me but I'm not too worried. We're in a transition - they've got to earn their stripes. But the way the trotting industry is going is worrying to me, and if my kids are going to develop I've got to leave some room for them."

"So to answer that question about the gallops, I believe that fundamentally I'm a horse trainer. I don't want to stay at the trots and drive badly, so I would like to recognize when I am not as competitive as I should be. I should then become only a horse trainer, not a horse driver. Now, if I'm a horse trainer, I should be training gallopers."

"*Why do you say that?*"

"Because there's a lot more money in it. Even for the bullshit, if you like, of the prestige. It's also a challenge for me to measure myself against those guys that seem to be good at it."

"One study has shown that the return on a dollar invested is higher in the Standardbred than in the gallopers."

"For the money spent on the horses? Sure it is. That's the point that should be argued by the administrators, and they seem to be very reluctant to do it. Standardbreds cost less, they're cheaper to keep, they race more often, and they earn more money. Now why shouldn't we be going a lot better?"

"It is a paradox: if the return on a dollar is better, why isn't pacing doing as well as galloping? But many people who become owners are more interested in prestige than return on a dollar. If you want a return on a dollar you wouldn't put money into either type of horse. Old timers are always telling me that at one stage the gallops were actually on the defensive against pacing."

"In West Australia, sure, we were beating the pants off them. The simple thing that happened was the Totalisator Agency Board (TAB). That murdered us, and is still choking us. Before that was introduced we had higher stakes, we had higher attendance, and we were turning over more money. Races was in real trouble."

"About what year?"

"I can't tell you, but it shows on the graph quite clearly. Now, one of the decisions when they brought in the TAB was that the races would be getting 60% of the funding distribution, and we'd get 40% of the distribution. We queried it at the time, and the reply was, 'Because we're going to bet on the Eastern States gallops, there's a bit more galloping content than harness racing content.'

"So you had Sydney, Melbourne and Perth gallops, and Perth trots. We were unhappy about it because we were better than them. We collected the figures and put our case to finance the TAB on a 50:50 basis. They said no, 60:40, and we had to agree to it. It didn't hurt us for three, four, five years, but then it started to kill us, and it is still killing us, to the stage now where they want to make it 70:30 and they can justify it on their figures."

"So the problem was that they didn't bet on Eastern states trots?"

"Yes. There have been several problems since; one is that races has grown because they get 50% more than we do every year, and the gap is widened and widened and widened. Now the credibility gap's widening with it, because they look to be better than us; we look to be in trouble, and we are now. Every year they get 50% more. In terms of how much money, it's many millions of dollars more have been given to them than to us, so naturally they have nicer, more attractive, more modern facilities. Our facilities have now fallen way behind par, and we've got no money to do anything about it. I can see that killing us."

One of the supreme ironies of this situation was explained to me by Ned Kersley: J.P. Stratton, regarded by many as the architect of the supremacy of trotting, was the one who pushed and pressured for the TAB. He pushed it as the future lifeblood of trotting.

I asked Fred about conditions at the time:

"If, at the time the TAB came in, someone had said to you, 'Why is pacing doing better than the gallops?' what would you have said were the reasons?"

"Several things. It was more spectacular. The track was the best racetrack in the Southern Hemisphere. That sounded very good in Perth in those days. Nothing else in Perth was better than anywhere else in the Southern Hemisphere. It was under lights, it was very spectacular. I think there were some other things that mattered. We didn't have TV, which has since arrived to keep people at home at night."

I remember as a young child going past Gloucester Park at night for the first time, and being astounded at the sheer brightness of the lights, all over the ground. It seemed to cast a carnival glow over that whole end of Perth. When, as an adult, I first went past the track at night, after some ten years on the other side of Australia, they seemed nowhere near so bright. I wondered if streetlighting and car lights had improved or if economy measures had cut the festive aura.

"Something that's on Saturday afternoon would be hit less by television than something that's on at night. TV effectively brings the best in the world into your home. Before all these communications systems, every village and town and city needed its own musicians, entertainers, racing etc. Now there can be one top act of each kind watched via satellite by the entire population of the world."

"Yes, and everything else drops off. Now how do you beat that? You can't beat that. There have been other changes. The video movies that are now freely available. I see people taking movies home: that hurts us. Also the change in the licensing hours. You could get a beer at the trots when the pubs had to shut early. There were no licensed restaurants like there are today. Friday or Saturday night in Perth, you can't get into a restaurant unless you book, unless it's a bad restaurant. There are thousands of those people that used to have to go to the trots."

"Yes, when I was a student, part of the reputation of the trots was a cheap, entertaining night out. One of the things that still dumbfounds me is that it's hard to get a seat at the trots in many areas. In the good old days, a lot of people were very fit, and they could stand up for hours, but not the modern person. They sit at a desk all day. They can't stand up very long. Ask the middle-aged

group who used to go to the trots or to the gallops a lot. Ask why they don't go now, and one of the most common things they'll say is, 'Oh, it's too tiring. It's so hard to get a seat."

"Yes, and who wants to go and stand out in the cold at the trots? They argue fiercely to keep a small track there, and an expanse of grass between the grandstand and the track. I said, 'You're keeping the people away from the action. Why don't we bring the track over here to the grandstands?' They said, 'We need the grass for people to stand and walk on'. Bullshit. Ladies who dress well don't want to walk around on grass with high-heeled shoes on. Not on grass which is damp with dew or rain. And right now we don't have any people anyhow so the grass just needs mowing. It really is a pain. There's no atmosphere."

So - shades of Wayne Lukas - Fred finds the challenge of another code of racing can be greater than trying to beat back a tough challenge in the code he has already proven himself in. In Fred's case there is also the bitterness and the anguish he feels at the decline of Standardbred racing because of a political decision taken in the 1960's. He knows the night time slot has had a greater increase in competition, but that only makes the original decision to 'help' Thoroughbred racing all the more unjust in its continued form. Now the funding should be rethought to 'help' pacing in Perth. Instead the changes in funding seem to be directed at killing off harness horse racing. There is a lesson for all racing people, in all codes, in what happened through that political intervention. Justice is not being done, nor will it be done unless the pacing brigade can muster some political clout, and present themselves as a voting block.

December 1988

In 1987 and 1988, Fred had been refused a license to train both gallopers and pacers. I again asked Fred about his desire to train gallopers.

"There are people training both gallopers and pacers in this state, by getting around the letter of the law. Are you still thinking of having a tilt at the gallops?"

"Yes but I would rather do it legally. I've had the odd galloper in the back yard, but I'm limited in as much as I am a publicly known person, and if I turn up at the training tracks, I'm noticed."

"My uncle Frank trained a double at the Flemington gallops. At that stage, before he came back to Perth, he was allowed to train both over there, and he was leaning more to the gallops. He seemed to think it was a better lifestyle. It's easier - no, hang on, I shouldn't say that because I don't think it is easier to train gallopers."

"It takes less time."

"You don't need all the equipment. You don't need to hassle yourself on gaiting, and gearing them, and shoeing them as carefully. The gallopers just have that sort of advantage. I think the disadvantage of gallopers is that it would be hard to get a successful galloper. They're a scarce commodity. To join in and get enough of them to be successful at a professional level, I'm sure that's the challenge."

"I've no doubt that as a professional horse trainer, the decision I should make is to train gallopers. What I have is a bit of loyalty, a comfort zone about training pacers - I know I can, and I'm happy doing it. I have to measure that against where I should be, and whether I can do it."

November 1989

Fred has obtained a dual license after three years of trying, and has started three individual Thoroughbred horses, for two wins, two seconds a third, and two unplaced runs. One was an eight-year-old called Little Hero, that had won his last race two years ago at Leonora. Leonora is the outback, the edge of the desert according to some, the middle of it in the opinion of others. Little Hero was given to Fred by his owner who no doubt felt Little Hope would have been a more appropriate name. That horse has had a midweek city win. Another was bought out of the paper; it has had three starts for a win and two seconds.

Fred's daughter Kellie and another girl ride the gallopers on a sand track that has been put in. Jockey Danny Miller calls in and does some riding. Judy says Fred's loving it, and he wants more. "That's the way he is thinking of going."

Fred himself was less optimistic. "When one of the gallopers wins, the phone doesn't ring off the hook. It has become evident I'm going to have to climb up the hard way, and find my own by leasing or buying cheaper horses. I'm not seen as a galloping trainer, I'm a trotting trainer who trains gallopers. They're a little bit 'thingy' the galloper trainers. For me to do well I'd have to stop training trotters."

"You'll have to drink beer in the members bar."

"Yes, that's one of my failures. I don't do that. I'm no good at that at all."

"You'll have to convert some of your trotting owners."

"One of them has bought a Thoroughbred yearling."

Writer Gino de Mori put it this way: "He's taken two old donkeys that could only win at Leonora or some place out the back of nowhere, and he has won in the city with them!"

14.1 Perfect conditions for him would be ?

The most important requirement for Fred would be a turn-around in the decline in crowds and purses in trotting in Western Australia. The fortunes of various codes of racing have risen and fallen over the years. However with the diversity of nighttime entertainment and forms of gambling now available, it is difficult to see how trotting in Perth could ever return to the glory days of the 1950's.

Another requirement for a return to perfect conditions for Fred would be a break in the slow financial strangulation of trotting by the government distribution formula for the profits from tote betting (pari-mutuel operation to an American). That is also unlikely.

Perhaps the most rewarding challenge for Fred will be in Thoroughbreds. However, because of the high cost of yearling gallopers, syndication is common. Fred hates the idea of running syndicates of owners.

Among the perfect possibilities for Fred would be a dramatic decline in the popularity of syndication in trotting. That would give Fred a chance of taking the training title back off Trevor Warwick. But is it likely to happen? Gino De Mori says,

"Fred keeps hoping some of Trevor's high priced horses will fail. And they do, every year. That doesn't stop people joining Trevor's syndicates. People know it's a high risk business."

14.2 Probabilities

Unless Fred takes a course in salesmanship, and reverses his attitude to syndicates, things will remain pretty much as they are. Trevor will remain Number One in trotting, and Fred will remain his main competitor. Fred will make steady but not dramatic headway in Thoroughbreds.

If he were to plunge enthusiastically into syndicates anything could happen. Fred Kersley has great horsemanship and training skills. He is still young compared to many of the great Thoroughbred trainers. Could he make it a unique double by one day becoming the number one Thoroughbred trainer in the state?

Fred and the mutts head off for coffee at 11am. Another morning's trackwork is done.

Differences in racing between America and Australia

Gambling in America has always been opposed by religious groups, which have a lot of power in that country. Gambling was illegal in many states. Racing, because of it's association with gambling, has also been opposed. Consequently, American racing in all it's forms, Quarter Horses, Standardbreds and Thoroughbreds, has been very restricted, and has a much lower public profile than in Australia.

In recent years however, the profitability of a government levy on gambling, coupled with the public's dislike of paying taxes, has led many states to legalise racing with gambling. As a result, the number of racetracks with betting has grown over the last 20 years.

Racetracks in America are mostly owned by individuals or companies, although some are owned by associations. Racetracks are bought and sold. In Australia the tracks are owned, or managed in trust, by bodies set up under special laws. They are not traded, although they may be sold if they cease to function as racetracks.

American racetracks generally race three to five times a week for two to twenty weeks and then either shut down for a lengthy period, or change to a different type of racing. The Meadowlands in New Jersey switches between gallopers and harness racing. Gallopers race every week in New York, but all the racing is at Belmont Park for most of the year, and at Saratoga or Aquaduct the rest of the year. Because of the snow and ice, many of the northern parts of the USA and Canada have no winter racing. Many horses and horsemen shift south for the winter.

Most Australian cities have two to four tracks for harness racing, and a similar number for gallopers. There is no Quarter Horse racing in the cities, but it is growing in the country areas of the eastern states. Usually there is racing on Saturday and one mid-week meeting. During the week there will be racing in country towns, and the city bettor can bet on these at government controlled 'shops'. There is no seasonal shifting or shutdown in Australia, because the climate is warmer.

At the Thoroughbred track in Australia, the difference Americans notice first is the absence of a dirt track. Gallops in the city are on turf. At all tracks they see bookmakers. 'Bookies' compete with the Totalisator Agency Board (TAB or 'Tote') for the punter's dollar. The Tote takes all the money bet on each horse and computes odds, which are displayed on screens around the track. All the money is paid out except for a government percentage to pay costs and make a profit for the government. American tracks have no bookmakers, only a Pari-Mutuel, which operates the same way as the Tote. Both pay a percentage into purses and track improvements.

In America the track is dirt because they race so many times per week that turf would be torn up. There is sometimes a turf track on the inside. Many of the stands in the northern part of the USA and Canada are glassed in because of the cold weather.

Harness racing in North America is almost all run over a distance of one mile. In Australia and New Zealand, mile races are short races, most races being around a mile and a half.

The most common race type in America is the claiming race, in which any horse entered can be bought for a stated sum. This results in frequent changes of a horse's owner and trainer. The most common races in Australia are restricted races and handicaps. Entry to restricted races is determined by the class of previous wins. In handicaps the track handicapper assigns the weight each horse will carry to try to have a close finish - to provide a good betting race. The trainers often disagree with the track handicapper's assessment of their horse. American trainers have only their own assessment of claiming class to blame.

In America almost all the competing horses are stabled at tracks. In Australia most horses are stabled off-track but there is a steadily increasing number stabled on-track, particularly in the cities. There are more races on an American card (program) and they are closer together. Probably because of the time pressure, the time taken for photos of winners in the winners circle is unbelievably short in the USA (make that *the* photo). American race books don't have the post time for each race, and tax is taken out of winnings, which have to be declared at income tax time.

Because of the extensive general press coverage of racing in Australia, the general public there is more aware of the names of top horses, drivers, jockeys and trainers.

Glossary

Above itself/ Above themselves

Term meaning the horse is so energetic it is prancing, bucking or playing around, and a bit difficult to handle.

Added money

Money added by the track to the purse for a race. Going back in time a few hundred years, prizemoney was whatever the owners put into a 'pot'. When racetracks appeared, and track owners wanted to attract the best horses, they 'added money' to the pot. They made that back from admissions. When tracks took over the betting, they used profits from that as well. The owners still have to put in, but the amount is usually aimed at discouraging horses with no chance of winning. A race will be advertised as '$50,000 added.'

Where there is no legalised betting, added money is hard to come by, and most purses consist of money put up by the owners. Futurities are a way of developing big purses, especially in states that don't allow betting.

Allowance race

Eligibility is determined by conditions. For example: three-year-old non-winners of $5,000 since March 1st. The horses entered in these races cannot be claimed, and in general, allowance races attract a better class of horse than claiming races. Weight carried by horses in the race may vary with past performances.

Assistant trainer

Trainer's employee who is second in charge or may be in charge of a branch of the stable at another track. Similar to a head lad in England, or a foreman in Australia.

Backside/Backstretch

The stable area at an American track. Usually has a lot of horses, often has staff accommodation and facilities that serve meals. Race commentators will occasionally speak of horses in the backstretch: 'As they go down the backside'.

Backstraight, Backstretch

Tracks usually have two straight sections and two curved areas. The straight on the opposite side to the stands is the backstraight or backstretch.

Blister

A blister is a compound that inflames the superficial tissues. Usually applied to some area of skin on the lower leg to induce healing in underlying tissues.

Blood count

Usually a blood test in which the red cell count is one of the most important measures taken.

Blood test

Usually means a series of tests done on the blood of horses that are performing poorly or sick. Done as a routine every 2 to 4 weeks by some trainers. Can be confused with the tests used to establish parentage and individuality OR pre- race drug tests.

Bookmaker, Bookie

Person who is licensed by the track to offer odds on the horses in a race. Anyone making a bet has fixed odds, as they were displayed or agreed at the time. When a bookie takes a lot of bets for one horse, he will usually change his board to offer poorer odds about that horse. If no money comes in for some horses, he will offer better odds on them to 'balance his book'. Handicappers like the fixed odds.

Black type

Refers to the bold type in yearling sales catalogues. The names of horses that win or place in certain races, usually stakes races, are printed in bold type in such catalogues. If a yearling has a lot of black type in it's catalogue pedigree, it means a lot of it's relatives won important races.

Bleeder

A horse that bleeds into it's lungs during or shortly after a race. Years ago a horse had to have blood appear at the nostrils to be called a bleeder. Later it was found that about 20% of harness horses and 80% of Thoroughbreds bleed into the lungs and bronchi, but in most of these cases it can only be seen with an endoscope passed down the airway.

Bloodworms

The most serious of the parasites of the horse, because it occasionally causes clots to form in major arteries of the gut. Unless surgery is attempted in these cases, the horse almost invariably dies.

Bottom

Putting bottom in a horse means developing it's stamina.

Bowed tendon

A rupture or microscopic tearing of the tendon at the back of the leg. Slow to heal, and the horse is usually a second or two slower when it does recover.

Bran

The husk of grains after the flour has been removed. Fed to horses to keep their bowel loose and moving.

Breeze

To breeze a horse is to send it a short distance at close to race pace.

Breezing

To run below fastest pace. In clocker's terms, slower than handily but faster than easily. It is a relative term, desribing the effort the horse makes, rather than something measured in seconds per furlong.

Brushing

Touching, rubbing, or lightly whipping the horse with the whip. A work with a near race-intensity finish.

Bute, Butazolidin

A medication for arthritis (inflamed joints). It is a pain- killing non-steroidal anti-inflammatory drug used a lot for horses with leg problems. Horses in some parts of America are allowed to race on low levels of Bute.

Calks, Caulks

Projection from the bottom of the shoe to help a horse get traction. Usually a screw-in stud in the heel of the shoe, which can be taken out after the race. Also called stickers.

Campaign

A horse's races from one spell (or turning out or let-up) to another, or for one season.

Canter

A slow gallop, used a lot in conditioning Thoroughbreds. In America it is usually called a gallop, which is very confusing for non-Americans.

Claimer, Claiming race

Claiming races make up the bulk of races in American racing - in Quarter Horses, Standardbreds and Thoroughbreds. Any horse entered can be claimed (bought) for the amount stated. A $1,000 claiming race is for very cheap, low class horses, at small tracks. A $50,000 claiming race is for high class claimers.

The claim has to be made before the race, sometimes before the previous race. At the time of the race, only the stewards know if there have been any claims. The previous owner gets any prizemoney, and the previous trainer gets the equipment. The new owner or the new trainer takes possession immediately. Usually the horse has to be run at a higher claiming price for some period like 30 days after a claim.

In Australia the number of claiming races is negligible. The majority of horses race through a series of classes, being eligible to win, say, two races in a class before they must move up and compete in the next highest class. A horse can skip classes, but usually if it wins at the higher class, it has to race at that class - ie it cannot go back and race at the lower classes. After a horse goes through the classes, it races in 'open class' or 'open company' races. Many horses reach a level where they cannot win, yet they cannot go back down the grades.

Classics, Classic races.

During the development of the Thoroughbred in England, three races for three-year-olds became known as the ones to win. The list was decided by an ill-defined mix of history, prizemoney, what previous winners went on to win, and the breeding success of previous winners. They were the Two Thousand Guineas, the Derby and the St Leger. These were usually won by colts, so the One Thousand Guineas and Oaks became the filly classics, parallel to the Two Thousand Guineas and the Derby.

In Australia, racing bodies in each state long ago set up their own classics, with the same names and distances. Harness racing also went in for Derbys and Oaks. American Thoroughbred racing also has Derbys and Oaks, but over 1¼m not

1½m. The Kentucky Derby became part of the Triple Crown. American harness racing developed it's own major events, and in recent years they too have become known as the Triple Crowns of trotting and pacing. Quarter Horse Derbys are mostly 400-440 yards.

Clocker

Someone who times horses' works with a stopwatch. In Australia they are usually employed by newspapers and racing papers. In America, horses that have not raced at all, or not recently, have to have a specified number of works timed before they can race. The idea is to give the bettor some line on the horse's ability and fitness. So the track employs a clocker.

Come from behind, Come from off the pace

Some horses like to drop back behind the leaders at the start of the race, and hope to overhaul them in the closing stages of the race. A useful strategy if there are some early speed horses in the race.

Condition

To get a horse fit and ready to race.

Conditioner

The trainer who gets the horse fit and ready to race.

Condition races

Races with some conditions of entry, such as non-winners of three races since ... These races are distinct from claiming races. These races are more common in harness racing in America, particularly at the small country tracks, because so many people breed and race a horse, and they don't want to risk losing it in a claiming race.

Conformation

The build of a horse, commonly used with particular reference to the correctness of alignment of the parts of the limbs.

Cooling out

Walking the horse after a race or work, until it cools down. This is taken much more seriously in America than Australia.

Cow hocked

Having the near part of the hocks turned towards the midline, turned-in like a cow's hocks often are.

Daily Racing Form

The American betting man's daily news. A daily newspaper, devoted entirely to racing, with great detail on past performances. Depending on the region, may contain information on Quarter Horse, Standardbred or Thoroughbred racing.

Dosage

A breeding theory that estimates a racehorse's best racing distance using numbers computed from the aptitudes of important sires in the pedigree.

Draw

To draw a horse before it's race is to take away it's hay and/or water. The reasoning is that when less hay and water is consumed, the dead weight carried by the horse is decreased.

Drench

To give a horse fluids, salts or medications via a stomach tube, which is passed up the horse's nostril, then down the throat into the stomach.

Fastwork

Training at race or near-race speeds

Firing

This is a controversial treatment for certain leg problems in horses. An area of the horse's leg is anesthetised, then a pattern of burns is made with a hot-pointed instrument. The area becomes painful and inflamed, and the horse is turned out (spelled). When I was a student, I remember a vet showing me Xrays from before and after treatment of a horse with bony outgrowths (osteophytes). The bony growths had disappeared. Some vets and especially trainers swear by it for results. Others say it is useless (and this was the conclusion of an English study), and since it inflicts pain on the horse, should be banned.

Foreman

Trainer's second in charge, main helper. Similar to assistant trainer in America and head lad in U.K.

Fractions, Fractional times

These are times for each quarter mile segment of the race. Many American handicappers are big on fractional times in the analysis of races (so am I) and American racetracks usually have timing apparatus every quarter mile. The times are flashed up on a screen, and are reported in the Daily Racing Form.

Fresh, Freshen up

A horse that has not been trained or raced hard has a lot of energy and enthusiasm, and is described as 'fresh'. To freshen a horse is to back off in it's training and racing, to allow it to recover it's enthusiasm.

Futurity

A race type in which the owner must make payments as the young horse grows, to keep it eligible. Very common in Quarter Horse racing, particularly in states that do not allow (or did not allow) gambling. Payments may start as early as before the horse is born, and continue at intervals. Some futurities accept entries from horses that were not paid up, on payment of a special fee. When Caesar Dominguez wanted to put Takin On The Cash in the All-American Futurity, it was going to cost owner Felipé Tiscareno $50,000. Mind you, first prize in 1990 was $1m, and the horse only had to make it into the trials and do better than 11th place to recover that money.

Gallop

Means very different things in different parts of the world. In Australia, New Zealand and the United Kingdom, it means a fast gallop. A slow gallop in those countries is called a canter. Americans seldom use the word canter because they use the word gallop for a slow gallop. A fast gallop at an American track is called a work or a breeze,

Gate, Gates, Starting Gates

The contraption used to make sure all horses in a race get away to as fair a start as possible. Often called the barrier, or barriers in Australia.

Good doer

A horse that eats well, especially when in training.

Grade 1 race, Grade 2, Grade 3 Abbrev. G1, G2, G3

This is the American version of the English Pattern system. The English graded their most important races by breeding significance. This made it easier for everyone to know which were the most significant races to win. It was handy for novices and foreigners. The English divided theirs into Group 1, 2, and 3. America has Grade 1, 2, 3. Now that all racing countries have grading systems, it is easy for those interpreting foreign pedigrees. You may have never heard of the races the horse won, but you know it was a good race if it was Grade 1, 2, or 3.

Grade - on a Quarter Horse's race record: see Speed Index

Grabs

Grabs are downward projections at the toe of the horseshoe to help the horse get better traction.

Groom

The person who looks after a horse day by day - waters, feeds, brushes and bandages it. In most stables they also muck out the stall. Most grooms have three horses to look after, but some have two and some unlucky ones may have half a dozen. They will say 'I rub 3 horses.'

Group 1 race, Group 2, Group 3 Abbrev. G1, G2, G3
See also Grade 1. Group races are the elite breeding races in the English grading system. The very best are classified as Group 1, and so on down the line. Similar gradings are now found throughout the world, in all forms of horse racing.

Handicap
To handicap a horse is to assess it's racing ability for betting purposes, or in the case of the track handicapper, to assign weights that will give all the horses an even chance, and make the race exciting.

Handicap race
One in which the horses carry weights that are assigned so all the horses will theoretically have an equal chance. This makes a race interesting to the betting public. They are very common in Australia.

Handle
The amount of money bet. Can refer to the amount bet on a single race, a day's card or a year's total. Usually called 'the pool' in Australia.

Home straight, Home stretch, Stretch.
The straight part of the racecourse nearest the stands. The finish line is at one end

Hots
Horses that have worked, that will be walked to cool them out, usually for 20 to 60 minutes. Most Australian trainers don't cool out their horses for more than a few minutes.

Hot walker
Has two meanings. To some it is a person who walks horses (Hand-walked). Hot walkers are only on the trainers premises for a few hours in the morning. To others it means a walking machine of the type with long radial arms. A typical machine has 6 arms, and upto 6 horses can be tied up to it. Usually a motor keeps the arms turning.

Jugging
An American term for giving fluids and drugs into the bloodstream, usually through the jugular vein in the neck. In America most jugging is done after the horse races, to speed it's recovery. Australian trainers call the same thing a 'drip' or an 'IV', abbreviations for an intravenous drip.

Jugs
The syringes or bottles, containing the drugs or fluids used in jugging.

Lasix barn
A barn near the saddling paddock where horses getting lasix are held, to ensure they get the drug. Another difference to Australia, where lasix is banned. Lasix is a medication for bleeders, but many trainers believe it makes horses faster.

Maiden
At the track, a horse, male or female, that has not won a race. At the stud, a maiden mare is a mare that has not had a foal.

Mainline
The main vein in the neck of the horse, the jugular, used for giving drugs or fluids directly into the bloodstream.

Meet, A meet
An American term for a season of racing at a track. May be two days, two weeks or seven months. The track usually has racing three to five days a week during a meet, then it closes down or switches to a different type of racing.

Meeting, Race meeting.
A day's racing in Australia. Most Australian main tracks have one meeting a week for most of the year.

Mutuel
The name for the computerised betting system in America. See Pari-Mutuel

Nick, Nicking
A nick is a cross of two lines in breeding that produces exceptional results.

Pari-mutuel, Mutuel
A computerised betting system in place at American tracks. Called Pari-mutuel because the first automated, centralised system in America, which did away with bookmakers, was modeled on a French system. Same as Totalisator or Tote in Australia.

Place bet
In America, to win a place bet the horse must come first or second. You win a show bet if the horse comes first, second, or third. In Australia, the horse must come first, second, or third to win a place bet.

Pony
At tracks it means the horse the trainer rides, or horses from which riders lead other horses. These can be horses that are being led for morning exercise, or a horse and rider being led to the start of a race.

Pre-race
Medications, intravenous drips, or jugs given to the horse before a race.

Quinella
To have the first two finishers in a race, in any order.

Raceway horse
A horse that is good enough to win ordinary races at the track, but not stakes races or classics.

Rating a horse
Controlling the horse's speed in a race, not letting it run all-out. This is very important in longer races. It can also refer to a handicapper's assessment of a horse, and may take the form of a number like speed ratings.

Router
American Thoroughbred term for a horse racing over a longer distance - over a mile. Not applicable in American harness racing because almost all races are run at a distance of one mile.

Selling race, Selling Plate
This is the English equivalent of a claiming race. The horses are for sale at the specified price. Horses that run in such races are called 'platers'.

Sore
A horse that is lame, or not free in it's movement.

Speed index
A system for comparing horses in Quarter Horse racing. At each track, the three best race times for each distance, each year for the previous three years are averaged. The average of those nine times becomes the 0100 rating on the grade system, for that distance at that track. If a horse runs faster than that average, points are added per hundredth of a second. For slower times points are deducted. Clearly, to have a grade above 0100 requires a very fast horse.

Grade refers to individual races. The highest grade result a horse has achieved, with the first 0's removed, is listed as its Speed Index. A lifetime best grade of 0090 becomes a Speed Index of 90. Horses going fast enough to get a Speed Index of 80 or above (grade of 0080), qualify for the Register Of Merit (ROM).

The Speed Index provides some measure of ability for comparing horses that run at different distances, in different years and on different tracks.

The main weakness of the system is the variation in the quality of horses running at different tracks. At a track with low quality horses, the nine fastest times that determine the magic 100 rating will be slower. Because of this, there is an American Quarter Horse Association minimum time for each distance. If the average of the nine best track times is slower than that minimum, the minimum is used instead. Too bad if your local track is a bog, but the alternative is to have horses at the top tracks sent out to the tracks with the lowest quality horses, to get an urealistically high Speed Index.

Speed rating
Figures used to compare horses for gambling purposes. Every handicapper has their own formula for computing a speed rating. A widely used formula in Thoroughbreds takes the track record as 100 points, and deducts a point for each 1/5 of a second the race time is over the record. That establishes the race winner's speed rating. The other horses in the race have a point deducted for each length they finish behind the winner, one length taking approximately 1/5 of a second in Thoroughbred racing.

Stakes race
Historically, races in which owners put up money. Now a quality race for which the track puts up almost all the money.

Stayer
Term for a horse which races in longer distance races. Equivalent of router in America, although Australians in Thoroughbred racing generally speak of sprinters, milers, and stayers.

Strapper
Person who cares for the horse. Same as groom.

Totalisator, Tote
Automated system in which all bets are taken and the odds calculated according to the pool on each type of bet on each horse. The odds change as the betting goes on, whereas with a bookmaker, the odds remain as they were when the bet was made.

Tout
Person selling information on horses, or tipping winners.

Weight-for-age race
A race in which the weight carried by each horse is determined by it's age and sex. The scale varies with the time of year and distance of the race. These races are common in Australia, and attract a high class of horse. Such races are important to breeders in helping to determine which are the best horses. The favorite usually wins. This differs from a handicap, in which the slower horses are given less weight. The favorite wins a handicap less often. Handicaps are more interesting to bettors, and attract a bigger betting pool or handle.

WINNING TRAINERS

by Ross Staaden

Published by Headway International Publishing

4 Gillon St, Karawara, Western Australia 6152

PO Box 1907, Barr St, Lexington, Kentucky, USA, Zip 40593-1907